After Herder

Philosophy of language has for some t
discipline of philosophy. But where di
identified as its father, but in fact its orig
that arose in eighteenth-century Germ
tradition. He also makes a case that th.

tradition was J. G. Herder. It was Herder who established such fundamental
principles in the philosophy of language as that thought essentially depends on
language and that meaning consists in the usage of words. It was he who on
that basis revolutionized the theory of interpretation ('hermeneutics') and the
theory of translation. And it was he who played the pivotal role in founding
such whole new disciplines concerned with language as anthropology and
linguistics. In the course of developing these historical points, this book also
shows that Herder and his tradition are in many ways superior to dominant
trends in more recent philosophy of language: deeper in their principles and
broader in their focus.

After Herder

Philosophy of Language in the German Tradition

Michael N. Forster

OXFORD
UNIVERSITY PRESS

UNIVERSITY PRESS

Great Clarendon Street, Oxford OX2 6DP
United Kingdom

Oxford University Press is a department of the University of Oxford.
It furthers the University's objective of excellence in research, scholarship,
and education by publishing worldwide. Oxford is a registered trade mark of
Oxford University Press in the UK and in certain other countries

First published 2010
First published in paperback 2012

British Library Cataloguing in Publication Data

Data available

Library of Congress Cataloging in Publication Data

Library of Congress Control Number: 2010923434

ISBN 978–0–19–922811–9
ISBN 978–0–19–965938–8 (Pbk)

Printed in the United Kingdom by
Lightning Source UK Ltd., Milton Keynes

To the memory of Michael Frede (1940–2007)

Acknowledgments

This volume and its companion volume *German Philosophy of Language from Schlegel to Hegel and Beyond* are dedicated to the memory of Michael Frede, who, shortly after retiring from the Chair in the History of Philosophy at Oxford University in 2005, died tragically while swimming in the sea near Delphi in the summer of 2007. Together with Raymond Geuss, he supervised my doctoral dissertation on Hegel's reception of ancient skepticism at Princeton University in the early 1980s. He was an intellectually inspiring and generous teacher, and remained a constant source of inspiration and generosity throughout the rest of his life. Michael is known, among many other things, for having helped to expand the horizons of ancient philosophers beyond the staple thinkers, Plato and Aristotle, to include in addition the riches of Hellenistic philosophy. This volume and its companion volume attempt to do something similar for work on German philosophy: to expand its horizons beyond such staple figures as Kant and Hegel in order to include in addition a group of less-well-known philosophers from the same period who shared a profound concern with language. I hope that Michael would have liked this project. There could be no surer criterion of its success.

This project also owes much to many other individuals and institutions. In a way it began its life at Oxford University in the late 1970s, where I was an undergraduate and had the good fortune to learn about German philosophy from the tutorials, lectures, and publications of Patrick Gardiner, Peter Hacker, Alan Ryan, Peter Strawson, Charles Taylor, and Ralph Walker. The project's second home was Princeton University in the early 1980s, where I benefited greatly from the teaching and publications of Michael Frede, Raymond Geuss, Saul Kripke, and the late Richard Rorty. Together with Michael Frede, Raymond Geuss deserves special mention in this connection. He inspired and nurtured my work on German philosophy when I was a doctoral student, and has continued to do so ever since. Another important early source of inspiration was a year I spent at Heidelberg University in 1984-5, where I especially benefited from the generous hospitality and erudition of Hans Friedrich Fulda. Subsequently, visits to the Friedrich-Schiller University in Jena—the original home of some of the intellectual developments discussed in this project—have been another invaluable source of intellectual stimulation. In this connection, I would especially like to thank Klaus Vieweg and Wolfgang Welsch for their warm hospitality and their rich learning. This book also owes a huge debt to the university at which I have taught for the past twenty-five years, the University of Chicago. The University of Chicago's extraordinary commitment to the life of the mind, and its encouragement of interdisciplinarity, have been a constant inspiration. So too have its faculty and students. I would especially like to thank the following faculty past and present: the late Arthur Adkins, Dan Brudney, Ted Cohen, Arnold Davidson, Dan Garber, Charles Larmore, Jonathan Lear, Brian Leiter, Leonard Linsky, Ian Mueller, Martha Nussbaum, Bob Richards, Howard Stein, Lina Steiner, Josef Stern, George Stocking, and Bill Tait. I would also like to thank the following past and present students (many of whom have now gone on to successful professional careers): Stephen Engstrom, Susan Hahn, Jim Kreines, Sheela Kumar, Alison Laywine, Stephen Menn, Nathana O'Brien, Gregg Osborne, Erich Reck, Tim Rosenkoetter, David Sussman, and Rachel Zuckert. In its later stages this project benefited greatly from the encouragement and generosity of the Dean of the Humanities Division, Martha Roth, and from a research fellowship held in 2008-9 at the University's Franke Institute for the Humanities, ably directed by Jim Chandler. So warm thanks to them as well. Other individuals who have contributed to the development of the project in one way or another, and whom I would also like to thank, include: Karl Ameriks, Andreas Arndt, Fred Beiser, Anne Birien, Paul Boghossian, the late Rüdiger Bubner, Thomas Erikson, Eckhart Förster, Kristin Gjesdal, Rolf-Peter Horstmann, John Hyman, Michael Inwood, Mark Johnston, Béatrice Longuenesse, John McDowell, Michael Rosen, Richard Schacht, Hans Sluga, Stelios Virvidakis, Pirmin Stekeler-Weithofer, Michael Williams, Allen Wood, and John Zammito. Institutions which have supported this project by hosting presentations of parts of it, or of closely related material, and which I would therefore like to thank, include the following: the Aristotle University in Salonica, the University of Athens, the University of California at Berkeley, the University of Chicago, Columbia University, the University of Crete, Drew University, the University of Georgia, Harvard University, the Humanities Institute of Osaka, the University of Illinois at Champaign-Urbana, the Internationale Hegel Gesellschaft, the Internationale Hegel Vereinigung, James Madison University, Johns Hopkins University, McGill University, the University of Michigan at Ann Arbor, New York University, the University of Notre Dame, Oslo University, the University of Patras, Princeton University, Temple University, and the University of Washington in Seattle.

I would also like to thank Oxford University Press and its Philosophy editor Peter Momtchiloff for bringing this project to fruition. Peter's support and advice during the project's development were extremely valuable. In particular, it was he who encouraged me to expand it from a rather haphazard collection of essays into the much more organized and comprehensive treatment that it now is.

About half of the essays in the present volume have been published before in some form. I would therefore like to thank the original publishers of the following essays for allowing me to re-publish them here: "Johann Gottfried von Herder" and "Friedrich Daniel Ernst Schleiermacher," *Stanford Encyclopedia of Philosophy*;[1] "Herder's Philosophy of Language, Interpretation, and Translation: Three Fundamental Principles," *The Review of Metaphysics*; "Gods, Animals, and Artists: Some Problem Cases in Herder's Philosophy of Language," *Inquiry* (by Taylor and Francis); "Herder's Importance as a Philosopher," *Von der Logik zur Sprache*, ed. R. Bubner and G. Hindrichs (Klett-Cotta, 2007); "The Liberal Temper in Classical German Philosophy: Freedom of Thought and Expression," *Internationales Jahrbuch des Deutschen Idealismus/International Yearbook of German Idealism*; "Schleiermacher's Hermeneutics: Some Problems and Solutions," *The Harvard Review of Philosophy*.

Last but not least I would like to thank my family for their love, support, and patience, especially my wife Noha, my daughter Alya, and my parents Michael and the late Kathleen Forster.

Notes

1. These articles are available online at <http://plato.stanford.edu/entries/herder/> and <http://plato.stanford.edu/entries/schleiermacher/> respectively.

Contents

The present volume will be followed by a companion volume *German Philosophy of Language from Schlegel to Hegel and Beyond*, whose contents will be as follows:

Introduction

Part I: Schlegel

1. Friedrich Schlegel
2. Friedrich Schlegel's Hermeneutics

Part II: Humboldt

3. Wilhelm von Humboldt
4. Herder, Schlegel, Humboldt, and the Birth of Modern Linguistics

Part III: Hegel

5. Hegel on Language
6. Hegel and Some (Near-)Contemporaries: Narrow or Broad Expressivism?
7. Hegel and Hermeneutics

Part IV: And Beyond

8. Philosophy of Language in the Nineteenth Century
9. Hermeneutics

Select Bibliography

Abbreviations

FSSW   *Friedrich Schleiermacher's sämmtliche Werke* (Berlin: G. Reimer, 1835–), references to division, volume, and page

G   *Johann Gottfried Herder Werke*, ed. U. Gaier et al. (Frankfurt am Main: Deutscher Klassiker Verlag, 1985–)

S   *Johann Gottfried Herder Sämtliche Werke*, ed. B. Suphan et al. (Berlin: Weidmann, 1877–)

WHGS   *Wilhelm von Humboldts Gesammelte Schriften*, ed. A. Leitzmann et al. (Berlin: B. Behr, 1903–)

All references are to volume and page unless otherwise stated.

Introduction

Herder famously (or: as should be famous) stands at the beginning of
classical German philosophy of language not only chronologically;
he is at the same time the "main source," so to speak, and the
constant, even if only implicit, reference point of the philosophy of
language. Fichte, Friedrich and A.W. Schlegel, Schleiermacher and
Schelling, Hegel and Humboldt all take over, directly or indirectly,
explicitly or tacitly, ideas of Herder's. That many of these ideas
often appear in these authors much more elaborated and better
proven than in Herder himself should not be allowed to obscure
the fact that they are already to be found in Herder at least in a
seminal form and that Herder in many respects simply made the
beginning.

E. Coseriu[1]

In the Anglophone philosophical tradition the philosophy of language has for
quite a long time now enjoyed something like the status of "first philosophy,"
having displaced in that central position such previous occupants as metaphysics
and epistemology. But where did the philosophy of language begin? Michael
Dummett claims that Frege is "the father of 'linguistic philosophy,' "[2] and
Anthony Kenny similarly maintains that "Frege gave philosophy its current
linguistic turn."[3] Assuming, as seems reasonable, that the expressions "linguistic
philosophy" and "[philosophy's] linguistic turn" here refer mainly to the
two doctrines that (1) thought is essentially dependent on and bounded by
language, and (2) meaning consists in the use of words, then these historical
claims are false. Long before Frege, a series of important German thinkers,
including Herder, Hamann, Schleiermacher, Friedrich Schlegel, Wilhelm von
Humboldt, and Hegel, had already espoused versions of these doctrines. And
far from introducing them, Frege actually reacted *against* them—backing off

the bold claim that thought is *essentially* dependent on and bounded by language and substituting for it the weaker claim that the dependence in question is only a contingent feature of the thought of human beings, as well as rejecting any equation of meaning with the use of words in favor of a Platonism about meaning (or "sense").[4] This volume and its companion volume *German Philosophy of Language from Schlegel to Hegel and Beyond* are concerned with the *real* beginnings of modern philosophy of language, in Herder and his tradition. One of their aims is thus to fill a major lacuna in Anglophone philosophy of language's knowledge of its own origins, and hence in its self-understanding.

These volumes do not purport to provide a full history of the tradition in question. Rather, they consist of essays on selected thinkers and topics within it. The essays make a number of ambitious and controversial historical claims in addition to the one just mentioned. One of these claims lies in a detailed vindication of Coseriu's rather isolated aperçu that it was *Herder* who played the most fundamental role within this tradition. A central part of the vindication, developed in the present volume, goes roughly as follows. Towards the end of the eighteenth century three striking revolutions occurred in the philosophy of language (here understood in the narrow sense of a set of fundamental issues concerning thought, meaning, and language, rather than in the broader sense used in these volumes' titles), the theory of interpretation (or "hermeneutics"), and the theory of translation. The revolution in the philosophy of language consisted in the development of three principles: (1) that thought is essentially dependent on and bounded by language, (2) that meaning consists in word-usage, and (3) a quasi-empiricist principle that meaning essentially depends on corresponding perceptual or affective sensations (though with two qualifications allowing for a converse dependence as well, and for the possibility of metaphorical extensions of the meanings that are directly anchored in sensations—hence the "quasi"). The revolution in hermeneutics largely consisted in grounding the methodology of interpretation in the three principles just mentioned along the following lines: due to principle (1), there is in fact no need for the interpreter to worry about the commonly assumed possibility that an author may have had thoughts which either altogether transcended or were only very imperfectly reflected in his capacity for linguistic expression; due to principle (2), the interpreter's primary task is one of determining an author's pattern of word-usage, and thereby his meaning; and due to principle (3), the interpreter must also somehow imaginatively recapture an author's semantically relevant sensations. The revolution in the theory of translation consisted in the development of what has recently been called a "foreignizing" approach to translation. This approach addresses the challenging task of reproducing the distinctive meanings of an author (especially an author from a remote historical period or culture) in translation by "bending" the usage of words in the target language in order thereby to approximate the usage of words and hence the meanings in the source language (this method rests on principle (2)), and also by imitating the musical aspects of the source text, such as meter, rhyme, assonance, and alliteration, as faithfully as possible (this method largely rests on principle (3), the thought being that the musical aspects of a text express fine nuances of an author's sensations, which, in light of principle (3), are internal to his meanings, so that reproducing a text's musical aspects in translation is important not only for other reasons but also for semantic ones). To the extent that these three revolutions have been noticed by the secondary literature at all, they have been noticed in isolation from each other, and the credit for them has been distributed among several people: the revolution in philosophy of language has commonly been credited to Hamann, the revolutions in hermeneutics and translation-theory to Schleiermacher.[5] I argue, to the contrary, that these revolutions are intimately interconnected (namely, in the ways just indicated), that the credit for them mainly belongs to a single individual, and that this individual was not Hamann or Schleiermacher but *Herder*. Moreover, I argue that Herder deserves the main credit here not only in the sense that he developed the relevant ideas first (despite the fact that Hamann was the older man) but also in the sense that for the most part his versions of them are philosophically superior to Hamann's and Schleiermacher's versions.[6]

Another ambitious and controversial historical claim developed in these volumes is that, besides laying the foundations for modern philosophy of language, hermeneutics, and translation-theory in the way just sketched, Herder also laid the foundations for such entirely new (closely related) disciplines as cultural anthropology and linguistics.[7]

These are some of the project's more dramatic historical claims. However, the project's purpose is not *only* historical, but also to a considerable extent systematic. The purpose is not only to set the historical record straight, but also to rescue and champion a tradition of thought about language which, in my opinion, gets many important things right that more recent philosophers concerned with language have tended to get badly wrong.

What do I find so admirable in this tradition as compared with more recent philosophy? Part of its achievement lies in the sheer philosophical *depth* of its ideas concerning language, including its ideas in the philosophy of language (in the narrow sense), hermeneutics, and translation-theory. These ideas often proleptically correct or improve on ideas which subsequently came to dominate both German and Anglophone philosophy in the twentieth century. Several of the essays in these volumes make a detailed case for such depth, so I shall not steal their thunder here by saying more about what it consists in than I already have. But one very general observation may be worth making here at the outset: This depth is not altogether surprising on reflection, for the following reason. To put it a little pointedly, compared with most recent philosophers, including most recent philosophers of language, the thinkers in this tradition *knew a lot* about language. In particular, they all had an impressive knowledge, not only of their native German and other modern European languages, but also of ancient languages (for example, they all had good Latin, Greek, and Hebrew, and several of them also knew Sanskrit), and in certain cases culturally distant living languages as well (for example, Humboldt knew several of these including the Kawi language of Java). Moreover, they were all deeply engaged in, and strikingly skilled at, the tasks of interpreting and translating texts, including not only texts from other modern European languages but also ones from historically-culturally distant languages. This intimate, skilled acquaintance with a broad range of languages and linguistic tasks could hardly but lend depth to their theoretical ideas about language.

In addition to sheer depth, though, another striking virtue of this tradition's ideas about language is their *breadth*—which contrasts sharply with the narrowness of most recent Anglophone philosophy of language. For example, besides such foundational questions in the philosophy of language as those concerning the relation between thought and language and the nature of meaning, these thinkers were also deeply interested in such further questions as the following: the extent of linguistic-conceptual variation across historical periods and cultures; the nature of interpretation, and how to accomplish it; the nature of translation, and how to accomplish it;[8] the nature of animal language and cognition; the nature of expression in such non-linguistic arts as sculpture, painting, and music; the role of genre in both linguistic and non-linguistic art; a broad range of ethico-political questions concerning language, including ones about the relation of alternative strategies of interpretation and translation to the contest between nationalistic and cosmopolitan ideals and ones about the importance of freedom of expression; and many further fascinating questions as well.

One sometimes hears Anglophone philosophers today sounding the death-knell of philosophy of language as the central core of the discipline of philosophy. This is not too surprising given the largely misguided and severely impoverished stock of ideas that currently constitute philosophy of language in the Anglophone world. One of my more ambitious hopes for this project is that it may help to revive philosophy of language in the Anglophone world by re-injecting into it some of the depth and the breadth of the Herderian tradition.

The essays in these volumes were for the most part originally written as discrete pieces rather than as parts of a whole, and I have attempted to preserve rather than to erase their original autonomy in putting them together here. Consequently, they do not form a continuous narrative, and they sometimes overlap. Nonetheless, by arranging them in a certain order and interspersing introductory encyclopedia-style essays on each of the main thinkers covered, I have endeavored to produce something that does at least approximate a whole with a continuous narrative. An energetic reader might therefore want to read through the essays of the two volumes in sequence from beginning to end. Alternatively, since each essay has sufficient autonomy to be read by itself, he or she might choose to "dip" selectively according to interest.

The essays in these volumes cannot claim to exhaust the wealth of the tradition they explore. However, it is my plan to complement them with further essays in the future, and my hope that they may also encourage other philosophers to venture into this extraordinarily rich and underdeveloped territory.

Notes

1. E. Coseriu, "Zu Hegels Semantik," *Kwartalnik neofilologiczny*, 24 (1977), p. 185 n. 8.
2. M. Dummett, *Frege: Philosophy of Language* (Cambridge, Mass.: Harvard University Press, 1981), p. 683.
3. A. Kenny, *Frege* (London: Penguin, 1995), p. viii.
4. This is not to deny that Frege made important contributions to the philosophy of language. He did—for example, his clear sense/referent distinction.
5. The secondary literature in question here saliently includes the following: for the philosophy of language, I. Berlin, *Vico and Herder* (New York: Viking Press, 1976) and *The Magus of the North* (New York: Farrar, Straus, and Giroux, 1993); for hermeneutics, M. Frank, *Das individuelle Allgemeine* (Frankfurt am Main: Suhrkamp, 1985) and *Das Sagbare und das Unsagbare* (Frankfurt am Main: Suhrkamp, 1990); and for translation-theory, A. Berman, *L'Épreuve de l'étranger* (Paris: Gallimard, 1984).
6. See esp. Essay 4.
7. See Essay 6 and *German Philosophy of Language*, Essay 4.

8. Anglophone philosophy of language has indeed invented pale substitutes for these inquiries into interpretation and translation, in particular Davidson's reflections on the nature of "radical interpretation" and Quine's on the "indeterminacy of translation." But these substitutes are highly abstract and largely misguided, so that they in the end have little to tell us about the real nature of interpretation or translation. Indeed, far from constituting or encouraging a serious treatment of these vitally important subjects by Anglophone philosophy, they have merely tended to displace it.

PART I
Herder

1

Johann Gottfried Herder

Johann Gottfried Herder (1744–1803) is a philosopher of the first importance.[1] This judgment depends heavily on the intrinsic quality of his ideas (of which this essay will try to give an impression). But another aspect of it is his intellectual influence. This has been immense both within philosophy and beyond it (much greater than is usually realized). For example, Hegel's philosophy turns out to be largely an elaborate systematic development of Herder's ideas (especially concerning the mind, history, and God); so too does Schleiermacher's (concerning language, interpretation, translation, the mind, art, and God); Nietzsche is deeply influenced by Herder as well (concerning the mind, history, and values); so too is Dilthey (especially concerning history); even John Stuart Mill has important debts to Herder (in political philosophy); and beyond philosophy, Goethe was transformed from being merely a clever but rather conventional poet into a great artist largely through the early impact on him of Herder's ideas.

Indeed, Herder can claim to have virtually established whole *disciplines* which we now take for granted. For example, it was mainly Herder (not, as has often been claimed, Hamann) who established fundamental ideas concerning an intimate dependence of thought on language which underpin modern philosophy of language. It was Herder who, through those same ideas, his recognition of deep variations in language and thought across historical periods and cultures, his broad empirical approach to languages, and in other ways, inspired Friedrich Schlegel and Wilhelm von Humboldt to found modern linguistics. It was Herder who developed modern interpretation-theory, or "hermeneutics," in ways that would subsequently be taken over by Schleiermacher and then more systematically formulated by the latter's pupil Boeckh. It was Herder who, by doing so, also contributed to establishing the methodological foundations of nineteenth-century German classical scholarship (which rested on the Schleiermacher-Boeckh methodology), and hence of modern classical scholarship generally. It was Herder who did more than anyone else to establish the general conception and the interpretive methodology of our modern discipline of anthropology. Finally, Herder also made vital contributions to the progress of modern biblical scholarship.

1. Life and Works

Johann Gottfried Herder (1744–1803) was born in Mohrungen in East Prussia. His father was a schoolteacher and he grew up in humble circumstances. In 1762 he enrolled at the University of Königsberg, where he studied with Kant, who accorded him special privileges because of his unusual intellectual abilities. At this period he also began a lifelong friendship with the irrationalist philosopher Hamann. In 1764 he left Königsberg to take up a school-teaching position in Riga. There he wrote the programmatic essay *How Philosophy Can Become More Universal and Useful for the Benefit of the People* (1765); published his first major work, concerning the philosophy of language and literature, the *Fragments on Recent German Literature* (1767–8); and also published an important work in aesthetics, the *Critical Forests* (1769). In 1769 he resigned his position and travelled—first to France, and then to Strasbourg, where he met, and had a powerful impact on, the young Goethe. In 1771 he won a prize from the Berlin Academy for his best-known work in the philosophy of language, the *Treatise on the Origin of Language* (published 1772). From 1771 to 1776 he served as court preacher to the ruling house in Bückeburg. The most important work from this period is his first major essay on the philosophy of history, *This Too a Philosophy of History for the Formation of Humanity* (1774). In 1776, partly thanks to Goethe's influence, he was appointed General Superintendant of the Lutheran clergy in Weimar, a post he kept for the rest of his life. During this period he published an important essay in the philosophy of mind, *On the Cognition and Sensation of the Human Soul* (1778); a seminal work concerning the Old Testament, *On the Spirit of Hebrew Poetry* (1782–3); his well-known longer work on the philosophy of history, the *Ideas for the Philosophy of History of Humanity* (1784–91); an influential essay on the philosophy of religion, *God: Some Conversations* (1787); a work largely on political philosophy, written in response to the French Revolution, the *Letters for the Advancement of Humanity* (1793–7); a series of *Christian Writings* (1794–8) concerned with the New Testament; and two works opposing Kant's critical philosophy, *A Metacritique on the Critique of Pure Reason* (1799) (directed against the theoretical philosophy of the *Critique of Pure Reason*) and the *Calligone* (1800) (directed against the aesthetics of the *Critique of Judgment*). In addition to the works just mentioned, Herder also wrote many others during his career.

Herder's earlier works are often his best. He himself wrote in *On the Cognition and Sensation of the Human Soul* that "the first uninhibited work of an author is . . . usually his best; his bloom is unfolding, his soul still dawn." Whether or not that is *generally* true, it does arguably apply to Herder himself.

2. Philosophical Style

In certain ways Herder's philosophical texts are easier to read than others from the period. For example, he avoids technical jargon, writes in a manner that is lively and rich in examples rather than dry and abstract, and has no large, complex system for the reader to keep track of. But his texts also have certain peculiarities which can impede a proper understanding and appreciation of his thought, and it is important to be alerted to these.

To begin with, Herder's writing often seems emotional and grammatically undisciplined in ways that might perhaps be expected in casual speech but not in philosophical texts. This is intentional. Indeed, Herder sometimes deliberately "roughed up" material in this direction between drafts. When writing this way he is often in fact using grammatical-rhetorical figures which can easily look like mere carelessness to an untutored eye but which receive high literary sanction from classical sources and are employed by him artfully (e.g. anacoluthon). Moreover, he has serious philosophical reasons for writing in such a way rather than in the manner of conventional academic prose, including the following: (1) This promises to make his writing more broadly accessible and interesting to people—a decidedly non-trivial goal for him, since he believes it to be an essential part of philosophy's vocation to have a broad social impact. (2) One of his central theses in the philosophy of mind holds that thought is not and should not be separate from volition, or affect, that types of thinking which aspire to exclude affect are inherently distorting and inferior. Standard academic writing has this vice, whereas spontaneous speech, and writing which imitates it, do not. (3) Herder is opposed to any grammatical or lexical straightjacketing of language, any slavish obedience to grammar books and dictionaries. In Herder's view, such straightjacketing is inimical, not only to linguistic creativity and inventiveness, but also (much worse), because thought is essentially dependent on and confined in its scope by language, thereby to creativity and inventiveness in thought itself.

Another peculiarity of Herder's philosophical texts is their *unsystematic* nature. This is again deliberate. For Herder is largely hostile towards systematicity in philosophy (a fact that is reflected both in explicit remarks and in many of his titles: *Fragments . . .* , *Ideas . . .* , etc.). He is especially hostile to the ambitious sort of systematicity aspired to in the tradition of Spinoza, Wolff, Kant, Fichte, Schelling, and Hegel: the ideal of a comprehensive theory whose parts display some sort of strict overall pattern of derivation. He has compelling reasons for this hostility: (1) He is very skeptical that such systematic designs can be made to work (as opposed to creating, through illicit means, an *illusion* that they do). (2) He believes that such system-building leads to a premature closure of inquiry, and in particular to disregarding or distorting new empirical evidence. Scrutiny of such systems amply bears out both of these concerns. Herder's well-grounded hostility to this type of systematicity established an important countertradition in German philosophy (which subsequently included, for example, Friedrich Schlegel, Nietzsche, and Wittgenstein).

On the other hand, unlike his friend Hamann, Herder is in *favor* of "systematicity" in a more modest sense: the ideal of a theory which is self-consistent and supported by argument.[2] He by no means always achieves this ideal (so that interpreting him calls for more selectivity and reconstruction than is the case with some philosophers).[3] However, his failures to do so are often more apparent than real: First, in many cases where he may seem to be guilty of inconsistency he is really not. For he is sometimes developing philosophical dialogues between two or more opposing viewpoints, in which cases it would clearly be a mistake to accuse him of inconsistency in any usual or pejorative sense. And (less obviously) in many other cases he is in effect still working in this dialogue-mode, only without bothering to distribute the positions among different interlocutors explicitly, and so is again really innocent of inconsistency (examples of this occur in *How Philosophy Can Become* and *This Too a Philosophy of History*). Moreover, he has serious motives for using this method of (implicit) dialogue: (1) Sometimes his motive simply lies in the fact that when dealing with religiously or politically delicate matters it permits him to state his views but without quite stating them as his own and therefore without inviting trouble. But he also has philosophically deeper motives: (2) He takes over from the precritical Kant an idea (inspired by ancient skepticism) that the best way for the philosopher to pursue the truth is by setting contrary views on a subject into opposition with one another in order to advance towards, and hopefully attain, the truth through their mutual testing and modification. (3) Also, he develops a more original variant of that idea on the socio-historical plane: analogously, the way for humankind as a whole to attain the elusive goal of truth is through an ongoing contest between opposing positions, in the course of which the best ones will eventually win out (this idea anticipates, and probably inspired, a central thesis of John Stuart Mill's *On Liberty*). This yields a further motive for the dialogue-method (even where it does not lead Herder himself to any definite conclusion), in effect warranting the rhetorical question, And what does it matter to the cause of humankind and its discovery of truth whether those various opposing positions are advanced by different people or by *the same* person? Second, Herder's appearance of neglecting to give arguments is often, rather, a principled rejection of arguments *of certain sorts*. For example, he has a general commitment to empiricism and against apriorism in philosophy which leads him to avoid familiar sorts of apriorist arguments in philosophy; and a commitment to non-cognitivism in ethics which leads him to refrain from familiar sorts of cognitivist arguments in ethics.

3. General Program in Philosophy

Hamann's influence on Herder's best thought has been greatly exaggerated by some of the secondary literature (e.g. Isaiah Berlin). But Kant's was early, fundamental, and enduring. However, the Kant who influenced Herder in this way was the *pre*critical Kant of the early and middle 1760s, not the critical Kant (against whom Herder later engaged in the—rather distracting and ineffective—public polemics of the *Metacritique* and the *Calligone*). Some of Kant's key positions in the 1760s, sharply contrasting with ones which he would later adopt during the critical period, were: a (Pyrrhonist-influenced) skepticism about metaphysics; a form of empiricism; and a (Hume-influenced) non-cognitivism in ethics.[4] Herder took over these positions in the 1760s and retained them throughout his career. It should by no means be assumed that this debt to the *early* Kant is a debt to a philosophically *inferior* Kant, however; a good case could be made for the very opposite.

Herder's 1765 essay *How Philosophy Can Become More Universal and Useful for the Benefit of the People* is a key text for understanding both his debt to Kant and the broad orientation of his philosophy. The essay was written under strong influence from Kant, especially, it seems, Kant's 1766 essay *Dreams of a Spirit Seer*, which Kant sent to Herder prior to its publication ("a sheet at a time," Herder reports).

Herder's essay answers a prize question set by a society in Bern, Switzerland: "How can the truths of philosophy become more universal and useful for the benefit of the people?" This question was conceived in the spirit of the *Popularphilosophie* that was competing with school-philosophy in the German-speaking world at the time. Kant himself tended to identify with *Popularphilosophie* at this period, and Herder's selection of this question shows him doing so as well. But in his case the identification would last a lifetime. Philosophy should become relevant and useful for the people as a whole—this is a basic ideal of Herder's philosophy.

Largely in the service of this ideal, Herder's essay argues in favor of two sharp turns in philosophy, turns which would again remain fundamental throughout the rest of his career. The first lies in a rejection of traditional metaphysics, and closely follows an argument of Kant's in *Dreams of a Spirit Seer*. Herder's case is roughly this: (1) Traditional metaphysics, by undertaking to transcend experience (or strictly speaking, and a little more broadly, "healthy understanding," which includes, in addition to empirical knowledge, also ordinary morality, intuitive logic, and mathematics), succumbs to unresolvable contradictions between claims, and hence to the Pyrrhonian skeptical problem of an equal plausibility on both sides requiring a suspension of judgment ("I am writing for Pyrrhonists," Herder says). Moreover (Herder goes on to add in the *Fragments* of 1767–8), given the truth of a broadly empiricist theory of concepts, much of the terminology of traditional metaphysics turns out to lack the basis in experience that is required in order even to be meaningful, and hence is meaningless (the illusion of meaningfulness arising through the role of *language*, which spins on, creating illusions of meaning, even after the empirical conditions of meaning have been left behind).[5] (2) Traditional metaphysics is not only, for these reasons, useless; it is also *harmful*, because it distracts its adherents from the matters which should be their focus: empirical nature and human society. (3) By contrast, empirical knowledge (or strictly speaking, and a little more broadly, "healthy understanding") is free of these problems. Philosophy should therefore be based on and continuous with this.

Herder's second sharp turn concerns ethics. Here again he is indebted to the precritical Kant, but he also goes somewhat further beyond him. Herder's basic claims are these: (1) Morality is fundamentally more a matter of sentiments than of cognitions. (Herder's sentimentalism is not crude, however; in subsequent works such as the *Critical Forests* and *On the Cognition* he acknowledges that cognition plays an important role in morality as well.) (2) Cognitivist theories of morality—of the sort espoused in this period by Rationalists such as Wolff, but also by many other philosophers before and since (for example, Plato and the critical Kant)—are therefore based on a mistake, and so useless as means of moral enlightenment or improvement. (3) But (and here Herder's theory moves beyond Kant's), worse than that, they are actually *harmful* to morality, because they weaken the moral sentiments on which morality really rests. In *This Too a Philosophy of History* and *On the Cognition* Herder suggests several reasons why: (a) Abstract theorizing weakens sentiments *generally*, and hence moral sentiments in particular (this is perhaps Herder's least interesting reason). (b) The cognitivists' theories turn out to be so *strikingly* implausible that they bring morality itself into disrepute, people reacting to them roughly along the lines: "If this is the best that even the *experts* can say in explanation and justification of morality, then morality must certainly be a sham, and I may as well ignore it and do as I please." (c) Such theories distract people from recognizing, and working to reinforce, the *real* foundations of morality: not an imaginary theoretical insight of some sort, but a set of causal mechanisms that inculcate and sustain the moral sentiments. (4) More positively, Herder accordingly turns instead to discovering theoretically and promoting in practice just such a set of causal mechanisms. In *How Philosophy Can Become* he mainly emphasizes forms of education and an emotive type of preaching. But elsewhere he identifies and promotes a much broader set of mechanisms as well, including: the influence of morally exemplary individuals; morally relevant laws; and literature (along with other forms of art). Literature is a special focus of Herder's theory and practice here. He sees literature as exerting a moral influence in several ways—for instance, not only through fairly direct moral instruction, but also through the literary perpetuation (or creation) of morally exemplary individuals (e.g. Jesus in the New Testament), and the exposure of readers to other people's inner lives and the consequent enhancement of their sympathies for them (a motive which lies behind Herder's epoch-making publication of the *Popular Songs* [*Volkslieder*] [1774], a collection of translations of poems from peoples around the world). Herder's development of this theory and practice of moral pedagogy was lifelong and tireless.

4. Philosophy of Language, Interpretation, and Translation

The *Treatise on the Origin of Language* from 1772 is Herder's best-known work in the philosophy of language by far. However, it is in certain respects both unrepresentative and inferior in comparison with other works, such as the *Fragments* and *On the Cognition*, and should not monopolize attention.

The *Treatise on the Origin* is primarily concerned with the question whether the origin of language can be explained in purely natural, human terms or (as Süßmilch had recently argued) only in terms of a divine source. Herder argues in support of the former position and against the latter. His argument is quite persuasive (especially when supplemented on its positive side from the *Fragments*). But this argument is unlikely to, and should not, constitute a modern philosopher's main reason for interest in Herder's views about language—deriving its zest, as it does, from a religious background that is, or should be, no longer ours.

Of far greater modern relevance are three related theories which Herder develops: a philosophy of language concerning the very nature of language, thought, and meaning; a theory of interpretation; and a theory of translation. These theories are found scattered through a large number of Herder's works. The following are their main features:

Philosophy of Language: Language, Thought, Meaning

Already in the mid-1760s—for example, in *On Diligence in Several Learned Languages* (1764) and the *Fragments* (1767–8)—Herder began advancing three fundamental theses in this area:

(1) Thought is essentially dependent on, and bounded in scope by, language—i.e. one can only think if one has a language, and one can only think what one can express linguistically.[6] (To his credit, Herder normally refrains from a more extreme, but philosophically untenable, version of this thesis, favored by some of his successors, which simply *identifies* thought with language, or with inner language.)

(2) Meanings or concepts are—not the sorts of things, in principle autonomous of language, with which much of the philosophical tradition has equated them, e.g. the referents involved, Platonic forms, or mental ideas, but instead—*usages of words*.[7]

(3) Conceptualization is intimately bound up with (perceptual and affective) sensation. More precisely, according to Herder's quasi-empiricist theory of concepts, sensation is the source and basis of all our concepts, but we are able to achieve non-empirical concepts by means of a sort of metaphorical extension from the empirical ones—so that all of our concepts ultimately depend on sensation in one way or another.[8]

The first two of these theses dramatically overturned the sort of dualistic picture of the relation between language, on the one hand, and thought/meaning, on the other, that had predominated during the seventeenth and eighteenth centuries. They thereby essentially founded the philosophy of language as we still know it today. Hamann has often been credited with introducing something like these two revolutionary theses and then passing them on to Herder (e.g. by Isaiah Berlin). But that is a mistake; Herder was already committed to them in the mid-1760s, Hamann only much later and under Herder's influence.

The third thesis, quasi-empiricism, would be far less widely accepted by philosophers of language today. However, it may well be correct too. (Contrary to first appearances, it need not conflict with thesis (2), the equation of meanings with word-usages. And the most likely modern ground for skepticism about it, namely a Fregean-Wittgensteinian anti-psychologism concerning meaning that is popular today, may well itself be mistaken.)

In addition to making a fundamental contribution to the philosophy of language, these three theses also underpin Herder's theories of interpretation and translation (as we are about to see).[9]

Theory of Interpretation

Herder's theory of interpretation rests on (and also in a way supports) a certain epoch-making insight:

(1) Whereas such eminent Enlightenment philosopher-historians as Hume and Voltaire had normally still held that, as Hume put it, "mankind are so much the same in all times and places that history informs us of nothing new or strange," Herder discovered, or at least saw more clearly than anyone before him, that this was false, that peoples from different historical periods and cultures vary *tremendously* in their concepts, beliefs, (perceptual and affective) sensations, and so forth.[10] He also recognized that similar, albeit usually less dramatic, variations occur even between individuals within a single period and culture. These two positions are prominent in many of Herder's works.[11] Let us call them together his principle of *radical difference*.

(2) Given this principle of radical difference, and the gulf that consequently often initially divides an interpreter's own thought from that of the person he wants to interpret, interpretation is often an extremely *difficult* task, requiring extraordinary efforts on the part of the interpreter.[12] (Note that, to his credit, Herder does not draw the more extreme—and misguided—conclusion to which some more recent philosophers, such as Donald Davidson, have been tempted that it would be *impossible*.)

(3) In particular, the interpreter often faces, and needs to resist, a temptation falsely to *assimilate* the thought which he is interpreting to someone else's,

especially his own. (This theme is prominent in *This Too a Philosophy of History*, for example.)

How, given these challenges, is the interpreter supposed to achieve accurate interpretation? Herder's answer comprises several points:

(4) The three above-mentioned theses with which he founds the philosophy of language undergird his whole theory of interpretation and entail certain aspects of the answer to the question just posed. It is an implication of Herder's thesis that all thought is essentially dependent on and bounded by language that an interpreted subject's language is in a certain sense bound to be a reliable indicator of the nature of his thought, so that the interpreter at least need not worry that the interpreted subject might be entertaining ineffable thoughts or thoughts whose character is systematically distorted by his expression of them in language. It is an implication of Herder's thesis that meaning consists in word-usage that interpretation essentially and fundamentally requires pinning down an interpreted subject's word-usages, and thereby his meanings. Finally, it is an implication of Herder's quasi-empiricist thesis concerning concepts that an interpreter's understanding of an interpreted subject's concepts must include somehow recapturing their basis in the interpreted subject's sensation.

Herder also espouses three further basic principles in interpretation-theory which contribute to answering the question posed above:

(5) A principle of *secularism* in interpretation: Contrary to a practice that was still common in Herder's day in relation to the Bible, the interpretation of texts must never rely on religious assumptions or means, even when the texts are sacred ones, but must instead rely only on secular ones. (This principle is already prominent in Herder's writings on biblical interpretation from the 1760s.)

(6) A principle of *generic* interpretation. In addition to the nature of a work's meanings, interpretation must also pay close attention to the nature of its *genre* (i.e. roughly, a set of general purposes and rules that it aspires to realize and conform to). As in the case of meanings, genres vary from age to age, culture to culture, and even individual to individual, and the interpreter therefore faces, and needs to resist, constant temptations falsely to assimilate a work's genre to others with which he happens to be more familiar (for example, to assimilate Shakespearean "tragedy" to Sophoclean "tragedy," or vice versa). (This principle is already prominent in the *Critical Forests* from 1769, but finds its classic statement in the essay *Shakespeare* from 1773.)

(7) A principle of *methodological empiricism* in interpretation: Interpretation must always be based on, and kept faithful to, exact observations of relevant linguistic (and other) evidence. This applies when the interpreter investigates word-usages in order to discover meanings;[13] when he makes conjectures

about an author's psychology;[14] and when he attempts to pin down a work's genre, or the purposes and rules that constitute it.[15]

So far, these principles will probably seem sensible enough. But beyond them, Herder also advances a further set of interpretive principles which are likely to sound much more "touchy-feely" at first hearing (the first of them rather literally so!). However, I want to suggest that they are in fact on the contrary quite "hard-nosed":

(8) Herder proposes (prominently in *This Too a Philosophy of History*, for example) that the way to bridge radical difference when interpreting is through *Einfühlung*, "feeling one's way in." This proposal has often been thought (for example, by Meinecke) to mean that the interpreter should perform some sort of psychological self-projection onto texts. However, that is emphatically *not* Herder's idea—for that would amount to just the sort of distorting assimilation of the thought in a text to one's own which he is above all concerned to *avoid*. As can be seen from *This Too a Philosophy of History*, what he has in mind is instead an arduous process of historical-philological inquiry. What, though, more specifically, is the cash value of his metaphor of *Einfühlung*? It has at least five components, which are quite various in nature: (a) Note, first of all, that the metaphor implies (once again) that the interpreter typically faces radical difference, a gulf, between his own mentality and that of the interpreted subject, making interpretation a difficult, laborious task (it implies that there is an "in" there that the interpreter must carefully and laboriously "feel his way into"). (b) The metaphor also implies more specifically (*This Too a Philosophy of History* shows) that the "feeling one's way in" should include thorough research not only into a text's use of language but also into its historical, geographical, and social context. (c) It also implies a claim—based on Herder's quasi-empiricist theory of concepts—that in order to understand an interpreted subject's language the interpreter must achieve an imaginative reproduction of his (perceptual and affective) sensations.[16] (d) It also implies (*This Too a Philosophy of History* again shows) that hostility in an interpreter towards the people whom he interprets will generally distort his interpretation, and must therefore be avoided (Herder is equally opposed to excessive *identification* with them for the same reason). (e) Finally, it also implies that the interpreter should strive to develop his grasp of linguistic usage, contextual facts, and relevant sensations to the point where it achieves something like the same immediacy and automaticness that it had for a text's original author and audience when *they* understood the text in light of such factors (so that it acquires for him, as it had for them, the phenomenology more of a *feeling* than a cognition).

(9) In addition, Herder insists (for example, in the *Critical Forests*) on a principle of *holism* in interpretation. This principle rests on several motives,

including the following: (a) Parts of a text taken in isolation are typically ambiguous in various ways (in relation to background linguistic possibilities). In order to resolve such ambiguities, one needs the guidance provided by surrounding text. (b) That problem arises *once* a range of possible linguistic meanings is established for a piece of text. But in the case of a text separated from the interpreter by radical difference, knowledge of such a range itself presents a problem. How is he to pin down the range of possible meanings, i.e. possible usages, for a word? This requires a collation of the word's actual uses and an inference from these to the rules that govern them, i.e. to their usages, a collation which in turn requires looking to remoter contexts in which the same word occurs (other parts of the text, other works in the author's corpus, works by other contemporaries, etc.), or in short: holism. (c) Authors typically write a work *as* a whole, conveying ideas not only in its particular parts but also through the way in which these fit together to make up a whole. Consequently, readings which fail to interpret the work as a whole will miss essential aspects of its meaning—both the ideas in question themselves and meanings of the particular parts on which they shed important light.

(10) In *On Thomas Abbt's Writings*, *On the Cognition*, and elsewhere Herder makes one of his most important innovations: interpretation must supplement its focus on word-usage with attention to authorial *psychology*. Herder implies several reasons for this: (a) As was already mentioned, he embraces a quasi-empiricist theory of concepts which implies that in order to understand an author's concepts an interpreter must imaginatively recapture the author's relevant sensations. (b) As Quentin Skinner has recently emphasized, understanding the linguistic meaning of an utterance or text is only a necessary, not a sufficient, condition for understanding it *tout court*; one needs, in addition, to establish the author's illocutionary *intentions*. For example, I meet a stranger by a frozen lake who tells me, "The ice is thin over there"; I understand his linguistic meaning perfectly; but is he simply informing me?, warning me?, threatening me?, joking? . . . (c) Skinner himself tends to imply that one can determine linguistic meanings prior to establishing authorial intentions. That may *sometimes* be so (e.g. in the example just given). But is it *generally*? Herder implies not. And this seems right, because commonly the linguistic meaning of a formula is ambiguous (in terms of the background linguistic possibilities), and in order to identify the relevant meaning one must turn, not only (as was already mentioned) to larger bodies of text, but also to hypotheses, largely derived therefrom, concerning the author's intentions (e.g. concerning the subject-matter that he intends to treat). This is a further reason why interpreters must invoke psychology. (d) Herder also (as was already mentioned) implies that an author often conveys ideas in his work, not explicitly in its

parts, but rather via these and the way in which they are put together to form a textual whole. It is necessary for the interpreter to capture these ideas, both for their own sakes and because doing so is often essential for resolving ambiguities at the level of the parts. (e) Herder also refers to the second half of his doctrine of radical difference—*individual* variations in mode of thought even within a single period and culture—as a source of the need for psychological interpretation. Why does any special need arise here? Part of the answer seems to be that when one is dealing with a concept that is distinctive of a particular author rather than common to a whole culture, one typically faces a problem of *relative paucity and lack of contextual variety* in the actual uses of the word available as empirical evidence from which to infer the rule for use, or usage, constitutive of its meaning. Hence one needs extra help—and the author's general psychology may provide this.

(11) In *On Thomas Abbt's Writings*, *On the Cognition*, and elsewhere Herder also indicates that interpretation, especially in its psychological aspect, requires the interpreter to use "divination." This is another principle which is liable to sound disturbingly "touchy-feely" at first hearing—in particular, it can sound as though Herder means some sort of prophetic process that has a religious basis and is perhaps even infallible. However, what he really has in mind here is (far more sensibly) a process of hypothesis, based on the meager empirical evidence that is available, but also going well beyond it, and therefore vulnerable to subsequent falsification, and abandonment or revision if falsified.

Finally, Herder also makes an additional important point concerning the general nature of interpretation:

(12) After Herder, the question was explicitly raised whether interpretation is a science or an art. Herder does not himself explicitly raise or address this question. But his strong inclination would clearly be to say that it is *like* rather than unlike natural science. He has several reasons for such an inclination: (a) He assumes (as indeed did virtually everyone at this period) that the meaning of an author's text is as much an *objective* matter as the subjects investigated by the natural scientist. (b) The *difficulty* of interpretation which results from radical difference, and the consequent need for a *methodologically subtle* and *laborious* approach to interpretation in many cases, make for further points of similarity between interpretation and natural science. (c) The essential role of "divination," qua *hypothesis*, in interpretation constitutes yet a further point of similarity between interpretation and natural science. Moreover, (d) even the subject-matter of interpretation is not, in Herder's view, sharply different from that dealt with by natural science: the latter investigates observable physical processes in nature in order to determine the forces that underlie and produce them, but similarly interpretation

investigates observable human verbal (and non-verbal) physical behavior in order to determine the forces that underlie and produce *it* (Herder explicitly identifying mental conditions, including conceptual understanding, as "forces").[17]

Herder's theory of interpretation had an enormous and beneficial impact on subsequent hermeneutics. His theory was taken over almost in its entirety by Schleiermacher in the latter's much more famous hermeneutics lectures, delivered during the first third of the nineteenth century. Admittedly, Schleiermacher's theory was also directly influenced by sources which he shared with Herder, especially Ernesti. However, such fundamental and famous positions in it as his supplementing of "linguistic" with "psychological" interpretation and his identification of "divination" as the main method of the latter are due entirely to Herder. Moreover, where Herder and Schleiermacher *do* occasionally disagree concerning interpretation, Herder's position almost always turns out to be philosophically superior on close inspection.

By decisively influencing Schleiermacher's hermeneutic theory Herder also exercised an indirect decisive influence on that of Schleiermacher's greatest pupil Boeckh, whose *Encyclopedia and Methodology of the Philological Sciences* (1877) essentially reproduced Schleiermacher's theory with only modest elaborations, and became the standard methodological work for classical scholars and others. Moreover, Boeckh's one significant departure from Schleiermacher's theory, namely his addition of *generic* interpretation to the aspects of interpretation which Schleiermacher had already distinguished, in effect simply took up and incorporated the strong emphasis that Herder had already placed on this.[18]

Theory of Translation

The following are some key theses concerning translation which Herder already developed in the *Fragments* of 1767–8, and which subsequently went on to have an enormous and beneficial impact on both the theory and the practice of translation in Germany:

(1) Translation faces a deep challenge due to the fact that radical mental differences—including in particular, conceptual differences—occur between different historical periods and cultures, and even to some extent between individuals within a single period and culture.

(2) As a result, translation is in many cases an extremely difficult undertaking.

(3) Again as a result, translation commonly confronts a choice between two possible approaches: what Herder calls a "lax" approach (i.e. one in which the

language and thought of the target text are allowed to diverge rather freely from those of the source text) and an "accommodating" approach (i.e. one in which the language and thought of the target text are made to accommodate to those of the source text).

(4) Herder rejects the former approach, largely because it entails sacrificing semantic faithfulness (arguably the most fundamental and commonly accepted goal of translation).

(5) He in particular rejects a certain rationale for it which Dryden and others had advocated, namely that a translation should provide *the work that the author would have written had his native language not been the one he actually had but instead the target language*. Herder objects to this that in such a case as that of translating Homer, for example, the author *could not* have written his work in the modern target language.

(6) So Herder urges that the translator should instead err in the other direction, towards "accommodating."

But how is this to be achieved?

(7) One necessary means to achieving it which Herder identifies is *interpretive* expertise in the translator. So Herder requires this.

(8) Another, much less obvious, means is a certain vitally important technique which Herder develops for overcoming conceptual discrepancies between the source language and the target language. That might seem simply impossible (indeed, some recent philosophers, such as Donald Davidson, have mistakenly assumed that it would be). But Herder, drawing on his novel philosophy of language, finds a solution: Since meanings or concepts are word-usages, in order to reproduce (or at least optimally approximate) in the target language a concept from the source language which the target language currently lacks, the translator should take the closest corresponding word in the target language and "bend" its usage for the course of the translation in such a way as to make it mimic the usage of the source word. This technique essentially requires that the source word be translated uniformly across its multiple occurrences in a work (and also that the single target word chosen not be used to translate any other source words). Such an approach is far from being common in translation practice, so far indeed that it is rarely found in translations. However, Herder scrupulously uses it in his own translations, as does an important subsequent tradition which has followed him in adopting it (including Schleiermacher, Rosenzweig, and Buber).

(9) Herder is well aware that using this "bending" approach will inevitably make for translations that are more difficult to read than those that can be produced by a more "lax" method (e.g. by using multiple words in the target language to translate a single word in the source language). However, he

considers this price well worth paying in order to achieve maximal semantic accuracy.

(10) Another key means which Herder espouses is to complement the goal of semantic faithfulness with that of faithfulness to the *musical form* of a literary work (e.g. meter and rhyme). As might be expected, his motives for doing this are partly extra-semantic: in particular, aesthetic fidelity, and fidelity to the exact expression of feelings which is effected by means of a literary work's musical features. But they are also in part semantic: in his view, musical form and semantic content are strictly inseparable, so that fully realizing even the goal of semantic faithfulness in fact requires that a translation also be faithful to the work's musical form. Why does he believe that form and content are inseparable in this way? He has two main reasons: First, musical forms often carry their own meanings (think, for example, of the humorous and bawdy connotations of the meter/rhyme-scheme of a limerick). Second, as was recently mentioned, Herder believes that musical form is essential to an exact expression of feelings; but, as we saw earlier, he also thinks that feelings are internal to meanings (this is part of the force of his quasi-empiricism in the philosophy of language); so that reproducing a work's musical form in translation turns out to be essential even for accurately conveying the meanings of its words and statements in translation.

(11) In addition to being necessary in order to achieve as fully as possible translation's traditional fundamental goal of exactly reproducing meaning (as well as aesthetic fidelity and fidelity in the expression of feelings), the more "accommodating" sort of translation that has just been described is also necessary, in Herder's view, in order to achieve certain further important goals. One of these lies in a potential that translation has for enriching the target language (both conceptually and in musical forms). Herder argues convincingly that, whereas "lax" translation forgoes this opportunity, "accommodating" translation exploits it.

(12) Another of these further goals lies in expressing, and cultivating in a translation's readers, a cosmopolitan respect for the Other—something which requires that the translation reproduce the Other's meanings and musical forms as accurately as possible.

(13) Herder holds that the preferred "accommodating" sort of translation requires the translator to be in a sense a "creative genius," i.e. skilled and creative enough to satisfy the heavy demands that this sort of translation imposes on him, in particular creative enough to invent the required new conceptual and musical forms in the target language.

(14) Despite his commitment to the central importance of this sort of translation (largely, as we have seen, due to its necessity for achieving translation's

traditional fundamental goal of faithfully reproducing meaning), Herder is also in the end quite liberal about the forms that translation—or interlinguistic transfer more generally, including, for example, what he sometimes distinguishes from "translation [*Übersetzung*]" proper as "imitation [*Nachbildung*]"—can legitimately take. He allows that its possible forms are quite various, and that which one is most appropriate in a particular case will largely depend on the author or genre in question and on the translator's purposes.

Herder's theory of translation (as just summarized), and his demonstration of its viability in practice, for example in his sample translations of Shakespeare in the *Popular Songs* [*Volkslieder*], had an enormous and beneficial impact on a whole generation of German translation theorists and practitioners—including Voss (the great translator of Homer), August Wilhelm Schlegel (the translation theorist, and great translator of Shakespeare), Goethe (an important theorist of translation), Wilhelm von Humboldt (a significant translator and theorist of translation), and Schleiermacher (an important theorist of translation, and Germany's great translator of the Platonic dialogues). Herder's principle of complementing semantic faithfulness with faithfulness in the reproduction of musical form had an especially powerful impact on these successors. His principle of "bending" word-usages in order to cope with conceptual incommensurabilities was less widely followed, but was adopted by Schleiermacher among others.[19]

Herder's philosophies of language, interpretation, and translation owe significant debts to predecessors—for example, his philosophy of language is significantly indebted to Leibniz and Wolff, his theory of interpretation to Ernesti, and his theory of translation to Abbt.[20] However, even his borrowings incorporate important refinements, and his overall contribution is enormous.

5. Role in the Birth of Linguistics and Anthropology

Herder's philosophies of language and interpretation made an important contribution to the birth of two whole academic disciplines which did not yet exist in his day but which we today take for granted. Through emphasizing thought's essential dependence on and bounding by language, the radically different forms of thought supported by different languages, the need for a rigorously empirical approach to the investigation of such differences, and in other ways, Herder made a fundamental contribution to the birth of modern linguistics. That birth occurred above all in two thinkers who were both profoundly influenced by Herder: Friedrich Schlegel, whose main work in this connection is his *On the Language and Wisdom of the Indians* (1808), and Wilhelm von Humboldt, whose main work in this connection is his *The Diversity of Human Language Structures and its Influence on the Mental Development of Mankind* (1836). Besides taking over the insights of Herder's already mentioned, Schlegel and Humboldt were also deeply motivated by two more specific theses that he had advanced in his *Ideas for the Philosophy of History of Humanity*: (1) that because of thought's essential dependence on and bounding by language and the radically different ways of thinking that are supported by different languages, the empirical study of languages in their difference from each other can afford a sort of window onto the radically different ways of thinking in question; and (2) that among the deep differences between languages which require investigation here are deep differences in their grammatical structures.[21]

Less obviously, but no less importantly, Herder's theories about language and interpretation (together with his distinctive values, especially the pluralistic form of cosmopolitanism to be discussed later in this essay) also played a fundamental role in the birth of modern cultural anthropology. Several of Herder's writings, especially the 10th Collection of the *Letters for the Advancement of Humanity*, contain a virtual blueprint for that future discipline. His specific contributions here were many and deep; but they include, for example, his principle of radical difference, his principle of thought's essential dependence on and bounding by language, and his principle of holistic interpretation. The channels through which such contributions influenced the development of the discipline centrally included the following. Franz Boas, the father of American anthropology, was German by birth and education, and had his intellectual roots in the German tradition, including not only Herder himself (whom he sometimes mentions by name) but also other German thinkers who were either directly or indirectly influenced by Herder in profound ways, such as Wilhelm von Humboldt, Steinthal, Bastian, Dilthey, and Wilhelm Wundt. Through Boas, this intellectual inheritance was passed on to his students in American anthropology (including Sapir, Lowie, Kroeber, Benedict, and Mead), and then to their students. On the other side of the Atlantic, Bronislaw Malinowski, the father of modern British anthropology (as a discipline grounded in intensive fieldwork), had deep German intellectual roots that lead back to Herder as well. Malinowski sometimes explicitly mentions Herder and Herder's follower Wilhelm von Humboldt in a positive way. But that is only the tip of the iceberg. Malinowski's father, who held the chair in Slavonic philology at the university Malinowski attended in Poland, was a German-trained expert in philology and comparative grammar with a special interest in collecting folksongs and folklore—an intellectual profile which immediately places him within Herder's sphere of influence. Also, Malinowski himself studied in Leipzig with Wilhelm

Wundt, the author of the massive work *Völkerpsychologie* (1900–9), and indeed even began writing a dissertation there on *Völkerpsychologie*. But Wundt's work has deep Herderian roots: the discipline of *Völkerpsychologie* had originally been founded by Lazarus and Steinthal under the influence of Herder and Wilhelm von Humboldt; Wundt himself frequently cites Herder with warm approval; and indeed it would hardly be an exaggeration to say that Wundt's work is just a sort of grand re-writing of Herder's *Ideas*. In short, Malinowski was deeply steeped in Herder's influence. He subsequently passed on his Herderian intellectual legacy to his students in British anthropology (including Evans-Pritchard, Firth, and Leach).[22]

6. Philosophy of Mind

In *On the Cognition* of 1778 and elsewhere Herder also develops an extremely interesting and influential position in the philosophy of mind. The following are some of its central features.

Herder's position is uncompromisingly *naturalistic* and *anti-dualistic* in intent. In *On the Cognition* he tries to erase the traditional sharp division between the mental and the physical in two specific ways: First, he advances a theory that minds consist in *forces* [*Kräfte*] which manifest themselves in people's bodily behavior—just as physical nature contains forces which manifest themselves in the behavior of bodies. (The general notion of mental "forces" was not entirely new with Herder, but can already be found before him in Rationalists such as Wolff and Süßmilch.) He is officially agnostic on the question of what force is, except for conceiving it as something apt to produce a type of bodily behavior, and as a real source thereof (not merely something reducible thereto). This, strictly speaking, absolves his theory from certain common characterizations and objections (for example, Beiser and Nisbet's characterization/objection that it is "vitalist"). But it also leaves his theory with enough content to have great virtues over rival theories: (1) The theory ties mental states conceptually to corresponding types of bodily behavior—which seems correct, and therefore marks a point of superiority over dualistic theories, and indeed over mind-brain identity theories as well. (2) On the other hand, the theory avoids *reducing* mental states to bodily behavior—which again seems correct, in view of such obvious facts as that we can be, and indeed often are, in particular mental states that happen to receive no behavioral manifestation, and which hence marks a point of superiority over outright behaviorist theories.

Second, Herder also tries to explain the mind in terms of the phenomenon of *irritation* [*Reiz*], a phenomenon which had recently been identified by

Haller, and which is paradigmatically exemplified by muscle fibers contracting in response to direct physical stimuli and relaxing upon their removal—in other words, a phenomenon which, while basically physiological, also seems to exhibit a transition to mental characteristics. There is an ambiguity in Herder's position here: Usually, he wants to resist physicalist reductionism, and so would be reluctant to say that irritation is purely physiological and fully constitutes mental states. However, in the 1775 draft of *On the Cognition*, and even in some parts of the published version, this *is* his position. And from a modern standpoint, this is arguably a further virtue of his account (though of course we would today want to recast it in terms of different, and much more complex, physiological processes than irritation).

This second line of thought might seem at odds with the first one (forces). But it need not be. For, given Herder's official agnosticism about what forces are, this second line of thought could, so to speak, fill in the "black box" of the hypothesized real forces, namely in physicalist terms. In other words, it turns out (not indeed as a conceptual matter, but as a contingent one) that the real forces in question consist in physiological processes.

Herder's philosophy of mind also advances a thesis that the mind is a *unity*, that there is no sharp division between its faculties. This thesis contradicts theorists such as Sulzer and Kant. However, it was not in itself new with Herder, having already been central to Rationalism, especially Wolff.[23] Where Herder (together with Hamann) is more original is in rejecting the Rationalists' reduction of sensation and volition to cognition; establishing the unity thesis in an empirical rather than apriorist way; and adding a normative dimension to it—this is not only how the mind *is* but also how it *ought* to be. This last feature can sound incoherent, since if the mind is this way by its very nature, what sense can there be in prescribing to people that it should be so rather than otherwise? However, Herder's idea is in fact the coherent one that, while the mind is indeed this way by its very nature, people sometimes behave as though one faculty could be abstracted from another, and try to effect such an abstraction, but this then leads to various malfunctions, and should therefore be avoided.

Herder's overall thesis of the mind's unity rests on three more specific doctrines concerning intimate mutual involvements between mental faculties, and malfunctions that arise from striving against them, doctrines which are in large part empirically motivated and hence lend the overall thesis a sort of empirical basis:

A first concerns the relation between thought and language: Not only does language of its very nature express thought (an uncontroversial point), but also (as noted earlier) for Herder thought is dependent on and bounded by language. Herder largely bases this further claim on empirical grounds (for example, concerning how children's thought develops in step with language acquisition). The normative aspect of his position here is that attempts (in the manner of some metaphysics, for example) to cut language free from the constraints of thought, or vice versa, lead to nonsense.

A second area of intimate mutual involvement concerns cognition and volition, or affects. The claim that volition is and should be based on cognition is not particularly controversial. But Herder also argues the converse, that all cognition is and should be based on volition, on affects—and not only on such relatively anemic ones as the impulse to know the truth, but also on much less anemic ones. He is especially concerned to combat the idea that *theoretical work* in philosophy or the sciences is or should be detached from volition, from affects. In his view, it never really is even when it purports to be, and attempts to make it so merely impoverish and weaken it. His grounds for this whole position are again mainly empirical in nature.

A third area of intimate mutual involvement concerns thought and sensation. Conceptualization and belief, on the one hand, and sensation, on the other, are intimately connected according to Herder. Thus, he advances the quasi-empiricist theory of concepts mentioned earlier, which entails that all our concepts (and hence also all our beliefs) ultimately depend in one way or another on sensation. But conversely, he also argues (anticipating much important twentieth-century work in philosophy) that there is a dependence in the other direction, that the character of our sensations depends on our concepts and beliefs. Normatively, he sees attempts to violate this interdependence as inevitably leading to intellectual malfunction—for example, as has already been mentioned, he thinks that metaphysicians' attempts to cut entirely free from the empirical origin of our concepts lead to meaninglessness. His grounds for this whole position are again largely empirical in character.

In a further seminal move in the philosophy of mind Herder argues that (linguistic) meaning is fundamentally social—so that thought and other aspects of human mental life (since these are essentially articulated in terms of meanings), and therefore also the very self (since this is essentially dependent on thought and other aspects of human mental life, and moreover defined in its specific identity by theirs), are so too. Herder's version of this position seems intended only as an empirically-based causal claim. It has since fathered a long tradition of attempts to generate more ambitious cases for stronger versions of the claim that meaning—and hence also thought and the very self—is at bottom socially constituted (for example, in Hegel, Wittgenstein, Kripke, Burge, and Brandom). However, it may well be that these more ambitious cases and versions do not work, and that Herder's original version is exactly what should be accepted.

Herder also, in tension though not contradiction with this principle of sociality, holds that (even within a single period and culture) human minds are as a rule deeply *individual*, deeply different from each other—so that in addition to a generalizing psychology we also need a psychology oriented to individuality. This is an important idea which has strongly influenced many subsequent continental thinkers (for example, Schleiermacher, Nietzsche, Proust, Sartre, and Manfred Frank). Herder himself advances it only as an empirical rule of thumb. By contrast, a prominent strand in Schleiermacher and Frank purports to establish it as an a priori universal truth. However, Herder's original version is again arguably the more plausible one.[24]

Finally, like predecessors in the Rationalist tradition and Kant, Herder sharply rejects the Cartesian idea of the mind's self-transparency—instead insisting that much of what occurs in the mind is unconscious, so that self-knowledge is often deeply problematic. This is another compelling position which has had a strong influence on subsequent thinkers.

This whole Herderian philosophy of mind owes much to predecessors, especially ones in the Rationalist tradition. But it is also in many ways original. The theory is important in its own right. And it exercised an enormous influence on successors (for example, on Hegel in connection with anti-dualism, the role of physical behavior in mental conditions, faculty-unity, and the sociality of meaning, thought, and self; on Schleiermacher in connection with anti-dualism and faculty-unity; and on Nietzsche in connection with the interdependence of cognition and volition, or affects, the individuality of the mind and the consequent need for an individualistic psychology, and the mind's lack of self-transparency).

7. Aesthetics

In the *Critical Forests* (1769, though the important fourth part was not published until the middle of the nineteenth century) Herder initially set out to argue for the following aesthetic theory: whereas music is a mere succession of objects in time, and sculpture and painting are merely spatial, poetry has a sense, a soul, a force; whereas music, sculpture, and painting belong solely to the senses (to hearing, feeling, and vision, respectively), poetry not only depends on the senses but also relates to the imagination; whereas music, sculpture, and painting employ only *natural* signs, poetry uses *voluntary and conventional* signs.

This theory was subsequently taken over (with only minor modifications) by Schleiermacher in his aesthetics lectures, and it has sometimes been touted as Herder's main achievement in aesthetics (for example, by Norton). But it is a naive theory, and Herder's real achievements in aesthetics are other than and contrary to it.

As we saw earlier, Herder's philosophy of language is committed to the two doctrines that thought is essentially dependent on and bounded by language, and that meaning is word-usage. This invites certain questions. These doctrines make a plausible break with an Enlightenment assumption that thought and meaning are in principle autonomous of whatever material, perceptible expressions they may happen to receive. Following Charles Taylor, we might call such a move one to "expressivism." But what form should expressivism take *exactly*? Is the dependence of thought and meaning on external symbols strictly one on *language* (in the usual sense of "language")? Or is it not rather a dependence on a broader range of symbolic media including, besides language, also such things as painting, sculpture, and music—so that a person might be able to entertain thoughts which he was not able to express in language but only in some other symbolic medium? Let us call the former position *narrow expressivism* and the latter *broad expressivism*.

Also, is Herder's own position narrow expressivism or broad expressivism? It might seem at first sight that his two doctrines themselves already answer this question in favor of narrow expressivism because of their reference to "language" and "words." However, matters are not quite so simple. For one thing, such terms easily lend themselves to broadened uses which might include media beyond language in the usual sense. For another thing, precisely such a broadening actually occurs in a philosopher closely connected with Herder: Hamann. In his *Metacritique on the Purism of Pure Reason* (written and circulated in 1784, but not published until 1800), Hamann is no less *verbally* committed to the two doctrines in question than Herder. But he embraces broad expressivism. And he does so quite consistently, because he understands the terms "language" and "word" as they occur in the doctrines in unusually wide senses—for example, he explicitly includes as forms of the "language" on which he says thought depends not only language in the usual sense but also painting, drawing, and music.

Nonetheless, Herder's considered position *is* in fact the narrow expressivism that his two doctrines initially seem to suggest (so that his verbal sharing of them with Hamann in fact masks a significant difference of philosophical position between the two men).

Moreover, after much wrestling with the subject, Herder eventually developed a particularly compelling version of narrow expressivism. The key work in this connection is again the *Critical Forests*. By the time of writing this work, Herder was already committed to the two doctrines in question, and, as this would suggest, from the start in the work he is committed to narrow expressivism. However, his commitment to it is initially unsatisfactory and even inconsistent. For one thing, it initially takes the extreme and implausible form of denying to the non-linguistic arts any capacity to express thoughts *autonomously* of language by denying that they can express thoughts *at all*. This is the force of the naive theory recently described which the work initially set out to develop. Adding outright inconsistency to this unsatisfactoriness, Herder is from the start in the work also committed to saying (far more plausibly) that visual art often *does* express thoughts—for example, he intervenes in a quarrel between Lessing and Winckelmann on the question of whether linguistic art (especially poetry) or visual art (especially sculpture) is expressively superior *in ways which tend to support Winckelmann's case for visual art*. This unsatisfactoriness and inconsistency mainly result from Herder's oversight of a single fact: that it is perfectly possible to reconcile narrow expressivism with the attribution of thoughts to non-linguistic art, namely *by insisting that the thoughts expressed by non-linguistic art must be derivative from and bounded by the artist's capacity for linguistic expression*. However, by the time Herder writes the later parts of the *Critical Forests*, he has found this solution. Thus in the third part, focusing on a particularly instructive example, he notes that the pictorial representations on Greek coins are typically allegorical in nature. And by the time of writing the fourth part he is prepared to say something similar about much painting as well, writing there, for example, of "the sense, the allegory, the story/history which is put into the whole of a painting." By 1778 he extends this account to sculpture as well. Thus in the *Plastic* of 1778 he abandons the merely sensualistic conception of sculpture that had predominated in the *Critical Forests* and instead argues that sculpture is essentially expressive of, and therefore needs to be interpreted by, a *soul*, but this no longer forces him into unfaithfulness to his principle that thought is dependent on, and bounded by, language, for he now conceives the thoughts expressed by sculpture to have a linguistic source: "The sculptor stands in the dark of night and gropes towards the forms of gods. *The stories of the poets are before and in him*." Subsequently, in the *Theological Letters* (1780–1) and the *Letters for the Advancement of Humanity*, Herder extends the same solution to music as well.

In the considered position at which he eventually arrives Herder also implies that "non-linguistic" art is dependent on thought and language in another way: In the fourth part of the *Critical Forests* he develops the point (already alluded to earlier in this essay) that human perception is of its nature infused with concepts and beliefs, and consequently with language—which of course implies that the same is true of the perception of "non-linguistic" artworks in particular. So "non-linguistic" art is really doubly dependent on thought and language: not only for the thoughts that it *expresses* but also for those that it *presupposes* in perception.

With Herder's achievement of this refined form of narrow expressivism and Hamann's articulation of his broad expressivism, there were now two plausible but competing theories available. Nineteenth-century theorists (e.g. Hegel, Schleiermacher, and Dilthey) would subsequently be deeply torn between them, and the dispute remains an important one today. While the philosophical issues involved are difficult, I believe that Herder's position is the correct one.[25]

Since for Herder thought and language play important roles not only in linguistic but also in "non-linguistic" art, both for him present similar interpretive challenges, requiring similar interpretive solutions. One aspect of this which deserves special emphasis is *genre*.

Herder believes, plausibly, that a work of art is always written or made to exemplify a certain genre, and that it is vitally important for the interpreter to identify its genre in order to understand it. Herder's basic conception of genre is that it consists in an overall purpose together with certain rules of composition dictated thereby. For Herder, genres are in large measure socially pregiven, but they always play their role in a work via the intention of the artist (not autonomously thereof), and he is not inexorably locked into them but rather can and sometimes does modify them.

Why does Herder believe that it is vitally important to identify a work's genre correctly in order to understand the work properly? He has three main reasons (all good ones): First, grasping a work's genre is itself an essential constituent of understanding the work and its contents (in much the same way as we would today say that grasping a sentence's illocutionary force is itself an essential constituent of understanding the sentence and its contents). Second, because an author intends his work to exemplify a certain genre, there will normally be aspects of the work's meaning which are expressed, not explicitly in any of its parts, but rather through its intended exemplification of the genre. For instance, Lessing had argued that the purpose of Aesop's fables as a genre was to illustrate through a concrete example a universal moral principle, whereas Herder argues that it was instead to illustrate general rules of life, experience, or prudence—so the full interpretation of any particular fable must include either the idea of a universal moral principle (if Lessing is right) or the idea of a general rule of life, experience, or prudence (if Herder is right). Or to cite a "non-linguistic" example, Herder argues that ancient Egyptian sculpture (unlike Greek) had the purpose as a genre of expressing certain ideas about death and eternity—so that the full interpretation of a piece of Egyptian sculpture must include this aspect of its meaning deriving from the genre. Third, correctly identifying the genre is also vitally important for accurately interpreting things that *are* expressed explicitly in parts of a work. Hence, for example, in the *Critical Forests* Herder argues that in order to achieve a proper understanding of "ridiculous" passages in Homer (such as the Thersites episode in *Iliad*, book 2) it is essential to understand them in light of the nature of the whole text and their contribution thereto.

Just as Herder insists on a scrupulous methodological empiricism in interpretation generally, so he insists on it in determining genres in particular. He therefore sharply rejects apriorism here—not only the absolute apriorism of refusing in one's definition of a genre to be guided by the observation of examples at all, but also the more seductive relative apriorism of allowing oneself to be guided by the observation of examples but excluding from these particular cases, or even whole classes of cases, to which the resulting genre-conception is to be applied in interpretation. The latter procedure is still disastrous, in Herder's view, because the superficial appearance of a similar genre shared by different historical periods or cultures, or even by different authors within one period and culture, or indeed even by a single author in one work and the same author in another commonly in fact masks vitally important differences. Herder identifies this sort of misguided apriorism in the definition of genres in many areas of interpretation. For example, in the essay *Shakespeare* (1773) he detects it in the French critics' approach to tragedy, an approach which assumes the universal validity of Aristotelian genre-rules that were originally derived exclusively from ancient tragedies (the critics sometimes even overlooking this empirical derivation), and consequently assumes that they provide an appropriate yardstick for interpreting Shakespearean tragedy as well, whereas the latter's genre-conception is in fact quite different. And in *This Too a Philosophy of History* and other pieces he detects it in Winckelmann's treatment of ancient Egyptian sculpture: Winckelmann implicitly assumes the universal validity of a genre-conception for sculpture which he has derived from the Greeks, namely one dominated by the genre-purpose of a portrayal of this-worldly life and beauty, and he then applies this in the interpretation of Egyptian sculpture, where the genre-conception is in fact quite different, in particular involving a contrary genre-purpose of conveying ideas of death and eternity.

In addition, Herder emphasizes that getting questions of genre right is vitally important not only for the correct *interpretation* of artworks, but also for their correct critical *evaluation*. The French critics not only make an *interpretive* mistake when they go to Shakespeare with a genre dogmatically in mind that was not his, but they also, on this basis, make an *evaluative* one: because they falsely assume that he somehow must be aspiring to realize the genre-purpose and -rules which Aristotle found in ancient tragedy, they fault him for failing to realize them, while at the same time they overlook the quite different genre-purpose and -rules which he really aspires to realize and his success in realizing these. Similarly, Winckelmann not only makes an *interpretive* mistake when he implicitly imputes to the Egyptians a Greek genre-conception for sculpture that was not theirs, but also, on this basis, an *evaluative* one: because he falsely assumes that the Egyptians somehow must be aspiring to realize the Greek genre-purpose and -rules, he faults them for failing to realize these, and at the same time he overlooks their success in realizing the very different genre-purpose and -rules which they really do aspire to realize.[26]

Nothing has yet been said about *beauty*, a subject that is often thought to be the central concern of aesthetics. Herder has several interesting ideas on this subject too. A first, which he develops in the *Critical Forests*, concerns the very concept of beauty. He argues, plausibly, that this concept's origin lies in *visual* experience, but that it has been extended from that domain to cover virtually "everything that has a pleasurable effect on the soul," that in this sense "sight . . . allegorizes the images, the representations, the conceits of the soul," and so *beauty* becomes our most general term of approval for whatever we find pleasing in relation to any of the senses and indeed to mental life more generally.

A second interesting idea of Herder's concerning beauty (prima facie somewhat at odds with the first one, but potentially reconcilable with it, and perhaps even encouraged by it) occurs in his later work the *Calligone*. There he suggests, in opposition to the great emphasis traditionally placed on beauty in the philosophy of art, that beauty is not in fact nearly as essential to art as it is often taken to be. In particular, he argues that art is much more essentially a matter of *Bildung*—cultural formation or education (especially in moral respects).

A third important idea of Herder's concerning beauty (both as it relates to art and more generally) is that standards of beauty vary greatly from one historical period and culture to another. This at least is his usual position, from early works such as *On the Change of Taste* to late ones such as the *Calligone* (where he invokes it against Kant's *Critique of Judgment*). Occasionally, a counterstrand surfaces in Herder's works in which he argues for a deeper unity in standards of beauty across historical periods and cultures (for example, in the *Critical Forests*). However, his former, usual position seems to be his considered one, and is much the more plausible one.

Finally, a position closely connected with the point recently mentioned that *Bildung* is the fundamental role of the arts: In *On the Effect of Poetic Art on the Ethics of Peoples in Ancient and Modern Times* (1778) and again later in the *Calligone* Herder argues more specifically that the fundamental role of the arts both has been historically and moreover should be one of moral character formation. He has a nuanced account of how the arts do and should perform this function. For example, in *On the Influence of the Beautiful Sciences on the Higher Sciences* (1781) he specifies three ways in which poetry and literature promote moral character formation: First, they do so "through light rules," in other words through subtly conveying ethical principles directly in explicit or implicit ways. Second, and more importantly, they do so by presenting in an attractive light good moral exemplars for people to emulate: "still better, through good examples." Third, they also convey a broad range of practical experience relevant to the formation of moral character which would otherwise have to be acquired, if at all, by the more arduous route of first-hand experience. In the *Calligone* Herder also notes concerning non-linguistic art that music has a power to affect moral character for good or ill depending on the principles with which it is associated, and that visual art has a power to make moral ideals attractive by presenting them blended with physical beauty. Herder's conception that it is and should be the primary function of art to form moral character serves him as a criterion for evaluating artworks. Thus when he observes in *On the Effect* that in contrast to earlier poetry modern poetry has typically lost this function, he means this as a serious criticism of modern poetry. And he even applies this criterion as a ground for criticizing certain works by his friends Goethe and Schiller which he considers immoral or amoral in content.

8. Philosophy of History

Herder's philosophy of history appears mainly in two works: *This Too a Philosophy of History* and the later *Ideas*.

His philosophy of history is initially likely to seem striking and interesting mainly for its development of a teleological conception of history as the progressive realization of "reason" and "humanity"—a conception which anticipated and strongly influenced Hegel, among others. However, this conception is highly dubious on reflection, and is arguably *not* one of Herder's main achievements in this area.

His most intrinsically important achievement in this area arguably rather lies in his development of the thesis already mentioned earlier—contradicting such Enlightenment philosopher-historians as Hume and Voltaire—that there exist radical mental differences between different historical periods (and cultures), that people's concepts, beliefs, sensations, etc. differ in deep ways from one period (or culture) to another. This thesis is already prominent in *On the Change of Taste* (1766) and persists throughout Herder's career. It had an enormous influence on successors such as the Schlegels, Schleiermacher, Hegel, Nietzsche, and Dilthey.

Herder makes the empirical exploration of the realm of mental diversity posited by this thesis the very core of the discipline of history. For, as has often been noted, he takes relatively little interest in the so-called "great" political and military deeds and events of history, focusing instead on the "innerness" of history's participants. This choice is deliberate and self-conscious. Because of it, *psychology and interpretation* inevitably take center-stage in the discipline of history for Herder.

Herder has deep philosophical reasons for this choice, and hence for assigning psychology and interpretation a central role in history. To begin with, he has *negative* reasons directed against traditional political-military history. Why *should* history focus on the "great" political and military deeds and events of the past, after all? There are several possible answers: (1) A first would be that they are fascinating or morally edifying. But Herder will not accept this. For one thing, he denies that mere fascination or curiosity is a sufficiently serious motive for doing history. For another thing, his anti-authoritarianism, anti-militarism, and borderless humanitarianism cause him to find the acts of political domination, war, and empire which make up the vast bulk of these "great" deeds and events not morally edifying but morally *repugnant*.[27]

This leaves two other types of motivation that might be appealed to for doing the sort of history in question: (2) because examining the course of such deeds and events reveals some sort of overall *meaning* in history, or (3) because it leads to *efficient causal insights which enable us to explain the past and perhaps also predict or control the future*. Herder is again skeptical about these rationales, however. This skepticism is perhaps clearest in the *Older Critical Forestlet* (1767–8) where, in criticism of rationale (2), he consigns the task of "the whole ordering together of many occurrences into a plan" not to the historian but instead to the "creator, . . . painter, and artist," and in criticism of rationale (3), he goes as far as to assert (on the basis of a Hume- and Kant-influenced general skepticism about causal knowledge) that with the search for efficient causes in history "historical seeing stops and prophecy begins." His later writings depart from this early position in some obvious ways, but they also in less obvious ways remain faithful to it. They by no means *officially* stay loyal to the view that history has no discernible meaning; famously, *This Too a Philosophy of History* insists that history does have an overall purpose, and that this fact (though not the *nature* of the purpose) is discernible from the cumulative way in which cultures have built upon one another, and the *Ideas* then goes on to tell a long story to the effect that history's purpose consists in its steady realization of "reason" and "humanity." However, Herder clearly still harbors grave doubts just below the surface. This is visible in *This Too a Philosophy of History* from the work's ironically self-deprecating title; Pyrrhonian-spirited motto; vacillation between several incompatible models of history's direction (progressive?, progressive and cyclical?, merely cyclical?, even regressive?); and morbid dwelling on, and unpersuasive attempt to rebut, the "skeptical" view of history as meaningless "Penelope-work." (A few years later in his *Theological Letters* of 1780–1 Herder would write that history is "a textbook of the nullity of all human things.") It is also visible in the *Ideas* from the fact that Herder's official account there of the purposiveness of history gets contradicted by other passages which insist on the *inappropriateness* of teleological (as contrasted with efficient causal) explanations in history. Herder's official position certainly had a powerful influence on some successors (especially Hegel), but it is this quieter counterstrand of skepticism that represents his better philosophical judgment. Concerning efficient causal insights, Herder's later works again in a sense stay faithful to his skeptical position in the *Older Critical Forestlet*—but they also modify it, and this time for the better philosophically speaking. The mature Herder does not, like the Herder of that early work, rest his case on a *general* skepticism about the role or discernibility of efficient causation in history. On the contrary, he insists that history *is* governed by efficient causation and that we should try to discover as far as possible the specific ways in which it is so. But he remains highly skeptical about the *extent* to which such an undertaking can be successful, and hence about how far it can take us towards real explanations of the past, and towards predicting or controlling the future. His main reason for this skepticism is that major historical deeds and events are not the products of some one or few readily identifiable causal factors (as political and military historians tend to assume), but are rather the products of chance confluences of huge numbers of different causal factors, many of which, moreover, are individually unknown and unknowable by the historian (for example, because in themselves too trivial to have been recorded, or, in the case of psychological factors, because the historical agent failed to make them public, deliberately misrepresented them, or was himself unaware of them due to their submersion in the hidden depths of his mind).[28]

Complementing this *negative* case against the claims of traditional political-military history to be of overriding importance, Herder also has *positive* reasons for focusing instead on the "innerness" of human life in history. (1) One reason is certainly just the sheer interest of this subject-matter (though, as was mentioned previously, that would not be a sufficient reason in his eyes). (2) Another reason is that his discovery of radical diversity in human mentality has shown there to be a much broader, less explored, and more intellectually challenging field for investigation here than previous generations of historians have realized. Two further reasons are moral in nature: (3) He believes, quite plausibly, that studying people's minds through their literature, visual art, etc. generally exposes one to them at their moral best (in sharp contrast to studying their political-military history), so that there are benefits of moral edification to be gleaned here. (4) He has cosmopolitan and egalitarian moral motives for studying people's minds through their literature, visual art, etc.: (in sharp contrast to studying unedifying and elite-focused political-military history) this promises to enhance our sympathies for peoples, and moreover for peoples at all social levels, including lower ones. Finally, doing "inner" history is also important as an instrument for our *non*-moral self-improvement: (5) It serves to enhance our self-understanding. One important reason for this is that it is by, and only by, contrasting one's own outlook with the outlooks of other peoples that one comes to recognize what is universal and invariant in it and what by contrast distinctive and variable. Another important reason is that in order fully to understand one's own outlook one needs to identify its historical origins and how they developed into it (this is Herder's justly famous "genetic method"—first prominently discussed by him in the *Fragments* in connection with language, but also applied by him much more broadly—which subsequently became fundamental to the work of Hegel, Nietzsche, and Foucault). (6) Herder believes that an accurate investigation of the (non-moral) ideals of past ages can serve to enrich our own ideals and happiness. This motive finds broad application in his work. One example is his exploration of past literatures in the *Fragments* largely with a view to drawing from them lessons about how better to develop modern German literature.[29]

Herder's decision to focus on the "innerness" of history's participants, and his consequent emphasis on psychology and interpretation as historical methods, strikingly anticipated and strongly influenced Dilthey. So too did his rationale for this decision, as described above, which is indeed arguably superior to Dilthey's, especially on its positive side. (Dilthey's positive reasons are alarmingly thin—mainly just that our interest in narrative is more fundamental than our interest in explanation; and that we can enrich our drab lives by encountering the different experiences of historical Others—whereas, as we have just seen, Herder's are rich and compelling.)

Finally, Herder is also impressive for having recognized, and, though not solved, at least grappled with, a problem that flows from his picture of history (and intercultural comparison) as an arena of deep variations in human mentality. This is the problem of *skepticism*. He tends to run together *two* problems in this connection: (1) the problem of whether there is any *meaning* to the seemingly anarchic and endless series of changes from epoch to epoch (or culture to culture); (2) the problem that the multiplication of conflicting viewpoints on virtually all subjects that is found in history (or in intercultural comparison) causes, or at least exacerbates, the ancient skeptic's difficulty of unresolvable disputes forcing one to suspend belief. Problem (1) has already been discussed. Here it is problem (2) that concerns us. This is a problem that Troeltsch would make much of in the twentieth century. But Herder had already clearly seen it.

Herder is determined to avoid this sort of skepticism. He has two main strategies for doing so, but they are inconsistent with each other, and neither in the end works: His first strategy is to try to defuse the problem at source by arguing that, on closer inspection, there is much more common ground between different periods and cultures than it allows. This strategy already occurs in the *Critical Forests*, where (as was mentioned earlier) Herder argues that different standards of beauty have an underlying unity, and it plays a central role in the *Ideas*, where in particular "humanity" is presented as a shared ethical value. Herder's second strategy is instead to acknowledge the problem in an unmitigated form and to respond with relativism: especially in *This Too a Philosophy of History* he argues that—at least where questions of moral, aesthetic, and prudential value are concerned—the different positions held by different periods and cultures are equally valid, namely for the periods and cultures to which they belong, and that there can be no question of any preferential ranking between them. The later *Letters for the Advancement of Humanity* vacillates between these two strategies.

Neither of these strategies is satisfactory in the end. The first, that of asserting deep commonalities, is hopeless (notwithstanding its seemingly eternal appeal to empirically underinformed Anglophone philosophers). It flies in the face of the empirical evidence—for example, Herder in this mode sentimentally praises Homer for his "humanity," and thereby lays himself open to Nietzsche's just retort in *Homer's Contest* that what is striking about Homer and his culture is rather their *cruelty*.[30] And indeed, it flies in the face of Herder's own better interpretive judgments about the empirical evidence—for example, his observation in *On the Change of Taste* that basic values have not only changed over the course of history but in some cases actually been inverted (an observation which strikingly anticipates a brilliant insight of Nietzsche's concerning a systematic inversion of Homeric ethical values that occurred in later antiquity with Socrates/Plato and especially Christianity).

Herder's alternative, relativist, strategy is more interesting, but is not in the end satisfactory either (even concerning values, where its prospects look best). There are several potential problems with it. One, which is of considerable historical interest but probably not in the end fatal, is this: Hegel in the *Phenomenology of Spirit* and then Nietzsche in his treatment of Christian moral values saw the possibility that one might accept Herder's insight that there are basic differences in values but nonetheless avoid his relativism by subjecting others' values to an *internal* critique, a demonstration that they are internally inconsistent. For example, Nietzsche (whose version of this idea is the more plausible) traced back such Christian values as love and forgiveness to a contrary underlying motive of resentment [*Ressentiment*]. However, in order to work, such a response would need to show that the inconsistency was *essential* to the values in question, not merely something contingent that could disappear leaving the values consistently held—and this it probably cannot do. A more serious problem with this strategy is rather a twofold one, which Nietzsche again saw: First, we cannot in fact sustain such a relativist indifference vis-à-vis others' values. Do we, for example, *really* think that a moral rule requiring the forcible burning of dead men's wives is no better and no worse than one forbidding it? (As Nietzsche memorably puts the point, "Is life not passing judgment, preferring, being unfair . . . ?") Second, nor does the phenomenon of fundamental value variations *require* us to adopt such an indifference. For, while it may indeed show that there are no universal or objective values, it leaves us with a better alternative to indifference: continuing to hold our values and to judge others' values in light of them *only now in a self-consciously non-universal, non-objective way*. (As Nietzsche puts it, "My judgment is *my* judgment." Or if we reject Nietzsche's extreme individualism, "Our judgment is *our* judgment," for some less-than-universal *us*.)

9. Political Philosophy

Herder is not usually thought of as a political philosopher. But he was one, and moreover one whose political ideals are more admirable, theoretical stances more defensible, and thematic emphases of more enduring relevance than those of any other German philosopher of the period. His most developed treatment of political philosophy occurs relatively late, in a work prompted by the French Revolution of 1789: the *Letters for the Advancement of Humanity* (including the early draft of 1792, which is important for its frank statement of his views about domestic politics).

What are the main features of Herder's political philosophy? Let us begin with his political *ideals*, first in domestic and then in international politics: In domestic politics, the mature Herder is a liberal, a republican, a democrat, and an egalitarian (this, it should be noted, in historical circumstances where such positions were by no means commonplace, and were embraced at a personal cost). His *liberalism* is especially radical in advocating virtually unrestricted freedom of thought and expression (including freedom of worship). He has several reasons for this position: (1) He feels that such freedom belongs to people's moral dignity. (2) He believes that it is essential for individuals' self-realization. (3) As was mentioned earlier, he believes that people's capacities for discerning the truth are very limited and that it is through, and only through, an ongoing contest between opposing viewpoints that the cause of truth gets advanced. (John Stuart Mill would later borrow from these considerations—largely via Wilhelm von Humboldt—to form the core of his case for freedom of thought and expression in *On Liberty*.)[31]

Herder is also committed to *republicanism and democracy* (advocating a much broader franchise than Kant, for example). He has several reasons for this position, ultimately deriving from an egalitarian concern for the interests of all members of society: (1) He feels it to be intrinsically right that the mass of people should share in their government, rather than having it imposed upon them. (2) He believes that this will better serve their *other* interests as well, since government *by* also tends to be government *for*. (3) He in particular believes that it will diminish the warfare that is pervasive under the prevailing autocratic political régimes of Europe, where it benefits the few rulers who decide on it but costs the mass of people dearly.

Finally, Herder's *egalitarianism* also extends beyond this. He does not reject class differences, property, or inequalities of property outright. But he does oppose all hierarchical oppression; argue that all people in society have capacities for self-realization, and must receive the opportunity to fulfill them; and insist that government must intervene to ensure that they do receive it, for example by guaranteeing education and a minimum standard of living for the poor.

Concerning international politics, Herder has often been classified as a "nationalist" or (perhaps even worse) a "German nationalist."[32] Some other philosophers from the period deserve such a characterization (for example, Fichte). But where Herder is concerned it is deeply misleading and unjust. On the contrary, his fundamental position in international politics is a committed *cosmopolitanism*, an impartial concern for *all* human beings. This is a large part of the force of his ideal of "humanity." Hence, for example, in the *Letters* he approvingly quotes Fénelon's remark, "I love my family more than myself; more than my family my fatherland; more than my fatherland humankind.''[33] Moreover, unlike Kant's cosmopolitanism, Herder's is genuine: Kant's cosmopolitanism is vitiated by a set of empirically ignorant and morally inexcusable prejudices that he harbors—in particular, racism, antisemitism, and misogyny. By contrast, Herder's is entirely free of these prejudices, which he indeed works tirelessly to combat.

Herder does indeed *also* insist on respecting, preserving, and advancing national groupings. However, this is entirely unalarming, for the following reasons: (1) For Herder, this is emphatically something that must be done for *all* national groupings *equally* (not just or especially Germany!).[34] (2) The "nation" in question is not racial but linguistic and cultural (in the *Ideas* and elsewhere Herder indeed rejects the very concept of race). (3) Herder does not seek to seal off nations from each other's influence or to keep them static; he recognizes as normal and welcomes interlinguistic and intercultural exchange, as well as linguistic-cultural development. (4) Nor does his commitment to national groupings involve a centralized, militarized state (in the *Ideas* and elsewhere he strongly advocates the disappearance of such a state and its replacement by loosely federated local governments with minimal instruments of force). (5) In addition, his insistence on respecting national groupings is accompanied by the strongest denunciations of military conflict, colonial exploitation, and all other forms of harm between nations; a demand that nations instead peacefully cooperate and compete in trade and intellectual endeavors for their mutual benefit; and a plea that they should indeed actively work to help each other.

Moreover, Herder has compelling reasons for this insistence on respecting national groupings: (1) The deep diversity of values between nations entails that homogenization is ultimately impracticable, only a fantasy. (2) Such diversity also entails that, to the extent that it *is* practicable, it cannot occur voluntarily but only through external coercion. (3) In practice, attempts to achieve it, for example by European colonialism, are moreover coercive from, and subserve, ulterior motives of domination and exploitation. (4) Furthermore, real national variety is positively valuable, both as affording individuals a vital sense of local belonging and in itself.

Indeed, Herder's pluralistic cosmopolitanism is a very important and attractive alternative to the homogenizing forms of cosmopolitanism, based on delusions concerning either the fact or the prospect of universally shared values, which have predominated since the Enlightenment and are still popular today, both among philosophers (especially in the Anglophone world) and in international political organizations such as the United Nations.

It might still be objected that all this does not yet really amount to a political *theory*—such as other philosophers have provided, including some of

Herder's contemporaries in Germany. In a sense that is true, but philosophically defensible; in another sense it is false. It is true in the following sense: There is indeed no grand metaphysical theory underpinning Herder's position—no Platonic theory of forms, no correlation of political institutions with "moments" in a Hegelian Logic, no "deduction" of political institutions from the nature of the self or the will à la Fichte or Hegel, etc. But that is quite deliberate, given Herder's skepticism about such metaphysics. And is this not indeed philosophically a good thing? Nor does Herder have any elaborate account purporting to justify the moral intuitions at work in his political position as a sort of theoretical insight (in the manner of Kant's theory of the "categorical imperative" or Rawls's theory of the "original position," for example). But that is again quite deliberate, given his non-cognitivism in ethics, and his rejection of such theories as both false and harmful. And is he not again right about this, and the absence of such an account therefore again a good thing? Nor is Herder sympathetic with such tired staples of political theory as the state of nature, the social contract, natural rights, the general will, and utopias for the future. But again, he has good specific reasons for skepticism about these things.[35] This, then, is the sense in which the objection is correct; Herder does indeed lack a "political theory" of *these* sorts. But he lacks it *on principle*, and is arguably quite right to do so.

On the other hand, in another sense it is false that he lacks a "political theory." For he *does* have a "political theory" of a different, and arguably much more valuable, sort. First, consistently with his general empiricism, his position in political philosophy is deeply empirically informed. For instance, as can be seen from the *Dissertation on the Reciprocal Influence of Government and the Sciences* (1780), his thesis concerning the importance of freedom of thought and expression, and the competition between views that it makes possible, for producing intellectual progress is largely based on the historical example of ancient Greece, and in particular ancient Athens (as contrasted with later societies which lacked the freedom and competition in question). And in the 1792 draft of the *Letters* he even describes the French Revolution and its attempts to establish a modern democracy as a sort of "experiment" from which we can learn (for example, whether democracy can be successfully extended to nations that are much larger than ancient Athens). Second, in conformity with his general non-cognitivism about morals, he is acutely aware that his political position ultimately rests on moral sentiments—his own and, for its success, other people's as well. For example, in the 10th Collection of the *Letters* he emphasizes that people's moral "dispositions" or "feelings" play a fundamental role as essential supports for his political position's realization. As has been mentioned, this standpoint absolves him of the need to do certain sorts of theorizing. Indeed, it not only precludes the need for cognitivist groundings of the moral intuitions in question, but also promises short, effective solutions to various other problems that might look like real brain-teasers to a cognitivist.[36] However, it also leads him to engage in theorizing of another sort, namely theorizing about how, and by which causal means, people's moral sentiments should be molded in order to realize the ideals of his political position. His discussion of moral "dispositions" in the 10th Collection is an example of such theorizing—concerning the *how*, rather than the causal means. Some of his extensive theorizing about causal means (education, exemplary individuals, laws, literature, etc.) has already been sketched earlier in this essay. *These* two sorts of political theorizing—empirical theorizing and theorizing about moral sentiments—*are* deeply developed in Herder. And they arguably have much more point than the sorts which are not.

In short, to the extent that Herder's political philosophy really is theoretically superficial, it is, to borrow a phrase of Nietzsche's, "superficial—*out of profundity*" (whereas more familiar forms of political philosophy are profound—out of superficiality). And in another, more important, sense it is not theoretically superficial at all.

10. Philosophy of Religion

In Herder's day German philosophy was still deeply committed to the game of trying to reconcile the insights of the Enlightenment, especially those of modern natural science, with religion, and indeed more specifically with Christianity. Leibniz, Kant, Hegel, Schleiermacher, and many others played this game—each proposing some new reconciliation or other. Herder was part of this game as well. This was not a good game for philosophers to be playing. But it was only in the nineteenth century that German philosophy found the courage to cut the Gordian knot and turn from apologetics for religion and Christianity to thoroughgoing criticism of them (the prime examples being Marx and Nietzsche). This situation imposes certain limits on the interest of Herder's philosophy of religion, as on that of the other reconciling philosophers mentioned.

Also, it should be mentioned that while Herder's philosophy of religion was generally very enlightened and progressive in both his early and his late periods, there was a spell in the middle, the years 1771–6 in Bückeburg, during which he fell into the sort of religious irrationalism that is more characteristic of his friend Hamann. This happened as the result of what we would today classify as a mild nervous breakdown (documentable from his correspondence at the time), and should basically be discounted.

Despite these qualifications, Herder did make important contributions to the philosophy of religion—that is, important in terms of their influence, their intrinsic value, or both. One of these (important mainly for its influence) lies in his neo-Spinozism. Herder's sympathetic engagement with Spinoza's work goes back at least as far as 1769. But its main expression is found in *God: Some Conversations* from 1787. Herder published this work in the wake of Jacobi's *On the Doctrine of Spinoza* (1785), in which Jacobi had revealed that the highly respected philosopher, critic, and dramatist Lessing—who was much admired by Herder in particular—had confessed to him shortly before his death that he had abandoned orthodox religious conceptions in favor of Spinozism. Jacobi had himself argued, sharply to the contrary, that Spinozism, and indeed all fundamental reliance on reason, implies atheism and fatalism, and should therefore be rejected in favor of a leap of faith to a conventional Christian theism. Jacobi's work (along with a reply by Moses Mendelssohn) caused a public furor. In *God: Some Conversations* Herder intervened. In this work he supports Lessing's side of the debate by developing a version of "Spinozism" which modifies the original in some significant respects, largely with a view to defusing Jacobi's objections. Herder shares with Spinoza the basic thesis of *monism*, and like Spinoza equates the single, all-encompassing principle in question with God (which of course calls into question Jacobi's charge of atheism). But whereas Spinoza had characterized this single, all-encompassing principle as *substance*, Herder instead characterizes it as *force*, or *primal force*. This fundamental modification involves several further ones which Herder also finds attractive, including the following: (1) Whereas Spinoza had conceived the principle in question as an *inactive thing*, Herder's revision rather turns it into an *activity*. (2) Spinoza's theory had attributed *thought* to the principle in question, but had rejected conceptions that it had *intentions* or was a *mind*. By contrast, Herder claims that it *does* have intentions. And since his general philosophy of mind identifies the mind with force, his identification of the principle in question with force also imports an implication that it *is* a mind (he does not yet quite say this in *God: Some Conversations*, but a few years later in *On the Spirit of Christianity* of 1798 he explicitly describes God as a *Geist*, a mind). In these ways, Herder in effect re-mentalizes Spinoza's God (thereby further undermining Jacobi's charge of atheism). (3) Whereas Spinoza had conceived nature mechanistically, in keeping with his Cartesian intellectual heritage (and had thereby invited Jacobi's charge of fatalism), Herder (though officially still agnostic about what force is) rather tends to conceive the forces at work in nature as *living*, or organic (a conception of them that he mainly owes to Leibniz). (4) Herder believes that Spinoza's original theory contained an objectionable residue of dualism (again inherited from Descartes), in its conception of the relation between God's two known attributes, thought and extension (and similarly, in its conception of the relation between *finite* minds and bodies). By contrast, Herder's own conception of God as a force (and of finite minds as likewise forces) is designed to overcome this alleged residual dualism. For forces are of their very nature expressed in the behavior of extended bodies. (5) Herder also sketches a more detailed account of nature as a system of living forces based in the primal force, God—an account which in particular ascribes an important role in this system to the sort of opposition between forces that is exemplified by the magnet, and characterizes the system as a self-development towards higher and higher forms of articulation.

During the last quarter or so of the eighteenth century and then well into the nineteenth century a wave of neo-Spinozism swept through German philosophy and literature: in addition to Lessing and Herder, further neo-Spinozists included Goethe, Schelling, Hegel, Schleiermacher, Hölderlin, Novalis, and Friedrich Schlegel. This wave was largely a result of Herder's embrace of neo-Spinozism in *God: Some Conversations* (and in Goethe's case, Herder's sympathy with Spinozism even before that work), and it largely took over Herder's modifications of Spinoza's position.

However, Herder's most *intrinsically* valuable contribution to the philosophy of religion rather concerns the interpretation of the Bible. In this connection, as has already been mentioned, he champions a strict *secularism*. This was already his position in the 1760s. At that period he argued firmly, in the spirit of Galileo, for disallowing revelation any jurisdiction over natural science—though he did so not in an anti-religious spirit but in the hope and expectation that an autonomous natural science would confirm religion. And he made a parallel case for the autonomy of *interpretation*: Religious assumptions and means have no business interfering in the interpretation of texts either, even when the texts are sacred ones. Instead, even the Bible must be interpreted as the work of human beings, and by means of the same sorts of rigorous hermeneutic methods that are employed for interpreting other ancient texts—any religious enlightenment coming as a *result* of such interpretation, not entering into the process itself. This whole position remained Herder's considered position in his later period as well.

The general principle that the Bible should be interpreted in the same way as other texts was by no means the commonplace in Herder's day that it has become since, but nor was it new with him. In adopting it he was self-consciously following the lead of several recent Bible scholars—in particular, Ernesti, Michaelis, and Semler. However, Herder's secularism is more consistent and radical than theirs.

This can be seen from a comparison with Ernesti (the most important of the Bible scholars just mentioned, and the one most consistently admired by Herder). Ernesti's great work, *Institutio interpretis Novi Testamenti* (1761), which Herder singles out for special praise, is a key statement of the sort of secularism in question. Initially, the work seems to advocate a secularism identical in spirit to Herder's, arguing that we must interpret biblical books in the same way as profane texts, and *thereby* learn whatever religious truth they contain. However, as the work develops, matters become much cloudier. In this connection, it is important to distinguish two questions which can be asked concerning the relation between divine inspiration and interpretation: (1) May readers of sacred texts rely on a divine inspiration of *themselves* (for example, by the Holy Spirit) bringing them to a correct interpretation rather than on more usual interpretive means? (2) May they assume in interpretation that because *the texts' authors* are divinely inspired the texts must be completely true and therefore also completely self-consistent? When Ernesti develops the details of his position it becomes clear that he has really only advanced as far towards secularism as consistently answering question (1) in the negative, *not question (2)*. His failure to give a consistently negative answer to question (2) lands him in flat contradiction with his official commitment to interpreting sacred texts in exactly the same way as profane texts (for, of course, as he himself implies, in interpreting profane texts we may *not* assume that the texts are throughout true and therefore also self-consistent). It also seems intellectually indefensible in itself—merely a rather transparent refusal to stop, so to speak, "cooking the books" in favor of the Bible when interpreting it. By contrast, the young Herder advances beyond Ernesti in his secularism because he consistently answers *both* questions in the negative, and thereby, unlike Ernesti, achieves a position which is both self-consistent and otherwise intellectually defensible. Moreover, Herder's actual interpretations of the Bible admirably conform to this theoretical position, not only refraining from any reliance on divine inspiration and instead employing normal interpretive techniques, but also frequently attributing false and even inconsistent positions to the Bible (both to the Old and to the New Testaments).

Another noteworthy aspect of Herder's strict secularism in interpretation is his insistence that interpreters of the Bible must resist the temptation to read the Bible as *allegory* (except in those relatively few cases—for example, the parables of the New Testament—where there is clear textual evidence of a biblical author's intention to convey an allegorical meaning). In *On God's Son, the World's Savior* (1797) Herder gives a perceptive general diagnosis of how the temptation to allegorical interpretation arises: over the course of history people's beliefs and values change, leading to discrepancies between the claims made by their traditional texts and their own beliefs and values, but they expect and want to find their traditional texts correct, and so they try to effect a reconciliation of them with their own beliefs and values by means of allegorical readings.

Herder's theoretical commitment to strict secularism in biblical interpretation led him to interpretive discoveries concerning the Bible which were themselves of great importance. For example, concerning the Old Testament, his commitment to applying normal interpretive methods enabled him to distinguish and define the different genres of poetry in the Old Testament in a way that was superior to anything that had been achieved before him. Also, the same commitment, and in particular his consequent readiness to find falsehood and even inconsistency in the Bible, allowed him to make such important interpretive observations as that the ancient Jews' conceptions about death, the afterlife, the mind, and the body had changed dramatically over time. (For these two achievements, see especially *On the Spirit of Hebrew Poetry*.) Again, the same commitment, and in particular Herder's consequent rejection of unwarranted allegorical interpretations, allowed him to substitute for the prevailing interpretation of the Song of Solomon as religious allegory an interpretation of it as simple erotic love poetry which is today generally accepted as correct. Similarly concerning the New Testament, Herder's commitment to applying normal interpretive methods, including his consequent readiness to discover falsehood and inconsistency, enabled him to treat the authors of the four gospels as individual human authors rather than as mere mouthpieces of the deity, to perceive inconsistencies between their accounts, to establish the relative dates of the gospels correctly for the first time (Mark first, Matthew and Luke in the middle, John last and late), and to give a broadly correct account of their genesis in oral sermon as well as of their likely relations to each other—achievements which he attained above all in two late works from 1796–7, *On the Savior of Mankind* and *On God's Son, the World's Savior*.

Herder's strict secularism in interpretation would shortly afterwards be adopted by Schleiermacher, who similarly embraced the principle that the interpretation of sacred texts must treat them as the works of human authors and apply exactly the same interpretive methods to them as are applied to profane texts, and who similarly followed through on this commitment, in particular finding not only falsehoods but also inconsistencies in the Bible.[37]

Herder's great achievements in this whole area also have something of the character of the early acts of an inexorable tragedy, however. As has been mentioned, he did not by any means intend his championing of the cause of intellectual conscience in insisting on the autonomy of natural science and interpretation to undermine religion in general or Christianity in particular;

on the contrary, his hope and expectation was that both sorts of autonomy would in the end support religion and Christianity. However, this hope has been sorely disappointed. Autonomous natural science has increasingly made religion generally and Christianity in particular look untenable. And Herder's policy of reading the Bible as a collection of human texts, with all the foibles of human texts, has increasingly led to an undermining of the Bible's claims to intellectual authority. Much of what Herder has ultimately achieved in this area would therefore be deeply unwelcome to him.

Notes

1. Two German editions of Herder's works have been used in this volume: *Johann Gottfried Herder Sämtliche Werke*, ed. B. Suphan et al. (Berlin: Weidmann, 1877–) and *Johann Gottfried Herder Werke*, ed. U. Gaier et al. (Frankfurt am Main: Deutscher Klassiker Verlag, 1985–). References to these editions will take the form of the primary editor's surname initial followed by volume and page number (e.g. S5:261 or G2:321).

2. This marks an important point of methodological contrast with Hamann, whom Herder already criticizes for failing to provide arguments in an essay from early 1765 (G1:38–9).

3. In this connection Charles Taylor wisely comments that "deeply innovative thinkers don't have to be rigorous to be the originators of important ideas" ("The Importance of Herder," in *Isaiah Berlin: A Celebration*, ed. E. and A. Margalit [Chicago: University of Chicago Press, 1991]). The converse is true as well: thinkers can be very rigorous without originating any important ideas. (Note for analytic philosophers.)

4. For some further discussion of these positions, esp. Kant's early Pyrrhonist-influenced skepticism about metaphysics, see my *Kant and Skepticism* (Princeton, NJ: Princeton University Press, 2008).

5. This diagnosis in terms of language seems to go beyond the precritical Kant. However, it has deep precedents and roots in the tradition of British Empiricism, especially Bacon and Locke.

6. This thesis is already prominent in *On Diligence in Several Learned Languages* (1764) and in the *Fragments*.

7. The positive side of this thesis and also its rejection of what Ian Hacking calls the "way of ideas" are already prominent in the *Fragments*.

For Herder's rejection of Platonic forms, see *Johann Gottfried Herder Briefe*, ed. W. Dobbek and G. Arnold (Weimar: Hermann Böhlaus Nachfolger, 1977), 1:179–80 (a letter from 1769). The *Fragments* and the *Treatise on the Origin* (including the latter's drafts) already develop several points which speak against equating concepts with referents (e.g. that language is originally and fundamentally expressive in nature rather than designative or descriptive, and that meaningful but empty names occur), and Herder later goes on to reject this equation explicitly in the *Ideas*.

8. For this thesis, see esp. *Treatise on the Origin* and *On the Cognition*.

9. For more details on Herder's philosophy of language, see Essays 2, 3, and 4.

10. "Normally" in this sentence does real work. For it is also possible to find anticipations of Herder's contrary position in Hume and Voltaire, as well as in other Enlightenment predecessors such as Montesquieu (whom he is himself more inclined to acknowledge as a forerunner in this connection) and Condillac, and even earlier in Montaigne.

11. See e.g. *On the Change of Taste* (1766), *This Too a Philosophy of History*, and *On the Cognition*.

12. See in this connection, for example, Herder's discussion of interpreting ancient Hebrew in *Treatise on the Origin*.

13. This point is already prominent in the *Fragments*.

14. See esp. *On Thomas Abbt's Writings* (1768).

15. See esp. *Shakespeare*.

16. In his writings on the Old Testament Herder astutely forestalls some likely objections here by noting that this reproduction need not involve actually *having* the sensations. His idea is rather that a sort of imaginative reproduction of an interpreted subject's sensations is possible which, while more than merely a dry propositional grasp of them, is also less than an actual sharing of them, and that it is only this that is required for interpretation.

17. The sort of position described in this paragraph has been stigmatized as "positivist" by Gadamer—but on the basis of some very dubious philosophical arguments. H.D. Irmscher in his "Grundzüge der Hermeneutik Herders," in *Bückeburger Gespräche über J.G. Herder 1971* (Bückeburg: Grimme, 1973), questions the sort of characterization of Herder's position that I have given here, arguing that Herder's position rather anticipates Gadamer's own conception of meaning as something

relative to a developing interpretive context. There are in fact certain passages in Herder—especially from his earliest and his latest periods—which tend to suggest such a view. However, it does not seem to me his usual or his best view.

18. For more on Herder's theory of interpretation, see Essays 2, 4, and 5, and *German Philosophy of Language*, Essay 9.

19. For more on Herder's theory of translation, see Essays 2, 4, and 12.

20. For philosophy of language see Essay 2, for theory of translation, Essay 12, and for theory of interpretation, *German Philosophy of Language*, Essay 9.

21. For more on Herder's role in the birth of linguistics, see *German Philosophy of Language*, Essay 4.

22. For more on Herder's role in the birth of anthropology, see Essay 6.

23. Herder's introduction to his 1775 draft shows that he is fully aware of this debt.

24. As I implied, the previous doctrine of the sociality of meaning, thought, and self might seem inconsistent with this doctrine of individuality, but it is really not. Even when the doctrine of individuality is pushed down as far as the level of meanings, as Herder pushes it, there need be no inconsistency here, provided that the doctrine of the sociality of meaning is only asserted as an empirically based causal claim, as Herder asserts it, rather than as a stronger doctrine about social practice constituting the very essence of meanings. Society is, as it were, causally required in order to provide a common semantic clay, which, however, then often gets molded in individual ways.

25. For more on this whole subject, see Essay 3 and *German Philosophy of Language*, Essay 6.

26. For more on Herder's views about genre, see Essay 5.

27. Here Herder's position is strikingly *continuous* with that of his arch-opponent in the philosophy of history, Voltaire, who also anticipates him by turning away from political-military history in favor of a history of culture.

28. Herder's arguments against these three rationales are all briefly summarized in Letters 121–2 of the 10th Collection of the *Letters for the Advancement of Humanity*, though they are more fully stated individually elsewhere.

29. As often in this essay, the reasons mentioned in this paragraph are culled from a large number of Herder's writings.

30. Needless to say, the interpretive issues here are far more complicated than can be conveyed in a single sentence.

31. For more on this subject, see Essay 7.

32. For example, by R. Ergang in *Herder and the Foundations of German Nationalism* (1931; repr. New York: Octagon Books, 1966); and by K.R. Popper in *The Open Society and its Enemies* (London: Routledge and Kegan Paul, 1945), who includes Herder in a sort of Hall of Shame recapitulating the rise of German Nationalism.

33. Admittedly, Herder does on occasion write in ways that appear to be more critical of cosmopolitanism, especially in *This Too a Philosophy of History*. However, there are special features of the passages in question which make them much less clearly at odds with the position ascribed to him above than they may initially seem, including (1) a restriction of his approval of exclusive forms of nationalism to nations *in early periods of history*, (2) a restriction of his hostility to cosmopolitanism to *specific forms* of it, namely forms which preclude commitment to a local culture and seek to efface cultural differences, and (3) a pursuit of a general rhetorical strategy of deflating smug Enlightenment assumptions, including cosmopolitanism, by championing contrary positions regardless of his own beliefs.

34. Herder did not claim or seek superiority for Germany. Instead, he emphatically rejected any such idea of a "Favoritvolk" (as he put it in the *Letters*). It is certainly true that he worked especially hard in Germany's interests over the course of his career. However, this was from a version of what we would today call the principle "Think globally, act locally" (hence when he lived in Riga, a Russian possession, during the 1760s his efforts were instead largely focused on benefiting *Russia*), and also from a (realistic) sense of Germany's current cultural and political inferiority in comparison with such powerful neighbors as France and Britain.

35. For some helpful discussion of this, see F.M. Barnard, *Herder's Social and Political Thought: From Enlightenment to Nationalism* (Oxford: Oxford University Press, 1965), pp. 54–5, 64–6, 105–6, 141.

36. e.g. How do you reconcile your cosmopolitanism with your respect for different nations when those nations turn out to have really inhumane practices towards their own members or other nations? This problem would probably strike a cognitivist as the discovery of an embarrassing contradiction in Herder's position. But to a non-cognitivist like himself

it instead merely looks like the sort of indeed practically challenging but theoretically quite unpuzzling conflict that can *always* in principle arise when a person has multiple sentiments, or commitments. How do you reconcile your devotion to Mary with your commitment to your career when your career requires you to neglect her? . . .

37. For a little further discussion of Herder's principles of biblical interpretation in relation to predecessors and successors, see *German Philosophy of Language*, Essay 9.

2

Herder's Philosophy of Language, Interpretation, and Translation: Three Fundamental Principles

A good case could be made that Herder is the founder not only of modern philosophy of language but also of the modern philosophy of interpretation ("hermeneutics") and translation, and that he has many things to say on these subjects from which we may still learn today. This essay will not attempt to make such a case,[1] but it will be concerned with some aspects of Herder's position that would be central to it: three fundamental principles in his philosophy of language which also play fundamental roles in his theory of interpretation and translation. The essay's aim is also threefold: first, to describe the principles in question and their roles in this theory; second, to explain their emergence in a way which helps to make clearer the nature of Herder's contribution (for example, I shall be making a case for Herder's priority over Hamann, and for his indebtedness instead to some less familiar influences); and third, to give at least a sense of their philosophical subtlety and defensibility. (A companion essay to follow will discuss Herder's views concerning some prima facie problem cases.[2])

I

As is well known, a model of thought, meaning, and language which predominated during the Enlightenment, saliently among the British Empiricists for example, conceived of thought and meaning in a sharply dualistic fashion as (at least in principle) separable and autonomous from whatever material, perceptible expressions they may happen to receive in language, and of language as merely a means to their communication that is quite inessential to their actual existence. Herder's first two fundamental principles in the philosophy of language contradict this model.

The first of these principles asserts that thought is essentially dependent on and bounded by language—that is, that one cannot think unless one has a language and one can only think what one can express linguistically.

This principle carries important consequences for interpretation. For example, in a certain and important sense it guarantees that a person's use of language is bound to be a reliable indicator of the nature of his thought (that the nature of his thought cannot radically transcend, or be discrepant with, his use of language).[3]

It is well enough known that Herder commits himself to a version of this principle in later works such as *A Metacritique on the Critique of Pure Reason* (1799) (henceforth: *Metacritique*) and the *Ideas for the Philosophy of History of Humanity* (1784–91) (henceforth: *Ideas*). For example, he writes in the latter work that "a people has no idea for which it has no word."[4] However, it is important to realize that he was already firmly committed to it much earlier. Thus, moving backwards chronologically, versions of it are already to be found in *On the Cognition and Sensation of the Human Soul* (1778) (henceforth: *On the Cognition*),[5] and in the *Treatise on the Origin of Language* (1772) (henceforth: *Treatise on the Origin*).[6] But even before that, it is already prominent in the *Fragments on Recent German Literature* (1767–8) (henceforth: *Fragments*), where Herder writes, for example:

[Language is] the form of cognition, not merely in which but also in accordance with which thoughts take shape, where in all parts of literature thought sticks [*klebt*] to expression, and forms itself in accordance with this . . . Language sets limits and contour for all human cognition.[7]

Indeed, Herder is already committed to a version of the principle as early as the essay *On Diligence in Several Learned Languages* (1764) (henceforth: *On Diligence*), where he writes:

What exactly is the connection between language and mode of thought? Whoever surveys the whole scope of a language surveys a field of thoughts and whoever learns to express himself with exactness precisely thereby gathers for himself a treasure of determinate concepts. The first words that we mumble are the most important foundation stones of the understanding, and our nursemaids are our first teachers of logic.[8]

Herder's mentor Hamann has often been credited with inventing this revolutionary doctrine and communicating it to Herder (for example, by Rudolf Haym, Fritz Mauthner, Josef Nadler, Roger Brown, Isaiah Berlin,

Fred Beiser, and Ian Hacking).[9] However, this seems to be a mistake. It is, of course, true that Hamann was the older man; began his career as an author first; was deeply interested in, and published some unusual ideas about, language first; nurtured Herder's intellectual growth generally and his interest in language in particular; taught Herder foreign languages; and so forth. But did Hamann invent and communicate to Herder this vitally important doctrine? That is a different question. And several considerations, put together, strongly suggest that he did not, that the influence must instead have been *the other way round*: (1) As I have mentioned, Herder was already committed to the doctrine in *On Diligence* of 1764 and very prominently so in the *Fragments* of 1767–8. (2) By contrast, Hamann's most famous and widely cited expressions of it—in his *Metacritique on the Purism of Pure Reason* (1784) (henceforth: *Metacritique*) and in his letters—come from the 1780s, that is, two decades later.[10] And while there are a number of places in which he articulates it before the 1780s, as far as I can see none of them is earlier than late 1771, that is, still about seven years after Herder had first stated the doctrine in print.[11] (3) The work of Hamann's that immediately precedes Herder's *On Diligence* and *Fragments*, namely the *Crusades of the Philologist* from 1762 (henceforth: *Crusades*), is clearly committed—as Dilthey already noticed—[12] to an entirely contrary conventional Enlightenment picture according to which thought is prior to and autonomous of language, and language is merely an instrument for thought's communication, moreover one which may only very imperfectly express the thought in question. Some representative passages:

The natural manner of thought has an influence on the language.[13]

[Language is] the means of conveying our thoughts and understanding others' thoughts.[14]

Each manner of thought which comes a little into fashion . . . tinges the expression of our concepts. The Christians' way . . . accordingly had to receive a new tongue and a holy manner of writing to distinguish them, likewise.[15]

To speak is to translate—from the tongue of angels into the tongue of men, that is, to translate thoughts into words—things into names—images into signs . . . This kind of translation (I mean, speech) resembles more than aught else the wrong side of a tapestry: "And shows the stuff, but not the workman's skill"; or it can be compared with an eclipse of the sun, which can be looked at in a vessel of water.[16]

Do the elements of the ABC lose their natural meaning, if in their infinite combinations into arbitrary signs they remind us of ideas which dwell, if not in heaven, then in our brains? But if we raise up the whole deserving righteousness of a scribe upon the dead body of the letter, what sayeth the spirit to that? Shall he be but a groom of the chamber to the dead letter, or perhaps a mere esquire to the deadening letter? God forbid![17]

(4) It is true (and this is presumably the main source of the mistaken orthodoxy in the secondary literature) that in his *Philological Thoughts and Doubts* from 1772 (henceforth: *Philological Thoughts*)—a critique of Herder's *Treatise on the Origin* from the same year—Hamann on the basis of the doctrine in question criticizes Herder's work for adopting what Hamann disparagingly calls a "Platonic" conception that inner language, or *Besonnenheit*, is prior to and the basis of outer language.[18] This critique of Herder, *if considered in isolation*, would certainly give the impression that Hamann was the real innovator in connection with the doctrine, who turned Herder away from a rather conventional Enlightenment picture of the relation between thought and outer language toward accepting the doctrine in his later works. However, it is essential to realize that the conventional Enlightenment picture in question is *peculiar to this one essay of Herder's, appearing no more in his preceding than in his subsequent works*. Consequently, it seems that all Hamann is really doing here is, in effect, adopting the doctrine which Herder had *himself* already developed in earlier works such as *On Diligence* and the *Fragments* and playing it back against the incompatible conventional Enlightenment position into which Herder had temporarily lapsed in *Treatise on the Origin*. In sum, it seems very probable that Herder embraced this key doctrine before Hamann and influenced Hamann to accept it rather than vice versa.

Moreover, Herder's formulations of the doctrine tend to be much more philosophically circumspect and defensible than Hamann's. Hamann is prone to wild formulations of it, such as: "reason is language, *logos*."[19] This sort of simplistic formulation is not going to be philosophically defensible. For one can think without in the process expressing what one thinks linguistically—for example, someone thinks that Jones is a fool, but never actually says so. And conversely, one can express language without in the process doing any corresponding thinking—for example, someone who does not understand English can say in a parrot-like fashion "It is a fine day" without thereby thinking of its being a fine day. To Herder's credit, he *avoids* this sort of simplistic formulation.[20]

Herder does occasionally adopt the only slightly more promising position that thought is *internal* speech.[21] This is still philosophically objectionable, albeit less obviously so. For one can think something without in the process expressing what one thinks in language even internally—for example, one is sitting upstairs at home working, having been told that John will be coming home before Mary, one hears the front door open and footsteps mount the stairs, Mary appears in the room and one says, quite truly, "I thought it was John," even though no such little formula had run through one's mind, merely a perception of the front door and the footsteps and a feeling of unsurprise. And conversely, one can express language even internally without in the process doing any corresponding thinking—for example, our person who does not understand English can say to himself internally "It is a fine day" without thereby thinking of its being a fine day.[22]

However, as the passages that I quoted earlier from the *Ideas*, the *Fragments*, and *On Diligence* show, Herder's *usual* position is instead the much more circumspect and philosophically defensible one that thinking is essentially dependent on language-possession and bounded in its scope by the thinker's capacity for linguistic articulation *simpliciter*.[23]

It would be a mistake, though, to infer from the fact that Herder does not owe this doctrine to Hamann that he therefore invented it ex nihilo. On the contrary, versions or close variants of it were already quite common among thinkers with whom Herder was familiar (an important point which has been strangely overlooked by the secondary literature). It was already a fairly widespread "paradigm" (or a fairly widespread counter-paradigm to the Enlightenment's more standard dualistic paradigm). The two most important examples of this, as far as direct influence on Herder is concerned, are the following.

First, the influential literary journal founded by Lessing, Mendelssohn, and Nicolai, *Letters concerning the Most Recent Literature* (1759–65) (henceforth: *Letters*),[24] on which Herder's *Fragments* provided a sort of commentary, had already made several examples of such a position known to Herder. In part 9, published in 1761, letter 144 by Mendelssohn reviews an author who cites and objects to a claim made by a certain Dr Löscher that "it is quite impossible that something can be thought without using words." The author in question had adduced a string of objections to this claim (we often think without words or signs; people thought before language was invented; a deaf-and-dumb person has concepts for which he has never heard a word; and what about angels?). But Mendelssohn answers them point by point, thus defending Löscher's claim (albeit with the qualification, which he introduces as part of his answer concerning the angels, that it may not be *simply impossible* to think without words or signs).[25] So we already here have two people advocating versions or close variants of the doctrine in question: Löscher and Mendelssohn. Again, in part 17, published in early 1764, letter 271 by Abbt (whom Herder greatly admired) takes up a claim made by Meier that, as Abbt puts it, "thoughts adhere and so-to-speak stick [*kleben*] to the expression." Abbt, far from disagreeing with this claim, only objects to Meier's implication of its originality, noting that it is a commonplace which he has himself long believed and which has appeared in many books.[26] Abbt goes on to object further that this correct claim makes Meier's use of the metaphor of "the relation of clothing to the body" to characterize the relation of expression to thought inappropriate: "For where thoughts are concerned, which are unthinkable without words, the expression relates to the thought at the very least like the skin to the body." Abbt subsequently adds that "one could say that a human being's wealth in thoughts is hence to be sought, as in Law's [commercial] system, in sheer word-shares. He has no idea except in accordance with the value of these words." Finally, Abbt insists on a minor revision in an answer that Meier had given to an objection that deaf-and-dumb people can achieve understanding without words, namely the answer that they do not and that if they did they would at least have to use other signs, referencing an example from Geneva in which they clearly did but also pointing out that this was indeed achieved through the use of other signs. So here we have two further people advocating versions or close variants of the doctrine in question: Meier and Abbt. Herder in his *Fragments* cites both of these letters, and in particular recurs repeatedly and approvingly to Abbt's formulation that "thoughts adhere and so-to-speak stick to the expression." It seems clear that these versions of the doctrine were what originally inspired Herder to adopt it in *On Diligence* and the *Fragments*.

A second important source of the doctrine for Herder was Süßmilch, who had adduced a version or close variant of it—specifically, one asserting that language is required for any *rational* thought—in order to refute naturalistic accounts of the origin of language according to which language is a human invention in his *Attempt at a Proof that the First Language received its Origin not from Man but solely from the Creator*, a work formally published in 1766 but already read before the Berlin Academy in 1756 (henceforth: *Attempt*).[27] Herder in his *Fragments* and *Treatise on the Origin* wrestles against Süßmilch's refutation itself, but in doing so he also quietly accepts this doctrine. That Süßmilch's influence on him in this connection was considerable is clear from several finer points of agreement between them in this area which are visible in Herder's texts from 1767 to 1772.[28]

Two further possible but more marginal influences are worth noting briefly as well: Third, as Hans Aarsleff has pointed out, the French tradition had also already developed versions or close variants of the doctrine in question—in particular, Rousseau in the *Discourse on the Origin of Inequality* (1755) and Condillac in *An Essay on the Origin of Human Knowledge* (1746).[29] It is possible that Herder was influenced to adopt the doctrine by these French authors as well as by the Germans mentioned above, though his explicit treatment of the former in *Treatise on the Origin* shows little evidence of this, and if anything suggests the contrary.

And fourth, Herder was probably also encouraged in his acceptance of this doctrine by the English poet Young, whose didactic poem *Night Thoughts* (1742) contains similar ideas. Thus, later in life Herder would quote the following lines from Young's poem in connection with the doctrine:

> Speech, Thought's Canal! Speech, Thought's Criterion too.
> Thought, in the Mine, may come forth Gold or Dross;
> When coin'd in Word, we know its *real* Worth.[30]

And that Herder was already dwelling on these ideas of Young's by as early as 1765 can be seen from an allusion to them in an essay which he wrote in that year for and about Hamann.[31]

This fairly widespread paradigm (or counter-paradigm) on which Herder was drawing had, for all practical intents and purposes, a single ulterior source: the Leibniz-Wolff tradition. Leibniz had already developed the doctrine that thought is deeply dependent on language in his *Dialogue on the Connection between Things and Words* (1677).[32] And under his influence Wolff had gone on to argue for a version of the doctrine more publicly before any of the people mentioned above, namely in his *Empirical Psychology* (1732),[33] and his *Rational Psychology* (1734).[34] The authors in the *Letters* all clearly stand under Wolff's dominating influence in their commitment to this doctrine.[35] Similarly, Süßmilch explicitly credits the doctrine and most of his arguments for it to Wolff.[36] And indeed, one can also find several further German representatives of the doctrine from the period who were similarly dominated by Wolff's influence—for example, Reimarus,[37] and (as Süßmilch notes) Reusch.[38] The French tradition leads back to Wolff as well—for Rousseau clearly got the doctrine from Condillac, and Condillac explicitly (albeit grudgingly) attributes it to Wolff.[39] Young—who is in any case a less clear example of the doctrine and probably less important as an influence on Herder—may have been influenced by Wolff as well (given his religious and philosophical interests and the dates). In sum, for all intents and purposes, the ultimate source was the Leibniz-Wolff tradition—and so one might reasonably speak in this connection of the *Leibniz-Wolff paradigm*, or the *Leibniz-Wolff counter-paradigm*.[40]

Wolff was himself rather ambiguous concerning exactly what *strength* to give this doctrine, however. Did it apply to *all* thought or only to certain sorts of thought, for example *rational* thought? Was the dependence on language a truly *essential*, or *necessary*, one or merely of some *weaker* sort? Most of the time he implies the latter, more modest, answers to these questions.[41] But there are also passages in which he at least seems to imply the former, more ambitious, answers—that language is truly *necessary* for *all* thought.[42]

Not surprisingly, therefore, the thinkers who worked within Wolff's paradigm are divided in similar ways. For example, at least Löscher and Abbt believe that the doctrine applies to all thought, whereas Süßmilch believes that it applies, not to all thought, but only to rational thought.[43] And whereas Löscher and Abbt think that the dependence is a truly necessary one, Mendelssohn explicitly questions this, and Süßmilch generally stops short of such a claim as well, instead characterizing (rational) thought's dependence on language merely in terms of the latter being the only existing causal means to the former.[44]

The tendency of *Herder's* version of the doctrine is toward the *stronger* claims, toward insisting, like Löscher and Abbt, that *all* thought is *essentially* dependent on language. That he tends to make the doctrine one about *all* thought is already evident from the formulations in *On Diligence* and the *Fragments* which I quoted earlier.[45] And that he believes the dependence in question to be *essential* becomes particularly clear in *Treatise on the Origin*, where this constitutes one of his main grounds of complaint against Süßmilch's weaker version of the doctrine.[46] This position that the dependence on language is exceptionless for all thought and essential seems intuitively plausible.

This still leaves the important question of what the *justification and explanation* for the doctrine might be, however.[47] The philosophers who had worked within Wolff's paradigm before Herder had already generated quite a number of arguments in its support. In particular, Wolff, Condillac, and Süßmilch had all offered multiple arguments for their versions of it, largely overlapping but also with some significant differences. Süßmilch's case is fairly representative, and was the one that most influenced Herder, so I shall focus on it here. Süßmilch had offered several arguments in support of his version of the doctrine, among which the following are the most important: (1) Following Wolff, he had observed in its support that deaf-and-dumb people lack reason insofar as they lack language (he concedes that they can have reason to the extent that they employ hand-signals, but he considers these to be both equivalent to and parasitic on language-use).[48] (2) Similarly (but now, he says, following Hobbes), he had noted in its support that a child's reason develops in step with its grasp of language.[49] (3) Again closely following an argument of Wolff's, he had argued that without the aid of signs it would be too difficult for people to recognize and abstract from the flux of experience the characteristic marks [*Charaktere*] that are required for the formation of general concepts, which are in turn required for any rational thought.[50]

Hamann makes no progress on the question of justification and explanation at all, instead simply admitting bafflement about it (in a famous late passage he writes, "For me these depths are still covered in darkness; I am still waiting for an apocalyptic angel with a key to this abyss").[51] But Herder's position is more complicated and interesting—and it is here that he makes his most original contribution.

Herder by no means *entirely* rejects Süßmilch's case. As early as the *Fragments* and then throughout his subsequent career he himself uses versions of Süßmilch's arguments (1), concerning the deaf-and-dumb, and (2), concerning children, in order to support the doctrine.[52] And (as we are about to see) at least in *Treatise on the Origin* he also accepts a version of Süßmilch's argument (3). So he clearly believes that these arguments do go *some* way towards justifying the doctrine.

However, he implies, rightly, that they are *insufficient* to justify or explain the version of the doctrine which he himself believes to be correct, namely the strong version according to which *all* thought is *essentially* dependent on language. This is the main thrust of his criticism of Süßmilch in this area in *Treatise on the Origin*.[53] It is noteworthy that the same complaint could be leveled with equal right against the arguments Wolff and Condillac had provided as well—all of which in particular share with Süßmilch's arguments the shortcoming of being in one way or another merely *empirical* rather than *conceptual* in character, and therefore incapable of justifying or explaining any claim of an *essential* dependence.[54] To have perceived this insufficiency, and the consequent need for a better justification and explanation of the strong version of the doctrine, is one of Herder's two main contributions in this area.

His other is to have actually succeeded in providing such a superior justification and explanation. However, that he did so is by no means obvious. For his most explicit and best known attempt, in the *Treatise on the Origin*, is a rather miserable failure. His strategy there is to take over Süßmilch's argument (3) but to modify it in two ways: His first modification in effect consists of maintaining that general concepts, and hence characteristic marks (which Süßmilch had called *Charaktere* and he himself calls *Merkmale*), are necessary conditions, not merely of all *rational* thought, but of *all* conceptualization and thought.[55] His second modification lies in turning argument (3) from being, like arguments (1) and (2), merely an empirical argument, which consequently shares with them the weakness of inevitably failing to prove or explain any *essential* dependence of (rational) thought on language, into a *conceptual* argument which consequently can prove and explain an essential dependence. His solution here is very quick: he simply identifies the fundamental aspect of (rational) thought whose practicability Süßmilch had claimed required the help of language, namely the recognition of characteristic marks, as *itself* language.[56]

However, the new argument that results from these modifications fails. The former modification, while not *obviously* correct, at least looks very plausible—so far so good.[57] But the latter modification is at bottom merely sophistical. It arguably succeeds in *one* sense: *if* it were legitimate to call the recognition of characteristic marks language, then the argument would now somewhat plausibly justify and explain a claim that *all* thought is *essentially* dependent on language, since it is indeed plausible to hold that all thought entails general-concept-possession, and that all general-concept-possession entails the recognition of characteristic marks.[58] But calling the recognition of characteristic marks language is *not* legitimate. It is merely an unacknowledged stipulative redefinition of the word "language," which, in thus seeming to make possible a justification and explanation of the doctrine that *all* thought is *essentially* dependent on language, in reality changes the meaning of that doctrine and deprives it of virtually all its original interest—which depended on "language" being meant in something like its usual sense. (It is, after all, no very great news—though it might not indeed be *completely* trivial—to be told that all thought is essentially dependent on certain fundamental aspects of thought!)

Herder soon recognized the weakness of this merely specious solution and abandoned it. Thus he already expresses general misgivings about the *Treatise on the Origin* as early as 1772.[59] And (perhaps moved by Hamann's criticisms of the essay on this score in the *Philological Thoughts* of 1772) he publicly retracts the work's key move of internalizing "language" in *On the Cognition* of 1778.[60]

However, there is also a second doctrine that can be found in Herder's texts, and which, besides being of immense importance for the philosophy of language and the theory of interpretation and translation in its own right, also makes possible—and indeed had already made possible for Herder even before he wrote the *Treatise on the Origin*—a much more satisfactory argument for the first doctrine.

II

This second doctrine consists in a denial that *meanings* or *concepts* are to be equated with the sorts of items, in principle autonomous of language, with which most of the philosophical tradition had equated them—for example, the objects to which they refer, Platonic "forms," or the mental "ideas" favored by the British Empiricists and many other philosophers in the seventeenth and eighteenth centuries—[61]and an equation of them instead with *usages of words*.

This doctrine has important consequences for Herder's theory of interpretation and translation: It is an immediate implication of the doctrine for the theory of interpretation that interpretation essentially and fundamentally involves determining word-usages. Accordingly, Herder writes in *On the Spirit of Hebrew Poetry* (1782–3): "Let us seek the word's concept not from etymologies, which are always uncertain, but according to the clear use [*Gebrauch*] of the name in its various times."[62] This doctrine also grounds a fundamental principle of Herder's in the theory of translation, namely that translation's basic goal of faithfully reproducing a work's meanings in a different language requires a reproduction of the original word-usages, which, if they are not already afforded by the target language (as they rarely will be in cases where historical or cultural distance is involved), must be achieved by a "bending" of the (closest) pregiven word-usages from the target language performed over the course of the translation.[63]

Hamann has again sometimes been credited with inventing a doctrine about meanings of this general sort and passing it on to Herder (for example, by Isaiah Berlin).[64] Hamann does certainly embrace such a doctrine during the 1770s and 1780s. Thus, as we saw earlier, he already speaks disparagingly of Platonism in a general way in his *Philological Thoughts* of 1772. And by 1781 he rejects not only the identification of concepts with Platonic forms but also the identification of them with their referents: "Plato's archetypes strike me like material ideas strike Reimarus. Nothing seems easier than the jump from the one extreme to the other, and nothing as difficult as uniting them in a middle."[65] Hamann also rejects any form of the seventeenth- and eighteenth-century "way of ideas." This can already be seen from his criticisms of Tiedemann in his 1771 review,[66] and from his criticisms of the *Treatise on the Origin*'s variant of such a theory in his *Philological Thoughts* of 1772.[67] It can also be seen from his *Metacritique* of 1784, which opens with warm applause for Hume's praise of Berkeley's attack on abstract ideas, which Hamann evidently (mis)understands as an attack on any conception of meanings or concepts which takes them to be ideas (as contrasted with words and particulars).[68] Accordingly, and more positively, in the same work Hamann implies that, rather than concepts being autonomous of and actively governing language, the opposite is in fact true,[69] that language is "without any other source of authority than tradition and usage,"[70] and that words get elevated from being mere objects of the senses into constituting "understanding and concepts" simply by the "spirit of their use and application."[71]

However, it again seems to me very probable that Herder is the source of this doctrine and Hamann the borrower. For at least until the early 1760s Hamann was still committed to a conventional dualistic conception of the relation between concepts and words which accorded the former priority and autonomy over the latter, whereas by the mid-1760s at latest Herder was already committed to the new doctrine in question. Thus, Hamann's first publication, the *Socratic Memorabilia* of 1759, is still committed to that conventional conception.[72] And his *Crusades* of 1762 is clearly still wedded to it as well (as the series of passages from the work that I quoted earlier—which should be reviewed at this point—shows). In contrast, by the mid-1760s at latest Herder is already committed to the new doctrine. Thus, concerning the positive equation of meanings or concepts with word-usages (and a consequent conception of interpretation as essentially involving the determination of word-usages), as we saw earlier, Herder already writes in *On Diligence* (1764) about the connection between language and thought:

Whoever learns to express himself with exactness precisely thereby gathers for himself a treasure of determinate concepts. The first words that we mumble are the most important foundation stones of the understanding.[73]

He already in *On the Change of Taste* (1766) uses the term "name" as a virtual synonym for "concept."[74] And he already in the *Fragments* (1767–8) insists on the "adhesion of the thought to the word" or the "expression," writes of the understanding of concepts that "the question is not how an expression can be etymologically derived and analytically determined, but how it is *used*,"[75] and accordingly advocates that in order, for example, to understand the changing nature of people's moral concepts one must closely scrutinize their changing word-usages.[76] So much for the doctrine's positive side.[77] Concerning its negative side, its rejection of more traditional accounts of meanings or concepts: It is already pretty clear that the passages just cited are in part deliberately directed against the Enlightenment's standard equation of concepts with mental "ideas," conceived in dualistic terms as prior to and autonomous of language.[78] Regarding the rejection of Platonic "forms," Herder already writes in a 1769 letter to Mendelssohn concerning the latter's Platonically inspired *Phaedo*:

Nothing in the world, I think, has produced more opinions and perhaps also more errors than that one has considered and hypostatized [*realisiert*] abstract concepts as individual existences. Thus do we hypostatize the word Nature, Virtue, Reality, Perfection. Originally these concepts were nothing but abstractions, relations of this to that, so to speak shadows and colors of things; we make them into things themselves, and hence imagine finished skill-things [*Fertigkeiten*], which the soul collects like gold pieces, realities which are only relations and which we think of as positions, perfections which we individualize and attribute as such to the soul. Let us . . . by analysis of the concepts get back to the origin of these words; and we will see in them substantived phenomena [*phenomena substantiata*].[79]

Finally, Herder also from an early period rejects any equation of meanings with referents. The *Fragments* and *Treatise on the Origin* already imply such a rejection, and develop several quite compelling arguments for it (to be discussed below). And Herder then goes on to articulate it more explicitly in the *Ideas* as follows:

No language expresses things [*Sachen*] but only names. Also no human reason therefore has cognition of things but it has only characteristic marks of them which it signifies with words.[80]

In sum, it seems very probable, once again, that this second doctrine was Herder's before it was Hamann's, and that it migrated from Herder to Hamann rather than vice versa.[81]

 As in the case of the first doctrine, the historical situation is more complicated than this, however. (We here come to another part of the story that has been entirely overlooked by the secondary literature.) For if Herder was probably not indebted to Hamann here, there are other people to whom he certainly was. Specifically, there was already a movement afoot in contemporary German biblical hermeneutics which emphasized the fundamental importance of word-usage for meaning. For example, Wettstein already wrote in a work on biblical hermeneutics first published in 1756:

The true meaning of words and phrases is not so much to be sought from etymology or from single words taken separately, but rather from usage and examples.[82]

Similarly, Ernesti's great work *Institutio interpretis Novi Testamenti* from 1761 already emphasized that a word's meaning depends on its usage, and that interpreting a word therefore essentially turns on determining its usage:

It is evident that the signification of words depends upon the *usage of language*; and that the latter being known, the former is known also.[83]

Like Wettstein, Ernesti especially contrasts this approach to determining meaning with a focus on etymology, which he considers to be unreliable.[84] Herder, who was in particular a great admirer of Ernesti's work, is clearly drawing on this school of biblical hermeneutics here.[85]

 What, if anything, does Herder's doctrine *add* to (Wettstein and) Ernesti's? Ernesti is basically advancing a doctrine about what determines, and hence how to discover, which meaning a word bears rather than a doctrine about what meaning *is*. Or as one might also roughly put it, he is advancing an *epistemological* doctrine rather than an *ontological* one. Thus, while he makes the points just cited, he nevertheless still conceives the nature of word-meaning in quite conventional Enlightenment terms as consisting in *a connection between a word and an idea*.[86] Herder, by contrast, and following him Hamann, develop Ernesti's merely epistemological doctrine into a corresponding and explanatory *ontological* one: a word's meaning depends on its usage, so that determining word-usage is the key to determining word-meaning, *because meaning just consists in word-usage*.

As I mentioned earlier, this second doctrine of Herder's is extremely important, not only in its own right, but also because it provides the basis for a much more satisfactory justification and explanation of his first doctrine (the doctrine that thought is essentially dependent on and bounded by a thinker's capacity for linguistic expression) than the one that he gives in the *Treatise on the Origin*. The argument is simple but compelling: Intuitively enough, thought is of its very nature articulated in terms of *concepts*, in terms of *meanings*. But now, if concepts or meanings *just are usages of words*, and grasping concepts or meanings therefore just is being competent in usages of words, thought's essential dependence on and boundedness by linguistic competence seems hereby both established and explained.

Herder himself gives this argument in several places. One occurrence is the following passage already quoted from *On Diligence*, which should now be reviewed in this light:

What exactly is the connection between language and mode of thought? Whoever surveys the whole scope of a language surveys a field of thoughts and whoever learns to express himself with exactness precisely thereby gathers for himself a treasure of determinate concepts. The first words that we mumble are the most important foundation stones of the understanding.[87]

Another, nearly identical, statement of the argument occurs in the *Fragments*, where Herder adds to his expression of the first doctrine (already quoted earlier)—his assertion that language is "the form of cognition, not merely in which but also in accordance with which thoughts take shape, where in all parts of literature thought sticks to expression, and forms itself in accordance with this"—the following justificatory-explanatory remark:

In being brought up we learn thoughts through words, and the nurses who form our tongue are hence our first teachers of logic; with all sensible concepts in the whole language of common life the thought sticks to the expression.[88]

Indeed, now that we know to look for it there, we can even see a version of this argument (albeit a distorted and problematic one) surviving in the *Treatise on the Origin*'s case that concepts (or their characteristic marks) *are* words, and that for this reason all thought, or "reflection," requires language.[89]

Although this Herderian argument for the first doctrine has in a way been very much "in the air" again since the later Wittgenstein, it is surprisingly difficult to find an explicit statement of it in recent philosophy. Especially when reinforced by the arguments for the second doctrine to be discussed below, it constitutes a much more compelling case for the first doctrine than several others which have been explicitly offered recently.[90]

This still leaves the question of what the *justification* for this second doctrine *itself* may be. Hamann nowhere gives one, as far as I can see; he merely rejects the various traditional models of meaning in a more or less unargued way and opts instead for equating meaning with word-usage again in a more or less unargued way. But here again Herder's position is more complicated and interesting. In addition to explicitly rejecting the notion that a term's meaning or concept is its referent (in passages such as the one recently quoted from the *Ideas*), he also develops at least three powerful considerations justifying such a rejection: (1) Already in the *Fragments*,[91] and especially at the start of the *Treatise on the Origin*, he argues that the original and fundamental roots of human language are *expressive* in nature rather than designative or descriptive, namely the expressive "language of sensation" which human beings share with animals—[92] a position which would be incompatible with equating meanings with referents. (2) Implicitly in the *Treatise on the Origin*, and then more explicitly in the *Metacritique*, he argues that even the meanings of singular referring terms essentially and fundamentally involve *general* concepts—[93] which again seems to preclude equating meanings with referents. (3) As can be seen, for example, from an early draft of the *Treatise on the Origin* where he criticizes our tendency to accept uncritically "linguistic concepts" which we receive from tradition but which are in fact empty,[94] Herder (like anybody who has a significant knowledge of the history of thought) is acutely aware of the phenomenon of meaningful referring-terms (proper names, general-kind-terms, and so forth) which happen to lack referents (for example, "Zeus," "centaurs")—a phenomenon which is again incompatible with an equation of meanings with referents.

This complex Herderian case against equating meanings with referents strikingly anticipates much important later philosophy of language. One classic later work directed against such an equation is Frege's essay *On Sense and Reference*.

But Herder's case is especially similar to the late Wittgenstein's: Wittgenstein too makes this equation a central target for attack.[95] For Wittgenstein too the expressive, as contrasted with the designative or descriptive, function of language—in his case, especially the (allegedly) expressive function of first-person psychological statements—is an important part of the argument against such a theory of meaning.[96] For Wittgenstein too a further important part of the argument is a thesis that singular referring uses of language—in particular, acts of ostension and proper names—presuppose a stage-setting of general concepts.[97] Finally, for Wittgenstein too the fact that referring-terms can be meaningful even though they happen to have no referents (or their referents have ceased to exist) constitutes yet another important point against the equation in question.[98]

Hegel in the *Phenomenology of Spirit* and the late Wittgenstein would develop an additional part of the case needed to justify Herder's doctrine, namely a part that refutes the "way of ideas" and the Platonic theory of "forms" and justifies an equation of meanings with word-usages instead. They give virtually the same argument, grounded in close reflection on our ordinary criteria for ascribing semantic understanding to people: If, as the "way of ideas" or Platonism holds, meaning consisted in a mental idea or a mental connection to a Platonic form, then one would expect that in cases where we assume that this occurs for a person our ordinary criteria for ascribing semantic understanding would tell us to ascribe semantic understanding to him no matter how wayward his linguistic behavior might be. But in fact, we find that if we assume that it occurs but also that he engages in very wayward linguistic behavior, our ordinary criteria dictate that we should *deny* him such understanding. Conversely, if the "way of ideas" or Platonism were true, then one would expect that in cases where we assume that a person engages in all the linguistic behavior typical of someone who semantically understands but that he lacks the relevant mental idea or mental connection to a Platonic form, our ordinary criteria would dictate that we should deny him semantic understanding. But in fact, we rather find that they dictate that we should *ascribe* it to him. By contrast, these facts concerning our ordinary criteria for ascribing semantic understanding accord perfectly with an equation of meaning with word-usage.[99]

Herder himself anticipates this twofold argument. Thus, recall his approving allusion (implicitly already in 1765, explicitly later) to Young's lines:

> Speech, Thought's Canal! Speech, Thought's Criterion too.
> Thought, in the Mine, may come forth Gold or Dross;
> When coin'd in Word, we know its *real* Worth.

More specifically, compare with the former part of the Hegel-Wittgenstein argument such passages in Herder as this one from the *Fragments*:

Who can express himself about all subjects . . . in the language of common life more fluently and correctly than the common man of good healthy understanding? But now, try in his case to separate the *thought* from the *expression*—you do not understand the word.[100]

And compare with the latter part of the Hegel-Wittgenstein argument Herder's remark in *On Diligence*:

Whoever learns to express himself with exactness precisely thereby gathers for himself a treasure of determinate concepts.[101]

III

Finally, Herder also advances a third important doctrine in the philosophy of language: a quasi-empiricist theory of meanings, or concepts, according to which all our meanings, or concepts, are of their nature based in (perceptual or affective) sensation.[102] Empiricist theories of concepts had of course already been espoused by predecessors such as Locke and Hume. Less famously, such a theory was also present, as one side of an ambiguous position, in the precritical Kant (to whom Herder is heavily indebted here).[103] But Herder's theory has two special features which distinguish it from these earlier theories (hence the "quasi-"), and which also arguably make it superior: (1) Plausibly anticipating much important work by more recent philosophers (for example, work by Norwood Hansen and Thomas Kuhn), Herder maintains that the dependence holds in the other direction as well, that our sensations also depend on our concepts (and beliefs and theories).[104] This is not, for Herder, to deny that *any* sensation can occur prior to conceptualization ("our" does some real work here). For example, in the *Treatise on the Origin* he acknowledges that animals and people just beginning to learn language do have sensations of a kind. But in his view, the process of language- and concept-acquisition transforms the nature of a person's sensations. Consequently, Herder's position is not, as for example Hume's was, that a person simply has the sensations which ground concepts first and then on that basis acquires the concepts afterwards. Rather, in Herder's view, the sensations which ground concepts inevitably undergo a transformation as the concepts are acquired, their final required nature being of a sort that they can only have along with the concepts. (2) Herder believes (again plausibly) that we are able to, and do, achieve concepts which are in a way non-empirical, namely by means of a sort of metaphorical extension from the empirical ones. Thus in his *Metacritique* he says that in a sense "the whole of language is allegory," and that language "can only connote the finest concepts of the understanding through 'the same, another,' 'in and outside,' 'before and after' . . . Throughout in language sensuous words connote the finest concepts of the understanding."[105] Consider, for example, the relation between the sensuous "in" of "The dog is in the garden" and the more abstract "in" of "John is in the Republican party," "Mary is in trouble," and so forth.[106] These two finer points leave it the case, however, that for this theory all concepts are of their nature grounded in corresponding sensations in one way or another.

This third doctrine has important consequences for Herder's theory of interpretation and translation. Concerning interpretation, it implies that in order to understand another person's concepts an interpreter must not only master the person's word-usage in an external way, but must also in some fashion recapture the person's relevant sensations.[107] (Due to qualification (1) above, the converse is true for Herder as well: in order properly to grasp a person's sensations an interpreter must also interpret his linguistic concepts.) Accordingly, Herder argues in the *Fragments* that in order really to understand the Greeks we must learn to *see* like them;[108] and he argues in *On the First Documents* (1769) that because people's concepts of happiness and pleasure are based on their distinctive "temperament," "feeling nature," "sense for rapture," in order really to understand the ancient Orientals' versions of those concepts we need to recapture these affective states of theirs imaginatively.[109] This is a large, and quite sensible, part of the force of Herder's notorious claim, in *This Too a Philosophy of History for the Formation of Humanity* (1774) and elsewhere, that interpretation, especially of culturally alien thought, requires an interpreter to employ *Einfühlung*, or "feeling one's way into" the other's standpoint. This third doctrine is also a major reason behind a key move which Herder makes in translation theory, namely towards insisting that the translation of poetry must aim to reproduce faithfully not only the original meaning but also the musical aspects of the poetry (for example, meter, rhyme, alliteration, and assonance). Achieving the latter is not, for Herder, merely a desirable luxury over and above the more fundamental goal of achieving the former. Rather, in Herder's view, the musical aspects of a poetic work give an interpreter indispensable clues to the exact nature of the sensations which are internal to the work's meanings and which the interpreter therefore needs to discover in order to arrive at an exact understanding of those meanings, so that a translation's failure to reproduce the musical aspects of the work will undermine the very *semantic* understanding of the work that readers of the translation can achieve.[110]

Herder's combination of his second doctrine (meaning is word-usage) with this third doctrine (meaning is of its nature based in sensation) may seem problematic at first sight. However, I want to suggest that it is really not. Here are some prima facie problems, together with suggested solutions: (1) Explaining meanings in terms of sensations can sound incompatible with equating meanings with word-usages because it can seem to make words and their usages *inessential* to meanings. This need not be so, however. For the explanation in terms of sensations may instead specify a *further* essential aspect of meanings (or alternatively—to anticipate my next point—an aspect that is already implicitly included in the relevant concept of word-usage). (2) Conversely, if we equate meanings with word-usages, does that not preclude any essential role in meanings for the possession of sensations? The answer is again: not necessarily. For a usage of anything is always implicitly relative to some *context* or other, and the relevant context here might very well essentially include the possession of certain sensations. (3) Anglophone philosophers are likely to be prejudiced against such a combination of positions by their familiarity with the late Wittgenstein's version of a "meaning as word-usage" doctrine. For Wittgenstein usually argues that such processes as having or imaginatively reproducing sensations are altogether inessential for conceptual understanding.[111] It is not clear that this is *always* his position (for one thing, he usually characterizes examples of conceptual understanding in a phenomenologically rich way that includes sensations and images).[112] But to the extent that he does hold it, it is a rather implausible position. We can and should grant *this* much to such a position: our ordinary criteria for ascribing conceptual understanding to a person do not require that in order to be properly ascribed conceptual understanding on a particular occasion he must, in addition to being then able to use relevant words with external competence, also have relevant sensations or images *occurring on that occasion*. This is something that Wittgenstein clearly wants to insist on,[113] and it seems clearly correct.[114] But would our ordinary criteria really sanction ascribing conceptual understanding to someone who, for example, thanks to some imaginable science-fictional mechanism or other, had arrived at an external competence in using the word "red" without *ever* having had sensations or images of redness—to someone whose external competence was (to put the point a little tendentiously) merely *robotic*? The answer seems to be pretty clearly No.[115] In sum, it seems on closer reflection that Herder's second and third doctrines are in fact perfectly compatible with each other, and that the third doctrine may well be correct.

IV

These, then, are three fundamental principles in Herder's philosophy of language, interpretation, and translation. From a modern standpoint, the first two of them, and the arguments he develops in their support, are pretty clearly of epoch-making importance. The third is likely to seem much more controversial today. However, it may well be that in thus refining rather than jettisoning the empiricist tradition's theory of concepts he developed yet a further insight from which we still have something to learn.[116]

Notes

1. For such a case, see Essay 4.
2. Essay 3.
3. Hence Herder writes at *A Metacritique on the Critique of Pure Reason* (1799), S21:19 that language is a "mirror of the human understanding." (As Herder points out, Leibniz had already said this before him.)
4. G6:347; cf. 138–42; *Metacritique*, S21:19, 88, 293–4; *On the Ability to Speak and Hear* (1795), S18:384 ff.
5. G4:356–9.
6. G1:727.
7. G1:556–7; cf. 177, 394–7, 403–4, 407–10, 426, 558, 606–8 (though contrast pp. 259, 404–6).
8. G1:27.
9. R. Haym, *Herder nach seinem Leben und seinen Werken* (Berlin: Gaertner, 1880), 1:137–8; F. Mauthner, *Beiträge zu einer Kritik der Sprache* (1902; 3rd edn. Berlin: Felix Meiner, 1923), 2:47; J. Nadler, *Johann Georg Hamann* (Salzburg: Otto Müller, 1949); R. Brown, *Wilhelm von Humboldt's Conception of Linguistic Relativity* (The Hague/Paris: Mouton, 1967), ch. 4; I. Berlin, *Vico and Herder*, pp. 165–7; F.C. Beiser, *The Fate of Reason* (Cambridge, Mass.: Harvard University Press, 1987), p. 16; I. Hacking, "How, Why, When, and Where Did Language Go Public?" and "Night Thoughts on Philology," in his *Historical Ontology* (Cambridge Mass.: Harvard University Press, 2002). Despite my disagreements with them on this and a few other points, I have found almost all of these works very helpful.
10. Hamann's *Metacritique* is indeed full of this doctrine—see e.g. *Hamanns Schriften*, ed. F. Roth (Berlin: G. Reimer, 1820–), 7:6, 9—but

belongs to 1784. So too does the oft-quoted letter to Herder in which Hamann writes: "Even if I were as eloquent as Demosthenes, I would merely have to repeat a single maxim three times: reason is language, *logos*. This is the bone I gnaw on, and on it I will gnaw myself to death. For me these depths are still shrouded in darkness; I am still waiting for an apocalyptic angel with a key to this abyss" (Johann Georg Hamann, *Briefwechsel*, ed. W. Ziesemer and A. Henkel [Wiesbaden: Insel, 1955–], 5:177; cf. pp. 108 [a letter from late 1783], and 210 ff.).

11. Hamann's first reasonably clear expression of the doctrine seems to occur in a review of a work by Tiedemann dated Dec. 27, 1771 in which it serves as his implicit ground for rejecting Tiedemann's standard Enlightenment picture of language as merely an instrument for the communication of representations (*Hamanns Schriften*, 4:3–5). Shortly afterwards, in 1772, Hamann invokes the doctrine again in a similar way in his *Philological Thoughts and Doubts* against Herder's *Treatise on the Origin* (see my following discussion). The earliest expression of the doctrine that I have found in Hamann's *letters* is the following remark in a 1774 letter to Kant: "So true is it that speaking [*Sprache*] and writing are the most essential instruments and conditions of all human instruction, more essential and absolute than light for seeing and sound for hearing" (Hamann, *Briefwechsel*, 3:87). There are two passages in *Crusades of the Philologist* (1762) that might look like exceptions to this general rule, but they both turn out not to be on closer inspection—concerning which, see Essay 9.

12. W. Dilthey, "Johann Georg Hamann," in his *Gesammelte Schriften* (Stuttgart: B.G. Teubner and Göttingen: Vandenhoeck and Ruprecht, 1914–), 11:32.

13. *Hamanns Schriften*, 2:122–3.

14. Ibid., p. 128.

15. Ibid., pp. 206–7. The image which follows this passage in the text of God's spirit abasing and expressing itself through the "human stylus" of holy men is also significant.

16. Ibid., pp. 262–4 (tr. H.B. Nisbet).

17. Ibid., p. 272 (tr. Nisbet). There are two potentially contrary-looking passages in the *Crusades* which will be considered and defused in Essay 9.

18. *Hamanns Schriften*, 4:59–60: "I have called this supernatural proof of the human origin of language a 'Platonic' one because it begins with the analogical term of art *Besonnenheit*, as a 'single and illuminating spark' of the complete system, and returns at the end to a Greek

synonymy [i.e. *logos*]; and because the Platonists rechewed *ad nauseam* the *logos endiathetos* or *enthumêmatikos* and *logos prophorikos*, the *inner* and *outer* word, like the Swedish goblin-seer [i.e. Swedenborg] *ab intra ad extra*."

19. Hamann, *Briefwechsel*, 5:177 (this remark is from 1784).
20. There are a few *apparent* exceptions to this rule. But when considered more closely they rather confirm it. For example, one might compare with Hamann's simplistic formulation just quoted a statement of Herder's which perhaps inspired it: "In the deepest languages . . . *reason* and *word* are only *one* concept, *one* thing: *logos*" (*On the Cognition*, G4:358). But Herder's statement is significantly less bald than Hamann's. For to approve other languages for showing insight into the intimacy of the relation between thought and language by using the same term and concept for both is not quite to say oneself that they are the very same thing. Again, Herder goes on in a part of the *Fragments* from which I quoted earlier to say that "in common life it is surely clear that thought is almost nothing else but speaking" (G1:558). But he does not quite say here that thought *is* speaking, only that it is "*almost* nothing else but" speaking; and indeed elsewhere in the *Fragments* he argues that even the conception that expression relates to thought like the skin to the body does not leave enough of a distinction between them (G1:404–6). His considered position in the *Fragments* in fact seems to be that thought and language are not identical or reducible in either direction, but instead interdependent (a position similar to that recently championed by Donald Davidson in "Thought and Talk," in his *Inquiries into Truth and Interpretation* [Oxford: Clarendon Press, 1991], p. 156).
21. Herder already comes close to saying this in the *Fragments*: "We think in language . . . and in common life it is surely clear that thought is almost nothing else but speaking" (G1:558). He holds a version of this position (albeit an idiosyncratic one) in *Treatise on the Origin*. And he holds it most explicitly in the *Metacritique*: "What is *thinking*? Speaking inwardly, that is, expressing to oneself the characteristic marks [*Merkmale*] which one has internalized" (S21:88, cf. 19).
22. For some reflections similar to the above against the outright identification of thought with either external or internal linguistic expression, see L. Wittgenstein, *Zettel* (Oxford: Blackwell, 1967), par. 100 and *Remarks on the Philosophy of Psychology* (Chicago: University of Chicago Press, 1980), vol. 2.

23. It is interesting to note that Schleiermacher would later run through all three of the positions just distinguished. At least in earlier work he sometimes adopts the crude Hamannian equation of thought with language (see e.g. F.D.E. Schleiermacher, *On the Different Methods of Translation*, in A.L. Willson ed., *German Romantic Criticism* [New York: Continuum, 1982], p. 20: "the internal and essential identity of thought and expression"), and at other times the only slightly better equation of thought with inner language (see e.g. F.D.E. Schleiermacher, *Hermeneutics and Criticism*, ed. A. Bowie [Cambridge: Cambridge University Press, 1998], p. 9: "Thinking is an inner speaking"). However, in his later work he instead tends to gravitate toward the more defensible third position.

24. *Briefe die neueste Literatur betreffend* (Berlin: Friedrich Nicolai, 1759–65).

25. Another expression of this sort of position by Mendelssohn occurs in the *Letters* at part 13, pp. 22 ff.: "Without the help of language we human beings can achieve no clear cognition and hence no use of reason . . . Our cognition becomes lively and fiery but also confused as soon as we perceive a number of characteristic marks at the same time, and if we want to distinguish them we must separate them and confer on each a particular sign or name from which symbolic cognition arises."

26. That the former point was no empty boast is proved by a text from 1758 in which Abbt already argues for a version of the claim in question (*Thomas Abbts vermischte Werke* [Frankfurt and Leipzig: Friedrich Nicolai, 1783], part 6, p. 111). For some examples of what the "many books" Abbt mentions might be, see my following points about Wolff.

27. J.P. Süßmilch, *Versuch eines Beweises, daß die erste Sprache ihren Ursprung nicht vom Menschen, sondern allein vom Schöpfer erhalten habe* (Berlin: Buchladen der Realschule, 1766).

28. Some examples: (1) As we shall see shortly, Herder's most explicit *arguments* for the doctrine turn out to be the same as Süßmilch's (the deaf-and-dumb lack reason, children acquire reason in step with their acquisition of language, and language is necessary for the acquisition of the characteristic marks from which general concepts are formed). (2) Herder and Süßmilch both make an exception to the doctrine in the case of God. (3) Herder also often echoes Süßmilch in conceding that some animals can think, though not rationally, despite lacking (relevant sorts of) language.

29. H. Aarsleff, *From Locke to Saussure: Essays on the Study of Language and Intellectual History* (Minneapolis: University of Minnesota Press, 1982), esp. pp. 150, 163–6.

30. S18:385.

31. G1:39.

32. In *Leibniz Selections*, ed. P.P. Wiener (New York: Charles Scribner's Sons, 1951). For example, we read there the following exchange between the dialogue's interlocutors: "B. This . . . makes me realize that in my thinking I never recognize, discover, or prove any truth without calling up to mind words or some other kind of signs. A. Quite so; yes, if there were no signs, we should never think or conclude anything intelligibly" (p. 9). Cf. Leibniz's *Unvorgreifliche Gedanken, betreffend die Ausübung und Verbesserung der deutschen Sprache* (1697).

33. C. Wolff, *Psychologia Empirica*, in his *Gesammelte Werke* (repr. Hildesheim: Georg Olms, 1968), esp. pars. 284–5, 342, 351, 368–9.

34. C. Wolff, *Psychologia Rationalis*, in his *Gesammelte Werke*, esp. par. 461. It is perhaps not so surprising that those parts of the secondary literature concerned with the Herder-Hamann doctrine we are considering which are not grounded in any thorough first-hand acquaintance with original sources, such as the works of Isaiah Berlin and Ian Hacking, should have overlooked the doctrine's origin in Wolff. But one is more surprised to see that even the learned scholar of Hamann, Rudolf Unger, not only overlooks but actually denies that the doctrine has such an origin (R. Unger, *Hamann's Sprachtheorie im Zusammenhange seines Denkens* [Munich: C.H. Beck, 1905], p. 214).

35. Mendelssohn was very heavily influenced by Wolff generally; Abbt and Meier were both students of Baumgarten, Wolff's most important student; the specific arguments for the doctrine which Mendelssohn and Abbt give are the same as, and clearly inspired by, Wolff's (for example, like Wolff, Mendelssohn in letter 144 and in part 13 saliently appeals to introspection, or the fact that if one tries to think without words or signs one finds oneself unable to do so, argues that without words or signs the soul cannot grasp "the first elements of thoughts, the separations," and also uses Wolff's terminology of "symbolic cognition" as contrasted with "intuitive cognition"; and like Wolff, Abbt in his 1758 remarks similarly appeals to introspection, and argues that words are required for abstract concepts and hence also for inference); and so on.

36. By contrast, the French were not a significant influence on Süßmilch; he had not read Condillac, and he only read the relevant parts of Rousseau late in the process of composing his own work.

37. H.S. Reimarus, *Die vornehmsten Wahrheiten der Religion* (1st edn. 1754, last rev. edn. 1766; latter repr. Göttingen: Vandenhoeck and Ruprecht, 1985). Reimarus was probably not a major influence on Herder's adoption of the doctrine itself, but, as we shall see in this and its companion essay, he did influence Herder on some significant finer points relating to the doctrine.

38. J.P. Reusch, *Systema logicum antiquiorum atque recentiorum item propria praecepta exhibens* (4th edn. Jena: Cröcker, 1760).

39. E.B. de Condillac, *An Essay on the Origin of Human Knowledge*, ed. T. Nugent (Gainsville, Fla.: Scholars' Facsimiles and Reprints, 1971), p. 136. Condillac's acknowledgment also comes after an extended discussion by him of two examples which, as he notes, he has borrowed from Wolff: one of a boy born deaf-and-dumb, the other of a boy reared by bears (cf. Wolff, *Psychologia Rationalis*, par. 461).

    Thus, in respect of this doctrine at least, Aarsleff's provocative but rather eccentric attempt in *From Locke to Saussure* to represent the French rather than the Germans as the originators of all the main ideas in the philosophy of language which arose in this period ultimately fails. (The French have a stronger claim to have been the leaders in important developments that took place at about the same period in the theories of interpretation and translation, however. See Essay 1 on their anticipation of the thesis of radical mental difference; Essay 5 on Voltaire's insight into the historicity of genres; and Essay 12 on d'Alembert's innovations in the theory of translation.)

40. Wolff's importance for philosophy generally and for the philosophy of language in particular tends to be underestimated today. For example, staying within the philosophy of language, he seems to have been a prime source, not only for the doctrine in question here, but also for the revolutionary idea in the Herder–Hegel tradition that language and hence conceptualization and thought are fundamentally *social*, as well as for the idea, later fundamental to Saussurean linguistics, that *difference* is at least as important for the constitution of concepts as *similarity*.

41. For example, at *Psychologia Empirica*, par. 284 he merely argues that our abstractions become clearer and more distinct by the use of words, and he actually expresses skepticism about people who infer from this that we cannot think without the use of words. Similarly, at *Psychologia Rationalis*, par. 461 he merely argues, under the significant heading "The dependence of the use of reason on the use of speech": "The use of reason is facilitated and amplified by the use of speech; without the use of speech the use of reason may scarcely be conceded."

42. For example, at *Psychologia Empirica*, par. 342 he concludes: "And thus the indispensable necessity of words for designating our perceptions and of an indissoluble connection between intuitive cognition and symbolic cognition becomes clear." And similarly, at *Psychologia Rationalis*, par. 461 he concludes: "Hence it is sufficiently shown how great is the necessity of words or other equivalent signs for the production of mental operations."

43. This observation about Süßmilch requires some qualification. At points he seems to be using the word "thought" in an extremely broad way (which Descartes had introduced) to refer to just about any mental process at all, including for example mere sensation. For instance, at *Attempt*, p. 35 he says concerning "sensations and imagings" that "we cannot deny the animals this sort of thoughts." Hence his disagreement with Löscher and Abbt here may be in part more verbal than substantive. However, at other points he conceives thought as a higher mental function than mere sensation and imaging. For example, at *Attempt*, p. 52 he describes the latter as merely "the first foundational beginnings of thought." And this side of his position puts him in substantive rather than merely verbal disagreement with Löscher and Abbt here.

44. See e.g. *Attempt*, preface and p. 5. Süßmilch is a little ambiguous about this, though—for instance, he does speak of "necessity" in this connection at p. 44.

45. This claim requires some qualification. After the works just mentioned, as Herder's position became less exclusively influenced by the authors in the *Letters* and more influenced by Süßmilch, it became more

LANGUAGE, INTERPRETATION, TRANSLATION   81

ambiguous on this score. For one thing, already in works from 1768–9
Herder, like Süßmilch, makes an exception of God, claiming that God
can think without language (see e.g. *On the Divinity and Use of the
Bible* [1768], G9/1:25–6; *On the First Documents* [1769], G5:27–9). For
another thing, in *Treatise on the Origin* Herder, again like Süßmilch,
often wants to say no more than that *rational* thought exhibits the
dependence in question, and is accordingly prepared to allow that
animals can think despite lacking (relevant sorts of) language (see e.g.
G1:718, 720–1, 772, 774).

However, that Herder does still *tend* to the stronger position can
be seen from such countervailing evidence as the following: (1) In
Treatise on the Origin he criticizes Süßmilch for allowing that lower
forms of reason can occur without language (G1:725–6). Süßmilch
had in fact only said that *non*-rational forms of *thought* could do so.
So it seems reasonable to see Herder as here really meaning to reject
the latter position. (2) Herder in *Treatise on the Origin* unequivocally
argues that all taking-awareness [*Besinnung*] and reflection [*Reflexion*]
requires language—which seems virtually equivalent to saying that
all thought does. (3) Accordingly, he at least says explicitly that all
"distinct thought" requires language (G1:727). (4) Several passages in
Treatise on the Origin imply—contrary to those mentioned above—that
animals, lacking (the relevant sort of) language, ipso facto lack, not
merely rational thought, but thought *tout court* (G1:728, 731). (5) Later,
in *On God's Son, The World's Savior* (1797), Herder retracts the idea
that God thinks without language, instead insisting that God's thought
does involve language (see esp. S19:295–7).

46. See esp. *Treatise on the Origin*, G1:725–6.
47. This remains very much a live question in the philosophy of language
     today—so that the observations which follow may be of more than
     merely historical interest. For, as Davidson notes, recent "philosophers
     have, for the most part, preferred taking a stand on the issue [of
     the relation between thought and talk] to producing an argument.
     Whatever the reason, the question of the relationship between thought
     and speech seems seldom to have been asked for its own sake"
     ("Thought and Talk," p. 156).
48. Süßmilch, *Attempt*, pp. 47–9, 56. Cf. Wolff, *Psychologia Rationalis*, par.
     461. Wolff's version of the doctrine had made room for the possibility
     mentioned in parentheses as well, namely by framing the doctrine in
     terms of "words or other equivalent signs" (a phrase which Süßmilch
     echoes).

49. *Attempt*, pp. 50–1. Wolff had *almost* made this argument as well, for he had emphasized that reason is not innate but is acquired by children (*Psychologia Rationalis*, pars. 458–9), and he had noted in support of the claim that reason depends on language that in cases in which children have been raised by bears and hence without language they have lacked reason until they subsequently began to acquire language (ibid., par. 461).

50. *Attempt*, pp. 33–4, 37–44. Cf. Wolff, *Psychologia Empirica*, par. 284; *Psychologia Rationalis*, par. 461. Wolff tends to make his version of this point without invoking a distinction between characteristic marks and general concepts—which seems philosophically preferable because characteristic marks are really *themselves* general concepts and the two-stage model really only applies to the special case of *complex* general concepts.

51. Hamann, *Briefwechsel*, 5:177.

52. See *Fragments*, G1:556 for an early version of the latter argument (children). See esp. *On the Cognition*, G4:357–8 for both arguments: "Those born deaf and dumb demonstrate in special tests how deeply reason, self-consciousness, slumbers, when they cannot imitate"; "Thus, as we see, does the child attain its mental constitution, it learns to speak . . . and precisely as a result and in the same way to think. Whoever has observed children, how they learn to speak and think, the peculiar anomalies and analogies which are expressed in the process, will hardly have any further doubts." For a later appeal to the deaf-and-dumb argument, see *Ideas*, G6:139, 347.

   Note, though, that Herder tends to advance his version of the deaf-and-dumb argument in an unqualified and consequently implausible-looking form—omitting Süßmilch's important qualification that the deaf-and-dumb can acquire reason even in the absence of language to the extent that they learn the use of other signs (as well as Süßmilch's saving observation that such signs are both equivalent to and parasitic upon language), and even at one point denying that they can do so (G6:347). A charitable reading of Herder's version of the argument would see it as really an elliptical or careless statement of Süßmilch's more carefully qualified and hence more plausible version which lies behind it.

53. See esp. G1:725–6.

54. Of course, this situation is not really surprising given that Wolff, Condillac, and Süßmilch were not—or at least not normally—committed to the strong form of the doctrine which Herder is espousing, and for which their arguments are inadequate.

55. G1:722–3: "[The human being] demonstrates reflection when he can not only recognize all the properties [of an object] in a vivid or clear way, but can in his own mind acknowledge one or several as distinguishing properties. The first act of this acknowledgment provides a distinct concept . . . What brought about this acknowledgment? A characteristic mark which he had to separate off." Cf. *Metacritique*, S21:208–9, 250–1, where Herder argues that general concepts are prior to (or at least coeval with) any recognition of particulars in human thought, language, or sensation. H.S. Reimarus had already argued for a priority of general concepts over particular concepts in his *Allgemeine Betrachtungen über die Triebe der Tiere* (1760; last rev. edn. 1762; latter repr. Göttingen: Vandenhoeck and Ruprecht, 1982), 1:35–6, and probably influenced Herder on this point.

56. G1:722–5, 733.

57. Much subsequent philosophy has followed this path of arguing that all conceptualization and thought, even about particulars, implicitly rests on general concepts. One example, directly influenced by Herder, is Hegel's argument concerning demonstratives such as *this*, *now*, and *here* in the "Sense-certainty" section of his *Phenomenology of Spirit*. Another example is the later Wittgenstein's position on the nature of both ostension and proper names.

58. With due regard to a point which I made about Wolff's position in a previous note (n.50): either because the general concept is complex and requires characteristic marks to constitute it or because it itself *is* a characteristic mark.

59. *Johann Gottfried Herder Briefe*, 2:130–4.

60. G4:357.

61. For an excellent account of this "way of ideas," see I. Hacking, *Why does Language Matter to Philosophy?* (Cambridge: Cambridge University Press, 1993), chs. 2–5.

62. G5:1007. Cf. *Fragments*, G1:322, 421–3. This is not to say that for Herder interpretation *only* involves determining word-usages. It is in fact one of his most important innovations in comparison

with predecessors such as Ernesti to have insisted that interpretation essentially involves determining much more as well—for example, besides linguistic meanings or word-usages, also aspects of authorial psychology and genre.

63. See e.g. *Fragments*, G1:199–200, 205; *Popular Songs* [*Volkslieder*] (1774), G3:26.

64. Berlin, *Vico and Herder*, p. 165: "Herder had derived from Hamann his notion that words and ideas are one" (cf. pp. 166–7). Similarly, Beiser argues that Hamann was already committed to an anti-Platonic nominalism in 1759 (*The Fate of Reason*, p. 25).

65. Hamann, *Briefwechsel*, 4:287 (this letter is from 1781). Strictly speaking, "material ideas" had been defined by Wolff as impressions from sensible objects occurring in the brain either via the senses or innately (*Psychologia Rationalis*, par. 112)—which is not quite the same as an identification of ideas with their referents. However, it is easy to see how an analytically cloudy mind like Hamann's would tend to conflate these two things (especially given that, in addition to the very expression's emphasis on the ideas' materiality, its definition also incorporates their reference to objects). And I take it that at least part of what Hamann means to reject here in rejecting "material ideas" is an equation of ideas with their referents.

66. *Hamanns Schriften*, 4:3–5.

67. Ibid., pp. 59–60.

68. Ibid., 7:3.

69. Ibid., p. 6: "Receptivity of language and spontaneity of concepts!"

70. Ibid.

71. Ibid., p. 13; cf. p. 14.

72. Beiser argues that Hamann already adopts a nominalist position in this work (*The Fate of Reason*, p. 25). But I do not find his argument convincing. The only evidence he cites is the work's ironic dedication "To the public, or nobody, the well known," which he reads as part of a nominalist attack on abstractions. But in the absence of any supporting evidence, such a reading seems a stretch. And the little that Hamann says in the text that is of clear relevance to this subject not only fails to provide any support but seems to imply a standard dualistic picture of the relation of concepts to their material expressions which accords the former priority and autonomy over the latter. In particular, he writes: "As the human being was created in God's image, likewise the body seems to be a figure or image of souls. If our skeleton is hidden to us because we are made in hiding, because we are formed below in

the earth, how much more are our concepts made in hiding, and can be considered limbs of our understanding" (*Hamanns Schriften*, 2:21).

73. G1:27.

74. G1:151: there are peoples "who are so different that they scarcely have a common name [i.e. concept] left." Cf. *Treatise on the Origin*, G1:733, where Herder approves of languages in which "*concept and word . . . share one name.*"

75. G1:421–3. Cf. *On the Spirit of Hebrew Poetry* (1782), G5:1007, as quoted earlier: "Let us seek the word's concept not from etymologies, which are always uncertain, but according to the clear use [*Gebrauch*] of the name in its various times."

76. G1:322 (Greek slightly amended): an interpreter must "trace the metamorphoses which in Greek the words *anêr, anthrôpos, agathos, kalos, philokalos, kalok'agathos, kakos, epicheirêtês*, and in Latin *vir, homo, bonus* and *melior* and *optimus, honestus, pulcher* and *liberalis, strenuus* and such national words have undergone, which were the honor of their age, and changed with it."

77. The late Herder remains committed to this positive position. Consider, for example, the following remark in the *Metacritique*: "No boy will . . . , once he has grasped the word's sense, seek this sense outside and behind the word, but will seek it in the word and take possession of it by means of the word" (S21:173—though it should be noted that this late work also contains a few passages which imply a contrary view, e.g. at pp. 120, 123–4).

78. Cf. Herder's later renunciation in *On the Cognition* of the version of such a theory which he had himself transiently lapsed into in *Treatise on the Origin*, as well as his criticism of Kant's relevantly similar theory of "schematism" in the *Metacritique*.

79. *Johann Gottfried Herder Briefe*, 1:179–80; cf. Herder's *Metacritique*, S21:172.

80. G6:348; cf. 348–50.

81. Once Hamann is deprived of the credit for these two revolutionary doctrines, the foundations of the—still widespread, but I think basically mistaken—conception that Hamann was the deep, obscure well from which Herder drew most of his best ideas (a conception still found in Berlin and Beiser, for example) really begin to crumble.

82. J.J. Wettstein, *Libelli ad crisin atque interpretationem Novi Testamenti* (1st edn. 1756; 2nd edn. Halle, Magdeburg: I.G. Trampe, 1766), p. 120.

83. *Ernesti's Institutes*, ed. C.H. Terrot (Edinburgh: Thomas Clark, 1832), 1:27, cf. 63.

84. Ibid., pp. 91, 97, 161.

85. Notice, for example, that Herder echoes not only Wettstein and Ernesti's idea that meaning depends on word-usage and their consequent injunction to determine meaning by determining word-usage but also their insistence that this is superior to a focus on etymologies, which are unreliable as a guide to meaning. Incidentally, the warning that it is only current word-usage, not etymology, that provides a reliable guide to current meaning is correct and very important. This insight seems somehow to have been lost in much of the later German philosophical tradition, where a fair amount of humbug has resulted from ignorance or neglect of it—e.g., Fichte's argument in his *Speeches to the German Nation* that because German is an "original" and hence etymologically transparent language, whereas the Romance languages are based on a different language, namely Latin, and are hence etymologically opaque, German produces thought that is clearer and better than that produced by the Romance languages; and also some of Heidegger's etymological musings.

86. *Ernesti's Institutes*, 1:15–17, 27. Note that Ernesti was an admirer of Locke.

87. G1:27.

88. G1:556–7; cf. pp. 394–7.

89. G1:722–3; cf. p. 733 for a more explicit identification of "*concept* and *word*."

90. For example, Donald Davidson in "Rational Animals" (*Dialectica*, 4 [1982]) and "Thought and Talk" develops an argument for a version of the first doctrine which goes roughly like this: (1) Having thoughts requires having beliefs. (2) Having beliefs requires possessing the distinction between true and false beliefs. (3) The concepts of belief and of an objective truth and falsehood are ones which we can only achieve through interpreting other people's language. (4) Therefore having thoughts requires being an interpreter of other people's language. This is not a very compelling argument for the first doctrine. For one thing, as Davidson himself notes, it would only establish thought's *dependence* on language, not its *boundedness* by language. For another thing, while premises (1) and (2) are plausible, premise (3) looks at least as questionable as the conclusion to be proved. For, absent a further argument, it would appear that a person might well be able to arrive at the concepts of belief and of objective truth and falsehood merely through possessing his own mental representations and occasionally experiencing their invalidation by the world. And

Davidson's only way of counteracting this appearance seems to be to wheel on his whole theory of meaning—which is certainly more dubious than the conclusion to be proved (and indeed, as I have argued elsewhere, pretty clearly false).

Again, Manfred Frank, at *Das individuelle Allgemeine*, pp. 174–5, attempts to justify the doctrine by appealing to Saussure's principle that meaning only arises through a system of oppositions. But, assuming this principle of Saussure's to be correct, why could not such a system of oppositions, and hence meaning, exist without language being involved at all?

91. G1:611.

92. The *Treatise on the Origin* famously resists attempts such as Condillac's to derive the whole of human language from this expressive "language of sensation," but it also insists that this is an original and fundamental *part* of human language.

93. See my earlier note on this subject (n.55) for some relevant passages in these two texts, and in a work by Reimarus which anticipates this line of argument.

94. S5:152–3.

95. See esp. L. Wittgenstein, *Philosophical Investigations* (Oxford: Blackwell, 1958), par. 1, where Wittgenstein famously associates it with Augustine.

96. See e.g. ibid., par. 244.

97. See e.g. ibid., pars. 28–30 (ostension), 79 (proper names).

98. See e.g. ibid., par. 40.

99. Wittgenstein's version of this two-part case is well known. For a discussion of Hegel's much less well-known version of it, see my *Hegel's Idea of a Phenomenology of Spirit* (Chicago: University of Chicago Press, 1998), chs. 2, 4. Hegel and Wittgenstein's *former* point is more immediately compelling than their *latter*, converse, one, which encounters intuitive resistance deriving from a concern that the person in question might be engaging in all the linguistic behavior typical of semantic understanding but in a merely *robotic* way. I am sympathetic to this resistance, and would suggest that it calls for the sort of inclusion of *sensations and images* as essential aspects of semantic understanding that we are about to see Herder championing. However, this situation in the end argues, not for rejecting the second Hegel-Wittgenstein point, but rather for (re)construing the notion of "all the linguistic behavior typical of someone who semantically understands" in a way that is rich enough to include the relevant sensations and images (though not a mental idea or a mental connection to a Platonic

form). In fact, this may not be quite as remote from Wittgenstein's intentions as it seems since, for one thing, as has often been pointed out, he himself tends to describe cases of semantic understanding in a phenomenologically rich way that includes sensations and images rather than in an austerely behavioristic way. And Hegel too seems to commit himself to something like the position in question through his endorsement at *Encyclopedia*, par. 8 of the pseudo-Aristotelian tag "There is nothing in the intellect which was not in the senses" (albeit that his endorsement comes with the qualification that the converse is true as well).

100. G1:395; cf. 556–7: because of the dependence of concepts on words, "How much one could sweep away here which we . . . think falsely because we said it falsely."

101. G1:27.

102. See e.g. *Journal of my Journey in the Year 1769*, S4:454–6; *On the Cognition*, G4:351–4; *Metacritique*, S21:96, 117–18, 120–1.

103. Although the fact is usually overlooked, the precritical Kant often commits himself to an empiricist theory of concepts in early works such as the *Universal Natural History and Theory of the Heavens* (1755) and *Dreams of a Spirit Seer* (1766) (though not, indeed, consistently). Herder originally took over his theory from this side of the precritical Kant. This debt is traceable in Herder's notes from Kant's metaphysics lectures from the early 1760s and in Herder's *Essay on Being* (G1:9–21) which he wrote for Kant in 1764.

104. e.g., in *Treatise on the Origin* he writes that "vision refines itself with reason" (G1:750; cf. 723: a lamb does not *appear* to other animals as it does to reason- and language-using humans). Cf. *On the Cognition*, G4:372 ff., noting esp. the section title there "What Effect does our Thought have on our Sensation?" Also, *Critical Forests* (4), G2:290, 296–7, 308, 324, where Herder argues for the role of implicit comparisons, measurements, and inferences in vision. Also, Herder's *Metacritique*, S21:96–7, 117–18, 183, where he argues that human sensation is infused with concepts and thoughts. Subsequently, Hamann saliently emphasizes this direction of dependence in his *Metacritique* as well (see *Hamanns Schriften*, 7:11). Note, though, that this Herder-Hamann position is not quite as novel as it may at first appear, given that the Rationalists had regarded sensation as a confused form of cognition.

105. *Metacritique*, S21:120, 184. Cf. *Fragments*, G1:181–4; *Treatise on the Origin*, G1:758–9.

106. Although Herder's idea that it is possible for concepts which are in a way non-empirical to arise through metaphorical extensions from empirical ones is original vis-à-vis Locke, Hume, and the precritical Kant, it can already be found before Herder in Condillac (see *An Essay on the Origin of Human Knowledge*, pp. 250–4), by whom Herder may be influenced here.

107. See e.g. *Treatise on the Origin*, G1:753–4. It is perhaps worth emphasizing: *relevant* sensations. There is nothing in this aspect of Herder's position that requires one to turn interpretation into a *wholesale* recapturing of a person's sensations. A version of the important Fregean distinction between sense [*Sinn*] and mere coloring [*Färbung*] can still be upheld (albeit a psychologistic version of which Frege himself would have strongly disapproved).

108. G1:559.

109. G5:74–5.

110. See e.g. G2:1159, where Herder argues that it is essential to preserve Shakespeare's rhymes in translation because of the semantically relevant nuances of feeling which only they convey exactly.

111. See e.g. *Philosophical Investigations*, pp. 182, 217, and par. 663, where such processes are characterized as merely inessential accompaniments of understanding. This position of Wittgenstein's is an intellectual inheritance from Frege.

112. Some more direct evidence for such a contrary side of Wittgenstein can be found at *Brown Book*, in *The Blue and Brown Books* (Oxford: Blackwell, 1975), pp. 78–9, 156–7; *Philosophical Investigations*, pars. 448–9, 545; and *Remarks on the Philosophy of Psychology*, vol. 1, pars. 162, 200, 609.

113. See e.g. *Blue Book*, pp. 3, 12; *Brown Book*, pp. 156–7.

114. This large grain of truth in the implausible position in question can easily be confused with the latter, and may sometimes have seduced Wittgenstein into accepting it.

115. For Wittgenstein's own sensitivity to this sort of point (at least sometimes), see e.g. *Brown Book*, p. 157; *Remarks on the Philosophy of Psychology*, vol. 1, pars. 162, 200, 609.

116. By this point in the essay the reader may well be wondering whether the appearance of the first two doctrines in Herder and Hamann followed by their reappearance in the late Wittgenstein is merely a coincidence or instead the result of influence. This is really a further topic, deserving of separate treatment. But the short answer is that we are not dealing with a mere coincidence here. A key figure in the transmission of

these doctrines from Herder and Hamann to Wittgenstein seems to have been Fritz Mauthner, whose *Beiträge zu einer Kritik der Sprache* (1st pub. 1902) Wittgenstein read even before writing the *Tractatus* (where he alludes to it, albeit somewhat critically). Mauthner's book prominently contains both of the doctrines in question (for the first doctrine, thought's dependence on and boundedness by language, see esp. 1:176–232; for the second, meaning as word-usage, see esp. 1:24–5), as well as copious explicit discussions of Herder, Hamann, and others influenced by them.

3

Gods, Animals, and Artists: Some Problem Cases in Herder's Philosophy of Language

In the previous essay I argued for roughly the following account of Herder's central contribution to the philosophy of language. It is mainly Herder (not, as has often been claimed, Hamann) who deserves the credit for developing two fundamental principles in the philosophy of language which overturned standard Enlightenment conceptions and were of epoch-making importance: (1) Thought is essentially dependent on and bounded by language—i.e. one can think only if one has a language, and one can think only what one can express linguistically. (2) Meanings or concepts are to be equated—not with such items, independent of language, as the referents involved, Platonic forms, or the mental "ideas" favored by the British Empiricists and others in the seventeenth and eighteenth centuries but—with word-usages.

Moreover, Herder also deserves the credit for developing a set of cogent arguments for these principles, saliently including a (proto-Wittgensteinian) argument for (2) which turns on the decisiveness of linguistic-behavioral criteria in our everyday attributions of conceptual understanding to people, and an argument for (1) in terms of (2) along roughly the following lines: intuitively enough, thought is of its very nature articulated in terms of *concepts*, in terms of *meanings*, but now, if, as (2) says, concepts or meanings *just are usages of words*, and grasping concepts or meanings therefore just is being competent in usages of words, then thought's essential dependence on and boundedness by linguistic competence seems both established and explained.

Herder had already developed this whole position very early in his career: by about the mid-1760s.[1] To quote some representative passages, already in *On Diligence in Several Learned Languages* (1764) he writes:

What exactly is the connection between language and mode of thought? Whoever surveys the whole scope of a language surveys a field of thoughts and whoever learns to express himself with exactness precisely thereby gathers for himself a treasure of determinate concepts. The first words that we mumble are the most important foundation stones of the understanding, and our nursemaids are our first teachers of logic.[2]

And already in the *Fragments on Recent German Literature* (1767–8) he writes:

[Language] is . . . the form of cognition, not merely in which but in accordance with which thoughts take shape, where in all parts of literature thought sticks [*klebt*] to expression, and forms itself in accordance with this . . . In being brought up we learn thoughts through words, and the nurses who form our tongue are hence our first teachers of logic; with all sensible concepts in the whole language of common life the thought sticks to the expression . . . Language sets limits and contour for all human cognition.[3]

Finally (though less crucially for our present purposes), already by the mid-1760s Herder had also developed a third principle: (3) a quasi-empiricist theory of meanings or concepts according to which all meanings or concepts are of their nature based in (perceptual or affective) sensation—but a theory which diverges from, and arguably improves on, more traditional empiricist theories of meaning in maintaining that (a) the dependence holds in the other direction as well, i.e. that our sensations also depend on our concepts (and beliefs and theories), and (b) we are able to achieve concepts that are in a way non-empirical, namely by means of metaphorical extensions from the empirical ones.

If this interpretation is correct, then it naturally invites the following question: After accomplishing so much so early in the philosophy of language, what if anything did Herder do for an encore? What if any significant additions or revisions did he make to his philosophy of language after this?

His famous *Treatise on the Origin of Language* (1772) might seem like the obvious place to look for an answer to this question (after all, it is his best known work in the philosophy of language by far). But, while it is certainly of some relevance (as we shall see), it is by no means the mine of advances that one might expect or hope for. On the contrary, it mainly represents, not progress, but rather a (temporary) lapse from the position just described back to a more orthodox and less philosophically interesting position, in particular one that makes thought and meaning prior to and autonomous of language very much as the standard Enlightenment view had done (albeit while obscuring this fact by in effect *relabeling* them as "language" or "word").[4] However, Herder's theory by no means simply trod (or swallowed) water after the mid-1760s; it did develop further, and indeed in a rather impressive way.

One good measure of a philosopher's intellectual quality, I would argue, is the extent to which, and the subtlety and success with which, he searches out and strives to cope with prima facie problems confronting his theories. It is one thing to develop a forceful argument for a theory; it is another, and equally important, thing to follow that up with a scrupulous search for, honest confrontation with, and convincing defusing of, prima facie objections to the theory that remains. This, I want to suggest, is the general nature of Herder's main achievement in the philosophy of language after the mid-1760s.

To be more specific: Already by the mid-1760s to early 1770s he identified certain problem cases which seemed to threaten principles (1) and (2) (or at least to call into question what their exact force should be): God, animals, and non-linguistic art. In each of these cases he initially developed a way of reconciling the phenomenon in question with principles (1) and (2) which was unsatisfactory. But in each case he went on to reflect further and eventually succeeded in developing a much more promising-looking reconciliation.[5]

This essay will discuss Herder's developing views concerning the three problem cases in question. While it is arguable that the first of them, God, is or should be no more than a matter of historical interest to philosophers today (there probably happening not to be a God), the cases of animals and non-linguistic art (which certainly do exist!) remain highly relevant for the philosophy of language, so that discussing Herder's treatment of them may prove to be not only historically but also philosophically instructive.

I

The first case that posed a prima facie problem for principles (1) and (2) was God. Can't God think and conceptualize without language?

Wolff and Süßmilch, who had already embraced versions or close relatives of principle (1) before Herder, arguing that at least rational thought is dependent on language,[6] had made an *exception* of God: unlike human beings, God thinks without language.[7] In early works from the late 1760s Herder took over this solution, making a similar exception of God: "[God] thinks without words."[8]

Because Wolff and Süßmilch, in their versions or close relatives of principle (1), did not (usually) want to claim anything as strong as an *essential* dependence of *all* thought on language, this was a somewhat tenable position for them to adopt. But Herder from an early period did normally hold, and argue for, such a strong version of principle (1).[9] And this made his God-exception very problematic indeed—really just a self-contradiction.[10]

Concerning principle (2), the principle that meanings or concepts just are word-usages, the coherence of the early Herder's God-exception with this principle was ultimately not much better. Obviously, the exception threatened to contradict this principle as well. The early Herder had a solution *of sorts* here: according to *On the First Documents* (1769), unlike our thought, God's thought is not articulated in terms of (general) concepts, but is instead somehow unitary.[11] However, this solution at best only forestalls the looming contradiction at the cost of positing an incomprehensible mystery, namely that of a thought not articulated in terms of concepts. Moreover, as I mentioned earlier, in his argument for (1) in terms of (2) Herder himself evidently assumes that thoughts are essentially articulated in terms of concepts. So once again there is probably in the end an implicit self-contradiction here.

In later works, by contrast, Herder copes with the case of God in a way that avoids this thicket of inconsistencies, namely by retracting the God-exception and affirming that, like human thought and concepts, God's thought and concepts are dependent on and bounded by language.

He does so on the basis of a new, and exegetically plausible, conception that the Bible is actually supportive of, rather than at odds with, such a position. Thus, in *On God's Son, The World's Savior* (1797) he focuses on the famous opening statement from John's Gospel, "In the beginning was the word, and the word was with God, and the word was God," and he defends this statement as faithful to the spirit of the Bible as a whole, pointing out, persuasively, that it is not, as it might seem and has seemed to many, merely a late incursion of new-fangled Hellenistic philosophy into the Bible, but is instead continuous and consistent with Old Testament ideas to the effect that God's creative power resides in His word.[12] Accordingly, he argues in explication and endorsement of John's statement that "God himself was what we call word, understanding, will of the deity; for in His essence nothing is separable."[13]

This revision in Herder's position between the late 1760s and the 1790s was also made possible by a change in his theology that had occurred in the intervening period—again (like his re-interpretation of the Bible) a change that was arguably for the better. The main theological motivation behind Wolff's, Süßmilch's, and the early Herder's God-exception had lain in a traditional dualistic conception of God's relation to the physical world which entailed that it would be incompatible with the nature and the dignity of God for God's thought, and hence for God Himself, to be dependent on the physical world—as would be implied by a conception of God's thought as dependent on and bounded by language. However, in *God: Some Conversations* (1787) Herder had come to argue for a variant of Spinoza's monism which identified (not only human minds and thoughts, but also) God's mind and thoughts with *force*,[14] and which conceived force as something that of its very nature required physical embodiment.[15] Hence a conception of God's thought as essentially dependent on and bounded by language now, far from being inconsistent with Herder's fundamental theological outlook, cohered with it perfectly.

This left Herder with a much more attractive philosophical position concerning God's bearing on principles (1) and (2)—not only eliminating the nest of inconsistencies that had afflicted his initial position, but also bringing his philosophy of language into pleasing alignment with what was arguably an improved interpretation of the Bible and an improved theology.

However, since philosophy's best estimate today is that there probably happens not to be a God, this position has little contemporary philosophical relevance. So let us, as it were, leave God for the birds.

II

For another set of difficult questions that arises in connection with principles (1) and (2) concerns animals (birds included). Do animals think? Do they have concepts? Do they have language? And if the answer to the former two questions is Yes, but that to the last No, then is this not flatly inconsistent with Herder's principles (1) and (2)?

Herder's (somewhat ambiguous) position in this area is heavily indebted to predecessors, in particular two philosophers from the Wolffian tradition who had already espoused versions or close relatives of principles (1) and (2), and who had devoted a lot of attention to animals: Süßmilch and Reimarus. (Herder discusses both men in the *Treatise on the Origin of Language* and elsewhere.) In order to understand Herder's position (and its ambiguity), it helps to see it in the light of this intellectual background.

It may be useful to begin with a general observation that applies to this whole group of thinkers: To their considerable intellectual credit, they all avoid a certain quick and hence tempting, but intrinsically implausible, way of avoiding the inconsistencies which threaten here, namely the Cartesian tack of denying that animals have any mental life at all. That Cartesian position had enjoyed a certain popularity in the seventeenth century, but it is very implausible,[16] and by the eighteenth century its implausibility was widely recognized by philosophers, including those in Germany. The German thinkers with whom we are concerned consequently stood in a roughly similar—and similarly salutary—intellectual situation vis-à-vis their Cartesian predecessors as many cognitive ethologists stand in today vis-à-vis the long, dark night of twentieth-century behaviorism concerning animals, from which they have only recently emerged to recognize that animals do have a mental life and that it permits and requires investigation.

Concerning Süßmilch specifically: Accordingly, Süßmilch in his *Attempt at a Proof that the First Language received its Origins not from Man but solely from the Creator* (published in 1766, but already presented before the Berlin Academy in 1756) holds that animals do have certain lower mental functions in common with mankind—including sensations, images, some memory, attention, recognition, distinguishing (e.g. of master from enemy), and cunning.[17] And he even allows that animals *think*, and hence presumably also that they employ concepts—though not that they do so in ways involving *universal* concepts, nor therefore *reason*.[18] On the linguistic side, he allows that (some) animals use signs for warning, attracting, expressing needs, indicating danger, etc.[19] But he denies that these signs are capable of supporting universal concepts or rational thought, on the grounds that, unlike the language of human beings, first, they are not voluntary or mutable, second, they are not diverse or numerous, and third, they do not include abstract, universal terms.[20] Indeed, he does not even seem to believe that animals' universal-concept*less*, *non*-rational thought and concepts are made possible by or depend upon this use of signs. So for him these signs are basically irrelevant for avoiding the sorts of inconsistencies that threaten here. Nevertheless, he does manage to avoid them, because his versions or close relatives of principles (1) and (2) only hold that *universal-concept-using, rational* thought and *universal* concepts depend on language, which is consistent with his concession to animals of universal-conceptless, non-rational thought and concepts.

Reimarus in his *The Most Exalted Truths of Natural Religion* (1754, final revised edition 1766) and his *General Observations on the Drives of Animals, Mainly on their Drives of Artifice* (1760, final revised edition 1762) develops a position that is largely similar to Süßmilch's but also different in several important respects.[21] Concerning, first, the similarities, Reimarus likewise rejects Cartesianism and concedes lower mental functions to animals,[22] and he likewise concedes to animals a use of signs while also insisting that this is too primitive to sustain (rational) thought and (universal) concepts, so that it is basically irrelevant to avoiding the inconsistencies that threaten here.[23] Concerning the differences, Reimarus disagrees with Süßmilch in three important respects: (a) Reimarus, in his versions or close relatives of principles (1) and (2), is inclined to say that proper language is required, not only for any rational thought or universal concepts, but for any thought or concepts *at all*.[24] (b) Accordingly, he denies, not only that animals have rational thought and universal concepts, but that they have *any* thought, *any* concepts.[25] So, like Süßmilch, he too succeeds in avoiding the inconsistencies that threaten here, but in this significantly different way. (c) Less crucially for our immediate purposes, Reimarus also qualifies the thesis that animals share lower mental functions with humans: because humans, unlike animals, possess proper language and hence thought and concepts, humans' versions of the lower mental functions differ from animals' versions of them—"they are articulated with a clear consciousness."[26]

Herder in his *Treatise on the Origin of Language* from 1772 agrees with these two predecessors' common ground. In particular, like both of them, he avoids the tempting Cartesian tack,[27] instead allowing that animals do have lower mental functions, and he grants that animals use signs to express needs and so forth, but considers this use too primitive to sustain (rational) thought and (universal) concepts, and hence basically irrelevant for avoiding the inconsistencies that threaten here. Beyond this, he is somewhat torn between Süßmilch and Reimarus on the first two points that separate them,[28] but overall he inclines more to Reimarus's positions than to Süßmilch's: (a) Although he is ambiguous about this, his considered inclination, in his versions of principles (1) and (2), is to say, not merely that all *rational* thought and *universal* concepts depend on language, but that all thought and all concepts do so.[29] (b) Reflecting both that ambiguity and that considered inclination: In some passages he agrees with Süßmilch that animals can think, only not rationally.[30] But due to the considered inclination just mentioned, such a position threatens to generate an inconsistency in Herder's case. And so, in other passages he tends to revise it towards saying that, while animals do have other sorts of mental life, they *cannot* think or possess concepts. Hence he implies that both taking-awareness [*Besinnung*], or reflection [*Reflexion*], and possessing concepts are distinctively human activities—[31] which effectively amounts to saying that both thought and conceptualization are distinctively human activities. And accordingly, he says that unlike human beings a parrot "speaks merely words without thoughts,"[32] and that, unlike a human being who "already possessed the art of thinking which created the art of speaking," "the ape always apes, but it has never imitated: never said to itself with awareness, 'I want to imitate that in order to . . .' For if it had ever done that, if it had been able to think even just a single time a single such reflection . . . then at that very moment it was no longer an ape!"[33] Because of the inconsistency with his considered inclination that otherwise looms, it is, I suggest, the latter of these two alternative positions—the denial to animals of any thoughts or concepts at all—that should be seen as Herder's considered position here. Consequently, his considered solution to the inconsistencies with principles (1) and (2) that threaten in connection with animals is the same as Reimarus's. (c) Less crucially for our purposes, again like Reimarus (but this time unambiguously), Herder rejects Süßmilch's position that we simply share lower mental functions with the animals, arguing instead that human beings' possession of language, concepts, and thought transforms the nature of their lower mental functions.

Herder in particular believes that because the sensations that we adult humans have are of their very nature infused with language, concepts, and thought, our possession of the latter items and animals' lack thereof entails that even our sensations are different in nature from animals'.[34] In short, Herder's considered position in the *Treatise on the Origin* is exactly the same as Reimarus's.

Within this tradition, therefore, there were two closely related but competing positions in play, each of which succeeded in preserving internal consistency concerning principles (1) and (2) and the case of animals in its own way: the Süßmilch position and the Reimarus-Herder position. It is the latter that really interests us here—not only because we are concerned with Herder, but also because the Reimarus-Herder position seems more philosophically compelling than Süßmilch's, since (as I argued in the previous essay) Herder succeeds in providing very plausible justifications for its stronger versions of principles (1) and (2). But *whichever* of the two positions is in question, and *especially* if it is the Reimarus-Herder position, empirical evidence about animals poses certain further problems which threaten to make such a position untenable and which therefore still need to be addressed.

One such problem can be seen from recent discoveries concerning the surprisingly extensive and sophisticated use of signs by certain species of animals in the wild (for example, vervet monkeys),[35] and by other species taught in captivity (for example, bonobo apes).[36] The latter cases are especially impressive, and become all the more so when one keeps in mind that competence in sign-use can be *passive* rather than *active* (or as animal researchers would put it, can consist in *comprehension* rather than *production*), for the empirical evidence suggests that trained animals' passive competence in sign-use often far outstrips their active competence (as is of course also the case with most human language-users).[37] Such discoveries call forcefully into question the Reimarus-Herder claim that animals do not think or have concepts (and perhaps even Süßmilch's claim that they do not engage in rational thought or possess universal concepts).[38]

Now there is certainly no shortage of recent philosophers and scientists who would want to hold the Reimarus-Herder line against this sort of argument by denying that animal sign-use constitutes real language or that it provides evidence of genuine thought and concepts.[39] However, their position and the cases they make for it are not very convincing.[40] It seems much more plausible to conclude that some sign-use by animals does indeed rise to a level that should be called language, and does indeed show that they possess (or, in cases where human training is involved, come to possess) thoughts and concepts.[41] Consequently, it seems that the Reimarus-Herder position (and perhaps even Süßmilch's position) concerning animals stands in need of significant revision.

However, the revision that is required here is a modest one in a certain and important sense. In particular, this sort of empirical evidence and the revision for which it calls do not threaten to re-establish the sorts of inconsistencies from which we began and which the Reimarus-Herder position had resolved, namely those between Herder's two principles in the philosophy of language, (1) and (2), on the one hand, and an ascription to animals of thoughts and concepts but a denial to them of language, on the other. Why not? Because the empirical cases in question here are precisely ones in which we are inclined to ascribe thoughts and concepts to animals *on the basis, and to the extent, of their competence in language*.

Now it is, I suggest, one of the impressive things about Herder that, having initially adopted the Reimarus-Herder position in his *Treatise on the Origin*, he later became aware of just the sort of empirical evidence that I have been discussing here and modified his position in precisely the way that such evidence requires. Thus, in the first book of the *Ideas for the Philosophy of History of Humanity* (1784) he notes that higher apes such as the orangutan sometimes develop a passive (though not, he argues, an active) grasp of human language,[42] and that they have "a mode of thought right on the border of reason."[43] And accordingly, in a footnote that he adds to the second edition of the *Treatise on the Origin* in 1789 he corrects a judgment that he had made in the first edition of 1772 that the orangutan's physical organs do not prevent it from speaking, arguing on the basis of more recent scientific dissections that this was a mistake based on now outdated science, and that there *is* in fact a physiological obstacle—[44] the implication being that where the first edition had seen a deep psychological impediment to the orangutan's use of language there is in fact only a superficial physiological one (one compatible with the orangutan's possession of a passive grasp of language).

This is almost exactly the position that is taken today by such leading researchers on ape communication as Savage-Rumbaugh (except that they have now found techniques for circumventing apes' lack of suitable speech organs in order to enable them to complement the sort of passive comprehension of language of which Herder was already aware with an active production of language—especially the use of lexigrams on a computer keyboard).[45]

Nor did this revision of Herder's produce any serious tensions with broader features of his philosophical position. Quite the contrary. For, whereas Süßmilch and probably even Reimarus would have felt a need to resist it for theological reasons which led them to expect, and want to find, a sharp division between animals and humans,[46] Herder is in general disposed to stress *continuity* between animals and humans—for reasons that are in part empirical, in part moral, and in part theological/metaphysical.[47]

There is, however, also a further class of empirical cases which might still seem to threaten the (revised) Herder-Reimarus position (and perhaps even Süßmilch's position), and to pose a more serious threat to Herder's two principles in the philosophy of language, (1) and (2). The cases in question are ones in which animals seem to possess (rational) thought and (universal) concepts *without* having any corresponding linguistic capacities, cases in which we are inclined to ascribe (rational) thought and (universal) concepts to animals despite their lack of (or at least in a way that significantly outstrips their) competence in sign-use, on the basis of their *non*-communicative behavior. Familiar examples are "intelligent" dogs, to which people often feel inclined to ascribe thoughts, concepts, and perhaps even reasoning, not mainly on the basis of, and certainly without any restriction to, whatever primitive sign-use they may engage in (barking, whining, tail-wagging, etc.), but rather on the basis of and in the specific ways suggested by their *other* behavior. But nature is also teeming with further examples. Such cases have encouraged even some quite hard-nosed contemporary philosophers and scientists to espouse the position that animals sometimes possess thoughts, concepts, and perhaps even reasoning despite lacking (or at least in ways that transcend) any linguistic competence.[48]

However, I would suggest that this threat to the (revised) Reimarus-Herder position (and perhaps even to Süßmilch's position), and to Herder's two principles in the philosophy of language (1) and (2), can be effectively answered in the general spirit of Herder's (revised) position, as follows. Although we certainly are sometimes tempted to ascribe thoughts, concepts, and even reasoning in such cases, it seems fair to say that overall our intuitions about whether or not to do so are torn and uncertain.[49] This situation is readily explicable in terms of the nature of the behavioral criteria for our prephilosophical concepts of thought, conceptual understanding, and reasoning. These concepts have their paradigmatic application to human beings who display certain characteristic patterns of (a) active linguistic behavior ("production"), (b) passive linguistic behavior ("comprehension"), and (c) non-linguistic behavior (for example, where conceptual understanding is concerned, perceptual-discrimination-behavior). However, *partial* realizations of this paradigmatic combination can and sometimes do occur as well. For instance, the apes that Herder already described do not display characteristic active linguistic behavior but they do display characteristic passive linguistic behavior and non-linguistic behavior; and "intelligent" dogs and the like often display characteristic non-linguistic behavior more or less without any characteristic linguistic behavior at all. It is quite natural that, prephilosoph-ically, we are prepared to extend the concepts in question to cover some of these non-paradigmatic cases, but without having any precise semantic rules governing which are and which are not included, just how close the approximation to the paradigmatic cases must be in order for something to be properly classified as an instance of these concepts. Cases such as Herder's apes are pretty close to the paradigmatic ones, so that, confronted with the relevant empirical evidence, we will be rather strongly inclined to ascribe thoughts, concepts, and perhaps even reasoning here. But cases such as "intelligent" dogs who display only characteristic non-linguistic behavior are quite remote from the paradigmatic cases, in a grey area between clear applicability and clear non-applicability of the concepts in question—which explains our prephilosophical ambivalence about whether or not to credit such animals with thoughts, concepts, and reasoning.[50] However, this prephilosophical indeterminacy in our judgment about such cases need not be the final word on the matter. For we may find compelling reasons for resolving this indeterminacy in one direction or the other. And I would suggest that Herder's arguments for his two principles (1) and (2)—especially, his argument, based on the behavioral criteria that we use in ascribing conceptual understanding, for equating meanings or concepts with word-usages, and his argument that thoughts are of their very nature articulated in terms of concepts and that because these just are word-usages thought is therefore dependent on and bounded by linguistic competence—constitute strong reasons for resolving the indeterminacy *against* extending the concepts in question to animals such as "intelligent" dogs which share with paradigmatic cases only characteristic non-linguistic behavior but not characteristic linguistic behavior.[51]

This still leaves an interesting and important further question, though, namely: How should we characterize the mental life of such animals *positively*? As Donald Davidson has pointed out, we do not have an alternative mentalistic conceptual vocabulary conveniently available here (this is no doubt one reason why we often find it hard to resist extending the concepts of thought, conceptual understanding, and even reasoning to such cases).[52] Also, it should be kept in mind that the non-linguistic behavior in such cases often really is quite strikingly like that involved in genuine cases of thought, conceptual understanding, and reasoning. I would suggest that these two considerations speak in favor of adopting one (or possibly more than one) of the following approaches: we might continue using the concepts of thought, conceptual understanding, and reasoning for such cases but now in a self-consciously *metaphorical* way; we might talk explicitly of states and processes *analogous* to thought, conceptual understanding, and reasoning (this would probably be better, for clarity's sake); or we might speak in terms of "proto-thoughts," "proto-concepts," etc. (this is similar to the preceding option, but perhaps even better, both for the sake of greater linguistic convenience and because it incorporates a gesture towards a plausible evolutionary theory).

Reimarus, in his *General Observations on the Drives of Animals, Mainly on their Drives of Artifice*, had already opted for the second of these three solutions (explicitly asserting analogousness). Since, as we have seen, Herder's considered position on animals is continuous with Reimarus's, one might reasonably expect that this would be his considered solution as well. In his *Treatise on the Origin* there is as yet little indication of such a solution. However, by the time he writes the *Ideas* he does embrace it—noting, for example, that "there is no virtue, no drive in the human heart of which there were not here and there in the animal world an analogon."[53] Indeed, at one point in this later work he even approximates the third (and I have suggested, optimal) solution, noting that animals have "prototypes [*Vorbilder*]" of human mental functions: "Thus everywhere we find prototypes [*Vorbilder*] of human modes of activity in which the animal is exercised . . . They have human-like thoughts, they exercise, forced to do so by forming nature, in human-like drives."[54] This, then, is another respect in which Herder's position concerning animals makes significant progress after its initial formulation.

III

A further set of difficult questions facing Herder's two principles in the philosophy of language arises in connection with the non-linguistic arts (painting, sculpture, music, etc.). Those two principles make a sharp and very plausible break with a common Enlightenment assumption that thought and meaning are autonomous of and prior to whatever material, perceptible expressions they may happen to receive. Following Charles Taylor, we might call such a move one to "expressivism."[55] But what form should expressivism take *exactly*? Is the dependence of thought and meaning on external symbols really one on *language* and *words* (in the usual sense of "language" and "words")? Or is it not rather a dependence on a broader range of symbolic media that includes, besides language and words (in the usual sense), also such things as painting, sculpture, and music—so that a person might be able to entertain thoughts and meanings which he could not express in language and words but only in some other symbolic medium? Let us call the former position *narrow expressivism* and the latter *broad expressivism*.[56]

Also, on second thoughts, is Herder's own position, as embodied in his two principles, narrow expressivism or broad expressivism? It certainly seems at first sight that the two principles commit him to narrow expressivism, because of their reference to "language" and "words." But matters may not be quite so simple. For one thing, such terms easily lend themselves to broadened uses which might include media beyond language and words in the usual sense. For another thing, precisely such a broadening actually occurred in a philosopher who was intimately associated with Herder: Hamann. In his *Metacritique on the Purism of Pure Reason* (1784) Hamann was just as much verbally committed to the two principles in question as Herder. But Hamann nonetheless embraced broad expressivism. And he did so quite consistently, because he understood the terms "language" and "word" as they occur in these two principles in unusually wide senses. For example, he explicitly includes as forms of the "language" on which he says thought depends not only language in the usual sense but also painting, drawing, and music.[57]

Fortunately, this further question that has intruded has a straightforward answer. Herder's considered position *is* in fact all along the narrow expressivism that his two principles seem to imply. (His verbal sharing of them with Hamann hence masks an important difference of philosophical position between the two thinkers.)

So the question that we need to consider is really just how defensible such a position is, especially in competition with broad expressivism. What I want to argue is basically this: Herder began his career with a naive version of it which is implausible, but through several years of struggle with the subject he eventually attained a refined version of it which is much more—indeed extremely—plausible. My hope is that considering this development may prove not only exegetically but also philosophically instructive.

The key work in this connection is Herder's *Critical Forests* from 1769 (though its important fourth and final part was not published until the middle of the nineteenth century). As we have seen, by that date Herder was already firmly committed to his two principles in the philosophy of language, and, as that would suggest, from the very start in the work he is committed to narrow expressivism. However, his commitment to it there initially takes a quite naive and unsatisfactory form in relation to the potentially threatening question of what to say about the non-linguistic arts. For one thing, his way of saving his narrow expressivist principles that thought is essentially dependent on and bounded by language and that meaning consists in word-usage in the face of the phenomenon of the non-linguistic arts is to deny the non-linguistic arts any capacity to express thoughts or meanings *autonomously* of language by denying that they can express thoughts or meanings *at all*. Thus, he initially sets out in the work to argue that whereas words and poetry have a sense, a soul, a force, by contrast music is a mere succession of objects in time, and sculpture and painting are merely spatial;[58] that whereas poetry not only depends on the senses but also relates to the imagination, by contrast music, sculpture, and painting belong solely to the senses (namely, to hearing, feeling, and vision, respectively);[59] and that whereas poetry uses *voluntary, conventional* signs, by contrast music, sculpture, and painting employ only *natural* ones.[60]

For another thing, exacerbating this unsatisfactoriness into outright inconsistency, Herder from the start in the work also has a set of intuitions that are sharply at odds with this form of narrow expressivism, and even with narrow expressivism generally—intuitions which imply, far more plausibly, that non-linguistic art *can* express thoughts and meanings after all, and which even imply in a broad expressivist spirit that it can do so in ways that are neither achieved nor achievable by language. For example, in the first part of the work he intervenes in a quarrel that had arisen between Lessing and Winckelmann concerning the question of whether, as Lessing thought, linguistic art (especially poetry) or, as Winckelmann thought, visual art (especially sculpture) is expressively superior *in ways which tend to support Winckelmann's case for visual art*.[61] In particular, he argues against Lessing and for Winckelmann that sculpture can express not only the temporally transitory but also the eternal;[62] that painting is capable of representing not only objects but also actions;[63] that the *visual* aspects of a work of dramatic poetry such as Sophocles' *Philoctetes* are as important to its meaning as its *verbal* aspects;[64] and that moreover all genuine poetry is "a sort of painting [*eine Art Malerei*],"[65] so that, for example, even in its *verbal* aspects the *Philoctetes* is "a series of acting, poetic paintings."[66]

This unsatisfactory, and indeed inconsistent, position at the beginning of the *Critical Forests* resulted mainly from a single oversight on Herder's part. This oversight lay in a failure to see any way of reconciling two strong, and both very plausible, intuitions which he had and which stand in tension (but not in fact contradiction) with each other: on the one hand, his intuition that thought is essentially dependent on and bounded by language and that meaning consists in word-usage, and on the other hand, an intuition that non-linguistic arts do nevertheless express thoughts and meanings. As a consequence of this oversight, when in the grip of the former intuition, he felt compelled to deny the latter one; and when in the grip of the latter intuition, he treated this as equivalent to abandoning the former one. What he had not yet realized was that it is perfectly possible to maintain both of the intuitions consistently with one another, namely *by insisting that the thoughts and meanings expressed by non-linguistic arts must be derived from and bounded by the artist's capacity for linguistic expression.*

However, by the time Herder wrote the later parts of the *Critical Forests* he had found this solution. Thus in the third part, focusing on a particularly clear and instructive example (i.e. one which illustrates with unusual clarity both that non-linguistic art does sometimes express thoughts and meanings, and that the thoughts and meanings in question have a prior linguistic articulation or articulability), he notes that the pictorial representations on Greek coins are typically allegorical.[67] And by the fourth part he is prepared to say the same about much painting as well, now writing for example of "the sense, the allegory, the story/history [*Geschichte*] which is put into the whole of a painting."[68] By 1778 at the latest he extends this account to sculpture as well. Thus, in the *Plastic* of 1778 he abandons the merely sensualistic conception of sculpture that had predominated in the *Critical Forests* and instead insists that sculpture is essentially expressive of, and therefore needs to be interpreted by, a *soul*.[69] But this no longer forces him into unfaithfulness to his two principles that thought is essentially dependent on and bounded by language and that meaning is word-usage, for he now conceives the thoughts and meanings expressed by sculpture to have a linguistic source:

The sculptor stands in the dark of night and gropes towards the forms of gods. *The stories of the poets are before and in him.*[70]

Similarly, in relation to music, Herder in the early 1780s moves away from the merely sensualistic conception of music that had predominated in the *Critical Forests* towards a conception which allows music intellectual content, but he does so in a way that is consistent with his principles that thought is essentially dependent on and bounded by language and that meaning is word-usage because he ties the content in question to a prior linguistic understanding: Whereas in *On the Effect of Poetic Art on the Ethics of Peoples in Ancient and Modern Times* from 1778 he is still only prepared to say that music is a dark expression of feelings,[71] by the time he writes the *Theological Letters* of 1780–1 he praises the power of the instrumental side of contemporary church music to express ideas as well, describing it with Luther—in a way that is significant both because it implies the music's expression of thoughts and meanings and because it implies that this intellectual content is derived from a prior linguistic expression—as a "second theology" (i.e. second only to actual theology), and giving specific examples of how the instrumental aspects of a work like Handel's *Messiah* express Christian ideas whose expression was originally linguistic:

What a great work this *Messiah* is, a true Christian epic in sounds! When you right from the start discern the gentle *voice of consolation* and hear *mountain and valley even out* in the whole of nature at the arrival of the Messiah, until *the exaltedness, the exaltedness of the Lord, reveals* itself and *the whole world beholds Him together* . . .[72]

Similarly, in the *Letters for the Advancement of Humanity* (1793–7) Herder goes on to argue that modern instrumental music more broadly (as it existed in his day!),[73] with its special emphasis on harmony and melody, developed out of Christian hymns, which were by contrast partly verbal and less harmonic-melodic, and that by means of its harmony and melody it succeeds in expressing a certain (quasi-Spinozistic) idea of the whole, including a harmonious whole of all peoples, which it took over from those hymns.[74]

There is also a further way in which Herder's considered position, at which he arrives by the end of the *Critical Forests*, implies that non-linguistic art involves thought and meaning, and hence language. The above points have been concerned with the fact that, like linguistic arts such as poetry, non-linguistic arts such as painting, sculpture, and music are heavily involved in the *expression* of thoughts and meanings. But by the time Herder writes the fourth part of the *Critical Forests* he also recognizes that thoughts and meanings, and hence language, are involved in non-linguistic arts in an even more fundamental way, namely as *presuppositions* of the very *perception* of such art (by the artist and his audience). For in the fourth part of the *Critical Forests* Herder begins to argue—anticipating much twentieth-century work on perception generally (for example, Hansen and Kuhn), and on the perception of non-linguistic art in particular (for example, Panofsky and Gombrich)—that human perception generally, and human perception of non-linguistic artworks in particular, is of its nature laden with concepts, beliefs, and theory, and hence implicitly dependent on language.[75] Consequently, on Herder's considered view, non-linguistic art is in fact *doubly* dependent on thought and meaning, and hence on language: not only for the thoughts and meanings that it *expresses* but also for those that it *presupposes* in perception.[76]

In sum, the considered position at which Herder eventually arrives is a refined form of narrow expressivism. It insists that thought is essentially dependent on and bounded by language and that meaning consists in word-usage (in the usual senses of "language" and "word"). But it also allows the non-linguistic arts a power both to presuppose and to express thoughts and meanings. And it reconciles these two seemingly incompatible stances by holding that this power is one that the non-linguistic artist (or perhaps one should really now use scare quotes there: "non-linguistic" artist) enjoys in virtue of, and in a manner bounded by, his linguistic capacity.[77]

This position has important implications not only for Herder's philosophy of language (our main concern here) but also for his philosophy of art. Concerning his philosophy of language, it shows that the narrow expressivism of principles (1) and (2) can be plausibly reconciled with a forceful intuition which threatens to conflict with it, namely the intuition that much non-linguistic art expresses thoughts and meanings. Concerning his philosophy of art, it implies that non-linguistic artworks are in important respects both similar to and dependent on language, and that the interpretation of the former is therefore in important respects both similar to and dependent on the interpretation of the latter.

With Herder's achievement of this position, and Hamann's achievement of his, there were now two incompatible, and both rather plausible, answers to the philosophical question raised at the start of this section available: the refined form of narrow expressivism at which Herder had eventually arrived, and a broad expressivism in Hamann's manner. The nineteenth-century German philosophical tradition—in particular, Hegel, Schleiermacher, and Dilthey—henceforth tended to vacillate between these two alternatives.[78] However, I would suggest that this vacillation is much less a symptom of the tradition's ineptitude than of the genuine difficulty of the philosophical choice between these two positions.

What *is* the correct position here? To backtrack a little for a moment, one thing that *can*, I think, be said with some confidence in this area is that the naive form of narrow expressivism from which Herder started out—the form which denies that non-linguistic arts express thoughts or meanings *at all*—is untenable. As we saw, Herder comes upon a *casus crucis* that shows this clearly enough: Greek coins. And he goes on to identify several further compelling examples as well, such as Greek sculpture. But the point can also be made by means of countless other examples—for instance, ancient Egyptian and Mesopotamian wall friezes depicting the events of specific wars and battles (or more recent equivalents such as the Bayeux tapestry); medieval and early modern religious paintings based on episodes from the Bible;[79] "program music" such as that composed by Liszt and Smetana (for example, the latter's cycle of symphonic poems *Ma Vlast* with its expression of thoughts about specific features of Czech geography and history);[80] and so on. To deny that such non-linguistic art expresses thoughts or meanings at all would pretty clearly be absurd. Indeed, in many cases—for example, the ancient wall friezes mentioned—that is arguably its *primary* function. If we are even for a moment tempted to imagine otherwise, that is probably only because we have been unduly influenced by a parochial experience of such things as twentieth-century abstract painting (e.g. Jackson Pollock) and instrumental music (e.g. Arnold Schönberg). In order to be at all plausible, therefore, narrow expressivism must instead take the more refined form that Herder eventually gave it.

But is refined narrow expressivism correct or is broad expressivism? This seems to me a far more difficult question to answer. What I want to suggest (albeit tentatively) is that refined narrow expressivism is indeed the more correct of the two positions, but that there are two important grains of truth in broad expressivism, one of which Herder himself perceives, but the other not.

In order to support the former of these suggestions—that refined narrow expressivism is the more correct of the two positions—I would like to say some things in support of Herder's refined narrow expressivist way of explaining instrumental music in particular. Since instrumental music seems an unusually favorable case for broad expressivism, and since most of my points could be extended to other non-linguistic artforms, this specific focus may serve as a means to make plausible a more general moral.

Instrumental music does seem to me an unusually potent source of a temptation to broad expressivism. For in contemplating this artform, we surely do often get a powerful sense that thoughts and meanings are being expressed which it is beyond the capacity of (existing or perhaps even any) language to capture. Accordingly, theories of this artform which attribute to it some sort of ineffable thought and meaning abound. Here are two examples: (a) The later Dilthey in his essay *Musical Understanding* treats instrumental music as a prime example of broad expressivism, arguing that while such music is indeed often expressive merely of linguistic thoughts, in its highest forms it also expresses non-linguistic ones, in particular ones about the nature of "Life" itself.[81] (b) Hanslick argues that music expresses strictly *musical* ideas,[82] and, following this lead, Stephen Bungay argues that it is just obvious that non-linguistic musical ideas and thinking occur.[83]

Despite the admitted seductiveness of the broad expressivist intuition about instrumental music, my strong suspicion is that Herder is in the end correct to judge that this artform should be explained in a narrow expressivist way. I would therefore like now to make a few points in support of such a view. (Similar points would apply to painting, and probably also to other non-linguistic arts.)

The intuition that instrumental music conveys thoughts and meanings which it is beyond the power of (existing or any) language to express can indeed seem very compelling, and I do not by any means want to suggest that it should be dismissed lightly. Nonetheless, it seems to me probable that it is illusory. (It may be salutary in this connection to recall the—presumable—illusion to which we often fall victim in waking from a dream that we have entertained thoughts and meanings in the dream that are linguistically inexpressible.)

Consider, first of all, Dilthey's attempt to vindicate this intuition. Dilthey believes that instrumental music in its higher forms expresses some sort of metaphysical or (quasi-)religious thought (about "Life"). This is a common enough conviction, and it may well be correct. But why should one take the thought in question to be linguistically inexpressible rather than—as Herder implies—linguistically expressible and perhaps, moreover, actually derived from linguistically expressed metaphysics or religion? Certainly, the sort of thought that Dilthey has in mind here may be only quite *vaguely* expressible in language. But is there really any reason to suppose that the music expresses it any *less* vaguely?

Bungay's attempt to vindicate the intuition in question is different. His claim is not that instrumental music expresses metaphysical or religious thoughts which transcend language, but rather that it expresses distinctively *musical* thoughts and ideas which transcend language. This claim strikes me as more plausible, but still in the end very questionable. It seems important to distinguish between two sorts of cases here. First, there are cases in which the relevant person, say a composer, possesses a linguistic or notational means of expressing the putative musical thoughts or ideas in question. In such cases it *does* seem to me appropriate to speak of his having musical thoughts and ideas. But then, these are also cases in which he can express them *linguistically* (even musical notation being plausibly considered a part of language). Second, there are certainly also cases in which a person develops putative musical thoughts or ideas *without* having any corresponding linguistic or notational means for expressing them. (Think, for example, of the once fairly common phenomenon of the skilled jazz or blues musician who does not read music and is verbally inarticulate to boot.) However, is it really so clear that in such cases we should speak literally of the person's having musical *thoughts and ideas*—rather than, say, of his creating/perceiving complex sound-patterns and -relationships? To my linguistic ear, at least, such a characterization would seem out of place if meant literally (though no doubt alright if only meant metaphorically).[84] In short, it seems to me that non-linguistic *musical* thoughts and ideas may well, again, be a will-o'-the-wisp.

However (turning now from refutation to diagnosis), I suspect that there are also deeper sources feeding the delusive temptation to suppose that instrumental music expresses linguistically inexpressible thoughts and meanings. Herder often suggests, very plausibly, that instrumental music is relatively inarticulate in the expression of thoughts and meanings (i.e. relatively as compared to language). For example (in an unusually extreme statement of such a position), he writes that music "gives the soul no determinate thought at all. Rather, as long as it is wordless, it leaves the soul free to retrieve what it likes from the treasure of memory."[85] He also often implies, again very plausibly, that instrumental music is relatively *articulate* in the expression of nuances of feeling or emotion (again, relatively as compared to language). For example, he writes that "suffering and joy, all of inner feeling in its breadth and depth, *can* only express itself harmonically, . . . *must* sound forth melodically."[86] What I want to suggest is that the temptation to suppose that instrumental music expresses linguistically inexpressible thoughts and meanings largely arises from its possession of this peculiar combination of inarticulateness and articulateness. For this combination of features can easily give rise to illusions that instrumental music expresses linguistically inexpressible thoughts and meanings in at least two ways: First, instrumental music often expresses a composer's *linguistically expressible* thoughts and meanings but in ways that are vague, making it hard for a listener to pin down the thoughts and meanings in question with any precision (from the music). This genuine presence of definite linguistically expressible thoughts and meanings which, however, the listener finds himself unable to pin down linguistically with any precision easily gets misconstrued by him as a presence of definite thoughts and meanings which cannot be linguistically expressed.[87] Second, music often expresses and communicates more precisely than could be done by language (alone) certain nuances of feeling and emotion—that is, certain psychological states which are other than thoughts and meanings but which can easily be mistaken for them (especially given that they do *involve* them,[88] and that other thoughts and meanings are expressed in the music as well).[89]

In sum, I suggest that when one considers the several possible closer specifications and sources of the intuition that instrumental music expresses linguistically inexpressible thoughts and meanings in this way, the intuition in the end proves to be illusory.

As I implied earlier, analogous points would hold for painting as well (and no doubt also for the other non-linguistic arts). For painting too sometimes expresses (vague) metaphysical or (quasi-)religious thoughts; it too involves technical "thoughts" and "ideas" which are sometimes linguistically expressible by the artist and sometimes not (for example, concerning perspective or color); and it too tends to combine relative inarticulateness in the expression of thoughts and meanings with relative articulateness in the expression of nuances of feeling and emotion (the former part of which point is obvious; concerning the latter, think for example of Rembrandt's self-portraits).

As I mentioned, though, I think that there are nonetheless two important grains of truth in broad expressivism—one of which Herder perceives, but the other not. The former, the one he *does* perceive, is difficult to capture correctly but can perhaps be articulated in three parts as follows: (a) As I recently suggested (and as Herder himself implies), non-linguistic art often succeeds in expressing fine nuances of feeling or emotion which language (alone) cannot.[90] (b) Moreover (a point which Herder anticipates in his account of music, and which has since been elaborated by other people), in many cases non-linguistic art not only expresses them but also in part *constitutes* them, in the sense that they could not exist without such expression.[91] (c) In consequence of these two points (as Herder himself implies), the expressibility and even the very existence of certain thoughts and meanings—most obviously, ones which actually refer to the feelings in question,[92] but also ones which depend on them in other ways in virtue of the sort of broad dependence of meanings on feelings posited by Herder's quasi-empiricist theory of meaning—depend on non-linguistic art's expression of the relevant feelings; whatever linguistic expressions of the thoughts and meanings may occur are parasitic on non-linguistic art's expression of the relevant feelings.[93]

This dependence of the expressibility and even the very existence of certain feelings, and hence of certain thoughts and meanings, on the expressive power of the non-linguistic arts comes quite close to what the broad expressivist had in mind. Nonetheless, I would suggest that it falls short of actually entailing broad expressivism, and remains consistent with narrow expressivism. This is so for two reasons: First (focusing on points (a) and (b)), the nuances of feeling which on this view can only be expressed, and are moreover in part constituted, by non-linguistic art are not themselves thoughts or meanings (only possible foundations for such).[94] And second (focusing on point (c)), it is consistent with this view that language should still be both *necessary for* and *able to express* the thoughts or meanings which these nuances of feeling support; it is just that language can only constitute and express them insofar as it is aided by relevant non-linguistic art in a certain way.[95]

The other important grain of truth in broad expressivism is one that Herder did *not* recognize, and recognizing it calls for a significant, though not huge, revision in his position. It seems to me that refined narrow expressivism, as it was standardly conceived by Herder and his tradition, rested on a certain mistaken assumption, and that it therefore needs to make a concession in the direction of broad expressivism—though one which can, and I suggest should, take the form of a modification of narrow expressivism bringing it slightly closer to broad expressivism rather than an abandonment of the former for the latter or even the adoption of a position mid-way between the two.

What is the mistaken assumption in question? The refined narrow expressivist in this tradition generally thinks of language in the usual sense as restricted to a very limited range of material-perceptual media: namely, audible noises made with the mouth (speech) and visible but non-pictorial marks on paper, wax, stone, or some other substance (writing). Herder in particular normally thinks of language in such a restrictive way—[96] and so too do other narrow expressivists influenced by him, such as Schleiermacher,[97] and Wilhelm von Humboldt.[98] But now, how, a broad expressivist may well ask, could these two sorts of material-perceptual media, among the many others that are conceivable (and perhaps even actual), possibly possess the sort of privilege as fundamental vehicles of thought and meaning which the refined narrow expressivist is attributing to them? Would this not be inexplicable, a sort of miracle?[99] Indeed, is it not, on reflection, *clear* that other material-perceptual media at least could, and perhaps even do, serve as fundamental vehicles of thought and meaning as well—for example, the sort of highly conventional, "unrealistic" pictures that are used to express ideas in ancient Egyptian painting (pictures distinct from, but closely related in form and function to, hieroglyphics),[100] or, beyond the sphere of art, sign-language as used by the deaf,[101] gestures,[102] and perhaps even more exotic media such as some animals may actually use (for instance, touch and chemical emissions)?[103]

I think that a refined narrow expressivist simply has to concede this point. That might seem like a huge concession for him to make to broad expressivism. However, I want to suggest that, on the contrary, he can and probably should make it in a way that allows him to claim that he is thereby only modestly revising his position rather than abandoning it for broad expressivism or even taking up a position mid-way between the two, namely on the following three grounds:

First, and perhaps most importantly, it seems plausible to say that such alternative material-perceptual media could only share with spoken and written language the function of serving as fundamental vehicles of thought and meaning to the extent that they took on the same sort of *highly rule-governed, conventional* character as spoken and written language have,[104] and thereby themselves became naturally describable as language in a sense of "language" which only barely, if at all, goes beyond the usual sense of the word. The case of deaf sign-language illustrates this fact—both in the sense that such sign-language displays the same highly rule-governed, conventional character as spoken and written language have and in the sense that it shows how naturally and seamlessly we extend our usual concept of "language" to cover a materially-perceptually unusual case provided only that this character is present.[105]

Second, this criterion *excludes*, rather than including, many forms and aspects of non-linguistic art, and moreover the very ones which we tend to think of as most responsible for making it *art*, namely those which are not guided by rules or conventions but instead issue from a sort of spontaneity and novelty. In other words, not only will any so-called "non-linguistic" medium that can serve as a fundamental vehicle for thought and meaning to the same extent turn out in fact to be language in something very much like the usual sense of the word "language," but in addition it will to the same extent turn out *not* to be art in the usual sense of the word "art."[106]

Third, while it does indeed seem clear that alternative material-perceptual media such as those recently mentioned *could* serve as fundamental vehicles of thought and meaning independently of spoken and written language, it seems doubtful that they do so to any great extent *in practice*. For example, the thoughts and meanings which the ancient Egyptian artist expressed through his conventional pictures were presumably in fact ones that he was already able to articulate in spoken (and perhaps also written) language; the heavy dependence of deaf sign-language on pre-existing spoken and written language is obvious as well (albeit that the exact degree and nature of the dependence are controversial questions); gesture too typically functions alongside equivalent spoken or written language rather than instead of it; and when one turns to animals' unusual material-perceptual media, even if one grants that these do sometimes sustain thoughts and meanings autonomously of spoken and written language (as I suspect one should), the thoughts and meanings in question seem likely to be quite limited in nature.

In sum, it seems to me that in the contest between the narrow and the broad forms of expressivism refined narrow expressivism does in the end prove to be more or less the correct position, but that in order to be *strictly* correct it needs to make two concessions to broad expressivism: first (as Herder saw), that language's expressiveness is in certain areas deeply dependent on that of the non-linguistic arts, and second (as he did not see), that *spoken and written* language is not the only possible fundamental vehicle for thought and meaning, but other forms of language, including some which at least border on art, could, and perhaps even to some extent actually do, serve as such fundamental vehicles as well.

If this is correct, then we may draw the following general morals for the philosophy of language (our main concern here) and also for the philosophy of art. The philosophy of language can in good conscience continue to advance Herder's two principles that thought is essentially dependent on and bounded by language and that meaning consists in word-usage (as long as it keeps in mind that the language and words in question may require extra-linguistic help and that they need not be restricted to *spoken and written* language and words); there is, after all, no need to make room for non-linguistic, non-verbal fundamental vehicles of thought and meaning as broad expressivism maintained. And concerning the philosophy of art, again very much as Herder's considered position implied, even many so-called "non-linguistic" artworks will in fact be dependent on language, so that their interpretation will be dependent on the interpretation of the latter; it will never be necessary to entertain the possibility that they express thoughts or meanings which transcend the artist's language; and indeed it will not usually even be necessary to entertain the possibility that they express ones which transcend his *spoken and written* language.

IV

These, then, have been three problem cases confronting Herder's two most fundamental principles in the philosophy of language which he himself identified and wrestled with. The general moral of the story I have told here is that, having initially developed ways of reconciling them with his two principles which were unsatisfactory, he subsequently searched for and eventually discovered far more satisfactory reconciliations, indeed reconciliations which (at least in the two cases that really require one: animals and non-linguistic art) seem broadly correct.

Notes

1. As I pointed out in Essay 2, this is much earlier than Hamann's commitment to a similar position, and also antedates Herder's own better known, but in my view anomalous and philosophically problematic, position in his *Treatise on the Origin of Language* (1772).
2. G1:27.
3. G1:556–7.
4. To be a little more precise, the *Treatise on the Origin of Language* relabels something which it considers to be a very fundamental aspect of all (human) thought and meaning, namely the isolation of "characteristic marks [*Merkmale*]," as "language" or "word." See esp. G1:723: "*This first characteristic mark of taking-awareness was a word of the soul! With it human language is invented.*"
5. There is also a fourth, and somewhat similar, problem case: human infants. However, Herder established a fairly plausible solution for this case early on and stuck with it thereafter: a child's thoughts and concepts are dependent on and develop in step with its development of language. Thus (as we saw) already in *On Diligence in Several Learned Languages* from 1764 Herder writes: "The first words that we mumble are the most important foundation stones of the understanding, and our nursemaids are our first teachers of logic" (G1:27). And similarly, in *On the Cognition and Sensation of the Human Soul* from 1778 we read: "Thus, as we see, does the child attain its mental constitution, it learns to speak . . . and precisely as a result and in the same way to think. Whoever has observed children, how they learn to speak and think, the peculiar anomalies and analogies which are expressed

in the process, will hardly have any further doubts" (G4:358). In light of work that has been done on infant psychology by Piaget and others in the twentieth century, this solution requires some revision. But the hope would be that it could largely survive the required revision. Some of Herder's own later and better thoughts concerning the analogous case of animals, as discussed below, are suggestive of ways in which this could be achieved.

6. Concerning these earlier versions or close relatives of principle (1), see Essay 2.

7. Thus Wolff only says that it is "any mortal [*ullus mortalium*]" who needs language for (rational) thought (*Psychologia Rationalis* [1734], par. 461). And Süßmilch argues explicitly that unlike human beings God has understanding without the use of any signs (Süßmilch, *Versuch eines Beweises, daß die erste Sprache ihren Ursprung nicht vom Menschen, sondern allein vom Schöpfer erhalten habe*, p. 5).

8. *On the Divinity and Use of the Bible* (1768), G9/1:25, cf. 25–6; also, *On the First Documents* (1769), G5:27–9.

9. Concerning this, see Essay 2.

10. There have, of course, been theological positions that have held that God can perform such feats as contravening logical laws and separating things from their essential properties. But Herder probably would not, and should not, have had the philosophical stomach for that.

11. G5:28.

12. S19:295–6, cf. 280.

13. S19:296–7.

14. G4:725 ff.

15. G4:774 ff.

16. After all, the behavior of animals affords us almost as good evidence for attributing mental states to them as the behavior of our fellow human beings affords us for attributing mental states to *them*.

17. *Versuch*, pp. 101–2.

18. Ibid., pp. 35, 52, 100–2. It is not *entirely* clear from the text that Süßmilch means this concession of thought to animals as an *additional* concession over and above the concession to them of some lower mental functions. For he at times uses the term "thought" in the very broad sense that Descartes had introduced, in which it applies to any mental content whatever, including such items as sensations and images (for example, he treats mere sensations and images as thoughts on p. 35). But that he at least sometimes means this as an additional concession is strongly suggested by the fact that at other points he conceives of

"thought" as a superior mental function over and above such things as sensations and images (e.g., at p. 52 he describes sensations and images as merely "the first foundational beginnings of thought"). Whether the thought that he concedes to animals is meant to be an addition to the *higher* among the lower mental functions—in particular, to attention, recognition, distinguishing, and cunning—is even less clear, but perhaps also matters less.

19. Ibid., p. 99.

20. Ibid., pp. 100–1.

21. H.S. Reimarus, *Die vornehmsten Wahrheiten der natürlichen Religion*, esp. vol. 2, essay 7; *Allgemeine Betrachtungen über die Triebe der Tiere, hauptsächlich über ihre Kunsttriebe*, esp. vol. 1, ch. 2. (There are some significant differences between Reimarus's positions in these two works, but I shall set these aside here.)

22. *Die vornehmsten Wahrheiten*, 2:531–2.

23. Ibid., pp. 521–2, 546.

24. Ibid., pp. 502, 532; cf. *Allgemeine Betrachtungen*, 1:50.

25. *Allgemeine Betrachtungen*, 1:24–5, 33–7, 45, 47, 50; cf. *Die vornehmsten Wahrheiten*, 2:532 n.

26. *Die vornehmsten Wahrheiten*, 2:531–2.

27. Cf. his statement later in the *Ideas for the Philosophy of History of Humanity* (1784–91): "To want to consider [animals] as machines is a sin against nature" (G6:110).

28. This ambiguity in his position persists in the *Ideas*—see esp. G6:138–42.

29. On this see Essay 2.

30. G1:718, 720–1, 772, 774 (for the concession that animals think); 725–6, 732–3 (for the denial that they do so with reason).

31. G1:722–3.

32. G1:728.

33. G1:731.

34. See esp. G1:717–19.

35. See D.L. Cheney and R.M. Seyfarth, *How Monkeys See the World* (Chicago: University of Chicago Press, 1990).

36. See S. Savage-Rumbaugh, S.G. Shanker, T.J. Taylor, *Apes, Language, and the Human Mind* (Oxford: Oxford University Press, 1998).

37. Concerning this subject, see ibid.; also, L.M. Herman and P. Morrell-Samuels, "Knowledge Acquisition and Asymmetry between Language Comprehension and Production: Dolphins and Apes as General Models

for Animals," in M. Bekoff and D. Jamieson ed., *Readings in Animal Cognition* (Cambridge, Mass.: MIT Press, 1996).

38. That the use of signs by certain animals constitutes strong evidence for their possession of thoughts and concepts, and also provides a promising route via which we may be able to access the content of the thoughts and concepts in question, has been plausibly argued especially by D.R. Griffin in *Animal Thinking* (Cambridge, Mass.: Harvard University Press, 1984), chs. 8–10; "Windows on Animal Minds," *Consciousness and Cognition*, 4/2 (1995); and *Animal Minds* (Chicago: University of Chicago Press, 2001). Interestingly, Griffin emphasizes that this point seems to apply far beyond the more obvious cases, such as monkeys, apes, and marine mammals, to include even such species as honey bees, and that the range of material-perceptual media of communication may extend well beyond the familiar cases of auditory and visual signs to include in addition such things as, for example, signs by touch and chemical-emissions. However, if the points I am about to make in what follows have force, Griffin has in one important respect under- and mis-stated his case: animals' competence in sign-use is not only *strong evidence* of their possession of thoughts and concepts but also a *conditio sine qua non* thereof.

39. See e.g. C. Taylor, "The Importance of Herder." Some further relevant literature that does not focus on Herder: J. Bennett, *Linguistic Behavior* (Cambridge: Cambridge University Press, 1976), pp. 202 ff.; N. Chater and C. Hayes, "Animal Concepts: Content and Discontent," *Mind and Language*, 9/3 (1994), esp. pp. 228 ff.; D. Davidson, "Rational Animals."

40. For example—even if one were to grant the validity of the various criteria to which they appeal, which often seem rather arbitrary—*pace* Taylor, "The Importance of Herder," there is good empirical evidence that sign-using animals do sometimes develop a sense of linguistic *rightness* (see e.g. Savage-Rumbaugh et al., *Apes, Language, and the Human Mind*); *pace* Bennett, *Linguistic Behavior*, there is good empirical evidence that animals do sometimes *intend* to communicate (see again the work by Savage-Rumbaugh et al. just cited; also, Griffin, *Animal Minds*, esp. pp. 173–4); *pace* certain other objectors, there is good empirical evidence that animals do sometimes employ a rudimentary *grammar* (see again the work by Savage-Rumbaugh et al. already cited); *pace* yet other objectors, there is good empirical evidence that animals are sometimes linguistically *creative* (see again ibid.); *pace* yet other

objectors, there is good empirical evidence that animals do sometimes refer to *absent* things and states of affairs (as Griffin points out, even bees do this). And so forth.

41. It is very much a further question what exactly the thoughts and concepts involved *are*. Especially in the natural cases, but even in those where human training is involved, it seems quite unlikely that they will be exactly the same as thoughts or concepts which *we humans* have and express in *our* languages. Davidson ("Rational Animals," pp. 319–21) and Chater and Hayes ("Animal Concepts: Content and Discontent," pp. 228 ff.) seem to me right to emphasize this. However, this does not, as they seem to suppose, constitute good grounds for skepticism that such animals *have* thoughts and concepts at all—any more than the fact that we usually face an analogous intellectual-linguistic gulf when we encounter the thoughts and concepts of historically or culturally alien *human beings* constitutes good grounds for denying that *they* have. In both cases, strenuous interpretive efforts are likely to be required if we are to achieve anything close to an exact understanding.

42. G6:117–18.

43. Ibid., p. 116. Cf. p. 141: "half human-reason." (Herder is still somewhat torn about this, though.)

44. The first edition of 1772 had said that "the ability is not impeded in this animal's case by the instruments" (G1:731). In the second edition of 1789 Herder adds the following self-correcting footnote: "It is clear from Camper's dissection of the orangutan (see his translated short writings) that this claim is too bold; however, formerly, when I wrote this, it was the common opinion of anatomists" (G1:1308). Herder already implies such a revision of his earlier position in 1784 at *Ideas*, bk. 1, G6:140–2 (though he still seems torn on the point there—thus contrast G6:117).

45. See e.g. Savage-Rumbaugh et al., *Apes, Language, and the Human Mind*, pp. 190, 213. Even Herder's—at first encounter merely quaint-sounding—speculation in the *Ideas* that it was human beings' upright posture that was the key to their development of reason (G6:125–30) because "only in an upright posture does true human language occur," since otherwise the "throat [gets] misformed," and although "several animals have vocal organs similar to humans' yet . . . none of them is capable of the *progressing* stream of speech from our elevated human breast, from our narrower and artfully closed mouth" (G6:141), turns out to contain much truth by current scientific lights. For, as Savage-Rumbaugh et al. note, it was evidently indeed their upright posture

that produced in human beings, unlike apes, a configuration of their vocal organs which made speech (and hence language, and hence reason) possible (*Apes, Language, and the Human Mind*, pp. 12–13).

46. See esp. Süßmilch, *Versuch*, pp. 103–4; also, Reimarus, *Die vornehmsten Wahrheiten*, 2:492–3, 567.

47. For this general disposition, see esp. the *Ideas*, bk. 1. Herder's *empirical* reasons lie in a multitude of physiological and behavioral continuities between animals and humans that he perceives (and that he outlines in *Ideas*, bk. 1). His *moral* reasons lie in an unusually high degree of moral respect and concern for animals (see e.g. *Ideas*, bk. 1, G6:156; *Fragments*, G1:611: mankind's early intercourse with animals was an "honor"; G7:743). His *theological/metaphysical* reasons lie in his strong sympathy with the old conception of a "great chain of being" (see e.g. *Ideas*, bk. 1, G6:105, 132, 147–8, 193), and in particular with the aspect of it that Leibniz had recast as his metaphysical principle of continuity in nature (see e.g. *Ideas*, bk. 1, G6:122, 166). (At least the first two of these three considerations should still have force for us today.)

48. See e.g. the following articles in *Erkenntnis*, 51/1 (1999): F. Dretske, "Machines, Plants, and Animals: The Origins of Agency" (which focuses mainly on birds); C. Allen, "Animal Concepts Revisited: The Use of Self-Monitoring as an Empirical Approach" (which focuses mainly on pigeons and pigs); G.G. Brittan, "The Secrets of Antelope" (which focuses mainly on antelope). See also Griffin, *Animal Thinking* and *Animal Minds* (which focus on a wide variety of species).

49. Concerning this point, cf. D. Davidson, "Thought and Talk," p. 155.

50. For a similar account of our conceptual situation here, see L. Wittgenstein, *Remarks on the Philosophy of Psychology*, vol. 2, pars. 186, 192.

51. Davidson has recently argued for a similar *conclusion* in "Rational Animals" and "Thought and Talk." But Herder's *arguments* seem to me much more compelling. For some critical assessment bearing on both their cases, see Essay 2.

52. D. Davidson, "The Emergence of Thought," *Erkenntnis*, 51/1 (1999), p. 11.

53. G6:109, cf. 127, 149.

54. G6:110.

55. C. Taylor, *Hegel* (Cambridge: Cambridge University Press, 1978), pp. 16 ff.; and "The Importance of Herder."

56. Opting for broad expressivism would in turn raise certain further interesting questions. For example, is the transcendence of language and words by a person's thoughts and meanings that can occur

merely a transcendence of *his* language and words, or can it also be a transcendence of language and words *tout court* (so that no amount of development in language and words could make the thoughts and meanings in question linguistically and verbally expressible)?

57. *Hamanns Schriften*, 7:10. Hamann indeed believes that, beyond such human expressive media, *the whole realm of nature* is an expressive "language," namely God's. Note that Herder can himself say in his own *Metacritique* that music is a "language" (S21:269).

58. *Critical Forests* (1), G2:193–4. Cf. Haym, *Herder nach seinem Leben und seinen Werken*, 1:241–6.

59. *Critical Forests* (1), G2:214–15. Cf. Haym, *Herder*, 1:258–9.

60. *Critical Forests* (1), G2:192–3. Cf. Haym, *Herder*, 1:246. This little theory of the arts has sometimes been touted as Herder's main achievement in aesthetics—e.g. by R.E. Norton in *Herder's Aesthetics and the European Enlightenment* (Ithaca: Cornell University Press, 1991). But, as I have already implied, and will in effect go on to argue in more detail, it is a naive and untenable theory, and Herder's real achievement in aesthetics is other than and contrary to it.

61. Cf. Haym, *Herder*, 1:233 ff.

62. *Critical Forests* (1), G2:131–8. Cf. Haym, *Herder*, 1:240.

63. *Critical Forests* (1), G2:200–1.

64. Ibid., p. 95. Cf. Haym, *Herder*, 1:234.

65. *Critical Forests* (1), G2:195. Cf. Haym, *Herder*, 1:242.

66. *Critical Forests* (1), G2:107.

67. *Critical Forests* (3), S3:396–7, cf. 419–20. In my view, this commonly disparaged and neglected third part of Herder's work thus takes a seminal step towards his considered and best aesthetic theory.

68. *Critical Forests* (4), G2:313, cf. 380. This represents a change of mind from *Critical Forests* (3), where Herder had argued that the presence of an allegorical sense in coins *distinguished* them from paintings, which by contrast offer a picture simply *as picture* (S3:419–20).

69. G4:296–301, 319. Cf. Haym, *Herder*, 2:69–70.

70. G4:317 (emphasis added). Cf. the 1778 essay *On the Effect of Poetic Art on the Ethics of Peoples in Ancient and Modern Times*, G4:172: Phidias' statue of Jupiter (i.e. Zeus) developed out of two Homeric verses. The *Ideas* repeats this solution concerning sculpture. Thus, on the one hand, the *Ideas* is firmly committed to the principles that thought is essentially dependent on and bounded by language and that meaning is word-usage: "A people has no idea for which it has no word" (G6:347). But on the other hand, the work also accords sculpture a capacity

to express thoughts and meanings, namely—preserving consistency with the principles just mentioned—ones which the sculptor has in virtue of a pre-existing linguistic capacity. For example, the work observes that Greek sculpture rests on Greek poetry (esp. Homer) and on Greek hero-legends (G6:529−33). For an even later formulation of this solution, see *Homer a Favorite of Time* (1795), S18:428−9, where Herder gives a slightly fuller statement of his view that Greek sculpture (and painting) expresses Homeric thought.

71. G4:201.
72. G9/1:554−5.
73. The restriction in parentheses is important, and concerns both the past and the future. This Herderian theory would be untenable as a theory about instrumental music *generally*. For some instrumental music antedates Christianity, and much twentieth-century instrumental music is anything but harmonic and melodic. However, concerning the former point, Herder was from an early date well aware that the ancients had already possessed instrumental music (see e.g. *Critical Forests* [4], G2:364), and is therefore here talking only about modern instrumental music, and indeed only about a certain type of it. (Cf. W. Wiora, "Herders Ideen zur Geschichte der Musik," in E. Keyser ed., *Im Geiste Herders* [Kitzingen am Main: Holzner, 1953], p. 108.) And concerning the latter point, Herder is of course not here talking about instrumental music as it would develop after his own lifetime.

The former of these defensive points is also relevant for answering another sort of objection that might be raised here: Isn't Herder's picture of the origin of language famously that it is born from music, and if so then how can music consistently be said to depend on language? This objection fails on two scores: First, as was just mentioned, Herder is here concerned only with a specific sort of modern instrumental music, so that even if his picture of origins were as just described his position here would be consistent with it. But second, his picture of origins is *not* in fact as just described. His real picture of origins is rather that "human beings have come to music no otherwise than via the path of language," that "singing language" is the "source of music" (*Critical Forests* [4], G2:360−3); or at least that singing and language were originally one (G1:612), and that if language was in a sense born from song, then this song was already identical with language (G1:741). In other words, far from being inconsistent with the account of instrumental music's relation to language in question here, his picture of origins would if anything tend to suggest it.

74. G7:454. None of this should be taken to imply that Herder believes that instrumental music is especially *adept* at expressing thoughts and meanings or should *primarily* serve that purpose. He often expresses skepticism on both scores (see e.g. S15:195, S23:567–73).

75. G2:290, 296–7, 308, 324. Herder here makes this point mainly in connection with *visual* perception.

76. For a strikingly similar recent theory of (visual) non-linguistic art, see E. Panofsky, *Meaning in the Visual Arts* (Chicago: University of Chicago Press, 1982), pp. 28–31.

77. It is admittedly a somewhat puzzling fact that Herder's last major work in aesthetics, the *Calligone* (1800), does not articulate this position clearly, but instead tends (albeit not consistently) to revert to the sort of sensualistic theory of the non-linguistic arts with which the *Critical Forests* had begun: music is merely concerned with expressing feelings (S21:63–4, 70–1, 186–90), sculpture does not express concepts (S21:169–71, 343–4), etc. However, I take this to be a sign, not that the interpretation of Herder's considered position given above is after all mistaken, but rather of the inferiority of this late work of his (an inferiority that is also manifested in other ways, as well as in other late works of his such as the *Metacritique*).

78. For an account of this vacillation, see *German Philosophy of Language*, Essay 6.

79. Panofsky, *Meaning in the Visual Arts* provides rich illustration of the general point from such cases. As Panofsky puts it, "In a work of [visual] art, 'form' cannot be divorced from 'content': the distribution of color and lines, light and shade, volumes and planes, however delightful as a visual spectacle, must be understood as carrying a more-than-visual meaning" (p. 168).

80. The idea of "program music," with its incorporation of thoughts and meanings into instrumental music, has come under attack from various quarters—e.g., E. Hanslick, *On the Musically Beautiful* (Indianapolis: Hackett, 1986), pp. 35, 43, 74–5, 78–9; and more recently R. Scruton, *The Aesthetics of Music* (Oxford: Oxford University Press, 1999), pp. 133–4. However, such attacks are not persuasive. Scruton develops his objection as follows: "The claim was made by Liszt, that music could be tied to a program, in such a way that it would be necessary to understand the program in order to understand the music. Such 'program music' must be heard as the unfolding of a poetic narrative . . . But was he right?" (p. 133). However, given the closeness of the connection between an author's intentions to express

such-and-such in his work and what he actually expresses in it, and hence between the former and what must be grasped in order to understand it—even if, as should be conceded, this closeness falls short of making the failure of his intentions a sheer impossibility (cf. L. Wittgenstein, *Philosophical Investigations*, p. 18: "Can I say 'bububu' and mean 'If it doesn't rain I shall go for a walk'?")—there is surely something a little paradoxical in the suggestion that a major composer like Liszt might simply be mistaken here. That is to say, one would surely need *very* strong and special reasons to justify overriding a major composer's own conception of what he is expressing in this way. What could these reasons be? Hanslick develops several which might potentially do the job, including (1) a purely evaluative argument to the effect that implementing the model in question makes for inferior music, (2) an argument that it violates the purely musical nature of music, and (3) an argument that it *cannot* occur. However, it seems to me that argument (1) comes to grief when confronted with a magnificent work like *Ma Vlast*, and that argument (2) does so as well (unless it is reduced to a secure but irrelevant tautology). As for argument (3), Hanslick's case seems to be that the very same music could equally well be associated with quite *different* thoughts and meanings. But this point surely carries little if any weight. For is not the same true of much if not all *linguistic* expression as well (where we do not for that reason question whether the expression of thoughts and meanings really occurs)? In short, program music seems to hold up well as an example against such attacks.

Unlike Hanslick and others who want to deny that instrumental music *ever* expresses linguistically capturable thoughts or meanings, S. Bungay, *Beauty and Truth* (Oxford: Oxford University Press, 1984), p. 137 concedes that it *sometimes* does, but considers it a disastrous mistake to suppose that it *always* does or should. This is a more modest position, and accordingly more plausible. However, it is reasonable to suspect that even this position is, if not strictly speaking false, then at least misleading, that instrumental music has the character in question a good deal more commonly than Bungay implies. Bungay cites the famous opening of Beethoven's Fifth Symphony as his star counterexample, claiming that Beethoven did not think up its famous theme in order to express a fateful mood, and that it is a matter of indifference "whether or not [listeners] think it represents the march of Fate, or anything else." I'm not convinced. It is significant in this connection that when asked about the meaning of his *Appassionata*

Sonata Beethoven replied, "Just read Shakespeare's *The Tempest*"
(Hanslick, *On the Musically Beautiful*, p. 37). *Pace* Bungay, it seems likely
that in composing the opening of the Fifth Symphony Beethoven did
in fact have thoughts of fate, human struggle (outer or inner), and
so forth in mind and did in fact mean to express those thoughts.
Consequently, it seems plausible to say that a listener who failed
to entertain such thoughts in some form would ipso facto have
a deficient aesthetic response to the music. In order to persuade
oneself that linguistically capturable thoughts and meanings are at
least not entirely irrelevant to the adequacy of a person's aesthetic
response in this case one might usefully ask oneself the question,
Could a listener have an adequate aesthetic response to this music if
he habitually thought of, say, clowns and their antics when he heard it
(i.e. had what one might—albeit tendentiously in this context—call
"inappropriate" thoughts)? The answer seems to be pretty clearly
No. I would suggest that the same answer applies if the question
is instead, Could the listener's aesthetic response to this music be
adequate if it included no linguistically capturable thoughts or meanings
at all, or none of the ones that Beethoven had in mind? (For a
defense of the principle that instrumental music expresses linguistically
capturable thoughts and meanings, cf. T.W. Adorno, *Aesthetic Theory*
[Minneapolis: University of Minnesota Press, 1997], esp. the "Draft
Introduction" on pp. 332–59.)

This issue is closely linked to another which has been much debated
in the literature, namely whether or not certain *feelings* or *emotions* are
expressed by instrumental music and therefore need to be captured by
listeners in some way if they are to understand the music properly. A
long tradition says Yes, but a significant one—including Hanslick, *On
the Musically Beautiful* and more recently D. Raffman, *Language, Music,
and Mind* (Cambridge, Mass.: MIT Press, 1993), pp. 57–9—says No.
Similar considerations to those just adduced concerning linguistically
capturable thoughts and meanings seem to me to show that the
correct answer here is Yes. For example (to focus first on the question
of what composers *intend* to express), Beethoven described himself
as being "incited by moods, which are translated . . . by me into
tones that sound, and roar and storm about me until I have set
them down in notes" and said that music should "strike fire in the
soul" (Hanslick, *On the Musically Beautiful*, p. 61; J.W.N. Sullivan,
Beethoven: His Spiritual Development [New York: Vintage Books, 1960],

p. 33). And if one conducts thought-experiments concerning emotions analogous to those that I recently suggested concerning thoughts and meanings—Would habitually having the "wrong" sort of emotional reaction to the opening of the Fifth Symphony, for example one of mirth, be compatible with an adequate aesthetic response to it? Would a sheer absence of emotional reaction, or an absence of the sort of emotional reaction intended by the composer?—they seem to confirm that a certain sort of emotive response is indeed internal to musical understanding. One reason why this further issue is closely linked to the previous one is that emotions require thoughts and meanings as intentional contents, so that allowing the latter a role in musical expression and understanding at least makes it easier to see—and might even be necessary for seeing—how the former can have one.

To sum up the positive picture of (much) instrumental music which seems to emerge from such considerations one can hardly do better than quote a—deeply uncharacteristic and (perhaps to some extent even internally) inconsistent—passage from its arch-opponent, Hanslick: "Thoughts and feelings run like blood in the arteries of the harmonious body of beautiful sounds. They are not that body . . . but they animate it" (*On the Musically Beautiful*, p. 82).

81. Dilthey, *Gesammelte Schriften*, 7:220 ff.
82. Hanslick, *On the Musically Beautiful*, pp. 10, 28.
83. Bungay, *Beauty and Truth*, p. 137.
84. It is not necessary for my philosophical purposes here to expect —perhaps unrealistically—that everyone or even most people will share this linguistic intuition about such cases. It is enough if these are cases in which our linguistic intuitions are uncertain, torn. For, provided that this is so, the philosophical arguments that support Herder's narrow expressivist principles, together with the plausibility of explaining away *other* apparent counterexamples to them such as the animal cases discussed earlier, can cumulatively create a justification for preferring the linguistic intuition which I am championing here over the contrary one. A similar situation holds in connection with the other main hard case that narrow expressivism confronts: the "intelligent" behavior of some non-language-using (or scarcely-language-using) animals. Of course, in neither of these cases (neither the musical nor the animal) need a decision to exclude the sort of performance in question from the sphere of *thoughts and ideas* properly so called involve any denial of its deep kinship with the latter, or any implication of its

superficiality in comparison with the latter. (On the contrary, it may well be the thoughts and ideas that are in a sense the more superficial relatives here.)

85. S15:195.
86. S23:561. In suggesting that instrumental music can express something about feeling or emotion that cannot be as accurately expressed by language (alone), Herder, and I in endorsing his position, are in agreement with a larger tradition that encompasses both composers and philosophers. For example, the composer Mendelssohn says that musical feeling is indescribable because it is too precise for words (Sullivan, *Beethoven*, pp. 20–1; Scruton, *The Aesthetics of Music*, p. 165). And the philosopher S. Langer develops a similar view in several works, including *Feeling and Form* (London: Routledge and Kegan Paul, 1953), *Problems of Art* (New York: Charles Scribner's Sons, 1957), and *Philosophy in a New Key* (Cambridge, Mass.: Harvard University Press, 1978) (though one should no doubt be skeptical of her specific explanation of this, à la Wittgenstein's *Tractatus*, in terms of a "logical form" shared between the feeling and the music).

The suggestion that instrumental music expresses feeling or emotion, and that it conveys nuances thereof more precisely than language (alone) can do, requires defense and qualification, however. For it is not always conceded that instrumental music expresses feeling or emotion at all, let alone that it does so more precisely than language (for example, Hanslick and Raffman both deny this). Perhaps the most serious objection to such a view is one that was first raised by Hanslick (*On the Musically Beautiful*, pp. 8–10): feelings and emotions of their very nature incorporate intentional objects, which seem beyond the reach of musical expression. Scruton (*The Aesthetics of Music*, pp. 165 ff.) provides a perceptive two-part response to this sort of objection which we can take over and build on here. First, he points out that instrumental music often *does* in fact express intentional objects (e.g. church music expresses the thought of God). Second, he argues that, despite the fact that emotions do essentially include intentional objects, it is in an important sense possible to identify emotions without pinning down their intentional objects—that if, for instance, one comes upon an unknown woman sitting on a bench in a park weeping, one may be able, by observing her behavior, to identify the character of her emotion without knowing the intentional object involved (e.g. whether she is weeping over the death of a parent, the thanklessness of a child, abandonment by a husband, or what not).

I would add, third, that in such cases it may also in a certain sense be possible to identify the emotion from observation of the person's behavior *more precisely* than could be achieved from a mere verbal description, that the person's complex behavior in its context may convey to one the quality of the emotion with a precision that could not be matched by a mere verbal description either of that behavior and context or of the emotion itself (though only "in a certain sense" because of course in another sense, namely that of pinning down the intentional object, the identification is ex hypothesi *less* precise). This situation suggests that, similarly, nuances of emotion may in a certain sense be expressed more precisely by instrumental music than could be achieved by language (alone) (even though in another sense, that concerned with the identification of the intentional object, they can usually only be expressed less precisely).

87. A variant of this illusion can arise in connection with a composer's *musically technical* thoughts and meanings, which are capable of linguistic or notational expression by him. These will be precisely graspable by a listener who has technical expertise in music. However, a layman will again often sense their presence but find himself unable to pin them down linguistically with any precision, and so be encouraged to imagine that linguistically inexpressible thoughts and meanings are involved.

88. Concerning this point, see n. 86, above.

89. There may well be further sources of the delusive temptation to ascribe ineffable thoughts and meanings to music in addition. For example, Raffman somewhat plausibly diagnoses such a temptation in terms of the existence of a sort of musical grammar, which leads to a false expectation of a musical semantics due to the conjunction of grammar with semantics in the linguistic case (*Language, Music, and Mind*, pp. 40–1).

90. I recently quoted a passage from Herder concerning musical harmony and melody to this effect (S23:561). Cf. G2:1159, where Herder implies that it is essential to preserve Shakespeare's *rhymes* in translation because of nuances of feeling which only they convey exactly. Also, recall in this connection Herder's claim in the *Critical Forests* that the *visual* aspects of a work like Sophocles' *Philoctetes* are as important to its overall meaning as its verbal aspects.

91. Herder's commitment to such a conception of the function of music can be seen from passages like the following: in music one has "inward essence, i.e. energetic force, pathos, how should I call it?, what

penetrates deeply into the soul: the world of a new feeling. All our sensations have become a string-play" (G2:406); "The song-tune steals into the heart and, unnoticed, tunes it to tones, to wishes, to strivings in this pitch, in this mode" (S23:343); "One feels oneself in the power of this soft and high law [of harmony], all one's feelings entwined in it" (S23:561). (Ancient Greek musical modes and modern Church music might be especially good examples to consider here.)

Similarly, the Schlegels and Hegel would later go on to suggest, intriguingly, that sculpture played an essential structuring role in the emotional lives of the ancient Greeks, so that in order to understand their emotional lives one needs to grasp that role.

More recently, R.G. Collingwood develops a similar conception of the function of non-linguistic art in his *The Principles of Art* (Oxford: Oxford University Press, 1969), esp. p. 274.

Another recent version of this sort of thesis is J.-P. Vernant's intriguing claim that the emergence of tragedy as a genre gives rise to a sort of "tragic consciousness" (it should be kept in mind here that although tragedy is a verbal art, its effects also depend heavily on visual and musical features).

92. For example, someone might describe himself as having felt in an "*Eroica* mood" today (though hopefully with a little self-irony!).

93. Such a position lies behind a central thesis of Herder's in translation theory: He insists that the translator (especially of poetry) must try to reproduce not only the meaning of a (poetic) text but also its musical aspects, and he sees this not merely as a desideratum over and above the more fundamental one of reproducing the meaning but rather (or also) as an essential requirement for achieving the latter, because he believes that it is often only the musical aspects of the text that reveal the exact nature of the feelings which are partly constitutive of the meanings expressed by the text. See e.g. G2:1159, where he implies that it is essential to preserve Shakespeare's rhymes in translation because of the semantically relevant nuances of feeling which only they convey exactly. Herder's point in the *Critical Forests* that the visual aspects of a dramatic work like Sophocles' *Philoctetes* are as important to its meaning as its verbal aspects should probably be interpreted as expressing this sort of position as well.

94. This point continues to hold true even if—as I think one should, and as I think Herder thinks one should—one includes among the nuances of feeling expressed and communicated by non-linguistic art

ones which are only imaginatively entertained rather than simply had (contrast actually feeling a certain sort of shame with merely imagining what it is like to feel it). Concerning Herder's own recognition of such a distinction, see e.g. *On the Spirit of Hebrew Poetry*, where he notes that the sort of *Einfühlung* by an interpreter into the feelings of the Psalms which he recommends need not, and indeed should not, involve actually *sharing* them, e.g. actually sharing David's hatreds and exultations (G5:1194).

95. The narrow expressivist's concession of this sort of dependence of certain areas of linguistic thought and meaning on non-linguistic art may seem less dramatic if it is kept in mind that linguistic thought and meaning are dependent on extra-linguistic matters in *many* ways (which is not, though, to deny that there is anything special about this case of dependence in particular; for one thing, it is a case of dependence on a certain sort of *expression*).

96. See e.g. *Ideas*, G6:347–55, where he attempts to account for what he takes to be the unique suitedness of speech as a vehicle for thought. (As will become clear shortly, my own view is that this is an attempt to account for something that is in fact false.)

97. In discussing the language on which he says thought depends (or with which he even says thought is identical) Schleiermacher hardly ever even considers the possibility of forms of language other than speech and writing. (One notable exception: his psychology lectures, in *Friedrich Schleiermacher's sämmtliche Werke* [Berlin: G. Reimer, 1835–], 3/4:46.)

98. See esp. W. von Humboldt, *On Language: On the Diversity of Human Language-Structure and its Influence on the Mental Development of Mankind* (Cambridge: Cambridge University Press, 1989), pp. 54–6, where Humboldt closely follows Herder's account in the *Ideas* of why speech is especially suited to be a vehicle of thought.

99. Herder himself perceives this oddity in a way, though without realizing that it constitutes an objection that he needs to address: "How strange that a moved breath of air should be the sole, or at least the best, medium of our thoughts and sensations!" (G6:347).

100. Concerning these, see E.H. Gombrich, *Art and Illusion* (Princeton, NJ: Princeton University Press, 1972), ch. 2 and pp. 123–4.

101. As I pointed out in Essay 2, Abbt and Süßmilch had rightly allowed that such sign-language can support (rational) thought, whereas Herder implausibly tends to resist doing so (see esp. *Ideas*, G6:347). We can

now in a way see *why* Herder inclines to this implausible position, namely because of his excessively restrictive conception of the possible material-perceptual media of language.

102. Already before Herder and his tradition, Condillac had plausibly argued that in certain cultures (Condillac focuses on the ancient Greeks and Romans) gesture takes on a far larger burden of communication than it does in our own (*An Essay on the Origin of Human Knowledge* [1746], pp. 199 ff.). Cf. Herder at *Fragments*, G1:613–14.

103. For an illuminating discussion of animals' use of diverse expressive media, and of the evidence these provide for animals' possession of thoughts and concepts, see Griffin, *Animal Thinking*, chs. 8–10; "Windows on Animal Minds"; and *Animal Minds*, esp. ch. 9.

104. This is admittedly vague. It would be no small or easy task to say exactly what sort of "highly rule-governed, conventional character" spoken and written language *do* have. But perhaps this large and difficult question may be bracketed here.

105. F. de Saussure, *Course in General Linguistics* (New York: McGraw-Hill, 1966), pp. 10–11 argues for a similarly liberal conception of the possible material-perceptual forms that language might take to the one I am advocating here.

106. Two cases on which one might try out this point: the Egyptian pictures mentioned above, and the Greek musical modes in their rigid association with certain occasions, ideas, and moods (cf. Hanslick, *On the Musically Beautiful*, p. 63).

4

Herder's Importance as a Philosopher

The title of this essay pays tribute to that of a well-known essay by Charles Taylor, "The Importance of Herder," with whose thesis that Herder is an important philosopher I am in the strongest agreement. However, my arguments for such an assessment will for the most part be quite different from Taylor's.[1]

Herder has been sufficiently neglected in recent times, especially among philosophers, to need a few words of introduction. He lived during the period 1744–1803; he was a favorite student of Kant's, and a student and friend of Hamann's; he became a mentor to the young Goethe, on whose development he exercised a profound influence; and he worked, among other things, as a philosopher, literary critic, Bible scholar, and translator.

As I mentioned, Herder has been especially neglected by *philosophers* (with two notable exceptions in the Anglophone world: Isaiah Berlin and Charles Taylor). This situation strikes me as very unfortunate.[2] Accordingly, I would like here to sketch a positive case for Herder's seminal importance in three closely connected areas of philosophy: the philosophy of language; the philosophy of interpretation (or "hermeneutics"); and the philosophy of translation.[3]

It has been widely recognized in the relevant literature that some very important and valuable developments took place in the philosophies of language, interpretation, and translation in late eighteenth- and early nineteenth-century Germany. However, this recognition has largely been distributed among commentators interested only in one or the other of these areas, and as a result the likelihood of deep interconnections between the developments has largely been overlooked. Also, the developments in the philosophy of language have usually been credited to Hamann, and those in the philosophies of interpretation and translation to Schleiermacher.[4] What I want to show in this essay is that these various developments are indeed deeply interconnected—in particular, that three revolutionary principles which were introduced in the philosophy of language at this period were also fundamental to the revolutions that occurred in the philosophies of interpretation and translation—and that in each case the main credit belongs, not to the other people just mentioned, but instead to Herder. Moreover, I want to suggest that, at least where the philosophies of language and interpretation are concerned, Herder's versions of the ideas in question are in important respects superior to these other people's versions of them, and indeed that they are still of importance today. Let me begin with the most fundamental of the three areas: the philosophy of language.

1. Philosophy of Language

Already in the mid-1760s, in his *On Diligence in Several Learned Languages* (1764) and *Fragments on Recent German Literature* (1767–8), Herder advanced two revolutionary doctrines which essentially founded modern philosophy of language as we have known it since: (1) Thought is essentially dependent on, and bounded in its scope by, language. That is to say: one can only think if one has a language, and one can only think what one can express linguistically. (2) Meanings, or concepts, are identical—not, as many philosophers before and even since have supposed, with such items, in principle independent of language, as objects referred to, Platonic forms, or mental ideas (à la Locke or Hume), but instead—with *word-usages*.[5]

Hamann has commonly been credited with introducing some such doctrines and then passing them on to Herder (for example, by Isaiah Berlin). However, I believe this to be a mistake; Herder already embraced them in the mid-1760s, Hamann only much later (mainly in his *Metacritique* of 1784, though there are also a few statements reaching back as far as the early 1770s). The intellectual debt is actually *the other way round!*[6]

Why have interpreters made this mistake? One reason is that Hamann's muddle-headed vanity and Herder's affable generosity have conspired to obscure this situation in their correspondence and their other writings. But the main reason lies in the following circumstances: In his best known (but not necessarily best) work in the philosophy of language, his *Treatise on the Origin of Language* (1772), Herder temporarily lapsed from his normal straightforward versions of the two doctrines in question into versions that watered them down into something much closer to a standard Enlightenment position that thought and meaning are prior to language. For in the *Treatise on the Origin* he in effect temporarily came to employ such terms as "language" and "word" merely as names for such mentalistic processes as the former (he was looking for a proof of the two doctrines, and temporarily imagined that this was a good way to obtain one, overlooking the fact that it had the unfortunate side-effect of virtually trivializing them, and so depriving them of their original interest). Hamann then published critiques of Herder's *Treatise on the Origin* in which he rejected such a move and implied a preference for the straightforward versions of the doctrines. Not knowing the full history, interpreters have taken this exchange, and Herder's subsequent turn (or in fact *re*turn) to the straightforward versions of the doctrines, as evidence of Hamann's seminal impact on Herder's development, whereas actually all that Hamann had done was to play back *Herder's own earlier position* against his temporary lapse from it![7]

However, it is not only a matter of chronological precedence here. For Herder's normal versions of the two doctrines are also *philosophically superior* to Hamann's. The following are four respects in which this is true:

(i) Hamann usually recasts the doctrine of thought's essential dependence on and boundedness by language in the form of the stronger claim of thought's outright *identity* with language. However, such a strong claim is not going to be philosophically defensible. For, one can think without in the process articulating the thoughts in question linguistically, even "in one's head" (for example, one is sitting upstairs at home expecting Mary to return home first, one hears someone at the front door who subsequently turns out to have been Peter, and one later says quite truly that one thought the person who came in was Mary, even though one had neither uttered not mentally entertained any such little formula as "Mary is here now," but merely heard the door and felt unsurprised). And conversely, one can articulate a sentence linguistically, indeed even "in one's head," without thereby doing any corresponding thinking (for example, one may watch television in a foreign language that one does not understand and repeat certain sentences, either explicitly or "in one's head," without thereby doing any corresponding thinking). Now, unlike Hamann, Herder is normally careful to avoid any such claim of an outright identity between thought and language. And he thereby holds the more philosophically defensible version of the doctrine.

(ii) Hamann has no *argument* for the doctrine—in a famous letter from the 1780s he writes that he is still waiting for an "apocalyptic angel" to illuminate him on this score! By contrast, Herder—indeed as early as the 1760s—develops an extremely plausible argument for it: thoughts are essentially articulated through concepts, but according to Herder's second doctrine concepts or meanings are (not referents, Platonic forms, or mental ideas, but) *word*-usages.

(iii) Unlike Hamann (who again has none), Herder also has plausible arguments for this second doctrine itself. His arguments against identifying meanings with referents include the following, all of which are plausible and important: (a) Referring-terms (i.e. referring by function even if not by actual performance) can be meaningful despite lacking any referent (e.g. the terms "Zeus" and "phlogiston"). (b) Language was originally *expressive* in nature rather than referring or descriptive, and indeed still includes many terms which, while meaningful, have an expressive rather than a referring or descriptive character (e.g. the term "Ah!"). (c) Singular referring terms do not acquire their meanings directly from or in an object referred to (the supposition that they do being one of the strongest sources of the temptation to equate meanings with referents), but only *via general concepts*. So much for the identification of meanings with referents. Herder's central argument against identifying them with Platonic forms or with mental ideas, and for instead equating them with word-usages, appeals to the *decisiveness of linguistic-behavioral criteria* for ascribing *understanding* to a person: that decisiveness would be incompatible with meaning consisting in a Platonic form or a mental idea (and understanding therefore in mental contact with such a form or containment of such an idea), but it accords perfectly with meaning consisting in word-usage (and hence understanding in competence in word-usage). In this connection, Herder is fond of quoting some lines from the poet Edward Young:

> Speech, Thought's Canal! Speech, Thought's Criterion too.
> Thought, in the Mine, may come forth Gold or Dross;
> When coin'd in Word, we know its *real* Worth.[8]

Consequently, meanings are not referents, Platonic forms, or mental ideas, but instead word-usages.[9]

(iv) Unlike Hamann, Herder in addition identifies a series of prima facie problem cases that seem to confront the two doctrines in question, i.e. cases in which thoughts or concepts seem to occur without any corresponding language use being involved: God, young children, animals, and non-linguistic art. And for each of these cases he develops a plausible way of saving the two doctrines in the face of it. For example, in the case of animals, his considered solution is roughly to say that higher primates such as apes sometimes acquire a rudimentary grasp of language and a commensurate ability to think and conceptualize, but that animals which lack language can only achieve pre-forms of such mental operations.[10] And in the case of non-linguistic art—sculpture, painting, music, etc.—his considered solution is to concede that such art often express thoughts and meanings, but to insist that the thoughts and meanings in question are dependent on and bounded by the artist's capacity for linguistic expression.[11]

Herder's two doctrines strikingly anticipate positions that would subsequently be held by the most important twentieth-century philosopher of language: the later Wittgenstein. This is not accidental; Herder (and Hamann) influenced Wittgenstein via Fritz Mauthner.[12]

But I think that a case could be made that Herder's philosophy of language is actually superior to Wittgenstein's in one important respect. For Herder also embraces a *third* doctrine in the philosophy of language: a quasi-empiricist doctrine which holds that meanings or concepts must of their very nature be anchored in (perceptual or affective) *sensations*, but which—unlike cruder traditional versions of such a position, for example Hume's—also incorporates two important qualifications (hence the "quasi-"): (i) that the dependence goes both ways, i.e. that the sensations of a concept-using human being also depend for their specific character on his concepts (it is not, as Hume supposed, simply a matter of a person's first having, say, the sensation of blue and then on that basis developing the concept of blue; rather, acquiring the concept affects the nature of the sensation); and (ii) that the dependence of concepts on sensations is loose enough to permit *metaphorical extensions* (so that, for example, the sensuous "in" found in a statement like "The dog is in his kennel" becomes the non-sensuous, or at least less-directly-sensuous, "in" found in a statement like "Smith is in legal trouble").[13]

Such a doctrine as this is likely to strike modern philosophical ears as misguided (it used to strike mine that way). This is mainly because of the intervening strong influence of Frege and Wittgenstein's anti-psychologism, or (precisely) exclusion of such mental items as sensations and images from any essential involvement in meaning and understanding. However, I want to suggest that Herder may well be right here. The following are some points in defense of his doctrine.

(a) One's confidence in Fregean-Wittgensteinian anti-psychologism should be at least a little undermined when one recalls another of Wittgenstein's doctrines: his very plausible doctrine that such concepts as "meaning" are in their prephilosophical state vague and fluid.[14] This doctrine makes it seem rather unlikely that our commonsense concept of meaning carries any such sharp partitioning of meaning from sensations and images as Fregean-Wittgensteinian anti-psychologism advocates. Indeed, Wittgenstein himself occasionally concedes that in excluding psychological items from meaning in this way, his conception of meaning as word-usage departs from the ordinary meaning of the term "meaning," selectively accentuating one strand of it to the neglect of other strands.[15]

(b) Herder's quasi-empiricist doctrine might seem incompatible with his and Wittgenstein's broadly shared identification of meaning with *word-usage*. Now, it is true that in Wittgenstein's version of this identification the concept of "word-usage" refers strictly to a pattern of linguistic competence in a sense that excludes any essential role for sensations or images. But that need not be true of *any* doctrine that meaning is word-usage. After all, a *usage* is of its very nature a usage in relation to some *context* or other, and there is no obvious reason why the context in question might not in this case essentially include *sensations* or *images*. So there is after all no real incompatibility here.

(c) Frege's anti-psychologism is based on a dubious Platonist ontology (the "third realm"). Wittgenstein's instead appeals, somewhat more plausibly, to arguments, similar to Herder's, concerning the criteria that we actually use for ascribing conceptual understanding to people: Wittgenstein argues that what is decisive here is their linguistic competence, not whatever sensations or images they may happen to have. However, there are two sides to Wittgenstein's case here which should be distinguished and which seem to me very different in their levels of plausibility: On the one hand, he argues that linguistic competence is *necessary* for understanding—and this seems *entirely* plausible. On the other hand, though, he also argues that it is in a sense *sufficient* for understanding, in particular that there is no need of any psychological process, such as having sensations or images, in addition—but this seems much less plausible. Suppose, for instance, that someone had never had a sensation of red and could not generate images of red (say, because he was congenitally blind or color-blind), but that we managed to teach him to make all of the right intralinguistic statements about red—for example, concerning its position in the color spectrum, its being a brighter color than grey, and so on—and that in addition we managed, by implanting a fancy electronic device in his brain, to enable him to apply the word "red" when and only when presented with something red (despite, let it be stipulated, still not having sensations or images of red).[16] Would we in such a case want to say that he fully understood the word "red"? It seems at least very plausible to say that we would *not*.

(d) Wittgenstein tirelessly points out that understanding a concept does not require that a person *currently* be having appropriate sensations or images. This seems very plausible. However, it is quite another thing to hold that understanding a concept does not require that a person have appropriate sensations or images *at all*. And this, it seems to me, is all that Herder is committed to denying.

(e) In the light of these considerations, someone might concede, *pace* Frege and Wittgenstein, that sensations or images are in *some* cases internal to concept-possession, but still deny that they *always* are, as Herder's doctrine holds. One class of apparent counterexamples that might be appealed to here would be terms like "chiliagon" or "God." However, such terms seem manageable by means of a strategy of analysis into sensorily instantiated sub-concepts with which earlier empiricists such as Locke were already very familiar. Another class of apparent counterexamples might be logical connectives, such as "and" and "not" (note that logic requires no more than these two). However, on reflection, these again fail to constitute convincing counterexamples. For instance, whenever one observes a certain state of affairs added to another (e.g. a chair being red and (then) having a cat sitting on it as well) one has a sensory illustration of "and"; and whenever one observes a certain state of affairs ceasing to obtain (e.g. the cat initially sitting on the chair but then jumping off it) one has a sensory illustration of "not."[17]

In sum, I would suggest that Herder's third doctrine is at least plausible, and that it may well constitute an important respect in which his philosophy of language is actually superior to Wittgenstein's.[18]

2. Philosophy of Interpretation (Hermeneutics)

Let us turn now to a further, but closely related, area of philosophy. Schleiermacher has commonly been credited with making major advances in the philosophy of interpretation, or "hermeneutics," in the early nineteenth century (for example, by Manfred Frank and Peter Szondi). I would agree that a huge advance in hermeneutics occurred at roughly this period (and also that, as Szondi implies, twentieth-century philosophical hermeneutics à la Heidegger and Gadamer has in contrast generally been a retrograde step rather than one of progress). However, I would suggest that almost everything that is distinctive and important in Schleiermacher's hermeneutics had in fact already been developed before him by Herder.[19] The following are some central examples:

(i) Schleiermacher famously argues in favor of a *general* hermeneutics, applicable to sacred texts as well as profane, modern as well as ancient, oral as well as written, and so on. But Herder had already moved strongly in this direction. For example, he had already argued in works from the 1760s against relying on divine inspiration when interpreting the Bible, and for instead interpreting the Bible in the same historically and philologically scrupulous manner as any other ancient text; and he had included modern as well as ancient texts in his own interpretive endeavors.

(ii) Schleiermacher makes the doctrine that thought is essentially dependent on and bounded by language (like Hamann, he goes as far as to say: identical with language) fundamental to his theory of interpretation. In consequence, he assumes that there is in fact no need to worry about a possibility alleged by some of his predecessors that an author may have entertained thoughts which he was unable, or only very approximately able, to express linguistically.[20] But, as we saw, Herder had already developed such a doctrine; and he too had made it fundamental to his theory of interpretation, in particular on this basis excluding the sort of worry just mentioned.

(iii) Schleiermacher equates meanings with word-usages, or rules of word-use, and accordingly makes pinning down the latter the central task of the linguistic side of interpretation. But, as we saw, Herder had already equated meanings with word-usages; and accordingly, he too had made pinning these down the central task of interpretation.

(iv) Schleiermacher famously emphasizes that interpretation needs to cope with a phenomenon of conceptual distinctiveness, not only between languages but also in the individual author vis-à-vis his background language; and he argues that largely for this reason interpretation needs to complement *linguistic* interpretation, which focuses on an author's background language, with *psychological* interpretation, which focuses on his individual psychology. But Herder had already argued along just these lines in *On Thomas Abbt's Writings* (1768) and *On the Cognition and Sensation of the Human Soul* (1778).[21]

(v) Schleiermacher famously argues for the need, especially on the psychological side of interpretation, to use a method of "divination," by which he means (with French rather than Latin etymology in mind: *deviner*, "to guess, to conjecture," rather than *divus* or *divinus*) a method of fallible, corrigible hypothesis based on but also going well beyond whatever meager empirical evidence is available. But Herder had already argued exactly the same in the two works of his just mentioned.

(vi) Schleiermacher argues for a form of methodological empiricism—i.e. working up to (general) conclusions from a careful consideration of empirical evidence—on both the linguistic and the psychological sides of interpretation. But Herder had already argued strongly for such a method as well.

(vii) Schleiermacher famously argues for a holistic approach to the available evidence—for example, for interpreting the parts of a text in light of the whole text to which they belong; the latter in light of the author's whole corpus; and all of these in light of the whole historical and social context to which they belong. But Herder had already argued for these sorts of holism as well (for instance, for the first in the *Critical Forests* [1769], and for the third in *This Too a Philosophy of History for the Formation of Humanity* [1774]).[22]

(viii) Schleiermacher famously addresses the problem of *circularity* which such holism seems to raise, arguing that (to take the first sort of holism as an example) the interpreter should begin by reading through the parts of a text in sequence, interpreting them as well as possible, then, having thereby reached an overview of the whole text, deploy this overview in order to refine his interpretation of the parts, whose refined interpretation can then produce a more exact understanding of the whole, and so on indefinitely (a solution whose key lies in the recognition that understanding is not an all-or-nothing matter, but instead comes in degrees). But, once again, Herder had already addressed the same problem and offered the same solution, namely in his *Critical Forests*.

Some of this mass of common ground between Schleiermacher's theory of interpretation and Herder's is probably due to the fact that they shared sources on the subject which they both respected, especially Ernesti's *Institutio interpretis Novi Testamenti* (1761). But much of it can only be due to Schleiermacher having borrowed from Herder—for example, the central ideas of complementing linguistic with psychological interpretation, especially in order to address the phenomenon of an author's conceptual distinctiveness, and of employing "divination," in the sense of fallible, corrigible hypothesis, particularly as the method of psychological interpretation (neither of which ideas had yet been developed by Ernesti).[23]

Moreover, where Schleiermacher's and Herder's theories of interpretation *do* differ, it almost always turns out that Herder's is philosophically superior. Here are some examples:

(a) Unlike Herder, Schleiermacher usually agrees with Hamann in opting for an ambitious "identity" version of the doctrine of thought's essential dependence on and boundedness by language (more specifically, for a doctrine that thought is identical with *inner* language). But, as we have already seen, unlike Herder's more restrained version of the doctrine, such an ambitious version is not philosophically tenable.

(b) Schleiermacher in some of his later work adds to his Herderian doctrine that meanings are word-usages, or rules of word use, a doctrine that they are Kantian empirical schemata, or rules for the production of images. However, Kant had conceived empirical schemata in the spirit of a sharp meaning-language dualism typical of the Enlightenment, and Schleiermacher's addition incorporates this feature. But this lands him, unlike Herder, in a contradiction with their shared fundamental conception of meanings as word-usages.[24]

(c) For Herder the phenomenon of individual conceptual distinctiveness in authors—which largely motivates his principle of complementing linguistic with psychological interpretation—is merely an empirically established rule of thumb. By contrast, Schleiermacher, in his *Dialectics* and *Ethics* lectures, argues for it in an a priori manner as a universal feature of all reason, or all meaning/understanding. However, this version of the position is much less plausible than Herder's: in its very a priori status, in the specific details of its a priori argument, and also in its highly counterintuitive consequence that strictly speaking nobody *ever* understands another person.[25]

(d) Whereas Herder conceives psychological interpretation as a broad exploration of an author's distinctive psychological traits, Schleiermacher usually attempts to specify it more narrowly as pinning down an author's "seminal decision [*Keimentschluß*]," which was present at his text's inception and unfolded itself as his text in a necessary fashion. However, this idea (inspired by Fichte's dubious metaphysics of the self) seems unhelpful as a general picture of the nature of texts and of how to interpret them. For how many texts are actually composed in this way (rather than, say, through a whole series of more or less distinct authorial decisions, serendipity during the process of composition, and so on)?[26]

(e) Whereas Herder allows the psychological side of interpretation to draw on both linguistic and non-linguistic behavioral evidence, Schleiermacher restricts it to linguistic evidence only. This again seems a retrograde step; *both* sources can in principle provide evidence of an author's psychology relevant to interpretation, and in some cases non-linguistic evidence may indeed be more telling than linguistic evidence. For example, if one is wondering whether the Marquis de Sade's writings emanate from a genuine sadism or instead merely affect it, say as a sort of literary pose adopted in order to attack a certain value system, then it surely helps to know something about his history of actual assaults on women.[27]

(f) Herder generally sees interpretive inquiries as similar to natural scientific ones, and in particular regards the role in interpretive inquiries of "divination," in the sense of fallible, corrigible hypothesis based on but also extending well beyond the limited empirical evidence available, as making them like natural scientific inquiries (see especially *On Thomas Abbt's Writings* [1768]). By contrast, Schleiermacher regards the role of "divination" in interpretation as making interpretation deeply *unlike* natural science: not a science but an art. Now, Herder and Schleiermacher both seem to me right in holding that a method of "divination," in the specified sense, is fundamental to interpretation. But I would suggest that Herder is correct in seeing this as a factor that makes interpretation like natural science, and Schleiermacher incorrect in seeing it as one that makes them unlike each other. For Schleiermacher's position here evidently rests on an assumption that natural science works exclusively with a method of plain induction, à la Hume (this first a is F, this second a is F, this third a is F, . . . therefore all a's are F),[28] so that the method of "divination," or hypothesis, on the psychological side of interpretation makes interpretation deeply unlike natural science. But since Poincaré and Popper we have come to realize that, on the contrary, natural science *very much* works by means of hypothesis rather than merely plain induction. At least to this extent, then, Herder's position concerning the degree to which interpretation and natural science are similar activities seems significantly superior to Schleiermacher's.[29]

(g) Another advantage of Herder's theory of interpretation over Schleiermacher's lies in its much greater emphasis on the vital importance for correct interpretation of identifying a work's *genre*, i.e. a set of purposes and rules (usually common to a number of works and authors) that regulate a work's composition. Herder emphasizes this not only in connection with linguistic texts (this is the focus of his classic essay *Shakespeare* [1773]), but also in connection with works of non-linguistic art, such as sculpture (see, for example, *This Too a Philosophy of History* [1774]). Two principles which he rightly emphasizes in this area are the following: First, genres, even when they share a single name (e.g. "tragedy" or "portrait sculpture"), often vary in important ways from epoch to epoch, culture to culture, individual author to individual author, or indeed individual work of an author to individual work, and it is vitally important for the interpreter to take this into account, and in particular to resist a consequent frequent and strong temptation falsely to assimilate one genre to another simply because they share a single name and certain common features (for example, to assimilate the genre of Shakespearean tragedy to that of ancient Greek tragedy, or the genre of ancient Egyptian portrait sculpture to that of ancient Greek portrait sculpture). Second, the identification of a work's genre (like that of word-usages or an author's psychology) needs to take place by scrupulous *empirical* means, not by means which are—at least relative to the work in question—apriorist (as tended to happen, for example, when seventeenth- and eighteenth-century French critics interpreted, and also negatively assessed, Shakespearean tragedy in terms of a conception of tragedy derived from Aristotle and ancient tragedy). Now, Schleiermacher does not *altogether* neglect the importance of identifying genre in interpretation and the difficulties involved in doing so.[30] But he does fail to give these the emphasis and attention they deserve, and his thoughts about them are merely pale reflections of Herder's.[31]

(h) Finally (and perhaps most controversially), I want to suggest that Herder's theory of interpretation has one further important point of superiority over Schleiermacher's. Famously, Herder argues that interpretation should employ a method of *Einfühlung* (literally: "feeling one's way into [the standpoint of the person interpreted]")—whereas by contrast Schleiermacher avoids this idea (preferring instead to speak merely of *placing* oneself in the position of the person interpreted). Herder's idea that *Einfühlung* plays an important role in interpretation combines several different facets, all of which, I think, turn out to be sensible on reflection, but one of which turns out to be especially significant. Among these facets, for example,[32] are a principle that interpretation commonly confronts a mental distance between the interpreted author and the interpreter which the latter needs to overcome by means of laborious historical and philological work (that there is, as it were, an "in" there into which he needs to feel his way by such means); and a principle that sound interpretation requires a measure of sympathy, or at least open-mindedness, towards the interpreted author.[33] (These two facets of Herder's ideal of *Einfühlung* are both prominent in his *This Too a Philosophy of History*, for instance.) But another central facet of his ideal of *Einfühlung*, and the one that I think deserves special emphasis, derives from his quasi-empiricism about meanings or concepts: because all meaning involves an aspect of (perceptual or affective) sensation, in order to understand another person's meanings it is essential that one grasp his relevant sensations (that one "feel one's way into" them).[34]

Aristotle had already implied something rather similar when he had written at *De Interpretatione*, 16a:

> Spoken words are the symbols of mental experiences and written words are the symbols of spoken words. Just as all men have not the same writing, so all men have not the same speech sounds, but the mental experiences, which these directly symbolize, are the same for all, as are also those things of which our experiences are the images.

But Herder's position differs from Aristotle's in at least three significant and attractive ways: First, whereas Aristotle restricts his thesis to perceptual sensations, Herder also includes affective ones (note that the verb *fühlen* and its cognates readily covers both cases).[35] Second, whereas Aristotle had strongly privileged vision over the other senses as a source of relevant perceptual sensations,[36] Herder does not.[37] Third, whereas Aristotle believes that people's relevant sensations are basically the same at all times and places, Herder believes that both perceptual and affective sensations vary markedly in their character between different historical periods and cultures, and indeed often even between different individuals within a single period and culture.[38] This makes the interpreter's task in this area far more challenging than Aristotle had supposed.

Herder's commitment to the importance of *Einfühlung* (in the relevant sense) for interpretation emerges in many passages. He especially emphasizes its importance in connection with the interpretation of other historical periods and cultures. For example, he writes in *This Too a Philosophy of History*:

> One would have first to *sympathize* with the nation, in order to feel a *single one* of its *inclinations* or *actions all together*, one would have to *find* a single word, to *imagine* everything in its fullness—or one reads—*a word!* . . . The *whole nature* of the soul, which *rules* through everything, which *models* all other inclinations and forces of the

soul *in accordance with itself*, and in addition *colors* the most indifferent actions—in order to share in feeling this, do not answer on the basis of the word but go into the age, into the clime, the whole history, feel yourself into everything—only now are you on the way towards understanding the word.[39]

Accordingly, concerning perceptual sensation specifically, he argues in the *Fragments on Recent German Literature* that in order really to understand the Greeks we need to learn to see like them.[40] And concerning affective sensation specifically, he argues in *On the First Documents* (1769) that because people's concepts of happiness and pleasure are based on their distinctive "temperament," "feeling nature," "sense for rapture," in order really to understand the ancient Orientals' versions of those concepts we must imaginatively recapture these affective states of theirs.[41]

However, Herder also represents *Einfühlung* (in the relevant sense) as essential for the interpretation of *individual* authors, whether or not they are historically/culturally distant from the interpreter. For example, in a section of *On the Cognition and Sensation of the Human Soul* titled "Our thought depends on sensation" he writes:

The deepest basis of our existence is individual, both in sensations and in thoughts . . . One ought to be able to regard every book as the offprint of a living human soul . . . The more modest wise man . . . seeks to read more in the spirit of the author than in the book . . . Every poem . . . is a . . . betrayer of its author . . . One sees in the poem not only, for instance, . . . the man's poetic talents, one also sees which senses and inclinations governed in him, by what paths and how he received images, how he ordered and adjusted them and the chaos of his impressions, the favorite sides of his heart . . . To be sure, not every soul from the gutter is worthy of such a study; but of a soul from the gutter one would also need no offprints, neither in writings nor in deeds. Where it is worth the effort, this *living reading*, this divination into the author's soul, is the *only* reading, and the deepest means of education. It becomes a sort of enthusiasm, intimacy, and friendship which is often most instructive and pleasant for us where we do not think and feel in the same way.[42]

Much of Herder's own interpretive work focuses heavily on precisely this task of recapturing the distinctive perceptual and affective sensations of a period/culture or individual. A good example of this in connection with periods/cultures is *This Too a Philosophy of History*. A good example in connection with the individual is *On Thomas Abbt's Writings*.

The exact techniques that Herder uses in order to accomplish this task would merit a detailed investigation, but one of them that is especially striking is the following. As can be seen both from the methodological remarks in *This Too a Philosophy of History* recently quoted and from his actual practice when interpreting historical periods and cultures within the same work, he believes that it is necessary to employ a *holistic* approach: an approach that considers a historical period or culture's distinctive environment, historical situation, activities, art objects, values, statements, etc. together, as an essential prerequisite for accurately identifying the nature of even a single one of its relevant sensations. He espouses this sort of holism in connection with interpreting individuals as well.

Now Herder's emphasis on the role of *Einfühlung* in interpretation may well sound misguided to modern philosophical ears. One reason for this is the widespread acceptance in contemporary Anglophone philosophy of anti-psychologism concerning meaning. However, as I have already argued, anti-psychologism itself seems a dubious doctrine on reflection. So *this* should not stand in the way of an acceptance of Herder's position.

Another reason why Herder's emphasis on *Einfühlung* can easily seem misguided is because it can sound as though he is here making it a condition of understanding that the interpreter *share* the (perceptual and affective) feelings of the period/culture or the individual interpreted, which would have absurd and even dangerous consequences. For example, it would imply that in order to understand Hitler's antisemitic effusions in *Mein Kampf* one needs to have antisemitic feelings oneself. However, Herder is not in fact committed to any such foolish position. In *On the Spirit of Hebrew Poetry* (1782–3) he explicitly argues that the sort of feeling-one's-way-into the standpoint of (say) David's psalms that is necessary in order to understand them does not require the interpreter actually to share David's hatreds and joys, and that this should not be his goal, but that his recapturing of David's feelings should instead take a different, imaginative form:

David had his affects and worries as a refugee and as a king. We are neither, and hence may neither curse enemies that we do not have nor exult over them as victors. But we must learn to understand and appreciate these feelings.[43]

Herder's position is therefore that a sort of imaginative recapturing of relevant sensations is possible which does not involve actually *having* or *having had* them, and that it is only *this* that is necessary for understanding.

I want to suggest that this is correct. For, (i) it seems true that some sort of recapturing of an author's sensations is necessary for interpretation. This is supported by Herder's case for quasi-empiricism, or the internal role of sensations in meaning. It also seems to be confirmed by our general experience in interpretation. For example, compare the sort of purely external account of ancient Greek religion that one finds in a book such as Walter Burkert's *Greek Religion* with the sort of, by contrast, sensation-rich account of it that one finds in Walter Otto's books on the subject:[44] despite the extraordinary sophistication and detail of Burkert's account, it seems true that one only really begins to understand the ancient Greeks' religious conceptions once one has complemented it with an account more in the manner of Otto's.[45] But (ii) it also seems true that one can achieve a kind of imaginative grasp of perceptual or affective sensations which, while more than a mere knowledge of them by description, is also less than a full-blooded possession of them; that this is indeed a routine feature of such processes as reading and understanding literature; and that this sort of imaginative grasp not only satisfies the requirement for interpretation just mentioned, but also does so while avoiding the sorts of absurdities described in the previous paragraph.

Furthermore, I would suggest that Herder's position also provides a key for solving certain important problems concerning interpretation which have been raised by more recent philosophers. Let me give two examples. First, Gadamer (appropriating and historicizing a position of Heidegger's) has argued that understanding essentially rests on "pre-understanding," a system of pre-cognitive perspectives on and attitudes towards the world, but that pre-understanding varies historically, so that, because one is restricted to one's own age's form of pre-understanding (or at least to a residue of it that still remains left over even after one has modified it in various ways), one could never exactly reproduce another age's understanding of its discourse.[46]

Now a Fregean-Wittgensteinian anti-psychologist would probably reject (Heidegger's and) Gadamer's very assumption here that understanding essentially rests on pre-understanding, on the ground that this amounts to a form of psychologism. But for reasons sketched earlier, I think that one should be skeptical about anti-psychologism, and that such a dismissal of Gadamer's problem would therefore be too quick; in some form or other, the idea that understanding essentially rests on pre-understanding is probably correct.[47] Nor does it seem plausible to try to forestall Gadamer's problem by questioning his thesis of the historical variability of forms of pre-understanding (and hence of forms of understanding); this thesis seems right as well.

Instead, I suggest that a better way of forestalling Gadamer's skeptical conclusion that an exact understanding of historical Others is impossible lies in Herder's insight that a type of imaginative access to another person's (perceptual and affective) sensations is possible which falls short of being the sort of *committed possession* of sensations that normally underlies our understanding of our own concepts, but which is nonetheless sufficient to support understanding. If all pre-understanding capable of supporting understanding had to have the character of committed possession, then a version of Gadamer's skepticism would indeed be inevitable, since one cannot simultaneously be in committed possession of one's own form of pre-understanding and of different, incompatible forms (for example, one cannot when perceiving trees both have one's own color experiences of them and the Greeks'; one cannot when insulted both have one's own emotional reactions and the Greeks'). But since a merely imaginative, non-committed sort of pre-understanding is sufficient to support understanding, Gadamer's skepticism can be avoided.[48]

Second, Anne Eaton has drawn attention to the following interesting problem that arises in connection with the interpretation of works of art: Understanding works of art often seems to require having affective sensations of a certain sort, but the affective sensations in question may in certain cases be morally reprehensible ones, so that the requirements of understanding and those of morality come into conflict. For example, it seems that Titian's *Rape of Europa* essentially expresses certain (by our lights) morally reprehensible feelings about rape which were typical of the period and culture to which Titian belonged, in particular a certain sort of male erotic titillation at and disdain for the victim of rape, so that in order fully to understand the work one would need to participate in such feelings.[49]

How, if at all, is this problem to be solved? Here again, an anti-psychologist will no doubt see the solution as lying in his sharp separation of understanding from feeling. But, for reasons already indicated, such a solution seems quite dubious on reflection. However, Herder's position once again makes a more plausible solution possible: What is required for understanding does indeed include recapturing feelings, but not necessarily in the form of actually *having* them, since an imaginative, non-committed recapturing of them is also possible and is sufficient to support understanding. And, unlike actually *having* an affective feeling, the imaginative, non-committed reproduction of it is motivationally inert, and hence morally unproblematic.

3. Philosophy of Translation

A third, and again closely related, area in which important developments occurred at this period is the philosophy of translation. Schleiermacher has received most of the credit for this too—in particular, for developing what has recently been aptly called a "foreignizing" (as opposed to "domesticating") approach to translation.[50] However, it seems to me that once again it is Herder who really deserves most of the credit.[51]

The following are some key theses of Herder's concerning translation that can already be found in his *Fragments on Recent German Literature* (1767–8), all of which Schleiermacher subsequently took over to form the core of his own theory of translation, especially in his classic essay *On the Different Methods of Translation* (presented as an address in 1813):

(i) Translation faces a deep challenge from the fact that there exist radical mental differences—including in particular, conceptual differences—between different historical periods and cultures, and indeed to some extent even between individuals within a single period and culture.

(ii) Consequently, translation is in many cases an extremely difficult undertaking.

(iii) Consequently again, translation commonly faces a choice between two possible approaches: what Herder calls a "lax" approach (i.e. one in which the language and thought of the target text are allowed to diverge rather freely from those of the source text) and an "accommodating" approach (i.e. one in which the language and thought of the target text are made to accommodate to those of the source text).

(iv) Herder basically rejects the former approach in favor of the latter—in large part because the former approach involves sacrificing semantic faithfulness (the most commonly accepted fundamental goal of translation).

(v) In particular, he rejects a certain rationale for the former approach which Dryden and others had advocated, namely that a translation should provide *the work that the author would have written had his native language not been the one he actually had but instead the target language*. Herder objects to this that in such a case as that of translating Homer, for example, the author *could not* have written his work in the modern target language.

(vi) So Herder urges that the translator should instead err in the other direction, towards "accommodating."

But how is this to be done?

(vii) One necessary means to achieving it which Herder identifies is *interpretive* expertise in the translator, so Herder requires this.

(viii) Another, much less obvious, means is a certain vitally important technique which Herder develops for overcoming conceptual discrepancies between the source language and the target language. That might seem simply impossible (indeed, some more recent philosophers, such as Donald Davidson, have mistakenly assumed that it would be). But Herder, drawing on his novel philosophy of language, finds a solution: Since meanings or concepts are word-usages, in order to reproduce (or at least optimally approximate) in the target language a concept from the source language which the target language currently lacks, the translator should take the closest corresponding word in the target language and "bend" its usage in such a way as to make it mimic the usage of the source word. This technique essentially requires that the source word be translated uniformly throughout its multiple occurrences in a work (and also that the single target word chosen not be used to translate any other source words). For example, if faced with the conceptual incommensurability between Homer's color word *chlôros*, which Homer sometimes applies to objects that we would classify as green (e.g. healthy foliage) but at other times to objects that we would classify as yellow (e.g. honey), and the closest counterpart color word(s) in modern English (say, *green* and *yellow*), such a translator will not use different English words for *chlôros* in different contexts (say, in some places *green* but in others *yellow*) but will instead choose a single word and stick with it throughout (say, *green*). Such an approach is far from being commonplace, so far indeed that it is rarely actually used in translations. But Herder scrupulously uses it in his own translations, as does an important tradition that has subsequently followed him in espousing it (including Schleiermacher, Rosenzweig, and Buber).

(ix) Herder is aware that using this "bending" approach will inevitably make for translations that are more difficult to read than those that can be produced by a more "lax" method (in particular, a method that uses multiple words in the target language to translate a single word in the source language). For example, it will produce passages in which honey is jarringly described as being green (or alternatively, healthy foliage as being yellow). But he considers this price worth paying in order to achieve maximal semantic accuracy.

(x) Another key means which Herder espouses is complementing the goal of semantic faithfulness with that of faithfulness to the *musical form* of a literary work (for example, meter and rhyme). His motives for doing this are in part extra-semantic: in particular, aesthetic fidelity, and fidelity to the exact expression of feelings which is effected by means of a literary work's musical features. But they are also in part semantic: in his view, musical form and semantic content are strictly inseparable, so that fully realizing even the goal of semantic faithfulness in fact requires that a translation also be faithful to the work's musical form. Why, though, does he believe that form and content are inseparable in this way? He has two main reasons: First, musical forms often carry their own meanings (think, for example, of the humorous and bawdy connotations of the meter/rhyme-scheme of a limerick). Second, as I just mentioned, Herder believes that musical form is essential to an exact expression of feelings. But, as we saw earlier, he also thinks that feelings are internal to meanings (this is the force of his quasi-empiricism in the philosophy of language). Consequently, reproducing a work's musical form in translation turns out to be essential even for accurately conveying the meanings of its words in translation.

(xi) The sort of "accommodating" translation that has just been explained, besides being necessary in order to achieve translation's traditional fundamental goal of faithfully reproducing meaning as fully as possible (as well as such goals as aesthetic fidelity and fidelity in the expression of feelings), is in Herder's view also necessary in order to realize certain further important goals. One of these lies in a potential which translation has for enriching the target language (both conceptually and in musical forms). Herder argues that whereas "accommodating" translation fulfills this potential, "lax" translation fails to do so.

(xii) Another of these further goals is expressing, and cultivating in the translation's readership, a cosmopolitan respect for the Other—something which requires that the translation reproduce the Other's meanings (and musical forms) as accurately as possible.

(xiii) Herder holds that the approved "accommodating" sort of translation requires the translator to be in a sense a "creative genius"—that is, skilled and creative enough to satisfy the heavy demands which this sort of translation imposes, in particular creative enough to invent the needed novel conceptual and musical forms in the target language.

(xiv) Despite his commitment to the centrality of this sort of translation (largely due to its necessity for achieving translation's traditional fundamental goal of faithfully reproducing meaning), Herder is also in the end quite liberal about the forms that translation (or interlinguistic transfer more generally, including for example what he sometimes distinguishes from translation proper as "imitation [Nachbildung]") can legitimately take. He allows that these forms are quite various, and that which one is most appropriate in a particular case will depend largely on the author or genre involved and on the translator's purposes.[52]

Herder's theory of translation (as just summarized), and his demonstration of its viability in practice, for example in his sample translations of Shakespeare in the Popular Songs [Volkslieder] (1774), had an enormous impact on a whole generation of German translation theorists and practitioners, including Voss (the great translator of Homer), A.W. Schlegel (an important translation theorist, and Germany's great translator of Shakespeare), Goethe (a significant theorist of translation), Wilhelm von Humboldt (an important translator and theorist of translation, especially in his 1816 translation of Aeschylus' Agamemnon and the theoretical preface to it), and Schleiermacher (an important theorist of translation, and Germany's great translator of the Platonic dialogues). Herder's principle of complementing semantic faithfulness with faithfulness in the reproduction of musical form had an especially powerful impact on these successors. His principle of "bending" word-usages in order to cope with conceptual incommensurabilities was less widely followed, but was adopted by Schleiermacher among others.

Schleiermacher was arguably the most theoretically sophisticated of these intellectual heirs, and the Herderian positions adumbrated above all survived to form the core of Schleiermacher's own powerful and influential theory of translation, as articulated especially in his essay *On the Different Methods of Translation* (1813). However, the situation in this case is slightly different from the one we encountered in interpretation theory. As we saw, in interpretation-theory Schleiermacher's borrowing of Herder's positions also involved a worsening of them. In this case, by contrast, Schleiermacher effected some genuine refinements. On the other hand, "refinements" is the right word, rather than say "innovations": Schleiermacher's improvements took the form of subtle modifications of Herder's positions rather than of anything fundamentally new. Let me run through Schleiermacher's main refinements in order to illustrate this situation.

(a) Schleiermacher radicalizes Herder's fundamental principles of mental (including in particular, conceptual) difference, and of the consequent extreme difficulty of translation in many cases, and he does so in three important respects. First, he emphasizes that reproducing semantic content and reproducing musical form are not only difficult tasks in themselves but also often stand in irreconcilable conflict with each other.[53] (Somewhat surprisingly, Herder had tended to ignore or downplay this.) Second, Schleiermacher develops a much more holistic conception of meaning than Herder's. For example, he regards the diverse usages of a single word which are normally distinguished by a dictionary entry as all implicitly internal to each of them, and hence to the word's meaning on any particular occasion of its use; he takes a similar view of families of cognate words; and he even regards a language's distinctive grammar as internal to its meanings. Consequently, in his view, translation, in order faithfully to reproduce meaning, needs to mimic much more than Herder had recognized. Third, Schleiermacher holds that a translation ought to convey where an author was being conceptually conventional in relation to his background language and where, by contrast, conceptually innovative, a task which can be accomplished to some extent according to Schleiermacher (namely by using relatively older vocabulary in the target language for the former cases and relatively newer vocabulary for the latter), but only to some extent (since, for example, it may turn out that the semantically closest equivalent in the target language for an author's conceptual innovation is a relatively old word).

(b) Schleiermacher thus sees the prospects of full success in translation as even dimmer than Herder already had. However, he also develops a simple but effective way of warding off sheer skepticism and despair here. His solution builds on an idea which Herder had already expressed in the *Fragments*, namely that if one cannot translate Homer with full adequacy then one should at least *approximate* it *as closely as possible*. Schleiermacher holds, similarly but more generally, that even if translation will inevitably fall short of full success, it should strive to realize its goals (i.e. semantic faithfulness, faithfulness to musical form, and now also reflection of an author's conceptual conventionalities and innovations) *as adequately as possible*.

(c) Schleiermacher sharpens Herder's "lax" vs. "accommodating" choice for translation (which he slightly recasts as a choice between moving the author towards the reader vs. moving the reader towards the author), arguing that the translator must opt unequivocally for one or the other, and that it must be the latter (whereas Herder had argued only for a *compromise erring towards* the latter). Although several insightful authors have argued to the contrary,[54] I think that Schleiermacher's position may be slightly preferable to Herder's here, for two reasons: First, the pole of "accommodating," or reader-towards-author, translation seems better suited than some sort of compromise between it and the opposite pole as an *ideal*, since it more effectively reminds the translator of what would be required for full realization of translation's fundamental goal of reproducing meaning, and so more effectively spurs him on to optimal performance (even if the best that he will ever actually be able to *achieve* will indeed be a sort of compromise). Second, Schleiermacher's sharp choice is also useful as an analytical tool for classifying translations, or parts of a translation, into two types, according as they tend towards the one extreme or the other.

(d) Schleiermacher develops a fuller argument against the "lax" (or author-towards-reader) alternative than Herder does. Like Herder, he makes the fundamental point that it fails by falling further short of translation's traditional fundamental goal of semantic faithfulness than is necessary. But he also makes a more elaborate case against Dryden's rationale for it, the rationale of providing *the work that the author would have written had his native language not been the one he actually had but instead the target language*. Building on Herder's objection to this, namely that it *could not have been the case* that (say) an ancient author like Homer wrote his work with a modern language as his native language, Schleiermacher more carefully distinguishes *two* good reasons why not (between which Herder had himself remained ambiguous): first, due to thought's essential dependence on and boundedness by language, together with the incommensurability of languages, an ancient author like Homer could not have had his original *thoughts* in such a case; and second, even *he* could not have existed, since "he" would then have lacked the language that was necessary for constituting the thoughts, desires, etc. which in essential part made him the person he was.[55]

(e) Turning to the favored "accommodating" (or reader-towards-author) approach, and in particular to its strategy of "bending" word-usages in the target language in order to reproduce word-usages and hence meanings from the source language, Schleiermacher develops a fuller case than Herder had done for rejecting some competing ways of dealing with problematic concepts which might be proposed. First, Schleiermacher considers the possibility of using different target language words in different contexts (as is very commonly done in practice), but he rejects this as needlessly distorting the meaning of the original. This seems right. Consider Homer's color-word *chlôros* again, for instance. Adopting the approach in question, a translator might translate this word sometimes as "green" and sometimes as "yellow," depending on the context. But note that this involves a severe distortion of the original meaning: in particular, it gives the false impression that Homer had *two familiar* concepts, whereas he in fact had only *a single unfamiliar* one. Second, Schleiermacher considers the possibility of what he calls "paraphrase"—that is, attempting to re-express the meaning of a word from the source language by capturing its extension correctly through piling up expansive or restrictive qualifications in the target language. He again rejects this as needlessly distorting the meaning of the original word, and this again seems right. For instance, a translator dealing with the word *chlôros* might in the spirit of this approach try using the phrase "green or yellow" in all contexts. But, besides obvious stylistic infelicity, this distorts the meaning severely, not only (as before) giving the modern reader the false impression that Homer here has *two familiar* concepts whereas he in fact has only *a single unfamiliar* one, but also giving him the false impression that Homer has a *disjunctive* concept whereas he in fact has a *non-disjunctive* one.

(f) Schleiermacher also defends the "bending" approach against certain further potential objections. First, as I mentioned earlier, Herder had recognized that this approach would make for translations that were harder to read, but he had considered this an acceptable price to pay in return for their greater semantic accuracy. Schleiermacher agrees, but he also adds the further point that their difficulty serves a *positive* function, namely that of alerting the reader to the fact that the "bending" approach is being used, and to where in particular it is being used (both things that he needs to know in order for the approach to work for him). For instance, in our Homeric example, the shock of finding honey described as "green" at certain points in the translation (or healthy foliage as "yellow") can serve to alert the reader to both of these things. Second, in the *Fragments* Herder had himself voiced a concern that the "bending" approach threatened to compromise the authentic nature of the target language (though he had evidently overcome this worry subsequently, since he had gone on to employ this approach in his own translations in the

Popular Songs). Schleiermacher explicitly answers this worry with two plausible points: (i) The high degree of linguistic liberty involved can, and moreover should, be confined to translators; it need not and should not infiltrate the broader language. (ii) A certain natural inertia in languages in any case ensures that any unnatural innovations that arise will not survive for long.

(g) Schleiermacher also develops a more elaborate account than Herder had given of certain conditions which must be fulfilled in order for the "bending" approach to be successful. First, translation of this sort must be done en masse (and systematically), both in order to accustom readers to its method and in order to provide them with a sufficient number of examples of a particular word's "bending" in a sufficiently wide variety of contexts so that they can identify the unfamiliar rule for its use which is being followed and communicated. Second, the "bending" approach can only work if there is sufficient flexibility in the target language, or, more precisely, in the attitude of target language users towards their own language. Schleiermacher plausibly sees such flexibility as a feature of German in his day, but not of French. Third, this approach requires for its success a fairly high level of interest in and knowledge of foreign cultures among the educated public. In short, this approach requires a rather specific historical-cultural *kairos* in order to achieve success.

These improvements in Schleiermacher's version of the theory are real enough. But, as we have seen, they occur against the background of a huge common core of theory which was Herder's achievement, and they have more the character of refinements than of innovations. Moreover, counterbalancing them, there are also certain respects in which Herder's version of the theory is arguably superior to Schleiermacher's. Here are two good candidates:

(i) Schleiermacher sees an exception to the rule of mental (and in particular, conceptual) difference in the area of vocabulary which merely refers to or describes items of sensory experience, and he therefore regards translation as easy and straightforward in such cases, so much so indeed that he does not even dignify it with the honorific name of "translation [*Übersetzen*]" at all, but instead distinguishes it as mere "interpreting [*Dolmetschen*]." However, the notion that there is such an exception to the rule of mental (and in particular, conceptual) difference is a mistake.[56] Indeed, *pace* Schleiermacher, vocabulary which refers to or describes items of sensory experience is arguably a paradigmatic area of conceptual discrepancy. For instance, Homer's word *Helios* and our word *sun* certainly refer to the same object but they clearly do not *mean* the same (e.g. the former carries implications of personhood whereas the latter does not); and Homer's color vocabulary is conceptually discrepant with our own, as the example of Homer's word *chlôros* illustrates.[57] Now, unlike Schleiermacher, Herder makes no such exception to the rule. To this extent, his theory of translation is superior.

(ii) As was mentioned earlier, although Herder accords a special status to "accommodating" translation, his considered position concerning translation (and other forms of interlinguistic transfer) is rather liberal: as he puts it in the late *Terpsichore* (1796), there are "*many* sorts of translation, depending on who the author is on whom one works and the purpose for which one represents him."[58] Schleiermacher is usually much less liberal, especially in his 1813 essay, where he argues that the only type of translation that is really possible is the approved reader-towards-author type, that everything else is mere imitation or paraphrase, and that these are only inadequate and unnecessary substitutes for translation proper.[59] I would suggest that the essay's argument against the very possibility of author-to-reader translation rests on an error (namely, an outright equation of this approach with the illegitimate *what the author would have . . .* rationale, which is in fact only *one* possible rationale for it), and that the essay's characterization of imitation and paraphrase as of their very nature merely failed attempts to achieve the same goal as translation is dubious as well. Moreover, and more positively, I would suggest that Herder's contrary intuition that, depending on the particular author and genre involved, and on the translator's particular purposes, one or other of these approaches might well be more appropriate than "accommodating," or reader-towards-author, translation is clearly right. For example, if one is translating Aristophanic comedy and one's purpose is to produce something that can be successfully performed on the modern stage, then one would be ill-advised to use the "accommodating," reader-towards-author, approach (as B.B. Rogers' translations of Aristophanes tend to do, for instance), and much better advised to use a "lax," author-towards-reader, or even an imitative, approach instead (as W. Arrowsmith does in his translation of Aristophanes' *Clouds*, for instance).[60] So this is another significant respect in which Herder's theory is arguably superior to Schleiermacher's.

4. Conclusion

This, then, has been a case for Herder's seminal importance in the philosophy of language, the philosophy of interpretation (or "hermeneutics"), and the philosophy of translation. As I have tried to show, the revolutionary developments that took place in these three areas in the late eighteenth and early nineteenth centuries were deeply interconnected (in particular, those in the philosophies of interpretation and translation largely rested on those in the philosophy of language); it was Herder, rather than other people who usually receive most of the credit, in particular Hamann and Schleiermacher, who was the real source of these developments; at least in the philosophies of language and interpretation his versions of these developments were also philosophically superior to those other people's versions of them; and in all of these areas he still has important things to teach us today. If this line of argument has been broadly correct, then Herder deserves much more attention from philosophers than he usually receives.

Notes

1. In particular, I do not follow, and would indeed firmly disagree with, Taylor's central claim that Herder's seminal contribution lies in his conception of *Besonnenheit* and of a related linguistic "rightness," as introduced in the *Treatise on the Origin of Language* of 1772, and that a whole family of further important and novel ideas somehow follows from that one.

   Incidentally, my title's addition of the qualification "as a philosopher" is not grudging in spirit but is on the contrary meant to flag the fact that Herder has claims to importance not only as a philosopher but also in several other disciplines.

2. The explanation of this neglect is complicated and of some interest. To mention a few of the relevant factors: (1) Herder often uses a passionate, unruly *Sturm und Drang* style, eschews systematicity, and seems to lack arguments and to tolerate inconsistencies. (2) He has managed (paradoxically enough) to acquire both a bad name with cosmopolitans for "nationalism" and a bad name with nationalists for a sort of cosmopolitan softness. (3) He fell out, in one way or another, with almost everyone who was anyone in his own day, especially his former teacher Kant, but also to some extent his former follower Goethe, Schiller, Fichte, and the Schlegels. As a result, he tended to be widely read and borrowed from by the generation(s) that succeeded him but *rarely credited*. (4) A further factor that has had a negative effect on Herder's reception by Anglophone philosophers is that his writings are linguistically challenging for non-Germans, and that there are relatively few reliable English translations available. Insofar as some of these factors, in particular (1) and (2), might seem to reflect badly

on Herder, that appearance rests on misconceptions which can easily be defused. For some of the required defusing, see Essay 1.

3. Similar cases could be made for his importance in several other areas of philosophy as well—including, philosophy of mind, aesthetics, philosophy of history, and political philosophy. I shall not go into these here, but for some relevant discussion see Essays 1 and 7.

4. See e.g., concerning the philosophy of language, Berlin, *Vico and Herder* and *The Magus of the North*; concerning the philosophy of interpretation, Frank, *Das individuelle Allgemeine* and *Das Sagbare und das Unsagbare*; and concerning the philosophy of translation, Berman, *L'Épreuve de l'étranger*, as well as the work of Lawrence Venuti influenced by it.

5. For details, including textual evidence, see Essay 2.

6. For details, see Essays 2 and 9.

7. For details, see Essays 2 and 9.

8. E. Young, *Night Thoughts*. To my knowledge, Herder's earliest allusion to this passage occurs in his *Dithyrambic Rhapsody on the Rhapsody of Cabbalistic Prose* (1764), G1:39. For a later quotation of it, see e.g. *On the Ability to Speak and to Hear* (1795).

9. For a more detailed discussion of points (i)–(iv), and a presentation of supporting textual evidence, see Essay 2.

10. This is roughly the solution that he eventually arrives at in *Ideas for the Philosophy of History of Humanity* (1784–91). It seems to me markedly superior to the solution he had offered earlier in the *Treatise on the Origin of Language* (1772), that only human beings can use language, think, or conceptualize—a position which Taylor praises at "The Importance of Herder," pp. 44 ff., but in my view mistakenly.

11. For more details concerning point (iv), see Essay 3.

12. See Essay 2, n. 116.

13. For more details about this third doctrine, including textual evidence, see Essay 2.

14. See my *Wittgenstein on the Arbitrariness of Grammar* (Princeton, NJ: Princeton University Press, 2004), pp. 137 ff.

15. See esp. *Wittgenstein's Lectures: Cambridge 1932–1935* (Chicago: University of Chicago Press, 1982), pp. 44, 47–8, 121.

16. The stipulation that he applies the term correctly but still lacks the sensation might be questioned on the ground that applying the term correctly is *sufficient* for having the sensation. However, I think that a little further reflection shows that this is not in fact true. Suppose, for example, that the electronic device in question worked by producing a sort of auditory buzzing in his head.

17. To forestall an objection that is likely to seem tempting here: Recall that, unlike cruder versions of a doctrine of concept-empiricism, Herder's version is not committed to claiming that such observations could be made *without* the concepts in question.

18. Two qualifications of these high claims on behalf of Herder's philosophy of language: (i) The three Herderian doctrines on which I have focused here were not entirely without precedents. In particular, the Leibniz-Wolff tradition had anticipated the doctrine of thought's essential dependence on and boundedness by language; Ernesti had anticipated the doctrine that meanings are word-usages (albeit only in an epistemological version); and Herder's quasi-empiricism is indebted not only to the empiricists themselves but also to the precritical Kant. Concerning these anticipations, see Essay 2. (ii) Important developments have certainly occurred in the philosophy of language since Herder. To mention a chronologically proximate one: Friedrich Schlegel and Schleiermacher subsequently introduced an important element of linguistic *holism* into the philosophy of language (*pace* Taylor, "The Importance of Herder," pp. 56–9, who gives the impression that such a move was already implied by Herder's position in *Treatise on the Origin*). Concerning this holism, see Essays 10–12 and *German Philosophy of Language*, Essays 1, 4, and 8.

19. One of the few people who have recognized Herder's importance for the development of hermeneutics is J. Wach, *Das Verstehen. Grundzüge einer Geschichte der hermeneutischen Theorie im 19. Jahrhundert* (1926–33; repr. Hildesheim: Georg Olms, 1966), 1:19–22, cf. 35–6, 72. However, Wach does not specify Herder's contributions in any detail, and does not identify what I would regard as some of his most important ones, such as complementing linguistic with psychological interpretation, and prescribing "divination" as the method especially of the latter.

20. For example, this sort of possibility had been alleged in an extreme form by Plato in the Seventh Letter, and by the early Hamann in a less extreme form in the following passage from the *Crusades of the Philologist* (1762): "To speak is to translate—from the tongue of angels into the tongue of men, that is, to translate thoughts into words—things into names—images into signs . . . This kind of translation (I mean, speech) resembles more than aught else the wrong side of a tapestry: 'And shows the stuff, but not the workman's skill'; or it can be compared with an eclipse of the sun, which can be looked at in a vessel of water."

21. Another theorist of hermeneutics from the period who was evidently influenced by Herder to incorporate a focus on authorial psychology

into interpretation is Friedrich Ast. Concerning this aspect of Ast's position, see Wach, *Das Verstehen*, 1:45–6, 49.

22. Here again, Friedrich Ast likewise follows Herder in emphasizing the need for such holism.

23. For some further details concerning the above points, see Essays 1, 2, and 11, and *German Philosophy of Language*, Essay 9.

24. On the other hand, a further aspect of this addition is more or less shared by Herder, namely its inclusion of sensations or images in meaning, and, as we have seen, while this is very controversial today (in particular, anathema to a Fregean-Wittgensteinian anti-psychologism), it may well be defensible.

25. For further discussion of points (a)–(c), see Essay 11.

26. It is an interesting minor symptom of the waywardness of this idea that presupposing it and applying it to the Platonic corpus as a whole led Schleiermacher into one of his gravest errors concerning that corpus: namely, that the *Phaedrus* (!) must be the earliest of the dialogues and the *Republic* the latest (since these two dialogues seem to share a certain family of fundamental ideas—about separate forms, a tripartite soul, etc.—in, respectively, a *seminal* and then a *fully-developed* manner). For fuller discussion and criticism of Schleiermacher's conception of the *Keimentschluß*, see Essay 11.

27. For further discussion of this question, see Essay 11.

28. Schleiermacher calls this a "comparative" method and sees it as prominent both in natural science and on the merely linguistic side of interpretation.

29. For some further discussion of this question, see Essay 11.

30. Concerning his occasional attention to this subject, see P. Szondi, "Schleiermacher's Hermeneutics Today," in his *On Textual Understanding and Other Essays = Theory and History of Literature*, vol. 15 (Manchester: Manchester University Press, 1986), p. 111.

31. By contrast, Schleiermacher's friend and colleague Friedrich Schlegel (together with his brother August Wilhelm Schlegel) paid more attention to the subject of genre, and has sometimes been seen as the person who really raised it to prominence in hermeneutics. For example, August Boeckh, who himself identified generic interpretation as one of the four fundamental types of interpretation, seems to credit the Schlegels as his main forerunners in this area in his *Encyklopädie und Methodologie der philologischen Wissenschaften* (1877; 2nd edn., Leipzig: B.G. Teubner, 1886), p. 253; and Szondi seems to take a similar view of Friedrich Schlegel's role in this area in his essay "Friedrich Schlegel's Theory of

Poetical Genres: A Reconstruction from the Posthumous Fragments,'' in *On Textual Understanding and Other Essays*. However, Herder raised the subject of the importance of identifying genre for interpretation to high prominence first, and he also did so in a more consistently defensible way than Friedrich Schlegel. (Concerning Friedrich Schlegel's theory of genre, see *German Philosophy of Language*, Essay 2.)

32. For a fuller list, see Essay 1.

33. "Open-mindedness" is perhaps the more accurate word for Herder's ideal, for just as he rejects negative prejudice as detrimental to sound interpretation so he rejects excessive sympathy as equally detrimental to it (see e.g. G5:1194).

34. A.W. Schlegel, taking over Herder's ideal of *Einfühlung*, pointed out that it would be possible to master the Greeks' use of a certain word "grammatically" but still not understand the word due to a failure to grasp the "intuitions" which underlay its use (see A. Huyssen, *Die frühromantische Konzeption von Übersetzung und Aneignung* [Zürich and Freiburg: Atlantis, 1969], pp. 69 ff., 89).

35. Indeed, in the *Treatise on the Origin* (1772) Herder holds that it is part of our original animal nature to *fuse* perceptual sensation with affective sensation (albeit that qua human beings we in a way manage to detach the former from the latter by means of language/reflection). See my *Herder: Philosophical Writings* (Cambridge: Cambridge University Press, 2002), pp. 88–9, 101–3, 137–8. Similarly, in *On the Cognition and Sensation of the Human Soul* (1778) he holds that the only healthy state for a human soul is one in which cognition includes affect, that any attempt to abstract cognition from affect amounts to a sort of pathology. See *Herder: Philosophical Writings*, pp. 226–9.

36. Cf. *De Anima*, 429a.

37. See esp. *On the Cognition and Sensation of the Human Soul* (1778), in *Herder: Philosophical Writings*, p. 204. This move is closely connected with Herder's tendency, in comparison with other thinkers, to demote vision in importance relative to the other senses, especially hearing (see e.g. ibid., pp. 97–9, 106–11).

38. See *Herder: Philosophical Writings*, pp. 114–15, 203–5, 217–23, 249–53, 291. Also G6:286 ff.

39. *Herder: Philosophical Writings*, p. 292.

40. G1:559.

41. G5:74–5.

42. *Herder: Philosophical Writings*, pp. 217–18. Cf. p. 291.

43. G5:1194.

44. See esp. Otto's four books *Die Götter Griechenlands*, *Dionysos*, *Die Manen*, and *Die Musen*.

45. Cf. again here A.W. Schlegel's observation (already mentioned in a previous note) that it would be possible to master the Greeks' use of a certain word "grammatically" but still not understand the word due to a failure to grasp the "intuitions" that underlay its use.

46. H.-G. Gadamer, *Truth and Method* (New York: Continuum, 2002).

47. Heidegger and Gadamer would of course be loath to equate pre-understanding with a subject's perceptual and affective sensations. They instead conceive it as something more "primordial" than either the subject-object distinction or the distinction between the theoretical and the practical. However, what is *plausible* in their position seems to me not badly (re)cast in such terms.

48. In qualifiedly endorsing Gadamer's notion of "pre-understanding" here, I mean to endorse his idea that it is a *necessary condition* of understanding, not the additional implication which the "pre- [*Vor-*]" sometimes seems to carry for him (though not for Heidegger) that it is something that takes place, or at least can take place, temporally *prior* to understanding. Herder's picture, which seems right to me, is that the sensations which support conceptual understanding are *inter*dependent with it—that not only are the concepts in question essentially infused with the sensations in question but also *vice versa*.

    This point should deter one from thinking of the sort of imaginative, non-committed grasp of another person's sensations that is being described here as a sort of *tool* for achieving understanding of the person's concepts, as though one could get hold of the tool first and then employ it to produce that result afterwards. The two things are too intimately connected to stand in such a relation, though the former remains a necessary condition of the latter.

    That consequence might sound disappointing. But if so, then the same point also carries a happier consequence. The above account naturally invites such questions (or perhaps, challenges) as the following: How can an imaginative grasp of a historical/cultural or individual Other's different sensations be achieved? And how can it be ascertained to have taken place correctly rather than incorrectly? The point just made suggests at least part of an answer to such questions: The interpreter can be guided towards a correct grasp of the Other's sensations by determining the extra-sensational aspects of the Other's usage of words, and to that extent the Other's concepts—which, since they are internal to the character of the Other's sensations, at least constrain viable intuitions concerning the character of the Other's sensations. And one can judge the interpreter's intuitions for correctness or incorrectness by seeing whether the extra-sensational aspects of his associated usage of words match up with those of the historical/cultural or individual Other whose sensations he is attempting to access, since their failure to do so will be enough to show that he has failed in the attempt (even if their success in doing so will not be enough to show that he has succeeded in the attempt).

49. A.W. Eaton, *Titian's "Rape of Europa": The Intersection of Ethics and Aesthetics* (University of Chicago doctoral dissertation, August 2003).

50. See esp. Berman, *L'Épreuve de l'étranger*; also L. Venuti, *The Translator's Invisibility: A History of Translation* (London: Routledge, 1995).

51. For a fuller discussion of this whole subject, including the textual evidence that I shall omit here, see Essay 12.

52. As in the philosophies of language and interpretation, Herder's positions here were to some extent anticipated by predecessors. For example, Thomas Abbt, whom he quotes with broad approval (but also some criticism) in connection with translation in the *Fragments*, had anticipated both his central approach of "bending" word-usages and that of complementing semantic faithfulness with faithfulness to musical form.

53. For example, the need to translate a single word by a single word throughout a poetic work in order to reproduce its semantic content by "bending" may conflict with the need to replicate the work's original rhyme scheme in the interests of preserving its musical form.

54. e.g. Rosenzweig, Huyssen, and Lefevere.

55. Schleiermacher also considers and rejects (correctly, I think, though with inadequate arguments) two possible revisions of Dryden's rationale, neither of which Herder had considered: first, providing the work that the author would have written if he had *added* to his native language a mastery of the target language and composed his work in the latter; and second, providing the work that the author would have written if he had added to his native language a mastery of the target language and himself *translated* his work from the former into the latter. For more on this, see Essay 12.

56. This mistake may be due in part to Schleiermacher's failure to draw a clear distinction between *referent* and *meaning*—a distinction which Herder had already pointed towards in his *Ideas for the Philosophy of History of Humanity*, which was being more explicitly articulated in Schleiermacher's day by Herder's disciple Wilhelm von Humboldt, and

which would later receive its classic statement in Frege's *On Sense and Reference*.

57. In addition to the peculiarities of this word already mentioned, it also incorporates an implication of moistness.

58. S27:275.

59. He adopts a more liberal position in his 1825 *Aesthetics* lectures, where he in particular welcomes imitation. This is why, despite the position described above, I implied earlier that he is ultimately sympathetic to Herder's liberalism.

60. *Pace* a confused contrary judgment of Schleiermacher's concerning the translation of ancient comedy in his 1813 essay.

5

Herder on Genre

One of the most striking inadequacies of contemporary Anglophone philosophy of language lies in its neglect of *genre*. This neglect largely rests on two seductive but grievous mistakes. First, it tends to be assumed that genres are confined to *literature* (e.g. epic poetry, lyric poetry, tragedy, comedy, the novel). This is by no means the case, however. Virtually all forms of linguistic communication, and many non-linguistic ones as well, essentially belong to one genre or another—the scientific article is as much a genre as the novel, the stump speech as much as either, the portrait sculpture as much as any of the preceding. Second, it tends to be assumed that genres are merely *species* of communicative activity (much in the way that cats and dogs are merely species of animals). They *are* that, but they are also *willed means* of communication—very much as expressions of concepts and illocutionary forces are not only species of communicative activity but also willed means of communication. (To put it another way: one can indeed classify certain utterances as expressions of the concept X, but they are so in virtue of the fact that their authors intend them to express the concept X; one can indeed classify certain utterances as assertions that Y, but they are so in virtue of the fact that their authors intend them to be assertions that Y; and likewise, one can indeed classify certain bodies of writing as novels, but they are so in virtue of the fact that their authors intend them to be novels.)[1]

German theorists of hermeneutics, and others influenced by them, have been far more sensitive to the importance of genre. Indeed, at least since the publication of August Boeckh's *Encyclopedia and Methodology of the Philological Sciences* (1877)—where Boeckh made the identification of genre one of the four fundamental types or aspects of interpretation that he distinguished (the other three being historical, linguistic, and individual—i.e. what Schleiermacher had called psychological—interpretation)—the central role that the identification of genre plays in interpretation has been widely recognized by that tradition.[2]

Boeckh himself seems to credit Friedrich and August Wilhelm Schlegel for elevating genre to its proper place in the theory of interpretation.[3] And some other modern theorists have implied a similar view—for example, Peter Szondi, in an essay that extols the importance of Friedrich Schlegel's theory of genre.[4] However, I want to suggest that it is really Herder who deserves most of the credit here, and that he developed a number of profound insights concerning genre which still repay serious consideration today.

I

A first point which deserves emphasis in this connection is simply that Herder focused on the question of genre to an almost unprecedented extent.[5] Beginning in his early essay *Of the Ode* (1764–5),[6] and then throughout the rest of his long career, he repeatedly took up the task of describing particular genres and sub-genres, explaining their genesis and development, and addressing various theoretical questions concerning them. Besides the essay just mentioned, further examples of this are his discussions of poetic genres in the *Critical Forests* (1769), tragedy in the essay *Shakespeare* (1773), the genres of Hebrew poetry in *On the Spirit of Hebrew Poetry* (1782–3),[7] the epigram in the *Scattered Leaves* (1785–97), and the fable, the fairy tale, the novel, the idyll, tragedy, and comedy in the *Adrastea* (1801–3).[8]

Perhaps especially noteworthy in this connection is his common practice of carefully distinguishing between a genre's various different sub-genres. He already does this in his early essay *Of the Ode*. Further examples of it are found in his later discussions of Hebrew poetry in general,[9] as well as of the Hebrew psalms in particular,[10] and of epigrams.[11]

II

Before discussing Herder's most important contributions to the theory of genre, it will be helpful to consider some preliminary questions. First of all, what *is* a genre? (And what *are* the particular genres?)

It is no part of Herder's project to attempt to provide a strict definition, i.e. non-trivial essential necessary and sufficient conditions, for the concept of genre (or for particular genre concepts).[12] However, nor is this omission at all embarrassing. For if twentieth-century philosophy of language has shown anything, it is that the—originally Socratic-Platonic-Aristotelian—prejudice that any legitimate general term must be definable by giving non-trivial essential necessary and sufficient conditions is illegitimate (this was a large part of the point of the later Wittgenstein's case that some general terms instead have only a "family resemblance" character).[13] It might in principle be a perfectly respectable answer to the question(s) just posed simply to say that a genre is *this* sort of thing: epic poetry, ode, sonnet, tragedy, comedy, novel, etc.[14] (or a tragedy *this* sort of thing: Aeschylus' *Agamemnon*, Sophocles' *Oedipus Rex*, Euripides' *Medea*, Shakespeare's *Hamlet*, etc.).

Herder does, though, in fact imply a somewhat more informative answer than that, a sort of informal definition: a genre is constituted by an overall *purpose* aimed at by a class of works, together with certain *rules of composition* which serve that purpose.[15] (Similarly, he sometimes gives informal definitions of particular genres.[16])

It may be worth pausing over this informal definition of genre for a while in order to try to bring out some of its strengths: (i) Some more recent authors on genre tend to efface Herder's inclusion of purposes in his conception of the constitution of genres, instead writing as though rules, or norms, alone constituted them.[17] Indeed, E.D. Hirsch has explicitly questioned the idea that genres have an overall purpose, or *telos*.[18] Now, if genres are as coarsely discriminated as they usually have been (so that, for example, Sophocles' *Oedipus Rex* and Shakespeare's *Hamlet* are both counted as belonging to a single genre of tragedy), then Hirsch's objection has a point, though even then *some* sort of shared overall purpose is normally identifiable, albeit perhaps a fairly thin one (for example, both Sophoclean and Shakespearean tragedy aim to provide a serious representation of a weighty human story by means of actors on a stage in order to entertain an audience and cause it to reflect). However, when genres are more finely discriminated (for example, so that just ancient tragedies are grouped together, or even just Sophoclean tragedies), and in proportion as this is done, then the idea of a shared overall purpose becomes increasingly compelling and contentful.[19] In short, Herder is probably right to see genres as constituted not only by rules but also by purposes.

(ii) Under the general heading of overall purpose and rules of composition, Herder employs a broad and diverse range of more specific criteria, including among other things type of thematic content.[20] This makes his position strikingly similar to that developed by the most thoughtful and sophisticated recent theorist of genre, Alastair Fowler, who not only like Herder gives an informal definition of genre in terms of overall purpose and rules of composition,[21] but also like Herder employs a broad and diverse range of more specific criteria, again including type of thematic content.[22]

(iii) Herder's account rightly implies that a work belongs to a certain genre not simply in virtue of having certain features but also in virtue of its author's having deliberately intended that it should have them: a work that merely *happened* to realize a certain purpose or to conform to certain composition-rules would not thereby instantiate the relevant genre; it only does so if it was produced by the author *in order to* realize that purpose and to conform to those rules.[23]

(iv) Some recent theorists of genre have tended to conflate genre with certain other important aspects of texts and discourse. For example, Hirsch in his well-known discussion of the subject tends to conflate it both with the *overall meaning* of a text and with *illocutionary force*.[24] Herder is normally innocent of such conflations, and this is an important virtue. Not everything that belongs to a text's overall meaning is also part of its genre, or vice versa (for example, its overall meaning may include lessons concerning a particular fictional character which are not part of its genre; and its genre may include a certain formal structure, as in the case of the sonnet, which is not part of its overall meaning). Nor should genre be conflated with illocutionary force. What distinguishes the two? Part of the answer to that question might simply consist in offering an informal definition of the contrast by means of examples: on the one hand, epic poetry, the ode, the sonnet, tragedy, comedy, the novel, etc. go together as genres; on the other hand, assertion, question, command, etc. go together as illocutionary forces. But it can also be said, somewhat more informatively, that whereas illocutionary force is a concept that applies to individual sentences, genre is a concept that only applies to whole works, which are usually (though not always) composed of multiple sentences.[25]

(v) Herder's informal definition in principle leaves open the possibility of genres which are only found in a single author or even only in a single work. This is quite deliberate, and again arguably a virtue. Although for Herder genres are typically shared by several works and several authors, he also allows (for example, in his essay *Shakespeare*) that there can be such a thing as a genre that is confined to a single author, and even such a thing as a one-off genre, a genre found only in a single work. For Herder, the great artist often develops new overall purposes and rules constitutive of new genres. It might be objected to this that the extreme case of a one-off genre is impossible because genres are of their very essence multiply instantiated. However, Boeckh—who basically shares Herder's position on these matters—argues very plausibly that what is essential to a genre is not multiple instantia*tion* but only multiple instantia*bility*.[26] (On the other hand, there are obviously powerful incentives for even a rather daring artist to conform, or at least stay close, to a pre-existing genre or genres—for example, besides limits to the artistic imagination, the desideratum of making a work intelligible and acceptable to an audience.[27])

(vi) There is an attractive side of Herder's reflections on genre which is skeptical of the idea that great art is guided by explicitly formulated genre rules, and which rather sees the great artist as guided by tacit sensibilities.[28] This need not conflict with, or restrict, Herder's standard account of genre in terms of overall purpose and rules of composition, but it does imply a certain qualification of it: namely, that when the great artist develops new (purposes and) rules, these are often ones that are not yet explicitly formulated by him. This position is intrinsically attractive, and also coheres nicely with a broader thesis that has been emphasized by some of the best recent literature on genre: namely, that the constituents of a genre, whether it is a new one or not, may sometimes be less than fully conscious.[29]

(vii) A final valuable feature of Herder's general conception of genre that is worth mentioning is the following. In the first draft of his essay *Shakespeare* he describes Shakespeare's plays as mixing "all the colors of the tragic, comic, etc."[30] Similarly, in the *Adrastea* he notes that Shakespeare's plays (and other genres) contain idyllic scenes.[31] He also characterizes the *Sakontala* of the Indian author Kalidasa as "epic drama."[32] Pushing this sort of position to an extreme, Friedrich Schlegel would in some of his fragments go as far as to advocate *replacing* a substantival use of genre-concepts with a merely adjectival one.[33] Herder here implies, and Schlegel characteristically overplays, an important point, namely that the basic genres (e.g. tragedy), once established, give birth to corresponding modes (e.g. being tragic) which can qualify works belonging to other genres.[34] For example, Fowler plausibly characterizes Hardy's novels as tragic novels (think, for instance, of *Jude the Obscure* and *Tess of the D'Urbervilles*).[35]

III

Continuing with some further preliminary points: Correct identification of a work's genre is vitally important for two main reasons, in Herder's view. First, it is essential for properly *understanding* the work, for *interpreting* it correctly.[36] Why is this so? Herder does not address this question very explicitly. But, from things he does say, one can infer at least three reasons: (i) Identifying a work's genre is in itself an essential aspect of fully understanding the work (rather as identifying an utterance's illocutionary force is in itself an essential aspect of fully understanding the utterance, even if one already knows the utterance's linguistic meaning).[37] (ii) There will normally be aspects of a work's *meaning* which are expressed, not so much by any of its particular parts, but rather through its exemplification, as a whole, of a certain genre. To illustrate this point with the help of a case discussed by Herder in his *Adrastea*: Lessing had argued that the function of Aesop's fables as a genre is to illustrate through a concrete example a universal moral principle, whereas Herder argues that it is rather to illustrate a general rule of life, experience, or prudence.[38] If *either* of these positions is correct, then the full interpretation of a fable should include the idea, drawn from the genre, of a universal moral principle (if Lessing is right), or of a general rule of life, experience, or prudence (if Herder is right).[39] (iii) Correct identification of a work's genre is also necessary in order properly to understand meanings that *are* expressed by the work's parts. In this spirit, Herder argues in the *Critical Forests* (1769) that in order to achieve a proper understanding of "ridiculous" passages in Homer, such as the Thersites episode in *Iliad*, book 2, it is necessary to understand them in light of the nature of the whole work and their contribution thereto.[40] The case just mentioned can serve to illustrate this point as well: whichever of the two accounts of Aesop's fables is correct, knowing it will enable one to infer from Aesop's descriptions of animals and their activities in a particular fable deeper specific meanings concerning a universal moral principle (if Lessing is right) or a general rule of life, experience, and prudence (if Herder is right).[41]

Second, in Herder's view, correctly identifying a work's genre is also essential for *evaluating* the work properly. This principle had already constituted one of Aristotle's main reasons for focusing on genre in the *Poetics*. Herder takes this principle for granted in such works as *Shakespeare* and *This Too a Philosophy of History*.[42] His more specific basis for it, again broadly shared with Aristotle, is the very plausible idea that the main way (or at least *a* main way) in which a work can fail is by failing to realize its genre-purpose or violating its genre-rules, and that the main way (or at least *a* main way) in which a work can succeed is by realizing its genre-purpose and conforming to its genre-rules—so that proper critical assessment of a work's value requires that the critic know the genre-purpose and -rules in question, i.e. know the work's genre.[43]

IV

I would like now to turn to what seem to me Herder's main contributions to the theory of genre. Important predecessors in the theory of genre such as Aristotle and Lessing would not, I think, have disagreed radically with any of the main features of Herder's theory discussed so far (his informal definition of genre, and his views concerning the relevance of the identification of genre for interpretation and evaluation). But certain further contributions that he makes would have seemed much less familiar and intuitive to them.

A first, and easily overlooked, such contribution lies in the fact that Herder extends the above model of what a genre consists in (overall purpose and rules of composition) and of why its identification is important (both for understanding and for critical evaluation) from its primary sphere of application, *linguistic* works of art, to include also *non-linguistic* works of art, such as sculpture. Accordingly, the various complications arising in connection with the task of identifying a work's genre that Herder recognizes (and that will be discussed in the following sections of this essay) are ones which, in his view, apply not only to linguistic works but also to non-linguistic works.

Thus, having applied the model to, and discussed those complications in connection with, tragedy in the essay *Shakespeare* (1773), he then goes on to apply it to, and to discuss the same complications in connection with, portrait sculpture in *This Too a Philosophy of History* (1774).[44]

Such an extension may seem quite natural to us today, and is indeed very compelling. But it rests on an assumption which is not altogether uncontroversial: namely that non-linguistic works of art are (at least often) broadly text-like. And that assumption, while correct, is one that Herder was not initially in a position to make, but had to earn (as it were). The reason for this is that in the *Critical Forests* (1769) he had initially committed himself to a theory of non-linguistic arts which made them radically different from linguistic ones: merely sensory in nature rather than expressive of meanings. The motive behind that theory lay in his deep commitment to a principle that at first sight seemed to preclude non-linguistic arts expressing meanings: the principle that all meaning is of its very nature linguistic, consisting in the use of words. This whole position put an obstacle in the way of any straightforward extension of his model of genre to non-linguistic art: in particular, any picture of a work of non-linguistic art as bearing *meanings* in virtue of its genre or as expressing *meanings* in particular parts which could only be understood in light of its genre was officially precluded. However, Herder eventually revised his view of non-linguistic art, coming to recognize, much more plausibly, that it *does* sometimes express meanings. A key move he made in this connection was to see that its doing so is *not* in fact incompatible with the principle that all meaning is of its very nature linguistic, consisting in the use of words. The apparent incompatibility disappears just as long as one insists that whatever meanings a work of non-linguistic (or perhaps better now: "non-linguistic") art expresses are expressed by it in virtue of the artist's linguistic capacities. Herder already began to shift to this new, and much more plausible, position on non-linguistic art in the later parts of the *Critical Forests*, and he developed it further in subsequent works.[45] By doing so he also made possible the full extension of his model of genre from linguistic to non-linguistic art. Accordingly, by the time he writes *This Too a Philosophy of History* (1774) he can apply his model of genre to sculpture, arguing in particular that Pharaonic portrait sculpture as a genre expresses ideas about death and eternity which are bound up with the ancient Egyptians' cult of the dead, and that such ideas are also part of the meaning of its particular features, such as the immobility of its figures.[46]

This step constituted important progress in the direction of generalizing the essential role that genre plays in communication and interpretation (concerning which, see my opening paragraph).

V

Herder also makes a further important contribution, or rather set of contributions, to the theory of genre. Famously, Plato, in such dialogues as the *Meno* and the *Republic*, holds that whenever language has a single general term, it connotes a single idea. In other words, contrary to the impression that one would receive by consulting commonsense linguistic intuitions or modern dictionary entries (where a single term will typically be assigned several distinct meanings or concepts), concepts are very sparse. This position is logically quite distinct from *another*, even better known, position of Plato's, namely that ideas are eternal objects separate from particulars. Now Aristotle famously rejects the latter sort of Platonism. But he is somewhat more sympathetic to sparseness-Platonism.[47] Accordingly, when he comes to a literary genre-term like "tragedy" he assumes there to be, and therefore attempts to identify, just a single idea or essence connoted by the term. This is the project of his *Poetics*.

The French dramatists and critics of the seventeenth and eighteenth centuries had largely followed Aristotle in this outlook, assuming there to be only a very limited set of genres, genre-terms such as "tragedy" connoting just one each. In addition, they had followed what they took to be Aristotle's actual definition of the essence of "tragedy." Even closer to home for Herder, Lessing had still espoused a similar position in his *Hamburg Dramaturgy* of 1767–9 (albeit while criticizing the French for misunderstanding the details of Aristotle's definition of tragedy).

Herder, in light of inspiration by some more insightful predecessors, and on the basis of more careful scrutiny of the literary works in question, took a quite contrary view. Already in *Of the Ode* (1764–5) he argued that the ode "has become a Proteus among the nations," to the point that it is doubtful that there is really a single thing there at all.[48] Subsequently, he took a similar position on epic poetry in the *Critical Forests* (1769). Voltaire had already argued in his *Essay on Epic Poetry* (1728) (a work which probably influenced Herder's thinking not only about epic poetry but also more broadly) that literary art forms were ever changing, and in particular that the various examples of "epic" poetry which history had generated (Homer's, Virgil's, Lucan's, Trissin's, Camoëns', Tasso's, de Ercilla's, Milton's, and so on) were in fact markedly different in kind from each other. Accordingly, in the *Critical Forests* Herder argued—in opposition to some remarks by Lessing in his *Laocoon* (1766)—that the different types of ancient Greek poetry were governed by sharply different purposes and rules, and moreover that different peoples had produced very different types of "epic" poetry (in particular, Homer, Ossian, Milton, and Klop-stock had each produced an "epic" poetry markedly different in kind from that of the others).[49] Similarly, and more famously, contrary to French and Lessingian assumptions of a single essence of "tragedy" already defined by Aris-totle, Herder argued in the essay *Shakespeare* (1773) that the genre-purpose(s) and -rules that constitute ancient tragedy are in fact sharply different from those that constitute Shakespearean tragedy, so that, despite sharing the same name, the genres are really different: "Sophocles' drama and Shakespeare's drama are two things, which in a certain sense scarcely share the same name."[50] In the late *Letters for the Advancement of Humanity* (1793–7) Herder sums up this whole position concisely as follows:

Homer's, Virgil's, Ariosto's, Milton's, Klopstock's works bear the single name of epic poetry, and yet, even according to the concept of art that lies in the works, let alone according to the spirit that ensouls them, they are quite different productions. Sophocles, Corneille, and Shakespeare share, as tragedians, only the name; the genius of their representations is quite different. Similarly in the case of all genres of poetry, down even as far as the epigram.[51]

Herder seems to me quite right about this. Indeed, if anything, I think he *understates* the differences between the various forms of "epic" and between the various forms of "tragedy." For example, concerning "epic," like Voltaire before him, he omits to mention some of the features which most sharply distinguish Homeric "epic" from later types of "epic"—in particular, the fact that Homer, unlike his later counterparts, intended his poetry to express truth throughout (all of its statements about the gods and about what had happened in the past included), and believed that this was possible because he was inspired by a divine Muse who knew everything;[52] and the fact that for Homer, unlike his later counterparts, another central purpose of his poetry was to perpetuate the renown, or *kleos*, of the heroes whose deeds he recounted (in a culture which set great value on the perpetuation of renown).

Similarly, in the case of "tragedy": Herder does argue somewhat plausibly that whereas ancient tragedy normally observed the unities of place, time, and action, Shakespearean tragedy routinely violates them.[53] He also implies, even more plausibly, that there are several other genre-differences here: ancient tragedy includes a chorus and music, whereas Shakespearean usually does not;[54] ancient tragedy requires its main protagonist to have a relatively high moral stature, whereas Shakespearean does not (an extreme example is *Richard III*);[55] ancient tragedy accords a central place to recognition scenes, whereas Shakespearean does not;[56] and ancient tragedy prohibits the inclusion of comedy, whereas Shakespearean permits it.[57] Even more impressively, he rightly implies that ancient tragedy had Dionysiac religious functions and civic-political functions which Shakespearean tragedy lacks.[58] However, as in the case of "epic," he omits to mention a still more profound point of contrast: whereas Shakespearean tragedy is in large part deliberately fictional, ancient tragedy in its great fifth-century versions, like its epic ancestor, was standardly conceived by the tragedians as an attempt to convey truth throughout, in particular as an attempt to re-enact and further develop true accounts of the past inherited from traditional myth.[59] Aristotle famously holds otherwise, interpreting ancient tragedy as—unlike history—deliberately fictional (*Poetics*, 1451a–b). But the case against Aristotle's interpretation is a strong one: in addition to the precedent for the thoroughly factual purpose of serious poetry that had been set by epic,[60] two very acute ancient authors who stand much closer in time, milieu, and intellectual orientation to the great tragedians of the fifth century than Aristotle does, namely Aristophanes and Plato, both provide compelling testimony to tragedy's factual purpose.[61] Moreover, Aristotle's mistake can be easily explained in terms of three causes: (i) the intervening introduction of forms of tragedy that were *indeed* fictional (rather than myth- or history-based); (ii) certain dubious philosophical assumptions that he makes about the nature of meaning and truth which force him in interpretation to assimilate others' beliefs to his own (a reading of tragedy as fictional in particular allows him to avoid ascribing to the tragedians beliefs about the gods which their plays seem to show them holding but which are incompatible with his own religious conceptions);[62] and most obviously, (iii) a desire to defend tragedy against Plato's accusation in the *Republic* that it propagates falsehoods concerning the gods and other matters.[63] In short, Herder's conception that there is a deep difference in genre between ancient and Shakespearean tragedy turns out to be even truer than he realized once one considers their sharply different attitudes to factuality/fictionality.[64]

Similarly concerning non-linguistic art, contrary to the tendency of the great eighteenth-century art historian Winckelmann to treat the ancient Greeks and the ancient Egyptians as sharing a single genre of portrait sculpture, Herder argues in *This Too a Philosophy of History* (1774) and again in his *Memorial to Winckelmann* (1777) that the genre-purposes and -rules were in fact very different in the two cases. In particular, he argues that whereas Greek portrait sculpture pursued the representation of this-worldly action, movement, and charm, Egyptian portrait sculpture, bound up as it was with the Egyptian cult of the dead, sought—precisely *not* to represent this-worldly action, movement, or charm, but instead—to serve as memorials for the dead, as eternal "mummies" (as Herder puts it), and accordingly to represent death and repose.[65]

This step would eventually make possible the sort of highly refined art history that we associate above all with such practitioners as E.H. Gombrich and E. Panofsky, in which superficially similar looking forms of visual art from different periods of history—for instance, depictions of nature in Pharaonic paintings vs. depictions of nature by Constable—are recognized to be in fact quite different in their genre-purposes and -rules.[66]

Indeed, Herder pushes this whole line of thought about both linguistic and non-linguistic art even further in a certain respect, especially in the drafts of his essay *Shakespeare*: Not only do such variations in genre occur across different periods of history and different cultures, but even at a single time and place two authors writing, say, "tragedy" may in fact be working with significantly different genres, and indeed even a single author, for example Shakespeare, may be doing so between distinct works of his which initially seem similar in genre.[67]

This further point incorporates an important insight that had already been developed by some of Herder's eighteenth-century predecessors (often in specific connection with Shakespeare), including Voltaire in his *Essay on Epic Poetry* (1728), Young in his *Conjectures on Original Composition* (1759), Johnson in his preface to his edition of Shakespeare's works (1765), and even Lessing at points in his *Hamburg Dramaturgy* (1767–9): it is characteristic of a literary genius, such as Shakespeare, to *break or transcend* genre-rules.[68] Herder accepts this position, but he also inflects it in a particular way: he normally conceives such breaking or transcendence, not as a matter of the genius abandoning rules altogether,[69] but rather of his creating new rules.[70]

This whole position concerning both linguistic and non-linguistic art leads Herder to some very important consequences concerning the interpretation and critical evaluation of such art. A first consequence is that, due to historical, cultural, and even individual distance, a work's genre will often be unfamiliar to the interpreter or critic, so that he will need to undertake an investigation of it in order to identify it correctly, and hence in order to understand or critically evaluate the work properly (given that correctly identifying the genre is a necessary condition for accomplishing either of these things). Accordingly, Herder himself devotes considerable time and energy to undertaking just such investigations of relatively unfamiliar genres—for example, the genre of Shakespearean tragedy in the essay *Shakespeare*, the genres of ancient Hebrew poetry in *On the Spirit of Hebrew Poetry*, and (turning to a non-linguistic case) the genre of ancient Egyptian portrait sculpture in *This Too a Philosophy of History* and the *Memorial to Winckelmann*.

It is part of Herder's position here that a genre is always rooted in a specific cultural context from a specific time and place, and that in order to identify it correctly (and hence in order to interpret or critically evaluate a work properly) one needs to see it in relation to its cultural context. Thus, already in *Of the Ode* (1764–5) he attempts to explain the various different types of ode that have been produced over the course of history in light of their respective cultural contexts,[71] and he demands that their future analyst should be someone who is an expert on antiquity and who knows the spirits of the relevant nations.[72] Similarly, in the essay *Shakespeare* he demands that the interpreter of dramatic works interpret them in light of the author "and his history and his time and his world."[73] For example, he himself interprets the three unities of place, time, and action which (in continuity with Aristotle, as he understands him) he believes regulated ancient tragedies as reflections of, and appropriate to, the relatively homogeneous social and psychological world of ancient Athens, and Shakespeare's contrasting disregard of the unities as a reflection of, and appropriate to, the more diverse social and psychological world of Elizabethan and Jacobean England.[74] Again (turning to non-linguistic art), in *This Too a Philosophy of History* and the *Memorial to Winckelmann* he interprets ancient Egyptian portrait sculpture's genre-purpose of expressing ideas about death and eternity as a reflection of the ancient Egyptians' religious cult of the dead.[75]

It is another part of Herder's position here that a narrowly defined genre's identity can normally only be fully determined in light of the origin and the diachronic development of the more broadly defined genre that generated it (assuming that one did). Herder already explicitly champions such a position in his early *Essay towards a History of Lyric Poetry* (1766), where he writes:

But it is not only delightful but also necessary to trace the origin of the objects that one wants to understand with a certain completeness. With that we obviously lose a part of the history, and how much does the history not contribute towards the explanation of the whole? And moreover, the most important part of the history, from which subsequently everything can be derived! For just as the tree from the root, so the progress and blossoming of an art must be capable of being derived from its origin. The origin contains in itself the whole essence of its product, just as the whole plant with all its parts lies wrapped up in the seed; and I will not be able to extract from the *later* condition the degree of explanation that makes my explanation *genetic*.[76]

This approach is already at work in Herder's historical treatment of the ode in *Of the Ode* (1764–5). It is also involved in his treatment of tragedy in *Shakespeare* (1773), where he discusses the development of ancient tragedy out of its simple beginnings in the chorus through successive additions of individual actors, in particular by Aeschylus and Sophocles, as well as the development of ancient tragedy into modern, and in particular Shakespearean, tragedy. It is also prominent in his treatments of further genres in later works, for example his treatment of the epigram in the *Scattered Leaves* (1785–97) and his treatments of the fable, the novel, and other genres in the *Adrastea* (1801–3).[77]

A second consequence is that interpreters and critics face a constant temptation falsely to assimilate a work's genre to other, more familiar genres, based on the superficial similarity of a shared name and/or a few shared features—a temptation to which they have indeed commonly succumbed, thereby vitiating both their understanding and their critical evaluation of works. For example, in the essay *Shakespeare* Herder argues that French interpreters and critics of Shakespeare have falsely assimilated Shakespeare's genre of "tragedy" to what Aristotle more or less correctly identified as the ancient genre of "tragedy," whereas in fact the two genres are importantly different—in particular, because ancient tragedy, as the product of a relatively simple social and psychological world, strives to preserve the unities of place, time, and action, whereas Shakespearean tragedy, as the product of a more complex social and psychological world, does not, but instead strives to provide a multifaceted "story/history [*Geschichte*]" of a "whole event [*Begebenheit*]." And Herder argues that French interpreters and critics have consequently both misunderstood Shakespearean tragedy and made misguided critical assessments of it—critical assessments that fault it for failing to fulfill certain genre-purposes and -rules which do not in fact belong to its genre (especially, conformity to the rules of the unities) and that omit to commend it for successfully fulfilling the genre-purposes and -rules which really do constitute its genre.[78] Similarly (turning to non-linguistic art), in *This Too a Philosophy of History* and the *Memorial to Winckelmann* Herder argues that Winckelmann's interpretation and critical assessment of ancient Egyptian portrait sculpture are both vitiated by a false assimilation of its genre to the genre of ancient Greek portrait sculpture. In particular, he argues that Winckelmann interprets Egyptian portrait sculpture as striving to achieve, and therefore criticizes it for failing to achieve, the sort of representation of this-worldly action, movement, and charm that Greek portrait sculpture really did strive and also manage to achieve, whereas in fact Egyptian portrait sculpture's genre-purpose was quite different and contrary, consisting—precisely *not* in the representation of this-worldly action, movement, or charm, but instead—in memorializing the dead, serving as their eternal "mummies," and so representing death and repose, in accordance with the religious cult of the dead to which it belonged, a purpose which it realized every bit as well as Greek portrait sculpture realized *its* purpose.[79]

These two major consequences—the frequent unfamiliarity of a genre to its would-be interpreter or critic, and his consequent need to work hard to identify it correctly; plus his need in particular to resist constant temptations to false assimilation—both seem to me correct and extremely important. For example, I would suggest that a large part of the challenge that we face when we set out to interpret or critically evaluate ancient Greek epic poems, tragedies, or comedies derives precisely from the facts that these are genres with which we are deeply unfamiliar, and that we are moreover obstructed in our attempts to identify them correctly by constant temptations falsely to assimilate them to superficially similar genres with which we are more familiar.[80]

A third consequence, which may be mentioned more briefly since it is rather implied by Herder's position than explicitly emphasized by him, is prospective in character: just as the past has seen the genesis of an almost endless variety of new genres as new periods, cultures, and individuals have come along to create them, so the future holds the possibility of an indefinite number of new genres as well.[81]

Finally, note that this whole situation concerning genre closely parallels one which Herder recognized in another area: conceptualization. There too a Platonist assumption of sparseness had dominated much earlier thought on the subject. There too Herder recognized that this assumption was incorrect, that continuity in the words used and/or other superficial similarities in fact mask myriad different concepts. And there too Herder saw that in consequence there is a major task of investigating unfamiliar concepts in order to identify them correctly, and thereby make proper interpretation (and evaluation) possible; a constant threat to achieving this deriving from a temptation falsely to assimilate alien concepts to ones with which the interpreter is already familiar and which superficially resemble them; and also a potential for an indefinite amount of conceptual innovation in the future, in continuation of that which has taken place in the past.

VI

A further important contribution that Herder makes to the theory of genre concerns the appropriate method to use in order to determine a work's genre (and thereby make proper interpretation and critical evaluation of the work possible). The situation just described—an anti-Platonist plethora of different genres, and the resulting challenges of identifying unfamiliar genres, and of resisting a pervasive temptation falsely to assimilate them to superficially similar familiar ones—was recognized by Herder largely thanks to his use of an empirical approach to determining genre. Likewise, he sees an empirical approach as the key to addressing the challenges that this situation involves. In this spirit, already in *Of the Ode* (1764–5) he enjoins that in constructing our aesthetic theories we should "begin not from the top but from the bottom."[82]

Accordingly, he sharply rejects apriorism in this area. One aspect of this rejection is his salutary avoidance of the sorts of apriorist schemas of possible genres that had already been developed before him by certain theorists (e.g. John of Garland), would soon be developed by some of his successors in the theory of genre (e.g. Goethe and Friedrich Schlegel),[83] and have continued to be developed, in ever more complicated versions, by recent theorists of genre (e.g. Frye, Scholes, and Hernadi).[84]

Another aspect of that rejection is Herder's repudiation of apriorism in determining the character of particular genres. This repudiation certainly precludes the *absolute* apriorism of undertaking to determine the character of a particular genre in isolation from any close observation of examples at all (say, on the basis of what Aristotle has told us a "tragedy" is). But it also precludes the *relative* apriorism of undertaking to do so under the guidance only of close observation of a limited range of examples without observation of further examples to which the resulting genre-conception is to be applied in interpretation or critical assessment. Even the latter procedure is disastrous, in Herder's view, because of the anti-Platonist fact that the superficial appearance of a single genre shared by different historical periods or cultures, or even by different authors within a single period and culture, or indeed even by a single author in one work and in another, typically masks important differences.

Herder detects such a misguided apriorism in the determination of genre in many areas of interpretation and criticism. For example, in the essay *Shakespeare* he sees it at work in the approach that the French dramatists and critics of the seventeenth and eighteenth centuries had usually taken to tragedy, an approach which essentially assumed the universal validity of an Aristotelian definition of tragedy that was originally derived by Aristotle exclusively from the observation of ancient tragedies—indeed, often without even noticing Aristotle's original empirical derivation of it—and which therefore took it for granted that this constituted an appropriate yardstick for interpreting and evaluating Shakespearean tragedy as well (whose genre is in fact sharply different). Herder argues (with a good nose for an ad hominem side-point) that Shakespearean tragedy needs a new Aristotle, i.e. someone who will define its genre(s) with the same sort of empirical care and thoroughness that Herder thinks Aristotle had applied to ancient tragedy.[85]

Similarly (turning to non-linguistic art), in *This Too a Philosophy of History* and the *Memorial to Winckelmann* Herder detects a misguided relative apriorism in Winckelmann's treatment of ancient Egyptian portrait sculpture: Winckelmann implicitly assumes the universal validity of a set of genre-purposes and -rules for portrait sculpture which he has derived from the particular case of Greek portrait sculpture, namely a set dominated by the genre-purpose of portraying this-worldly action, movement, and charm, and he then applies this in his interpretation and critical assessment of ancient Egyptian portrait sculpture, whose genre was in fact sharply different, in particular involving a quite contrary genre-purpose of conveying ideas of death and eternity.

More positively, Herder's own empirical approach to determining genre is multi-faceted. First and foremost, it includes careful analysis of the relevant works themselves in order to discover the operative genre-purposes and -rules. But it also includes further aspects. One of these, which has already been touched on, lies in consideration of the cultural context of the genre in question, and of the origin and diachronic development of a more broadly defined genre to which it belongs and which produced it. Another lies in consideration of *theoretical* discussions of the genre by the relevant artists and their contemporaries. Thus in the essay *Shakespeare* Herder considers Shakespeare's attribution of a certain taxonomy of dramatic genres to the character Polonius in *Hamlet*,[86] and, while he is skeptical that this provides any guide to Shakespeare's own dramatic genres, that is not because he considers such evidence to be in principle irrelevant—his discussion implies the opposite—but merely because he does not believe that Polonius' remarks reflect Shakespeare's own views.[87]

This methodological empiricism in determining genre accords well with Herder's approach in other areas of interpretation, and indeed in other forms of inquiry. For example, his approach to determining a person's meanings or concepts is, similarly, a thoroughgoing methodological empiricism: an exact scrutiny of patterns of word use.[88] And indeed, his general approach to intellectual inquiry normally rejects apriorism in favor of methodological empiricism.[89]

Note, finally, though, that Herder's methodological empiricism in determining genre is by no means inherently conservative. This is his approach for *discovering* the genres of *existing* works of literary and non-linguistic art, not an approach for *deciding* what genres to use in *future* ones. He does believe that such decisions for the future are likely to be made better if informed by a correct conception of the genres that have been used in the past. But that is not because he holds that these should be imitated. On the contrary, his standard position—a very sensible one—is that in deciding what form future works of art should take we have much to learn from a correctly interpreted past but should *not* slavishly imitate it.

VII

The foregoing are, in my view, Herder's central positions and achievements in the theory of genre. However, I would like now to conclude by making a few additional points in modest revision or extension of his positions.

To begin at the beginning, as I mentioned earlier, Herder's basic conception of a genre is that it is constituted by an overall *purpose* aimed at by a class of works, together with certain *rules of composition* which serve that purpose. However, this conception arguably requires certain revisions and developments:

(i) Herder normally implies the *singularity* of the purpose involved. Boeckh subsequently did so even more emphatically.[90] However, this position seems dubious on reflection, and potentially quite misleading. For example, the overall purposes of Homeric epic poetry were surely multiple (including, for instance, conveying religious, ethical, and historical truths, entertaining an audience, and perpetuating the renown or *kleos* of heroes). And similarly, ancient tragedy surely pursued multiple purposes (including, for instance, reenacting and developing accounts of the past drawn from traditional myths, Dionysiac religious purposes, civic-political purposes, and serving as a forum for innovative moral reflection).[91]

(ii) It is also very doubtful that *all* overall purposes and rules of composition which govern a work, or a set of works, belong to its genre. For example, an author's purpose of winning patronage or payment would normally not;[92] nor would his purpose of giving an account of such-and-such a specific fictional character's life; nor would certain rules of composition imposed by official censorship. Herder's explanation of genre in terms of overall purposes and rules of composition therefore needs qualification along these lines as well.

(iii) It also seems doubtful that the rules of composition constitutive of a genre should always be seen as serving its purpose(s) (except perhaps in a trivial sense to be mentioned in a moment). No doubt, they often do—at least in the modest sense that the purposes are better served by these rules than they would be by obvious alternatives. For example, in ancient tragedy the rule of including a chorus is well suited as a means of encouraging the audience's emotional involvement in the performance and hence realizing the performance's Dionysiac and civic-political purposes, and also as means of providing guidance as to the playwright's position on the moral issues whose exploration is another of the performance's purposes. But in other cases they seem not to—except perhaps in the trivial sense that they function as ends or purposes in themselves. Examples of this situation would be the very precise composition rules for the sonnet (at certain periods of its history), or the rule of composition observed in early modern tragedy that a tragedy should consist of five acts.

(iv) Friedrich Schlegel would later go on to point out that genres are often implicitly interdependent, forming a sort of system.[93] This is an important point (though Schlegel overdoes it, positing a single system of all genres). There are many obvious cases of the essential dependence of one genre on another—for example, parody and other forms of critical or humorous reaction to a pre-existing genre (as in the works of Cervantes, Swift, and Fielding, for instance); or ancient Greek tragedy in its relation to epic poetry. But genres also essentially depend on one another in myriad subtler ways. For example, as Friedrich Schlegel implies in his Cologne lectures on German language and literature (1807), and as his brother August Wilhelm implies in his *Course of Lectures on Dramatic Art and Literature* (1809), ancient Greek tragedy and comedy are in part implicitly defined by their exclusion of each other (as is shown, for instance, by the fact that humor is strictly excluded from ancient tragedy, unlike modern tragedy).[94] And one might plausibly argue that ancient Greek tragedy and history are likewise in part defined by relations of mutual exclusion (though identifying exactly how would not be a simple task).[95]

Another question that deserves further consideration concerns the critical evaluation of works of linguistic and non-linguistic art. Herder's central point here—that this is often vitiated by failing to identify their genres correctly, and consequently faulting them for not realizing genre-purposes and -rules which it was no concern of theirs to realize, and omitting to credit them for realizing ones which it *was* their concern to realize—is well taken and very important. But it also prompts the questions of how much room for a critical evaluation of works of art Herder means to leave, and of how much room he should leave. Clearly, he is not here committing himself to the absurd position that all works of art are equally good; on the contrary, a large part of his purpose in making this point is precisely to make it possible for differential evaluations of works of art to proceed in a more accurate way (accordingly, in his own activity as a critic of literature and non-linguistic art he is far from shy about making differential evaluations). However, what is less clear is whether he is leaving room, and whether room should be left, for *other* sorts of differential evaluations of works of art than ones in terms of their success or failure in realizing their own genre-purposes and -rules.[96] In particular, where does he stand, and where should one stand, on the question of whether or not there can be better or worse *genres*, and therefore grounds for saying that a work which optimally realizes one genre is better or worse than a work which optimally realizes another?

Much of what Herder says about genres—for example, his observations concerning ancient Greek tragedy vs. Shakespearean tragedy in *Shakespeare*, and concerning ancient Greek portrait sculpture vs. ancient Egyptian portrait sculpture in *This Too a Philosophy of History*—seems to imply a negative answer to that question: there can indeed be better or worse realizations of a particular genre's purposes and rules, but not better or worse genres themselves. However, he is sometimes more equivocal about this. For example, in the *Critical Forests* while he does write similarly that each type of poetry must be judged "within its borders, from its means and its purpose," he also says that "each introduced kind of poetry has its own ideal—*one a higher, more difficult, greater than another.*"[97]

Nor would a negative answer to the question be easy to sustain on reflection. It is no doubt often true that different genres are equally good (for example, the novel and the epic poem, the symphony and the concerto, the landscape painting and the portrait painting). But do we really want to say that they *always* are (for example, that the limerick is as good as the epic poem, the pop song as good as the concerto, the cartoon as good as the portrait painting)? Certainly, the idea that some genres rank higher than others has a very long history behind it.[98] And it is also interesting to note that the most sophisticated recent theorist of genre, Fowler in *Kinds of Literature*, while he officially embraces a Herderian refusal to rank genres,[99] at points slips back into the assumption that some genres are higher than others.[100]

It is in fact possible to think of certain ways of resisting the problematic conclusion that genres never differ in value while still staying well within the spirit of Herder's basic theoretical framework. One way of achieving this is to note that genre-rules can serve corresponding genre-purposes either more or less effectively, that genre-rules can be either more or less consistent with each other, and (at least once we recognize that genre-purposes are often multiple) that genre-purposes can be either more or less consistent with each other. Herder himself sometimes exploits this sort of possibility. For example, in *Of the Ode* he in effect argues that modern attempts to fulfill the ode's purpose of expressing *warm feeling* by means of a *heavy regulation* by composition-rules constitutes a sort of contradiction between the genre-rules and the genre-purpose which they are supposed to serve.[101] Similarly, in the essay *Shakespeare* he criticizes imitative, rule-bound French tragedy for undermining rather than serving its purpose of arousing feelings.[102] Similarly, in the *Letters for the Advancement of Humanity* he argues that the principle of mixing deliberate fiction with supposed religious fact that is characteristic of the poetry of Tasso and Milton has the fault of undermining the serious religious effect that the poetry aims at.[103] Fowler identifies further cases in which a work is vitiated because there is something like a conflict among its genre-rules and -purposes.[104]

Another way that stays within Herder's basic theoretical framework—though one which Herder exploits less often—is to note that genre-rules and -purposes can cohere with, or contribute to realizing, a *broader range* of purposes which the author or his culture has either more or less well. For example, in the *Letters for the Advancement of Humanity*, shortly after writing against the idea of a ranking of the genres of one age or nation over those of another,[105] Herder goes on rather to contradict such impartiality, arguing that there is in fact such a thing as progress in genres through history, and that this is measured by the degree to which they cast off crudeness of feeling and false ornamentation in favor of an orientation to "the center of all human strivings . . . , namely the genuine, whole, moral nature of the human being."[106]

However, it is difficult to resist the intuition that there is also room for a sort of comparative evaluation of genres that fits less easily into Herder's basic theoretical framework: an assessment of genre-rules, genre-purposes, and indeed also the broader authorial and cultural purposes to which they relate on aesthetic, moral, or prudential grounds that are *external* to the author and his culture. For example (assuming, as seems plausible, that Herder is mistaken when he implies a universally shared commitment to humanity in passages such as the one just quoted), someone might well want to pass negative judgment on certain genres of Aztec visual art because of their intimate link with the Aztec institution of human sacrifice, an institution that we, though not they, find morally repugnant. Herder is usually opposed to such external evaluation (markedly so in *This Too a Philosophy of History*, for example).[107] However, he does occasionally seem to resort to it himself. For example, in the *Adrastea* he passes negative judgment on the novels of chivalry of the late Middle Ages on what seem to be external moral grounds, including in particular a moral objection to the sort of class inequality that they presuppose and endorse.[108] And in the *Letters for the Advancement of Humanity* he criticizes the sort of personal satire that Butler and Swift wrote for such weaknesses as one-sidedness, exaggeration, injustice to its targets, and a limiting of the poetry's interest to its own age—criteria which appear to be more external than internal (i.e. accepted by the poets themselves).[109] It seems to me that such external evaluation may well be both inevitable and defensible.[110]

A further respect in which Herder's position on genre would benefit from revision or extension is the following (already touched on at the start of this essay). For Herder, as for the tradition of theorizing about genre that preceded him, the paradigm examples of genres are works of linguistic art. As we saw, he extends the concept of genre to cover works of non-linguistic art as well. However, further extensions should also be made. In particular, not only artistic uses of language but also *non-artistic* ones have their genres: genres include not only the epic poem, the ode, the sonnet, the tragedy, the novel, and so on, but also the history book, the scientific article, the newspaper report, the newspaper editorial, the advice column, the instruction manual, the shopping list, the love letter, and so on. And not only written uses of language but also *oral* ones have their genres: genres include not only all of the things just mentioned, but also the military order, the instruction to an employee, the confession, the paternal advice, the casual conversation, the story, the stump speech, the joke, and so on.[111] Indeed, most, if not all, linguistic acts, whether artistic or not, whether written or spoken, are performed with the intention and the awareness that they instantiate one existing genre or another. And if they are to be either fully understood or properly evaluated, it is essential that the interpreter or critic identify—not only their linguistic meaning and their illocutionary force (assertion?, question?, imperative?, etc.) but also—their genre. In the normal course of things, both the author's intention and the audience's identification are achieved so naturally and effortlessly that they are easily overlooked; but their role in communication is nonetheless pervasive and fundamental, and once noticed ought to strike the theorist with the force of a revelation. It follows from this situation that the whole Herderian theory of genre that has been expounded in this essay so far actually has an even broader and deeper significance than he himself realized.[112]

A final issue that deserves further consideration is the following. As I implied in passing earlier, Herder, while he normally thinks of all works of literature (and non-linguistic art) as belonging to particular genres, even if sometimes highly individual ones, is occasionally—for example, in the first draft of his essay *Shakespeare*—[113] tempted to take the position (already championed by Voltaire, Young, Johnson, and even Lessing) that a genius, such as Shakespeare, transcends genre altogether. The same ambiguity recurs in Friedrich Schlegel, who sometimes insists that a work of literature must belong to a definite genre,[114] but at other times wants to overcome genre-classifications altogether (in favor of a merely adjectival use of genre-concepts),[115] or at least to insist that they only apply to ancient or classical works, not to modern or romantic ones.[116] Similar misgivings about the (general) applicability of genre-classifications to literature have become commonplace in the twentieth century—for example, in Croce and recent champions of a "non-genre literature."[117] One recurrent idea that lies behind this whole counterstrand of skepticism about genre is that writing in a genre would restrict an author's creative freedom in a way that is both unacceptable in itself and incompatible with artistic greatness.[118]

The following points should be noted in this connection: (i) It is important to distinguish between, on the one hand, the question of whether genre-conceptions should be invoked in interpreting and evaluating works of art from the past, and on the other hand, the question of whether decisions about how to produce works of art in the future should invoke genre-conceptions. Even if the answer to the latter question were No (which is in fact doubtful), the answer to the former might still be a firm Yes. Indeed, it is hard to imagine that it could be anything *but* a firm Yes, given that at least the great majority of past works of art clearly were produced in order to instantiate one or another genre.

(ii) It is true, and also important, that much literature and non-linguistic art in the past has worked by deliberately reacting against, modifying, or developing pre-existing genres in various ways.[119] For example, in epic poetry, besides the many cases of innovation already noted by Voltaire and Herder, Byron's *Don Juan* is another;[120] in drama, the early history of Greek tragedy already involved multiple steps of innovation (for instance, one consisting in the initial development of a distinction between the chorus and an actor with a speaking part, and others consisting in increases in the number of actors involved),[121] and Shakespeare's *Troilus and Cressida*, *Henry IV* plays, and late "romances" all have a strikingly transformative character in relation to pre-existing genres as well;[122] Shakespeare was similarly transformative in relation to the sonnet;[123] concerning the novel, Cervantes, Fielding, Novalis, and the modernists Proust, Joyce, Woolf, and Mann all self-consciously modify pre-existing forms of the genre;[124] and indeed there are also literary works which it would be difficult to classify in relation to earlier genres at all, for instance Ariosto's *Orlando Furioso*,[125] and Sterne's *Tristram Shandy*. However, it is easy to exaggerate the frequency of past novelty in genre by focusing on such cases as these. For one thing, it is important to recall the multitudes of unoriginal minor artists who make up the great bulk of artistic life but are quickly forgotten. For another thing, there are many cases of even great artists who were not especially innovative in genre (though they were innovative in *other* ways)—for instance, Hardy in relation to the novel,[126] and Brahms in relation to the symphony.[127] For yet another thing, the cases recently listed are all from Western societies, which are highly *individualistic*, and in particular have a highly *individualistic aesthetic*. The overall picture of literature and non-linguistic art would change considerably if one also included art that belongs to less individualistic, more traditionalist societies, such as Pharaonic Egypt and China. For yet another thing, innovation in genre looks much less common when one includes not only literature and non-linguistic art but also non-artistic genres of writing and oral genres (such as those recently discussed). Finally, and perhaps most importantly, even when innovations such as those listed above *do* occur, they normally produce a *new* genre rather than no genre at all.[128]

(iii) Contrary to the concern that writing in a genre restricts an author's creative freedom, this is arguably no more true than that writing in *meanings* restricts his creative freedom. In both cases, doing so is a precondition of writing anything intelligible, and therefore in particular anything freely creative, at all. Also, writing in a genre is perfectly consistent with writing in a *new* genre (just as writing in meanings is perfectly consistent with writing in *new* meanings).[129] Moreover, even a failure to innovate in genre (like a failure to innovate in meanings or concepts) still leaves ample room for innovating in *other* ways.

(iv) Finally, it should be noted that there seems to be a sort of paradox involved in the German Romantics' ideas of a literature that transcends genre, and in similar recent ideas of a "non-genre literature." If such literature were to succeed in becoming anything intelligible or interesting at all, would it not inevitably constitute a *genre* or *genres* of "genre-transcending" or "non-genre" literature? Indeed, is that not precisely how we now view the Romantics' attempts in this direction, such as Schlegel's *Lucinde* and Novalis's *Heinrich von Ofterdingen*: as a certain *genre* or *genres*?[130] This is not quite to go as far as to say that it would be *impossible* to write without any overall purposes or rules of composition, and hence without any genre. But it is to suggest that doing so would be bound to incur the cost of a sort of unintelligibility and a loss of any real interest or value.[131]

Notes

1. Concerning these two points, cf. T. Todorov, *Genres in Discourse* (Cambridge: Cambridge University Press, 1990), pp. 9–10, 17–19.
2. Boeckh, *Encyklopädie und Methodologie der philologischen Wissenschaften* (citations are from the 2nd edn. of 1886). More recent theoretical

work on interpretation that has recognized the central role played by identifying genre includes E.D. Hirsch, *Validity in Interpretation* (New Haven and London: Yale University Press, 1967), esp. ch. 3; A. Fowler, *Kinds of Literature: An Introduction to the Theory of Genres and Modes* (Cambridge, Mass.: Harvard University Press, 1982), esp. ch. 14; T. Todorov, *Genres in Discourse*; and M.M. Bakhtin, "The Problem of Speech Genres," in his *Speech Genres and Other Late Essays* (Austin: University of Texas Press, 1986).

3. Boeckh, *Encyklopädie*, p. 253.

4. P. Szondi. "Friedrich Schlegel's Theory of Poetical Genres: A Reconstruction from the Posthumous Fragments."

5. In order to find a comparable level of focus, one would probably have to go back as far as Scaliger's *Poetices libri septem* (1561).

6. G1:57 ff.; cf. S27:163 ff. for a later treatment of the same topic.

7. See esp. G5:976–9.

8. Irmscher complains that it is surprising that Herder only gets to the novel—the rising star among genres in his age—this late in his career (H.D. Irmscher, *Johann Gottfried Herder* [Stuttgart: Reclam, 2001], p. 146). However, Herder had in fact already discussed the novel in his *Letters for the Advancement of Humanity* (1793–7) (see G7:548), and moreover in a way that was to prove seminal for the German Romantics' conception of the novel. Concerning this seminal influence, see *German Philosophy of language*, Essay 1.

9. G5:976–9.

10. G5:1196 ff.

11. S15:345 ff.

12. For some actively skeptical remarks about such a project, see the first draft of the essay *Shakespeare*, at G2:522–4. Cf. *Of the Ode*, where Herder opens with some remarks directed against the possibility of defining the ode (G1:77–8). (Note, though, that Herder's ultimate goal in the latter work was to provide, via a history of the ode and its relation to other forms of poetry, a sort of *Ersatz* for a definition of it: "finally, try to determine the ode in relation to other types of poetry, and to explain it philosophically" [G1:99].)

13. Wittgenstein, *Philosophical Investigations*, pars. 65 ff. For a similar rejection of demands for a strict definition of genre(s), and invocation of Wittgensteinian "family resemblance," cf. Fowler, *Kinds of Literature*, pp. 35 ff.

14. Herder's pupil Goethe raised two objections to such traditional lists of genres—the list he himself considers is: allegory, ballad, cantata, drama,

elegy, epigram, epistle, epic, narrative, fable, heroic verse, idyll, didactic poem, ode, parody, novel, romance, and satire—in his *Noten und Abhandlungen zu besserem Verständnis des West-östlichen Divans* (*Johann Wolfgang von Goethe Werke: Hamburger Ausgabe* [Munich: Deutscher Taschenbuch Verlag, 1988], 2:187): (i) they include classes at different levels, some being sub-classes of others; and (ii) the criterion of identity varies, sometimes being an internal characteristic, sometimes content, only rarely "essential form." Neither of these objections is forceful, however. Objection (i) simply brings out an important positive feature of genres, namely that, like classes, they often stand in relations of inclusion to one another. For example, within the broad genre of poetry one can distinguish the genre of lyric poetry (along with epic poetry, tragedy, etc.), within the genre of lyric poetry the genre of the sonnet (along with the ode, the elegy, the epigram, etc.), and within the genre of the sonnet still further genres or sub-genres (such as those distinguished by Fowler at *Kinds of Literature*, pp. 112−13). Objection (ii) is sufficiently answered by assimilating the concept of "genre" to family-resemblance concepts such as "game."

15. See e.g. G1:59−60; G4:23−4; S3:153−4; S15:372.
16. e.g. "the epigram poetically represents or applies and interprets a present object for a single determinate point of doctrine or of feeling" (S15:372); the idyll is "representation or narration of a human mode of life according to its natural condition, with its elevation to an ideal of happiness and unhappiness" (S23:303).
17. e.g. C. Guillén, *Literature as System: Essays toward the Theory of Literary History* (Princeton, NJ: Princeton University Press, 1971).
18. Hirsch, *Validity in Interpretation*.
19. Cf. Fowler, *Kinds of Literature*, p. 274.
20. See esp. *Of the Ode*, G1:59−60.
21. Fowler, *Kinds of Literature*, p. 55.
22. Ibid., pp. 60−74. The inclusion of thematic content among the criteria deserves explicit mention because it goes against a long tradition that has sought to define genres in purely formal terms (the "essential form" for which Goethe seems to be looking at *Noten und Abhandlungen*, p. 187).
23. Cf. Hirsch's distinction in *Validity in Interpretation* between a work's *intrinsic* genre and its merely extrinsic genres (i.e. features which it merely happens to have, but was not deliberately intended to have). Cf. also Guillén, *Literature as System: Essays toward the Theory of Literary History*, pp. 123, 386; and Todorov, *Genres in Discourse*, pp. 9−10.

24. Hirsch, *Validity in Interpretation*, ch. 3. Wittgenstein similarly runs together genre and what we would today call illocutionary force at *Philosophical Investigations*, par. 23. Bakhtin is almost guilty of the same conflation in "The Problem of Speech Genres," but astutely avoids it by in effect distinguishing illocutionary force from genre as "primary" vs. "secondary" genre. Todorov in *Genres in Discourse*, ch. 2 is careful about the distinction as well (though he does develop a questionable hypothesis to the effect that each genre has its origin in a corresponding illocutionary force).

25. This is not to deny that there are any significant similarities or connections between genre and a work's whole meaning, or between genre and illocutionary force. Nor is it to insist that the distinctions between them are always sharp (for example, as Todorov points out at *Genres in Discourse*, p. 20, *prayer* seems to be both an illocutionary force and a genre).

26. Boeckh, *Encyklopädie*, p. 141.

27. Boeckh holds that the genius often makes his own genre, but he also notes that when the genius does so it is often difficult to tell what belongs to the new genre (ibid., pp. 241–2).

28. Cf. K. Gjesdal, "Reading Shakespeare—Reading Modernity," *Angelaki*, 9/3 (2004), pp. 26–7. See for this esp. Herder's essay *Shakespeare*, and S3:360–1. Such ideas already had precedents in Voltaire's *Essai sur la poésie épique*, Edward Young's *Conjectures on Original Composition*, and Samuel Johnson's preface to his edition of Shakespeare, and they would subsequently have a famous afterlife in Kant's theory of genius in the *Critique of Judgment*.

29. Cf. Fowler, *Kinds of Literature*, pp. 25, 52, 60.

30. G2:525; cf. 520.

31. S23:303, 305.

32. G8:64.

33. See Szondi, "Friedrich Schlegel's Theory of Poetical Genres," pp. 91 ff.

34. Cf. Fowler, *Kinds of Literature*, pp. 106 ff.

35. Ibid., p. 167. Note, however, in complication and qualification of Fowler's own development of this point, that the temporal priority of the genre to the mode arguably concerns *possession* rather than *instantiation* of the modal concept. For example, Richmond Lattimore has somewhat plausibly characterized the *Iliad* as a tragic epic—on the ground that it focuses on the tragic story of Achilles—despite the fact that the *Iliad* (but not Lattimore!) antedates the genre of tragedy.

It may, though, still be true that instantiations of a modal concept which postdate the corresponding genre are thereby able to instantiate it in a *pre-eminent* sense. Similar questions and points apply concerning applications of modal concepts in cases where influence by the genre in question is precluded not by the wrong relation of temporal priority but instead by cultural distance or simply a contingent absence of influence.

36. Similarly, Fowler sees genre as primarily a means of communication, an instrument for conveying meaning, so that identifying a work's genre is essential for interpreting the work correctly (*Kinds of Literature*, pp. 20–2, 256 ff.). However, Fowler leaves the details about this rather unclear, and the following three points drawn from Herder may help to add some desirable precision to it.

37. This is the least explicit part of Herder's answer. The evidence that he believes it lies partly in the fact that his commitment to the fundamental importance of identifying genre for interpretation seems to extend beyond his appeal to the sorts of instrumental reasons for this which I am about to mention ((ii) and (iii)).

38. S23:260 ff.

39. Similarly, to give an example from a genre of non–linguistic art: Herder argues in *This Too a Philosophy of History* that Pharaonic portrait sculpture as a genre connotes ideas of death and eternity.

40. Or to give a more dramatic Homeric example: I would argue that it belongs to the genre of Homeric (and Hesiodic) epic poetry that it is intended by the poet to provide *truths* throughout, this being possible in the poet's view because he is inspired by a divine Muse who knows everything. If that is so, then interpretations which (as commonly happens) assume a contrary conception of the genre as, at least in part, *deliberately fictional* will mistakenly read many of the particular statements that occur in the poems in the poet's own voice as meant to be false, whereas someone with the correct conception of the genre will properly read them as meant to be true.

    Concerning the general point that the identification of a work's genre can deeply affect the interpretation of the meanings of its parts, cf. Hirsch, *Validity in Interpretation*, pp. 94–8; H. Dubrow, *Genre* (London/New York: Methuen, 1982), pp. 1 ff.

41. Or to give an example from non-linguistic art: Herder implies in *This Too a Philosophy of History* that when, and only when, one grasps that it belongs to the genre of Pharaonic portrait sculpture to express ideas about death and eternity one will come to understand that the

immobility in the representation of a particular human being in such a sculpture connotes his death and eternity.

42. G2:498 ff.; G4:23−4.

43. Cf. Boeckh, *Encyklopädie*, p. 242. Boeckh also makes an additional interesting point concerning genre and evaluation which is in tension, though not contradiction, with the point made here: Determining the pre-existing genre to which a work belongs (if any) can be important for evaluating the work because it enables the critic to assess what goes to the credit of the individual work and its author, as opposed to the pre-existing genre as a whole. Roughly speaking, if it turns out that the work's inclusion of some impressive-looking feature was already business-as-usual in a pre-existing genre to which the work belonged, then the work and its author deserve less credit for including it than they otherwise would.

44. G4:23−4; cf. *Memorial to Winckelmann* [*Denkmal Johann Win[c]kelmanns*] (1777), G2:664−6; also S27:163. Boeckh would later follow this whole line too (see esp. *Encyklopädie*, pp. 255−6).

45. For a fuller account of this whole development, see Essay 3 and *German Philosophy of Language*, Essay 6.

46. G4:23−4; cf. *Memorial to Winckelmann* (1777), G2:664−6. This Herderian way of making the extension of his model of genre to non-linguistic art possible is not, of course, the only conceivable way; the key requirement, that non-linguistic art be text-like, and in particular express meanings, might be vindicated in other ways, for example by dropping his principle that all meaning is linguistic, consists in the use of words, or revising it so as to include other symbolic media in addition to language and words in the usual sense. However, I believe that Herder's principle is correct as it stands (see on this Essay 3 and *German Philosophy of Language*, Essay 6), so that his way of making room for the extension of his model of genre is the proper one.

47. Only *somewhat* more, for it is actually one of Aristotle's distinctive features in comparison with Plato that he characteristically distinguishes several different senses of a term (think, for example, of his famous distinction between four types of "cause").

48. G1:79; cf. 79−88.

49. S3:153−4.

50. G2:499−500 (by "name" Herder here means, as he often does, *concept*). A.W. Schlegel would later develop this theme much more fully in his *Course of Lectures on Dramatic Art and Literature* (1809; New York: AMS Press, 1973).

51. G7:575−6.
52. This feature is shared with Hesiod.
53. This is a central theme in all three drafts of the essay *Shakespeare*, where Herder also makes the interesting suggestion that it was ancient tragedy's origin in the unified image of the chorus that gave rise to the unities in the first place, so that Shakespeare's usual dispensing with the chorus deprives them of their rationale. Herder's contrast is problematic, however, both because the theory of the three unities that is commonly attributed to Aristotle was not in fact his, since he only insists on one of the unities in question, namely that of action, and because paradigmatic ancient tragedies sometimes violate the other two unities, e.g. Sophocles' *Ajax* includes a shift in place (cf. A.W Schlegel, *Course of Lectures on Dramatic Art and Literature*, lect. 17; S. Halliwell, *Aristotle's Poetics* [Chicago: University of Chicago Press, 1998], esp. p. 287).
54. G2:506−7, 523, 528, 540; S23:346−8.
55. G2:528, 540.
56. G2:528.
57. G2:525, 539. Herder could have added that whereas ancient tragedy prohibits violence on the stage, Shakespearean permits it.
58. G2:516: "regular temple-prayer before [the stage]," "arrangements for the public aspect of the stage"; cf. 500−5; S23:346−7. I say "more impressively" because, unlike the other features of ancient tragedy just mentioned, these two are hardly touched on by Aristotle, if not indeed deliberately suppressed by him (concerning his suppression of the religious dimension of tragedy, cf. Halliwell, *Aristotle's Poetics*, pp. 146−8). It was only with Nietzsche's *The Birth of Tragedy* (1872) that the extent of Aristotle's omissions and distortions in his account of tragedy, especially his virtual omission of the Dionysiac religious aspect of tragedy, began to be widely realized by scholarship. Much of the best recent scholarship on ancient tragedy has emphasized and clarified both that religious aspect and tragedy's civic-political functions. See e.g. *Nothing to Do with Dionysos?*, ed. J.J. Winkler and F.I. Zeitlin (Princeton, NJ: Princeton University Press, 1990); *The Cambridge Companion to Greek Tragedy*, ed. P.E. Easterling (Cambridge: Cambridge University Press, 1997); and J.-P. Vernant and P. Vidal-Naquet, *Myth and Tragedy in Ancient Greece* (New York: Zone Books, 1990).
59. The ever intellectually daring Friedrich Schlegel already implies this point in his *History of the Poetry of the Greeks and Romans* (1798) and

in several subsequent works, though his brother August Wilhelm does not follow him in it. Cf. *German Philosophy of Language*, Essay 2.

60. Epic poetry had conceived itself not as fictional but as conveying truths throughout, including in particular historical truths about gods and men. Hence, for example, the appeals in epic poetry to the Muses for inspiration in order to enable the poet to make his account accurate (e.g. at the start of both Homer's *Iliad* and Hesiod's *Theogony*) and in particular historically accurate (see e.g. besides the start of the *Iliad* also and especially the appeal to the Muses in the interest of achieving accuracy at the opening of the relentlessly historical Catalogue of Ships in *Iliad*, bk. 2).

61. Aristophanes does so in the following brief but telling passage from the *Frogs*: "EURIPIDES. Is then this account about Phaedra which I composed untrue? AESCHYLUS. No, by Zeus, it is true; but the poet must hide from view what is base" (ll. 1052–3). Plato gives even more compelling testimony. For Plato's extended attack on epic and tragic poetry in *Republic*, bks. 2 and 3 consists largely of the charge that they give factually false accounts of the gods and heroes and their activities—a charge which only makes sense on the assumption that epic and tragic poetry *purport* to give *factually true* accounts of these matters. And Plato's account of epic and tragic poetry in *Republic*, bk. 10 as aimed at an exact copying or mirroring of reality implies the same assumption.

62. See on this my "On the Very Idea of Denying the Existence of Radically Different Conceptual Schemes," *Inquiry*, 44/2 (1998), esp. pp. 154–6, including n. 98.

63. In the *Republic*, bk. 10 Plato had explicitly thrown down a challenge to the friends of tragedy to defend it against his attack. It seems pretty clear that Aristotle conceived his *Poetics* largely as a response to that very challenge. Explaining the tragedians' (in Plato's view and in Aristotle's own view) false historical claims about gods and heroes and their activities as merely fictional in intent rather than factual was one essential part of Aristotle's defense. (Another was his reply to Plato's charge in bk. 10 that tragedy stirs up such irrational emotions as pity and fear: it indeed does so, but only in the service of the quite contrary and beneficial goal of their eventual catharsis.)

64. It might be wondered whether Herder does not similarly understate the differences between ancient and Shakespearean tragedy in connection with the catharsis of pity and fear. This is a complicated question. Here again he follows Aristotle, namely in regarding catharsis as indeed

the main purpose of ancient tragedy, and he holds that Shakespearean tragedy shares the same purpose (see esp. G2:508; his attribution of this purpose to both ancient and Shakespearean tragedy is also prominent in the *Adrastea*). But here again it might seem tempting to accuse Aristotle of getting ancient tragedy wrong (as A.W. Schlegel later would). Specifically, it might seem tempting to accuse him of having here invented an all-too-convenient ad hoc defense of it against Plato's accusation in the *Republic* that it stirs up such dangerous emotions as pity and fear: it does indeed stir them up, but only in the interest of their eventual catharsis. However, it seems to me probable that Aristotle has in fact captured something important about the nature of ancient tragedy here. The key to seeing this is to remember that (a) ancient tragedy is a Dionysiac rite, and (b) Dionysiac rites, such as the notorious seasonal revelries of the god's female followers through nature, seem *generally* to have had a cathartic dimension, temporarily releasing socially disruptive emotions and impulses in the interest of eliminating or taming them and so preventing their disruption of society. Though Aristotle suppresses this religious basis for his account, it shows through in his choice of the religiously charged verb *kathairein* (cf. *Politics*, 1341b–1342a). Indeed, one of Herder's more impressive achievements in this area is to have perceived this religious background and the consequently genuine basis of the Aristotelian doctrine that ancient tragedy's main function consists in the catharsis of pity and fear (see esp. *Adrastea*, S23:355–6, 385, where he notes that the ordering of the passions which tragedy effects through its arousal of pity and fear is "as happens in the orgiastic mysteries by means of a reconciliatory sacrifice"). Therefore, if Herder *does* understate the difference between ancient and Shakespearean tragedy in this area—as he still very well may—then this is probably not because he is wrong in attributing the purpose of catharsis to ancient tragedy but rather because he is wrong in attributing it to *Shakespearean* tragedy.

65. *This Too a Philosophy of History*, G4:23–4; *Memorial to Winckelmann*, G2:664–6.

66. Herder explicitly looks forward to such an art history at G2:666.

67. G2:524–5; cf. 519–20. For recent developments of this point in relation to Shakespeare, see R.L. Colie, *Shakespeare's Living Art* (Princeton, NJ: Princeton University Press, 1974) and L. Danson, *Shakespeare's Dramatic Genres* (Oxford: Oxford University Press, 2000).

68. Later in the century Kant would pursue a version of this idea in his influential theory of genius in the *Critique of Judgment*.

69. Herder does occasionally seem sympathetic to such an idea in the first draft of the essay *Shakespeare*, though (see G2:522 ff.).

70. Thus note that even in the first draft of the essay *Shakespeare* Herder writes: "From its origin, it seems to me, the stage has so altered with each of its main geniuses and changed into a new form that one would have to find for almost each original author of another people and for each of his original works a new name, *and so a new canon of rules*" (G2:524, emphasis added; cf. G5:1195).

    Boeckh would later take a similar position, arguing that genius makes its own genre (but adding that it is often difficult to tell what belongs to it, and that this is discerned by intuition rather than concepts) (*Encyklopädie*, pp. 241–2). Illuminating research has recently been done into the processes by which new genres arise. See esp. Fowler, *Kinds of Literature*, chs. 9 and 10; Guillén, *Literature as System* (which is esp. illuminating on the picaresque novel); and concerning Shakespeare specifically, Colie, *Shakespeare's Living Art* and Danson, *Shakespeare's Dramatic Genres*.

71. G1:79 ff.; cf. G2:507–8.

72. G1:98.

73. G2:548.

74. G2:499 ff., 507–9, 515, 545–6 (where Herder also implies an explanation of ancient tragedy's commitment to the unities in terms of the simplicity of its origins in the dithyrambic chorus). Cf. *Of the Ode*, esp. G1:85 concerning a growth in the variety of social subjects and in psychological complexity that takes place over the course of history, and its bearing on the changing nature of poetry.

75. G4:23–4 and esp. G2:664–6.

76. S32:86–7.

77. A fuller development of this sort of position would allow room for such diachronic processes as reactions against earlier genres, fusions of more than one genre, and so on. Cf. Fowler, *Kinds of Literature*, chs. 9 and 10.

78. To mention another literary example, in *On the Spirit of Hebrew Poetry* Herder points out that there is a strong temptation falsely to assimilate the genre of David's psalms to that of Pindar's odes or to that of modern lyric poetry, and consequently to fall victim to false interpretations and critical assessments of David's psalms (G5:1194–5; cf. already G1:65).

79. G4:23–4; G2:664–6.

80. Cf. Fowler, *Kinds of Literature*, esp. pp. 259–62, 273. Herder's and Fowler's positions in a way complement rather than simply reduplicate each other, for Fowler emphasizes the former point more (genre-unfamiliarity), whereas Herder emphasizes the latter point more (the temptation to false assimilation).

81. Friedrich Schlegel would later emphasize this prospective point more than Herder does, arguing that an "infinity" of new genres is possible (see Szondi, "Friedrich Schlegel's Theory of Poetical Genres," pp. 76–8). German Romanticism, especially in its literary dimension, was indeed largely concerned with exploiting this possibility by writing in new genres, as for example in the case of Schlegel's own *Lucinde* or Novalis's *Heinrich von Ofterdingen* (though here the idea of actually transcending genre also came into play).

82. G1:97.

83. In *Noten und Abhandlungen*, Goethe, despite a measure of sympathy with Herderian empiricism in determining genres, gives an apriorist argument that there are only three possible basic genres: epic, lyric, and drama (pp. 187–9). For a convincing criticism of this position, see Fowler, *Kinds of Literature*, p. 236. Similarly, Friedrich Schlegel sometimes rejects an empirical approach to determining the range of possible genres, as well as the nature of the particular genres, instead demanding an apriorist or "deductive" approach (see Szondi, "Friedrich Schlegel's Theory of Poetical Genres" p. 80). However, Schlegel's efforts in this direction—in particular, his classification of lyric poetry as subjective, drama as objective, and the novel as subjective/objective—again carry little conviction.

84. See Fowler, *Kinds of Literature*, pp. 235 ff. Fowler provides a thorough and withering attack on such apriorist schemas.

85. G2:548. For a similar position on determining the genre of David's psalms, see G5:1195.

86. *Hamlet*, act 2, sc. 2, Polonius speaking: "The best actors in the world, either for tragedy, comedy, history, pastoral, pastoral-comical, historical-pastoral, tragical-historical, tragical-comical-historical-pastoral, scene individable, or poem unlimited."

87. G2:519–20, 523–4, 530–2. Herder's readiness in principle to include this last sort of evidence anticipates a position that has been taken more recently by such theorists of genre as R. Cohen and Fowler (see *Kinds of Literature*, pp. 260–1).

88. See e.g. G1:322, 421–3, and G5:1007.

89. See Essay 1.
90. *Encyklopädie,* pp. 82, 132–3, 143 ff.
91. I am here stating what I take some of the main purposes of these genres actually to have been, not merely repeating a conventional view of what their purposes were.
92. There might be exceptions, though, e.g. the Pindaric ode.
93. See Szondi, "Friedrich Schlegel's Theory of Poetical Genres," pp. 78, 87. Cf. for this point Guillén, *Literature as System,* esp. ch. 9; also, pp. 131 ff., 495 ff. (though Guillén focuses more on systematicity in *theories* of genres than in genres themselves). Also, Fowler, *Kinds of Literature,* pp. 251 ff.
94. For a recent, but somewhat disappointing, attempt to develop a similar thesis, see M. Meyer, *Le Comique et le tragique: Penser le théâtre et son histoire* (Paris: Presses universitaires de France, 2003), pp. 9–62.
95. In particular, one would need to avoid giving the superficially attractive explanation which Aristotle's account in the *Poetics* suggests: that this is because history purports to be historically factual whereas tragedy purports to be historically fictional.
96. Cf. Fowler, *Kinds of Literature,* pp. 275–6.
97. S3:154, emphasis added. Cf. G1:60 and S15:392.
98. See Fowler, *Kinds of Literature,* pp. 216 ff. Fowler notes, for example, that in the field of literature epic poetry was for a long time ranked at the top of a hierarchy of literary genres, and that since the nineteenth century the novel has tended to displace it in that position.
99. See ibid., esp. p. 233 where Fowler writes disparagingly of "genre prejudice" in this connection.
100. See ibid., p. 275 where Fowler invokes "generic height."
101. G1:89–90.
102. G2:503 ff. For such a criticism of a certain type of epigram, cf. S15:355 ff.
103. G7:535–6.
104. See *Kinds of Literature,* pp. 158–9, 189, where he in particular criticizes *Lady Chatterley's Lover* and *Bleak House* in roughly these terms.
105. G7:573–5.
106. G7:578. The moral universalism that Herder implies here is not always his position and is probably not his best position. However, what interests me here is simply his appeal in this passage to an ideal that belongs to a genre's own culture but is not definitive of the genre itself as a criterion for assessing the genre. Such an appeal might also be made without any implication of universalism.

107. Cf. *Essay towards a History of Lyric Poetry* (1766), S32:125–6. Note that, by contrast, he has no objection to evaluating works of art in moral terms per se. On the contrary, he often does this.
108. S23:284–5.
109. G7:536–7.
110. For a little further discussion of this sort of issue as it arises in connection with value more generally, see Essay 1, where I defend such a stance in a way that stays fairly close to the general spirit of Herder's position, namely as self-consciously expressive of a subjective, non-universal standpoint. Such a defense contrasts sharply with more ambitious defenses, which are legion but seem implausible. For example, Friedrich Schlegel sometimes defends such a stance by means of a series of ambitious arguments, including an argument that there are in fact certain transhistorical genres, and an argument that certain genres can be given a "deduction," in particular that the superiority of epic poetry or the novel over other genres can be shown by means of the schema "lyric poetry = subjective, drama = objective, epic poetry or the novel = subjective/objective," which places epic poetry or the novel at the culmination of the other genres (see Szondi, "Friedrich Schlegel's Theory of Poetical Genres," pp. 79–81, 85–9). Likewise, Hegel defends such a stance by ranking genres on the basis of their allegedly different manners and degrees of success in expressing a metaphysical truth that he takes it to be their function to express.
111. Cf. Todorov, *Genres in Discourse*, pp. 9–10; Bakhtin, "The Problem of Speech Genres."
112. A similar point applies to Herder's hermeneutics at a more general level: he extends hermeneutics beyond its traditional focus on the interpretation of the Bible, so that it comes to include secular texts as well as sacred ones, modern texts as well as ancient ones, and even non-linguistic art. But he arguably could and should have gone even further. In particular, he could and should have included oral uses of language along with written ones (a potential which Schleiermacher would subsequently exploit in his own project of developing a more truly universal hermeneutics).
113. G2:522 ff.; cf. 519–20; also, *Of the Ode*.
114. See Szondi, "Friedrich Schlegel's Theory of Poetical Genres," p. 82.
115. Ibid., p. 93.
116. Ibid., pp. 93–4. Schlegel and other German Romantics accordingly sometimes attempted to break the bounds of genre in their own literary

works—e.g. Schlegel in his *Lucinde* and Novalis in his *Heinrich von Ofterdingen*.

117. See e.g. J. Culler, "Toward a Theory of Non-Genre Literature," in *Theory of the Novel*, ed. M. McKeon (Baltimore and London: Johns Hopkins University Press, 2000).

118. Cf. McKeon's observations at ibid., p. 3.

119. Cf. Fowler, *Kinds of Literature*, ch. 10; Guillén, *Literature as System*; and Dubrow, *Genre*.

120. Cf. Hirsch, *Validity in Interpretation*, p. 106.

121. Herder himself notes this in *Shakespeare* (G2:500, 524–5).

122. See Danson, *Shakespeare's Dramatic Genres*, esp. pp. 6–7, 98, 140–1. Cf. Colie, *Shakespeare's Living Art*.

123. See Dubrow, *Genre*, pp. 14 ff. Cf. Colie, *Shakespeare's Living Art*.

124. Cf. Guillén, *Literature as System*, pp. 125 ff., 146 ff.

125. Cf. ibid., pp 121–2.

126. Hardy did lend the novel a tragic modulation (as Fowler notes at *Kinds of Literature*, p. 167), but he arguably did little to change the genre as such.

127. *Pace* Fowler, ibid., p. 23.

128. Cf. Todorov, *Genres in Discourse*, pp. 14–15.

129. As Danson points out, Shakespeare—in this spirit—saw genres not as limiting but instead as opportunities for inventiveness (*Shakespeare's Dramatic Genres*, p. 143).

130. Cf. Fowler, *Kinds of Literature*, pp. 104–5, who makes a similar point concerning postmodern works.

131. Cf. ibid., pp. 31, 278.

6

Herder and the Birth of Modern Anthropology

If philosophy's viewpoint gets changed in the manner in which the Copernican system developed from the Ptolemaic system, what new fruitful developments must not occur here, if our whole philosophy becomes anthropology [*Anthropologie*].

Herder, *How Philosophy Can Become More Universal and Useful for the Benefit of the People* (1765)[1]

Herder did not in this passage mean by "anthropology" exactly what we would mean by it today.[2] And one might also reasonably balk at the prospect of the *whole* of philosophy becoming anthropology. Still, it would probably be a very good thing if, in the general spirit of this remark of Herder's, anthropology at least came to play a much bigger role in philosophy than it currently does.[3]

However, this paper is not really about that. Rather, it is about Herder's role in the very birth of the modern discipline of anthropology—or more precisely, *cultural* anthropology. (I shall simply set aside *physical* anthropology—a discipline that was for a long time yoked to cultural anthropology by what since the early twentieth century has increasingly come to look like little more than a bad pun.[4])

John Zammito, in an excellent book titled *Kant, Herder, and the Birth of Anthropology*, has argued that Herder played a vital role in the emergence of modern anthropology (in both its cultural and its physical versions).[5] According to Zammito, the precritical Kant developed a naturalistic, empiricist, anti-metaphysical, pragmatically oriented conception of philosophy as anthropology, which then decisively influenced his star student of the time, Herder. On Zammito's account, Kant went on in his later years to turn sharply away from all this in favor of a subordination of anthropology within philosophy, and moreover one which made anthropology fundamentally anti-naturalistic, apriorist, metaphysical, and moralized. However, Herder stayed faithful to the earlier conception of the discipline, and developed it further—in particular, on the cultural side of things, emphasizing the need for an empirical investigation of humankind in its great cultural (and individual) diversity, and the need to deploy for this purpose a historicist hermeneutics.

I find this account of Zammito's very compelling. My purpose in this essay is not so much to disagree with it, but rather to develop it further in certain ways in relation to cultural anthropology specifically—ways which will, though, shift its center of gravity a little, giving less of the credit to Kant and more to Herder (hence my dropping of Kant's name from the title of this essay).

By far the greater part of Zammito's book is devoted to explaining Kant's development (but subsequent abandonment), and Herder's subsequent continuation, of a conception of philosophy as anthropology, and of a naturalistic, empiricist, anti-metaphysical, pragmatic approach to humankind in that anthropology. Now, this was undoubtedly a very important step *viewed against the background of the metaphysical and apriorist extravagances of the German Rationalist tradition which had preceded it*, and which had indeed been continued by the precritical Kant himself until the early 1760s. But one might, I think, reasonably argue that it brought Kant and Herder no closer to establishing modern cultural anthropology, indeed rather less close, than a number of predecessors in other intellectual traditions had already come—for example, Hume in Britain; Montaigne, Montesquieu, and Voltaire in France; Vico in Italy; or indeed for that matter, Herodotus and Protagoras in ancient Greece.

It is really only when one reaches the last chapter of Zammito's book, where he discusses Herder's distinctive contributions of a focus on human mental diversity and a corresponding historicist hermeneutics, that one encounters anything that looks like progress towards modern cultural anthropology *tout court* (as opposed to progress towards it *within the German tradition* merely). It is therefore this particular part of Zammito's account that I would like to pick up and elaborate on here.

In further justification of the shift in emphasis and credit from Kant to Herder, I would also emphasize another fact somewhat more than Zammito does.[6] Once Kant abandoned his early conception of philosophy as anthropology (which, as I have just suggested, had temporarily brought him close, though not quite up, to the level of certain British, French, Italian, and ancient Greek forerunners of modern cultural anthropology), he then went on to develop a conception of anthropology which was to a great extent not only irrelevant to modern cultural anthropology but downright antithetical to it.[7] Concerning mere irrelevance, Kant's mature version of anthropology is far more focused on individual psychology than on cultures. Concerning downright antithesis, its purpose is much more "pragmatic," or utilitarian, than purely theoretical; it assumes a fundamentally homogenizing position concerning the mental outlooks of different cultures (for instance, Kant considers them all to be implicitly committed to a single moral principle, the "categorical imperative");[8] it shows little or no interest in the interpretation of cultural Others, or appreciation of the difficulties attendant on such interpretation;[9] its method is largely apriorist rather than empirical;[10] it usually ignores the deep dependence of thought and other aspects of mental life on language,[11] and the consequent need to investigate other cultures via their languages; it accords great significance to racial differences, and purports to explain the distinctive mental characteristics of different cultures as innate racial differences;[12] and finally, despite Kant's official cosmopolitanism, it devotes a good deal of space to disparaging non-European races for what Kant alleges to be their racially determined negative characteristics (for example, the Caribs of South America and the Jews).[13] These several features of Kant's mature version of anthropology are not merely different from but downright antithetical to the methodology, the results, and the values of modern cultural anthropology.[14]

In short, if we are interested in discovering a German contribution to the development of modern cultural anthropology *tout court* (rather than merely *in the German context*), then it is not to Kant that we should look, but rather to Herder.

I

So much for the main anticipation of my theme in the history-of-philosophy literature. But there is an equally important anticipation of it in the history-of-anthropology literature. In a pathbreaking and outstanding series of works on the history of American and British anthropology, George Stocking has placed great emphasis on the role of the German intellectual tradition in the development of modern anthropology on both sides of the Atlantic.[15] And his former student Matti Bunzl has extended part of Stocking's account further, and into even closer proximity to Herder, in an excellent article which emphasizes the important role played by the Humboldt brothers as influences on Franz Boas and thereby on the birth of modern American anthropology: "Franz Boas and the Humboldtian Tradition: From *Volksgeist* and *Nationalcharakter* to an Anthropological Concept of Culture."[16]

Here again, my argument in this essay will be marked above all by strong agreement with Stocking and Bunzl (as well as heavy indebtedness to them), but there will also be a certain shift in emphasis: While Stocking and Bunzl do both accord Herder a significant role in the development of modern anthropology, they tend, in my opinion, to underestimate it. For example, Stocking in his book *Victorian Anthropology* very plausibly ascribes to Herder a role in the emergence of nineteenth-century British anthropology, including the contribution of such seminal ideas as that of the variety of national spirits and that of a comparative study of languages,[17] but he does not pursue the same point in relation to twentieth-century British anthropology, which is arguably more important (I shall attempt to do so below); he omits to mention quite a number of further ideas central to British anthropology which can plausibly be traced back to Herder (I shall discuss a number of these below); and he misleadingly characterizes Herder as a source of "racialism,"[18] whereas Herder in fact sharply criticized the very concept of race (in his *Ideas for the Philosophy of History of Humanity* [1784–91]),[19] and emphatically rejected all racial discrimination (see especially the 10th Collection of his *Letters for the Advancement of Humanity* [1793–7]).[20] Similarly, Bunzl in his article very plausibly traces a number of the fundamental positions espoused by Franz Boas, the effective founder of modern American anthropology, back to the Humboldt brothers (for example, positions concerning language, and concerning the value of holistic descriptions of particular cases as contrasted with explanations in terms of universal laws), and he also acknowledges the Herderian background of some of these positions, but he arguably underestimates the great extent to which on such fundamental matters the Humboldts were merely following Herder, and there are also a number of additional debts to Herder in Boasian anthropology which he omits to mention (I shall discuss some of these below).

II

My thesis, then, could be put roughly like this: by developing Zammito's account of Herder's contribution to the birth of anthropology more fully and further forward in time, and by developing Stocking and Bunzl's account of the German roots of modern American and British anthropology more fully and further back in time, we can come to see that it was *Herder* who was the father of modern anthropology.

In order to try to make this rather ambitious thesis plausible, let me begin by offering a few general remarks concerning Herder's most relevant works and some of the likely channels of his influence on modern American and British anthropology, before then going on to identify a series of distinctive Herderian ideas which came to play fundamental roles in modern American and British anthropology.[21]

From an early period of his career, Herder was deeply interested in, and developed an impressive knowledge of, the ethnographic literature of his day, especially travel descriptions.[22] Among his own works, the following are especially significant for their contribution towards the development of modern cultural anthropology: the *Journal of my Journey in the Year 1769* (including, and indeed especially, the separate pages appended in Suphan's edition);[23] the *Popular Songs* [*Volkslieder*] (1774, and especially the edition of 1778–9); *This Too a Philosophy of History for the Formation of Humanity* (1774); the *Ideas for the Philosophy of History of Humanity* (1784–91), especially chapters 6–8 and 11; and the *Letters for the Advancement of Humanity* (1793–7), especially the 10th Collection, with its sketch of a "natural history of humanity."

Also important in this connection are certain contemporaries who were strongly influenced by Herder. Herder frequently mentions the scientist, anthropologist, and traveler Reinhold Forster respectfully for his ethnographic work. The latter's more famous son Georg Forster, who shared his father's ethnographic interests, in his turn became an enthusiastic follower of Herder's on these and other matters. Similarly, Wilhelm von Humboldt borrowed and developed many of Herder's key ideas, including ones that bear on the development of cultural anthropology, thereby contributing greatly to their broad and lasting influence. The works of Humboldt's that are most important in connection with cultural anthropology include his linguistic works—especially his famous Kawi introduction, *On the Diversity of Human Language-Structure and its Influence on the Mental Development of Mankind* (1836)—which are firmly grounded in Herder's ideas concerning the dependence of thought on language, the deep variability of languages and hence of modes of thought, and the consequent need to access a people's distinctive mode of thought via an investigation of its distinctive language; *Plan of a Comparative Anthropology* (written some time during the period 1795–7, though not published until 1903), which pursues ideas that Herder had developed on the same topic, notably in his sketch for a "natural history of humanity" in the 10th Collection of the *Letters*;[24] and *On the Task of the Historian* (1822), which again pursues ideas of Herder's, in particular concerning the need to penetrate the different mental characters of different peoples by means of an accurate understanding of them.[25]

Through which later channels did Herder exercise an influence on the development of modern cultural anthropology, though? A full answer to that question would be extremely complicated, and will not be attempted here. But two general channels which were clearly of decisive importance can be mentioned: First, Franz Boas, the father of American anthropology, was German by birth and education, and had his intellectual roots in the German tradition, including not only Herder himself (whom he occasionally mentions by name), but also other German figures who were either directly or indirectly influenced by Herder in profound ways, such as Wilhelm von Humboldt, Steinthal, Bastian, Dilthey, and Wilhelm Wundt.[26] Boas subsequently passed on this intellectual inheritance to his students in American anthropology, and to their students—including his own students Sapir, Lowie, Kroeber, Benedict, and Mead, and Sapir's student Whorf.

Second, on the other side of the Atlantic, Bronislaw Malinowski, the father of modern British anthropology as a discipline grounded in intensive fieldwork (rather than the armchair discipline that it had previously been with Tylor and Frazer) also had deep German intellectual roots that ultimately lead back to Herder. Malinowski on occasion explicitly mentions Herder and his follower Wilhelm von Humboldt in a positive spirit.[27] But that is really only the tip of a much deeper iceberg. Malinowski's father, who held the chair in Slavonic philology at the university Malinowski attended in Poland, was a German-trained expert in philology and comparative grammar who had a special interest in collecting folksongs and folklore—[28] an intellectual profile that immediately places him within Herder's sphere of dominating influence. Moreover, Malinowski himself studied in Leipzig with Wilhelm Wundt, the author of the massive work *Völkerpsychologie* (1900–9), and indeed began writing a dissertation there on *Völkerpsychologie*, which he subsequently went to London with the intention of completing.[29] Now, Wundt's work has deep Herderian roots (as can indeed already be seen from its title, *Völkerpsychologie*). The discipline of *Völkerpsychologie* had originally been founded by Lazarus and Steinthal under the influence of Herder and Wilhelm von Humboldt.[30] And the fundamental indebtedness of Wundt's work to Herder can also be seen from such more specific features of it as its theses that human society and language are interdependent, that language is fundamental to thought, that both differ deeply from society to society, and that because of language's fundamentalness to thought the exploration of language in its diversity can reveal the diversity of thought;[31] as well as from its overall theory of cultural development, especially its vision of "humanity" as the goal of history—[32] all of which clearly show the influence of Herder, and especially of Herder's most famous work, the *Ideas*. In fact, it would scarcely be an exaggeration to say that Wundt's work is essentially just a sort of grand re-writing of Herder's *Ideas*. In short, Malinowski was deeply steeped in Herder's influence. Malinowski then subsequently passed on his Herderian intellectual legacy to his students in British anthropology—notably, Evans-Pritchard, Firth, and Leach.[33]

III

Which specific ideas of Herder's were involved in this molding of modern anthropology? The two that Zammito mentions—mental diversity and a historicist hermeneutics—are among the most important ones, and are a fairly good place to start. It will help, though, to preface each of them with another relevant idea of Herder's.

(1) *Psychology as the central subject-matter of anthropology*. Already from an early stage of his career, Herder developed the project of a broad investigation into humankind in all its variety, an investigation that included, though it was not restricted to, the peoples today treated by cultural anthropology,[34] and he identified as the central focus of this investigation the distinctive *psychology* of the various peoples found in different times and places. For example, already in his 1769 *Journal* he writes:

> Let the human soul, in itself and in its appearance on this earth, its sense-instruments and concerns and hopes and pleasures and characters and duties and everything that can here make human beings happy, be my first concern. Let everything else merely be set aside . . . For this purpose I want to collect data in the history of all times: each time should supply me with the image of its own ethics, customs, virtues, vices, and happinesses.[35]

And he prominently includes in this project the sorts of so-called "savage" peoples on which modern anthropology would later come to concentrate:

> And in Asia, Africa, America? "Oh, those peoples are savages"; and savage peoples should, I think, be studied most to find out what their ethics, habits, and distinctive characteristics are.[36]

In *This Too a Philosophy of History* he represents the central task involved here as closely analogous to that of expressing

> the distinctive individuality of a human being—to be able to say what distinguishes him in a distinguishing way, how he feels and lives, how different and idiosyncratic all things become for him once *his* eyes see them, *his* soul measures them, *his* heart feels them.[37]

Herder faithfully adheres to this principle of emphasizing the distinctive psychology of different peoples in his two great systematic expositions of the sort of broad investigation of humankind in question: *This Too a Philosophy of History* and the *Ideas*. And he retains the same principle in his late sketch of such a "natural history of humanity" in the *Letters*. After Herder, the same emphasis appears in Wundt's conception of a *Völkerpsychologie*, and in other nineteenth-century German positions relevant to the birth of modern anthropology, including Dilthey's conception that the human sciences in general should be primarily concerned with interpreting people's mental "expressions" by means of psychology and hermeneutics. Now, this emphasis on penetrating the distinctive psychology of different groups has been retained by modern anthropology. Thus, to begin with the American side of the discipline, as Stocking has convincingly argued, Boas's anthropological work has just this sort of emphasis.[38] So too (indeed even more obviously) does the "culture and personality" work of several of Boas's most important students, especially Ruth Benedict. Indeed, so too does the work of the most recent doyen of American anthropology, Clifford Geertz. Similarly on the British side of modern anthropology, Malinowski conceived anthropology as fundamentally a form of psychology (very much in the spirit of Wundt and thereby Herder). For example, in his most famous work, *Argonauts of the Western Pacific*, Malinowski writes that the anthropologist must capture the facts of native life "not by a superficial registration of details, as is usually done by untrained observers, but with an effort at penetrating the mental attitude expressed in them"; that it is necessary for him to "find out the typical ways of thinking and feeling, corresponding to the institutions and culture of a given community"; and that "the final goal, of which an ethnographer should never lose sight," is "to grasp the native's point of view, his relation to life, to realize *his* vision of *his* world."[39]

(2) *Mental diversity*. Herder, while he insists that there does exist such a thing as a common human nature, involving fundamentally identical mental functions such as language-use and reasoning (in opposition to polygenetic theories which would divide humankind into distinct species, for example),[40] also emphasizes—contradicting a dominant Enlightenment tradition, exemplified by the philosopher-historians Hume and Voltaire—that human mental life varies deeply across historical periods and cultures (in concepts, beliefs, values, perceptual and affective sensations, etc.), and indeed that similar, albeit usually less dramatic, variations occur even between individuals living within a single historical period and culture.[41] Boas, Malinowski, and their followers again strongly echo this position. Thus, just like Herder, Boas insists (in opposition to polygenetic theories) that all historical periods and cultures exhibit a common human nature with fundamentally identical mental functions (including the use of language and reasoning),[42] but he also insists that deep mental differences occur across historical periods and cultures (for example, in concepts and values),[43] and he insists that there are even significant variations between individuals within a single historical period and culture.[44] Benedict follows

Boas in all of these respects, insisting on the unity of human nature, but also emphasizing human mental diversity across periods and cultures,[45] and (an aspect of her position that is often overlooked) insisting that significant individual differences occur as well.[46] In the British tradition, Malinowski's position is fundamentally similar: he too insists on a common human nature,[47] but also emphasizes that deep mental differences occur across historical periods and cultures,[48] and indeed that even within a single period and culture much individual variation is found.[49]

(3) *Understanding, rather than explaining, as the goal of anthropology.* As I have argued elsewhere, Herder, in keeping with his identification of the distinctive psychology of peoples from different periods and cultures as the central focus of his investigation of humankind, developed a principle that the fundamental task of such an investigation lies in *understanding* historical and cultural Others' statements, deeds, and works in their cultural and individual distinctiveness, rather than in *explaining* them, say in terms of efficient causal laws or in terms of a supposed overall purpose in history (a task which was for him secondary, and about whose feasibility he harbored significant doubts).[50] This principle was subsequently taken over from Herder by many other people, including Wilhelm von Humboldt, Droysen, and most famously Dilthey.[51] Now, Boas essentially adopted this principle too. This can already be seen from his early essay "The Study of Geography" (1887),[52] where he explicitly and sympathetically mentions the strongly Herder-influenced Goethe and Alexander von Humboldt as advocates of versions of it in application to both history and physical nature,[53] and where he also shows signs of approving of Dilthey's application of it to history.[54] Boas did indeed initially cherish hopes that the sort of focus on understanding cultures in their distinctiveness which he advocated would eventually lead to the discovery of explanatory laws governing them; but as time went on such hopes receded,[55] leaving him with a position that was virtually identical to Herder's and Dilthey's. This privileging of understanding over explanation still persists in the best recent American anthropology, for example the "hermeneutic" anthropology of Geertz. On the British side of the discipline, Malinowski's position was quite similar: for him too, anthropology's primary scientific task consisted in *understanding* other cultures, rather than in explaining them by means of general laws; and while he too cherished hopes of ultimately achieving the latter task as well,[56] in practice this aspiration did not play a prominent role in his empirical work.[57]

(4) *Historicist hermeneutics.* In connection with interpretation, Herder insists on (i) the importance of understanding the Other's viewpoint accurately,[58] but he notes (ii) that the phenomenon of deep mental diversity entails

that interpreters attempting to understand Others from the remote past or from alien cultures face formidable challenges,[59] and in particular (iii) that interpreters need to resist a constant temptation to assimilate such people's concepts, beliefs, values, etc. to their own, or to others with which they happen already to be familiar (for example, in the case of a modern classicist, the Greeks').[60] Now all three parts of this hermeneutic position are taken over by modern anthropology in both its American and British versions: The insistence on interpreting the Other's viewpoint accurately is fundamental to the work of both Boas and Malinowski.[61] So too is the recognition that deep mental diversity poses formidable challenges to the interpreter. And Boas and Malinowski in particular both emphasize the need to resist constant temptations to assimilate other people's viewpoints to one's own or to other viewpoints with which one happens already to be familiar. For instance, Boas emphasizes this in connection with temptations to impute one's own concepts or ideas to other people whose concepts or ideas are in fact different;[62] to project grammatical features of one's own language or of other languages with which one is already familiar onto languages which in fact lack them;[63] and to impute one's own perceptual experiences to other people whose perceptual experiences are in fact different.[64] And Malinowski emphasizes the same need in connection with the temptation falsely to assimilate the Trobrianders' concept of wealth to ours, their motives in working to ours, and so on.[65]

So much for the two Herderian contributions to modern anthropology which Zammito identifies (mental diversity and historicist hermeneutics), together with two additional contributions closely connected with them. But the continuity between Herder's position and that of modern anthropology, and the indebtedness of the latter to the former, also extends much further than this. So I would like now to identify a number of further Herderian principles which likewise went on to constitute foundations of modern anthropology:

(5) *Methodological empiricism in interpretation.* Herder strongly emphasizes throughout his (rather scattered) theory of interpretation that interpreters must not rely on apriorist assumptions but must instead work bottom-up from the relevant empirical evidence.[66] Accordingly, he insists on just this sort of empirical scrupulousness when interpreting the diverse outlooks of different historical periods and cultures, including primitive ones.[67] Boas and Malinowski self-consciously insist on, and implement, the same policy.[68]

(6) *Language fundamental.* As I have explained in detail elsewhere, Herder developed two revolutionary principles in the philosophy of language: that all thought is essentially dependent on and bounded by language; and that meanings consist (not in such items, potentially separable from language, as referents,

Platonic forms, or individual mental "ideas" à la Locke and Hume, but instead) in word-usages.[69] In addition, he argued that *all* human mental states and activities (including, for instance, our perceptions, emotions, and desires) are of their very nature implicitly articulated through language.[70] In consequence of these positions, for Herder discovering the nature of other peoples' distinctive ways of thinking, meaning, and indeed engaging in mental activity generally requires the penetration of their distinctive languages and word-usages.[71] Wilhelm von Humboldt subsequently took over this whole Herderian position, and made it the most fundamental rationale for a new science of linguistics. He also built on Herder's insights in a further way: In the *Ideas* Herder had already introduced the additional thesis that languages differ in important ways, and thereby affect modes of thought, even at the very fundamental level of their grammatical structures.[72] Humboldt takes over this thesis, and he develops it more prominently and in much greater empirical detail.[73] Now, Boas and his followers made this whole Herder-Humboldt position the foundation of their own anthropological approach.[74] In particular, this was the basis of Boas's approach to the study of native American languages.[75] And Boas's star student Sapir, together with *his* star student Whorf, made it even more central to their anthropological approach, namely in the form of what has become known as the "Sapir-Whorf hypothesis," the hypothesis that specific language structures determine specific worldviews.[76] Similarly on the British side of things, the Herder-Humboldt position lies behind Malinowski's equation of meaning with the use of words,[77] his thesis that language is fundamental to culture,[78] and his insistence (which he followed scrupulously in his own practice) that the anthropologist must attain facility, and must work, in the language of the natives he studies.[79] And through Malinowski the Herder-Humboldt position became part of the British anthropological tradition more broadly, for example recurring in Evans-Pritchard.[80]

(7) *Interpretive holism.* The early Herder of the 1760s had already insisted that individual passages in a text must always be interpreted in light of the whole text to which they belong. Similarly, Herder in the 1770s went on to insist that the sayings and doings of people belonging to a culture need to be interpreted in light of the whole culture to which they belong.[81] As he puts it in *This Too a Philosophy of History* (1774):

The whole nature of the soul, which rules through everything, which models all other inclinations and forces of the soul in accordance with itself, and in addition colors even the most indifferent actions—in order to share in feeling this, do not answer on the basis of the word but go into the age, into the clime, the whole history, feel yourself into everything—only now are you on the way towards understanding the word.[82]

Or as he puts it later in the *Letters* (1793–7):

Each nation must . . . be considered solely in its place with everything that it is and has—arbitrary separatings, slingings into a confused jumble, of individual traits and customs yield no history. With such collections one enters into a charnel house, and equipment and clothes closet, of peoples, but not into living creation.[83]

This principle of holism in interpreting the sayings and doings of a culture subsequently became central to modern anthropology. Boas insisted on it. For example, this was the ground on which, in a famous early dispute concerning the proper way to organize the ethnological materials at the United States National Museum, he objected to the then prevailing practice of putting similar-looking artifacts from different cultures together, arguing that instead all of the materials belonging to a particular culture should be displayed together.[84] But Boas also gave the principle a much wider application.[85] Boas's student Benedict insisted on this holistic principle too, indeed even more emphatically, for example in *Patterns of Culture*.[86] On the British side of things, Malinowski was also a firm proponent of this principle,[87] which he had evidently learned largely from Wundt,[88] and thereby indirectly from Herder.[89] And from Malinowski it passed to other British anthropologists, such as Evans-Pritchard.[90]

(8) *Participant-observation*. Remarkably, Herder, in the *Letters*, in the course of sketching a plan for a "natural history of humanity" which sounds almost like a blueprint for modern cultural anthropology, advocates what would today be called the method of participant-observation. Writing approvingly of De Pagès, the author of *Voyage autour du monde* (1783), Herder says:

Let one read his depictions of the characters of several nations in America, of the peoples of the Philippines, . . . how he sought to, so to speak, incorporate into himself the manner of thought of the Hindus, of the Arabs, of the Druse, etc. even through participating in their manner of living. Travel descriptions of such a sort . . . expand our horizon and multiply our sensitivity for every situation of our brothers.[91]

The method of participant-observation subsequently became central to modern anthropology. Boas and his followers (in particular, Lowie, Benedict, and Mead) advocated and practiced it to some degree.[92] And it was advocated and practiced even more assiduously in the British tradition, first by Malinowski (who coined the expression "participant-observation"), and then by his students, including Evans-Pritchard.[93]

(9) *Culture*. Herder also played a leading role in developing the distinctive concept of *culture* that lies at the heart of modern anthropology. His anticipation of this concept does not take the form of his use of a single German word,

but rather consists in a certain striking theoretical picture which he articulates with the help of several words, none of which by itself yet exactly captures the modern concept—including the words *Bildung, Kultur, Volk,* and *Nation.*[94] By means of such words Herder develops the striking theoretical picture of (i) a large number of distinctive, linguistically grounded sets of concepts, beliefs, modes of feeling, values, and artforms each of which is broadly shared by a people at a certain time and place; (ii) each of these sets being causally determined, besides by humankind's common biological nature, not by a people's race, but in part by its physical environment, and mainly by its history and enculturation;[95] (iii) these sets incorporating considerable variation at the level of individuals,[96] and constant change in the character of the set itself,[97] among other things due to the influence of other such sets;[98] and (iv) moreover, without there being any differential ranking between such sets.[99] Now it was precisely this whole Herderian picture that Boas came to express by means of his concept of "culture," and made fundamental to his own conception of the discipline of anthropology (where it forms the third and crowning part of the discipline, as reflected in the division of his famous essay collection *Race, Language, and Culture*).[100] In particular, just like Herder, Boas conceived cultures (i) to be multiple, to be sets of concepts, beliefs, modes of feeling, values, and artforms broadly shared by a people, and to be essentially linguistic;[101] (ii) to be causally determined, over and above humankind's common biological nature, not by race,[102] but in part by physical environment, and mainly by history and enculturation;[103] (iii) to leave room within the set of concepts, beliefs, etc. constitutive of a particular culture for considerable variation at the level of individuals,[104] constant change in the set itself,[105] and in particular change due to the influence of other such sets;[106] and (iv) to be free of any differential ranking between them.[107] Moreover, in his early essay "The History of Anthropology" (1904) Boas explicitly credits Herder with having played a seminal role in the development of the modern concept of culture:

To [the second half of the eighteenth century] belong Herder's *Ideen zur Geschichte der Menschheit* [*sic*], in which, perhaps for the first time, the fundamental thought of the development of the culture of mankind as a whole is clearly expressed.[108]

The same general picture and concept of "culture" was subsequently taken over from Boas by his students, for example by Benedict in *Patterns of Culture* and by Mead.[109] On the British side of things, Malinowski too made the concept of "culture" central to anthropology, conceiving it in a similar way.[110] For example, he too conceives of cultures as multiple; as sets of concepts, beliefs, etc.; as essentially linguistic;[111] as containing much variety at the level of individuals;[112] and as unranked. Through Malinowski's influence this concept of culture became central to subsequent British anthropology as well.[113]

(10) *Value variation, relative appropriateness, and incommensurability.* In *This Too a Philosophy of History* and other works Herder famously argued that ethical, aesthetic, and other values vary dramatically from period to period, and culture to culture, that in each case the values in question can be seen to be somehow appropriate to the period and culture to which they belong, and that indeed there is no acceptable way of adjudicating between them or ranking them.[114] These positions all reappear in Boas and his followers.[115] It was indeed Boas who coined the expression that has come to sum them all up: "cultural relativism."[116] Especially clear statements of them can be found in Benedict's *Patterns of Culture*,[117] and in Mead's *Coming of Age in Samoa*.[118] On the British side of anthropology, Malinowski adopted such positions as well. For example, *The Sexual Life of Savages*, chapter 13 contains explicit observations on value diversity, the relative appropriateness of different values to their respective contexts, and value incommensurability. And the positions in question are also reflected in his defense of such Trobriand practices as the polygamy of chiefs and orgiastic sexual festivals against interference by colonial administrators and missionaries with contrary values. (There are, to be sure, some tricky philosophical problems in this area. In particular, the third position involved, the renunciation of any adjudication or ranking of competing values, runs into philosophical difficulties. Herder himself does not *consistently* stick to such a position;[119] nor does Boas;[120] nor does Benedict.[121] More importantly, nor can one. For, as Nietzsche memorably put it, "Is life not passing judgment, preferring, being unfair . . . ?"[122] Still, even if continuing to prefer certain values over others is psychologically inevitable, the first two positions listed above may still reasonably move one *in the direction* of the third one.[123])

(11) *Pluralist cosmopolitanism.* Herder had no patience with the sort of *homogenizing* cosmopolitanism—or granting of equal ethical consideration to all human beings on the basis of an illusion that they all share a great deal in common mentally, and particularly in values—that was championed by many Enlightenment thinkers before him, including his own teacher Kant, that is indeed still championed by many ethicists and worthy organizations today, including for instance the United Nations, and that even finds favor with the occasional anthropologist, for example Levi-Strauss.[124] However, Herder embraced a distinctive ethical stance which might in contrast be called *pluralist* cosmopolitanism: a commitment to the equal value of all peoples, despite, and indeed in part because of, the diversity of their mental outlooks and

in particular their values. For example, in his plan for a "natural history of humanity" in the 10th Collection of the *Letters* he writes:

Above all, let one be unbiased . . . ; let one have no pet tribe, no favorite people on the earth . . . The nature-investigator presupposes no order of rank among the creatures he observes; all are equally dear and valuable to him. Likewise the nature-investigator of humanity . . . Nature developed the form of the human type as manifoldly as her workshop required and allowed . . . The negro, the [native] American, the Mongol has gifts, talents, preformed dispositions that the European does not have . . .[125]

In consequence of this position, Herder is a severe critic of imperialism and colonialism—a stance which he again prominently articulates in the 10th Collection of the *Letters*. This pluralist cosmopolitanism, and consequent strong opposition to imperialism and colonialism, went on to become the fundamental ethical outlook of modern anthropology. On the American side of the discipline, Boas took it over. His pluralist cosmopolitanism can be seen, for example, in a letter he wrote to the *New York Times* in 1916 protesting what he saw as American bias in the First World War, where he appeals to "the fundamental idea that nations have distinctive individualities, which are expressed in their modes of life, thought, and feeling" and to a principle that one should "seek to understand and to respect the individualities of other nations."[126] And in consequence of this stance, Boas was also a strong opponent of imperialism and colonialism.[127] From Boas pluralist cosmopolitanism and opposition to imperialism and colonialism passed into American anthropology more generally. For example, pluralist cosmopolitanism formed the ethical basis for a famous protest which the American Anthropological Association lodged in 1947 against the homogenizing cosmopolitanism of the United Nations' Universal Declaration of Human Rights.[128] And it remains the characteristic position of most American anthropologists today.[129] A similar point applies to the British side of the discipline: Malinowski too championed pluralist cosmopolitanism, under the name of a "new humanism"—[130] a name that points back to Wundt's *Völkerpsychologie* with its dominant ideal of "humanity,"[131] and thereby to Herder, from whom Wundt borrowed that ideal. Indeed, Malinowski characterizes the ideal of tolerating other peoples despite their mental, and in particular their ethical, distinctiveness as one of the main reasons for engaging in anthropology.[132] Connectedly, Malinowski's fundamental stance towards imperialism and colonialism is one of opposition.[133]

(12) Finally, in *This Too a Philosophy of History* and elsewhere Herder empha-sizes that one important reason for investigating other periods and cultures lies in the increase in our *self*-understanding, and the consequent improvement in

ourselves, that this makes possible—especially, in the recognition that certain traits of ours which we had assumed to be universal are in fact merely specific to us, and the consequent taking-to-heart of our own cultural limitations and weaknesses. For example, he writes in an essay from 1783:

When we have turned grey in certain ethical customs and modes of representation, and are consequently so grown-together with them that we believe them essential to humanity and so quite inseparable from it, how often have I been quite beneficially amazed and ashamed to find that a few levels further up or down [on the scale of peoples] whole peoples know nothing of these modes of representation and ethical customs, have never known anything of them, often cherish the very opposite ones just as dearly, and yet despite this are in a tolerably good condition and as comfortable as the fragile clay from which humanity is formed, together with the necessary expenses which each person incurs from without, could allow.[134]

And similarly, he writes in the *Ideas*:

The soul experiences a noble expansion when it dares to place itself outside the narrow circle that clime and education have drawn around us and at least learns amid other nations what one can dispense with. How much one there finds dispensed with and dispensable that one long considered essential! Notions that we often took to be the most universal axioms of human reason disappear here and there with the clime of a place, as dry land disappears like a cloud for someone sailing out to sea.[135]

Once again, this motive for engaging in anthropology was subsequently taken over by both the American and the British traditions of the discipline. On the American side, Boas took it over.[136] So too did his students Benedict and Mead.[137] Similarly on the British side of the discipline, this sort of motive lay behind much of Malinowski's anthropology,[138] which in particular challenged our modern European assumptions concerning economic and sexual life. And from Malinowski it then passed to others in the British tradition—for example, Evans-Pritchard.[139]

IV

So much by way of a sketch of Herder's seminal influence on the development of modern anthropology in both its American and its British versions. It might, however, be objected to this account that, even granting that Herder contributed the ideas in question and that they were subsequently taken over and developed by modern anthropologists in the ways suggested, still there is much more to modern anthropology than this, and a lot of the "much more" involved is either quite divorced from or indeed opposed to Herder's influence.

In one way this objection strikes me as right, but in another, more important, way as wrong. It is certainly true that much of the work that has been done under the name of "anthropology" over the past century or two has been divorced from, or contrary to, Herder's influence. But I want to suggest that the parts of modern anthropology in question are precisely those that turn out to be most dubious. In other words, I want to suggest that Herder's ideas have not only exercised a huge influence on the development of modern anthropology but also constitute a sort of "true center" of the discipline from which it has certainly on occasion strayed but only to its detriment.

In order to try to make this suggestion plausible, let me briefly discuss some of the "much more" in question.

(a) *Evolutionism*. This was the position espoused by such nineteenth-century armchair anthropologists as Tylor and Frazer. There had actually been an evolutionist *strand* in Herder himself, especially in the *Ideas*,[140] which subsequently reappeared in Wundt's *Völkerpsychologie*. However, evolutionism is at odds with Herder's more distinctive and original position, as it has been explained above. One of Boas's most important critical achievements was to demonstrate the implausibility of evolutionism, and by implication the superiority of Herder's more distinctive and original position. He did this, among other things, by showing that what had seemed to evolutionists to be common features shared by different cultures usually turn out when examined more closely to be in fact strikingly different across cultures;[141] that when common features do occur they often have different causes in different cultures;[142] and that there is no ladder of ascent in complexity between cultures, but in certain respects supposedly "higher" cultures are often *less* complex than supposedly "lower" ones, for example in their language structure or in their musical rhythms.[143] Malinowski was likewise an implacable and trenchant critic of evolutionism (for example, criticizing the evolutionists' doctrine of "survivals").[144]

(b) *Concept universalism*. A position of this sort was espoused by one of Boas's teachers in Germany, Bastian, who held that all cultures share a certain fixed set of basic concepts ("elementary ideas [*Elementargedanken*]"), only sometimes more purely and sometimes less so. And this sort of position continues to exercise a strong fascination over a certain type of anthropologist even today, especially in the USA (a recent example is Berlin and Kay in their work on color conceptualization), but also in other anthropological traditions (Levi-Strauss's structuralism would be an example). Such positions are again sharply at odds with Herder's standard view. But here again, it was arguably one of Boas's great virtues to have realized that when the relevant linguistic and behavioral evidence is examined carefully, the appearance that certain concepts are universally shared proves to be an illusion.[145]

(c) *Monolithic cultural spirit.* A position of this sort was adopted within the American anthropological tradition by one of Boas's students, Kroeber, in his theory of the "superorganic." Similar positions can be found in the French tradition (Durkheim) and the British (Radcliffe-Brown). Such positions are sharply at odds with Herder's, which—some common misconceptions about it to the contrary notwithstanding—emphasizes that individuality plays a vitally important role within a culture, and that cultures vary sharply in their degrees of integration. For example, concerning individuality, he already writes in *This Too a Philosophy of History*:

No one in the world feels the weakness of general characterizing more than I. One paints a whole people, age, region of the earth—*whom* has one painted?[146]

And concerning integration, in a section of the *Letters* titled "Do we still have the public and fatherland of the ancients?" he contrasts the relatively well-integrated cultures of the ancients with the relatively *dis*integrated culture of modern Germany.[147] Boas follows Herder in allowing for considerable individuality and lack of integration within a culture.[148] So too (despite some superficial appearances to the contrary) do Boas's students Benedict[149] and Mead.[150] Similarly on the British side of anthropology, Malinowski sharply rejects notions of a monolithic cultural spirit (Durkheim is his main target), insisting instead that even primitive cultures always combine collectiveness with individuality.[151] It seems clear that ideas of a monolithic cultural spirit are indeed mistaken, and that the contrary position shared by Herder, Boas, Benedict, Mead, and Malinowski is the correct one.[152]

(d) *Structural-functionalism.* Twentieth-century British anthropology developed two versions of "functionalism": the plain "functionalism" of Malinowski, and the "structural-functionalism" of Radcliffe-Brown. Malinowski's plain functionalism comprises three main theses: (i) All of a society's characteristic features—including, for example, its activities, implements, products, and institutions—are present within it because they serve either its members' basic biological needs or their socially derived needs (incidentally, this was Malinowski's main reason for rejecting the evolutionists' doctrine of "survivals"). (ii) In order to understand the *meaning* of any particular social feature, that feature must be considered in the context of the *whole* of social features to which it belongs. (iii) Each social feature is also *causally* interdependent with all of the others.[153] This whole position is quite similar to that of Herder, who would agree with theses (i) and (ii), and probably also with thesis (iii).[154] The position is not beyond dispute or free of ambiguity—for example, one might worry that there are certain forms of collective irrationality which constitute counterexamples to thesis (i); one might wonder whether thesis (ii) should

THE BIRTH OF MODERN ANTHROPOLOGY 217

take the strong form of a holism about interpretation based on a holism about meaning or the weaker form of a holism about interpretation alone; and one might argue against thesis (iii) that certain features of a society are causally independent of each other. Still, it is a position that seems broadly plausible and likely to be defensible in some form, albeit perhaps a suitably qualified form. Radcliffe-Brown's structural-functionalism is a very different matter, however. It has two distinguishing features: (a) a thesis that social structure (including, for example, the system of kinship relations) completely determines the individual, and (b) a thesis that consequently the anthropologist should focus on social structure alone, to the exclusion of psychology, meaning, and culture. These two theses would be sharply rejected both by Herder and by Malinowski. As we have already seen, contra thesis (a) they would deny that social structure fully determines the individual, instead insisting that individuals exercise a large measure of autonomy from society. And contra thesis (b) they would reject the proposal that anthropology should focus exclusively on social structure, both for the same reason, and because in their view excluding psychology, meaning, and culture from anthropology would amount to excluding the main *point* of the discipline. Moreover, Herder and Malinowski would, I think, be correct on all these scores.

(e) *Rousseauian Romanticism.* Just as Rousseau idealized the "noble savage," certain modern anthropologists have tended to do so as well—for example, Mead in *Coming of Age in Samoa,* and the young Levi-Strauss in his search for savage purity and simplicity in *Tristes Tropiques.* Herder was opposed to this sort of thing; he was no less skeptical of treating past or alien cultures as models than he was of treating modern European culture in that way. For example, already in his *Journal* of 1769, where he announces the plan to "collect data in the history of all times: each time should supply me with the image of its own ethics, customs, virtues, vices, and happinesses," he immediately goes on to add:

The human species has happiness as its result in all its ages, only in each in another way; we in our age err when, like Rousseau, we praise times that no longer are and never were, when, to our own discontentment, we create fictional images [*Romanbilder*] out of them and cast ourselves aside so as not to enjoy ourselves.[155]

Accordingly, while in *This Too a Philosophy of History* he enjoins a measure of sympathy when interpreting alien cultures, he also wisely counterbalances that advice in *The Spirit of Hebrew Poetry* with warnings against excessive identification with them.[156] This Herderian counter-position seems much more judicious than the sort of Rousseauian romanticism espoused by Mead and Levi-Strauss.[157] And the best anthropologists of the twentieth century—for example, Boas, Malinowski, Evans-Pritchard, and Geertz—have all rejected Rousseauian Romanticism in favor of a position more like Herder's.

(f) *Abstractionism*. By this I mean tearing individual features of a culture out of their context in order to use them as data for the construction of grand overall theories. Tylor and Frazer did this sort of thing in the service of their evolutionist theories, as did Bastian in the service of his theory of conceptual universalism, and so did Durkheim in the service of his social determinist theory of totemism. A more recent example would be Levi-Strauss's dragooning of aspects of native mythology into the service of his structuralist theory. As we have seen, Herder already sharply and convincingly opposed this sort of approach on the grounds that the interpretation of individual features must take their whole cultural context into account in order to be at all accurate. And it was on precisely the same grounds that Boas and Malinowski ably opposed it early in the twentieth century as well (in its evolutionist and conceptual universalist incarnations).

(g) *Apriorism*. By this I mean, not so much *absolute* apriorism (an approach that hardly anyone in modern anthropology would take seriously, though Freud comes close to it in his feeble *Totem and Taboo*), but rather the sort of *relative* apriorism that consists in paying insufficiently scrupulous attention to the data constituted by natives' linguistic and other behavior in its context, with a view to then building ambitious theories on this inadequate evidential foundation. Examples of such insufficiently scrupulous attention to the data include the sort of abstractionist reliance on other people's reports about it that one finds in the purely armchair theorizing of Tylor, Frazer, Durkheim, and Levi-Strauss (in whom it serves their evolutionist, social determinist, and structuralist theories respectively);[158] the work of Radcliffe-Brown, who did have some fieldwork experience, but whose ambitious structural-functionalist theory left it far behind;[159] and also the sort of crude question-and-answer fieldwork grounded in an inadequate knowledge of the native languages that Malinowski complains about.[160] Such (relative) apriorism is quite contrary to the sort of scrupulous empirical approach to interpretation, grounded in a thorough knowledge of the relevant language, informed by a knowledge of the whole cultural context, and achieved through participant-observation, which Herder championed. And all of the best twentieth-century anthropologists—including Boas, Malinowski, Evans-Pritchard, and Geertz—have sharply rejected such apriorism, in favor of this Herderian approach.[161]

(h) *Postmodernism (for want of a better term)*. Much recent anthropology—as reflected, for example, in the influential collection of essays *Writing Culture*, edited by Clifford and Marcus—[162] has been dominated by the following five features: (i) Inspired by such continental philosophers as Gadamer and Derrida, it has become deeply skeptical about the possibility of achieving an objective understanding of the Other at all.[163] (ii) Bearing in mind the imperial-colonial context within which most modern anthropology was done, it has come to suspect that anthropological investigation of the Other is an inherently imperialist, exploitative activity.[164] (iii) Inspired in large part by the work of Edward Said, it has undertaken to deconstruct the traditional anthropological concept of "culture": what one actually finds in the field, it is argued, is not a unified culture but rather a shifting plethora of contesting groupings and individuals;[165] to the extent that a culture exists at all, it is always fluid and changing,[166] and affected by external influences;[167] moreover, the concept of culture is an intrinsically divisive one.[168] (iv) In response to such concerns as these, recent anthropology has increasingly turned away from its traditional role of investigating the Other towards instead criticizing anthropological texts about the Other.[169] (v) It has also in some cases substituted for the sort of plain, limpid descriptive prose that was characteristic of anthropology's main nineteenth- and twentieth-century representatives a deliberately playful, reflexive, and obscure writing style more characteristic of recent continental philosophers such as Derrida.[170]

These five postmodern developments together constitute a sharp departure from the sort of "natural history of humanity" that Herder first envisaged, and the corresponding form that modern anthropology took during most of the twentieth century. However, it seems unlikely to me that they either should or will in the long run turn the discipline very far from that traditional Herderian course. The following are some points to note in this connection.

Ad (i) (skepticism concerning the possibility of objective understanding), as I have argued in detail elsewhere, it turns out on inspection that Gadamer and Derrida's denials of the possibility of an objective understanding, and reconception of understanding as instead merely an open-ended relative process, are quite groundless, indeed deeply confused.[171] It is particularly important here to insist on preserving the traditional distinction (which Gadamer would have us efface) between, on the one hand, *understanding* the Other's meaning (something which, at least prima facie, need not in principle involve any "filtering" through distinctive features of the interpreter's own outlook) and, on the other hand, *explicating*, *applying*, or *translating* it (activities which *do* essentially involve such a "filtering").

Ad (ii) (concerns about imperialism), the situation seems complicated and ambiguous but by no means damning. It is certainly true that nineteenth-century evolutionary anthropology was deeply implicated in imperialism and colonialism.[172] It is also certainly true that modern fieldwork-based anthropology, in both its American incarnation (Boas and his students) and its British

(Malinowski and his students), took place within and was only possible due to an imperial/colonial context, and moreover usually to some extent served or at least cooperated with the relevant imperial/colonial powers (this was true of Boas, Malinowski, and Evans-Pritchard, for example). However, some exceptions and individual ambivalence aside,[173] it is also strikingly true that most twentieth-century anthropologists, including such central figures as Boas and Malinowski—like Herder before them, and under his influence—were themselves strong champions of precisely the anti-imperial/colonial values which motivate the postmodernists' concern here, and that their intention in doing their anthropological work was accordingly far less one of supporting imperialism or colonialism than one of subverting it from within, or at least mitigating it.[174] Nor, I think, do attempts such as Fabian's to identify an imperialist-colonialist orientation in mainstream twentieth-century anthropology at a more fundamental, "transcendental" level, in an alleged "allochronicity" and privileging of visual representation, have much plausibility.[175] So the postmodernists' concern here would presumably in the end have to be, not so much that twentieth-century anthropology deliberately supported imperialism/colonialism (even at a subconscious "transcendental" level), but rather that, despite its strong contrary intentions, it had this *effect*. However, one wonders whether even that much is really true. After all, the wheels of empire and colonialism were already running pretty smoothly before the fieldwork anthropologists got involved. And at least on the British side of things, what followed their arrival was not some great new flowering of the Empire but rather its *dissolution*. It would no doubt be implausible to give much of the credit for that dissolution to anthropology (other causes, such as Britain's exhaustion by two world wars and the resistance of the colonized themselves, were obviously more important). But anthropology at least did not hinder it, and it does not seem far-fetched to suggest that it may even have contributed to it, in particular by promoting the sort of enhanced recognition of the Other among the British public that made the Empire come to seem a questionable undertaking (why, for instance, did the British government not simply have Ghandi shot?). On balance, then, it seems arguable that, not only in intention but also in effect, modern anthropology has stood less in the service of imperialism than against it.

Ad (iii) (deconstruction of the concept of "culture"), it seems unlikely that this concept, understood in the sense conferred on it by the tradition of Herder, Boas, and Malinowski, should be dispensed with. Concerning the postmodernists' first objection (individuality and contesting groups), as we have seen, that tradition had in fact already incorporated into its concept of culture strong qualifications concerning the large role played within any given culture by individuality, and the varying degrees of cultural integration to be found in different cases (thus stealing most of the postmodernists' thunder here). Nor are such complexities in themselves any objection to the propriety of the concept. Or is one by parity of reasoning also to deny the propriety of using such a concept as "German" or "French" simply because of differences in idiolect and dialect? The complexities in question would only constitute an objection to the concept if it turned out that the broadly shared features found among a particular group of people were normally much less striking and significant than the discrepancies found among them, so that the concept of a common culture hardly ever had a useful application. But that is arguably not the case. Concerning the postmodernists' second objection (that cultures are fluid and changing, and that they also influence each other), Herder, Boas, and others had in fact already acknowledged both of these points, which therefore constitute no objection at all to their concept of "culture," but only to a crude caricature of it. Finally, concerning the postmodernists' third objection (that the concept of culture is intrinsically divisive), while it is no doubt true that this concept, like any other that distinguishes between human beings (e.g. men/women, Christians/Jews, employers/workers), *can* be used in divisive ways, it is difficult to see why it, any more than they, *must* be. Indeed, it seems much more plausible to say that *forgoing* the concept would be likely to have divisive consequences, since, for example, without it we (*any* we) would be unable to explain or excuse behavior by an individual or group which conflicts with our own initial expectations and values as the product of the individual's or group's different culture.

Ad (iv) (the reflexive turn in anthropology), this is no doubt salutary as a moment of disciplinary self-criticism, but, largely for the reasons just given, it seems unlikely that it either should or will continue to dominate the discipline at the expense of its more traditional outward-looking concerns to the extent that it presently does. Nor does the increasing disappearance of the relatively isolated, static cultures on which anthropology traditionally focused entail otherwise; cultures under external influence and in a state of flux are no less suitable as objects of outward-looking anthropological research than relatively isolated, static ones.[176]

Ad (v) (the change in anthropologists' style of writing), this turn towards a self-indulgent, obscurantist writing style imitating continental philosophical models is fortunately still only a minority fashion, and will no doubt be short-lived.

In short, there seems to be nothing in the recent postmodernist movement in anthropology that either should or is likely to shift the discipline far from its traditional Herderian course for long.

V

To sum up the moral of this paper in one sentence: Not only did Herder make a decisive contribution to the birth of modern anthropology as a discipline, but in addition his principles arguably constitute a sort of "true center" of the discipline, which it abandons only to its detriment.

Notes

1. *Herder: Philosophical Writings*, p. 29.
2. Nor, though, did he mean by it something as remote from what we English-speakers would mean by it today as would a German-speaker today—for whom the word *Anthropologie* usually means either *physical* anthropology or else a certain sort of philosophical theory, not an investigation into the outlooks of other peoples (which would normally instead be called *Ethnologie*). Herder's meaning here presumably reflects that assigned to the word by his teacher, Kant, for whom *Anthropologie* did at least *include* that sort of investigation.
3. For a little further elaboration of this thought, see my "A Wittgensteinian Anti-Platonism," *Harvard Review of Philosophy*, 15 (2009).
4. They were still yoked together for Franz Boas, though he already foresaw their separation. More surprisingly, they are not even yet completely separated for the young Clifford Geertz (see e.g. his essay "The Growth of Culture and the Evolution of Mind," in C. Geertz, *The Interpretation of Cultures* [USA: Basic Books, 1973]).
5. J.H. Zammito, *Kant, Herder, and the Birth of Anthropology* (Chicago: University of Chicago Press, 2002).
6. Cf. ibid., pp. 344–5.
7. See I. Kant, *Anthropology from a Pragmatic Point of View* (The Hague: Nijhoff, 1974).
8. See e.g. I. Kant, *Groundwork of the Metaphysics of Morals* = *The Moral Law* (London: Hutchinson University Library, 1972), p. 67: "The ordinary reason of mankind . . . always has the aforesaid principle [i.e. the categorical imperative] before its eyes."
9. Kant's interpretations of earlier philosophers and of the New Testament inspire little confidence in his interpretive accuracy or in his appreciation of the difficulties involved in interpreting remote viewpoints.

10. Cf. Zammito, *Kant, Herder, and the Birth of Anthopology*, pp. 299–301.
11. Kant for the most part thinks and writes in the spirit of an orthodox Enlightenment assumption of the separability and autonomy of thought from language. Hence, for example, his pervasive preoccupation in the *Critique of Pure Reason* with such things as representations, judgments, concepts, and ideas, with scarcely a mention of sentences or words. There is, though, an interesting counterstrand in his writings which acknowledges some sort of dependence of thought on language (see e.g. Kant's *Anthropology from a Pragmatic Point of View*, p. 34; Reinhard Brandt and Michael Wolff have recently emphasized this strand in Kant's texts, citing a number of additional passages). For a detailed explanation of Kant's ambiguous position, see my "Kant's Philosophy of Language?" (forthcoming).
12. Kant's *Von den verschiedenen Racen der Menschen* (1775) is a seminal text in the development of the very dubious modern discipline of racial typology.
13. Cf. Zammito, *Kant, Herder, and the Birth of Anthropology*, pp. 344–5.
14. Similar points apply to Hegel's discipline of "anthropology." For example, like Kant's "anthropology," Hegel's is largely concerned with aspects of individual psychology, rather than with cultures and their differences. Moreover, when it does touch on the latter, it shares Kant's unfortunate emphasis on race and on the role of race in determining national character (see esp. Hegel's *Encyclopedia*, pars. 393–4).
15. Concerning American anthropology, see G.W. Stocking Jr., *Race, Culture, and Evolution: Essays in the History of Anthropology* (Chicago: University of Chicago Press, 1982), *The Ethnographer's Magic and Other Essays in the History of Anthropology* (Madison: University of Wisconsin Press, 1992), and *Delimiting Anthropology: Occasional Inquiries and Reflections* (Madison: University of Wisconsin Press, 2001). Concerning British anthropology, see G.W. Stocking Jr., *Victorian Anthropology* (New York/London: Free Press, 1987) and *After Tylor: British Social Anthropology 1888–1951* (Madison: University of Wisconsin Press, 1995).

It should be noted that Stocking's emphasis on the vitally important role played by German influences was anything but conventional wisdom at the time when he developed it. For example, Evans-Pritchard's elaborate genealogy of the discipline of anthropology in E.E. Evans-Pritchard, *Social Anthropology and Other Essays* (New York: Free Press of Glencoe, 1962) and *A History of Anthropological Thought* (New York: Basic Books, 1981) depicts the discipline as essentially the achievement of French and British theorists, with hardly even a mention of Germans. (Of course, the historical context in which Evans-Pritchard was writing—shortly after two devastating world wars fought against Germany—encouraged this exclusion.)

16. In *Volksgeist as Method and Ethic*, ed. G.W. Stocking Jr. (Wisconsin: University of Wisconsin Press, 1996).

17. Stocking, *Victorian Anthropology*, pp. 20–1.

18. Ibid., pp. 20, 25. Cf. *Race, Culture, and Evolution*, p. 214. Also, Bunzl, "Franz Boas and the Humboldtian Tradition: From *Volksgeist* und *Nationalcharakter* to an Anthropological Concept of Culture," p. 73.

19. G6:255–6: "Finally, I would also not like to see exaggerated the distinctions which have been interpolated into the human species from praiseworthy zeal for synoptic science. Thus some have, for example, dared to name *races* [*Rassen*] four or five divisions of the species which were originally made according to regions or even according to colors [Herder is almost certainly thinking here of Kant and his 1775 work on races—M.N.F.]; I see no reason for this name. 'Race' suggests a difference of descent, which here either does not occur at all or in each of these global regions within each of these colors includes the most diverse races. For each people is a people [*jedes Volk ist Volk*]: it has its national formation [*Bildung*], and its language. To be sure, the clime has spread over all of them here an impress there only a thin veil—which, though, does not destroy the original basic structure of the nation. This extends even to families, and its transitions are as variable as they are hard to discern. In short, there are neither four or five races nor exclusive varieties on earth. The colors blend into one another; the formations [*Bildungen*] serve the genetic character; and overall everything turns out to be only a shading of one and the same great picture that extends through all places and times on earth."

20. See the translation of the 10th Collection in *Herder: Philosophical Writings*.

21. Given the vastness of the terrain to be covered, my account will inevitably be sketchy and suggestive rather than probative, leaving much room for people whose purposes are more purely historical than mine to "connect dots."

22. For details, see G. Broce, "Herder and Ethnography," *Journal of the History of the Behavioral Sciences*, 22 (1986).

23. To quote just one relevant passage from this early material: Herder, fascinated by Montesquieu's work, complains, nevertheless, that

Montesquieu has paid insufficient attention to empirical evidence concerning the breadth and depth of the variety among nations that occurs, and he asks in particular, "And in Asia, Africa, America? 'Oh, those peoples are savages'; and savage peoples should, I think, be studied most to find out what their ethics, habits, and distinctive characteristics are" (S4:466).

24. Concerning the date of composition of the *Plan*, I suspect the latest date in the range (1797), since I suspect that the work was stimulated by Herder's project of a "natural history of humanity" in the 10th Collection of the *Letters*, published in 1797. However, the relevant ideas could also have come from earlier works of Herder's such as the *Ideas*.

25. Cf. Bunzl, "Franz Boas and the Humboldtian Tradition."

26. For some details, see Stocking, "The Boas Plan for the Study of American Indian Languages," in *The Ethnographer's Magic*, pp. 87 ff., and Bunzl, "Franz Boas and the Humboldtian Tradition."

27. See e.g. B. Malinowski, "A Scientific Theory of Culture," in *A Scientific Theory of Culture and Other Essays* (Chapel Hill: University of North Carolina Press, 1944), p. 147; and *Coral Gardens and their Magic* (New York/Cincinnati/Chicago: American Book Company, 1935), 2:x.

28. See M.W. Young, *Malinowski: Odyssey of an Anthropologist 1884–1920* (New Haven/London: Yale University Press, 2004), pp. 11–13.

29. See ibid., pp. 139–41, 147. Malinowski often refers to Wundt in his published writings. And it is striking how many of Malinowski's favorite topics already played a prominent role in Wundt's work, including: kinship; law; magic; gardening and magic; the soul; religion; myth; and humanity.

30. Cf. Bunzl, "Franz Boas and the Humboldtian Tradition," p. 28.

31. See e.g. W. Wundt, *Elements of Folk Psychology* (London/New York: Allen and Unwin/Macmillan, 1916), pp. 52–3: "A horde . . . is a human herd . . . Between the members of a horde . . . there exists a relation that is lacking in the animal herd . . . This relation is established and preserved through a community of language. Herder, therefore, truthfully remarks that man was from the beginning a 'herding animal,' in so far as he possessed social instincts. Even in the formation of language these social instincts were operative . . . Language is bound up with thought. From the phenomena of language, therefore, we may draw inferences concerning the most general characteristics of thought. Such fundamental differences of language as exist . . . imply . . . that

there are divergent directions and forms of thought." Cf. pp. 58, 67 ff.,
490, 493.

32. For example, Wundt opens the concluding chapter of his *Elements
of Folk Psychology*, titled "The Development to Humanity," with the
following remarks: "The ambiguity of the word 'humanity' is such that
it may signify human weakness as well as human sympathy and other
virtues. It was in the latter, more favourable, sense of the term that
Herder, even in his day, attempted, in his *Ideas*, to portray the history
of mankind as an 'education to humanity' . . . In using this phrase
to sum up the meaning of history Herder meant that the striving
which underlies all history was not merely for the development of
the qualities of humanity [*Menschlichkeit*], in the highest sense of the
term, but also essentially for their gradual extension to the whole of
mankind [*Menschheit*]" (ibid., pp. 470–2; cf. p. 519 where Wundt
praises Herder for having here basically freed himself from religious or
transcendentally teleological conceptions of the course of history).

33. Cf. T.H. Eriksen and F.S. Nielsen, *A History of Anthropology* (London:
Pluto Press, 2001).

34. Herder did not cordon off anthropology, say as the investigation of
small, non-literate, contemporary societies, from the investigation of
large, literate, or past societies; all were included. This might seem to
divide his position sharply from that of modern cultural anthropology.
However, that is not clearly the case. For example, Malinowski's
position that ethnology is part of "a general science of Man in
his mental and social nature" is strikingly—and it is reasonable to
suspect, not accidentally—similar (B. Malinowski, "Ethnology and
the Study of Society," *Economica* 6 [1922], p. 215). Moreover, there
is much to be said in favor of such a broad conception of the
discipline. For instance, only this could make possible the eventual
drawing of general conclusions about humankind. And certainly,
tendencies towards a more restricted definition of the discipline have
led to some rather arbitrary-looking boundary lines. For example,
does it really make sense that E.W. Lane's *Manners and Customs of
the Modern Egyptians* (1836), which to anyone standing outside the
modern discipline of anthropology looks like a superb early example of
participant-observation anthropology grounded in years of fieldwork
and a deep knowledge of the natives' language, should be virtually
ignored by the discipline, presumably just because it concerns a large
society some parts of which are literate?

35. S4:364; cf. 466, 472–3.

36. S4:466.
37. *Herder: Philosophical Writings*, p. 291; cf. p. 292.
38. Stocking, "Polarity and Plurality: Boas as a Psychological Anthropologist," in *Delimiting Anthropology*.
39. B. Malinowski, *Argonauts of the Western Pacific* (Long Grove, IL.: Waveland Press, 1984), pp. 19, 23, 25 (note the probable echo here in the *"his . . . his . . . "* of Herder's *This Too a Philosophy of History* as quoted above). Cf. Stocking, *Victorian Anthropology*, p. 321; *After Tylor*, pp. 233–4, 277.

There were, no doubt, also a number of *non*-German influences at work on Malinowski influencing his psychological emphasis, e.g. W.H.R. Rivers, who was a working psychologist as well as a (psychological) anthropologist. However, this fact does not undermine the point made above. For one thing, multiple influences are simply the rule in intellectual history rather than the exception. For another thing, Rivers was himself heavily German-influenced.

It might be supposed that there is at least one important difference between Boas and Malinowski, on the one hand, and Herder, on the other: Boas's interest in psychology includes a strong interest in the unconscious (see Stocking, "Polarity and Plurality," p. 59; "Franz Boas and the Culture Concept," in *Race, Culture, and Evolution*, pp. 221, 226–7; and Bunzl, "Franz Boas and the Humboldtian Tradition," pp. 70–1), and Malinowski's conception of anthropological understanding similarly emphasizes that in order to achieve it the anthropologist needs to penetrate deeper than the native himself, thus again involving the unconscious (Boas and Malinowski were both interested in, though also critical of, Freud). In fact, however, Herder—like the Rationalists and his teacher Kant before him—was already deeply committed to, and interested in, the role of unconscious mental processes (see e.g. *On the Cognition and Sensation of the Human Soul* [1778]). So even here Boas and Malinowski are still working well within the general orbit of Herderian ideas.

40. See esp. *Ideas*, bks. 4, 7.
41. Classic statements of this position can be found in the following works among others: *On the Change of Taste* (1766), *This Too a Philosophy of History* (1774), and *On the Cognition* (1778).
42. See F. Boas, *The Mind of Primitive Man* (New York: Macmillan, 1916), pp. 104 ff., 247; *Primitive Art* (New York: Dover, 1955), pp. 1–2.
43. See F. Boas, *The Mind of Primitive Man*, pp. 98, 143 ff., 197 ff.; *Race, Language, and Culture* (Chicago: University of Chicago Press, 1982),

pp. 635–6; *A Franz Boas Reader*, ed. G.W. Stocking Jr. (Wisconsin: University of Wisconsin Press, 1996), pp. 71, 243 ff.

44. See Boas, *The Mind of Primitive Man*, pp. 112–14; *Race, Language, and Culture*, pp. 260–8.

45. R. Benedict, *Patterns of Culture* (Boston: Houghton Mifflin, 2005), *passim*.

46. See e.g. ibid., ch. 8. It is easy to overlook this aspect of Benedict's position, but it is in fact central to her rationale for anthropology, which explains the significance of the discipline largely in terms of the fact that individuals often find themselves psychologically at odds with the general tenor of their own cultures and that they can mitigate this uncomfortable situation by encountering other cultures to which they would be better suited.

47. See e.g. Malinowski, "A Scientific Theory of Culture," pp. 39–41, 55 ff., 72. Cf. Stocking, *After Tylor*, pp. 276–7.

48. See e.g. Malinowski, *Argonauts of the Western Pacific*, pp. 510–13; *Coral Gardens and their Magic*, 1:198–210.

49. See e.g. B. Malinowski, *Crime and Custom in Savage Society* (New York: Humanities Press, 1951), pp. 3–4, 56; "Baloma: the Spirits of the Dead in the Trobriand Islands," in *Magic, Science, and Religion and Other Essays* (Prospect Heights, IL.: Waveland Press, 1992), pp. 240–54.

50. See Essay 1. As I show there, Herder developed a number of cogent arguments supporting this principle on both its positive and its negative sides.

51. Concerning Dilthey, see my discussion in Essay 1, where I point out that Herder's arguments for the principle were in certain respects superior to Dilthey's, especially on the positive side. Concerning the versions of this principle in Wilhelm von Humboldt, Droysen, and Dilthey, cf. Bunzl, "Franz Boas and the Humboldtian Tradition."

52. In *Volksgeist as Method and Ethic*, pp. 9 ff.

53. Goethe and Alexander von Humboldt were both profoundly influenced by Herder in this as in other areas (in Goethe's case directly, in Alexander von Humboldt's both directly and via the influence of his brother). Concerning Alexander von Humboldt's views, cf. Bunzl, "Franz Boas and the Humboldtian Tradition," pp. 38–40.

54. Concerning Boas's probable debt to Dilthey here, see Stocking, "From Physics to Ethnology," in *Race, Culture, and Evolution*, pp. 152, 154. In addition to the evidence cited by Stocking, an additional piece of evidence supporting the hypothesis that Boas is already indebted to Dilthey here lies in Boas's criticism in the essay of Buckle's contrary

position that history is concerned with discovering physiological and psychological laws—a position Dilthey had already criticized along similar lines in a well-known review from 1862. Boas later on explicitly mentions Dilthey's work with approval.

55. Stocking has emphasized this trajectory in the development of Boas's thought.

56. Cf. Young, *Malinowski*. The late work "A Scientific Theory of Culture" is a striking example of this.

57. Except, perhaps, in the modest sense that his empirical studies served the negative function of *discrediting false* general laws—for example, in the case of *Argonauts*, ones concerning the nature of human (or primitive human) economic activity.

58. In this spirit, he demands in the *Popular Songs* "that one give us whole, faithful natural history of peoples in their own monuments with some completeness, . . . not speak oneself, but let them speak, not always ask 'what the good of that is' but, good or not good, present it, not beautify, not trim and distort it with the hood of religion or classical taste, but give it as it is, and with faithfulness, joy, and love" (G3:62).

59. See on this, e.g., his *Treatise on the Origin of Language*, in *Herder: Philosophical Writings*, p. 114.

60. See on this, e.g., *This Too a Philosophy of History*.

61. See e.g. Boas, *A Franz Boas Reader*, p. 185; Malinowski, *Argonauts*, p. 25.

62. Boas, *The Mind of Primitive Man*, pp. 197 ff.

63. See on this Stocking, "The Boas Plan for the Study of American Indian Languages," pp. 79–80.

64. See F. Boas, "On Alternating Sounds," *American Anthropologist*, 2 (1889). The occurrence of perceptual variations across cultures and the need to take these into account had already been important parts of Herder's position (see e.g. *On the Change of Taste* [1766]; *On the Cognition* [1778]; and the *Ideas*, G6:286 ff.).

Stocking has rightly emphasized the importance of this early essay of Boas's. One aspect of its importance, I would suggest, lies in the fact that the essay's argument is in a way emblematic of Boas's whole approach to anthropology, and indeed of the discipline more generally: just as in this essay it turns out that our initial perception of vacillations in the sounds of natives' words is in reality a sort of illusion produced by our different ways of perceptually classifying sounds, their sounds really being no less coherent than our own, merely in accordance with a different system of perceptual classification, so likewise in other psychological areas (e.g. conceptualization) the anthropologist's initial perception of confusion in native practices gives way under closer examination to a recognition that such a perception was really illusory, that there is a coherent system present after all, only one that is significantly different from his own.

65. Zammito himself includes in his conception of Herder's interest in a "historicist hermeneutics" a further idea, which I have excluded here: an awareness of the unavoidable historical situatedness of the interpreter's own standpoint. This idea really belongs not to Herder but instead to certain later hermeneutic theorists, especially Gadamer. Indeed, as we have just seen in (iii), Herder's normal hermeneutic position—found in such works as *On Thomas Abbt's Writings* (1768) and *This Too a Philosophy of History* (1774), for example—is antithetical to such an idea: a *prohibition* on interpreting in ways that are infused by the interpreter's own distinctive standpoint. It is true that the German scholar Irmscher has made a sophisticated case that Herder already anticipates the idea in question (H.D. Irmscher, "Grundzüge der Hermeneutik Herders"). However, his case mainly rests on unrepresentative material—for example, Herder's very early work *On Diligence in Several Learned Languages* (1764), where he was still a relative neophyte in foreign languages and in consequence naively thought of understanding them as inevitably a process of translating them into one's native tongue; and his late *Christian Writings* (1794–8), which sometimes choose to interpret the Bible flexibly with an eye to modern applications due to the specifically religious-moral nature of the subject-matter involved. Moreover, the further hermeneutic idea in question is intrinsically dubious. This is a tricky subject which I have discussed elsewhere (see *German Philosophy of Language*, Essays 7 and 9), and so shall not broach in any detail here. But one point to note is that it seems a grievous mistake to efface—as Gadamer does—the traditional distinction between, on the one hand, *understanding* a text, discourse, etc. and, on the other hand, *explicating, applying*, or *translating* it; prima facie at least, understanding need not in principle involve the mediation of any distinctive "filter" contributed by the interpreter, whereas explicating, applying, or translating must do so. Finally, however these historical and philosophical matters stand, the further hermeneutic idea in question has been of little relevance for the development of modern anthropology (at least until very recently). For these several reasons, therefore, I exclude it here.

66. See e.g. *On Thomas Abbt's Writings* (1768) concerning the need to interpret individuals' minds not through general psychological theories but by paying painstaking attention to their words and deeds; the *Fragments on Recent German Literature* (1767–8) on the need to determine different periods' and cultures' varying ethical concepts by paying scrupulous attention to their varying word-usages; and the essay *Shakespeare* (1773) on the need to determine literary genres not through a priori theories but through a careful empirical investigation of the purposes and rules that the age or author is actually following.

67. See e.g. S4:465–6.

68. See e.g. Boas, *A Franz Boas Reader*, pp. 184–5; Malinowski, *Argonauts*, p. 399; "Ethnology and the Study of Society," pp. 215 ff. Cf. Eriksen and Nielsen, *A History of Anthropology*, p. 39.

69. See Essay 2.

70. See e.g. Herder, *Treatise on the Origin*.

71. See e.g. *Ideas*, G6:353–4.

72. Ibid.

73. See *German Philosophy of Language*, Essay 4.

74. Cf. R.L. Brown, *Wilhelm von Humboldt's Conception of Linguistic Relativity* (The Hague/Paris: Mouton, 1967), pp. 12–16. Also, Bunzl, "Franz Boas and the Humboldtian Tradition," pp. 63 ff. As Bunzl argues, it is likely that Boas imbibed this position largely through Steinthal, whom he knew personally, credits in print, and imitates in his aspiration to generate native American texts for philological and linguistic analysis (this aspiration was modeled on Steinthal's approach to African languages in his *Die Mande-Neger Sprachen* [1867]).

75. See e.g. Boas, *A Franz Boas Reader*, pp. 157 ff., 183–8. Cf. *Volksgeist as Method and Ethic*, pp. 63 ff., 215 ff. Some qualifications: (1) As Stocking has pointed out—"The Boas Plan for the Study of American Indian Languages," pp. 88–9—Boas's remarks in this area exhibit a certain tension, some of them implying that language determines thought, but others that it does not. The latter remarks may seem inconsistent with the former, and at odds with the Herder-Humboldt tradition. However, this is not straightforwardly so. One point Boas is often concerned to make when he denies that language determines thought is that a language can always *expand* in ways which enable it to express thoughts which it was at the outset unable to express, so that in *this* sense language does not determine or limit its possessor's thought (see e.g. *The Mind of Primitive Man*, pp. 148 ff.). But that point is compatible

with the sort of determining or limiting of thought by language that was championed by the Herder-Humboldt position, namely a limiting in the sense that a person can only think at any given time what he can express linguistically at that time. Indeed, it is really only a mild version of an even bolder point which Humboldt had himself made, namely that any language can be made to express any thought. On the other hand, when Boas denies that language determines thought he sometimes has in mind a different point which is more problematic. For example, he writes in one passage that "languages [are] molded by thought, not thought by languages" (*The Mind of Primitive Man*, p. 248). This may in the end be inconsistent with the passages in which Boas favors the determination of thought by language and with the corresponding Herder-Humboldt position. However, even here there is at least this much continuity with that position: Humboldt had himself held not only that languages determine the nature of a nation's mind *but also conversely* (cf. Bunzl, "Franz Boas and the Humboldtian Tradition," pp. 32–3, 69–70). (2) Boas's profound continuity with the Herder-Humboldt tradition on the fundamental issues in question here did not prevent him and his followers from disagreeing with Humboldt sharply on some further issues. For example, they essentially rejected Humboldt's characterization of American Indian languages as "incorporative" (see Stocking, "The Boas Plan for the Study of American Indian Languages," pp. 77–84).

76. Cf. Eriksen and Nielsen, *A History of Anthropology*, pp. 65–6. That Sapir was directly acquainted with and influenced by the Herder-Humboldt position can be seen from a review of Herder's *Treatise on the Origin* that he published in 1907 while still a young man, in which he sympathetically discusses Herder and Humboldt, as well as other people influenced by them, such as Grimm and Steinthal. See E. Sapir, "Herder's 'Ursprung der Sprache,'" *Modern Philology*, 5/1 (1907).

77. Malinowski, "The Problem of Meaning in Primitive Languages," in C.K. Ogden and I.A. Richards, *The Meaning of Meaning* (New York: Harcourt, Brace, and Co., 1945), pp. 321–2: "When a savage learns to understand the meaning of a word, this process is . . . [accomplished] by learning to handle it. A word *means* to a native the proper use of the thing for which it stands, exactly as an implement *means* something when it can be handled and means nothing when no active experience of it is at hand." (Malinowski here somewhat confuses the use of a *word* with the use of the *thing* for which a word stands, e.g. an implement.) *Coral Gardens*, 2:vii: "Language exists only in actual use within the

context of real utterance." (It should be noted, though, that Dewey was also a strong influence on Malinowski here.)

78. Malinowski, *Coral Gardens*, 2:21; "A Scientific Theory of Culture," p. 132.

79. As Malinowski put it: "Three-quarters of the success in fieldwork depends on the right equipment and attitude to language [*sic*]"; "No language, no penetration!" (Young, *Malinowski*, p. 48). Cf. B. Malinowski, *The Sexual Life of Savages* (New York: Harcourt, Brace, and World, 1929), pp. 464–5.

    Malinowski will have absorbed the Herder-Humboldt position via such channels as (i) his father's deep immersion in it; (ii) his own grounding in Lazarus, Steinthal, and Wundt's discipline of *Völkerpsychologie*, where it plays a central role (note, in addition to his indebtedness to Wundt, his crediting of Lazarus and Steinthal in connection with linguistic matters at *Coral Gardens*, 2:x, as well as the similarity between his collection in that work of Trobriand texts and provision of them with philological/linguistic analyses in the manner of classical texts and Steinthal's treatment of African materials in his *Die Mande-Neger Sprachen* [1867]); and (iii) his direct acquaintance with Humboldt's work (which he mentions at *Coral Gardens*, 2:x and at "The Problem of Meaning in Primitive Languages," p. 297).

    It should be noted, though, that Malinowski is not a slavish or unequivocal follower of the Herder-Humboldt position. For example, in *Coral Gardens*, which is in some ways the most impressive manifestation of his affiliation with it, he also goes out of his way to argue *against* the idea that all thoughts are reflected in language and all concepts in words (2:6, 65–8, 73). And elsewhere he remarks on the unreliability of native language use as a guide to the character of native thought and practice (see e.g. *The Sexual Life of Savages*, pp. 464–5; and esp. *Argonauts*, pp. 176 ff.). It is an interesting question how severe a contradiction or qualification of the Herder-Humboldt position such remarks really represent. But I shall not pursue that question here.

80. See Evans-Pritchard, *Social Anthropology*, pp. 79–80. This genealogy of the linguistic strand in modern British anthropology requires a little qualification, however. While British anthropology before Malinowski had indeed largely failed to accord language the sort of fundamental place within the discipline that he and his followers assigned to it, there had been some exceptions, including F.M. Müller, and at points in their careers also E.B. Tylor and W.H.R. Rivers. However, after Müller the tendency had been for the focus on language to recede as the

nineteenth century wore on. And more importantly, all three of these exceptions were people who themselves had strong ties to Germany (for example, Müller was an immigrant to England from Germany) and who had therefore themselves been strongly influenced by the Herder-Humboldt tradition. For some further details, see Stocking, *Victorian Anthropology* and *After Tylor*.

81. This thesis concerning interpretation should be distinguished from the different (though not incompatible) thesis that all aspects of a culture are causally or functionally interdependent—a thesis which, as Evans-Pritchard explains in *Social Anthropology*, has long roots reaching back before Herder, especially in the French tradition.

82. *Herder: Philosophical Writings*, p. 292.

83. Ibid., p. 395.

84. See Boas, *A Franz Boas Reader*, pp. 4–5, 57 ff. Cf. Stocking, "From Physics to Ethnology," in *Race, Culture, and Evolution*, p. 156; Bunzl, "Franz Boas and the Humboldtian Tradition," pp. 56 ff.

85. See e.g. Boas, *Primitive Art*, pp. 128–9, 336.

86. Benedict, *Patterns of Culture*, pp. 46 ff., 242–4.

87. See e.g. Malinowski, *Argonauts*, p. xvi; "Ethnology and the Study of Society," p. 218; *Magic, Science, and Religion and Other Essays*, p. 238; *A Scientific Theory of Culture and Other Essays*, pp. 33–5, 149, 154.

88. For an example of Wundt's own commitment to it, see his *Elements of Folk Psychology*, pp. 285–6; cf. p. 298.

89. Cf. Eriksen and Nielsen, *A History of Anthropology*, p. 41. Another influence here may have been Rivers, who likewise advocated holism in interpretation (cf. Stocking, *After Tylor*, p. 123). But since Rivers was himself intimately acquainted with the German tradition, this qualification is not in the end a big one.

90. See e.g. Evans-Pritchard, *Social Anthropology*, p. 80.

91. *Herder: Philosophical Writings*, p. 397. It would be an exaggeration to say that Herder ever practiced participant-observation himself, but he did at least approximate it. For example, he acquired a certain amount of first-hand experience of Eastern European cultures as a young man, and his 1769 journey to France involved something like participant-observation as well.

92. Concerning Boas himself, see Stocking, "Boas and the History of Humanistic Anthropology," in *Delimiting Anthropology*, pp. 72–3.

93. There is an interesting difference between Malinowski's and Evans-Pritchard's conceptions of this method, however. Evans-Pritchard tends to write as though the participant-observer sheds the concepts

and ways of thinking of his own culture, plunges into the natives' way of life, and then translates the new concepts and ways of thinking thus acquired back into his own culture's as well as he is able to: "He goes to live among a primitive people and learns their way of life. He learns to speak their language, to think in their concepts, and to feel in their values. He then lives the experience over again critically and interpretatively in the conceptual categories and values of his own culture" (Evans-Pritchard, *Social Anthropology*, p. 61). Malinowski occasionally characterizes the process in a similar way (see e.g. a passage quoted by Young at *Malinowski*, p. 49). However, in more considered reflections he instead implies that the process initially involves much interpreting of the natives' thoughts and doings by the anthropologist in terms of his own concepts and ways of thinking, these only gradually being shed as the process of enculturation advances (*The Sexual Life of Savages*, p. xxv). The latter account seems by far the more realistic of the two (the former account really is vulnerable to C. Geertz's swipe against participant-observation at *Works and Lives* [Stanford: Stanford University Press, 1988], p. 83 that it is more a wish than a method, whereas the latter account—and Malinowski was Geertz's intended target—is not). Note, however, that neither account implies that at the end of the interpretive process preparatory to anthropological writing the natives' thoughts and actions will inevitably be understood by the anthropologist through a "filter" of his own concepts and modes of thought. The apt metaphor with which to capture the goal in Malinowski's account is not one of standing atop a ladder formed of one's own concepts and ways of thinking, but rather one of ascending with the aid of such a ladder to a hay loft which the natives have reached by another route, and then letting the ladder fall away.

94. The former two words fall short of encapsulating the whole concept of culture because Herder normally uses them only in the singular, not in the plural (though "Bildungen" does occur in the irrelevant sense of physical formations); the latter two words he does often use in the plural, but they are rather too narrowly socio-political in emphasis to capture the whole concept. For an illuminating general discussion of the concept of culture in the German tradition, see R. Geuss, "*Kultur, Bildung, Geist*," in his *Morality, Culture, and History* (Cambridge: Cambridge University Press, 1999).

95. See e.g. *Ideas*, bks. 2, 7–9. Cf. D. Mühlberg, "Herders Theorie der Kulturgeschichte in ihrer Bedeutung für die Begründung der

Kulturwissenschaft," *Jahrbuch für Volkskunde und Kulturgeschichte*, 12 (1984), pp. 21–3.

96. See e.g. *This Too a Philosophy of History*, in *Herder: Philosophical Writings*, p. 291.

97. See e.g. S4:467.

98. Much of Herder's detailed discussion of history and culture emphasizes the role of such influences (see e.g. *Ideas*, bk. 11 on the influence of Chinese culture on surrounding cultures). His normative stance towards them is ambivalent, but by no means mainly negative. He is indeed opposed to the slavish imitation of one culture by another. But he considers other forms of influence natural and desirable. As he already puts it succinctly in 1769: "False imitation and mixing with other peoples has always corrupted nations . . . But a nation remains imperfect when it does not imitate at all" (S4:477).

99. Cf. Broce, "Herder and Ethnography," p. 161; Mühlberg, "Herders Theorie der Kulturgeschichte," p. 22.

100. Cf. Bunzl, "Franz Boas and the Humboldtian Tradition," pp. 68–73. Bunzl understates the continuity with Herder, however, by implying, mistakenly, that Herder's position had been hierarchical and even racialist.

101. Boas does insist on a *certain sort* of independence of culture from language, namely on the possibility of a single culture being shared by groups with different languages (*The Mind of Primitive Man*, pp. 132–3). But that does not imply that there could be a culture that was not grounded in language—which is the crucial point here.

102. See e.g. ibid., pp. 127 ff. Among the arguments that Boas uses in this connection are the empirical observations that when children from one race are raised by another they acquire its culture, and that two peoples identical in race will often have quite different cultures.

103. See e.g. ibid., pp. 159 ff.

104. See e.g. ibid., pp. 112–14.

105. See e.g. *Primitive Art*, pp. 6–7.

106. See e.g. ibid. on the constant exchange of visual art forms, myths, etc. that occurs between cultures.

107. Cf. Stocking, "Franz Boas and the Culture Concept," p. 229. Boas's inheritance and development of all these Herderian principles was evidently in part mediated by T. Waitz, author of *Anthropologie der Naturvölker* (1859) (cf. Bunzl, "Franz Boas and the Humboldtian Tradition," pp. 44 ff.).

108. Boas, *A Franz Boas Reader*, p. 24. Cf. *Reinventing Anthropology*, ed. D. Hymes (New York: Vintage, 1974), p. 19. Hymes points out that Boas's students Kroeber, Lowie, and Sapir make similar explicit tributes to Herder.

109. It has sometimes been argued that the concept of "culture" in American anthropology had more homegrown roots, e.g. in the work of F.H. Cushing. For a balanced contrary assessment, however, see Bunzl, "Franz Boas and the Humboldtian Tradition," pp. 72–3.

110. See esp. B. Malinowski, "Culture," *Encyclopaedia of the Social Sciences*, 4 (1931); and "A Scientific Theory of Culture."

111. See e.g. "A Scientific Theory of Culture," pp. 132 ff.

112. See e.g. "Baloma; the Spirits of the Dead in the Trobriand Islands," pp. 240–54.

113. It might be supposed that the modern anthropological concept of "culture" had older roots in Britain, and therefore did not need to wait for an infusion of Germanic influence through Malinowski in order to develop. In particular, Tylor had already given the following famous definition of "culture" in the 1870s: "Culture or Civilization, taken in its wide ethnographical sense, is that complex whole which includes knowledge, belief, art, morals, law, custom, and any other capabilities and habits acquired by man as a member of society" (E.B. Tylor, *Primitive Culture: Researches into the Development of Mythology, Philosophy, Religion, Language, Art, and Custom* [1873; repr. New York: Henry Holt and Co., 1877], 1:1). However, as Stocking argues in "Franz Boas and the Culture Concept," pp. 200 ff. and *Victorian Anthropology*, pp. 302 ff., Tylor's concept of "culture" is in fact very different from the modern one in a number of important ways. For instance, it is not normally conceived as plural, nor as fundamentally linguistic, nor as free of ranking (but rather as involving hierarchy).

114. *Herder: Philosophical Writings*, pp. 282–4, 296–7. For an earlier statement of some of these ideas, see Herder's *On the Change of Taste* (1766), in *Herder: Philosophical Writings*; for a later statement of them, see his *Letters* (1793–7).

115. Cf. Stocking, "Franz Boas and the Culture Concept," pp. 229–30.

116. Cf. Eriksen and Nielsen, *A History of Anthropology*, p. 40.

117. Benedict, *Patterns of Culture*, esp. pp. 51, 223.

118. M. Mead, *Coming of Age in Samoa* (New York: Harper Collins, 2001), p. 170.

119. For example, in the *Ideas* he passes highly differential judgments on various cultures and their values (for instance, negative ones on the Romans and their values, but positive ones on the Greeks and theirs).

120. Cf. Stocking, "Franz Boas and the Culture Concept," pp. 230–1; "Anthropology as *Kulturkampf*: Science and Politics in the Career of Franz Boas," pp. 110–11.

121. Cf. Geertz, *Works and Lives*, p. 116.

122. F. Nietzsche, *Jenseits von Gut und Böse*, in *Kritische Studienausgabe* (Munich/Berlin: Deutscher Taschenbuch/de Gruyter, 1988), vol. 5, par. 9. The force of Nietzsche's point perhaps tended to be missed by the leading field anthropologists of the twentieth century due in part to the fact that most of their fieldwork was done in a colonial context. Since the colonial powers had already done much to suppress the most severe violations of western values that occurred within the native societies in question by the time the anthropologists arrived there (e.g. aggressive cannibalism), it was far easier for the anthropologists to take a laissez faire attitude to the non-western values they found in operation there than it would have been had they arrived under pre-colonial conditions.

123. In particular, they may force one to recognize that, like other people's, one's own values are local and subjective rather than universal and objective, and they may thereby encourage one to be more tolerant of others' values than one would be if one believed one's own to be universal and objective—for example, to respect them except in cases where they come into outright conflict with one's own on really grave matters. In other words, although the third position cannot stand quite as it is, the revision required in order to make it defensible may still leave something similar in spirit.

124. For Herder's rejection of this sort of cosmopolitanism, see e.g. *This Too a Philosophy of History*.

125. *Herder: Philosophical Writings*, pp. 394–5. One of Herder's earliest statements of this sort of position occurs in the separate pages for his *Journal of My Journey in the Year 1769*: "A great article . . . It presupposes that each nation has its riches and distinctive features of spirit, of character, as of country. These must be sought out, and cultivated. No human being, no land, no people, no history of a people, no state is like the other, and consequently the true, the beautiful, and the good is not alike in them. If this is not sought, if another nation is blindly taken as a model, then everything suffocates" (S4:472).

126. Boas, *A Franz Boas Reader*, pp. 332 ff.

127. Cf. Stocking, "Anthropology as *Kulturkampf*," p. 104.

128. Concerning this protest, see Eriksen and Nielsen, *A History of Anthropology*, p. 77. The United Nations still persists in grounding its cosmopolitanism on the empirically false claim of universally shared ethical values to this day (see e.g. its recent publication *Crossing the Divide*).

129. For example, it has recently been explicitly championed by Paul Rabinow (see *Writing Culture*, ed. J. Clifford and G.E. Marcus [Berkeley and Los Angeles: University of California Press, 1986], p. 258).

130. See Malinowski, "Ethnology and the Study of Society" (the name "new humanism" connotes for Malinowski not only this ethical stance but also a certain theoretical project connected with it). Cf. Stocking, *After Tylor*, pp. 267, 396; Young, *Malinowski*, pp. 547, 556.

131. Cf. Malinowski, "Ethnology and the Study of Society," p. 217.

132. Malinowski, *Argonauts*, pp. 518–19.

133. Cf. Stocking, *After Tylor*, pp. 414–15. This is true despite Malinowksi's history of pragmatic cooperation with colonial authorities. It is reflected, for example, in his contempt for most colonial administrators and missionaries.

134. S15:138.

135. G6:304.

136. See e.g. Boas, *Race, Language, and Culture*, pp. 258–9, 636. Cf. Stocking, "Anthropology as *Kulturkampf*," pp. 103, 112.

137. See Benedict, *Patterns of Culture*, pp. 249–50; Mead, *Coming of Age in Samoa*, pp. 10–11, 144–60.

138. See e.g. Malinowski, "Ethnology and the Study of Society," p. 219: "It is not so far-fetched an idea as [it] might seem, to appeal to the savage for some light to be shed on our own nature. For nothing stimulates research and understanding so much as contrast and comparison."

139. See e.g. Evans-Pritchard, *Social Anthropology*, p. 129.

140. Cf. Broce, "Herder and Ethnography," p. 163.

141. See Boas, *The Mind of Primitive Man*, pp. 188 ff.; and for a vivid specific example, *Race, Language, and Culture*, p. 274 concerning the different uses and meanings that *masks* have in different cultures.

142. Boas, *The Mind of Primitive Man*, pp. 184 ff.

143. Ibid., pp. 193 ff.

144. Cf. Eriksen and Nielsen, *A History of Anthropology*, p. 44; Young, *Malinowski*.

145. Concerning Boas's critique of Bastian on this score, see Stocking, "Polarity and Plurality," p. 59. Cf. Eriksen and Nielsen, *A History*

of Anthropology, pp. 166–8. The substantive issue at stake here is of course a very contentious one (not only in anthropology but also in philosophy). In my view, it can only be decided in the end by means of extensive close examination of relevant empirical evidence concerning the linguistic and other behavior of people in different historical periods and cultures. For a discussion of some of the general questions involved, and also a critique, in the light of relevant empirical evidence, of Berlin and Kay's conclusions which is designed to illustrate the sort of contrary picture that emerges once the required close examination of relevant empirical evidence is undertaken, see my "On the Very Idea of Denying the Existence of Radically Different Conceptual Schemes."

146. *Herder: Philosophical Writings*, p. 291. Cf. *Letters*, G7:493, 584–5.

147. G7:301 ff.

148. See e.g. Boas, *Primitive Art*, pp. 84–5; *Race, Language, and Culture*, pp. 256, 258, 268–9, 285. Cf. Stocking, "Polarity and Plurality," pp. 59–61.

149. See e.g. Benedict, *Patterns of Culture*, ch. 8. Individuality and lack of full integration within a culture in fact constitute one of her main rationales for engaging in anthropology in the first place: individuals often find themselves deeply at odds with the general tenor of their own culture, and may therefore find consolation and inspiration by encountering another which is in relevant respects more congenial to them.

150. See Mead, *Coming of Age in Samoa*, ch. 11.

151. See Malinowski, *Crime and Custom in Savage Society*, pp. 3–4, 56; *Magic, Science, and Religion and Other Essays*, pp. 240–54. Cf. Young, *Malinowski*, pp. 238–40, 429, 433–4.

152. It is perhaps worth mentioning here that some of the best recent work in cognitive ethology—in particular, work by Donald Griffin—has shown that even among groups of animals there is often far more individual variation than used to be assumed.

153. For this whole theory, see esp. "A Scientific Theory of Culture." Malinowski tends to run theses (ii) and (iii) together due to his equation of meaning with use or function, but this seems to depend on a confusion between the function of a *word* and the function of an *item* referred to by a word (see "The Problem of Meaning in Primitive Languages," pp. 321–2, as quoted in a previous footnote). So the two theses are probably best distinguished. For a concrete example of (ii) and (iii), one might consider Malinowski's complex account

of such Trobriand institutions as the practice of brothers farming for their sisters and sending most of their agricultural produce to the latter, the chief's polygamy, the chief's wealth, the chief's largesse, the chief's prestige and influence, and overall social discipline within the community. As Malinowski conceives matters, the intelligibility of each of these institutions ultimately requires a consideration of each of the others, and indeed the very existence of each ultimately depends on the existence of each of the others.

154. As Evans-Pritchard points out in *Social Anthropology*, idea (iii) has long historical roots reaching back even before Herder, especially in the French tradition.

155. S4:364.

156. G5:1194. (Herder does, though, have the occasional Rousseauesque moment—e.g., his discussion of an Iroquois plan for peace in the 10th Collection of the *Letters*.) Cf. Broce, "Herder and Ethnography," p. 165.

157. Mead's idyllic picture of Samoan life has since been convincingly challenged on empirical grounds by D. Freeman, *Margaret Mead and Samoa: The Making and Unmaking of an Anthropological Myth* (Cambridge, Mass.: Harvard University Press, 1983). For a gentle exposure of the romantic fantasy and empirical ignorance at the core of Levi-Strauss's work, see Geertz, *The Interpretation of Cultures*, ch. 13.

158. Concerning Levi-Strauss in particular, see Geertz, *The Interpretation of Cultures*, ch. 13—an exquisitely ironic critical discussion of how, by his own account in *Tristes Tropiques*, the young Levi-Strauss went to Brazil in search of natives untainted by modern civilization, but when he eventually reached some was quite unable in the short time he spent with them to penetrate their mode of thought, which would have required the long, hard work of mastering their language and living with them as a participant-observer, and so gave up and instead went back to Paris to invent structuralism.

159. Cf. Stocking, *After Tylor*, ch. 7.

160. See Malinowski, *The Sexual Life of Savages*, pp. 464–5, 502 ff.; cf. 282 ff., 480.

161. See e.g. Boas, *A Franz Boas Reader*, pp. 184–5; Malinowski, *The Sexual Life of Savages*, pp. 282 ff., 464–5, 480, 502 ff.; Evans-Pritchard's pithy equations in a letter to Malinowski: "no fieldwork / Durkheim's views," "limited fieldwork / Radcliffe-Brown's views," "exhaustive fieldwork / Malinowski's views" (Stocking, *After Tylor*, p. 425; admittedly, Evans-Pritchard sometimes took a different view of

Radcliffe-Brown and Malinowski's relative merits); and Geertz, *The Interpretation of Cultures*, ch. 13.

162. *Writing Culture*, ed. J. Clifford and G.E. Marcus.

163. See e.g. J. Clifford, "On Ethnographic Authority," *Representations*, 1/2 (1983); and work by S. Tyler, such as "Post-Modern Ethnography: From Document of the Occult to Occult Document," in *Writing Culture*.

164. See e.g. *Reinventing Anthropology*, ed. Hymes, pp. 48 ff.; J. Fabian, *Time and the Other* (New York: Columbia University Press, 2002), *passim*; E.W. Said, *Culture and Imperialism* (London: Vintage, 1994), p. 184.

165. See Said, *Culture and Imperialism*, pp. 376–7, 407–8; *Orientalism* (New York: Vintage, 1979), pp. 45–6, 154–5, 229, 298, 325, 332–3, 347, 350.

166. See Said, *Orientalism*, pp. 332–3; *Culture and Imperialism*, p. 376.

167. See Said, *Culture and Imperialism*, pp. 15, 384 ("all culture [is] hybrid").

168. See Said, *Orientalism,* pp. 45–6, 154–5, 229, 298, 325, 332–3, 347, 350; *Culture and Imperialism*, pp. 407–8.

169. See e.g. the work of Clifford.

170. Examples of this can be found in the work of Tyler, Crapanzano, and Silverstein.

171. See *German Philosophy of Language*, Essays 7 and 9.

172. See Stocking, *Victorian Anthropology*, p. 273.

173. An arguable exception: Evans-Pritchard. An arguable case of individual ambivalence: Malinowski.

174. Cf. Stocking, *Victorian Anthropology*, p. 289; *After Tylor*, pp. 414–20 and *passim*. A similar point applies to some twentieth-century anthropologists who stand outside the Herderian tradition in anthropology, e.g. Radcliffe-Brown and Levi-Strauss.

175. Fabian, *Time and the Other*. Do we not constantly use timeless characterizations of people in our *own* culture as well (e.g. "Schoolteachers strive to keep order in the classroom in order to make learning possible")? And are they not just as likely to be positively valorizing or neutral as negatively valorizing? And do not analogous points apply concerning visual representations of people? The answer seems in each case to be Yes. There is indeed a *grain* of truth in Fabian's position, in that anthropology's use of such characterizations and representations has *sometimes* been negatively valorizing of the Other, especially when "allochronicity" took the very specific form given it by the evolutionists. But this grain of truth falls far short of demonstrating

the sort of "transcendental" flaw in the discipline that Fabian alleges.

176. Malinowski himself eventually came to recognize this (cf. Stocking, *After Tylor*, p. 276 n.; Young, *Malinowski*, p. 470). For a recent discussion of anthropology's potentials in this direction, see *Reinventing Anthropology*, ed. Hymes, pp. 30 ff.

7

The Liberal Temper in Classical German Philosophy: Freedom of Thought and Expression

Consideration of the German philosophy and political history of the past century might well give the impression, and often does give foreign observers the impression, that liberalism, including in particular commitment to the ideal of free thought and expression, is only skin-deep in Germany. Were not Heidegger's disgust at *Gerede* (which of course *really* meant the free speech of the Weimar Republic) and Gadamer's defense of "authority," "tradition," and "prejudice" more reflective of the real instincts of German philosophy than, say, the Frankfurt School's heavily Anglophone-influenced championing of free thought and expression? Were not the Kaiser and Nazism more indicative of Germany's true political nature than the liberalism of the Weimar Republic (a desperate, ephemeral experiment undertaken in reaction to Germany's disastrous defeat in the First World War) or the liberalism of (West) Germany since 1945 (in effect forced on the country by the victorious Allies after the Second World War)?

It can therefore come as a surprise—and an extremely heartening one—to learn that liberalism, including the ideal of free thought and expression, has long, deep roots in German philosophy and political history. In particular, during the classical period of German philosophy Kant, Herder, Georg Forster, Schiller, the young Fichte, the young Friedrich Schlegel, Schleiermacher, Wilhelm von Humboldt, and even Hegel all championed versions of liberalism, including freedom of thought and expression.[1] Also (and connectedly), liberalism, including commitment to freedom of thought and expression, constituted a central strand in nineteenth-century German politics.[2]

That much is beyond serious dispute. But I would like in this essay to argue for a more radical and controversial thesis (albeit in a somewhat tentative and sketchy way). A grudging Anglophone observer might concede what has just been said but reply along roughly the following lines: "To be sure, classical German philosophy embraced liberal political ideals. But it basically just took these over from the English and French Enlightenment. And (aside from some implausible and unhelpful metaphysical elaborations) it contributed little to their development. Where, for example, is the J.S. Mill of German philosophy?" What I want to suggest is that such a reply is in fact deeply mistaken. For one thing (and I merely mention this without elaborating on it), the Germans in question were by no means simply borrowing from the English and the French; they also had their own native tradition of liberalism going back at least as far as, and forcefully expressed in, the Reformation (in connection with freedom of thought and speech, Luther is the central figure). For another thing (and this is the point I want to elaborate on here), these German thinkers contributed *greatly* to the development of the ideas in question. In particular, the very Anglophone philosopher mentioned in this grudging reply, J.S. Mill, turns out to owe most of his (justly) famous case for freedom, including freedom of thought and expression, to the German tradition. Indeed, important aspects of his case for freedom of thought and expression only become fully intelligible and plausible once its original German form is retrieved and used to supplement or correct what is in effect an incomplete or inferior reproduction of it by Mill. Moreover, there are important additional arguments for freedom of thought and expression which the German tradition either preserved or developed but which Mill omits, whereas there is little if anything of importance in Mill's case which was not already in the German tradition. In short, unbeknownst to most of us, a vital, if wobbly, cornerstone of Anglophone liberal theory rests on firmer and broader German foundations.[3]

In order to perceive this situation, however, it is essential to look at the *right part* of the classical German philosophical tradition. Initially, focus is likely to turn to the best known philosophers of the period: Kant, Fichte, and Hegel. All three did in one way or another support liberalism generally and freedom of thought and expression in particular. It is probably also true that the predominant philosophical influence on the liberalism in nineteenth-century German politics was theirs.[4] However, it is quite doubtful that they achieved genuine theoretical advances in this area (deeply entangled as they indeed were in questionable metaphysics).[5] And it is even more doubtful that the Anglophone liberal tradition ever found much to learn from them (healthily skeptical as it has always been of such metaphysics).

The German thinkers to whom one *should* look for important theoretical advances in this area which proved influential on the Anglophone tradition are instead, I suggest, a roughly contemporary group dominated by

Herder—including, besides Herder himself, Wilhelm von Humboldt, Georg Forster, Schiller, Goethe, and Schleiermacher.[6]

I

J.S. Mill's *On Liberty* clearly owes a large debt to this group of thinkers for its general liberalism.[7] Wilhelm von Humboldt's *Ideas towards an Attempt to Fix the Limits of the State's Operation* was written in 1792, but was only published in German in 1851 and in an English translation in 1854. Mill began writing *On Liberty* in 1854, publishing it in 1859. Both in *On Liberty* itself and in his *Autobiography* (1873) he pays rich tribute to Humboldt's work and to its influence on his own.

In *On Liberty* Mill in particular acknowledges a debt to Humboldt's central principle of *individuality*.[8] In his *Autobiography* he adds Goethe and "a whole school of German authors" as further influences on *On Liberty*'s adoption of this principle of individuality.[9]

Herder is the real father of this ideal of individuality.[10] For, while all the members of the group listed above embraced it, they did so mainly as a result of Herder's leading influence. Herder had from an early period especially championed the individuality of *cultures*—for example, in *This Too a Philosophy of History for the Formation of Humanity* (1774). But he had also championed the individuality of *persons within* a culture—for example, in *On Thomas Abbt's Writings* (1768) and *On the Cognition and Sensation of the Human Soul* (1778).[11] The combined impact of these two Herderian positions was mainly responsible for the deep commitment to individuality that is found in this whole group of thinkers.

However, Mill's debt to these German thinkers in *On Liberty* clearly also extends well beyond this principle of individuality which he explicitly credits to them.[12] Two further examples, both, like the principle of individuality, fundamental to the work's general liberalism: First, Mill mainly applies this principle of individuality in order to justify maximal freedom of *action*.[13] But in doing so he is again following Humboldt. For in his work Humboldt had written that "that on which the whole greatness of a human being in the end rests, for which the individual human being must strive eternally, and which he who wants to affect human beings may never lose sight of, is individuality [*Eigentümlichkeit*] of force and culture," and that "this individuality is effected through freedom of action."[14] (Mill quotes from the former part of this passage, but obscures the latter part,[15] and thereby the identity of Humboldt's argument with his own.)

Second, Mill famously in *On Liberty* articulates what he goes as far as to call the "one very simple principle" which it is "the object of this essay . . . to assert," namely "that the sole end for which mankind are warranted, individually or collectively, in interfering with the liberty of action of any of their number, is self-protection. That the only purpose for which power can be rightfully exercised over any member of a civilized community, against his will, is to prevent harm to others. His own good, either physical or moral, is not a sufficient warrant."[16] Mill disallows treating mere annoyance to others (in contrast to harm) as a ground for interference: "There are many who consider as an injury to themselves any conduct which they have a distaste for, and resent it as an outrage to their feelings . . . But there is no parity between the feeling of a person for his own opinion, and the feeling of another who is offended at his holding it."[17] And he also includes consensual acts between more than one person in the protected sphere: this sphere is one "comprehending all that portion of a person's life and conduct which affects only himself, or if it also affects others, only with their free, voluntary, and undeceived consent and participation."[18] Now this whole principle again comes from Humboldt's work (with only slight modification).[19] Thus Humboldt writes that "every effort of the state is to be rejected to interfere in the private affairs of the citizens anywhere where they do not have immediate relation to the injury of the rights of the one person through the other,"[20] and that "to punish actions which bear solely on the agent or happen with the consent of the person they affect is forbidden by just the same principles which do not even permit them to be limited; and therefore, not only may none of the so-called crimes of the flesh (except rape), whether they annoy or not, attempted suicide, etc. be punished, but even the murder of another person with his consent would have to remain unpunished were it not that in this last case the too easy possibility of a dangerous misuse made a punishing law necessary."[21]

In this particular case the ulterior debt via Humboldt to Herder is weaker than in the case of individualism, but it is still significant. For, while one side of Herder is at odds with Humboldt's position here, namely a side which, insofar as it endorses the state, conceives the state in more paternalistic terms, for example as having some of the functions of a modern welfare state, another side of Herder very much anticipates Humboldt's position, and probably helped to inspire it, namely passages in which Herder looks forward to a sort of withering away of the state.[22]

This whole situation surely suggests the possibility that *On Liberty* may owe even *further* debts to the German thinkers in question which Mill fails to acknowledge explicitly. In this essay I want to argue that that is indeed the case, particularly in connection with the work's arguments for *freedom of thought and expression.*

II

As I read Mill's *On Liberty*, the work gives four main arguments for freedom of thought and expression, which can be roughly summarized as follows: (1) The "one very simple principle" protects all thought, and thereby, due to an intimate connection between thought and expression, virtually all expression too. (2) Freedom of thought and expression is necessary in order to make possible progress in knowledge of truth and avoidance of error. (3) Freedom of thought and expression is necessary for individualism. (4) Freedom of thought and expression is necessary for autonomy and hence for (moral) excellence. (Officially, these arguments are all supposed to be subsumable under a higher utilitarian principle of maximizing happiness.)

It seems to me that all four of these arguments are indebted to the Herderian tradition, which moreover in certain respects develops them in ways that are superior to Mill's. In order to show this, let me consider each of them in turn.

Mill's first argument goes like this: He argues that, since thought is purely inner, the "one very simple principle" that only harm to others can justify limiting a person's freedom guarantees complete freedom of thought. He then adds that this entails that freedom of expression is guaranteed as well because freedom of expression is "practically inseparable" from freedom of thought.[23]

We have already seen one important respect in which this argument is indebted to the Herderian tradition: namely, for the "one very simple principle," which Mill borrows from Humboldt. But I would like now to focus on a further debt.

What is the basis of Mill's claim that freedom of expression is "practically inseparable" from freedom of thought? That they *are* practically inseparable is by no means obvious. Locke, for example, had argued that, at least on certain matters, freedom of thought ought to be allowed but freedom of public expression not.[24]

Part of Mill's implicit answer to this question seems to lie in a plausible thesis that agility in thought is causally dependent on practice in linguistic expression. In this spirit, he notes in his *Autobiography* that "among the ordinary English . . . the habit of not speaking to others, nor much even to themselves, about the things in which they do feel interest, causes . . . their intellectual faculties to remain undeveloped."[25]

A further part of Mill's answer can be seen from his *System of Logic* (1843). On a standard Enlightenment model of the relation between thought and linguistic expression (assumed by Locke, for example), they had been conceived in sharply dualistic terms: thought was (at least in principle) capable of occurring in complete separation and autonomy from linguistic expression, and the latter was merely a contingent means for its communication, perhaps indeed a radically inadequate one. On such a model, it would naturally seem that (at least in principle) thought might quite well go its own merry way whithersoever it liked without linguistic expression even needing to occur at all, let alone in similar ways. However, in his *System of Logic* Mill rejects that standard Enlightenment view, committing himself instead to a contrary principle that thought is deeply dependent on and bounded by linguistic expression.[26]

Now it seems to me that here again Mill's argument is deeply indebted to the Herderian tradition. Herder and his tradition had certainly already recognized the *causal* principle to which Mill appeals. For example, Herder's essay *On the Ability to Speak and to Hear* (1795) is full of this principle.[27]

But more strikingly, it was also Herder and his tradition who had introduced the revolutionary principle, sharply at odds with most of the Enlightenment, that thought is deeply dependent on and bounded by linguistic expression. To quote one of Herder's early statements on this subject, from his *Fragments on Recent German Literature* (1767–8): language is "the form of cognition, not merely in which but also in accordance with which thoughts take shape, where in all parts of literature thought sticks to expression, and forms itself in accordance with this . . . Language sets limits and contour for all human cognition."[28]

Moreover, Herder had himself already pointed out precisely the sort of consequence of these two principles for freedom of expression to which Mill implicitly appeals, namely that facility in thought requires facility in linguistic expression, so that in order for the former to be really free the latter must be so as well. For example, in *On the Ability to Speak and to Hear* Herder writes in that vein:

Hagedorn says: whoever may think freely, thinks well. Ought one not to say with equal right: "Whoever *can* and *may* speak correctly, purely, appropriately, forcefully, concisely, cannot but think well"? If the language of a human being, of a human society, is sluggish, hard, confused, forceless, indeterminate, uncultured, then certainly the mind of these human beings is so too, for of course they think only in and with language.[29]

Nor did Herder and his tradition merely develop these considerations *first*; they also did so *more deeply* than Mill. Unlike Mill, Herder has sophisticated and compelling arguments for the principle of thought's deep dependence on and boundedness by language. In particular, he grounds it on an equally important and revolutionary further principle which he introduces, namely that meanings or concepts are to be identified—not, as many previous philosophers had believed, with such items, independent of language, as the referents involved, Platonic forms, or mental "ideas," but—with *usages of words* (a further principle for which he in turn develops several subtle and plausible arguments).[30]

Besides thus providing deep arguments for this principle which are missing from Mill's case, Herder also supplies something else that is missing from it. Mill's insight into thought's dependence on and boundedness by language might reasonably still leave one asking the following question: Granted that linguistic expression is required for thought in this way, why could it not take the form of merely *private* linguistic expression? Why is it not compatible with refraining from expressing oneself to *other people*? Unlike Mill, Herder has an answer to this question. Already in his *Treatise on the Origin of Language* (1772) he argues plausibly that linguistic expression has a social *telos*. And in later works such as *On the Cognition and Sensation of the Human Soul* (1778) he plausibly adds that linguistic expression's very foundation is social as well.[31]

One reason why this second debt in Mill's argument deserves special emphasis is the following. As has sometimes been pointed out by critics,[32] Mill's argument is problematic: If thought seems to be protected by the "one very simple principle" because it is purely inner, but then on closer scrutiny turns out to be inseparable from expression, which is not purely inner and so may well harm others, is not the proper conclusion to draw that freedom of thought is after all *not* protected by the principle *either* (rather than that, because it is, and because expression is inseparable from thought, freedom of expression is so as well)?[33] This problem indeed even threatens to undermine the "one very simple principle" itself, namely by calling into doubt whether there are any significant general categories of activity which it would protect after all.[34] However, even if Mill's argument does succumb to this problem, and indeed even if this problem (or another one) does damn the "one very simple principle" itself, he has still made one very important and plausible point here, namely that because thought and expression are "practically inseparable," the right to freedom of thought either stands or falls together with a right to freedom of expression, so that anything which really does establish the former thereby also establishes some version of the latter. For there may well be other considerations besides the "one very simple principle" which establish the right to freedom of thought, and whose extension in this manner to establish a right of freedom of expression does *not*, like the attempt so to extend the "one very simple principle," prove self-defeating. Examples might be the arguments for freedom of thought from *individuality* and *autonomy* to be discussed below, or the simpler consideration (also discussed below) that freedom of thought is just *intrinsically valuable*.

Mill's second, and perhaps central, argument for freedom of thought and expression in *On Liberty* is a quite different one. Famously, it is that freedom of thought and expression are vitally important because they make possible *progress in knowledge of truth and avoidance of error*.

Mill assumes that human cognition is of its nature profoundly fallible. Given this assumption, he identifies several main ways in which freedom of thought and expression are essential for advancing knowledge of truth and avoidance of error: (1) Both the genesis and the communication of new truths require that inquirers be and feel free to think and express them. Thus Mill writes that "genius can only breathe freely in an *atmosphere* of freedom,"[35] and that denying people freedom is robbing mankind of the opportunity to exchange error for truth.[36] (2) Free criticism and controversy are required in order to expose and correct old errors.[37] (3) Free testing of the truth by criticisms and even errors is necessary in order for people's grasp of it to achieve clear understanding, sureness, and vitality.[38]

Now it is a striking fact that Herder had already argued for freedom of thought and expression in almost exactly the same terms. Thus, Mill's assumption of the deep fallibility of human cognition was also Herder's.[39] And like Mill, Herder on the basis of this assumption gave the above three arguments for the vital importance of freedom of thought and expression for advancing knowledge of truth and avoidance of error: (1) Like Mill, he emphasized the importance of such freedom for the genesis and communication of new truths.[40] (2) Like Mill, he emphasized its importance for eliminating errors through criticism.[41] (3) Finally, like Mill, he emphasized the vital importance of a free testing of the truth through criticisms and errors for any clear understanding and sure grasp of it.[42] A more compressed form of Herder's case for freedom of thought and expression can also be found in Forster and Humboldt.[43]

One cannot be certain of an influence here. It is possible that Mill simply came up with the same line of argument independently of Herder and his tradition. Also, there are even earlier sources of such a line of argument which might have influenced Mill (and Herder too). One is Milton's *Areopagitica* (1644).[44] Another is Helvétius.[45] Nonetheless, I suspect that Herder and his tradition *did* influence Mill here.[46]

However, Herder's case is again not only prior but also arguably superior to Mill's in certain ways. Mill does not offer the above considerations in an a priori spirit. Rather, that freedom of thought and expression is important for advancing knowledge and avoiding error is for him basically an empirical claim made in the light of historical evidence, the above considerations constituting his explanation of why the empirically observable connection has obtained and can be expected to obtain in the future.[47] Accordingly, in *On Liberty* he adduces three historical examples of periods in which he alleges that freedom of thought and expression proved fecund for new ideas: the post-Reformation period, the second half of the eighteenth century on the Continent, and the Goethe-Fichte period in Germany.[48]

He implies that in contrast the ancient republics did not respect freedom generally, or the freedom of thought and expression in particular, instead requiring individuals to conform to their notion of social excellence.[49] In this connection he cites the case of Socrates, whose death sentence illustrates that "we do not now inflict so much evil on those who think differently from us, as it was formerly our custom to do."[50]

This whole part of Mill's case is problematic.[51] There are four main problems with it. The first two concern the modern periods mentioned by Mill, for it is by no means clear that these support his claim of a correlation between freedom of thought and expression, on the one hand, and advances in knowledge of truth and avoidance of error, on the other. First, concerning the post-Reformation period (and especially the scientific revolution), while there are some cases that favor Mill's claim, such as Boyle and Newton, what about such cases as Copernicus, Galileo, and Descartes, all of whom rather accomplished what they accomplished in the face of persecution for their thought and expression?

Second, the Goethe-Fichte period in Germany is a strangely equivocal case for Mill to appeal to. For, on the one hand, it is not exactly clear that major advances in knowledge of truth were achieved then, at least in the natural sciences (Goethe can no doubt wave the human intermaxillary bone in feeble triumph, but really . . .). And on the other hand, this was anyway by no means a period of unbridled freedom of thought and expression.[52]

Third, *On Liberty*'s negative assessment of the ancient republics seems both factually false and a huge missed opportunity for its empirical case: Athens in its heyday was in fact strongly and self-consciously committed to the ideal of individual freedom, including freedom of thought and expression (as can be seen from Pericles' Funeral Speech, for example). Nor does Socrates' trial constitute convincing evidence to the contrary: Socrates was a principled enemy of democracy,[53] and of freedom, including freedom of expression in particular.[54] Also, he had mentored two of the leaders of the recent anti-democratic, anti-liberal putsch by the Thirty Tyrants (Critias and Charmides). And it seems pretty clear that his trial was basically punishment for these political positions and activities (conducted under the cover of specious charges trumped up due to an amnesty which had prohibited prosecution for aiding the Thirty

Tyrants).[55] Moreover, the fact that classical Athens was normally a committed champion of freedom of thought and expression opens up a vital opportunity for someone like Mill who is seeking an empirical correlation between freedom of thought and expression, on the one hand, and advances in knowledge of truth and avoidance of error, on the other. For what richer source of such advances (in science, philosophy, history, politics, art, etc.) could one think of than Athens in the classical period?[56]

Fourth, in order to make a convincing empirical case, Mill would have had to show, not only that freedom of thought and expression was historically correlated with advances in knowledge of truth and avoidance of error, but also that its *absence* was historically correlated with the *absence* of such advances. But he fails to do this.

Now Herder's position in this whole area had been significantly different from, and far more plausible than, Mill's. In his *Dissertation on the Reciprocal Influence of Government and the Sciences* (1780) Herder too had sought to develop an empirical case for a connection between freedom (of thought and expression) and advances in knowledge of truth and avoidance of error. But his case has marked advantages over Mill's:

First, Herder is well aware of the sort of prima facie counterevidence from the post-Reformation period that I recently mentioned poses a problem for Mill (Copernicus, Galileo, and Descartes).[57]

Second, nor is Herder tempted to misrepresent the Goethe-Fichte period as clear evidence for the connection. For one thing, he has a humbler and more realistic assessment of the advances in knowledge achieved in this period than Mill does.[58] For another thing, he is innocent of Mill's illusion that this is a period of great freedom of thought and expression.[59]

Third (and most importantly), Herder recognizes that classical Athens was committed to freedom, including freedom of thought and expression, and he uses the correlation between this freedom and the great Athenian advances in knowledge as his central piece of empirical evidence. For example, he writes in his essay:

It is evident that the specifically Greek sciences and arts, unsurpassed by those of any other age or peoples after more than two thousand years, have been daughters of Greek legislation, Greek political institutions, and especially of Greek freedom.[60]

Fourth (and relatedly), Herder complements his more plausible case for a correlation between freedom of thought and expression and advances in knowledge of truth and avoidance of error with a plausible case for a correlation between its *absence* and the *absence* of such advances. For in his essay, he argues plausibly that with the curtailing of such freedom in Athens toward the end of the fourth century BC, the sciences (and arts) lost their vitality, and that this sorry combination continued during the Roman period.[61]

The jury should perhaps still be out on the question of whether or not there is a strong empirical correlation between freedom of thought and expression, on the one hand, and advances in knowledge of truth and avoidance of error, on the other. But Herder at least makes a much more compelling case for such a correlation than Mill does.

An additional arguable superiority of Herder's case over Mill's can be seen from the passages recently quoted from Herder as well: Unlike Mill, Herder embeds his argument in support of the importance of freedom of thought and expression for advancing knowledge of truth and avoidance of error within a broader argument in support of its importance for cultural progress more generally ("sciences *and arts*"). Progress in the arts is not (primarily) a matter of progress in knowing truths and avoiding errors, but is it not (virtually) as valuable, and is it not equally dependent on freedom of thought and expression (as the case of classical Athens again illustrates)?

A third argument for freedom of thought and expression which Mill gives draws on the principle of *individuality* discussed earlier. Mill primarily bases his case for freedom of thought and expression on the other arguments considered above, and then invokes the ideal of individuality as a reason for protecting freedom of *action* as well. However, it is probable that he here means freedom of "action" in a broad sense that *includes* freedom of thought and expression, so that he is (among other things) implying a self-standing argument for freedom of thought and expression based on the ideal of individuality. (Thus it is in this context that he writes that "genius can only breathe freely in an *atmosphere* of freedom."[62]) And it is at least clear that this *should* be his position.[63]

Now not only had Humboldt, inspired by Herder, already developed the ideal of individuality to which Mill is appealing here, and Mill's primary application of it to argue for freedom of action (as we saw), but he had also already developed this Millian application of it to argue for freedom of thought and expression. Thus Humboldt argues in his essay that free inquiry is vital for producing "self-activity," "autonomy" in thought and action,[64] and that individualities require a free reciprocal self-revelation to and influencing of one another for their development.[65] Such an argument can also be found in Herder. For example, in *On the Ability to Speak and to Hear* he writes that people who are not permitted to speak and hear about subjects inevitably have souls which remain "unpolished and clumsy in these areas," whereas "every lover of the *individuality* [*Eigentümlichkeit*] of human thoughts proceeded on this path; indeed every human being who wants to become truly and many-sidedly cultured [*gebildet*] knows no other."[66]

Finally, Mill in *On Liberty* has a fourth argument for freedom of thought and expression, closely connected with, but distinguishable from, his argument from individuality: such freedom is required for *autonomy*,[67] which is in turn required for (moral) excellence. Mill articulates this argument in the course of paying tribute to Humboldt.[68]

Mill is here once again drawing on an argument from the Herderian tradition, namely an argument to the effect that freedom of thought (and expression) is a precondition of the sort of autonomy in decision-making that is required for genuine moral virtue (or for that matter, vice); so that, since genuine moral virtue is of immense positive value, freedom of thought (and expression) is so as well. This argument is salient in Forster and Humboldt. For example, Forster writes in support of freedom of thought and expression that "*self-determination*, or in other words moral freedom, is the sole possible source of human virtue, and all the functions of the laws . . . must limit themselves exclusively to its protection."[69] Similarly, as we saw, Humboldt argues in the essay already discussed that free inquiry is essential for producing "self-activity" and "autonomy" in thought and action. And in a slightly earlier essay, *On Religion* (1789), he argues more elaborately that freedom of thought (and expression) is vital for generating reflection, self-consistency, and deep grounding in the principles that guide our actions, as well as for self-activity as opposed to reliance on foreign authority; that in these ways it is essential for moral character;[70] and that, since man's very raison d'être lies in his development of moral character, freedom of thought (and expression) is therefore of vital importance too.[71] Here again, though, it is arguably Herder who is the ultimate source of the argument. For already in his *Letters concerning the Study of Theology* from 1780–1 he had written in support of freedom of thought and expression:

Freedom is the foundation stone . . . of all voluntary virtue in the human heart . . . "But surely a freedom with laws?" Certainly with laws, but ones which the sound understanding recognizes as such, which freedom *elects* for itself.[72]

III

Now that we have seen the great extent to which Mill's arguments for freedom of thought and expression resemble and derive from the Herderian tradition's, it should also be noted that there are several further compelling arguments for freedom of thought and expression which play no significant role in Mill's work but which the Herderian tradition had rightly emphasized.

A first such argument is the extremely simple, but also extremely important, one that freedom of thought and expression should be protected because they are *intrinsically* valuable. I suspect that if one had asked the average ancient Athenian why he valued freedom in general, or freedom of thought and expression in particular, he would have given an answer of just this sort: they are valuable in themselves.[73]

Philosophers often tend to overlook such simple but vitally important possibilities. Mill in *On Liberty* does so in an extreme way, in effect arguing that respect for freedom of thought and expression is required in order to abide by the "one very simple principle," advance knowledge of truth and avoidance of error, promote individuality, establish the autonomy required for (moral) excellence, and via these things maximize human happiness, but *not* that it is valuable in its own right.[74]

By contrast, Herder and his tradition show much more sensitivity to this simple but important argument. For example, Herder writes in such a vein:

Should not . . . precisely in the spirit of the ancients, the voice of each citizen, even assuming that it appeared in print, be considered a freedom of the fatherland, a holy court of ostracism? The poor man was perhaps able to do nothing else than write . . .—do you want to rob the sighing man of his breath that goes forth into desolate emptiness?[75]

A further argument neglected by Mill in *On Liberty* but properly emphasized by the Herderian tradition is that freedom of thought and expression is valuable because it helps to curb tyranny. Predecessors such as Hume had already given an argument of this sort.[76] In *On Liberty* Mill *in a way* accepts it, but he claims that it has become less relevant due to the securely democratic environment of his own day.[77] However, this claim is surely dubious even by his own lights, given his recognition of the importance of *sustaining* democracy, and also his deep concern about democracy's *own* tyrannical potentials.

Herder, by contrast, keeps faith with this important traditional argument. His *Dissertation on the Reciprocal Influence of Government and the Sciences* is especially significant in this connection, for (as the "Reciprocal" hints) he argues there, not only that liberal republicanism benefits freedom of thought and expression and hence the sciences and arts, whereas despotism undermines them, but also that freedom of thought and expression and the consequent health of the sciences and arts benefit liberal republicanism, whereas their absence facilitates despotism: "Free states owe themselves to enlightenment, to science."[78]

A final important line of argument which Mill lacks but which is rightly emphasized by the Herderian tradition concerns, not so much the principle of respecting freedom of thought and expression per se, but rather its extension on an international plane.

Mill's case for respecting freedom, including freedom of thought and expression, does extend beyond national boundaries, but only to a severely limited degree. According to *On Liberty* and *A Few Words on Non-Intervention* (both 1859), a nation must respect the freedom (of thought and expression) of other "civilized" nations, but, in sharp contrast, this does not hold for "barbarians," who should instead be treated with benevolent despotism, or even benevolent aggression. Thus in *On Liberty* Mill writes concerning his "one very simple principle":

[It] is meant to apply only to human beings in the maturity of their faculties. We are not speaking of children . . . For the same reason, we may leave out of consideration those backward states of society in which the race itself may be considered as in its nonage . . . Despotism is a legitimate mode of government in dealing with barbarians, provided the end be their improvement, and the means justified by actually effecting that end. Liberty, as a principle, has no application to any state of things anterior to the time when mankind have become capable of being improved by free and equal discussion. Until then, there is nothing for them but implicit obedience to an Akbar or a Charlemagne, if they are so fortunate as to find one.[79]

One problem with this position of course lies in its naive faith in the noble motives and the beneficial effects of (a significant number of) colonialists and imperialists. (*A Few Words on Non-Intervention* is a sort of paean to the decent motives and beneficial effects of British colonialism in general and the East India Company in particular, of which Mill was a high-ranking official.[80]) We are unlikely to find this faith plausible today; nor should we.[81] The main problem with Mill's position, though, lies in its insidious conflation of a laudable principle of intervention with a very dubious one, turning on a conflation of importantly different senses of the "civilized"/"barbarous" distinction. To the extent that Mill conceives this distinction as something like a distinction between, on the one hand, nations in which people's basic freedoms are protected or at least not habitually and severely violated, and on the other hand, nations in which they *are* habitually and severely violated, his principle concerning intervention seems defensible, and indeed important. After all, *shouldn't* we have intervened coercively in Rwanda? The problem is that he runs together with such a conception of the distinction something much more like a distinction between nations which share our European culture and nations which do not, and in consequence turns his principle of intervention into one that would warrant our riding roughshod, not only over the freedom (of thought and expression) enjoyed by Rwanda's murderous thugs and their ilk, but equally over that enjoyed by, say, the Amazonian shaman and his tribe as they rather harmlessly go about their own quirky business and beliefs.[82]

Herder's position is strikingly different and much more attractive. He is quite properly very cynical about both the underlying motives and the effects of European colonialism (especially British colonialism, including in particular that of the East India Company).[83]

Moreover, he has a much more attractive position on the question of intervention than Mill does. On the one hand, he preserves, but also improves on, the good side of Mill's position, in his *Adrastea* (1801–4) approving of intervention in foreign nations in order to stop native oppression there in principle, but also entering the strong caveat that such intervention usually in practice substitutes even *worse* oppression and so proves unjustified.[84] On the other hand, he entirely avoids the pernicious side of Mill's principle of intervention (its sanctioning of intervention in non-oppressive but culturally "backward" nations). For, as I mentioned earlier, he is at least as concerned to protect *cultural* individualism as the individualism of persons within a culture, and accordingly, he extends his defense of freedom of thought and expression to intercultural cases, arguing quite as strongly against the coercive interference by one culture in another's thought and expression as he does against a single state's or culture's interference in that of its own members. For example, he writes in the *Letters for the Advancement of Humanity*:

What, generally, is a foisted, foreign culture, a formation that does not develop out of [a people's] own dispositions and needs? It oppresses and deforms, or else it plunges straight into the abyss. You poor sacrificial victims who were brought from the South Sea Islands to England in order to receive culture—you are symbols of the good that Europeans communicate to other peoples generally![85]

This, then, is a further respect in which the Herderian tradition's case for freedom of thought and expression is fuller and deeper than Mill's.

IV

Someone might perhaps grant all that I have said so far but still want to argue that there remain some important and valuable features of Mill's case for freedom of thought and expression which are absent from the Herderian tradition's case. However, I am skeptical, and would therefore like now to conclude by briefly discussing some of the potential candidates.

One obvious candidate is the fact that Mill ultimately subsumes the sorts of considerations that were discussed earlier under a utilitarian umbrella. Thus after presenting his "one very simple principle," he goes on to note: "It is proper to state that I forgo any advantage which could be derived to my argument from the idea of abstract right, as a thing independent of utility. I regard utility as the ultimate appeal on all ethical questions; but it must be utility in the largest sense, grounded on the permanent interests of man as a progressive being."[86] One can reasonably infer that he officially takes the same view of the other considerations to which his arguments for freedom of thought and expression appeal as well: knowledge of truth and avoidance of error, individualism, and autonomy. Ultimately, all of these receive their authority from the higher court of utility.[87]

This certainly constitutes a *difference* between Mill and the Herderian tradition (which tends to be quite skeptical about forms of utilitarianism). But it seems highly doubtful that it constitutes a point of *superiority* on Mill's side, and much more likely that it constitutes one of *inferiority*.

One obvious reason for this is the dubiousness of utilitarianism itself (though this is too large a topic to go into here). Another reason is the tenuousness of Mill's assumption that the several factors to which he appeals more directly—the "one very simple principle," knowledge of truth and avoidance of error, individualism, and autonomy—can all ultimately be warranted in utilitarian terms, that is, as requirements for maximizing happiness. Prima facie at least, that seems unlikely. Thus, as C.L. Ten has argued, the idea that utility would justify (unrestricted) commitment to the "one very simple principle" seems implausible.[88] And as Nietzsche memorably pointed out, the assumption that knowledge of truth and avoidance of error serve utility seems dubious as well.[89] And similar points apply to individualism and autonomy.[90]

Mill has a standard twofold strategy in this area, which might be characterized, a little unsympathetically, as follows: first (assuming an intuitive sense of "happiness") argue that the factor in question is justified by its serving happiness *instrumentally*, but then (in case that seems doubtful) shift to a thesis that the factor in question is instead or also an essential *constituent* of happiness (conceived now in a less intuitive sense). For example, in this spirit he both argues that individuality is required for "experiments in living" which make possible the maximization of happiness in the long run, and that it is an essential constituent of genuine happiness ("one of the principal ingredients of human happiness, and quite the chief ingredient of individual and social progress").[91] There need be no inconsistency in such a combination of positions; they could be married. The real problem with it is rather that the former (instrumental) arguments turn out to look very dubious (as has already been mentioned), while the latter (constitutive) claims turn utilitarianism into little more than a misleading reformulation of a traditional pluralism about values.[92]

The fact that Mill commits himself to an ulterior utilitarian framework in his arguments, whereas the Herderian tradition does not but instead rests content with a frank commitment to a plurality of values and with framing its arguments in terms of these, therefore in the end constitutes, not a point of superiority in Mill's case, but rather yet another point of inferiority.[93]

A further area where someone might suspect an important difference between Mill's position and the Herderian tradition's position which tells in Mill's favor is the following. Famously, Mill is not only or even primarily concerned with restrictions on freedom of thought and expression (or on freedom generally) by *authoritarian* governments, but also and especially by *democracies*: the sort of "tyranny of the majority" of which de Tocqueville had already written in *Democracy in America*. Does *this* not distinguish Mill sharply from the Herderian tradition to his advantage?

The answer is No. Herder is just as much in favor of republicanism and democracy over other forms of government as Mill is. But he is also like Mill acutely aware of their potentials for tyranny. For example, in the *Ideas for the Philosophy of History of Humanity* he says that it was understandable that, having tried out all sorts of other constitutions, people in more modern times returned to hereditary rulers, "for the tyranny of the aristocrats is a hard tyranny and *the commanding people is a true Leviathan*,"[94] and that "the word despotism . . . does not only apply to monarchy but occurs in all misused, ill-administered governments."[95]

Another famous and striking feature of Mill's position is that he does not see the threat to freedom of thought and expression (or to freedom generally) as coming only from *government* but is equally concerned about a threat to it posed by *society*. Is *this* not a point of difference and superiority in comparison with the Herderian tradition?

The answer is again No. For Herder's position is in fact very similar, and indeed in certain ways deeper. Herder is concerned about a societal threat too. For example, in *On the Ability to Speak and to Hear* he discusses differences between "regions [of Germany] where people spoke better because one was allowed to speak, because people knew how to hear without anger" and "others over which a fearful distrust, a deaf-and-dumb confinement of thoughts, spread its dark wings, and a word-shy, timid, so to speak stammering manner of thought held sway," as well as analogous differences between Germany's social classes.[96]

Moreover, Herder identifies some important and interesting types of societal threat which Mill overlooks. In particular, he argues that in certain cases the social conventions governing language itself constitute an unacceptable constraint on expression and hence thought. He focuses on three sorts of cases: First, there are cases in which linguistic conventions are simply too rigid.[97] Second, there are cases in which extraneous languages are accorded privileges over a native language—as Herder (correctly) believed occurred with Latin and French in relation to German in the Germany of his day.[98] Third, there are cases in which extraneous languages excessively influence a native language—as Herder (plausibly) believed also occurred with Latin and French in relation to German in his day.[99]

Clearly, there has to be *some* level of conformity to (shared) linguistic rules in order for there to be a (shared) language at all, and no doubt an even higher level than that minimum can be justified in functional terms. But this does not invalidate Herder's worry, which in effect concerns levels of regulation exceeding these. Why does he find such excess regulation objectionable? One reason, which applies even to the first type of case, is that it inhibits intellectual innovation, including conceptual innovation.[100] Another reason is that (like other constraints on freedom of thought and expression) such excessive regulation of language is often intertwined with, and supportive of, broader exercises of coercive power. This is a major source of his concern about the second and third types of case, in particular about the undue privileges enjoyed by Latin and French in Germany and their undue influence on German.[101]

A final feature of Mill's position to which someone might point as a differentia and virtue over the Herderian tradition's position is Mill's radicalism in his provision for freedom of thought and expression: He protects all thought and most expression as well. By contrast, Herder sometimes seems more cautious. For example, in his *Dissertation on the Reciprocal Influence of Government and the Sciences* he argues that governments may and should impose certain limits on freedom of thought and expression for the greater good.[102] Does this not constitute a difference between Mill and Herder that speaks in Mill's favor?[103]

There *is* a difference here. However, it is less sharp than it may seem, and does not tell clearly in Mill's favor. The following are some points to note in this connection: (i) Herder is normally quite as strident as Mill in his defense of freedom of thought and expression.[104] (ii) Herder's considered view seems to be, like Mill's, that freedom of thought should be entirely unrestricted.[105] (iii) Even Mill imposes some restrictions on expression—for example, disallowing the slandering of a tradesman before an unruly mob gathered outside his house.[106] Indeed, any reasonable position must do so. (iv) The difference between Mill and Herder therefore only concerns *exactly how much* limitation there should be on *expression*. (v) Herder's considered position on this question includes a principle that at least all plain, sincere expressions of (putative) truths should be protected.[107] Mill would agree with that. (vi) The disagreement between them therefore reduces still further to exactly how much limitation there should be on expressions *of other sorts*. (vii) Their main disagreement here concerns Mill's inclination to outlaw only expressions likely to cause immediate, readily identifiable harm (as in the tradesman case), whereas Herder is also inclined to outlaw some that promote immorality or even irreligion.[108] But is this so clearly a virtue on Mill's side? Perhaps not. For one thing, Mill is himself torn about the matter—for example, he seems inclined to ban procuring.[109] For another thing, it is not obvious that there should *not* be a ban on certain forms of expression promoting immorality (even if we may not agree with all of Herder's candidates).

V

In sum, many central aspects of Mill's justly celebrated case for freedom of thought and expression in *On Liberty* were originally developed by Herder and his tradition, and in certain respects in a superior form; in addition, there are further important and valuable arguments preserved or developed by Herder and his tradition which Mill neglects or rejects; and moreover, there is little if anything of importance and value in Mill's case that had *not* already been articulated by Herder and his tradition.

Reflecting back on the points made at the start of this essay about the uneasy relation in which recent German philosophy and political history stand to liberalism, and about the suspicions that this uneasy relation gives rise to among Anglophone observers, let me conclude with the following thoughts: Would it not be healthy for German culture and politics if this authentic German contribution to liberalism were better known in Germany? And would it not be healthy for relations between Germany and the Anglophone world if it were better known in the latter too?

Notes

1. For an excellent account of liberalism in this period of German philosophy, see F.C. Beiser, *Enlightenment, Revolution, and Romanticism* (Cambridge, Mass.: Harvard University Press, 1992).

2. Some helpful literature on this subject: J. de Grandvilliers, *Essai sur le libéralisme allemand* (Paris: M. Giara, 1914); J.J. Sheehan, *German Liberalism in the Nineteenth Century* (Chicago: University of Chicago Press, 1978); and R. Hinton Thomas, *Liberalism, Nationalism, and the German Intellectuals (1822–1847)* (Cambridge: W. Heffer, 1951).

   Points similar to the above apply to several further enlightened political ideals as well, such as republicanism, democracy, and cosmopolitanism: A focus on German philosophy and political history in the twentieth century might well, and often does, give the impression that these too are only skin deep in Germany. But classical German philosophy, and to some extent also nineteenth-century politics (for example, the Revolution of 1848), again suggest otherwise.

3. A similar point could probably be made in connection with Locke's liberalism, which likewise owes debts to Germany. For some helpful hints about this, see M. Cranston, "Liberalism," in *The Encyclopedia of Philosophy*, ed. P. Edwards (New York and London: Macmillan/The Free Press, 1967), 4:459.

4. See de Grandvilliers, *Essai sur le libéralisme allemand*, pp. 143–4; G. de Ruggiero, *The History of European Liberalism* (London and New York: Oxford University Press, 1927), pp. 23, 352–3.

5. There is no denying that Kant, Fichte, and Hegel—inspired by the Enlightenment and the French Revolution—all make *freedom* a strikingly central ideal in their philosophies, including their philosophies of politics, law, and society. But, rhetorical support aside, how much do they really accomplish for liberalism?

   Kant's political philosophy bases legislation on a principle of reconciling individuals' freedoms with one another (I. Kant, *The Metaphysics of Morals* [Cambridge: Cambridge University Press, 1996], pp. 30, 112). But Kant faces an embarrassing question here: On a Kantian view, all that legislation could possibly hope to affect or effect is some sort of *phenomenal* freedom. But what relevance does that have for the *noumenal* freedom which, on Kant's official theory, underpins morality and is what really matters? If, on the other hand, in order to avoid this problem, one detaches Kant's idea that the point of legislation is the reconciliation of individuals' freedoms from the official theory that causes the problem, is it any longer really a new idea?

   Kant's main arguments for freedom of thought and expression specifically seem to be threefold: First, this is required for enlightenment, in the sense of thinking for oneself (I. Kant, *What Is Enlightenment?*, in *Kant: On History*, ed. L.W. Beck [Indianapolis: Bobbs-Merrill, 1980], pp. 4–5). Second, it is required for self-government, since enlighten-ment is in its turn required in order to make people competent for self-government (ibid., p. 10). Third, (in the meantime) freedom of expression is required in order to keep authoritarian but benevolent and open-minded rulers adequately informed (I. Kant, *On the Proverb: That May Be True in Theory But Is of No Practical Use*, in *Immanuel Kant: Perpetual Peace and Other Essays*, ed. T. Humphrey [Indianapo-lis: Hackett, 1983], pp. 82–3). The first two of these arguments are sensible but unoriginal. The third is, in its assumption of monarchical benevolence and open-mindedness, and of the consequent efficacy of simply informing a monarch, merely a naive and obsequious variant of a much more plausible and important traditional argument to the effect that part of the value of freedom of thought and expression lies in the constraint which it imposes on arbitrary governmental pow-er (a variant which Kant was evidently seduced into embracing by the limitation of his experience to the very atypical case of Freder-ick the Great, an unusually benevolent and open-minded monarch). On the other hand, Kant *cannot*, it seems, really claim credit for an important argument which has sometimes been credited to him (for example, by B. Mitchell, *Law, Morality, and Religion in a Secular Society* [Oxford: Oxford University Press, 1978], p. 93; cf. J. Gray, *Mill on Liberty: A Defence* [London: Routledge, 1996], p. 78), and which will be considered further later: that freedom of thought and expression is required for autonomy and hence for moral responsibility. Kant did probably influence the general idea here that moral responsibility requires self-given laws. But he also says that the absence of freedom of thought and expression is a "self-incurred tutelage," the result of "laziness and cowardice" (*What Is Enlightenment?*, p. 3), i.e. *already* an exercise of autonomy and hence morally blameworthy.

J.G. Fichte's *Foundations of Natural Right* of 1796–7 (Cambridge: Cambridge University Press, 2000) attempts to establish an elaborate system of liberal rights by showing them all to be "deducible" from the principle of the self's self-positing (itself a sort of freedom). This "deduction"—Fichte's most distinctive theoretical contribution—is extremely implausible. If, on the other hand, one detaches his system of rights, and his detachable arguments for them, from this highly implausible foundation, then they constitute a mixed bag—some conventional others not, some attractive others not.

Concerning freedom of thought and expression in particular, in an early essay, *Demand for the Return of Freedom of Thought from the*

Princes of Europe, who hitherto Suppressed It from 1793 (*J.G. Fichte Gesamtausgabe*, ed. R. Lauth and H. Jacob [Stuttgart–Bad Cannstatt: Frommann, 1964], vol. 1), Fichte maintained that freedom of thought is an inalienable right (pp. 174, 180, 187), and gave several arguments for this: it is purely inner (p. 174), it defines what it is to be a human being (p. 175), and (more specifically) it is part of our rational nature (pp. 182–3). Also, he argued that free expression was a right, derivable from a more basic right each of us has to hear others' opinions (pp. 177, 183). This early position seems very questionable. It relies on a naive theory of natural rights (borrowed uncritically from the French revolutionaries). Also, it raises more questions than it answers. For example, why would pure innerness entail an inalienable right? And even if a measure of freedom in thinking were essential to human nature, or more specifically to rationality, might this not be a measure consistent with all the limitations on freedom of thinking that despots ever want to impose? Later, in the *Foundations of Natural Right* of 1796–7, Fichte takes the starkly different position that there can be no right to freedom of thought (only a duty), since it is something inner beyond the power of others (pp. 51, 102). His reasoning here seems dubious (surely, thought is all too vulnerable to various sorts of coercion by others), and the elimination of any right to freedom of thought retrograde, indeed disastrous. Finally, in an even later period Fichte showed little respect for freedom of thought and expression, instead embracing very paternalistic views. (Concerning this, see I. Berlin, "Two Concepts of Liberty," in his *Liberty* [Oxford: Oxford University Press, 2002], pp. 195–7. Berlin's essay also contains some penetrating criticisms of Kant's and Hegel's forms of liberalism which complement the criticisms sketched here.)

Despite the centrality of a notion of "freedom" in his system, Hegel is not as readily classifiable as a liberal. Still, his recognition of a set of characteristically liberal institutions and rights (for example, protection of property, political representation, separation of church and state, religious toleration, and a significant measure of freedom of thought and expression) does perhaps warrant such a classification. Hegel's overall liberalism is vulnerable to a criticism similar to that just leveled against Fichte's, however. In his *Philosophy of Right* (Oxford: Oxford University Press, 1976) Hegel in effect offers a twofold metaphysical grounding for his system of liberal rights: first, a "deduction" of it from the nature of the will (this is Hegel's counterpart to Fichte's "deduction" from the self's self-positing, by which it was indeed clearly inspired) and, second, a "deduction" of it from the structure of the "Idea" (as expounded in Hegel's *Logic*). Both "deductions" are highly implausible (in the latter case on two levels). If, on the other hand, one detaches Hegel's set of liberal institutions and rights, and his detachable arguments for them, from this dubious foundation, while they certainly then look more sensible, they also form a miscellany of quite variable originality and quality.

This is also true of Hegel's liberalism concerning thought and expression in particular. His metaphysical explanation and justification of this institution is primarily that (like monarchy) it represents the modern state's principle of *subjectivity*, a principle derived from the Idea (*Philosophy of Right*, p. 295). That could only be an impressive rationale if one accepted the strange metaphysics of the Idea. Abstracting from this, his rationale for the institution appeals rather to such diverse and variably impressive considerations as the following: First, free thought and speech are important in order for individuals to come to understand why the legal-ethical principles which they observe deserve recognition (ibid., p. 294). Second, people want some share in debate and decision-making, and will put up with more impositions put upon them if they get it (ibid.). Third, the strong rationality of the modern state can tolerate such freedom, since, and as long as, such freedom remains without any real effect (ibid., pp. 173, 206). The first of these arguments is sensible but unoriginal; the second either sensible but unoriginal or disturbingly cynical, depending on whether the emphasis is on its former half or its latter; the third cynical and unedifying.

In sum, when one sees past their rhetoric and their dubious metaphysics, the liberalisms of Kant, Fichte, and Hegel look startlingly short on substance. Perhaps nineteenth-century German liberalism's lamentable lack of staying power was not unconnected with its tendency to follow these false prophets of liberalism.

6. There are several further subject areas in and connected to philosophy concerning which a similar moral applies. For example, if one is interested in the birth of modern philosophy of language, interpretation theory ("hermeneutics"), translation theory, or anthropology, Kant, Fichte, and Hegel provide rather slim pickings; but if one turns instead to Herder and his group one finds riches.

7. For some suggestive points about the essay's resemblances and debts to the ideas of this group, see F.M. Barnard, *Herder's Social and Political Thought*, pp. 77–8, 167–8.

8. Mill uses a passage from Humboldt on this principle as his motto for *On Liberty*: "The grand, leading principle, towards which every argument unfolded in these pages directly converges, is the absolute and essential importance of human development in its richest diversity" (*The Collected Works of John Stuart Mill* [henceforth: *Collected Works*], ed. J.M. Robson [Toronto and London: University of Toronto Press and Routledge, 1963–91], 18:215). He also explicitly credits Humboldt for this principle in the main body of the work, quoting further passages from Humboldt on it (ibid., pp. 261–2).

9. *Autobiography*, in *The Essential Works of John Stuart Mill*, ed. M. Lerner (New York: Bantam, 1965), p. 150.

10. Since this essay will largely be devoted to tracing Mill's ideas concerning liberty back to Herder, it may be worth noting here at the outset that Mill's *general* philosophical profile strikingly reminds one of Herder's. In addition to the liberalism discussed in this essay, some further areas of striking agreement between Mill and Herder are: empiricism; recognition of thought's intimate dependence on and boundedness by language; sentimentalism in ethics; recognition of the importance of poetry for cultivating the moral sentiments; commitment to republicanism and democracy; feminism; cosmopolitanism; and the ideal of progressing "humanity." How much of this agreement is merely accidental, how much merely the result of shared influences, and how much the result of Herder's (indirect) influence on Mill? The answer is not entirely clear. However, my suspicion is that the role of (indirect) influence is significant. Mill's works contain a number of explicit references to Herder (see the index to *Collected Works*); there are also a fair number of arguable allusions to Herder, including for example the reference just quoted to "a whole school of German authors"; and by Mill's day Herder's influence on European thought had become so widespread that indirect influences are often likely even where Mill was not conscious of them. One example of a case in which a conscious influence can be identified with some confidence: Mill's late ideal of a "religion of humanity," in the sense of a conviction in and commitment to the progressive improvement of humanity over the course of history (*Collected Works*, 10:420 ff.). This ideal has usually been seen as an inheritance from Comte (see e.g. A. Ryan, *J.S. Mill* [London and Boston: Routledge, 1974], ch. 8; G. Himmelfarb, *On Liberty and Liberalism* [San Francisco: ICS Press, 1990], pp. 88 ff.), and no doubt there is much truth in this. But note that Mill was quite critical of Comte's relevant views, and observe that by contrast already in

his essay *Coleridge* from 1840 he praised "that series of great writers and thinkers, from Herder to Michelet, by whom history, which was till then 'a tale told by an idiot, full of sound and fury, signifying nothing,' has been made a science of causes and effects; who, by making the facts and events of the past have a meaning and an intelligible place in the gradual evolution of humanity ["Humanity" is a distinctive and central Herderian term, concept, and ideal.—M.N.F.], have at once given history, even to the imagination, an interest like romance, and afforded the only means of predicting and guiding the future, by unfolding the agencies which have produced, and still maintain, the present" (*Mill's Essays on Literature and Society*, ed. J.B. Schneewind [New York and London: Collier Books, 1965], p. 316; Mill's approving remarks on Herder's philosophy of history continue over pp. 316–17). Indeed, Mill had already alluded approvingly to Herder and his school of historical writing in *The Spirit of the Age* from 1831 (see ibid., p. 52; also, note that the very title of this essay is a Herderian coinage [*Zeitgeist*], and that the essay's relativistic defense of the Middle Ages and criticisms of hereditary monarchy are indebted to Herder's historical writings).

11. For instance, in *On Thomas Abbt's Writings* Herder says that "a human soul is an individual in the realm of minds: it senses in accordance with an individual formation, and thinks in accordance with the strength of its mental organs . . . My long allegory has succeeded if it achieves the representation of the mind of a human being as an individual phenomenon, as a rarity which deserves to occupy our eyes" (*Herder: Philosophical Writings*, p. 167).

12. It was not for nothing that Mill suggested in letters to Gomperz and Ruge that the essay was needed less in Germany "than here" (*Collected Works*, 14:539, 598).

13. *Collected Works*, 18:260 ff.

14. *Wilhelm von Humboldts Gesammelte Schriften* [henceforth: WHGS], ed. A. Leitzmann et al. (Berlin: B. Behr, 1903–), 1:107.

15. *Collected Works*, 18:261. Mill does, however, note that for Humboldt individuality has "two requisites, 'freedom and variety of situations.'"

16. Ibid., p. 223. It is by no means clear that this really is the "one very simple principle" of the essay. For example, what about the recently mentioned ideal of individuality? (In his *Autobiography* Mill indicates that *that* is the "single truth" of which *On Liberty* is "a kind of philosophical textbook" [p. 149].) And what about knowledge of truth (as we will see shortly, another central concern of the essay's)? And what about (moral) autonomy (as we will see later, yet another concern of

the essay's)? And what about the essay's officially overarching principle of utility? Still, the principle in question is at least *an* important principle of the essay's.

17. *Collected Works*, 18:283.

18. Ibid., p. 225.

19. The main modification consists in the fact that whereas Humboldt is exclusively concerned with the right of the *state* to interfere, Mill is also concerned with the right of groups or individuals within a state to do so.

20. WHGS 1:111; cf. 129, 134.

21. WHGS 1:207; cf. 182, 190.

22. See e.g. the following censored and unpublished passage from the *Ideas for the Philosophy of History of Humanity* (1784–91): "The people needs a lord as long as it has no reason of its own. The more it acquires this and knows how to govern itself, the more the government must soften or finally disappear. The noblest purpose of government is therefore that it become dispensable and that each person govern himself" (S13:456).

23. "[Liberty] comprises, first, the inward domain of consciousness; demanding liberty of conscience in the most comprehensive sense; liberty of thought and feeling; absolute freedom of opinion and sentiment on all subjects, practical or speculative, scientific, moral, or theological. The liberty of expressing and publishing opinions may seem to fall under a different principle, since it belongs to that part of the conduct of an individual which concerns other people; but, being almost of as much importance as the liberty of thought itself, and resting in great part on the same reasons, is practically inseparable from it . . . From [the liberty of thought] it is impossible to separate the cognate liberty of speaking and of writing" (*Collected Works*, 18:225–7).

24. J. Locke, *An Essay on Toleration*, in his *Political Essays,* ed. M. Goldie (Cambridge: Cambridge University Press, 2000), pp. 141–2.

25. *Autobiography*, p. 43. Similarly, in *Grote's History of Greece [II]* (1853) Mill approvingly quotes Grote's opinion that the distinctive ancient Greek tradition of public speaking was an essential causal factor in the extraordinary development of ancient Greek thought (*Collected Works*, 11:297–8).

26. Thus Mill begins the book with a chapter significantly titled "Of the necessity of Commencing with an Analysis of Language" in which he argues that so commencing is necessary because (1) "reasoning, or inference . . . is an operation which usually takes place by means of words, and in complicated cases can take place in no other way,"

and especially (2) "a proposition . . . is formed by putting together two names . . . , is *discourse, in which something is affirmed or denied of something*" (*Collected Works*, 7:19–21).

27. Kant articulates a version of it in *What Does it Mean to Orient Oneself in Thinking?* (1786) as well, very likely under Herder's influence (Kant had published two reviews of Herder's *Ideas for the Philosophy of History of Humanity* shortly before, in 1784–5).

28. G1:556–7. Several other thinkers in the Herderian tradition embraced versions of this principle as well, including Humboldt and Schleiermacher. For a discussion of the history of this principle, see Essays 2 and 3, and *German Philosophy of Language*, Essay 8.

29. S18:384–5; cf. 386–7.

30. See Essays 2 and 3.

31. Herder does not, indeed, advance the latter thesis in the very strong form which some subsequent thinkers have given it—e.g. Hegel, later Wittgenstein, Kripke, and Burge, all of whom have argued in one way or another that communal language-use is *essential* to linguistic meaning. Rather, he advances it as a simple claim of causal dependence. However, this may well in the end put him on firmer philosophical ground than they are on. And even in this modest form, his thesis can serve to plug the gap in Mill's case mentioned above.

32. e.g. J.W.N. Watkins, "John Stuart Mill and the Liberty of the Individual," in *Political Ideas*, ed. D. Thomson (Harmondsworth: Watts, 1975), pp. 159–60.

33. It is indeed tempting to accuse Mill of an outright inconsistency in the argument: in order to justify freedom of thought, he starts out assuming a conventional Enlightenment picture of thought as radically inner, but then, in order to extend his argument to justify freedom of expression as well, he assumes a quite contrary picture of thought as deeply dependent on outer expression.

34. The principle may well be problematic for other reasons too—for example, the notorious difficulty of defining its notion of "harm" satisfactorily.

35. *Collected Works*, 18:267. Mill had already developed this point much more fully in *Grote's History of Greece [II]* (1853) (*Collected Works*, 11:320–1).

36. *Collected Works*, 18:229.

37. Ibid., pp. 231–3.

38. Ibid., pp. 229, 243–52, 258.

39. For example, in the *Ideas for the Philosophy of History of Humanity* Herder argues that just as we only learn to walk by falling so we only progress towards the truth through error (G6:145).

40. For example, in the *Letters for the Advancement of Humanity* (1793–7) Herder writes: "Should not . . . the voice of each citizen, even assuming that it appeared in print, be considered a freedom of the fatherland . . . ? . . . [Especially] valuable for the man of understanding are the hints and looks of those who see further. They inspire to activity when everyone is asleep; they sigh perhaps when everyone is dancing. But they do not only sigh; they show higher results in simpler equations by means of a certain art. Do you want to make them be silent because you calculate merely according to the common arithmetic? They go silent easily and continue to calculate; but the fatherland counted on these quiet calculators. *A single* step of progress that they successfully indicated is worth more than ten thousand ceremonies and eulogies" (*Herder: Philosophical Writings*, pp. 376–7).

41. For example, in the *Letters for the Advancement of Humanity* Herder writes: "Free investigation of the truth from all sides is the sole antidote against delusion and error of whatever sort they may be . . . The river current of human cognition always purifies itself through oppositions, through strong contrasts. Here it breaks off, there it starts; and in the end a long and much-purified delusion is regarded by human beings as truth" (ibid., pp. 370–1). Cf. Herder's point there in support of "the communication of thoughts" that "the mistake gets discovered, the error gets corrected" (ibid.); also, S18:385 and S24:92–3.

42. For example, in the *Letters for the Advancement of Humanity* Herder writes: "Let the deluded person defend his delusion, the person who thinks differently his thought; that is *their* business. Even if both of them fail to be corrected, for the unbiased person there certainly arises out of every criticized error a new reason, a new view of the truth" (*Herder: Philosophical Writings*, p. 370). Cf. *On the Ability to Speak and to Hear*, where he notes in support of freedom of expression: "We see everywhere that men in whom there was a great drive to become acquainted with the truth from *all* sides sought even on remote sides intercourse with people *who dared to speak freely*" (S18:386). Cf. also S24:92.

43. For example, Forster writes in his *Fragment of a Letter to a German Author on Schiller's "Gods of Greece"* (1789): "If there is a universal truth which is to be acknowledged by all then no other path leads

to it but this: that each person says and defends what *seems* to him to be the truth. From the free expression of all diverse opinions, and their equally free testing, it is inevitable that in the end—to the extent that this limited, shortsighted species is capable of such a cognition at all—the pure truth will emerge as a result intelligible and welcome to each sense, filling each sense, will be *voluntarily* accepted by all, and will then govern us in peace alone" (G. Forster, *Werke in vier Bänden* [henceforth: Forster, *Werke*], ed. G. Steiner [Frankfurt am Main: Insel, 1967–70], 3:33). Similarly, Humboldt in the work already cited notes that part of the "harm of limiting freedom of thought" concerns "the results of inquiry," "incompleteness or incorrectness in our scientific cognition" (WHGS 1:160).

44. Milton's *Areopagitica* had already made the cause of knowing truth and avoiding error the core of its case for freedom of thought and expression, and had indeed already developed versions of points (1)–(3). See J. Milton, *Areopagitica*, in his *Areopagitica and Of Education*, ed. K.M. Lea (Oxford: Clarendon Press, 1973), esp. pp. 5, 23, 32–3, 40 for (1); pp. 14, 35–6, 41 for (2); and pp. 29–30, 41 for (3).

45. Helvétius had already argued for freedom of thought and expression in terms of its necessity for discovery of the truth, and had (in still closer anticipation of Mill) added that discovery of the truth was important because it promoted human happiness. See K. Martin, *French Liberal Thought in the Eighteenth Century* (Boston: Little, Brown, and Co., 1929), pp. 184–5.

46. The closest thing to direct evidence of this that I have found occurs in Mill's essay *Coleridge* (1840), where he explicitly discusses Herder and his tradition, and where he writes: "Among the truths long recognized by Continental philosophers, but which very few Englishmen have yet arrived at, one is, the importance, in the present imperfect state of mental and social science, of antagonistic modes of thought; which, it will one day be felt, are as necessary to one another in speculation, as mutually checking powers are in a political constitution. A clear insight, indeed, into this necessity, is the only rational or enduring basis of philosophical tolerance; the only condition under which liberality in matters of opinion can be anything better than a polite synonym for indifference between one opinion and another" (*Mill's Essays on Literature and Society*, p. 295).

47. This is an example of the "inverse deductive method" which Mill advocates for the social sciences—that is, a method in which a law is first suggested by some factual evidence that it is adduced to explain

but then verified by reference to higher-level law(s) (see Mill, *System of Logic*, in *Collected Works*, 8:911 ff.). In the spirit of this method, Mill praises de Tocqueville for combining, on the one hand, a reliance on empirical evidence with, on the other hand, an "a priori" explanation of the phenomena thus empirically discovered (meaning by this, roughly, an explanation in terms of general psychological laws) (*Mill's Ethical Writings*, ed. J.B. Schneewind [New York and London: Collier Books, 1965], p. 108).

48. *Collected Works*, 18:243.

49. Ibid., p. 226.

50. Ibid., p. 241. Cf. p. 235.

51. Its weakness was already perceived by one of Mill's earliest critics, James Stephen, who in his *Liberty, Equality, Fraternity* (repr. Indianapolis: Liberty, 1993) argued that commitment to, and success in, discovering truth have been at least as common in societies which have lacked freedom of thought and expression as in ones which have enjoyed it.

52. Think, for example, of Fichte's *Atheismusstreit*, Herder's struggles with the censors when writing his *Ideas for the Philosophy of History of Humanity* and *Letters for the Advancement of Humanity*, and Kant's problems with censorship in connection with his *Religion within the Bounds of Reason Alone*.

53. For example, in Plato's *Apology* and *Crito* Socrates argues that in matters of virtue it is the advice of the one or few experts, not that of the many, which should be followed; and in the latter work he holds up Sparta and Crete, two of the most authoritarian states in the Greek world, as his models of good government.

54. For example, in Plato's *Apology* Socrates champions a principle of obedience to betters; Xenophon reports revealingly on his special liking for the Thersites episode in the *Iliad*; and Plato's *Republic* depicts him discussing freedom, including freedom of speech, in the most disparaging terms (557b–c).

55. For a plausible historical argument along these general lines, see I.F. Stone, *The Trial of Socrates* (Boston and Toronto: Little, Brown, and Co., 1988). Stone is not a professional classicist or classical philosopher, but his book is much more illuminating than most of the more professional literature on this topic (e.g. work by Kraut and Vlastos).

56. It is one of the mysteries about *On Liberty* that just a little earlier, in the review essay *Grote's History of Greece [II]* (1853), Mill had followed Grote in taking an almost diametrically opposed position on classical Athens—agreeing with Grote, on the basis of such evidence

as Pericles' Funeral Speech, that classical Athens had been emphatically committed to freedom, including freedom of thought and expression, and that it had therefore richly illustrated the value of such freedom for progress in knowledge (*Collected Works*, 11:318–21, 324–5). Why did Mill abandon this earlier, correct position for the incorrect one in *On Liberty*? One factor to consider here is an intervening misinterpretation of the historical Socrates and his trial. It seems that Mill, on the basis of evidence in such dialogues as the *Apology* and the *Phaedo*, arrived at a picture of Socrates as a champion of free thought and expression (see e.g. *Grote's Plato* [1866], in *Collected Works*, 11:424–5). Such a picture is almost certainly a mistake (it is one thing to complain bitterly that people are trying to muzzle you, and to encourage members of your own coterie to challenge your ideas, quite another to be committed to a general principle of freedom of thought and expression). However, given that Mill came to see Socrates in such terms, he would then have been tempted to see the Athenians' trial of Socrates as an attempt to suppress freedom of thought and expression (as he does in *On Liberty*), rather than as the (perhaps misguided) attempt to defend such freedom that it really was. And he would then also, by a further shaky step of inference, have been tempted to see the trial (so interpreted) as reflecting a more general anti-liberal trait in Athenian democracy (as he again does in *On Liberty*).

57. For example, Herder writes in his essay: "The first inventions and experiments were the undertakings of private persons, for genius is fated to make its own way ... Descartes was banished from his fatherland; Copernicus revealed his system of the heavens only on the day of his death; and Galileo had to bear chains because of his discoveries in the heavens" (S9:351).

58. For example, Herder is critical of Goethe's ethical views, has no sympathy with Fichte's theories, and is highly skeptical of Kant's critical philosophy.

59. Herder was himself a victim of censorship, and was acutely aware of its burdens on his fellow Germans at this period. If he was not *entirely* gloomy about it, this was because he believed that the political fragmentation of Germany limited its effectiveness to a local level (see S24:108).

60. *J.G. Herder on Social and Political Culture*, ed. F.M. Barnard (Cambridge: Cambridge University Press, 1969), p. 239. Cf. S9:330. Humboldt too interprets the historical nature of ancient Athens in this more correct way, even overstating the point: the ancients enjoyed "unlimited

freedom of thought, boundless tolerance" (*On Religion* [1789], in WHGS 1:51).

61. *J.G. Herder on Social and Political Culture*, pp. 239–40. Herder also argues (perhaps more questionably) that in the modern period lands in which the Inquisition has been active have seen less scientific advances than lands in which it has not (S9:358).

62. *Collected Works*, 18:229.

63. There is a link between this argument for freedom of thought and expression and the preceding one (concerning knowledge of truth and avoidance of error). For Mill, individuality is in some sense intrinsically valuable, and its intrinsic value justifies the freedom of (action and) thought and expression that is required for its realization. But individuality is also valuable as a means towards discovery of truth (and better ways of living), so that this instrumental value justifies the freedom of (action and) thought and expression that is required for its realization as well. Thus Mill writes that one reason why "individuality is a valuable element in human affairs" is because "there is always need of persons . . . to discover new truths, and point out when what were once truths are true no longer" (ibid., p. 267).

64. WHGS 1:160.

65. WHGS 1:122–3, 128. An argument of this sort is also central to Schleiermacher's essay *Toward a Theory of Sociable Conduct* (1799).

66. S18:386–7.

67. Concerning Mill's commitment to an ideal of autonomy, cf. Gray, *Mill on Liberty: A Defence*, pp. 55, 74 ff. In order to see that the two ideals of individuality and autonomy are distinct, notice that the latter could in principle be achieved even if everyone in fact thought and acted in the same way, whereas the former, individuality, could not.

68. "The human faculties . . . , and . . . moral preference, are exercised only in making a choice. He who does anything because it is the custom, makes no choice. He gains no practice either in discerning or in desiring what is best. The mental and moral, like the muscular powers, are improved only by being used. The faculties are called into no exercise by doing a thing merely because others do it, no more than by believing a thing only because others believe it . . . It really is of importance, not only what men do, but also what manner of men they are that do it. Among the works of man, which human life is rightly employed in perfecting and beautifying, the first in importance surely is man himself. Supposing it were possible to get houses built, corn grown, battles fought, causes tried, and even churches erected

and prayers said, by machinery—by automatons in human form—it would be a considerable loss to exchange for these automatons even the men and women who at present inhabit the more civilized parts of the world, and who assuredly are but starved specimens of what nature can and will produce" (*Collected Works*, 18:262–3).

69. *Fragment of a Letter to a German Author on Schiller's "Gods of Greece,"* in Forster, *Werke*, 3:34.

70. WHGS 1:73–4.

71. WHGS 1:76.

72. S11:202.

73. Cf. R. Rhees, who writes (somewhat overstating the point): "For the man devoted to liberty, there is nothing which *makes* liberty important. And he has no reasons for his devotion" (R. Rhees, *Without Answers* [London: Routledge, 1969], p. 84).

74. In *The Subjection of Women* Mill does come *closer* to giving an argument of the latter sort, pointing out that freedom (of thought and expression) is a basic human want and a part of happiness: "After the primary necessities of food and raiment, freedom is the first and strongest want of human nature . . . He who would rightly appreciate the worth of personal independence as an element of happiness, should consider the value he himself puts upon it as an ingredient of his own" (J.S. Mill, *The Subjection of Women* [Indianapolis: Hackett, 1988], pp. 103–4; cf. *On Liberty*, in *Collected Works*, 18:270). However, as is inevitable given his official utilitarianism, this is still not quite a claim of its intrinsic value, but rather of its value as a means to happiness (albeit a constitutive rather than merely a causal means).

75. *Herder: Philosophical Writings*, p. 376.

76. D. Hume, *Of the Liberty of the Press*, in his *Essays Moral, Political, and Literary*, ed. E.E. Miller (Indianapolis: Liberty, 1985), p. 12. As Himmelfarb notes, Bentham, James Mill, and even the young J.S. Mill himself had all used this argument too (Himmelfarb, *On Liberty and Liberalism*, pp. 33–4).

77. *Collected Works*, 18:228.

78. S9:383.

79. *Collected Works*, 18:224. Cf. *A Few Words on Non-Intervention*: "To go to war for an idea, if the war is aggressive, not defensive, is as criminal as to go to war for territory or revenue; for it is as little justifiable to force our ideas on other people, as to compel them to submit to our will in any other respect. But there assuredly are cases in which it is allowable to go to war, without having been ourselves attacked, or

threatened with attack . . . There is a great difference (for example) between the case in which the nations concerned are of the same, or something like the same, degree of civilization, and that in which one of the parties to the situation is of a high, and the other of a very low, grade of social improvement" (*Collected Works*, 21:118).

80. In a similar spirit, Mill in *Grote's History of Greece |II|* gives a very positive assessment of the motives and effects of ancient Athenian imperialism (*Collected Works*, 11:321 ff.).

81. Concerning effects, one only has to think of the partitioning of India or the present-day misery of black Africa, for example.

82. In this connection, observe how Mill writes about such peoples in his late essays on religion: he speaks of "Patagonians, or Esquimaux, or something nearly as brutal," of "a Bosjesman or an Andaman islander, or something still lower," and opines that "savages are always liars" (*Collected Works*, 10:390, 459, 395).

83. See e.g. *Letters for the Advancement of Humanity*, 10th Collection (in *Herder: Philosophical Writings*); also, S23:496–505.

84. S23:502–3.

85. *Herder: Philosophical Writings*, p. 382. Herder is strongly opposed to interference in other cultures not only by means of brute coercion, but also by means of such subtler instruments as addictions and luxuries. e.g., in *This Too a Philosophy of History for the Formation of Humanity* he writes: "*Whither* do European colonies not *reach*, and whither *will* they not reach! Everywhere the savages, the more they become fond of our brandy and luxury, become *ripe* for our *conversion* too! Everywhere approach, especially through brandy and luxury, *our culture*. Will soon, God help us!, all be human beings *like us*!" (ibid., p. 325).

86. *Collected Works*, 18:224.

87. *On Liberty* itself makes this position fairly clear in connection with individualism and autonomy. Concerning knowledge of truth, note that Mill writes elsewhere: "If religion, or any particular form of it, is true, its usefulness follows without other proof"; "The knowledge of every positive truth is a useful acquisition" (*Collected Works*, 10:403–5).

88. C.L. Ten, "Mill's Defence of Liberty," in *J.S. Mill: On Liberty in Focus*, ed. J. Gray and G.W. Smith (London: Routledge, 1991), esp. p. 213.

89. For example, were not the gentle, anthropomorphizing falsehoods of Greek mythology or Christianity's consoling myths of an afterlife more promotive of happiness than the hard, "disenchanted" truths of modern science?

90. This fact that *On Liberty* appeals to a wide variety of considerations which are not at all easily squared with Mill's official utilitarianism finds a large part of its explanation in the fundamental thesis of the present essay that the work is heavily indebted to multiple arguments drawn from the Herderian tradition.

91. *On Liberty*, in *Collected Works*, 18:261.

92. Concerning the latter problem, cf. Isaiah Berlin's plausible argument that Mill's utilitarianism unwittingly collapses into a form of value-pluralism ("John Stuart Mill and the Ends of Life," in Berlin, *Liberty*, pp. 225 ff.).

93. Two additional observations loosely connected with the preceding: (1) Isaiah Berlin tends to interpret Mill as a pluralist and an open-ended historicist about values, and to see his case for freedom of thought and expression as resting on these positions, and properly so (Berlin, "Two Concepts of Liberty" and "John Stuart Mill and the Ends of Life," both in *Liberty*). However, if there is a good philosophical case of such a sort to be made, it is much less likely to be found in Mill—who is officially neither a pluralist nor an open-ended historicist about values—than in Herder—who is officially both. (2) John Gray has argued that Mill's case for freedom (of thought and expression) founders on the indefensibility of an underlying assumption that he makes of universalism, or precisely *lack* of historicism, in values (Gray, *Mill on Liberty: A Defence*, "Postscript"). In ascribing such an assumption to Mill, Gray interprets him more accurately than Berlin, and Gray's rejection of universalism is also highly plausible. However, Herder's construction of a strikingly similar case for freedom (of thought and expression) but on a historicist foundation suggests that there may in fact be no deep incompatibility between these two things (and that a Millian could recast his case in historicist terms, much as Herder had already done).

94. S13:386 (emphasis added).

95. S13:454.

96. S18:387.

97. e.g., in the essay just mentioned Herder is concerned about "people who may not communicate with each other, on whom language itself imposes a constraint, a ceremonial" (S18:387–8).

98. This was a lifelong preoccupation of Herder's.

99. The following passage from the *Letters for the Advancement of Humanity* combines all three sorts of concerns: the Greeks, Romans, and French, Herder says, had glorious, independent languages, "And the language

of the Germans, which our ancestors called a language of tribal stem, pith, and heroes, should pull the victory car of others like a conquered prisoner, and in the process still give itself airs in its clumsy empire- and court-style? Throw it away, this oppressive finery, you matron squeezed in contrary to your will, and be what you can be and formerly were: a language of reason, of force and truth" (*Herder: Philosophical Writings*, p. 387). Cf. S24:376 ff.

100. On Herder's (arguably correct) philosophy of language, introducing new concepts consists in introducing new usages of words. But if the latter is prohibited or strongly discouraged, people will tend not to do it.

101. Herder remarks at one point—with special reference to Greek, Latin, Arabic, Spanish, and French—that a refined, influential language gives a nation "a secret domination" (S16:604). See also the quotation in n. 99.

Some relevant facts to keep in mind in this connection: (1) Latin's source in Germany's Roman conquerors, its longstanding association with an oppressive Catholic Church, and its use in the universities, which held a dominating monopoly over much of Germany's intel- lectual life; (2) the association of French with France's general cultural domination of Germany in the eighteenth century, and with the despotic court, bureaucracy, and cultural institutions of Frederick the Great.

A close modern counterpart to Herder's concern here would be the concern that many people in the non-Anglophone world have today about the undue privileges enjoyed by (American) English in their countries and its undue influence on their native languages, interconnected as these things are with the oppressive or intrusive influence of American military bases, economic power, fast-food chains, movies, and so on.

102. See e.g. S9:358–9, 400–1. In one uncharacteristically illiberal passage in the *Adrastea* Herder even implies that immoral plays and anti-Christian expression should be banned (S24:174–6).

103. Beiser suggests so at *Enlightenment, Revolution, and Romanticism*, pp. 210, 400.

104. e.g., the *Dissertation* just mentioned also includes statements like the following: "In the realm of truth, in the realm of thoughts and minds, no earthly power can or should decide; the government cannot, let alone its cowled censor" (S9:358). Cf. Herder's statement in the *Letters for the Advancement of Humanity* that "one may . . . rob the public of no

opinions, not even the craziest ones, in that the state, when they seem false or dangerous to *it*, may rather occasion their public refutation, so that darkness may be conquered by light for the world's advantage" (provided only that an author insults no one and gives his own name) (*Herder: Philosophical Writings*, p. 373).

105. e.g. in the late *Adrastea* Herder writes that "persecution for *thoughts*, whatever subject these may concern, is not the spirit of Christianity" (S24:92), and although he imposes some restrictions on expression, he in the process leaves the thoughts untouched (S24:176: "let him [i.e. the offender] satisfy himself in his chaotic darkness—in quiet"). (This marks a revision in standpoint since the *Dissertation on the Reciprocal Influence of Government and the Sciences*. Contrast there S9:358.)

106. *Collected Works*, 18:260.

107. See e.g. S9:358, 360–1, 401. Note that in his *Adrastea* Herder, a devout Christian, makes a forceful case for according freedom of thought and expression to "freethinkers," including outright atheists (S24:91 ff.). (S24:175–6 seems anomalous.)

108. See S9:400–1; S24:174–6.

109. *Collected Works*, 18:296–7.

PART II
Hamann

8

Johann Georg Hamann

Johann Georg Hamann (1730–88) is by any measure an interesting figure in the history of German philosophy: a friend of both Kant and Herder; a passionate defender of religion against the Enlightenment; and the author of a number of bizarre but influential works concerned with language and other topics. He has often been seen as much more than just interesting: as the seminal thinker in the philosophy of language during this period. But whether such a view is really justified is something we will need to consider. This article attempts to provide an overview of Hamann's philosophical work under the following headings:

1. Life and Writings
2. Philosophical Style
3. Epistemology
4. Philosophy of Language
5. Philosophy of Mind
6. Aesthetics
7. Philosophy of History
8. Political Philosophy

1. Life and Writings

Johann Georg Hamann (1730–88) was born at Königsberg in Prussia in 1730, the son of a barber-surgeon. His father was a Lutheran with Pietist leanings. After being tutored at home and attending schools, the young Hamann enrolled at the University of Königsberg in 1746—initially to study theology, though he later switched to law. He left university in 1752 without a degree, and became tutor to the sons of some minor nobility on the Baltic.

In 1756 he joined the family firm of his friend Christoph Berens in Riga, and was sent on a secret mission to London. On the way there, he visited

Berlin, where he met several figures of the Berlin Enlightenment, including Moses Mendelssohn. In London his secret mission failed, and he turned to a life of dissipation which used up the money that had been entrusted to him and included a homosexual relationship that ended in disaster and humiliation. During 1758, out of money and friends, he spent many months in a London garret rereading the Bible in its entirety, recovering his previous Christian faith in a more radical form, and writing an extensive commentary on the Bible in which he worked out its meaning for his own life, the *Biblical Reflections*, as well as the autobiographical *Thoughts on the Course of My Life*, and the philosophically oriented *Fragments*.

Late in 1758 he returned to Riga, where the Berenses forgave him. There he fell in love with Christoph Berens's sister, but the family refused him permission to marry her. In 1759 he returned to Königsberg to live in his father's house, where he remained for most of the rest of his life. In the same year Christoph Berens, a devotee of the Enlightenment, undertook an expedition to Königsberg in order to attempt, with the help of the (not yet famous) philosopher Immanuel Kant, to cure Hamann of his extreme religiosity. The attempt failed, and provoked Hamann to publish his *Socratic Memorabilia* (1759), a work in which he defiantly reaffirmed his radical religious standpoint, likening his own pious resistance to the Enlighteners Berens and Kant to Socrates' pious resistance to the Sophists.

This work was followed by *Crusades of the Philologist* (1762), a collection of miscellaneous short pieces, several of which had been published previously. In 1763 he began an intimate relationship with a peasant woman who had been taking care of his father, Anna Regina Schumacher, which never led to marriage, but produced four children. During this period he worked in Königsberg as a low-level civil servant (despite achieving some prominence as an intellectual through his publications, friendships, and letters, he would never work as an academic or cleric).

In 1764 he began tutoring, and befriended, the young Johann Gottfried Herder. In the summer of that year he went on travels abroad, which lasted for several years. In 1766 his father died while he was still away. In 1767 he returned to Königsberg and became clerk and translator for the General Excise Administration, a tax farming agency in the Prussia of Frederick the Great which was run by a French consortium. In 1772 Herder published his prize-winning *Treatise on the Origin of Language*, which made a case that the origin of language was human rather than divine. This provoked Hamann to write a series of bitterly critical pieces in response: *The Last Will and Testament of the Knight of the Rose-Cross*, *Philological Thoughts and Doubts*, and *To the Solomon of Prussia* (only the first of which was published at the time).

In 1773 Hamann published an engagingly whimsical piece called *New Apology of the Letter h*, in which he defended unpronounced occurrences of the letter *h* against a recent proposal that they should be eliminated, writing part of this piece under the assumed persona of the letter *h* itself. During this period he also wrote two political satires in French, the preferred language of Frederick the Great, against whose French Enlightenment-dominated state the satire was largely directed: *Lost Letter of a Savage of the North to a Financier at Peking* (1773) and *The Worm of the North* (1774).

In 1774 Herder published a much more religiously committed work about the Old Testament, *Oldest Document of the Human Species*, to which Hamann responded more positively than to the *Treatise on the Origin of Language*, both in letters and in the publication *Christiani Zacchaei Telonarchae Prolegomena on the Most Recent Interpretation of the Oldest Document of the Human Species* (1774).

In 1775 Hamann wrote another work concerned with religion, *Hierophantic Letters*, and one largely on sex and marriage, *Essay of a Sibyl on Marriage*. In 1777 he pursued the theme of sex and marriage further in *Skirts of Fig Leaves*. He was also promoted to Superintendant of the Customs Warehouse at this time. In 1779 he produced the work *KONXOMPAX*, which contains a satire on Lessing's sharp distinction between the knowledge of God and the knowledge of the accidents of history. In 1780 he worked on a translation of Hume's *Dialogues concerning Natural Religion*, but did not publish it due to the emergence of a competing translation.

In 1781 Kant published his *Critique of Pure Reason*, which Hamann already read at the proof stage. Hamann immediately wrote a review (unpublished at the time). In 1784 he would go on to write a longer and more critical response to Kant's book, the famous *Metacritique on the Purism of Reason*. Though not published until 1800, this was already circulated among friends at the time, including Herder.

In 1782 Hamann began an extensive correspondence with Friedrich Heinrich Jacobi, notable for its warmth and its philosophical content. In 1784, besides writing the *Metacritique*, he published *Golgotha and Sheblimini!*, a critical response to Mendelssohn's *Jerusalem*, a work that had sought to defend Judaism in the spirit of Enlightenment ideas about natural religion. In 1786 he wrote *Disrobing and Transfiguring*, which continues his critique of Mendelssohn.

In 1787 he petitioned to leave his post, and was discharged from it. He then traveled to Münster to stay with an admirer of his work, the Princess Gallitzin, and at last visited Jacobi. He died at Münster in 1788.

Hamann's intellectual outlook is distinguished above all by three features. First, he was a committed Christian of a Lutheran and somewhat Pietist bent, and a theist who had no sympathy at all with Enlightenment natural religion or deism—a stance which dominates all areas of his thought. (His religion was idiosyncratic, however. For example, he showed little interest in the afterlife, and reveled in sexuality and sensualism.) Second, and relatedly, he was a firm opponent of the Enlightenment, in particular its exaltation of reason. Third, he had an unusually strong interest in and involvement with language: he possessed a broad knowledge of languages, both ancient and modern; translated much, including both academic texts and commercial ones (the main languages involved were English, French, and German); taught languages to other people (including Herder); and developed unusual philosophico-religious ideas about language (for example, that nature and history are texts composed by God).

Hamann rubbed shoulders with many of the most prominent intellectuals of his day, including Kant, Herder, Jacobi, Lavater, and (in an indirect way) Goethe. His intellectual influence was considerable—especially, on Herder in connection with language; on Jacobi, Schleiermacher, and Kierkegaard in connection with the fundamental role of faith or feeling, rather than reason, in religion; and on the Romantics in connection with the religious significance of art, and the role of genius in its creation.

The perception of Hamann's importance was enhanced soon after his death by Goethe's enthusiastic discussion of him in his autobiography *Poetry and Truth* and by a respectful review of his collected works which Hegel wrote. Their posthumous acknowledgment of Hamann was qualified, however; Goethe noted that in reading his idiosyncratic works "one has to forgo altogether what is usually meant by understanding," and Hegel judged him incapable of *developing* his insights.

2. Philosophical Style

In sharp contrast to many other eighteenth- and early nineteenth-century German philosophers, Hamann has no pretensions to systematicity. Some of his titles indeed draw attention to the unsystematic nature of his works (e.g. *Fragments* [*Brocken*] and *Two Mites* [*Zwei Scherflein*]). His rationale for this stance varies. He initially espoused it largely due to a sense that he was personally unable to produce a system.[1] However, he also had some more principled reasons. Already in the *Biblical Reflections* and the *Fragments* he takes the view, motivated by religious humility, that all of our knowledge and understanding is only partial. And later on he explicitly embraces unsystematicity on the grounds that systematicity is an obstacle to truth.[2]

Besides being unsystematic, Hamann's writings are typically short; occasional in nature (often written in response to other people's publications—e.g.

Herder's *Treatise on the Origin of Language*, Kant's *Critique of Pure Reason*, and Mendelssohn's *Jerusalem*—or, more idiosyncratically, as self-reviews of his own); adorned with mysterious visual symbols (e.g. the figure of Pan), and enigmatic titles, subtitles, and mottos; authored with an adoption of strange identities (e.g. in the *Socratic Memorabilia*, Socrates, and in the *New Apology of the Letter h*, the letter h itself); extremely obscure in content; lacking in developed argument;[3] full of quotations from ancient and modern works left in their various original languages, as well as citations and allusions, many of whose significance is left unclear; prone to the use of German archaisms, especially the vocabulary and constructions of Luther's German Bible; bombastic and dramatic; crude, sometimes to the point of obscenity; humorous and satirical, often in cruel ways; and rich in metaphors. As Goethe already observed, the cumulative effect of such features (especially for a modern reader deprived of the help that was supplied by the contemporary context) is to preclude satisfactory understanding. Indeed, for most normal people (especially today) reading Hamann is a form of intellectual torture.

Hamann did not *have* to write in this way; his early *Biblical Reflections*, a long work, is written clearly and even elegantly, and his letters throughout his life often show similar virtues. Why, then, did he *choose* to write in this way? Part of the explanation lies in his principled contempt for reason, and therefore for the conventional ways of writing that rely upon it. Another part of the explanation lies in a deep disaffection with his age and its "public"—rooted in his unpopular religious position, but also exacerbated by more mundane grievances, including, for example, his lowly employment and inadequate salary—which leaves him uninterested in being understood by most of his contemporaries, and indeed keen to mystify them.[4] Yet another part of the explanation lies in a motive that is in tension with the preceding one: a wish to cultivate a strikingly distinctive authorial individuality.[5] Yet another part of the explanation lies in a fear that his ideas were not original or cogent (in his letters he voices a fear that he got all his main ideas from the poet Edward Young,[6] and laments the weakness of his own intellect, e.g. in comparison with Kant's),[7] and in a resulting desire to mask his intellectual nakedness. It is difficult to have much sympathy with these motives.

3. Epistemology

Hamann does not have a systematic epistemology. However, his views in this area do have a consistently skeptical or negative tendency.

One of his most significant works concerned with epistemological issues is the *Socratic Memorabilia* of 1759. In this work he inverts the picture, widespread during the Enlightenment (as it still is today), of the historical Socrates as a rationalist in the manner of the Enlightenment itself. Instead, he interprets—and closely identifies with—Socrates as an opponent of rationalism, who encountered and combated rationalism in the form of Sophism, and himself instead relied on divine inspiration. Despite the thinness of the evidence on which Hamann based this interpretation (he mainly drew on a few secondary sources and the pseudo-Platonic *Second Alcibiades*, only beginning a real study of Plato later, in 1761),[8] there is probably much truth to it.[9]

Hamann's own epistemological stance in the *Socratic Memorabilia* is a sort of fusion of this Socratic pious humility (human reason cannot achieve knowledge, our only source of insight is divine inspiration) with a Hume-inspired conception that since reason leads nowhere we must instead rely on feeling and faith (Hamann extends Hume's idea that all our convictions must ultimately rest on experience, custom, or belief, to include *religious* belief, faith).[10] This position would subsequently have great influence on two other German philosophers from the period who were concerned to defend Christian religion against Enlightenment rationalism: Jacobi and Schleiermacher.

Over the course of his career Hamann's critical stance on reason became multi-faceted, somewhat subtle, and quite interesting. The following ideas should be distinguished: (1) Hamann adopts a basic skepticism about the power of reason.[11] In early works such as the *Socratic Memorabilia* this skepticism tends to be extreme and unqualified. However, in later works such as the *Metacritique* it tends to turn into the more moderate position that reason is legitimate and even indispensable, but only provided that it remains *dependent on and subordinate to* experience and faith.[12] (2) Hamann develops a corresponding genetic thesis: in the *Crusades* (1762) he argues that such features of discourse as rhythm, emphasis, and metaphor are historically prior to logic and reason;[13] and in *Doubts and Thoughts about a Miscellaneous Piece of News* (1776) he implies that faith/revelation and sensory experience are prior to reason.[14] (3) Hamann opposes the hypostatization of "reason": this is really just a name for a collection of activities or relations, not a thing.[15] (4) In the *Metacritique* and elsewhere Hamann insists on several further deflations of conventional conceptions of reason which represent it as "pure" or exalted: not only is it a mistake to suppose that reason can dispense with experience (or faith), but it is also a mistake to suppose that it can operate independently of language, or that it can be detached from cultural tradition (so that Enlightenment pretensions to a reason that is common to human beings at all times and places are in error).

Another noteworthy feature of Hamann's epistemology is his emphasis—again in the spirit of Socrates—on the fundamental importance but also
the great difficulty of *self*-knowledge. Already in the *Fragments* (1758) he claims
that self-knowledge is required for *any* knowledge;[16] in the *Crusades* (1762) he
asserts that for us human beings self-knowledge holds the key to becoming
divine;[17] and in a later letter he adds that self-knowledge is the key to genuine
authorship.[18] But he also emphasizes both the epistemological and the emotional difficulty of achieving self-knowledge.[19] On the epistemological side,
the difficulty (Hamann sometimes goes as far as to say: impossibility) is due to
the fact that Cartesian conceptions of the mind's immediate self-transparency
are radically false. Hamann argues in the *Fragments* (1758) that self-knowledge
can instead only be achieved via a knowledge of others, both other people and
God; and that in particular we need to see ourselves in others' eyes, as in a
mirror.[20] In *The Wise Men from the East in Bethlehem* (1761) he adds that the
nature of the self is only revealed to itself by its actions, which are the work
of Providence or God (rather than of immediately self-transparent motives).
On the emotional side, Hamann in the *Crusades* describes self-knowledge as
a "descent into hell."[21] He is presumably thinking here largely of his own
experience—in particular, of how his lapse into dissolute activities during his
visit to London, and the disapproving reactions which this provoked in the
eyes of others, including Berens and (in Hamann's view) God, increased his
self-knowledge but only in a most painful way.

4. Philosophy of Language

This subject will be discussed in detail in the next essay, and will therefore
be treated only briefly here. Hamann has sometimes been credited with
introducing two seminal doctrines concerning the relation between thought
or concepts, on the one hand, and language, on the other, both of which were
in opposition to the sharply dualistic and subordinating conception of that
relation that had typified the Enlightenment, and with subsequently passing
these doctrines on to Herder, thereby founding the philosophy of language
as we have known it since: (1) that thought is essentially dependent on and
bounded by language (Hamann goes as far as to say: identical with it); and (2)
that concepts or meanings consist—not in referents, Platonic forms, mental
"ideas," etc., but—in word-usages.

Hamann did indeed eventually come to espouse such doctrines in the
1770s and 1780s, especially in the *Metacritique* of 1784. However, before that

time—for example, in *Biblical Reflections* (1758) and the *Crusades* (1762)—he himself held standard dualistic, subordinating views. By contrast, Herder had already adopted such doctrines considerably earlier, namely in writings from the mid-1760s. The influence here was therefore in fact the opposite of that commonly supposed: Herder on Hamann, not Hamann on Herder.

Moreover, Hamann's versions of these two doctrines turn out to be philosophically inferior to Herder's. For example, unlike Herder, Hamann *identifies* thought with language outright, which is not a philosophically tenable position; whereas Herder has compelling arguments for both doctrines, Hamann offers no real argument for either; unlike Herder, Hamann does not seriously consider, or attempt to defend the doctrines against, some important prima facie counterexamples, such as "intelligent" but languageless animals; unlike Herder, Hamann allows the terms "language" and "word" as they occur in the two doctrines a far broader range of applications than is usual (including, for example, music and painting), and thereby arguably lends the doctrines a greater flexibility than in the end turns out to be philosophically justified; and unlike Herder, Hamann infuses these doctrines with a mystifying religious dimension, in the spirit of the *logos* of St John's Gospel.

Somewhat similarly: Hamann in the course of his critique of Herder's *Treatise on the Origin of Language* (1772) insists on the fundamental sociality of language and reason (an important thesis which has found much favor in recent philosophy). However, Herder had himself already advanced the same thesis in the *Treatise*, albeit inconsistently (and would later repeat it consistently in *On the Cognition and Sensation of the Human Soul* [1778]).

Somewhat similarly again, Hamann's rejection of Herder's naturalistic theory of the origin of language in the *Treatise* in favor of a divine origin rests on misconceptions about the nature of Herder's position, and introduces a highly dubious counter-theory that the explanation of language's origin lies in the fact that everything that Adam encountered in the Garden of Eden was God's language.

Another significant idea of Hamann's in this area is his critique of metaphysics as a pseudo-discipline that arises from abuses of language, including excessive abstraction from experience, the hypostatization of general concepts (e.g. "reason"), and outright linguistic solecism (e.g. Spinoza's conception of God as a *causa sui* flouts the fact that the term "cause" implies a relation between two distinct entities or events). However, here again Hamann is deeply indebted to predecessors—especially, the British philosophers Bacon and Locke, and also Herder's *Fragments on Recent German Literature* (1767–8).

Two further, closely related areas in which Hamann has sometimes been claimed to have had important ideas are the theories of interpretation and translation. However, here again his achievements turn out to be either dubious or modest. Concerning interpretation, he is notable for a strong commitment to reading the Bible in ways which rely on divine inspiration and impute widespread allegory—traditional interpretive approaches that it was one of Herder's and Schleiermacher's greatest achievements as theorists of interpretation to criticize and reject.

Concerning translation, Hamann correctly recognizes that discrepancies between the conceptual resources of different languages often force the translator to opt either for what would today be called "domesticating" or for what would today be called "foreignizing" translation; and he prefers translation which errs in the latter direction rather than the former. This is an attractive position. However, he does little to justify his preference or to explain in any detail how "foreignizing" should be achieved—fronts on which Herder and Schleiermacher, by contrast, would both develop highly sophisticated and cogent positions.

The above negative points, which are of fundamental importance for an assessment of Hamann's philosophy of language, will be discussed in more detail in the next essay. Here it may be appropriate to conclude by appending a few less fundamental but still significant points about particular works:

Hamann's philosophically significant *Metacritique* of 1784 accuses Kant in the *Critique of Pure Reason* of (a) mistakenly conceiving reason as "pure," or independent, from language, instead of essentially dependent upon it (this is one of three types of "purity" that Hamann accuses Kant of mistakenly ascribing to reason—the other two being purity from experience and from mutable tradition); and (b) basing his philosophical position on abuses of language (this is an example of Hamann's usual diagnosis of the sources of metaphysical illusion). The first of these accusations is half right, but only half right. Kant's psychological rather than linguistic way of casting the subjects of the *Critique of Pure Reason* (e.g. in terms of "representations," "concepts," "ideas," "judgments," and "principles," rather than, say, "words" and "sentences") does indeed bespeak a strong continuity with conventional Enlightenment dualism and subordination. But as Reinhard Brandt and Michael Wolff have recently pointed out, there is also a striking series of remarks scattered through Kant's works in which he rather affirms some sort of strong dependence of thought on language, and of concepts on words. The truth is that Kant has one foot in the predominant dualistic, subordinating camp of Enlightenment predecessors such as Locke and Hume, but another foot in the camp of people like Leibniz and Christian Wolff who had already broken with that dualism and subordination in the direction of something more like doctrines (1) and

(2). Hamann's criticism of Kant therefore has *some* justification, but is also guilty of an oversimplification.[22]

One of Hamann's most attractive works concerned with language—a favorite of Kant's—is his *New Apology of the Letter h* from 1773. This work cannot claim any great philosophical importance, but it does in certain ways show Hamann both at his most characteristic and to his best advantage. The work is directed against a proposal that had been made by a certain C.T. Damm that the unpronounced "h" which was a common feature of German spelling at the time be dropped. Hamann comes to the defense of the letter "h," at one point whimsically adopting the identity of the letter itself in order to do so. Hamann makes several sober and intelligent points against Damm's proposal—for instance, that there are many other letters in German spelling which are likewise unpronounced (e.g. the second "n" in "Mann"), so that a consistent application of Damm's principle would cause widespread havoc in the language; and that even if unpronounced, such letters may still serve the useful function of distinguishing for readers between the different senses of phonetic homonyms. But Hamann's defense of the letter "h" also rests on a series of considerations which are more characteristic and interesting, while also being more questionable. These include the following: (i) Damm's proposal derives from an erroneous rationalist idea that language, as well as reason and religion, can do without arbitrary assumptions. (ii) Moreover, it represents the general tyranny of the rationalizing Enlightenment with its institutions over the idiosyncratic individual. (iii) Rejecting the letter "h" simply because it is unpronounced is an example of preferring the *letter* to the *spirit* (i.e. preferring what is perceptible and mundane to what is less tangible but divine). (iv) Combating the unpronounced letter "h" is also an attack on the language of Luther's Bible.[23]

5. Philosophy of Mind

Until the 1770s Hamann's conception of the relation between the mind and the body was sharply dualistic, in the usual manner of the Enlightenment.[24] Hamann was agnostic about the further details, though; for example, in a letter from the period he leaves open the question of whether there is a pre-established harmony or a "physical influx" (albeit while implying some preference for the former theory).[25] However, beginning in the early 1770s his usual position instead became monistic in tendency. For example, in the *Philological Thoughts and Doubts* (1772) he observes concerning mind and body that "the philosophers have always divorced themselves from the truth by divorcing what nature has put together."[26] One striking feature of this new position was Hamann's emphasis on the role that the sexual side of bodily life plays in determining the life of the mind. For example, he says in one place that he has never been able to imagine a creative mind without genitals.[27]

Hamann also espouses a doctrine of the unity of the mental faculties. As we have already seen, he identifies reason and language. He also regards reason and sensation as profoundly interdependent. (Both of these positions are prominent in the *Metacritique*.) And a third intimate connection on which he insists concerns cognition and volition, or affect: in his view, nothing significant can be achieved in the sphere of cognition that is not rooted in volition, or affect (including, as we just saw, sexual affect).[28]

These positions—mind/body monism and a doctrine of the unity of the mental faculties—are part of what Hamann means to convey when he embraces the "principle of the coincidence of opposites [*principium coincidentiae oppositorum*]" (which he attributes to Giordano Bruno but which more properly belongs to Nicholas of Cusa).[29]

Herder essentially agreed with Hamann's positions concerning mind/body monism and the unity of the mental faculties. Herder's classic statement of such positions is found in his *On the Cognition and Sensation of the Human Soul* (1778, though a good draft had already been written by 1775).

Since Hamann's shift to these positions only occurs in the late 1760s and early 1770s, it is not entirely clear which of the two men can claim the most credit for them. The conventional view would be that it is Hamann, and this may be correct. But the points already made above concerning the philosophy of language should put us on our guard here.

6. Aesthetics

Hamann was not very well versed in literature or art—for example, he had little knowledge even of contemporary German literature. He was also modest about his talent for such subjects—for example, he bemoaned his poor musical-metrical ear and his poor vision.[30] After showing an early interest in aesthetics, especially in his famous *Aesthetica in Nuce*, which appeared as part of the *Crusades* (1762), and in his *Five Shepherd's Letters concerning School Drama* (1763), he showed little interest in the subject during the last twenty-five years of his career.

Nonetheless, he did espouse a number of ideas in this area which became quite influential, and some of which may also have significant intrinsic value.

A first is the idea, initially articulated in the *Aesthetica in Nuce*, but later echoed in the *Metacritique* as well, that music is older than speech, and painting than writing.[31] This idea had precedents, especially among British thinkers and scholars.[32] But its introduction in Germany had a powerful impact on subsequent theorists, including Herder.

Closely connected with that idea is a further one which becomes especially salient in the *Metacritique*, namely that such apparently non-linguistic arts as music and painting ought really themselves to be classified as forms of *language*, as employments of *words*. This position contrasts with that taken by Herder, who did not usually classify such arts in this way. And this difference entails an important difference in the force of their versions of the two doctrines in the philosophy of language mentioned earlier: (1) that thought is essentially dependent on and bounded by language; and (2) that concepts or meanings consist in word-usages. The difference can be captured by saying that whereas Hamann is a broad expressivist, Herder is a narrow expressivist. Which of these two positions is the correct one is a very important question both for the philosophy of language and for aesthetics, and a very difficult question to decide. My own view is that Herder's narrow expressivism is in the end the superior position. But it should at least be conceded that Hamann has staked out an important alternative possibility. His alternative position would later play an important role in the Romantics Wackenroder and Tieck, as well as in Hegel (who, although he does not usually call non-linguistic arts "language" or "words," does similarly think of them as in certain cases sufficient vehicles for thoughts and concepts).

Closely connected with the position just described is Hamann's commitment to the *cognitive* value of such arts as music and painting—their expression of meanings and thoughts (i.e. candidates for truth and falsehood). Herder's competing position can ascribe a cognitive value to such arts as well, and in its mature version does so (namely, by regarding the meanings and thoughts in question as parasitic on the artist's language, in the usual, narrow sense of "language"). The general conception that such arts have a cognitive value seems clearly true of many cases. It would later assume great importance in the aesthetic theories of the Romantics and Hegel (who, though, were somewhat torn between Hamann's and Herder's specific ways of holding it).

Another idea of Hamann's, closely related to the preceding one, and to his fundamental religious motivation, is that art needs a *religious* basis.[33] This idea too would have an important impact on the Romantics and Hegel.

Another central idea of Hamann's in aesthetics is the concept of genius, the concept of the great mind who destroys existing rules and, by establishing a new model, gives rise to new ones: "A genius must come down to shake rules . . ."[34] Hamann's first salient use of this concept occurs in the *Socratic Memorabilia* of 1759. Not surprisingly, he there understands genius in religious terms, conceiving Socrates' *daimonion* as a paradigmatic example of it (along with his own religiously inspired standpoint). But already in the same work, as well as later, two of his other favorite examples of genius are Homer and Shakespeare—which also lends the concept a more aesthetic, and even secular, dimension.[35] Hamann would later go on to champion this conception of genius as essentially involving the violation of existing rules against the sort of advocacy of rule-following that he saw as typical of much Enlightenment aesthetics, in particular Mendelssohn's concept of good "taste."

Hamann's concept of genius is strikingly similar to one that was developed at around the same time by his favorite poet Edward Young in *Conjectures on Original Composition* (like the *Socratic Memorabilia*, from 1759), and the focus on Homer and Shakespeare as examples represents another striking point of similarity with Young. There has therefore been some debate in the secondary literature concerning whether Hamann developed these ideas independently of Young or under his influence. Rudolf Unger basically prefers the *former* view (while acknowledging that Hamann may have added the examples of Homer and Shakespeare under Young's influence, and that he came to equate his own and Young's positions soon after the *Socratic Memorabilia*). Unger's main arguments for this lie in certain anticipations of the genius-concept in Hamann's works from 1758, and in the lateness of Young's work.[36] I am myself more inclined to the *latter* view. For the anticipations in the works from 1758 are not close in their details, and evidence in a letter to his father from December, 1758 shows that Hamann had already received a (presumably early) copy of Young's work by that date.[37]

Be this as it may, Hamann's introduction of this concept of genius into Germany had a considerable impact on subsequent aesthetic theory there, including Kant's theory in the *Critique of Judgment* and the Romantics' theory.

Finally, and in close connection with this concept of genius, Hamann during the 1780s came to place increasing emphasis on the importance of *individuality* in authors, artists, and their works.[38] In particular, he came to emphasize his *own* individuality as an author.[39] Since Herder had already been emphasizing both the fact and the importance of individuality—including the individuality of authors and artists—in works from the late 1760s and 1770s, it is reasonable to suspect that this is another area in which Hamann is borrowing from Herder rather than influencing him. Be that as it may, their shared idea(l) of individuality would subsequently have an enormous impact on successors such as Schleiermacher, the Schlegels, Wilhelm von Humboldt, and Nietzsche.

7. Philosophy of History

For Hamann, the history of the ancient Jews is a paradigm for understanding all history, and the history of the ancient Jews is to be understood from the Bible.[40] As Unger points out, Hamann's explanation of history as a whole employs two different models, both of them religious: first, an interpretation of it as symbolic of otherworldly religious facts; and second, an interpretation of it as the realization of a divine plan for human salvation.[41] None of this should be of great interest to a philosopher of history today, though, given the untenability of the religious assumptions involved.[42]

Of somewhat more enduring interest are two further ideas which Hamann espouses, albeit without developing them much. One of these is an idea that doing history, like knowing the future, requires prophecy.[43] This idea has an interesting aspect and also a more dubious one. The interesting aspect is the thought that because the concepts, beliefs, etc. of past ages are often profoundly different from our own, it requires exceptional talent on the part of an historian to understand such ages. This is the thought that Friedrich Schlegel later had in mind when he echoed Hamann by claiming that history is a sort of backward prophecy. However, Hamann's main point is rather that an understanding of past ages must always be in terms of the future to which they eventually lead, that it is in *this* sense that history requires prophecy (his model here is the interpretation of the events and statements in the Old Testament in terms of their "fulfillment" in the New Testament). This point seems far more dubious. Certainly, its religious version should no longer be taken seriously. But even in a secularized version, the sort of "Whiggishness" that it entails is very questionable; good history is surely at least as much a matter of *abstracting from* what we now know to have been a period's eventual results as of explaining it in terms of them, if not more so.

A second interesting idea of Hamann's is that *language* is of central importance for history.[44] This idea eventually comes to rest on his versions of the important principles in the philosophy of language that (1) thought is essentially dependent on and bounded by language and (2) concepts or meanings are word-usages. If these principles are correct, as they probably are, then the historian, as someone who seeks to penetrate the distinctive thoughts and meanings of past ages, must indeed examine their linguistic expressions closely in order to do so. Historians have no doubt always paid some attention to linguistic evidence from the past ages with which they were concerned, but Hamann here develops a specific rationale for doing so which is especially compelling and which requires that the attention paid be especially close.

8. Political Philosophy

Hamann does not really have a political philosophy. However, he does have certain views about politics.

Perhaps the most striking of these is a deep hatred of the regime of Frederick the Great—against whom much of his political satire is directed. It is important to understand his reason for this hatred, however. His reason is not, as one might suppose, an opposition to monarchy as such, or a commitment to republicanism or democracy.[45] On the contrary, monarchy seems to have been his preferred form of government, and he was no friend of republicanism or democracy.[46] Rather, his main reason was that Frederick stood for the importation of the ideas and values of the French Enlightenment, especially its rationalism and its deism or atheism (Hamann especially hated Frederick's favorite, the rationalist and deist Voltaire, with a passion).

Hamann was also bitterly critical of Kant's essay *What is Enlightenment?* (1784), which conceived Enlightenment as man's release from self-incurred tutelage, distinguished between a "public" (i.e. scholarly) and a "private" (i.e. professional) use of reason, and restricted freedom of expression to the former.[47] Hamann's hostility derived partly from the fact that he had a stronger aversion to paternalism and commitment to freedom of expression than Kant's (in this Hamann showed himself to be a true heir of Luther).[48] However, it also had a more specific source: Hamann perceived Kant as here suppressing the fact that the real problem of the age lay not in a self-incurred tutelage but instead in Frederick the Great's tutelage, and as moreover cravenly coming to the aid of that tutelage (as the toadies of the Berlin Enlightenment did) by advocating a hypocritical and cowering confinement of one's freedom of expression to the "public" domain.[49] In other words, Hamann's hostility was in large part a continuation of his attack on the regime of Frederick the Great, and continuous with the latter in its motivation.

Another area in which Hamann can appear to be more politically enlightened than he really is concerns his attitude towards women. The fact that his first venture in publishing, the journal *Daphne* for which he wrote as a student, was intended for women, his lifelong devotion to his common-law wife and their daughters, his impatience with what he rightly saw as Kant's condescending attitude towards women, his late friendship with the Princess Gallitzin, and so on can easily give the impression that he had an enlightened view of women. There is a grain of truth in this. However, his fundamental conception of women's role in society remained profoundly sexist, squarely in the spirit of the Old Testament's conception of Eve's subordination to Adam. As he put it: "The man relates to God as the woman to the man."[50]

In sum, Hamann's political philosophy is undeveloped, and what there is of it is largely unattractive.

Notes

1. See e.g. *Johann Georg Hamanns Briefwechsel*, 1:431.
2. See e.g. *Briefwechsel*, 6:276.
3. Herder already criticized Hamann for this feature in an essay from 1765 (see G1:38–9).
4. Concerning Hamann's inclination to hermeticism, cf. T.J. German, *Hamann on Language and Religion* (Oxford: Oxford University Press, 1981), ch. 1.
5. Concerning Hamann's interest in his own individuality as an author, see e.g. *Briefwechsel*, 7:43.
6. *Briefwechsel*, 2:433.
7. *Briefwechsel*, 5:108.
8. See R. Unger, *Hamann und die Aufklärung* (Jena: Eugen Diederichs, 1911), pp. 503–4.
9. For a reading of the historical Socrates' project which tends to support Hamann's intuitions about it, see my "Socrates' Demand for Definitions," *Oxford Studies in Ancient Philosophy*, 31 (2006), and "Socrates' Profession of Ignorance," *Oxford Studies in Ancient Philosophy*, 32 (2007).
10. This position is already foreshadowed in works from 1758: the *Fragments* already rejects apriorism and instead insists that knowledge must be based on experience (*Johann Georg Hamann Sämtliche Werke*, ed. J. Nadler [Vienna: Verlag Herder, 1949], 1:298; cf. later *Briefwechsel*, 6:281), while the *Biblical Reflections* and *Reflections on Church Hymns* already reject reason and instead advocate a reliance on faith (see e.g. *Sämtliche Werke*, 1:167, 224, 246, 264, 269, 291, 296–7).
11. This skepticism tends to include an opposition not only to philosophy but also to natural science. This contrasts sharply with Herder's strong sympathy with, and interest in, natural science.

12. Cf. *Briefwechsel*, 5:265: reason needs to be a servant to experience and revelation, not a lawmaker; 7:165: faith needs reason as much as reason needs faith.

13. *Sämtliche Werke*, 2:124, 197.

14. *Sämtliche Werke*, 3:191.

15. See e.g. *Briefwechsel*, 7:26, 172–3.

16. *Sämtliche Werke*, 1:299.

17. *Sämtliche Werke*, 2:164.

18. *Briefwechsel*, 6:343.

19. See e.g. *Briefwechsel*, 1:374; *Fragments*, at *Sämtliche Werke*, 1:300; also *Crusades*, at *Sämtliche Werke*, 2:164.

20. *Sämtliche Werke*, 1:300–2. Given the alleged fundamentalness of self-knowledge for all knowledge, this presumably means that there is an *inter*dependence here.

21. *Sämtliche Werke,* 2:164.

22. For a fuller discussion of this issue, see my "Kant's Philosophy of Language?" (forthcoming).

23. For similar ideas, cf. *Two Mites on the Most Recent German Literature* (1780), at *Sämtliche Werke*, 3:240–2.

24. See e.g. *Sämtliche Werke*, 1:85, 234, 300, 305, 309; 2:139, 198; *Briefwechsel*, 1:377, 393.

25. *Briefwechsel*, 1:377.

26. *Sämtliche Werke*, 3:40. Cf. on this topic German, *Hamann on Language and Religion*, pp. 63–4, 68–9, 75–7, 80.

27. *Briefwechsel*, 2:415.

28. See e.g. ibid., pp. 415, 417.

29. See e.g. *Briefwechsel*, 4:287; 5:327. Cf. on this subject R. Unger, *Hamanns Sprachtheorie im Zusammenhange seines Denkens* (Munich: C.H. Beck, 1905), pp. 105–10.

30. See *Sämtliche Werke*, 2:377–9. Cf. Unger, *Hamanns Sprachtheorie*, p. 239.

31. See *Crusades* at *Sämtliche Werke*, 2:197; *Metacritique* at *Sämtliche Werke*, 3:286.

32. See Unger, *Hamann und die Aufklärung*, p. 246.

33. Cf. ibid., pp. 258–62.

34. *Five Shepherd's Letters* (1763), at *Sämtliche Werke*, 2:362.

35. Cf. Unger, *Hamann und die Aufklärung*, pp. 287–8, 309–11.

36. Ibid., pp. 275 ff.

37. *Briefwechsel*, 1:286: "I received the Young properly today."

38. See e.g. *Briefwechsel*, 6:19–20. Cf. on this subject Unger, *Hamanns Sprachtheorie*, pp. 250–2; *Hamann und die Aufklärung*, pp. 209–10.

39. See e.g. *Briefwechsel*, 7:43.

40. Cf. Unger, *Hamanns Sprachtheorie*, pp. 111 ff.

41. Ibid., pp. 122−3.

42. Unger arrives at a similar conclusion. However, his route to it, namely a complaint that Hamann lacks a model of "development," seems hardly better than Hamann's own position.

43. *Sämtliche Werke*, 2:175−6. Cf. German, *Hamann on Language and Religion*, p. 123.

44. See already Hamann's early remarks at *Briefwechsel*, 1:393. Cf. German, *Hamann on Language and Religion*, p. 132.

45. *Pace* I. Berlin, *The Magus of the North* (New York: Farrar, Straus, and Giroux, 1993), p. 108.

46. Cf. Unger, *Hamann und die Aufklärung*, p. 180.

47. See *Briefwechsel*, 5:289−92.

48. Cf. *Two Mites on the Most Recent German Literature* (1780), at *Sämtliche Werke*, 3:232−5; also, 4:261−3.

49. See *Briefwechsel*, 5:289−92.

50. *Essay of a Sybil on Marriage*, at *Sämtliche Werke*, 3:200.

9

Hamann's Seminal Importance for the Philosophy of Language?

Some readers of this volume may have formed the impression that, in treating Herder first and at considerable length, then turning to Hamann only second and much more briefly, I am committing a sort of terrible *hysteron proteron*. Are not Hamann's ideas in the philosophy of language chronologically prior to, and of more seminal importance than, Herder's?

A whole series of eminent and influential commentators has, in one way or another, implied such a view, depicting Hamann as the deep well of seminal ideas in the philosophy of language which were only later adopted and publicized by Herder. This series of commentators includes Rudolf Haym, Fritz Mauthner, Josef Nadler, Roger Brown, Isaiah Berlin, Frederick Beiser, and Ian Hacking.[1]

In particular, these commentators have claimed or implied that two revolutionary doctrines which essentially founded modern philosophy of language were first invented by Hamann and then passed on by him to Herder: (1) that thought is essentially dependent on and bounded by language; and (2) that meanings, or concepts, are—not referents, Platonic forms, or mental "ideas," but instead—word-usages.

However, I believe that this common picture is fundamentally mistaken. Neither in connection with these two doctrines nor indeed in any other major connection can Hamann claim seminal importance for the philosophy of language. My seeming *hysteron proteron* is therefore only an illusion.

In order to make a case for this controversial position, I shall first discuss the two key doctrines just mentioned at some length. I shall then consider some further ideas in the philosophy of language more briefly. Finally, I shall say something about the closely related topics of the theories of interpretation and translation.

I

It is, of course, true that Hamann was older than Herder; that he began his career as an author first; that he became deeply interested in, and published some unusual ideas about, language first; that he nurtured Herder's intellectual growth generally and his interest in language in particular; that he taught Herder foreign languages; and so forth.

It is also true that Hamann articulated versions of the two doctrines mentioned above in his *Metacritique* of 1784,[2] as well as in several other places, and that by doing so he helped to win widespread acceptance for them, thereby contributing to the growth of the philosophy of language.

However, Herder had already developed these two doctrines first and passed them on to Hamann. In other words, the influence was just the opposite of that claimed by the series of commentators recently mentioned. Moreover, Hamann's versions of the doctrines are markedly inferior to Herder's in several important respects. So for both of these reasons, my seeming *hysteron proteron* turns out to be an illusion.

Let me begin by discussing the question of the direction of influence (before going on to discuss that of inferiority). The following facts, put together, show that Herder was the real innovator in connection with these doctrines and Hamann the follower, rather than conversely:

1. *The main evidence for Hamann's commitment to his versions of the two doctrines that is cited by the commentators mentioned above comes from the 1780s*—especially from the *Metacritique* of 1784,[3] and a series of letters that Hamann wrote in the 1780s.[4] Hamann's commitment to the doctrines does extend a little further back in time than that, but *not further back than the early 1770s*. Thus, his first expression of a commitment to doctrine (1) occurs in a review of a work by Tiedemann from late 1771, where this doctrine serves as his implicit ground for rejecting Tiedemann's standard Enlightenment picture of the relation between language and thought as a sharp duality in which the former is subordinate to the latter as merely an instrument for its communication (by contrast, the review looks forward approvingly to the imminent publication of Herder's *Treatise on the Origin of Language* of 1772).[5] Shortly afterwards, Hamann in his *Philological Thoughts and Doubts* of 1772 again implicitly invokes the doctrine, this time against Herder's *Treatise* itself. Hamann's first *explicit* statement of a version of the doctrine occurs in a letter to Kant from April 1774 which is

concerned with Herder's recent *Oldest Document of the Human Species* (1774), and reappears shortly afterwards unchanged in Hamann's published version of his letters to Kant on this subject, *Christiani Zacchaei Telonarchae Prolegomena on the Most Recent Interpretation of the Oldest Document of the Human Species* (1774):

So true is it that speaking [*Sprache*] and writing [*Schrift*] are the most essential instruments [*Organa*] and conditions of all human instruction, more essential and absolute than light for seeing and sound for hearing.[6]

Somewhat similarly concerning doctrine (2): Prior to his fairly explicit commitment to it in the *Metacritique* of 1784,[7] Hamann does at least already imply the inadequacy of the main alternative theories of meaning that had been developed by previous philosophers—including the equation of meanings with referents, the Platonic theory of forms, and the Enlightenment's "way of ideas"—during the 1770s and early 1780s.[8] But as far as I can see, he does not explicitly equate meanings with word-usages until the *Metacritique* itself (and even then not very clearly).

2. *Until the 1770s Hamann's standard position concerning the thought-language and meaning-word relations was instead a sharply dualistic and subordinating one in the conventional spirit of the Enlightenment.*[9] (Not coincidentally, so too was his standard position concerning the mind-body relation.[10]) Thus Hamann holds a conventional sharply dualistic and subordinating conception of those relations in his *Biblical Reflections* of 1758,[11] and he is still emphatically committed to such a conception of them in his *Crusades of the Philologist* from 1762. The following are a number of specific points to note in the latter connection: (i) The *Crusades* gives the following definition of language, completely in the spirit of Enlightenment dualism and subordination: language is "the means of conveying our thoughts and understanding others' thoughts."[12] (ii) The topic of the *Crusades*' opening "Essay on an Academic Question" is a prize question set by the Berlin Academy concerning the influence that language and opinions have on each other. This topic would have cried out for an enunciation of doctrines (1) and/or (2) if Hamann had been at all inclined to accept them at the time. However, far from enunciating them, he there presents the thought-language and meaning-word relations in sharply dualistic and subordinating terms throughout (the subordination is reflected, for example, in the fact that he says a great deal more about the influence of thought on language than vice versa).[13] (iii) The *Crusades* contains a whole series of specific passages which clearly imply a conventional dualistic and subordinating

picture of the relations between thought and language, and between meaning and word:

The natural manner of thought has an influence on the language.[14]

Each manner of thought which comes a little into fashion . . . tinges the expression of our concepts. The Christians' way . . . accordingly had to receive a new tongue and a holy manner of writing to distinguish them, likewise.[15]

To speak is to translate—from the tongue of angels into the tongue of men, that is, to translate thoughts into words—things into names—images into signs . . . This kind of translation (I mean speech) resembles more than aught else the wrong side of a tapestry: "And shows the stuff, but not the workman's skill"; or it can be compared with an eclipse of the sun, which can be looked at in a vessel of water.[16]

Do the elements of the ABC lose their natural meaning, if in their infinite combinations into arbitrary signs they remind us of ideas which dwell, if not in heaven, then in our brains? But if we raise up the whole deserving righteousness of a scribe upon the dead body of the letter, what sayeth the spirit to that? Shall he be but a groom of the chamber to the dead letter, or perhaps a mere esquire to the deadening letter? God forbid![17]

(iv) There are just two lonely passages in the *Crusades* that might give a contrary impression (indeed, these are the only passages in all of Hamann's writings before the 1770s that might do so).[18] One of these occurs in the "Latin Exercise" concerning dreams, originally from as early as 1751, which Hamann includes in the *Crusades*:

Assuredly, it is a defect of our station that we are unable to do without these material ideas and likewise words [*ut materialibus istis ideis perinde ac verbis carere nequeamus*] if we want to be conscious of our own thoughts.[19]

This sentence might sound like an impressive early expression of doctrine (1). However, it is in fact merely a mechanical and ephemeral repetition by the student Hamann in 1751 of a theory that had already been advanced by Wolff in his *Empirical Psychology* of 1732 and his *Rational Psychology* of 1734,[20] which had indeed *itself* prefigured doctrine (1) in a significant way.[21] The second passage occurs in a section of the *Crusades* titled "Miscellaneous Remarks." There Hamann writes that "the riches of all human cognition rest on the exchange of words," and in a footnote cites Edward Young's line from his poem *Night Thoughts*, "Speech, thought's canal! Speech, thought's criterion too."[22] However, while Hamann would *in later years* cite Young's line in support of doctrine (1), there is nothing to suggest that he is already doing so here. Instead, his focus here is merely on the causal importance of verbal communication for the growth of knowledge.[23] On closer inspection, then, neither of the two passages which might seem to constitute exceptions to the rule of the *Crusades'* commitment to a conventional Enlightenment conception of the thought-language and meaning-word relations in terms of dualism and subordination really does so. So much for the *Crusades* of 1762. Finally, it should also be noted that Hamann's private letters before the 1770s at several points likewise express a conventional dualistic and subordinating conception of the thought-language and meaning-word relations,[24] and that they nowhere even so much as hint at an anti-dualistic, non-subordinating conception of them in the spirit of doctrines (1) or (2).

3. *In sharp contrast, Herder was already firmly committed to the two doctrines in question by as early as the mid-1760s.* For example, concerning doctrine (1), he already writes in *On Diligence in Several Learned Languages* from 1764:

What exactly is the connection between language and mode of thought? Whoever surveys the whole scope of a language surveys a field of thoughts and whoever learns to express himself with exactness precisely thereby gathers for himself a treasure of determinate concepts. The first words that we mumble are the most important foundation stones of the understanding, and our nursemaids are our first teachers of logic.[25]

And he already writes in the *Fragments on Recent German Literature* of 1767–8:

[Language is] the form of cognition, not merely in which but also in accordance with which thoughts take shape, where in all parts of literature thought sticks to expression, and forms itself in accordance with this . . . Language sets limits and contour for all human cognition.[26]

Similarly, concerning doctrine (2), Herder already reflects such a doctrine in the passage just quoted from *On Diligence* of 1764 (review especially the stretch "whoever learns . . . of the understanding"). And he already insists in the *Fragments* of 1767–8 not only (as just quoted) that "thought sticks to expression," or to word, but also that concerning the understanding of concepts "the question is not how an expression can be etymologically derived and analytically determined, but how it is *used*."[27]

4. The chronological facts described above are enough by themselves to warrant at least a very strong suspicion that the direction of influence concerning doctrines (1) and (2) was the opposite of that commonly supposed: Herder on Hamann, not Hamann on Herder.[28] But this strong suspicion hardens into virtual certainty when the following additional evidence is noted: (i) Hamann had already read Herder's *Fragments*, in which the two doctrines in question are prominent, by 1766 in manuscript.[29] As I mentioned before, in Hamann's review of Tiedemann from late 1771, where he implies an

acceptance of doctrine (1) for the first time, namely by rejecting Tiedemann's commitment to the sort of conventional dualistic, subordinating conception of the language-thought relation to which he had himself previously likewise been committed,[30] he in sharp contrast explicitly heralds the imminent publication of Herder's *Treatise on the Origin of Language*. This is evidently because he assumes that Herder, having already championed a version of doctrine (1) in the *Fragments*, will do so again in that forthcoming work. In other words, *Hamann's very first expression of a commitment to doctrine (1) has Herder in mind as its source*. (ii) When Herder's *Treatise* actually appeared, Hamann got a surprise. Searching for a strong proof of doctrines (1) and (2), Herder had now in effect reconceived the "language" and "words" to which the doctrines refer in terms of certain *internal mental processes*—an unfortunate move, which in effect only preserved the doctrines *verbally*, while in *substance* returning Herder's position to a conventional model of dualism and subordination (and which he would therefore abandon soon afterwards, especially in *On the Cognition and Sensation of the Human Soul* [1778]). Hamann in his *Philological Thoughts and Doubts* of 1772 therefore rejected this position transiently adopted by Herder in the *Treatise*, accusing Herder of a "Platonism" which distinguishes between an inner and an outer *logos*:

I have called this supernatural proof of the human origin of language the Platonic proof because it starts with the neological term of art *Besonnenheit* . . . and at the end returns to a Greek synonymy [i.e. *logos*], and because the Platonists rechewed to the point of disgust the *logos endiathetos* or *enthumêmatikos* and *logos prophorikos*, the inner and outer word, like the Swedish coop-prophet [i.e. Swedenborg].[31]

But the point to note here is that in doing this Hamann was in effect merely playing back the theoretical position from Herder's own *Fragments* against Herder's (temporary) new position in the *Treatise*! (iii) It will be recalled that Hamann's first *explicit* statement of doctrine (1), in a letter to Kant from April 1774 concerning Herder's *Oldest Document*, and in his published version of his letters to Kant on that subject from the same year, reads as follows:

So true is it that speaking [*Sprache*] and writing [*Schrift*] are the most essential instruments [*Organa*] and conditions of all human instruction, more essential and absolute than light for seeing and sound for hearing.

Now, the details of this formulation strikingly echo prior statements of the doctrine by *Herder*. Thus, Hamann's formulation of the doctrine here in terms of "speaking [*Sprache*] and writing [*Schrift*]" echoes Herder's formulations of it in the *Oldest Document* itself.[32] Hamann's statement that "*Sprache* and writing are the most essential . . . conditions of all human instruction" echoes such previous statements of the doctrine by Herder as his already-quoted statement in the *Fragments* that *Sprache* is "the form of cognition, not merely in which but also in accordance with which thoughts take shape, where in all parts of literature thought sticks to expression, and forms itself in accordance with this . . . Language sets limits and contour for all human cognition." And Hamann's reference to speaking and writing as "*Organa* . . . of all human instruction" echoes Herder's previous characterization of language in the *Treatise* as the "*Organ* of the understanding."[33] (iv) Although Hamann nowhere explicitly credits Herder for inspiring him with doctrines (1) and (2) specifically, he does at least credit Herder for inspiring him with ideas in this general area. For example, he writes in a letter to Herder: "Your theme of language, tradition, and experience is my favorite idea, my egg, which I brood over—my one and all—the idea of humanity and its history."[34] (v) Finally, Herder in his *Treatise* of 1772 draws attention to what he considers to be the significant ambiguity of the Greek word *logos*, meaning both "word" and "reason" or "concept":

In more than one language *word* and *reason*, *concept* and *word* . . . also share one name, and this synonymy contains its whole genetic origin . . . The Greek word *alogos* comprises both [*nonrational* and *dumb*].[35]

As we already saw in passing, Hamann in his *Philological Thoughts and Doubts* of 1772 criticizes Herder for that idea:

I have called this supernatural proof of the human origin of language the Platonic proof because it starts with the neological term of art *Besonnenheit* . . . and at the end returns to a Greek synonymy [i.e. *logos*].

However, this very idea would later become a central feature of Hamann's *own* statements of doctrine (1)! For example, he writes in a letter from 1784: "Reason is language, *logos*."[36] This peculiar sequence of events shows an additional respect in which Hamann's version of doctrine (1) is indebted to Herder, albeit a minor one. But it is also symptomatic of the character of Hamann's relation to the doctrine more generally: he actually owes it to Herder, but instead of publicly crediting Herder for it, tends only to criticize him publicly in connection with it.

5. Why did the myth of Herder's debt to Hamann for doctrines (1) and (2) arise in the first place? Why have commentators so often failed to see that the debt is the other way round? Several factors seem to have played a role here. (i) The general fact that Hamann was older, theorized about language first, taught Herder languages, and so on already lends a certain superficial plausibility to the conventional story. (ii) So too does Hamann's tendency

to imply ownership of the doctrines in question and to fail to give Herder credit for them, combined with Herder's deferential and generous tendency to overlook this injustice to himself. (iii) So too does Hamann's public criticism of Herder's *Treatise* for what is in spirit (if not letter) a conventional dualistic, subordinating picture of thought/language and meaning/word, and Herder's subsequent (re)turn in works such as *On the Cognition and Sensation of the Human Soul* (1778) to a genuine commitment to doctrines (1) and (2). Not knowing the broader history involved here—in particular, the facts that Hamann launched his critique from the standpoint of Herder's own earlier *Fragments*, and that Herder's subsequent turn to the doctrines was merely a *return*—commentators have been misled by this sequence of events into thinking that Hamann was the innovator and Herder the follower. (iv) Finally, that impression was no doubt reinforced by the fact that later on Hamann wrote his *Metacritique* of 1784 and this was then followed by Herder's own *Metacritique* of 1799, which echoed not only the former work's title but also several of its specific doctrines, and its use of them to attack Kant's *Critique of Pure Reason*. These events again encouraged the impression that Hamann was the innovator and Herder the follower. In this *particular* case there is obviously some truth to the impression. However, it is not *generally* true. And indeed, even in this case, it is not ultimately true concerning such central ideas common to both of the works in question as doctrines (1) and (2) and the related doctrine of the tradition-bound nature of language and reason, all of which doctrines, as we have seen, were originally Herder's achievements before Hamann incorporated them into his *Metacritique*.

II

However, concerning doctrines (1) and (2), it is not *only* a matter of Herder's priority over Hamann as an influence. In addition, Herder's versions of these doctrines are greatly superior to Hamann's. Let me briefly indicate a number of respects in which this is true. (Since I have already discussed most of these issues in detail in other essays, I shall be brief here.)

1. Herder's formulations of doctrine (1) normally restrict themselves to a claim that thought is essentially dependent on and bounded by language. By contrast, Hamann's formulations radicalize this into a claim that thought *is* language: "Reason is language, *logos*."[37] This radicalization no doubt makes for a striking slogan, but it is not good philosophy. For a person can very well think without in the process using language (even internally), and conversely,

a person can very well use language (even internally) without thereby doing any corresponding thinking.[38]

2. Hamann has no justification or explanation for his version of doctrine (1); in a letter from 1784 he famously writes, "I am still waiting for an apocalyptic angel with a key to this abyss."[39] By contrast, Herder does develop an impressive justification and explanation—perhaps the most compelling part of which justifies and explains doctrine (1) in terms of doctrine (2).[40]

3. Hamann has no justification for doctrine (2) either. By contrast, Herder develops compelling arguments in support of this doctrine as well—perhaps the most important of which turns on the observation that in our ascriptions of an understanding of meanings or concepts to people the decisive criterion lies in their competence in word-usage.[41]

4. Herder is acutely aware of the existence of a whole series of prima facie problem cases facing doctrines (1) and (2), cases which seem to constitute counterexamples to the doctrines by showing that thoughts and meanings can in fact occur even in the absence of language or words: in particular, God, human infants, animals, and non-linguistic art. And he accordingly undertakes a major, and eventually successful, project of addressing and defusing each of these problem cases.[42] By contrast, Hamann neither perceives nor tackles these problem cases.

5. Hamann's way of understanding doctrines (1) and (2) is significantly different from Herder's. For Herder, the terms "language" and "word" as they occur in these doctrines are meant in their usual senses. By contrast, for Hamann they are meant in senses which include as "language" and "word" not only language and word in the usual sense, but also (as Hamann's *Metacritique* shows) such things as music, painting, and drawing,[43] and indeed (as other works show) the whole of nature and history (since Hamann conceives nature and history as God's language).[44] This makes the real force of doctrines (1) and (2) significantly different for Herder and Hamann—a difference which might be captured by saying that Herder commits himself to *narrow* expressivism, whereas Hamann commits himself to *broad* expressivism.[45] Both of these positions deserve to be taken seriously, and the disagreement between them is a difficult one to resolve. However, I believe, and have elsewhere argued, that Herder's narrow expressivism is in the end the correct position.[46] So here again Hamann's position in the end seems inferior to Herder's.

6. Finally, Herder's versions of doctrines (1) and (2) are perfectly secular in spirit. By contrast, Hamann's versions involve a Christian religious mysticism, broadly in the spirit of St John's Gospel ("In the beginning was the word, and the word was with God, and the word was God"). For example, one of Hamann's statements of doctrine (1) in a letter from 1786 says, "Reason and

writ are at bottom one: the language of God."[47] This is another respect in which Hamann's versions of the doctrines are inferior to Herder's.

In sum, Herder's versions of doctrines (1) and (2) are not only chronologically prior to and the source of Hamann's, but are also markedly superior to Hamann's.

III

That is the core of my case. Let me, though, now turn to consider more briefly three further topics in the philosophy of language concerning which Hamann has sometimes been thought to have made seminal contributions.

The first of these topics is the question of the origin of language. Hamann both develops negative criticisms of Herder's position on this question in the *Treatise on the Origin of Language* and offers an alternative position of his own. However, in neither case do his ideas contribute much of value. His negative criticisms of Herder's position largely rest on misunderstandings. For example, one of his key objections is that language, rather than being purely human in origin, is *both* human and divine.[48] However, that had in fact been precisely Herder's own position in the *Treatise* (though Hamann would not be the last person to overlook this fact). Herder had written the work in the spirit of a principle which his teacher Kant had championed in his *Universal Natural History and Theory of the Heavens* (1755) to the effect that explanations of natural phenomena in terms of natural laws are no less compatible with God's fundamental role in nature than explanations of them in terms of violations of natural laws (i.e. in terms of miracles), and are indeed better proofs of God's fundamental role in nature than the latter. Thus Herder writes in the *Treatise*:

The human origin shows God in the greatest light: *His work, a human soul, creating and continuing to create a language through itself because it is His work, a human soul.*[49]

Accordingly, Herder quite properly replied to Hamann's objection in a letter that the position Hamann was championing against him was in fact the same as his own.[50] Another of Hamann's objections to Herder's position in the *Treatise* is that Herder contradicts himself by both asserting that humans are distinguished from animals by a certain freedom from instinct manifested in their use of language and asserting that *Besonnenheit*, and hence language, constitutes a natural distinguishing characteristic of the human species—that is, Hamann triumphantly infers, an *instinct*. However, this objection is again superficial, for Herder's former assertion was really only meant as a denial that humans are governed, like animals, by instincts that are highly limited and limiting in function, which in his view *Besonnenheit* and language are not.[51] Moreover, when one turns from Hamann's negative criticisms to his own positive theory of the origin of language, his position is even weaker. For what he offers here is a theory that in the Garden of Eden everything that Adam and Eve encountered was God's word, so that the origin of human language was easy —[52] which ought surely to strike us today as nothing more than a religious fairy story.[53]

A second topic is a thesis that language and reason are fundamentally *social* — a thesis which has found great favor in one form or another in more recent philosophy.[54] Hamann does advance such a thesis in the course of his critique of Herder's *Treatise* in *Philological Thoughts and Doubts* (1772). However, this is a thesis which Herder had *himself* advanced in the *Treatise* (albeit alongside certain incompatible remarks), and which he would later do so again (this time more consistently) in *On the Cognition and Sensation of the Human Soul* (1778).[55]

A third topic is the critique of metaphysics as a discipline resting on linguistic error. Especially during the 1780s Hamann developed a fairly extensive attack on metaphysics, grounded in the general idea that metaphysics rests on various sorts of abuses of language — including, in particular, terminological abstraction from experience,[56] hypostatization (for example, "reason"),[57] and sheer linguistic solecism (for example, Hamann argues that Spinoza's conception of God as a "causa sui" involves a misuse of the concept of cause, which *implies* a relation between two distinct things).[58] Hamann famously directs this sort of linguistic criticism of metaphysics against Kant's *Critique of Pure Reason* in the *Metacritique* of 1784, but he also brings it to bear against a broader range of metaphysical theories during the 1780s.[59] This project is important and interesting, both in its general conception and in some of its specific details. However, it is again doubtful that Hamann deserves *very* much credit here. For one thing, the British philosophical tradition, especially Bacon and Locke, had already developed similar linguistic critiques of metaphysics.[60] For another thing, closer to home Herder had already done so as well, namely in his *Fragments* of 1767–8.[61]

IV

Let us turn next to the theory of interpretation. This is another area in which Hamann has sometimes been thought to have broken new ground. However, his record in this area is actually less one of achievement than of underachievement.

Hamann does, admittedly, from time to time articulate interesting and potentially fruitful ideas in this area. For example, he notes that words (like numerical digits) receive their value not intrinsically but rather from their position in relation to other words;[62] that the concepts expressed by words change with time and place;[63] that in order to discover a word's meaning an interpreter needs to proceed like a natural scientist, experimenting by placing and examining it in different relations;[64] that the interpreter needs to put himself into the intellectual and affective position of the person whom he is interpreting;[65] that few authors understand themselves, so that the interpreter needs to see beyond what the author himself sees;[66] that doing history is difficult, requiring a sort of "prophecy," just as knowing the future does;[67] and that a past people's *language* is a central clue for the historian.[68]

However, these valuable ideas are isolated and undeveloped. Moreover, they are counterbalanced and indeed outweighed by a set of much more pervasive and prominent ideas of a much more dubious character. Let me explain.

Among Herder's and Schleiermacher's greatest achievements in the theory of interpretation was the establishment of the following principles: 1. The interpreter must above all focus closely on word-usage. 2. He must interpret an author's words in the light of a thorough investigation of their historical, geographical, etc. context. 3. He must approach the author and his text with a certain sort of open-mindedness, trying to be sympathetic but also avoiding excessively close identification. 4. When interpreting sacred texts such as the Bible, he must not base his interpretation on an assumption that the text in question is divinely inspired, or that he himself is divinely inspired; instead, he must interpret it in a strictly secular fashion like any other ancient text. 5. When interpreting sacred texts, he must in particular resist the temptation to read them as allegories, except in those relatively few cases where there is good textual evidence of the author's intention to convey an allegorical meaning (e.g. the parables of the New Testament).

Now Hamann's standard positions concerning interpretation are just about *diametrically opposed* to these. Indeed, he is a sort of one-man embodiment of almost everything that Herder's and Schleiermacher's theories of interpretation set out, quite rightly, to combat. Thus, among Hamann's central principles concerning interpretation are the following: 1. Especially in connection with biblical interpretation, Hamann is often contemptuous of the philologist's close focus on words (in favor of what he calls "spirit").[69] 2. Again especially in connection with biblical interpretation, Hamann is often contemptuous of paying close attention to an author's historical, geographical, etc. context.[70] 3. Hamann insists that the interpreter must interpret with passion, or in the manner of a friend—[71] a position that might sound like an anticipation of

Herder's, but in fact rejects it in favor of the sort of excessive identification with an author that Herder warns against. 4. Hamann in interpreting the Bible rests his interpretation both on an assumption that the text is divinely inspired and on an assumption that he is himself divinely inspired as its interpreter. 5. Hamann insists on interpreting the Bible as pervasively allegorical (e.g. he interprets the Song of Solomon in this way).[72]

V

Finally, let us consider the theory of translation. Here again it seems to me that Hamann deserves some credit, but not very much.

Isaiah Berlin has attributed to Hamann two positions concerning translation: (i) a denunciation of it, on the grounds that it loses what distinguishes one type of inner experience from another;[73] (ii) a view that all translation distorts, since sense and word are one.[74]

However, as far as I can see, Hamann nowhere holds position (i).[75] Also, it would be a surprising position for him to have held, given that he himself often translated academic works (for example, Dangeuil from French into German, and Hume from English into German), and indeed made his living largely by translating (mainly from German into French).[76] He *may* have come to hold some version of position (ii) once he adopted Herder's equation of meaning with word-usage in the 1770s–1780s. But even that is not clear.

By contrast, a position which he certainly *does* hold concerning translation is a preference for what would today be called "foreignizing" over "domesticating" translation—that is, a preference for translation that attempts to bridge the conceptual gap that typically exists between the source language and the target language by distorting the latter rather than misrepresenting the former.[77] Herder essentially agreed with this preference, arguing in the *Fragments* that translation should steer a middle course but one that errs towards foreignizing; and Schleiermacher would later agree with it as well in *On the Different Methods of Translation*.

However, Hamann does not get much beyond this rather vague and inchoate principle, and in that respect his position again falls far short of Herder's. In particular, Hamann lacks Herder's sophisticated and compelling case for preferring foreignizing over domesticating translation—a case which appeals to the greater semantic faithfulness to the source text that foreignizing makes possible; the greater opportunities for enriching the target language that it affords; and the greater respect for the Other that it both expresses and encourages. And Hamann also lacks Herder's insightful, indeed revolutionary, account of exactly what foreignizing translation must involve—in particular, a "bending" of word-usages in the target language undertaken in order to mimic those in the source language and thereby reproduce the source language's concepts as accurately as possible, and an attempt (especially when translating poetry) to reproduce not only the semantic content of the original work but also its musical form.

In short, while Hamann's theory of translation is of *some* interest, it falls far short of the sophistication and power of Herder's.

VI

In sum, the common picture of Hamann as a deep well of seminal ideas in the philosophy of language, who inspired Herder to reproduce and publicize them, and thereby founded a whole intellectual tradition, is basically a myth. Herder was the real innovator here, and his ideas are also greatly superior to Hamann's in substance.

Recognizing this situation corrects a historical mistake and redresses a historical injustice (to Herder). It may also help to discourage a certain false and pernicious tendency in more recent German and continental philosophy to equate intellectual originality and depth with obscurity and obscurantism (a tendency prominent in Heidegger, Derrida, and their followers, for instance). For this tendency arose in no small part due to the erroneous picture of obscure Hamann as the original genius and clear Herder as his mere epigone.

Notes

1. See Haym, *Herder nach seinem Leben und seinen Werken*; Mauthner, *Beiträge zu einer Kritik der Sprache*; Nadler, *Johann Georg Hamann*; Brown, *Wilhelm von Humboldt's Conception of Linguistic Relativity*; Berlin, *Vico and Herder* and *The Magus of the North*; Beiser, *The Fate of Reason*; Hacking, "How, Why, When, and Where Did Language Go Public?" and "Night Thoughts on Philology."

    Significantly, Rudolf Unger, the author of what is still the most thorough and best treatment of Hamann's philosophy of language, *Hamanns Sprachtheorie im Zusammenhange seines Denkens*, takes a contrary view. See esp. pp. 258–63.

2. Concerning doctrine (1), see e.g. *Metacritique*, at *Johann Georg Hamanns Sämtliche Werke*, 3:284: "language, the only, first, and last organon and criterion of reason." Concerning doctrine (2), see e.g. ibid., pp. 284, 288: language has "no credentials but tradition and usage"; "by the spirit of their institution and meaning, [words] belong to the understanding and concepts"; "words . . . become determinate objects for the understanding only through their institution and meaning in usage."

3. See n. 2, above.

4. See esp. *Johann Georg Hamanns Briefwechsel*, 5:95, 108, 177, 360; 6:168; 7:49, 156.

5. *Sämtliche Werke*, 3:15–16.

6. *Briefwechsel*, 3:87; *Sämtliche Werke*, 3:130.

7. See n. 2, above.

8. For his rejection of the equation of meanings with referents, see a letter from 1781 at *Briefwechsel*, 5:287. For his rejection of the Platonic theory of forms, see *Philological Thoughts and Doubts* from 1772, at *Sämtliche Werke*, 3:47, and a letter from 1781 at *Briefwechsel*, 5:287. For his rejection of the Enlightenment's "way of ideas," see his 1771 review of Tiedemann, at *Sämtliche Werke*, 3:15–16. Essay 2 contains a little more discussion of this subject.

9. Dilthey already noted this fact briefly in passing in his article "Johann Georg Hamann," at *Gesammelte Schriften*, 11:32. Cf. Unger, *Hamanns Sprachtheorie*, pp. 144–51.

10. See e.g. *Sämtliche Werke*, 1:85, 234, 300, 305, 309; 2:139, 198; 3:350; *Briefwechsel*, 1:377, 393.

11. See esp. *Sämtliche Werke*, 1:29, 220.

12. *Sämtliche Werke*, 2:125. Note that this is virtually identical to Tiedemann's definition, which Hamann will subsequently criticize. Contrast with it Hamann's more elaborate *later* definition of language in a letter to Lindner from 1783, which is instead in the spirit of doctrine (1): language is the "true art of thinking and acting or of communicating and of understanding and interpreting others" (*Briefwechsel*, 5:25).

13. *Sämtliche Werke*, 2:119–26.

14. Ibid., p. 122.

15. Ibid., p. 170.

16. Ibid., p. 199.

17. Ibid., p. 203.

18. Cf. Unger, *Hamanns Sprachtheorie*, pp. 130, 214, 225.

19. *Sämtliche Werke*, 2:222.

20. See Wolff, *Psychologia Rationalis*, esp. pars. 112, 461.

21. See Essay 2. Oddly, and uncharacteristically, Unger overlooks the fact, and indeed even denies, that Wolff had prefigured the doctrine in this way (see *Hamanns Sprachtheorie*, p. 214).

22. *Sämtliche Werke*, 2:129.

23. This is a theme that Young's line can very aptly be called on to support; indeed, if one reads it in its original context in *Night Thoughts*, its spirit is considerably closer to this message than to an expression of doctrine (1).

24. See e.g. *Briefwechsel*, 1:354, 393.

25. G1:27.

26. G1:556–7; cf. 177, 394–7, 403–4, 407–10, 426, 558, 606–8.

27. G1:421–3. Cf. later *On the Spirit of Hebrew Poetry* (1782), G5:1007: "Let us seek the word's concept not from etymologies, . . . but according to the clear use of the name in its various times."

28. In saying this, I do not mean to exclude the possibility that other influences may have helped move Hamann towards these doctrines as well. We have already encountered two likely ones in passing: Wolff and the poet Young. For a broader range of relevant possibilities see Essay 2.

29. See *Briefwechsel*, 2:376–7, a letter from Hamann to Herder on this subject from August 1766.

30. Hamann quotes Tiedemann's definitions of *language* as "an accumulation, a collection of sounds through whose connection and sequence people can communicate their thoughts to each other," and of *word* as "a noise or a sound with which the person who produces it connects a certain representation," and he accuses these definitions and the rest of Tiedemann's theory of being "insipid and shallow" (*Sämtliche Werke*, 3:15–16).

31. Ibid., p. 47.

32. See e.g. G5:269, 276–8.

33. G1:733. Hamann would later sometimes repeat this idea of language being an *organon* of thought or reason in close connection with Young (see e.g. *Briefwechsel*, 7:49). But Young had not used the word in this context, as Herder had. Likewise, note that Hamann's routine later casting of doctrine (1) in terms of "reason" (rather than, say, "thought") again points to Herder as an influence rather than to Young. For Herder had commonly cast the doctrine in terms of "reason" whereas Young had nowhere done so (he did use the word "reason" in *other* contexts, but in this context instead wrote of "thought").

34. *Briefwechsel*, 6:127; cf. 108.

35. G1:733.
36. *Briefwechsel*, 5:177. Cf. Unger, *Hamanns Sprachtheorie*, p. 235.
37. *Briefwechsel*, 5:177.
38. For more details, see Essay 2.
39. *Briefwechsel*, 5:177.
40. For more details, see Essay 2.
41. For more details, see Essay 2.
42. For details, see Essay 3.
43. "The oldest language was music . . . The oldest writing was painting and drawing" (*Sämtliche Werke*, 3:286).
44. See e.g. *Crusades of the Philologist*, "Aesthetica in Nuce," at *Sämtliche Werke*, 2:203–4.
45. Concerning this difference, see *German Philosophy of Language*, Essay 6.
46. See Essay 3 and *German Philosophy of Language*, Essay 6.
47. *Briefwechsel*, 6:296.
48. *Sämtliche Werke*, 3:27.
49. G1:809.
50. *Briefwechsel*, 3:10–11.
51. Cf. Unger, *Hamanns Sprachtheorie*, p. 177.
52. See esp. *Sämtliche Werke*, 3:31–2.
53. Nor is Hamann's merit in proposing it enhanced by the fact that through mercilessly browbeating Herder at a time when the latter was emotionally vulnerable, he eventually managed to convert him to it for a while—the main public symptom of this being Herder's *Oldest Document* of 1774. Fortunately, Herder soon afterwards returned to a more sensible naturalistic position.
54. For a claim that Hamann was important in this connection, see e.g. Hacking, "How, Why, When, and Where Did Language Go Public?"
55. For a little more discussion of this subject, see my *Hegel's Idea of a Phenomenology of Spirit*, p. 222, n. 56.
56. See on this already the *Crusades* of 1762, at *Sämtliche Werke*, 2:206–7. But esp. the *Metacritique*. Also, *Briefwechsel*, 5:265–6.
57. See e.g. *Briefwechsel*, 7:26, 172–3.
58. See *Briefwechsel*, 5:326.
59. See e.g. *Briefwechsel*, 5:264–6, 272; 6:296.
60. Cf. Unger, *Hamanns Sprachtheorie*, pp. 228–33.
61. See G1:557–8. Like Hamann, Herder stands under the influence of the British in this area, especially Bacon.
62. See *Socratic Memorabilia* (1759), at *Sämtliche Werke*, 2:71. Cf. German, *Hamann on Language and Religion*, pp. 44–5.

63. See e.g. *Socratic Memorabilia*, at *Sämtliche Werke*, 2:71; and *Crusades*, at *Sämtliche Werke*, 2:170.

64. See *Briefwechsel*, 1:270. Cf. German, *Hamann on Language and Religion*, pp. 44–5.

65. See e.g. *Biblical Reflections*, at *Sämtliche Werke*, 1:8. Cf. German, *Hamann on Language and Religion*, pp. 123, 130–1.

66. *Briefwechsel*, 6:22: "Only very few authors understand themselves, and a proper reader must not only have the ability to understand his author, but also to achieve an overview [*übersehen*] of him." This remark of Hamann's from 1785 echoes a famous similar comment of Kant's concerning the interpretation of Plato at *Critique of Pure Reason*, A314/B370. It is closely connected with Hamann's commitment to the unconscious, and to the consequent difficulty of self-knowledge (a commitment Kant basically shares). Later on, Friedrich Schlegel and Schleiermacher would famously make similar statements concerning interpretation. Hamann's version is especially close in spirit to Friedrich Schlegel's version.

67. See *Sämtliche Werke*, 2:175–6. Friedrich Schlegel would later say something that sounds very similar. However, Hamann's point is less the interesting and important one that Schlegel later had in mind, namely that due to the deep discrepancy in mental outlook between different historical ages, doing history requires a sort of interpretive-philological genius, than the much more dubious one that history needs to be interpreted teleologically in light of the future, as when Christians interpret events in the Old Testament in light of events in the New.

68. See *Briefwechsel*, 1:393: "In the language of each people we find its *history*. Since the gift of speech belongs among the distinguishing advantages of humankind, I am surprised that no one has yet made an attempt to investigate the history of our species and our soul more closely from this angle." Cf. German, *Hamann on Language and Religion*, p. 132.

69. See e.g. *Crusades*, at *Sämtliche Werke*, 2:203. Note that this is not Herder and Schleiermacher's similar-sounding but much more sensible suggestion that the interpreter's close focus on words should be *complemented* by a focus on the spirit, or mind, of the *human* author. Rather, it is a suggestion that the interpreter's close focus on words should be *replaced* by a responsiveness to a *divine* spirit.

70. See e.g. ibid., pp. 211–13. Hamann adopts the two dubious positions just described largely in opposition to the Old Testament philologist Michaelis. In fairness, it should be noted that Hamann also has some

more legitimate complaints against Michaelis (e.g. for a certain sort of anachronistic rationalistic reading of the Old Testament).

71. See e.g. ibid., pp. 171, 208–9.

72. *Pace* Nadler, *Johann Georg Hamann*, pp. 195, 247, who strangely claims that Hamann renounces allegorical interpretation in favor of literal. Concerning features 4 and 5 here, see e.g. *Biblical Reflections*, at *Sämtliche Werke*, 1:128, 157–9; *Crusades*, at *Sämtliche Werke*, 2:203–4, 211–13; *Hierophantic Letters* (1775), at *Sämtliche Werke*, 3:151–2. Cf. Unger, *Hamanns Sprachtheorie*, pp. 48–61; *Hamann und die Aufklärung*, pp. 230–1.

73. Berlin, *The Magus of the North*, p. 89.

74. Ibid., pp. 77–8, 130.

75. The only evidence that Berlin cites in this connection, from the "Essay on an Academic Question" in the *Crusades*, is not even about translation, but rather about writing in a foreign tongue, and does not exactly denounce even that (ibid., p. 89).

76. He also writes balanced critical reviews of translations, positive as well as negative, and at one point rather carefully reviews a work by Johnson on the history of translation—all of which again speaks against any simple rejection of translation.

77. See e.g. *Biblical Reflections*, at *Sämtliche Werke*, 1:124; *Briefwechsel*, 1:390.

PART III
Schleiermacher

10

Friedrich Daniel Ernst Schleiermacher

Friedrich Daniel Ernst Schleiermacher (1768–1834) perhaps cannot be ranked as one of the very greatest German philosophers of the eighteenth and nineteenth centuries (like Kant, Herder, Hegel, Marx, or Nietzsche). But he is certainly one of the best second-tier philosophers of the period (a period in which the second-tier was still extremely good). Nor was he only a philosopher; he was also an eminent classical scholar and theologian. Much of his philosophical work was in the philosophy of religion, but from a modern philosophical point of view it is his hermeneutics (i.e. theory of interpretation) and his theory of translation that deserve the most attention. This article will attempt to provide a fairly broad overview of his philosophical thought. One thing that will emerge from this is that although he has important philosophical debts to many predecessors and contemporaries (including Spinoza, Kant, and Friedrich Schlegel), he was above all following in the philosophical footsteps of one predecessor in particular: Herder.

1. Life and Works
2. Philosophy of Language
3. Philosophy of Mind
4. Hermeneutics (i.e. Theory of Interpretation)
5. Theory of Translation
6. Aesthetics
7. Dialectics
8. Ethics
9. Political and Social Philosophy
10. Philosophy of Religion

1. Life and Works

Friedrich Daniel Ernst Schleiermacher (1768–1834) was born in Breslau as the son of a clergyman of the reformed church. His earlier education took place in institutions of the Moravian Brethren (Herrnhuter), a strict pietist sect. However, while there he also pursued broader humanistic interests. Largely as a result of skepticism about certain Christian doctrines taught there, he moved to the more liberal University of Halle in 1787. However, he continued in theology (with philosophy and classical philology as minor fields). He passed his theological examinations in Berlin in 1790. This was followed by a period as a private tutor, which ended in 1793, partly, it seems, due to friction caused by his sympathy with the French Revolution, to which his employer was opposed.

During the periods just mentioned he was heavily occupied with the study and criticism of Kant's philosophy. This work culminated in several unpublished essays— *On the Highest Good* (1789), *On What Gives Value to Life* (1792–3), and *On Freedom* (1790–3)—which rejected Kant's conception that the "highest good [*summum bonum*]" requires an apportioning of happiness to moral desert, and Kant's connected doctrine of the "postulates" of an afterlife of the soul and God, while developing an anti-Kantian theory of the thoroughgoing causal determination of human action and of the compatibility of this with moral responsibility. In 1793–4 he wrote two essays about Spinoza: *Spinozism* and *Brief Presentation of the Spinozistic System*. The main catalyst for these essays was Jacobi's work *On the Doctrine of Spinoza, in Letters to Mr. Moses Mendelssohn* (1785), which was highly critical of Spinozism. But they also show the influence of Herder's work *God: Some Conversations* (1787), which championed a modified form of Spinozism. In his two essays Schleiermacher himself embraces a modified form of Spinoza's monism similar in character to Herder's (in particular, like Herder, he is inclined to substitute for Spinoza's single substance the more active principle of a single fundamental force). He also attempts to defend this position by showing it to be reconcilable with central features of Kant's theoretical philosophy (notably, Kant's doctrine of things in themselves). This neo-Spinozistic position would subsequently be fundamental to Schleiermacher's most important work in the philosophy of religion, *On Religion: Speeches to its Cultured Despisers* (1799). However, in thus rejecting Jacobi's anti-Spinozism, Schleiermacher seems also to have absorbed something from Jacobi that would be equally important for his future philosophy of religion: the idea (for which his Pietist background no doubt made him receptive) that we enjoy a sort of immediate intuition or feeling of God.

During the period 1794–6 Schleiermacher served as a pastor in Landsberg. In 1796 he moved to Berlin, where he became chaplain to a hospital. In Berlin he met Friedrich and August Wilhelm Schlegel as well as other Romantics, became deeply engaged in the formation of the Romantic movement, and collaborated with the Schlegel brothers on the short-lived but important literary journal *Athenaeum* (1798–1800). Among Schleiermacher's contributions to this journal was the short proto-feminist piece *Idea for a Catechism of Reason for Noble Ladies*. During the period 1797–9 he shared a house with Friedrich Schlegel. Encouraged by the Romantic circle to write a statement of his religious views, in 1799 he published his most important and radical work in the philosophy of religion, *On Religion: Speeches to its Cultured Despisers* (revised editions followed in 1806, 1821, the latter including significant "explanations," and 1831). This work sought to save religion in the eyes of its cultured despisers (prominent among them some of the Romantics) by, inter alia, arguing that human immortality and even God are inessential to religion; diagnosing current religion's more off-putting features in terms of its corruption by worldly bourgeois culture and state-interference; and arguing that there are an endless multiplicity of valid forms of religion. The book won Schleiermacher a national reputation. In the same year (1799) he also published an essay on the situation of the Jews in Prussia, *Letters on the Occasion of the Political-Theological Task and the Open Letter of Jewish Householders*. In this work he rejected an expedient that had been proposed of effecting the Jews' civil assimilation through baptism (which would, he argues, harm both Judaism and Christianity) and instead advocated full civil rights for Jews (on certain reasonable conditions). The same year also saw Schleiermacher's composition of the interesting short essay *Toward a Theory of Sociable Conduct*, which is important as his first significant discussion of the art of conversation (an art that would later be central to his discipline of dialectics). Finally, 1799 also saw his publication of a highly critical review of Kant's *Anthropology*. The review in particular took Kant to task for his dualistic philosophy of mind, and his superficial, disparaging attitude towards women and other peoples.

During the following several years Schleiermacher complemented *On Religion* with two substantial publications which were more ethical in orientation: the especially important *Soliloquies* (1800; second edition 1810) and the *Outlines of a Critique of Previous Ethical Theory* (1803). In 1800 he also defended his friend Friedrich Schlegel's controversial and arguably pornographic novel *Lucinde* from the same year in his *Confidential Letters Concerning Friedrich Schlegel's Lucinde*—a shared proto-feminism constituting a large part of his reason for sympathizing with Schlegel's book. During the period 1799–1804 Schleiermacher developed together with Schlegel the project of translating

Plato's dialogues. As time went on, however, Schlegel left this work to Schleiermacher, which contributed to increasingly difficult relations between the two men after 1800. Schleiermacher's translations appeared during the period 1804–28 (though not all of the dialogues were translated in the end), and are still widely used and admired today.

While in Berlin Schleiermacher developed romantic attachments to two married women, Henriette Herz and Eleonore Grunow—the latter of which attachments led to scandal and unhappiness, eventually causing Schleiermacher to leave the city. He spent the years 1802–4 in Stolpe. By 1804 he was teaching at Halle University. During the period 1804–5 he began lecturing on ethics (as he would do repeatedly until 1832). In 1805 he also began his famous and important lectures on hermeneutics (which he delivered repeatedly until 1833). In 1806 he published the short book *Christmas Eve*, a literary work which explores the meaning of Christian love by depicting a German family's celebration of Christmas Eve. This is in keeping with *On Religion*'s ideal of (Christian) religion as family- rather than state-centered. In 1806–7 he left Halle as a result of the French occupation, and moved back to Berlin. From this time on he began actively promoting German resistance to the French occupation, and the cause of German unity. In 1808 he married Henriette von Willich (a young widow), with whom he had several children. In 1808–9 he became preacher at the Dreifältigkeitskirche, in 1810 professor of theology at the University of Berlin, and by 1811 also a member of the Berlin Academy of Sciences.

After becoming a member of the Academy he often delivered addresses before it, among which several on ethics, one on translation from 1813, one on the philosophy of Socrates from 1815, and one on Leibniz's idea of a universal language from 1831 are especially significant.

In 1811 he lectured on dialectics for the first time (as he would do repeatedly until his death, at which time he was in the early stages of preparing a version for publication). In 1812 he began lecturing on the history of philosophy (as he would again repeatedly in subsequent years). In 1813 he delivered as an address and then published as an essay *On the Different Methods of Translation*—a very important work in translation theory deeply informed by his experience as a translator. In 1818 he lectured on psychology for the first time (as he would do repeatedly until 1833–4). In 1819 he lectured on aesthetics for the first time (as he subsequently did on two further occasions, the last of them in 1832–3). In the same year he also began lecturing on the life of Jesus (as he did again on four further occasions over the following twelve years)—thereby inaugurating an important genre of literature on this subject in the nineteenth century.

In 1821–2 he published his major work of systematic theology, *The Christian Faith* (revised edition 1830–1). In 1829 he published two open letters on this work (nominally addressed to his friend Lücke), in which he discusses it and central issues in the philosophy of religion and theology relating to it in a concise and lucid way.

Schleiermacher died in 1834.

As can be seen even from this brief sketch of his life and works, a large proportion of Schleiermacher's career was taken up with the philosophy of religion and theology. However, from the secular standpoint of modern philosophy it is his work in such areas as hermeneutics (i.e. the theory of interpretation) and the theory of translation that is most interesting. Accordingly, this article will begin with these more interesting areas of his thought, only turning to his philosophy of religion briefly at the end.

2. Philosophy of Language

Since the topics of language and psychology are central to Schleiermacher's hermeneutics and theory of translation, it may be appropriate to begin with some discussion of his philosophies of language and mind. Schleiermacher nowhere presents his philosophy of language separately; instead, it is found scattered throughout such works as his lectures on psychology, dialectics, and hermeneutics. The following eight positions—all but the last of which are heavily indebted to Herder—are especially worth noting:

(1) In his lectures on psychology, Schleiermacher takes the following position on the question of the origin of language (virtually identical to Herder's in the *Treatise on the Origin of Language* [1772]): The origin of language is not to be explained in terms of a divine source. Nor is it to be explained in terms of the primitive expression of feelings. Rather, the use of inner language is simply fundamental to human nature. It is the foundation of, and indeed identical with, thought. It is also the foundation of other distinctively human mental characteristics, in particular self-consciousness and a clear distinguishing of perception from feeling and desire.

(2) Language (and hence thought) is fundamentally social in nature. More precisely, while inner language is not dependent on a social stimulus (so that even in the absence of this children would develop their own languages), it does already involve a tendency or implicit directedness towards social communication.

(3) Language and thought are not mere additions to other mental processes which human beings share with the animals. Rather, they are infused

throughout, and lend a distinctive character to, all human mental processes. In particular, they structure human beings' sensory images in distinctive ways.

The next five of the eight positions are especially important for Schleiermacher's hermeneutics and theory of translation (to be discussed below):

(4) Schleiermacher already in early work postulated an identity of thought with linguistic expression. He often equates thought more specifically with *inner* language (e.g. he already does so in his 1812–13 ethics lectures). His main motive behind such a refinement can be seen from the lectures on psychology, where he discusses cases in which thought occurs but without arriving at any outward linguistic expression. It has been claimed in some of the secondary literature that he eventually gave up this whole position. He does retreat from it somewhat, but in his psychology lectures of 1830 we still find him writing of "the activity of thought in its identity with language."

(5) Schleiermacher adopts a view of meaning which equates it—not with such items, in principle independent of language, as the referents involved, Platonic forms, or the mental "ideas" favored by the British Empiricists and others, but—with word-usage, or rules for the use of words. For example, in the hermeneutics lectures he says that "the . . . meaning of a term is to be derived from the unity of the word-sphere and from the rules governing the presupposition of this unity."

(6) In his psychology lectures, Schleiermacher argues that although thought and conceptualization are not *reducible* to the occurrence of sensuous images (since that would conflict with the position that the former require or are identical with language), the latter are an essential *foundation* for the former. This position is also reflected in his strong attraction, in some of his later hermeneutics and dialectics lectures, to Kant's theory of empirical schemata—according to which empirical concepts are grounded, or consist, in unconscious rules for the generation of sensuous images—and to turning it into an account of the nature of all concepts. (This invites the question whether there do not also exist strictly a priori concepts, as Kant had held. In his psychology lectures Schleiermacher vacillates in his answer to this question: sometimes implying so, but at other points instead implying—more consistently with the position just described—that it is merely the case that some concepts are *more* distantly abstracted from sensory images than others. The latter is his normal answer in the dialectics lectures as well.)

(7) Human beings exhibit, not only significant linguistic and conceptual-intellectual similarities, but also striking linguistic and conceptual-intellectual differences, especially between different historical periods and cultures, but even to some extent between individuals within a single period and culture. (In this connection, Schleiermacher argues, plausibly, that the phenomenon of

the linguistic and conceptual-intellectual development of cultures over time is only explicable in terms of linguistic and conceptual-intellectual innovations performed by individuals, which get taken over by the broader culture, becoming part of its common stock.)

(8) Importantly, Schleiermacher develops a much more *holistic* conception of meaning than his predecessors (this is the one major respect in which his philosophy of language goes beyond Herder's). At least three aspects of his semantic holism can be distinguished: (a) As can already be seen from a passage quoted above, he espouses a doctrine of "the unity of the word-sphere." This doctrine in effect says that the various specific senses that a single word typically bears, and that will normally be distinguished by any good dictionary entry (e.g. the different senses of "impression" in "He made an impression in the clay," "My impression is that he is reluctant," and "He made a big impression at the party"), always form a larger semantic unity to which they each essentially belong (so that any loss, addition, or alteration among them entails an alteration in each of them, albeit possibly a subtle one). (b) He holds that the nature of any particular concept is partly defined by its relations to a "system of concepts." In this connection, the dialectics lectures emphasize a concept's relations as a species-concept to superordinate genus-concepts, relations as a genus-concept to subordinate species-concepts, and relations of contrast to coordinate concepts falling under the same genus-concepts. However, other types of conceptual relationships would be included here as well (e.g. those between "to work," "worker," and "a work"). (c) He holds that the distinctive nature of a language's *grammatical* system (e.g. its system of declensions) is also partly constitutive of the character of the concepts expressed within it. (This last position was also developed at around the same time by Friedrich Schlegel, for whom it constituted one of the main rationales for a new discipline of "comparative grammar" which he conceived in his *On the Language and Wisdom of the Indians* [1808]. Shortly afterwards, it was taken over and used to similar effect by another of the founders of modern linguistics, Wilhelm von Humboldt.)

As I mentioned earlier, with the sole exception of this final feature (semantic holism), Schleiermacher's entire philosophy of language is heavily indebted to Herder's. However, it arguably weakens Herder's in certain respects. For example, whereas Herder's version of doctrine (4) normally restricted itself to a claim that thought is essentially dependent on and bounded by language, Schleiermacher's version asserts the outright *identity* of thought with language, or with inner language. But such a strong version of the doctrine is philosophically problematic—vulnerable to counterexamples in which thought occurs without any corresponding (inner) language use, and vice versa. Again, as we saw, in later works Schleiermacher tends to add to the Herderian doctrine (5) a thesis that concepts are empirical schemata à la Kant (see (6)). This is likely to seem problematic because of its inclusion of sensory images in meaning. But that is arguably not so: Herder had already included them as well in a way; contrary to first appearances, doing so need not conflict with a suitably construed doctrine of meanings as word-usages; and the currently popular Fregean-Wittgensteinian attack on such "psychologism," which is likely to make such a position seem suspect, may well itself be misguided. What *is* problematic about Schleiermacher's thesis is rather that Kant's theory of empirical schemata had implied a sharp distinction between meanings, conceived as something purely psychological, and word-usages, so that Schleiermacher's unmodified reintroduction of the theory implies the same, and hence conflicts with doctrine (5), the doctrine that meaning is word-usage. Finally, whereas for Herder doctrine (7) was merely an empirically established rule of thumb and admitted of exceptions, Schleiermacher in his lectures on ethics and dialectics attempts to give a sort of *a priori proof* of linguistic and conceptual-intellectual diversity even at the level of individuals as a *universal* fact—a proof that is dubious in its very a priori status, in its specific details, and in its implication of the extremely counterintuitive consequence (often explicitly asserted by Schleiermacher) that, strictly, no one can ever understand another person.

3. Philosophy of Mind

Schleiermacher's philosophy of mind is found mainly in his lectures on psychology. It is too extensive to present in detail here. But the following four central principles—all of which have their roots in Herder, and especially in Herder's main work on the philosophy of mind, *On the Cognition and Sensation of the Human Soul* (1778)—are especially striking and important:

   (a) Schleiermacher argues for a strong dependence of the soul (or mind) on the body, and indeed for their identity. However, he resists reductionism in either direction, arguing that both what he calls "spiritualism" (i.e. the reduction of the body to the mind) and "materialism" (i.e. the reduction of the mind to the body) are errors. He refers to the sort of non-reductive unity of mind and body that he instead champions as "life."

   (b) Schleiermacher also identifies the soul (or mind) with "force." Thus already in *On Freedom* (1790–3) he writes that the soul is "a force or a composite of forces."

(c) Schleiermacher also argues strongly for the unity of the soul (or mind) within itself; the soul is not composed of separate faculties (e.g. sensation, understanding, imagination, reason, desire). He himself often works with a twofold distinction between what he refers to as the mind's "organic" (i.e. sensory) and "intellectual" functions, but he holds these too to be at bottom identical.

(d) Schleiermacher argues that human minds, while they certainly share similarities, are also deeply different from each other—not only across social groupings such as peoples and genders, but also at the level of individuals who belong to the same groupings. The deep distinctiveness of individual minds periodically exercises an important influence on the development of society at large—both in the political-ethical sphere (where Schleiermacher calls the individuals who play such a role "heroes") and in the sphere of thought and art (where he calls them "geniuses"). The distinctiveness of individual minds cannot be explained by any process of calculation (in particular, it is a mistake to suppose that all human minds begin the same and only come to differ due to the impact of different causal influences on their development, which might in principle be calculated). It can, however, be understood by means of "divination" (concerning which more anon).

Finally, one feature of Schleiermacher's philosophy of mind which *distinguishes* it from Herder's, and from other predecessors', is also worth noting: Schleiermacher says relatively little about *unconscious* mental processes, and when he does mention them often seems skeptical about them. For example, he argues that thought cannot be unconscious, and that so-called "obscure representations" are in fact merely sensuous images which do not involve thoughts.

4. Hermeneutics (i.e. Theory of Interpretation)

Some of Schleiermacher's most important philosophical work concerns the theories of interpretation ("hermeneutics") and translation. Friedrich Schlegel was an immediate influence on his thought here. Their ideas on these subjects began to take shape in the late 1790s, when they lived together in the same house for a time. Many of their ideas are shared, and it is often unclear which of the two men was the (more) original source of a given idea. But since Schlegel's surviving treatments are much less detailed and systematic than Schleiermacher's, the latter take on prime importance.

Schleiermacher's theories of interpretation and translation rest squarely on three of the Herder-inspired doctrines in the philosophy of language that were described above: (4) thought is essentially dependent on and bounded by, or even identical with, language; (5) meaning is word-usage; and (7) there are deep linguistic and conceptual-intellectual differences between people. Doctrine (7) poses a severe challenge to both interpretation and translation, and it is the main task of Schleiermacher's theories to cope with this challenge. Schleiermacher's most original doctrine in the philosophy of language, doctrine (8) (semantic holism), is also highly relevant in this connection, for, as Schleiermacher perceives, semantic holism greatly exacerbates the challenge to interpretation and translation posed by (7).

Schleiermacher lectured on hermeneutics frequently between 1805 and 1833. The following are his main principles:

(a) Hermeneutics is strictly the theory of *understanding* verbal communication—as contrasted, not equated, with explicating, applying, or translating it.

(b) Hermeneutics should be a *universal* discipline—i.e. one that applies equally to all subjects areas (such as the Bible, law, and literature), to oral as well as to written language, to modern texts as well as to ancient, to works in one's own language as well as to works in foreign languages, and so forth.

(c) In particular, the interpretation of sacred texts such as the Bible is included within it—this may not rely on *special* principles, such as divine inspiration (either of the author or of the interpreter).

(d) Interpretation is a much more difficult task than is generally realized: contrary to a common misconception that "understanding occurs as a matter of course," "misunderstanding occurs as a matter of course, and so understanding must be willed and sought at every point." (This position derives from Schleiermacher's version of principle (7): deep linguistic and conceptual-intellectual diversity.)

How, then, is interpretation to be accomplished?

(e) Before the interpretation proper of a text or discourse can even begin, the interpreter must acquire a good knowledge of its historical context. (The suggestion found in some of the secondary literature that Schleiermacher thinks historical context *irrelevant* to interpretation is absurd.)

(f) Interpretation proper always has two sides: one linguistic, the other psychological. Linguistic interpretation's task (which rests on principle (5)) consists in inferring from the evidence consisting in particular actual uses of words to the rules that are governing them, i.e. to their usages and thus to their meanings; psychological interpretation instead focuses on an author's psychology. Linguistic interpretation is mainly concerned with what is common or shared in a language; psychological interpretation mainly with what is distinctive to a particular author.

(g) Schleiermacher implies several reasons why an interpreter needs to complement linguistic interpretation with psychological in this way. First, he sees such a need as arising from the deep linguistic and conceptual-intellectual distinctiveness of individuals. This distinctiveness at the individual level leads to the problem for linguistic interpretation that the actual uses of words which are available to serve as evidence from which to infer an author's exact usage or meaning will usually be relatively few in number and poor in contextual variety—a problem which an appeal to authorial psychology is supposed to help solve by providing additional clues. Second, an appeal to authorial psychology is also required in order to resolve ambiguities at the level of linguistic meaning that arise in particular contexts (i.e. even after the range of meanings available to the author for the word(s) in question is known). Third, in order fully to understand a linguistic act one needs to know not only its linguistic meaning but also what more recent philosophers have called its "illocutionary force" or intention. For example, if I encounter a stranger by a frozen lake who says to me, "The ice is thin over there," in order fully to understand his utterance I need to know not only its linguistic meaning (which in this case is clear) but also whether it is being made as a factual observation, a threat, a joke . . . (Schleiermacher himself emphasizes the first of these three considerations most. However, if, as he does, one wants to argue that interpretation needs to invoke psychology *generally*, and if, as I hinted earlier, linguistic and conceptual-intellectual distinctiveness is not in fact the pervasive phenomenon that he usually takes it to be, then it is arguably the latter two considerations that should be considered the more fundamental ones.)

(h) Interpretation also requires two different methods: a "comparative" method (i.e. a method of plain induction), which Schleiermacher sees as predominating on the linguistic side of interpretation, where it takes the interpreter from the particular uses of a word to the rule for use governing them all; and a "divinatory" method (i.e. a method of tentative, fallible hypothesis based on but also going well beyond available empirical evidence; the etymology to keep in mind here is not so much Latin *divinus* but rather French *deviner*, to guess or conjecture), which he sees as predominating on the psychological side of interpretation. (The widespread notion in the secondary literature that "divination" is for Schleiermacher a process of psychological self-projection into texts contains a tiny grain of truth, in that it is his view that interpretation requires *some* measure of psychological commonality between interpreter and interpreted, but is basically mistaken.)

(i) Ideal interpretation is of its nature a holistic activity (this principle in part rests on but also goes well beyond Schleiermacher's *semantic* holism). In particular, any given piece of text needs to be interpreted in light of the whole text to which it belongs, and both need to be interpreted in light of the broader language in which they are written, their larger historical context, a broader pre-existing genre, the author's whole corpus, and the author's overall psychology. Such holism introduces a pervasive circularity into interpretation, for, ultimately, interpreting these broader items in its turn depends on interpreting such pieces of text. Schleiermacher does not see this circle as vicious, however. Why not? His solution is not that all of these tasks should be accomplished simultaneously—for that would be beyond human capacities. Rather, it lies in the (very plausible) thought that understanding is not an all-or-nothing matter but something that comes in *degrees*, so that it is possible to make progress towards full understanding in a piecemeal way. For example, concerning the relation between a piece of text and the whole text to which it belongs, Schleiermacher recommends that we first read through and interpret as best we can each of the parts of the text in turn in order thereby to arrive at an approximate overall interpretation of the text, and that we then apply this approximate overall interpretation in order to refine our initial interpretations of the particular parts, which in turn gives us an improved overall interpretation, which can then be re-applied towards further refinement of the interpretation of the parts, and so on indefinitely.

Schleiermacher's debts to Herder in this theory of interpretation extend far beyond the framework-principles (4), (5), and (7) mentioned earlier. Indeed, Schleiermacher's theory as it has just been described is almost identical to Herder's. Some of this commonality is admittedly due to shared influences, especially Ernesti. But Schleiermacher's theory owes exclusively to Herder the two central moves (often wrongly thought to have been original with Schleiermacher) of supplementing "linguistic" with "psychological" interpretation and of identifying "divination" as the predominant method of the latter. (Herder had already made these two moves mainly in *On Thomas Abbt's Writings* [1768] and *On the Cognition and Sensation of the Human Soul* [1778].) Schleiermacher's theory as it has just been described for the most part merely draws together and systematizes ideas that already lay scattered throughout a number of Herder's works.

There are some significant exceptions to this rule of continuity, however—respects in which Schleiermacher's theory deviates from Herder's. But it is precisely here that the theory tends to become more problematic. To begin with two deviations which are *not* problematic: First, as was previously mentioned, Schleiermacher exacerbates the challenge to interpretation which principle (7) already poses by introducing principle (8), semantic holism. Second, Schleiermacher's theory explicitly introduces principle (b), the *universality* of hermeneutics. This principle is very much in the spirit of Herder's theory, but does go beyond its letter.[1]

Turning now to deviations which *are* problematic, we already noted several examples of such problematic deviations concerning the exact force of the three principles in the philosophy of language which underpin Schleiermacher's theory of interpretation, principles (4), (5), and (7). But in addition: Whereas Herder rightly emphasizes the vital importance in interpretation of correctly identifying a work's genre, and also the great difficulty of doing so in many cases, especially due to the constant changes in genres that take place and the consequent pervasive temptation falsely to assimilate unfamiliar genres to more familiar ones, Schleiermacher pays relatively little attention to this subject. Again, unlike Herder, Schleiermacher, especially in his later work, more closely specifies psychological interpretation as a process of identifying, and tracing the necessary development of, a single authorial "seminal decision [*Keimentschluß*]" that lies behind a work and unfolds itself as the work in a necessary fashion. However, this seems an unhelpful move to make, for how many works are actually composed, and hence properly interpretable, in such a way? Again, whereas Herder includes not only an author's linguistic behavior but also his non-linguistic behavior among the evidence relevant to psychological interpretation, Schleiermacher normally insists on a restriction to the former. But this too seems misguided; for example, the Marquis de Sade's recorded *acts* of cruelty seem no less potentially relevant to establishing the sadistic side of his psychological make-up, and hence to interpreting his texts in light of this, than his cruel statements. Again, unlike Herder, Schleiermacher regards the central role of "divination," or hypothesis, in interpretation as a ground for sharply distinguishing interpretation from natural science, and hence for classifying it as an art rather than a science. However, he should arguably instead have regarded it as a ground for considering interpretation and natural science *similar*. (His mistake here was evidently caused by a false assumption that natural science works by a method of plain induction—i.e. roughly: this first a is F, this second a is F, this third a is F, . . . therefore all a's are F—rather than by hypothesis.)

Schleiermacher's theory also tends to play down, obscure, or miss certain important points concerning interpretation which Friedrich Schlegel had already made. Schlegel's treatment of hermeneutic matters, in such texts as his *Philosophy of Philology* (1797) and the *Athenaeum Fragments* (1798–1800), largely resembles Schleiermacher's. But it also includes the following three points which are either less bold, obscured, or altogether missing in

Schleiermacher: (i) Schlegel emphasizes that (at least superior) texts often express *unconscious* meanings: "Every excellent work . . . aims at more than it knows" (*On Goethe's Meister* [1798]). Schleiermacher sometimes implies a similar-looking view, most famously in his doctrine that the interpreter should aim to understand an author better than the latter understood himself, but Schlegel's version of it is more radical, envisaging indeed an "infinite depth" of meaning largely unknown to the author. (ii) Schlegel emphasizes that a work often expresses important meanings, not explicitly in any of its parts, but rather through the way in which these are put together to form a whole. This is a very important point. Schleiermacher perhaps *in a way* makes it as well, but if so, then only as incorporated into and obscured by his more dubious doctrine of the "seminal decision." (iii) Unlike Schleiermacher, Schlegel emphasizes not only that works typically contain confusions which the interpreter needs to identify, but also that the interpreter needs to explain them when they occur: "It is not enough that one understand the actual sense of a confused work better than the author understood it. One must also oneself be able to know, *characterize*, and even *construe* the confusion even down to its very principles." This is another very important point.

Be these shortcomings in the details of Schleiermacher's hermeneutics as they may, his pupil Boeckh, an eminent classical philologist, subsequently gave a broadly faithful and even more systematic re-articulation of Schleiermacher's hermeneutics in lectures that were eventually published as the *Encyclopedia and Methodology of the Philological Sciences* (1877), and through the combined influence of Schleiermacher's and Boeckh's treatments it achieved something very much like the status of the official hermeneutical methodology of nineteenth-century classical and biblical scholarship.[2]

5. Theory of Translation

As was already mentioned, Schleiermacher also develops his theory of translation on the foundation of the Herder-influenced principles (4), (5), and (7), together with (8), his own semantic holism, which exacerbates the challenge to translation already posed by (7).

Schleiermacher was himself a masterful translator, whose German translations of Plato are still widely used and admired today, about two hundred years after they were done. So his views on translation carry a certain prima facie authority. He explains his theory of translation mainly in the brilliant essay *On the Different Methods of Translation* (1813). The following are some of his main points:

(a) Translation usually faces the problem of a conceptual gulf between the source language and the target language (as the latter currently exists). (This is an application of principle (7).)

(b) This situation makes translation an extremely difficult task, posing a major obstacle to the attainment of translation's traditional primary goal, the faithful reproduction of meaning. In this connection, Schleiermacher in particular notes the following problem (which might be dubbed the paradox of paraphrase): If, faced with the task of translating an alien concept, a translator attempts to reproduce its intension by reproducing its extension with the aid of an elaborate paraphrase in his own language, he will generally find that as he gets closer to the original extension he undermines the original intension in other ways. For instance, faced with Homer's color word *chlôros*, a word which Homer sometimes applies to things that we would classify as green (e.g. healthy foliage) but at other times to things that we would classify as yellow (e.g. honey), a translator might attempt to reproduce the extension correctly by translating the word as "green or yellow." But in doing so he would be sacrificing the original intension in other ways—for Homer did not *have* either the concept green or the concept yellow (only the concept *chlôros*), and in addition for Homer *chlôros* was not a *disjunctive* concept.

(c) Schleiermacher also identifies a number of further challenges which commonly exacerbate the difficulty of translation. For example, he notes that in the case of poetry it is necessary to reproduce not only the semantic but also the musical aspects of the original, such as meter and rhyme—and this not merely as a desideratum over and above the main task of reproducing meaning, but also as an essential *part* of that task, because in poetry such musical features serve as essential vehicles for the precise expression of meaning. And he argues that in addition to reproducing meaning a translation should attempt to convey to its readership where an author was being conceptually conventional and where conceptually original—for example, by using older vocabulary from the target language in the former cases and relative neologisms in the latter. But he notes that in both of these connections the added requirement or desideratum involved will frequently stand in tension with that of finding the closest semantic fit—for example, it will turn out that the word which would best reproduce a rhyme or best reflect a concept's vintage is not the one that is closest in meaning to the word in the original.

(d) Because of this great difficulty, the translator needs to possess real interpretive expertise, and to be an "artist," if he is to cope with the task of translation at all adequately.

(e) The conceptual gulf that poses the central challenge here might in principle be tackled in one of two broad ways: either by bringing the author's linguistic-conceptual world closer to that of the reader of the translation or vice versa. The former approach had been championed, among others, by Luther in his classic *Letter on Translation* (1530) and practiced by him in his translation of the Bible (he called it *Verdeutschung*, "Germanizing"). However, Schleiermacher finds it unacceptable, mainly because it inevitably distorts the author's concepts and thoughts. Schleiermacher therefore champions the alternative approach of bringing the reader towards the linguistic-conceptual world of the author as the only acceptable one.

But how can this possibly be accomplished?

(f) According to Schleiermacher, the key to a solution lies in the plasticity of language. Because of this plasticity, even if the usages of words, and hence the concepts, expressed by the target language *as it currently exists* are incommensurable with the author's, it is still possible for a translator to "bend the language of the translation as far as possible towards that of the original in order to communicate as far as possible an impression of the system of concepts developed in it." (This solution presupposes principle (5).) For instance, the translator faced with the task of translating Homer's word *chlôros* would select the closest counterpart in the target language, say "green," but then modify its usage over the course of the translation so that it gets applied not only to things which are green (e.g. healthy foliage) but also to things which are yellow (e.g. honey).

(g) This approach entails a strong preference for translating any given word in the original in a uniform way throughout the translation rather than switching between two or more different ways of translating it in different contexts.

(h) This approach also makes for translations that are considerably less easy to read than those that can be achieved by the alternative approach (*Verdeutschung*). However, this is an acceptable price to pay given that the only alternative is a failure to convey the author's meaning at all accurately. Moreover, the offending peculiarities have a positive value in that they constantly remind the reader of the conceptual unfamiliarity of the material that is being translated and of the "bending" approach that is being employed.

(i) In order to work at all effectively, though, this approach requires that large amounts of relevant material be translated, so that the reader of the translation becomes habituated to it and acquires enough examples of a particular word's unfamiliar use in enough different contexts to enable him to infer the unfamiliar rule for use involved.

(j) Even this optimal approach to translation has severe limitations, however. In particular, it will often be impossible to reproduce the holistic aspects of meaning—the several related usages of a given word, the systems of related words/concepts, and the distinctive grammar of the language. And since these holistic features are internal to a word's meaning, this will entail a shortfall in the communication of its meaning by the translation. Reading a translation therefore inevitably remains only a poor second best to reading the original, and the translator should think of his task as one of striving to approximate an infinite, never fully realizable, ideal.

(k) Translation is still amply justified, though—not only for the obvious reason that it is needed in order to make works available to people who want to read them but are not in the fortunate position of knowing the original languages, but also for the less obvious reason that through its "bending" approach it effects a conceptual enrichment of their language (and through its reproduction of musical features a musical enrichment).

(l) Nor (Schleiermacher adds in answer to a worry which Herder had expressed) need we fear that this enrichment will deprive our language of its authentic character. For in cases where a real conflict with that character arises, the enrichments in question will soon wither from the language.

Here again (as in the case of interpretation), not only the framework principles (4), (5), and (7), but *most* of these ideas about translation come from Herder. In particular, Schleiermacher's central strategy of "bending" the target language in order to cope with conceptual incommensurability, and his point that it is also important to convey the musical aspects of an original (poetic) text in order to convey its meaning accurately, both do so. (Relevant Herderian sources here are the *Fragments on Recent German Literature* [1767–8] and the *Popular Songs* [*Volkslieder*] [1774].) However, unlike Schleiermacher's theory of interpretation, which as I mentioned often worsens Herder's, this theory of translation tends to refine Herder's in some modest but significant ways. Among the ideas just adumbrated, examples of this occur in (b), where Schleiermacher's paradox of paraphrase is largely novel; (c), where his ideal of making clear in a translation at which points the author was being conceptually conventional and at which points conceptually original is novel in comparison with Herder; (h), where his point that the oddities resulting from the "bending" approach are not only an acceptable price to pay but can actually serve a positive function is novel; (i), which is a novel point; (j), where his point about the principled limitation on the successfulness of translations posed by semantic holism is novel; and (l), which plausibly contradicts Herder.[3]

6. Aesthetics

Schleiermacher tended to be quite self-deprecating about his sensitivity to and knowledge of art, and hence his aptitude for aesthetics (e.g. in *On Religion* and the *Soliloquies*, where he is clearly rather in awe of the greater talent and expertise in this area enjoyed by such Romantic friends as the Schlegel brothers), and accordingly tended to shy away from discussing the subject in detail in his earlier work. However, he did eventually bring himself to confront the subject systematically, namely in his lectures on aesthetics (first delivered in 1819, and then again in 1825 and 1832–3).

Part of his motivation behind this eventual confrontation with the subject—and part of the reason why it remains interesting today—derives from the fact that the phenomenon of art, and in particular the phenomenon of non-linguistic art (e.g. painting, sculpture, and music), prompts a certain theoretical question which is of fundamental importance, not only for the philosophy of art itself, but also for hermeneutics or the theory of interpretation, and for the philosophy of language that underlies it: Do non-linguistic arts such as painting, sculpture, and music express thoughts and meanings, and if so how? This question is obviously important for the philosophy of art. But it is also important for hermeneutics, or the theory of interpretation, because it brings in its train such further issues as whether the theory of interpretation ought not to treat additional forms of expression besides the linguistic ones treated by Schleiermacher's own hermeneutics, what the appropriate methods of interpretation might be in such additional cases, and how such additional cases and their interpretive methods might relate to linguistic ones. Moreover, the question mentioned is also important for the philosophy of language that underpins Schleiermacher's theory of interpretation, as embodied in principles (4) and (5). For a positive answer to this question might well seem to threaten those two principles, or at least to show that they need radical revision.

In his last cycle of aesthetics lectures (1832–3) Schleiermacher initially pursued a very simple strategy for dealing with these issues concerning non-linguistic art. However, he eventually realized that the strategy in question is untenable, and abandoned it for a more promising but also more ambiguous position.

His whole train of thought there closely followed one that Herder had already pursued in the *Critical Forests* (1769), and so it may be useful to begin with a brief sketch of the latter. By the time of writing the *Critical Forests* Herder was already committed to his own versions of principles (4) and (5). Accordingly, in reaction to the phenomenon of the non-linguistic arts the book initially set out to argue for a theory of their nature which would preserve consistency with those principles, and it did so in a very straightforward way, denying the non-linguistic arts the ability to express thoughts or meanings *autonomously* of language by denying them the ability to express thoughts or meanings *at all*: whereas poetry has a sense, a soul, a force, music is a mere succession of objects in time, and sculpture and painting are merely spatial; whereas poetry not only depends on the senses but also relates to the imagination, music, sculpture, and painting belong solely to the senses (to hearing, feeling, and vision, respectively); whereas poetry uses *voluntary and conventional* signs, music, sculpture, and painting employ only *natural* ones. However, as Herder proceeded with his book he came to realize that this simplistic solution was untenable: in the third part of the book he stumbled upon the awkward case of ancient coins, which, though normally non-linguistic, clearly do nonetheless often express thoughts and meanings in pictorial ways. This realization did not lead him to abandon his versions of principles (4) and (5), however. Instead, it brought him to a more refined account of the non-linguistic arts which was still consistent with those principles: the non-linguistic arts do sometimes express thoughts and meanings, but the thoughts and meanings in question are ones which are *parasitic on a prior linguistic expression or expressibility of them by the artist*. In the fourth part of the book (not published until the middle of the nineteenth century, and hence unknown to Schleiermacher) Herder already extended this solution from coins to painting; and in subsequent works he extended it to sculpture and music as well.

Schleiermacher's aesthetics lectures follow a strikingly similar course. He initially sets out to develop a version of the theory that Herder had initially developed in the *Critical Forests*, correlating the several non-linguistic arts with the different senses as Herder's theory had done (his only significant revision here consists in modifying Herder's correlation of sculpture with the sense of touch to include vision as well as touch). Like Herder's initial theory, Schleiermacher's is largely motivated by his prior commitment to principles (4) and (5), which, again like Herder's initial theory, it seeks to vindicate in a naive way: non-linguistic arts, such as music and sculpture, do not express thoughts or meanings *autonomously* of language because they do not express them *at all*. For example, Schleiermacher argues that music merely expresses physiologically based "life-conditions [*Lebenszustände*]," not representations or thoughts. However, rather like Herder with his ancient coins, in the course of developing this naive solution Schleiermacher stumbles upon a case which forces him to the realization that it is untenable: He develops his naive solution smoothly enough for the cases of music and painting, but in the middle of his discussion of sculpture he suddenly recalls Pausanias' account that the very earliest Greek sculptures were merely rough blocks whose function was to serve, precisely, as symbols of religious *ideas* (oops!). He subsequently goes on to note that an analogous point holds for other non-linguistic arts, such as painting, as well. Accordingly, at this stage in his lectures he changes tack. He now acknowledges that non-linguistic arts *do* (at least sometimes) express thoughts and meanings after all, and he goes on to vacillate between two new, and mutually conflicting, accounts of that fact: (a) The arts in question do so in such a way that the thoughts and meanings involved are at least sometimes not (yet) linguistically articulable. (In particular, he suggests that the early Greek sculpture just mentioned expressed religious ideas which only *later* got expressed linguistically.) This account would entail abandoning or at least severely revising principles (4) and (5). (b) The arts in question do so in virtue of a pre-existing linguistic articulation or articulability of the same thoughts and meanings in the artist. (Schleiermacher actually only says in virtue of "something universal," "a representation," but a dependence on language seems clearly implied.) This account is similar to Herder's final account, and, like it, would preserve principles (4) and (5). In the end, then, having renounced his initial—clearly untenable—position, Schleiermacher is left torn between these two more plausible-looking positions, which, however, contradict each other.

The eighteenth- and nineteenth-century German hermeneutic tradition as a whole was similarly torn between these two positions. As has already been mentioned, (b) was the considered position at which Herder eventually arrived. But (a) had strong champions as well—in particular, Hamann, Wackenroder and Tieck, Hegel (concerning architecture and sculpture), and the later Dilthey. The choice between these two positions is a genuinely difficult one, philosophically speaking.[4]

Where does this leave Schleiermacher in relation to the several issues bearing on his theory of interpretation and his philosophy of language which, I suggested, encouraged him to undertake this investigation of non-linguistic art in the first place? Concerning the primary question, whether the non-linguistic arts express thoughts and meanings and if so how, he has now realized that they do indeed (at least sometimes) express thoughts and meanings, but he remains torn on exactly how they do so. Concerning his theory of interpretation, that realization is already important, because it shows that interpretation theory does indeed need to extend its coverage beyond linguistic cases to include at least some that are non-linguistic. But he remains torn on the further issues in this area—in particular, on whether, as (a) implies, there will be cases in which the interpretation of non-linguistic art will transcend the interpretation of any associated language or, as (b) implies, it will always be dependent on and restricted by the interpretation of associated language. Finally, concerning the philosophy of language which underpins his theory of interpretation, he remains torn about whether the thoughts and meanings expressed by non-linguistic art are always parasitic on language (position (b)), so that principles (4) and (5) can be retained without qualification or modification, or are instead sometimes independent of language (position (a)), so that principles (4) and (5) will either have to be abandoned or (with Hamann in his *Metacritique* [1784]) (re)construed in a way that stretches their reference to "language" and "words" to include not-strictly-linguistic-or-verbal symbol use in the non-linguistic arts.

Another motive behind Schleiermacher's treatment of art in his late aesthetics lectures concerns its cultural status, especially relative to religion. It was an abiding concern of Schleiermacher's from early in his career until the very end of it to subordinate art to religion. The final cycle of the aesthetics lectures from 1832−3 is merely the last in a long line of attempts to achieve this goal. It seems to me, however, that, partly for reasons already touched on, this last attempt turns out to be oddly and interestingly self-subverting.

Let me first briefly review Schleiermacher's series of attempts to subordinate art, and then explain how this last one proves self-subverting. It was already one of the early Schleiermacher's primary goals to turn contemporary culture, and especially the Romantic movement, away from the then fashionable idea that art was the highest possible form of insight towards the idea that religion was. This is an important part of the project of *On Religion* (1799), where he criticizes the sort of elevation of art above religion that Goethe and Schiller had begun and the Romantics had accentuated, complains of the trivial nature of modern art, and argues that art ought to subserve religion as Plato had thought.[5] The ethics lectures of 1812−13 continue the same project in a certain way. There Schleiermacher represents art as of its very nature a collective expression of religious feeling (one which differs in accordance with the differences between religions). In other words, he represents art as only true to its own nature when it subserves religion. The 1830 psychology lectures play an interesting variation on the same theme. There Schleiermacher argues that the perception of beauty is a feeling but one which has a certain sort of deep cognitive content in that it expresses the relation of intelligence to Being. This makes it sound very much like religious feeling, and indeed in these lectures it is treated as a sort of close second-in-command to religious feeling. It might seem as though, from Schleiermacher's standpoint, there was a danger here of art acquiring too independent and exalted a status. However, that danger is in part averted by the fact that he is here talking primarily about *natural* beauty, and only secondarily about artistic beauty.

The 1832−3 aesthetics lectures continue this sort of art-demoting project, but in a different way. Schleiermacher's initial intention there, it seems, was to demote art (in comparison with religion) in two ways: First, as we saw, the lectures initially set out to give an account of non-linguistic arts (music, painting, and sculpture) which represents them as merely expressive of sensuous feelings and non-cognitive in character. Second, the lectures give an account of poetry which represents it as merely national and indeed merely individual in nature (not universal). Thus the lectures argue that art generally, and therefore poetry in particular, is national in nature, not universal like science and (in a way) religion, and more radically that poetry indeed has the function of expressing individuality, of resisting even the commonality of a national language (thereby making explicit a potential which is also present, though less fully realized, in normal language-use). However, as I suggested, this twofold strategy for demoting art turns out to be curiously self-subverting. For one thing, as we saw, the model of non-linguistic art as merely sensuous and non-cognitive in the end proves unsustainable. Moreover, not only does non-linguistic art turn out to have a cognitive content after all, but in addition that fact becomes clear from a case (the earliest Greek sculpture) in which the content in question is not trivial but deeply religious in character. Furthermore, this self-subversion would be even more extreme if position (a) won out over position (b) in the end. For another thing, poetry's function of expressing individuality implies that for Schleiermacher it represents the *highest ethical value* (for more on individuality's high status in Schleiermacher's ethics, see below). In short, what was intended as a demotion of art turns willy-nilly into a sort of cognitive-religious and ethical exaltation of it.

7. Dialectics

Most of Schleiermacher's earliest philosophical work was in areas of the subject which might reasonably be described as peripheral in comparison with such central areas as metaphysics and epistemology (in particular, ethics, philosophy of religion, and hermeneutics). This fact, together no doubt with the imposing presence of several competitors who had recently made or were making contributions in those central areas (including Kant, Fichte, Schelling, and Hegel), seems to have spurred Schleiermacher to develop his own treatment of them. The result was his "dialectics," which he began presenting in lecture-form in 1811. (The subject-title calls to mind relevant positions not only in Plato and Aristotle, but also in Kant and Hegel.)

Accordingly, Schleiermacher's dialectics in some ways carries the marks of a discipline which he felt forced to develop, rather than one for which he had a clear, compelling vision (as he had for his philosophy of religion and his hermeneutics, for instance). For one thing, the nature of the discipline undergoes a striking shift between its two earliest versions (the lectures of 1811 and 1814–15)—which have the character of fairly conventional treatments of metaphysical and epistemological issues, already concerned indeed to a certain extent with resolving disagreements, but in a purely theoretical way—and its two main later versions (the lectures of 1822 and the book-fragment from 1833), which make the art of actually resolving disagreements through conversation the core of the discipline (albeit that "conversation" here includes not only the paradigm case of oral communication but also written communication and even dialogue internal to a single person's mind). With some qualification, this shift might be described as one from a more Aristotelian to a more Socratic-Platonic conception of "dialectics."

For another thing, in all of its versions Schleiermacher's dialectics has an oddly rag-bag appearance, including as it does not only material that would naturally be classified as metaphysics and epistemology, but also large helpings of philosophy of mind, logic (especially the logic of concepts and judgments; Schleiermacher treats the logic of syllogism in a reductive and rather deprecatory way), philosophy of science, and philosophy of religion.

In its final versions (on which I shall henceforth focus here), the discipline has roughly the following character: Its concern is with what Schleiermacher calls "pure thought," as distinguished from the thought of everday affairs or art—that is, with thought which aims at truth, rather than merely at achieving practical ends or inventing fictions.[6]

According to Schleiermacher, genuine knowledge of its very nature requires, not only (1) correspondence to reality, but also (2) systematic coherence with *all* knowledge and (3) universal agreement among people. (The main motive behind this elaborate position seems to derive from the thought that there is in principle no way to determine the fulfillment of condition (1) *directly*, so that believers need to rely on guidance by the fulfillment of conditions (2) and (3).) [7]

Not surprisingly given the strength of the three conditions just mentioned, Schleiermacher considers genuine knowledge to be only an "idea" towards which we can make progress, not something that we can ever actually achieve. (His position here strongly resembles his official positions in hermeneutics and translation theory that the correct understanding of another person and the correct translation of a text are only things to which we can approximate, not that we can ever actually achieve.)

Schleiermacher's dialectics is largely conceived as a methodology for making such progress. This project proceeds relatively smoothly in connection with conditions (1) and (2). For example, in connection with (1), he develops certain principles concerning how to form concepts correctly rather than incorrectly (i.e. in such a way that—to borrow a more recent idiom—they, their superordinate genus-concepts, their subordinate species-concepts, and their contrasting coordinate concepts "carve nature at the joints"). And in connection with (2), while he acknowledges that the task of forming a totality of knowledge is of its nature incompletable, he nonetheless prescribes what he calls "heuristic" and "architectonic" procedures for, respectively, amassing pieces of knowledge and forming them together into a coherent whole.

However, the project runs into deeper difficulties in relation to condition (3). There are two main problems here. First, in addition to the obvious and avowed impossibility of actually accessing all people in order to come to agreement with them, Schleiermacher also identifies a further obstacle in the way of reaching, or even making significant progress towards, agreement with them: the deep differences that occur between different languages and modes of thought. The dialectics lectures themselves fail to find any very promising way of coping with this problem. The 1822 version attempts two ways, but neither looks hopeful. Its first approach consists in hypothesizing a domain of "innate concepts" common to everyone (with certain qualifications, for example that these concepts require sensations in order to be actualized). This would certainly solve the problem, but only by contradicting Schleiermacher's normal, and philosophically superior, position, from which the problem arose in the first place, that there *is no* such conceptual commonality across all different languages (or even, Schleiermacher normally adds, between all individuals who in some sense share a language). The second approach attempted is an argument that we need to develop a complete history of the differences in question and of how they arose. However, this seems beside the point—a distraction from the problem rather than a solution to it. In the 1833 book-fragment Schleiermacher at points seems close to giving up on this problem, saying in one place that because of it dialectics must restrict itself to a specific "linguistic sphere." But at other points he evidently still clings to the hope of finding common ground uniting different "linguistic spheres." What sort of solution does he have in mind? The answer can perhaps be seen from an 1831 address that he gave on Leibniz's idea of a universal language. In this address he in effect argues that it was a mistake on Leibniz's part to suppose that there was *already* a conceptual common ground shared by everyone, which could be captured in a universal language (this also amounts to a rejection of his own dubious idea in the 1822 lectures of common "innate concepts"), but that the sort of conceptual common ground that Leibniz had thus wrongly envisaged as *already* existing can nonetheless be *achieved* (or at least approached) for the sciences, namely by cultivating an attitude of openness to the borrowing of conceptual resources from other languages as such resources prove themselves useful for the sciences (a process which, according to Schleiermacher, is in fact already heavily underway, and which is realizable either through outright borrowing of the foreign words in question or through translation of them into one's language in the sort of sensitive way that his theory of translation advocates). Schleiermacher points out that this solution requires an (in any case healthy) shedding of prejudices about the superiority of one's own language, mode of thought, and people over others. This looks like Schleiermacher's most promising solution to the problem in question. He did not, however, live long enough to develop it in detail or to build on it towards a more complete method for resolving interlinguistic disagreements.

Second, and perhaps more surprisingly, Schleiermacher's dialectics lectures do not even develop a substantive account of how to resolve disagreements through conversation *within* a "linguistic sphere." However, here again it is fortunately possible to supplement the dialectics lectures with extraneous material which goes further in such a direction. One important text in this connection is Schleiermacher's early essay *Toward a Theory of Sociable Conduct* (1799), which is precisely concerned with the art of conversation within a linguistic sphere. This early essay emphasizes the importance of finding (conceptual) "content" that one shares with one's interlocutor(s), and restricting one's conversation to this. Schleiermacher accordingly recommends in the essay that one begin a conversation guided by a sort of minimal estimate of such content arrived at from one's knowledge of such things as the profession, the educational background, and the class of one's interlocutor(s), but that one thence tentatively and experimentally work outwards towards identifying and exploiting further shared content—a process which he recommends one should undertake, not by the heavy-handed method of introducing doubtfully shared content directly, but rather by the subtler method of introducing it indirectly in the form of a dimension of allusion and satire which one adds to one's treatment of already established shared content (after which, if the response is positive, it can join the previously established shared content as a proper subject-matter for direct treatment). Another helpful source in this connection is Schleiermacher's hermeneutics lectures, which implicitly revise the earlier account just described in two respects: (a) In that account conversation was to be restricted to conceptual content that was already shared between interlocutors. But as we saw previously, by the time Schleiermacher writes the hermeneutics lectures he is skeptical that people *ever* really share conceptual content. Consequently, he would presumably now set the bar for fruitful conversation somewhat lower than strict sharing. (b) Also, it seems reasonable to infer from his conception of hermeneutics that he would now place less emphasis on discovering pre-existing commonalities, or near-commonalities, and more on refining those found and establishing further ones—in both cases, with the help of adept use of the art of hermeneutics.

Finally, Schleiermacher's hermeneutics lectures also supply a further part of his seemingly missing solution to the problem of reaching agreement through conversation, both in inter- and in intra-linguistic contexts. Clearly, any art of reaching agreement through conversation is going to depend on an art of interpreting interlocutors. Accordingly, the dialectics lectures explicitly assert the dependence of dialectics on hermeneutics (as well as vice versa), Schleiermacher's conception of hermeneutics as a universal discipline ensures its applicability to conversations, and Schleiermacher mentions in the hermeneutics lectures that he sometimes applies his own hermeneutical principles in conversational contexts. In short, Schleiermacher's hermeneutics itself constitutes an important component of his art of reaching agreement through conversation.

In sum, whereas Schleiermacher's final conception of dialectics as a discipline leads one to expect it to provide a fairly detailed set of procedures for resolving both inter- and intra-linguistic disagreements in conversation (analogous to the detailed set of procedures for interpretation that one finds in his hermeneutics), this expectation is largely disappointed by the dialectics lectures themselves. However, one can supplement the dialectics lectures from other texts in order to see how Schleiermacher might have envisaged a fuller solution to this task.

One last point which also deserves mention in this connection is the following. Schleiermacher's most prominent motive for developing such an art of conversation is the epistemological one described above. That may or may not be a good motive in the end. However, Schleiermacher also has further and independent motives behind this art which are more obviously attractive. Thus, the 1831 address on Leibniz implies two additional motives behind the intercultural side of the art: first, Schleiermacher's cosmopolitan concern for humanity as a whole in all its diversity constitutes a moral reason for promoting fruitful intercultural dialogue; and second, his sense that insight, far from being our monopoly, is dispersed among many cultures constitutes another reason for us to engage in such dialogue. (Schleiermacher would presumably say that analogous considerations help to justify the intracultural side of the art as well.) Again, the essay *Toward a Theory of Sociable Conduct* emphasizes an additional motive behind the intracultural side of the art. In this essay Schleiermacher does not mention his later epistemological motive at all, but instead focuses on more direct benefits which he expects from fruitful conversation between members of society, in particular the individual's enrichment of his own limited perspective through incorporation of the different perspectives of other people. (Schleiermacher would presumably say that an analogous consideration helps to justify the intercultural side of the art as well.) In short, even if it were to turn out that Schleiermacher's predominant epistemological motive for developing an art of inter- and intra-cultural conversation were unpersuasive, such an art might still be valuable for other reasons which he also has in mind such as these.

Finally, it is also worth mentioning a few further positions from Schleier-macher's dialectics briefly. One rather striking position is a denial that any concepts, thoughts, or cognitions are either purely a priori in nature or purely empirical, either the product of the "intellectual" function alone or of the "organic" function alone. All are the product of *both* functions—though the *proportions* in which they are involved vary from case to case.

More specifically, as Schleiermacher conceives the situation, all are located on a continuum that stretches between the maximally "intellectual" ideas of Being or God and the maximally "organic" chaos of sensations. These two extremes do not themselves involve mixture: Being or God is purely intellectual, while the chaos of sensations is purely organic. However, they do not for that reason constitute counterexamples to the position just mentioned, because they are not themselves strictly speaking concepts, thoughts, or cognitions.

As I mentioned previously, Schleiermacher's theory of concepts also says that they are in each case defined by relations of subsumption under higher concepts, contrast with correlative concepts similarly subsumed, and subsumption of further concepts under them. Subsumption under the non-concept Being and the subsumption of a class of primitive judgments about sensations constitute special cases at the two extremes of this conceptual hierarchy.

Another position which Schleiermacher holds is that the (Kantian) distinction between analytic and synthetic judgments is a merely "relative" one. One reason for this position seems to lie in his view that all judgments are partly empirical in nature (a consideration which anticipates Quine). But what he mainly seems to have in mind is that it is always in some sense up to us to decide how many and which characteristic marks to build into any given subject concept, and therefore how many and which judgments in which that subject concept features will count as analytic or as synthetic.

A last feature of Schleiermacher's dialectics is more puzzling. Schleiermacher notes at one point that he wants to chart a sort of middle course between ancient dialectics, which had the virtue of openness but the vice of courting skepticism, and the dogmatism of the scholastics, for whom everything of importance was pre-decided in an assumed religious principle. His concession to the former position has in effect already been described above. But what about his concession to the latter? This takes the form of positing a "transcendental ground" or God which is (1) beyond all oppositions, including those of thought/reality, thought/volition, and concept/judgment, (2) beyond Being (even though Being is itself beyond such oppositions), (3) an essential impulse behind, and accompaniment of, all attempts to know, and (4) not thinkable or linguistically expressible but instead felt. This is all rather mysterious. For example, the philosophical rationale for positing such a "transcendental ground" or God as beyond rather than identical with Being is obscure, and so too is the exact way in which it is supposed to be the impulse behind and accompaniment of all attempts to know.

8. Ethics

Schleiermacher's ethical thought divides into two overlapping chronological phases: The first phase—which stretched from the late 1780s until about 1803—was mainly critical in character. Early in this phase, the three unpublished essays *On the Highest Good* (1789), *On What Gives Value to Life* (1792–3), and *On Freedom* (1790–3) mounted a sustained attack on Kant's ethical theory, and at the end of this phase the longer published work *Outlines of a Critique of Previous Ethical Theory* (1803) developed that attack into a more comprehensive and systematic critique of previous ethical theories. The second phase—which began around 1800—was by contrast mainly constructive in character. To this phase belong the *Soliloquies* (1800), the *Draft of an Ethics* (1805–6), and Schleiermacher's mature ethics lectures (including the complete draft from 1812–13, as well as a number of later partial drafts).

The three early essays *On the Highest Good*, *On What Gives Value to Life*, and *On Freedom* criticize and reject central tenets of Kant's moral philosophy: in particular, Kant's inclusion in the "highest good [*summum bonum*]" of an apportioning of happiness to moral desert; Kant's position that this must be believed in as a presupposition of morality, so that its own implicit presuppositions, an afterlife of the soul and a God, must be so too (the doctrine of the "postulates"); and Kant's incompatibilism concerning causal determinism and the freedom required for moral responsibility, and consequent recourse to the causally indeterministic noumenal realm as the locus for freedom (*On Freedom* argues for the causal determination of all human actions, but for the compatibility of this with the freedom required for moral responsibility).

A further area of disagreement with Kant forms the hinge on which Schleiermacher's development of his own constructive ethical theory turns. Kant's fundamental moral principle, the "categorical imperative," consisted according to its central formula in a requirement that an agent's moral maxim (or intention) be consistent when universalized, and was conceived by Kant to apply uniformly to *all* human beings. Schleiermacher rejects this position in two ways. First, already in *On What Gives Value to Life*, and then especially in the *Soliloquies*, he argues against the latter idea of uniformity in ethics—instead asserting, in the spirit of Herder (and others influenced by him, such as Goethe, Schiller, and fellow Romantics), the value of *diversity* or *individuality* even in the moral sphere. In this connection, Schleiermacher champions not only a (moral) distinctiveness of different human societies vis-à-vis the human species as a whole (this had been Herder's main cause), but also a (moral) distinctiveness of the individual vis-à-vis his society (this had also been Herder's cause). (In *On Religion* Schleiermacher makes an analogous case for both societal and individual diversity in religion. His positive evaluation of societal and individual diversity naturally also extends beyond morals and religion.)

Second, Schleiermacher also rejects the content of Kant's "categorical imperative" as specified by its central formula: the requirement of consistency of a maxim under universalization. In *On Religion* and the *Soliloquies* he is rather inclined to champion Kant's subordinate formula of a commitment to the welfare of *humanity*, though not in Kant's sense of a common rational nature, but instead in Herder's sense of all human beings in their diversities as well as their commonalities. (In *On Religion* he discusses the historical dimension of this principle of humanity in a Herderian vein, like Herder in his *Ideas for the Philosophy of History of Humanity* [1784–91] emphasizing the important role played by (Christian) religion in advancing it, and interpreting history as its progressive realization.)

This double position of Schleiermacher's might seem to court the following sort of problem: What if the moral values of a society or an individual conflict with the ideal of humanity? What, for example, if the society is Nazi Germany or the individual Hitler? In the *Soliloquies* Schleiermacher forestalls this sort of problem by limiting the forms of moral distinctiveness and individuality that he supports to those that are compatible with, or even promotive of, the ideal of humanity. Thus he expresses his commitment to moral distinctiveness or individuality in such formulas as that a person should be an individual "without violating the laws of humanity," that "each human being should represent humanity in his own way," and that what is valuable is a person's "distinctive being and its relation to humanity." Similarly, Schleiermacher's championing of (moral) diversity or individuality is always combined with requirements of a measure of conformity with a broader species-wide or societal whole.

This constructive tension between "distinctive [*eigentümlich*]" and "universal" sides of ethics survives to constitute the central principle of Schleiermacher's mature ethics lectures. There he begins by arguing that very general forms or analogues of such a constructive tension exist as universal facts of nature—that all finite beings exhibit such a tension, more specifically that all life does so in the form of a tension between autonomy and social commonality, and more specifically still that all human mental life does so in this same form. He then goes on to derive from this a moral duty to realize such a tension in one's own person.

This position provokes certain questions, to which the answers are not entirely clear. First, is Schleiermacher not here guilty of the so-called "naturalistic fallacy," of attempting to deduce an "ought" from an "is"? The answer to this question would depend on the exact nature of his derivation of the moral duty from the universal facts of nature, which is obscure. Second, how can a synthesis of commonality with individuality both be an unavoidable fact about human nature (e.g. because we can never quite share *any* concepts, we also can never quite share any moral concepts in particular) and be a moral duty? There are two possible answers to this puzzle. One would appeal to Schleiermacher's determinism and compatibilism; that a mode of existence or behavior is inevitable does not for him preclude its moral obligatoriness. The other would instead appeal to the fact that the sort of synthesis in question can come in varying degrees; it might be that *some* degree of moral individuality is indeed inevitable for the reason mentioned but that the degree which is morally required is greater.

In addition to the central principle just discussed, three further aspects of the mature ethics lectures are worth mentioning briefly: (a) As was reflected in the argument just sketched, Schleiermacher's mature conception of ethics is that it is fundamentally ontological rather than merely prescriptive in character: it is based on the immanence of "reason" in "nature," and is hence more fundamentally a matter of an "is" than of an "ought." (b) Accordingly (with an eye to the role of "reason" just mentioned), for Schleiermacher ethics is not fundamentally a matter of sentiments—these, he says, simply vary—but instead of cognitions, or more exactly, of something that grounds both ethical sentiments and ethical cognitions. (Here Schleiermacher is close to agreement with Kant.) (c) Accordingly again (but this time with an eye to the predominance of ontology over prescription just mentioned), Schleiermacher divides his ethics into a Doctrine of Goods, a Doctrine of Virtue, and a Doctrine of Duties, treating them in this sequence in order to reflect what he takes to be the greater fundamentalness of goods over virtues and of virtues over duties.

Despite these intriguing lines of thought, Schleiermacher's ethics lectures are not a great success. They contain a rather unholy mixture of, not only ethics in the usual sense, but also political philosophy, metaphysics, epistemology, and philosophy of mind; lurch back and forth between claims of startling dubiousness and claims of startling banality (with too little in between); and hold all this together with a thick stain of obscurantism and a thin varnish of systematicity. One often gets the impression that, having put the more critical phase of his work in ethics behind him, Schleiermacher found that he did not really have enough constructive to say about the subject to fill up the hours in the lecture hall.

9. Political and Social Philosophy

Schleiermacher's political and social philosophy is found scattered throughout a considerable number of works from different periods. Its most systematic, but not necessarily most interesting, statement occurs in his lectures on the theory of the state, delivered between 1808–9 and 1833.

Concerning international politics, Schleiermacher's fundamental position is thoroughly Herderian: a cosmopolitan commitment to equal moral respect for all peoples in their diversity. This position is already articulated in *On What Gives Value to Life* (1792–3); it is central to *On Religion* (1799) and the *Soliloquies* (1800), in the form of a commitment to the Herderian ideal of "humanity"; and it survives in later works as well (for example, in the 1831 address on Leibniz's idea of a universal language).

Concerning domestic politics: Schleiermacher was always somewhat reticent about fundamental constitutional questions. To judge from his early enthusiasm for the French Revolution, and his republican-democratic model of an ideal church in *On Religion*, the early Schleiermacher was strongly attracted to republicanism and democracy (like Herder and the young Friedrich Schlegel). However, his later position—while it still makes consent a conditio sine qua non of any genuine state—is more sympathetic to aristocratic and monarchical forms of government. Thus in his lectures on the theory of the state from 1829–33 he argues that whereas smaller and "lower" states are naturally democratic, large and "higher" ones are naturally aristocratic or monarchical.

However, Schleiermacher's domestic politics is more consistently radical in another respect: liberalism. (Here again he is heavily indebted to Herder.) Already in 1799 the essay *Toward a Theory of Sociable Conduct* argues that there should be a sphere of free (by which Schleiermacher means especially: state-free) social interaction, in order to make possible the development and communication of individuality; and *On Religion* argues strongly against state interference in religion, making the liberation of religion from such interference a fundamental part of its program for developing individualism in religion, and diagnosing some of the worst vices of current churches and religion in terms of such interference. This liberalism remains prominent in the ethics lectures of 1812–13, which add to the positions just mentioned a proscription of state interference in the universities. And it is still central to Schleiermacher's political thought in his (otherwise much more conservative) late lectures on the theory of the state from 1829 to 1833, where he argues that the three spheres of sociality, religion, and science (e.g. the universities) lie beyond the legitimate power of the state, and notes critically that the current (Prussian) state falls short of this ideal.[8] Schleiermacher's reasons for his broad liberalism are severalfold, but a fundamental one is the need to free up a domain in which the basic good of *individuality* can develop.

Schleiermacher devotes especially close attention to the question of *religion's* proper relation to the state (and to other socio-political institutions). As was mentioned, in *On Religion* he indicates two main reasons for wanting to see religion freed from state interference: first, because he values individualism in religion, the autonomous development of a multiplicity of forms of religion; and second, because he believes that state interference corrupts the nature of religion by, for example, attracting the wrong sorts of people into leadership positions within the church (men with worldly skills and motives rather than religious ones) and foisting alien political functions onto religious mysteries such as baptism and marriage. He argues that the true socio-political center of religion should instead be the family—a position which he subsequently goes on to illustrate in *Christmas Eve* (1806), a work which depicts in a literary way a sort of ideal interweaving of (Christian) religion with family life.

One especially interesting case to which he applied his general insistence on the freedom of religion from state interference was that of Prussia's Jews. (Once again, Herder had already set the tone here—both by developing a very sympathetic interpretation of ancient Judaism and by forcefully criticizing modern anti-semitism.) In an early work on the subject of Jewish emancipation in Prussia, *Letters on the Occasion of the Political-Theological Task and the Open Letter of Jewish Householders* (1799), Schleiermacher argues that Jews should receive full citizenship and civil rights, provided only that they compromise in their religious observances to a point allowing them to meet their duties to the state, and that they give up such politically threatening commitments as those to a coming messiah and to their status as a separate nation. He argues that Jews should not have to resort to the expedient of baptism as a means for achieving citizenship and civil rights (as some (Jewish) contemporaries had proposed), on the grounds that this expedient would be detrimental both to the Jews and their religion and to Christianity. In the latter connection his main expressed concern is that it would further water down an already rather watery church. But another concern is that it would in effect amount to yet more interference by the state in a religious mystery (baptism). It is significant to note that Schleiermacher adopts this strikingly liberal position concerning the Jews despite himself being rather critical of Judaism as religion: in *On*

Religion he argues that Reimarus's conception that there are deep continuities between Judaism and Christianity is mistaken, and that although Judaism was a beautiful religion in its day it has long since become corrupted and is now effectively moribund (unlike vibrant Christianity).

A further important aspect of Schleiermacher's socio-political philosophy, especially in its earlier phases, is his proto-feminism (in which he is strongly influenced by Friedrich Schlegel, but probably also by Herder, who was arguably the pioneer in this area). This proto-feminism has several sides. First, Schleiermacher encourages women to strive for goods which have traditionally been the monopoly of men. For example, in his short *Idea for a Catechism of Reason for Noble Ladies* (published in the *Athenaeum*) he enjoins women, "Let yourself covet men's culture, art, wisdom, and honor." Second, as a special case of this, he encourages women to seek sexual fulfillment, and to free themselves from inhibitions about discussing sex. This is one of the central themes of his *Confidential Letters Concerning Friedrich Schlegel's Lucinde* (1800). Third, he identifies women as a source of valuable moral and intellectual resources for the benefit and improvement of society as a whole. One example of this is their natural aversion to the sorts of insensitivity and violence to which men are commonly prone, and their potential ability to restrain instead of permitting or encouraging these. In such a vein the *Idea for a Catechism* enjoins women, "You should not bear false witness for men. You should not beautify their barbarism with words and works." Another (more local) example, discussed in *Toward a Theory of Sociable Conduct*, is the ability of women, due to their broad educations but their freedom from the narrow confines of the professions, to direct social conversation away from limited professional concerns towards deeper and more broadly shared ones (Schleiermacher is thinking here especially of the hostesses of salons of the period that he attended). Another example can be seen in an argument which Schleiermacher develops in his ethics lectures to the effect that women are by nature more attuned to recognizing and respecting individuality, whereas men are more attuned to recognizing and respecting abstract generalizations, and that accordingly one of the key functions of marriage is to bring about a valuable blending of these (equally important) intellectual-moral qualities in each partner.[9]

At the risk of repetition, it is worth underscoring that in its broad cosmopolitan concern for other peoples, Jews, and women Schleiermacher's socio-political philosophy was continuing a paradigm which was above all the achievement of a single predecessor: Herder.

A final noteworthy feature of Schleiermacher's socio-political philosophy, especially prominent in the works from 1799 to 1800, is a broad critique of some central modern socio-economic institutions and a set of proposals for remedying their negative effects. (The *Soliloquies* casts this critique in the form of an attack on the self-satisfaction of the Enlightenment that is very reminiscent of Herder's attack on the same in *This Too a Philosophy of History*.) Three parts of Schleiermacher's case are especially interesting: First, in *Toward a Theory of Sociable Conduct* he implicitly criticizes modern division of labor for the way it blinkers people, inhibiting their development of their own individuality and their sense for the individuality of others. His solution here is the development of a sphere of "sociability"—that is, a sphere of free conversation and social intercourse, in which such one-sidedness can be overcome. Second, in *On Religion* he criticizes the deadening repetitive labor typical of modern economies as an obstacle to spiritual, and in particular religious, self-development. His solution here is mainly a hope that advances in technology will free people from the sort of labor in question. Third, in *On Religion* and the *Soliloquies* he criticizes the hedonism, utilitarianism, and materialism of the modern age for preventing people's spiritual and religious self-development. His main solution here is the sort of revival of a vibrant religious and moral life for which *On Religion* and the *Soliloquies* argue.

10. Philosophy of Religion

Schleiermacher's most radical and important work in the philosophy of religion is his *On Religion: Speeches to its Cultured Despisers* of 1799. (Later editions of this work, and his later theological treatise *The Christian Faith*, strive for greater Christian orthodoxy, and are consequently as a rule less interesting from a philosophical point of view.)

As its title implies, the project of *On Religion* is to save religion from the contempt of Enlightenment and especially Romantic skeptics about religion, "its cultured despisers." At least where the Romantics were concerned, the work was strikingly successful in this regard, in the sense that several of them, especially Friedrich Schlegel, did turn to religion in the years following the book's publication (though admittedly not to quite the sort of religion that Schleiermacher had envisaged). Schleiermacher's later philosophy of religion is similarly motivated. In his 1829 open letters to Lücke he especially emphasizes the pressing need to defend religion against the twin threats posed to it by modern natural science and modern historical-philological scholarship.

This project of defending religion against educated skeptics is reminiscent of Kant's similarly motivated critical philosophy. Schleiermacher is also sympathetic to Kant's general strategy in connection with religious matters of "deny[ing] knowledge in order to make room for faith" (*Critique of Pure*

Reason, Bxxx), and in particular to Kant's attack on traditional proofs of the existence of God; Schleiermacher himself denies that religion is a form of knowledge or can be based on metaphysics or science. However, as can already be seen from his early unpublished essays *On the Highest Good* (1789) and *On What Gives Value to Life* (1792–3), Schleiermacher's strategy is in other respects defined more by opposition to than by agreement with Kant's. In particular, Schleiermacher sharply rejects Kant's alternative *moral* proof of an otherworldly God and human immortality (i.e. Kant's proof of them by showing them to be necessary presuppositions of morality); for Schleiermacher religion can no more be based on morality than on metaphysics or science.

As this stance already suggests, Schleiermacher has a large measure of sympathy with the skeptics about religion whom he means to answer. But the early Schleiermacher's sympathy with them also goes far deeper than this. In *On Religion* he is skeptical about the ideas of God and human immortality altogether, arguing that the former is merely optional (to be included in one's religion or not depending on the nature of one's imagination), and that the latter is positively unacceptable. Moreover, he diagnoses the modern prevalence of such religious ideas in terms of the deadening influence exerted by modern bourgeois society and state interference in religion. He reconciles this rather startling concession to the skeptics with his ultimate goal of defending religion by claiming that such ideas are inessential to religion. This stance strikingly anticipates such later radical religious positions as Mauthner's "godless mysticism." (Schleiermacher's subsequent religious thought tended to backtrack on this radicalism, however, restoring God and even human immortality to a central place in religion.)

This naturally leaves one wondering what the content and the epistemological basis of religion *are* for the early Schleiermacher. As can already be seen from the 1793–4 essays *Spinozism* and *Brief Presentation of the Spinozistic System*, and then again from *On Religion*, he follows Spinoza in believing in a monistic principle that encompasses everything, a "one and all." However, he also modifies Spinoza's conception in certain ways, partly under the influence of Herder (whom he mentions by name in the essays on Spinoza). In particular, whereas Spinoza had conceived his monistic principle as a substance, Schleiermacher follows Herder in thinking of it rather as an original force and the unifying source of a multiplicity of more mundane forces. (Later on Schleiermacher distanced himself from this neo-Spinozistic position. He explicitly denied that he was a follower of Spinoza. Accordingly, in the dialectics lectures he argued that there was an even higher "transcendental ground" *beyond* the Spinozist *natura naturans* or the Herderian highest force. His main motive behind this change of position was evidently a desire to avoid the heavily charged accusations of Spinozism and pantheism—which is hardly an impressive motive philosophically speaking.)

So much for the content of religion, as the early Schleiermacher envisages it. What about its epistemological basis? As I mentioned, for Schleiermacher religion is founded neither on theoretical knowledge nor on morality. According to *On Religion*, it is instead based on an intuition or feeling of the universe: "Religion's essence is neither thinking nor acting, but intuition and feeling. It wishes to intuit the universe."

The term "intuition" here is both revealing and problematic. As Kant had defined it, "*intuition* is that through which [a mode of knowledge] is in immediate relation to [objects]" (*Critique of Pure Reason*, A19). So part of what Schleiermacher means to convey here is evidently some sort of immediate cognitive relation to some sort of object, namely the universe as a single whole. On the other hand, the term "intuition" also imported certain implications which Schleiermacher in fact wanted to avoid. In particular, Kantian pure or empirical intuition required the addition of concepts in order to constitute any sort of real insight ("intuitions without concepts are blind"—*Critique of Pure Reason*, A51), whereas Schleiermacher had in mind a sort of insight unmediated by concepts. In the later editions of *On Religion* he therefore retreated from speaking of "intuition" in connection with religion (instead reserving this term for science), and instead spoke simply of "feeling." In accordance with this change, *The Christian Faith* went on to define religion more specifically as a feeling of absolute dependence, or what Schleiermacher also described in his open letters to Lücke as the immediate consciousness of "an immediate existence-relationship."

A further aspect of the "feeling" on which Schleiermacher bases religion should also be mentioned: its inclusion of *motivating* force, its self-manifestation in *actions*. The wish to include this aspect was one of Schleiermacher's reasons for supplementing religious "intuition" with "feeling" even in the first edition of *On Religion*. And his later work emphasizes this dimension of religious "feeling" as well.

This whole epistemological position looks suspiciously like philosophical sleight-of-hand, however. "Feelings" can be of two very different sorts: on the one hand, non-cognitive "feelings," such as physical pains and pleasures; on the other hand, "feelings" which incorporate beliefs, for example a feeling that such and such is the case. Whereas the possession and awareness of non-cognitive feelings such as pains and pleasures may indeed be conceptually unmediated, beyond mediation by reasons for or against, and in a sense infallible, the possession and awareness of feelings which incorporate beliefs, for instance the feeling that such and such is the case, does require conceptual mediation, is subject to reasoning for or against, and is fallible. As can be seen from the neo-Spinozistic content that Schleiermacher's religious intuition or feeling was originally supposed to have, his original characterization of it as an intuition in the Kantian sense of an immediate cognitive relation to an object, his later characterization of it as representing "an immediate existence-relationship," and so on, he does not mean religious feeling to be merely non-cognitive, but to incorporate some sort of belief. However, he also helps himself to the apparent epistemological advantages which belong only to non-cognitive feelings: non-mediation by concepts, transcendence of reasons for or against, and infallibility. In short, it looks as though his epistemological grounding of religion in "feeling" depends on a systematic confusion of these two crucially different sorts of cases.

Turning more briefly to some additional features of Schleiermacher's philosophy of religion in *On Religion*: He recognizes a potentially endless multiplicity of valid religions, and strongly advocates religious toleration. However, he also arranges the various types of religion in a hierarchy, with animism at the bottom, polytheism in the middle, and monotheistic or otherwise monistic religions at the top. This hierarchy is understandable given his fundamental neo-Spinozism.

More internally problematic, however, is a further elaboration of this hierarchy that he introduces: he identifies Christianity as the highest among the monotheistic or monistic religions, and in particular as higher than Judaism. His rationale for this is that Christianity introduces "the idea that everything finite requires higher mediation in order to be connected with the divine" (i.e. the higher mediation of Christ). But this looks contrived. Even if one granted that "higher mediation" was a good thing, why do other monotheistic religions such as Judaism not share in this putative advantage as well, namely in the form of their prophets? And if the answer is because prophets are not themselves divine, then why is the mediator's divinity supposed to be such a great advantage?

Furthermore, Schleiermacher remarks on the distinctively *polemical* nature of Christianity, the striking extent to which Christianity's religious and moral standpoint is defined by a hostile opposition to other standpoints, and even to other dissenting positions within Christianity itself. This is an extremely insightful observation. (Think, for example, of Nietzsche's brilliant explanation of Christian values as a deliberate inversion of Greek and Roman values motivated by *Ressentiment*, and of the revealing fact that the Christian word "demon" was originally the Greeks' most generic word for a deity; also of the bloody early internal history of Christianity, the Crusades, the Inquisition's treatment of Jews and witches, and many similar horrors—all of which only stopped, or receded, when Christianity became politically impotent in the modern period.) But then, how can a proponent of religious pluralism and toleration like Schleiermacher consistently see this striking trait of Christianity as anything but a very serious vice?

On the (flimsy) basis of this perception of Christianity's superiority, Schleiermacher tries to reconcile his neo-Spinozism with traditional Christian doctrines as far as possible. This project already begins in a modest way in *On Religion*, where for example he works to salvage the Christian doctrine of miracles in the modified form of a doctrine that includes *all* events as miracles (insofar as viewed from a religious perspective). A similar project is pursued much more elaborately (and tediously) in *The Christian Faith*.

Notes

1. There were, however, other more explicit precedents—e.g. in van der Hardt, Chladenius, Pfeiffer, Grosch, and Meier.
2. For further discussion of Schleiermacher's hermeneutics, see Essay 11 and *German Philosophy of Language*, Essay 9.
3. For further discussion of Schleiermacher's theory of translation, see Essay 12.
4. For more on this subject, see *German Philosophy of Language*, Essay 6.
5. The early Schleiermacher was in a way strikingly successful in achieving his goal: after 1799, largely under his influence, the leading Romantics did increasingly turn away from art towards religion, and to some extent the same was also true of German culture more broadly.
6. Schleiermacher denies, though, that the former is sharply divorced from the latter two; rather, it is to some degree implicit in them and vice versa.
7. In his well-known early interpretation of Schleiermacher's dialectics in *Das individuelle Allgemeine* the German scholar Manfred Frank accentuated condition (3), attributing to Schleiermacher on this basis a consensus theory of truth. However, in his subsequent edition of Schleiermacher's dialectics lectures Frank rightly admits that this interpretation overlooked the realism implied by condition (1). This correction of Frank's early reading of Schleiermacher's dialectics also undercuts Frank's equally well-known early reading of Schleiermacher's hermeneutics in *Das individuelle Allgemeine*, which built upon this ascription to Schleiermacher of a consensus theory of truth an ascription to him also of a (roughly

Gadamerian) conception of interpretation as an ongoing construction of facts about meaning through the development of interpretations.

8. Cf. Schleiermacher's similarly liberal Augsburg Confession sermons from 1830.

9. It should be noted, though, that Schleiermacher later on tended to become more conservative in his views about women.

11

Schleiermacher's Hermeneutics: Some Problems and Solutions

Schleiermacher is widely regarded as the father of modern hermeneutics, or interpretation theory. That title may in the end more properly belong to his predecessor Herder. But whichever of them deserves the greater credit (a question I shall set aside here),[1] the theory which they both develop is arguably not only the ancestor of, but also philosophically superior to, its more metaphysically pretentious descendant in Heidegger and Gadamer, and is of great intrinsic interest.[2]

The purpose of this essay is to explore some central aspects of Schleiermacher's hermeneutics and to suggest how they should be interpreted and assessed.[3] My general strategy will be to point up rather than to play down some inconsistencies and other problems in his position—in part simply because I believe that they are there and that exegesis therefore ought to recognize them, but more because reflecting on them seems to me philosophically fruitful. The interpretive and philosophical suggestions I will be offering are provisional and tentative in spirit.

1. Philosophy of Language

Schleiermacher's hermeneutics rests on several important principles in the philosophy of language. It may therefore be appropriate to begin with a discussion of these.

(1) Herder had already advanced a doctrine that thought is essentially dependent on and bounded in its scope by language—i.e. that one can only think if one has a language, and one can only think what one can express linguistically.[4] This doctrine is quite important for interpretation, because it in a certain sense guarantees that a person's use of language is a reliable indicator of the nature of his thought, that these cannot be radically discrepant.

Schleiermacher takes over this doctrine and makes it fundamental to his hermeneutics.[5] However, he is also tempted to make it bolder in a certain way: Sometimes he merely advances it in the form just stated.[6] But often he instead elevates it to a doctrine of the outright *identity* of thought and language,[7] or of thought and inner language.[8] Commentators have commonly approved of this—for example, Heinz Kimmerle seems to like the identification with language,[9] Richard Niebuhr and Manfred Frank that with inner language.[10] But it is philosophically untenable, in either version. For, I can think something without expressing it linguistically; and I can express something linguistically without doing any corresponding thinking (for example, if I happen not to understand the language that I am using). And likewise, I can think something without using language even internally (for example, having been told to expect John home before Mary, I hear the door open and footsteps mount the stairs, Mary appears and I say quite truthfully "I thought it was John," even though no such little formula had run through my mind, merely a feeling of unsurprise), and I can use language internally without doing any corresponding thinking (for example, if it happens to be a language I do not understand). So Schleiermacher should have stuck with the more cautious Herderian formulation of the doctrine (here, as elsewhere, he has *implausibly overspecified* a plausible position which he has inherited from Herder). On the other hand, rather to his credit, in his later work he seems at least somewhat inclined to retreat from the identity-versions back towards that superior formulation.[11]

(2) Some further important positions concern the nature of *meaning*. Ernesti, Herder, and Hamann had collectively moved away from traditional philosophical theories which took meanings to be items in principle independent of language—such as the referents involved, Platonic forms, or mental ideas—and towards identifying them instead with *word-usages*, or *rules of word use*.[12] It follows from this move that interpretation essentially and centrally involves pinning down word-usages, or rules for the use of words. Schleiermacher adopts this whole position. Hence, for example, he says that "the . . . meaning of a term is to be derived from the unity of the word-sphere and from the rules governing the presupposition of this unity."[13]

(3) However, Schleiermacher eventually attempts to combine with this position a further one which entails that a capacity to have *images* plays an essential role in meaning as well. Specifically, he tries to explain meaning in terms of Kantian (empirical) schemata: rules for the production of images.[14] This combination of positions is again in a way continuous with Ernesti, Herder, and Hamann, who had rather similarly combined with their emphasis on the role of word-usage in meaning an essential role for Lockean ideas

(Ernesti) or sensations (Herder and Hamann). Such combinations are likely to seem unhappy to us today at first hearing, but they may not be. Here are some prima facie problems: (a) Explaining meanings in terms of such mentalistic processes as having images might sound incompatible with equating meanings with word-usages, because it might seem to make words and their usages *inessential* to meanings. However, it need not do so; it might instead be specifying a *further* essential aspect of meaning (or perhaps—to anticipate my next point—one already implicitly included in the relevant concept of word-usage). (b) Another way in which there might seem to be an incompatibility between the two doctrines is this: If we equate meanings with word-usages, then does that not preclude any essential role in meaning for the capacity to have images? The answer is again: Not necessarily. For a usage of anything always involves some *context* or other, and that context might very well in this case essentially include having images. (c) Anglophone philosophers are likely to be prejudiced against such a combination of doctrines by more recent and familiar versions of the "meaning as word-usage" doctrine, in particular the later Wittgenstein's version. Wittgenstein purports to show, by examining our actual criteria for ascribing conceptual understanding to people, that having images and similar mental processes is neither sufficient nor necessary for conceptual understanding.[15] His arguments for the former conclusion are extremely compelling, but his arguments for the latter much less so. We may certainly grant him that our linguistic intuitions do not require that in order properly to ascribe conceptual understanding to someone at a particular time the person must, in addition to using words with external competence, have images actually occurring at that time. But would our linguistic intuitions really sanction ascribing conceptual understanding to someone who, for example, had, by some science-fictional means or other, say by the implanting of a device in his brain, arrived at an external competence in using the word "red" without ever having had sensations of red or being able to generate an image of red—to someone whose external competence was (to put the point a little tendentiously) merely *robotic*?[16] The answer seems to be No. In short, some version of the sort of combined position to which Schleiermacher—like Ernesti, Herder, and Hamann before him—is attracted may well be both self-consistent and philosophically defensible. On the other hand, there is a problem with Schleiermacher's *specific way* of introducing such a combination, namely by appealing to Kant's conception of empirical schematism. For Kant had conceived schemata in sharply dualistic terms as purely mental, involving no essential relation to language, and Schleiermacher's appropriation of the conception of schemata takes over this sharp dualism.[17] This really does threaten to generate an inconsistency with the doctrine that meanings consist in word-usages, in the manner of prima facie problem (a) above.

(4) Although Schleiermacher does not himself make this point, note that doctrine (2), the doctrine that meanings are word-usages, promises an *explanation and justification* of doctrine (1), the doctrine of thought's essential dependence on and boundedness by linguistic competence. For, uncontroversially enough, thought is of its very nature articulated in terms of concepts, or meanings, but then if meanings turn out *to be usages of words*, one can see immediately why thought would be essentially dependent on and bounded by a thinker's linguistic competence.[18]

(5) There remains, though, an important further question which leaves the exact force of doctrines (1) and (2) in some doubt: Must thought and meaning be articulable by a thinker in language in the usual sense of "language" (let us call such a position *narrow expressivism*), or can other symbolic media play this foundational role for thought and meaning as well, for example sculpture or music (let us call such a position *broad expressivism*)? Schleiermacher's commitment to doctrines (1) and (2) might seem already to imply the former answer to this question. But it really does not, or at least not clearly. For the terms "language" and "word" in those doctrines might be bearing unusually broad senses.[19] Indeed, they actually *had* done so in Hamann's version of the same doctrines in his *Metacritique* of 1784. And Schleiermacher himself on occasion includes such media as instrumental music under the term "language."[20] Perhaps the best place to look for Schleiermacher's considered answer to our question is his lectures on aesthetics. The lectures on aesthetics initially set out to develop a position on art that would imply narrow expressivism, or the fundamentalness of language (in the usual sense) to thought and meaning, and they do so in an extremely simple way: (a) Arts, such as sculpture and music, which are not linguistic (in the usual sense) do not express thoughts *at all* (for instance, music expresses physiologically based *Lebenszustände* but not representations or thoughts). This theory is untenable, however. And Schleiermacher abruptly realizes this in the course of developing it when, discussing sculpture, he suddenly recalls Pausanias' account that the very earliest Greek sculptures were merely crude blocks whose main function was to serve, precisely, as symbols of religious ideas (oh dear!).[21] At this point Schleiermacher changes tack, acknowledging now that such non-linguistic arts *do* at least sometimes express thoughts after all, and he then vacillates between two new and mutually inconsistent explanations of this: (b) They do so in such a way that the thoughts in question are (at least in certain cases) not (yet) linguistically articulable (for example, he suggests that the early Greek sculpture just mentioned expressed religious ideas which only *later* got

expressed linguistically).[22] (c) They do so but in virtue of a pre-existing linguistic articulation of the same thoughts in the artist (actually, Schleiermacher only says in virtue of "something universal," "a representation," but the dependence on language seems clearly implied).[23] In the end, then, having rightly rejected the clearly untenable position (a), Schleiermacher is left torn between two more sensible positions which, however, give contradictory answers to our question: position (b), which entails broad expressivism (a position that had already been espoused by Hamann, and that was also adopted by Hegel and the later Dilthey); and position (c), which entails narrow expressivism (a position that Herder had eventually arrived at).[24] Both of these positions deserve to be taken seriously, philosophically speaking. But Schleiermacher does not really decide between them. He thereby also leaves the exact force of doctrines (1) and (2) uncertain.

(6) As we already saw in passing, Schleiermacher advances a thesis of "the unity of the word-sphere."[25] The force of this thesis seems to be that there is something like a *single meaning* common to all of the uses of a word.[26] Consequently, the interpretation of a word is for Schleiermacher a two-stage process: first, one infers from the known actual uses of the word to particular usages, or rules for use; and then one infers from the latter to a single, all-embracing rule for use which covers them all.[27] At first sight, this thesis seems to take sharp issue with Ernesti, who had emphasized the *multiplicity* of a word's usages, and hence meanings.[28] It also seems to conflict sharply with our usual assumptions about these matters, according to which, for example, the various different entries for a word in a dictionary give *different meanings*. Indeed, at first sight, the thesis seems to involve a hopeless coarsening of our usual criteria of meaning-identity—hopeless not only in that, as just noted, it would force us to override our strong commonsense intuitions that the same word often bears different meanings, but also in that it would force us to endorse contradictions. For example, suppose that "Smith is sitting on a [river] bank" is true and "Smith is sitting on a [financial] bank" is false; will we not by this thesis have to say that the *same proposition* is both true and false? Can anything be said in Schleiermacher's defense here? There is, I think, one rather small class of cases for which a form of the objection that he is unacceptably violating our commonsense intuitions about meaning does in fact hold up in the end: cases which we would normally classify as ones of *sheer* polysemy ("bank" is a plausible example; such cases sometimes arise when two or more unrelated etymologies lie behind a word). He should probably just concede that there are such exceptions to his thesis.[29] But his thesis is really concerned with the much larger class of cases in which we would intuitively want to say that, although there are different meanings involved, they are in some degree

related (for example, *impression* in "He made an impression in the clay," "My impression is that he is reluctant," and "He made a big impression at the party"). And our commonsense intuition of a diversity of meanings, as well as our need to preserve consistency, in these cases are in fact amply *respected* by Schleiermacher's thesis. How so? This is because he in effect distinguishes between two different sorts or senses of "meaning," and allows that against the background of the single meaning$_1$ postulated by his thesis a word may indeed have several different meanings$_2$.[30] Accordingly, he is himself by no means shy about detecting ambiguities in individual words.[31] Therefore, the charge that he hopelessly coarsens our criteria of meaning-identity turns out to be mistaken. Indeed, it turns out that the upshot of his thesis is actually the very *opposite* of that. For his thesis involves a *holism* to the effect that the meanings$_2$ of a word are always dependent for their exact character on the single overarching meaning$_1$ which they together compose.[32] Consequently, if the overall pattern of particular usages is altered in any respect, this modifies each of them, each meaning$_2$. And that makes for extremely *fine-grained* criteria of identity for meaning$_2$.[33] Accordingly, Schleiermacher claims that, contrary to common assumptions, there are never any real synonyms in a language,[34] or between two different languages.[35]

(7) Finally, it is worth making a more general observation about Schleiermacher's theory of meaning and conceptual understanding: Such features of his theory as his inclusion of the meaning-holism just mentioned do arguably still conflict with our usual criteria for meaning-identity and conceptual understanding, albeit not in the crude way in which the doctrine of "the unity of the word-sphere" initially seemed to. After all, in the case in question my expression "extremely fine-grained" implied *more fine-grained than we would usually accept*. This may appear objectionable if one assumes a certain picture (fairly common in recent Anglophone philosophy) about the nature of meaning and our cognitive relation to it: that meaning is a sort of single natural kind whose character can be distilled consistently and determinately from our usual linguistic intuitions concerning it. However, such a picture is in fact pretty implausible. An alternative and better way to think about the concept of meaning is as a concept, or perhaps a range of concepts, constituted by pre-given linguistic intuitions which are often inconsistent, indeterminate, and no doubt inadequate in other ways as well, a concept or range of concepts which we therefore may and should refashion more consistently, determinately, and otherwise adequately in order to serve our various purposes, doing which will sometimes involve transcending and even contradicting those pregiven linguistic intuitions.[36] From this perspective, such features of Schleiermacher's theory escape the sort of residual objection just envisaged, and can indeed begin

to look quite attractive (for example, developing more fine-grained criteria of meaning-identity than we currently employ might serve our purposes very well in activities such as interpretation).[37]

2. Misunderstanding Occurs as a Matter of Course

Let us turn now to Schleiermacher's hermeneutics, or theory of interpretation, itself. Schleiermacher famously holds that, contrary to a common assumption that "understanding occurs as a matter of course," "misunderstanding occurs as a matter of course, and so understanding must be willed and sought at every point."[38] What is the basis of this position?

The points that I have just made suggest that part of the answer to this question may be that Schleiermacher presupposes a certain (arguably justified) "raising of the bar" of our usual criteria for meaning-identity, and therefore for exact conceptual understanding, which he has effected. There is some truth in this. However, he clearly conceives the position in question as more a discovery than merely a byproduct of his own conceptual innovations. So wherein lies the putative discovery?

Schleiermacher has two very different lines of reasoning underpinning this position—one of them apriorist, the other empirical. (Officially, he aspires to overcome the very distinction between a priori and empirical knowledge.[39] But at least in this case, what he ends up with is rather a vacillation between the two than a synthesis.)

The *apriorist* explanation is dominant in the lectures on hermeneutics, and has been heavily emphasized by Wilhelm Dilthey and Manfred Frank. As Dilthey observes,[40] in the *Ethics* Schleiermacher argues in an a priori fashion that all living reason combines identity with *difference*. Similarly, as Frank notes,[41] in the *Dialectics* Schleiermacher argues in an a priori fashion that all meaning and understanding involve, along with a universal aspect, an *individual* aspect coming from the subject. These positions entail that whenever an interpreter attempts to understand another person there is *always and ineliminably* an obstacle of difference or individuality present.

On this first line of reasoning, then, the problem of misunderstanding is *entirely general*. In particular, it is not especially due, and is not restricted, to cases of historical or cultural distance—as Schleiermacher indeed explicitly says at one point in his hermeneutics lectures.[42] Moreover, on this line of reasoning, it is impossible for exact understanding of another person *ever* to occur; understanding of another person can only ever be *approximate*—as Schleiermacher again says explicitly at points.[43]

The contrasting *empirical* line of reasoning occurs especially in Schleiermacher's classic essay *On the Different Methods of Translation* from 1813. According to this essay, there are two common sources of conceptual incommensurability between an interpreter and the text he interprets, and these are especially troublesome when they both occur together: (1) historical or cultural distance, which causes the standard conceptual resources of languages to diverge;[44] and (2) an author's own conceptual innovations.[45] (Ernesti and Herder had both already emphasized these two sources of difficulty for the interpreter.)

On this second line of reasoning, it may indeed be the case that the obstacles in question occur more frequently than is usually recognized—for example, Schleiermacher would say that interpreters dealing with distant periods or cultures confront conceptual divergence more commonly than they usually realize;[46] and he thinks that conceptual innovation by authors is a less rare phenomenon than we often suppose as well (to the point, in the essay mentioned, of actually considering it a sine qua non of great literature or philosophy, literature or philosophy that deserves to be heard beyond its own time and place).[47] But they will not *always* be present. Indeed, the essay in question argues that there is one whole area of language in which historical and cultural distance *never* generates conceptual incommensurability, namely everyday referring and descriptive language concerning items of sensory experience (as heavily used in commercial contexts, travel literature, and so forth);[48] and the essay certainly sees authorial conceptual originality as something exceptional, not ubiquitous.[49] Again, on this second line of reasoning, there is no question of exact understanding being *impossible* (not only because, as was just mentioned, there are cases in which the relevant obstacles do not arise at all, but also because when they *do* arise they can often be overcome by careful interpretation).[50]

I want to suggest that Schleiermacher's empirical line of argument is far superior to his a priori line of argument. For (1) the a priori line of argument rests on dubious a priori theories about the nature of reason or the subject (dubious both in their a priori status and in their specific details), and (2) its consequence that exact understanding of another person is always impossible is radically counterintuitive.

If we *do* read Schleiermacher's position concerning the difficulty of understanding in the empirical way that I am advocating, then certain further issues take on importance. As I mentioned, *On the Different Methods of Translation* implies that there is one large area of exceptions to conceptual variation: referring and descriptive language concerning sensory items. However, at other points Schleiermacher seems to align himself rather with a (Herderian) position which emphasizes the *variability* of sensory experience and its language.[51]

And of course his official apriorist position that we *always* conceptualize in an individual way would also imply that there are no real exceptions here. Likewise, in his *Dialectics* he identifies a second area of putative exceptions: everyone shares the same concept of *being*.[52] However, he is again ambivalent about this. Thus the *Dialectics* virtually retracts it by adding the qualification that this is not strictly a case of "thought." And in a more straightforward way *On the Different Methods of Translation* questions whether this case constitutes an exception as well.[53] Also, Schleiermacher's official apriorist position that we *always* conceptualize individually would again preclude any real exception here.

Now I want to suggest that Schleiermacher should have *dropped* this whole idea of exceptions. As a matter of philology, sensory discourse, far from being an area of exceptions, turns out to be a *paradigmatic* area of conceptual variations. Consider, for example, the discrepancy in sense between such co-referring sensory words as the Greek word *Helios* and our own word *sun* (for one thing, the former carries an implication of personhood that the latter lacks), or the deep discrepancies between Homeric color conceptualization and our own.[54] And in light of Charles Kahn's recent work on the verb *to be* in ancient Greek, even the concept of *being* looks variable.[55]

Another issue is this: The philosophically superior empirical strand of argument that I have been highlighting (in opposition to its neglect by the secondary literature) coheres with an admirable empirical approach in several other key areas of Schleiermacher's theory as well (where it has similarly been neglected or even denied by the secondary literature). Here are two examples:

(1) Dilthey and Gadamer claim that Schleiermacher's basic method of interpretation is a sort of empathetic self-projection onto texts, that it is in this sense at least apriorist rather than empirical. But on the contrary, Schleiermacher explicitly rejects apriorism both on the linguistic (or grammatical) and on the psychological (or technical) sides of interpretation:

Grammatical [interpretation]. The elements of a language as presentations of a specifically modified capacity for intuition cannot be constructed a priori, but only recognized via comparison of a great number of individual cases. In the same way on the technical side, one cannot construct the differing individualities a priori.[56]

His position is instead that one must proceed "bottom up" from empirical evidence, in linguistic interpretation beginning from the examples of a word's actual uses, classifying these into particular usages, and then looking for their all-embracing unity; and in psychological interpretation starting with the (linguistic) evidence furnished by the author, and then inferring from that to a psychological portrait of the author.

(2) Dilthey and Kimmerle claim that Schleiermacher excludes consideration of a text's *historical context* from interpretation.[57] This is an extraordinary misunderstanding of his position. He does say that the consideration of a text's historical context must precede interpretation proper.[58] But the force of this is not to say that interpretation should *dispense* with it, but on the contrary to insist that it is *absolutely indispensable* to interpretation, a sine qua non of any interpretation worthy of the name taking place at all.[59]

3. Linguistic versus Psychological Interpretation

Schleiermacher famously distinguishes between two essential sides of all inter-pretation: on the one hand, linguistic (or grammatical) interpretation, and on the other hand, psychological (or technical) interpretation.[60]

There has been a lengthy debate in the secondary literature concerning this subject which should be addressed here briefly at the outset: Dilthey and Gadamer characterized Schleiermacher's theory as fundamentally psychologistic and empathetic. Kimmerle then, on the basis of a detailed investigation of the hermeneutics manuscripts, argued that this was only true of the late Schleiermacher, but that the early Schleiermacher had believed in the identity of thought and language and had made interpretation focus on language. More recently, Frank and Bowie have argued that there is really no great change here: both early and late Schleiermacher give roughly equal weight to language and psychology.

I basically agree with this last view. The Dilthey-Gadamer account is hope-lessly one-sided and misleading. But nor is Kimmerle's view correct. For, (a) the later Schleiermacher continues to assume at least the dependence of thought on language,[61] and continues to devote roughly as much space to linguistic (or grammatical) as to psychological (or technical) interpretation.[62] Moreover, (b) Schleiermacher's earliest manuscripts already emphasized psy-chological (or technical) interpretation as well as linguistic (or grammatical).[63] (In connection with point (b), it should be noted that this earliness of Schleier-macher's commitment to complementing linguistic with psychological (or technical) interpretation becomes much less surprising when one realizes—as commentators have invariably failed to—that he did not himself invent the idea of doing so but instead inherited it from Herder.[64])

What is Schleiermacher's rationale for his distinction between the linguistic and the psychological sides of interpretation? One rationale that is prominent in the texts is the following:

(1) This distinction corresponds to Schleiermacher's distinction between the *identical,* or shared, and the *individual*, or idiosyncratic, aspects of a text. What is shared in a text's use of language, especially what is shared conceptually, is to be investigated by linguistic interpretation (using a predominantly "comparative" method); what is individual in a text's use of language, in particular individuality in concepts, is to be investigated by psychological interpretation (using a predominantly "divinatory" method). This rationale has been emphasized by Frank,[65] and it is indeed prominent in Schleiermacher's texts.[66] To be more specific, a central part of this rationale seems to be as follows: Recall Schleiermacher's conception that meanings are rules for the use of words, and that accordingly the fundamental task of interpretation is to infer from observed actual uses of words to the underlying rules which are guiding them. Now in the case where an interpreter is attempting to discover the meaning that a word bears in a common language—the task of linguistic interpretation—there will typically be a large number of examples of the word's use in a rich variety of contexts available to serve as the evidential basis from which to infer the underlying rule. Accordingly, in such a case all the interpreter usually needs to do in order to arrive at a reasonably sure and accurate estimation of the underlying rule is to gather these examples together and infer directly from them to the character of the underlying rule which is guiding them by means of a "comparative," or in other words a plain-inductive, method. However, in cases where an interpreter is trying to discover the novel usage or meaning which a conceptual innovator has conferred on a word, the task is typically much less simple. For in such cases the number of actual examples of the usage in question that are available will usually be much smaller,[67] and the variety of contexts in which they occur much more limited.[68] Consequently, merely collecting and "comparing," or doing plain-induction on, the examples will usually not by itself be enough to enable the interpreter to pin down with any confidence or precision the underlying rule in accordance with which the author is using the word. What, therefore, is the interpreter to do in such a case? Schleiermacher notes, sensibly, that he should first examine the common background language (since, for one thing, the author will usually be *modifying* a pre-existing rule for the word, rather than wholly departing from it, or coining a sheer neologism).[69] But that only minimizes the original problem rather than solving it. Schleiermacher believes that what is needed in addition is to call to aid a knowledge of the innovative author's *psychology*, that knowing his psychology can facilitate the task of estimating his new rule

SCHLEIERMACHER'S HERMENEUTICS 373

for the use of the word from the meager evidence available of how he has actually used it. This idea is at least somewhat plausible. For example, suppose that an author has gone as far as to coin a new term, which he uses on only three occasions in his extant works, each time in (serious) application to women. In such a case, the knowledge that he was a *misogynist* might be of considerable help towards more closely determining what the term was likely to mean. In particular, such knowledge would more or less exclude the possibility that it connoted a virtue, and make it likely that it connoted a vice.

However, it would not be satisfactory for Schleiermacher to make this first rationale *the* rationale for the distinction between linguistic and psychological interpretation. For one thing, as I have mentioned, he often acknowledges that conceptual originality occurs only *sometimes*, and moreover this *should* be his position. But in that case, if this rationale were *the* rationale for psychological interpretation, how could psychological interpretation *always* be required, as he says it is? For another thing, even where conceptual originality does occur, it is hard to believe that recourse to the author's psychology in the general manner of the imaginary example just given is going to be necessary and helpful *in all cases*, and this still further diminishes the range of cases for which this rationale would justify psychological interpretation.

It is therefore of some importance that there are also at least two further rationales for psychological interpretation that can be found in Schleiermacher:

(2) He sometimes indicates that (as their very names suggest) linguistic interpretation is oriented to *language* whereas psychological interpretation is oriented to the underlying *thoughts* conveyed by language.[70] This might sound unhelpful at first hearing, but is arguably not. For one thing, does it not violate Schleiermacher's doctrine of an intimate connection between thought and language? The answer is: not once the crude "identity" version of that doctrine is rejected, as it must be anyway. For another thing, is determining thoughts not something that linguistic interpretation *already* does in determining the *meanings* of words and sentences? Here the answer is that Schleiermacher has *further* aspects of "thought" in mind. As Quentin Skinner has recently emphasized, in order fully to understand an utterance or text one needs to do more than just determine its linguistic meanings; one needs in addition to pin down the author's illocutionary intentions. To borrow an example of Skinner's, if one encounters a stranger by a frozen lake who tells one, "The ice is thin over there," one may understand the linguistic meaning of his utterance perfectly, but yet still not fully understand the utterance, because one remains uncertain what he intends to do with it—simply inform one?, warn one?, threaten one (say, by alluding to the expression "You're skating on

thin ice")?, joke (by stating the obvious)?, etc. This, I suggest, is part of what Schleiermacher is getting at when he writes that "the possession of the whole spirit of the utterance is only achieved via the technical; for dealt with merely grammatically the utterance always remains just an aggregate"; and that "every utterance corresponds to a sequence of thoughts and must therefore be able to be . . . understood via the nature of the utterer, his mood, his aim . . . [This] we call technical interpretation."[71]

(3) In addition, Schleiermacher suggests a further rationale for complementing linguistic interpretation with an appeal to the author's psychology. Skinner tends to write as though one can fix linguistic meaning prior to establishing any additional authorial intentions. That may be so in *some* cases—for instance, in that of the frozen lake example just given. But is it *generally* so? Schleiermacher implies, very plausibly, that it is not, because in order to fix the linguistic meaning of words and sentences one often needs to address problems of semantic and syntactic *ambiguity*, and that can only be done by appeal to conjectures about the author's intentions (e.g. about the subject-matter that he intends to treat). This, I take it, is Schleiermacher's point in the following passage:

> The technical side is presupposed for the completion of the grammatical side. For in order to determine what is grammatically indeterminate, knowledge of the whole . . . as a sequence of thoughts . . . is presupposed. And in the case of ambiguity the sequence of thoughts is always one of the determining factors, even in relation to details.[72]

I would suggest that rationales (2) and (3) work much better as fundamental rationales for always complementing linguistic with psychological interpretation than does rationale (1). For, unlike the task identified by (1) of dealing with conceptual innovation, which seems very limited in occurrence, the tasks identified by (2) and (3) really can plausibly claim to be more or less *ubiquitous* in interpretation. And unlike the former task, they can plausibly claim to require an appeal to the author's psychology for their solution not only sometimes but *always*.

However, it would be a mistake to exaggerate the opposition between these rationales. For rationale (1) can certainly stand as a *further* part of Schleiermacher's full case for complementing linguistic with psychological interpretation.

Indeed, there are arguably additional, similarly subordinate (i.e. again less-than-universally-applicable), rationales as well. Here is one example:

(4) Schleiermacher's friend and colleague Friedrich Schlegel had already made the important point that a text will sometimes communicate thoughts

over and above those that it expresses explicitly in its parts, but via the latter and the way in which they are put together to form a whole.[73] And it could be argued that Schleiermacher himself retains a version of this very plausible point in his (otherwise dubious) doctrine of a "seminal decision [*Keimentschluß*]" that underlies, and unfolds itself in a necessary fashion as a whole text (concerning which dubious doctrine more in a moment).

Actually, the idea of complementing linguistic with psychological interpretation, and even the several rationales for doing so which have just been distinguished above, were not entirely new with Schleiermacher, but can largely already be found in Herder, especially in his *On Thomas Abbt's Writings*, *On the Cognition and Sensation of the Human Soul*, and *Critical Forests*.

Unlike Herder, however, Schleiermacher also develops the theory of psychological interpretation in certain more specific ways which seem unhelpful. The following are two examples.

Herder had included among the evidence on which an interpreter should draw for psychological interpretation both an author's verbal and his *non-verbal* behavior. Schleiermacher occasionally implies the same—for example, he refers at one point in this connection to "the totality of the person's acts."[74] But more usually he implies that the evidence adduced should only include verbal behavior, or even only writings.[75] The former, Herderian position seems clearly the correct one. For example, in our imaginary case of the misogynist, his record of nasty *deeds* against women might be the only or the best evidence for his misogyny. And of course, a restriction to written evidence would make no sense at all in many contexts of interpretation (for instance, when one is interpreting members of a preliterate culture).

However, *something* can perhaps be salvaged from Schleiermacher's standard view: He occasionally implies that, although there may be no *universal* requirement that an interpreter restrict himself to verbal or written evidence, there is at least an important subset of cases for which this is normally advisable, namely *ancient* texts, where we usually lack reliable biographical evidence beyond what is supplied by the author's own texts.[76]

Another respect in which Schleiermacher develops the theory of psychological interpretation more specifically but unhelpfully concerns the doctrine, recently mentioned, of a "seminal decision" made by an author from which his text unfolds in a necessary fashion, and which it is the interpreter's job in psychological (or technical) interpretation to identify and trace in its necessary development.[77] This doctrine was absent from Schleiermacher's earliest version of his theory of psychological (or technical) interpretation, but eventually acquired a central role in the theory.[78]

This seems to me another example of Schleiermacher implausibly overspecifying a very plausible position inherited from Herder. The doctrine of the seminal decision faces at least three prima facie problems:

(1) As Dilthey points out, the doctrine was originally inspired by Fichte's theory of the necessary generation of the world of experience out of the self's original act of self-positing.[79] Such an extravagant and implausible metaphysical theory is surely an inauspicious birthplace for a doctrine about the nature and interpretation of texts.

(2) Schleiermacher's doctrine is from the start afflicted by an ambiguity between two models of *generation* which were competing in biology at the time: the preformationist model (according to which all the parts of a mature organism are already present in the seed in microcosm) and the epigenetic model (according to which they are not, but only develop subsequently). In the *Introductions to the Dialogues of Plato*, where he applies the theory of the seminal decision to the Platonic corpus as a whole, Schleiermacher goes back and forth between these two models. Clearly, however, they would entail very different versions of the doctrine (not only with respect to the nature of the seminal decision itself but also with respect to the nature of the supposed "necessity" of its further development in a text), with very different consequences for interpretation. Moreover, each alternative has serious drawbacks: It seems very unlikely that a version of the doctrine based exclusively on the preformationist model would be generally applicable.[80] And the epigenetic model has the disadvantage that it leaves the nature of the supposed "necessity" of the further development involved quite obscure.

(3) Most importantly, *whichever* model of generation is in question, the doctrine of the seminal decision is surely very implausible as a general doctrine about how texts emerge and function. For texts often arise through *multiple* decisions, often, moreover, ones made at *different stages* in the process of composition, and often with a lot of *serendipity* influencing the process along the way as well. Something like Schleiermacher's picture may *occasionally* apply to texts, but surely not very often, let alone always.

In fairness, it seems to me that Schleiermacher eventually in a way recognized that the doctrine faced problems of these sorts. They should really have caused him to abandon it, or at least demote it to the status of a subordinate principle with only limited application (a further subordinate rationale to add to those already mentioned above), but instead he clung to it doggedly, and tried to qualify it in ways that would enable it to cope with them. Thus, in partial recognition of, and answer to, problem (1), the 1832 version of his *Hermeneutics* makes an effort to confront, and reconcile, the doctrine with the empirical character of various sorts of texts.[81] (But the reconciliation is not effective.) In partial recognition of, and answer to, problem (2), the 1832 version in effect says that the seminal decision is sometimes more of the preformationist sort and sometimes more of the epigenetic sort.[82] (But this leaves the doctrine extremely vague, and it still leaves the nature of the supposed "necessity" in the epigenetic cases quite obscure.) And in partial recognition of problem (3), the 1832 version acknowledges that multiple decisions are sometimes involved at different points in the process of composition,[83] that serendipity often plays a role in the process of composition,[84] and more generally that works do not always contain everything essential in a seminal decision[85]—but it attempts to hold on to the doctrine of the seminal decision in the face of these concessions by implying that when multiple decisions are involved they somehow *follow from* a seminal one,[86] that the results of serendipity are merely *secondary* thoughts,[87] and that when there is no containment of everything in a seminal decision the work is *imperfect* [*unvollkommen*].[88] (But these face-saving qualifications are surely very dubious and ad hoc.)

4. The Comparative Versus the Divinatory Methods

Schleiermacher holds that a "comparative" method predominates in linguistic interpretation's inferences from actual word uses to the rules that govern them, but a "divinatory" method in psychological interpretation's inferences from linguistic (and perhaps other) evidence to the psychological traits of the author. However, he also allows that the "comparative" method plays a role in psychological interpretation, and that the "divinatory" method does in linguistic interpretation.[89] His idea in the latter case is that this happens especially when the available evidence consisting of a word's actual uses is relatively meager in amount and in contextual variety, as for example when the interpreter is a young child first learning a language,[90] or when the subject interpreted is a conceptual innovator.[91]

What does this distinction between methods amount to? As I have already mentioned, Schleiermacher essentially conceives the "comparative" method as a method of *plain induction* (this first a is F, this second a is F, this third a is F . . . therefore all a's are F), whereby one infers from a collection of a word's actual uses to a general rule governing them (for example, one perceives the word *rouge* applied on multiple occasions to red things without exception, and one infers that the rule governing its use is that it applies to all and only red things).[92]

But what does Schleiermacher mean by a "divinatory" method? There are several possible answers:

(1) Dilthey and Gadamer understand it to consist in a sort of psychological self-projection by the interpreter onto the person interpreted (or his texts).[93] There is a certain amount of textual evidence that seems to support such a reading: (a) Schleiermacher writes that the divinatory method "depends on the fact that every person, besides being an individual himself, has a receptivity for all other people. But this itself seems only to rest on the fact that everyone carries a minimum of everyone else within himself, and divination is consequently executed by comparison with oneself."[94] And (b) he also commonly speaks of the interpreter "put[ting] himself 'inside' the author" or "in the position of the author."[95] However, I want to suggest that these passages should really be understood in the following way. As (a) shows, Schleiermacher does believe that interpretation by divination involves psychological self-projection to this extent: it involves presupposing that the people whom one interprets share *something* in common with one mentally. However, that is a fairly modest and uncontroversial thesis (after all, interpretation surely at least requires that the interpreter presuppose that, like himself, the people whom he interprets *think* and *mean* things). The important question is whether Schleiermacher also means to be advocating more ambitious forms of psychological self-projection, for example a projection of one's own concepts and beliefs. I think that the answer is No. Talk of the interpreter "put[ting] himself 'inside' the author" or "in the position of the author" might seem to suggest this. But this cannot be Schleiermacher's considered position, and it would not be a defensible position. For Schleiermacher, very plausibly, identifies such assimilation of texts to one's own manner of thought as the deepest source of *misunderstanding*, and strictly *prohibits* it:

Misunderstanding is either a consequence of hastiness or of prejudice. The former is an isolated moment. The latter is a mistake which lies deeper. It is the one-sided preference for what is close to an individual's circle of ideas and the rejection of what lies outside it. In this way one explains in or explains out what is not present in the author [*sic*].[96]

I therefore suggest that when Schleiermacher speaks of the interpreter "put[ting] himself 'inside' the author" and the like, this is really little more than a metaphor for a not-thereby-more-closely-specified process of interpretation.[97] Indeed, one can sometimes *see* that this is the force of such remarks from the fact that he goes on to explain them in terms of a complex process of interpretation having nothing to do with self-projection.[98] And it is also significant in this connection that alongside such metaphors of an interpreter's self-transposition into the author Schleiermacher just as often uses metaphors of an interpreter's self-*effacement* and self-*transformation*—for example, writing that the interpreter should "step outside of [his] own frame of mind into that of the author" and that he should "transform himself, so to speak, into the author."[99]

(2) Another possibility is suggested by the Latin etymology of the word "divination" (*divus* [n.], a god; *divinus* [adj.], of a god, divinely inspired, prophetic; *divinus* [n.], a prophet), which might lead one to infer that Schleiermacher means *prophecy*, that is, some sort of immediate insight having a divine basis and perhaps also infallibility. Schleiermacher does occasionally write in ways that encourage such a reading. For example, at one point in the hermeneutics lectures he initially wrote *prophetisch* before substituting *divinatorisch*.[100] However, this would obviously again be a very unattractive position philosophically speaking. Moreover, it clearly does not reflect Schleiermacher's considered view. For one thing, he is in fact strongly opposed to any interpretation of texts (including sacred texts) that relies on a supposed divine inspiration.[101] For another thing, he emphasizes that "divination" is based on scrutiny of available evidence, and is fallible.[102] His main reasons for evoking a kinship with prophecy here are merely that he thinks that "divination" radically transcends the available evidence, and that the sort of grasp of a person's psychology at which it aims includes hypothetical and predictive knowledge about how the person would or will behave in such-and-such circumstances.[103]

(3) A more helpful etymological clue is the French verb *deviner*, meaning to guess or conjecture.[104] For Schleiermacher's considered conception of "divination" does in fact turn out to be a (perfectly secular) process of guesswork, conjecture, or hypothesis, based on close scrutiny of the available evidence, but also going well beyond it, and hence open to either additional support or falsification by further evidence. Thus he writes at one point that divination is required in order to construct "a complete image of a person from only scattered traces," noting that "we cannot be too careful in examining from every angle a picture that has been sketched in such a hypothetical fashion. We should accept it only when we find no contradictions, and even then only provisionally."[105] This is Schleiermacher's considered conception of "divination," and it is obviously a far more philosophically attractive one than either of the two preceding alternatives.

Finally, it is worth noting here that Herder had already advocated the use of a method of "divination," especially on the psychological side of interpretation, and that he too had fundamentally conceived this as a process of fallible hypothesis based on meager empirical evidence.[106]

5. Is Interpretation a Science or an Art?

There are two important points of similarity between interpretation and natural science which Schleiermacher would certainly concede: (1) He assumes (as did virtually everyone else at this period) that interpretation, in its attempts to discern what an author means in his text, is as much concerned with the discovery of *objective facts* as natural science is in its attempts to discern the workings of physical nature. There has indeed been some controversy about this in the secondary literature, some scholars reading Schleiermacher in this way (e.g. Gadamer, Betti, and Hirsch), but others instead reading him as anticipating Gadamer in conceiving meaning as something constructed in interaction with an indefinitely expandable audience of interpreters (e.g. Frank and Bowie).[107] However, the latter reading is without textual justification,[108] and anachronistic.[109]

(2) As can be seen from his position that misunderstanding is the interpreter's natural condition, and from his development of an elaborate hermeneutic methodology in order to cope with this problem, Schleiermacher believes that interpretation, at least in many cases, is a very *difficult* undertaking, requiring *methodologically informed* and *laborious* solutions—just like natural science!

Nonetheless, Schleiermacher famously infers from the central role of "divination" in interpretation that interpretation is an *art*. And the main force of this position is precisely to say that it is *not* a science. That this is so can be seen from the fact that this position arose in response to a question that had been posed by Friedrich Schlegel: Is interpretation an art or a science?[110]

I think that Schleiermacher is quite right to emphasize the role of "divination," qua hypothesis, in interpretation, but that he should have been moved by this insight towards precisely the opposite conclusion on the art versus science question: this again makes interpretation very much *like* natural science. For since the work of Poincaré and Popper, we have come to realize that this sort of method is *paradigmatic* of natural science.[111] I suggest that Schleiermacher was seduced into his error here by an assumption—common at the time, but basically mistaken—that the method of natural science is one of plain induction (this first a is F, this second a is F, this third a is F . . . therefore all a's are F).[112] Had he not made this mistaken assumption, he might well have been moved to draw the correct conclusion.[113]

In sum, ironically enough, we can extract from Schleiermacher himself at least three good reasons for *resisting* the sort of sharp distinction between interpretation and natural science that he himself argued for and that he perhaps did more than anyone else to establish in the subsequent German tradition, where it became and has remained virtually a knee-jerk assumption.[114]

Notes

1. For a discussion of this question tending in Herder's favor, see Essay 4 and *German Philosophy of Language*, Essay 9.
2. See *German Philosophy of Language*, Essay 9. Cf. P. Szondi, *On Textual Understanding and Other Essays*, p. 97 for a similar assessment.
3. The essay will be very selective, omitting a number of other central aspects of Schleiermacher's theory. For example, I shall not here discuss his famous conception that hermeneutics should be a *universal* science, or his famous position that the parts of a text/discourse must be interpreted through larger wholes of various sorts, or his solution to the problem of hermeneutic circularity that such holism seems to involve.
4. See esp. Herder, *Fragments on Recent German Literature* (1767–8).
5. Like Herder before him, Schleiermacher normally in such contexts thinks of language as consisting in speech or writing. However, he does occasionally entertain a broader conception of the "linguistic" which would include further media in addition (see esp. his psychology lectures, *Friedrich Schleiermacher's sämmtliche Werke* [henceforth: FSSW], 3/6:46, 539–40; cf. *On Religion: Speeches to its Cultured Despisers* [1799] [Cambridge: Cambridge University Press, 1996], p. 166 on instrumental music). This vacillation leaves a certain indeterminacy in the exact force of the doctrine, concerning which more soon.
6. See e.g. *Hermeneutics: The Handwritten Manuscripts* [henceforth: *The Handwritten Manuscripts*], pp. 97–8, 193.
7. See e.g. *On the Different Methods of Translation*, p. 20: "the internal and essential identity of thought and expression."
8. See e.g. *Hermeneutics and Criticism*, p. 9: "thinking is an inner speaking."
9. See *The Handwritten Manuscripts*, p. 34.
10. R.R. Niebuhr, *Schleiermacher on Christ and Religion* (New York: Scribner, 1964), p. 81; M. Frank, *Das individuelle Allgemeine*, p. 250.
11. Heinz Kimmerle's well-known characterization of the later Schleiermacher as someone who broke with the identity thesis (see *The Handwritten Manuscripts*, p. 36) contains an important element of truth, but is somewhat overstated. Schleiermacher's inclination to distance

himself from the identity thesis can be seen, not only by comparing earlier and later versions of his hermeneutics lectures (as Kimmerle does), but also by comparing the 1818, 1830, and 1833–4 versions of his psychology lectures. However, it would be an exaggeration to say that he ever unequivocally gave up the identity thesis. For example, to focus on the psychology lectures, while the sort of emphatic statement of the identity thesis that is found in the lectures of 1818—for instance, "inner speaking . . . is completely identical with thinking" (pp. 446–7)—does indeed recede by the time Schleiermacher gives the lectures of 1830 and 1833–4, he can still at one point in the 1830 lectures talk of "the activity of thought in its identity with language" (p. 263).

12. In this context, it should not be assumed that the rules in question are formulated, and perhaps not even that they are in all cases formulable.

13. *The Handwritten Manuscripts*, p. 50. The more specific doctrine of "the unity of the word-sphere" which appears here will be discussed later.

14. *Hermeneutics and Criticism*, pp. 234 ff., 271 ff.

15. See esp. the *Blue Book* and the *Philosophical Investigations*.

16. It might be objected here that to hypothesize external competence in using the word "red" *is* to hypothesize having sensations of red or the ability to generate images of red. However, I would suggest that a little further reflection on the range of possible hypothetical cases shows otherwise. For example, imagine that the device implanted in the person's brain produced his external competence by generating a sort of auditory buzzing in his head when the word was to be applied.

17. See e.g. his psychology lectures, pp. 147–8, where he seems to think of schemata as constituting meanings autonomously of language, language merely being required for the *communication* of meanings.

18. This seems to me a much more satisfactory explanation and justification of doctrine (1) on Schleiermacher's behalf than the one suggested by Frank at *Das individuelle Allgemeine*, pp. 174–5 in terms of Saussure's conception of meaning as arising through a system of oppositions. For, absent some further argument to the contrary, such a system of oppositions, and hence meaning, might arise without language being involved at all.

19. Think, for example, of Nelson Goodman's recent book title *Languages of Art*.

20. See e.g. *On Religion*, p. 166. Cf. psychology lectures, pp. 46, 539–40.

21. Aesthetics lectures, FSSW 3/7:579–80.

22. Ibid., pp. 584–5. Cf. the similar position that Schleiermacher had already adopted earlier concerning instrumental music in *On Religion*, p. 166.

23. Aesthetics lectures, pp. 587–8. Such a rejection of (a) and vacillation instead between (b) and (c) can, it seems, already be found in Schleiermacher's treatment of music in *Christmas Eve* [*Die Weihnachtsfeier*] (San Francisco: Edwin Mellen Texts, 1990), pp. 46–7.

24. In the *Critical Forests* of 1769—a work that clearly formed the foundation for Schleiermacher's aesthetics lectures—Herder had been similarly torn between several incompatible positions on the question at issue, but had eventually worked his way towards a version of position (c), which he thenceforth retained as his considered view. See on this Essay 3.

25. *The Handwritten Manuscripts*, pp. 50, 79; *Hermeneutics and Criticism*, pp. 33–4, 36–7, 247.

26. This thesis can therefore be seen as a sort of appropriation of a similar doctrine in Plato (concerning whose version of it, see my "Socratic Refutation," *Rhizai,* 3/1 [2006]), who was of course one of Schleiermacher's main philosophical preoccupations at the time. However, as I am in effect about to show, Schleiermacher's appropriation of it also involves a fairly radical reworking of Plato's cruder version of it.

    Pace Frank, *Das individuelle Allgemeine*, pp. 187, 213–14, Schleiermacher's thesis has nothing to do with the *intersubjectivity* of meaning. Nor is it even a matter of the identity of meaning in metaphorical uses (ibid., pp. 215–16), though that is much *closer* to what Schleiermacher has in mind.

27. *The Handwritten Manuscripts*, p. 79: "Once one has a number of clear and distinct usages by collecting analogies or by referring to dictionaries, the rule for discovering the unity is to put together these contrasting meanings" (cf. pp. 62, 121–2).

28. *Ernesti's Institutes*, p. 11. Certainly, *pace* Kimmerle (*The Handwritten Manuscripts*, p. 31), Schleiermacher should not be seen as *borrowing* from Ernesti in this thesis. Ernesti does indeed deny that words have multiple meanings *in particular occurrences* (*Ernesti's Institutes*, pp. 20–1), but that is an entirely different point.

29. He fails to do this. See e.g. *Hermeneutics and Criticism*, p. 247: it is a "necessary . . . principle . . . that two schemata are not the basis of one and the same word."

30. For example, at *The Handwritten Manuscripts*, p. 76 he contrasts with the "essential meaning" of the connected family of usages of a word

the "particular meanings" of the specific usages. Cf. *Hermeneutics and Criticism*, pp. 35, 233–4. He often distinguishes the two sorts of meaning terminologically as, respectively, *Bedeutung* and *Gebrauch*.

31. See e.g. Schleiermacher, *Introductions to the Dialogues of Plato* (Cambridge and London: Pitt Press, Deighton, and Parker, 1836), pp. 69, 113, 120–1.

32. Hence, strictly, "one must be in command of the unity of the linguistic value to arrive at the multiplicity of manners of use" (*Hermeneutics and Criticism*, p. 37).

33. There are also further aspects of meaning-holism in Schleiermacher which make for still further fine-grainedness in his criteria of identity for meaning$_2$. These concern, not other usages of the same word, but families of cognate words and the internality of a language's grammar to word-meaning. See e.g. *On the Different Methods of Translation*.

34. *Hermeneutics and Criticism*, pp. 247–8.

35. See psychology lectures, pp. 173–4. Schleiermacher's whole line of thought in this thesis is very similar to one that has motivated more recent linguists to speak of a word's "semantic field"—see e.g. E. Nida, *Toward a Science of Translating* (Leiden: Brill, 1964), pp. 37–40. (Nida adds an important point which is at least less clear in Schleiermacher, namely that what is essential to specific word meanings is not only what the "unity of the word-sphere"—to use Schleiermacher's terminology—*comprises* but also how it is *structured* [ibid., pp. 89 ff.].) I therefore disagree with Szondi's judgment that Schleiermacher's conception of the unity of the word-sphere stands in sharp *contradiction* with modern linguistics (Szondi, *On Textual Understanding and Other Essays*, p. 107).

36. For some further discussion of this subject, see my *Wittgenstein on the Arbitrariness of Grammar*, ch. 6.

37. I shall bracket here the interesting question of the extent to which this methodological perspective is Schleiermacher's *own*. However, note that his emphasis on conceptual variations across and also within cultures at least coheres well with it (since he would surely have to include the concepts of *meaning* and *conceptual understanding* in such variations).

38. *The Handwritten Manuscripts*, pp. 109–10; *Hermeneutics and Criticism*, pp. 21–2.

39. *Hermeneutics and Criticism*, p. 279. Cf. psychology lectures, p. 20: "All approximation to knowledge must be a reciprocal working of the a priori into the a posteriori and vice versa."

40. W. Dilthey, "Schleiermacher's Hermeneutical System in Relation to Earlier Protestant Hermeneutics," in his *Hermeneutics and the Study of History* (Princeton, NJ: Princeton University Press, 1996), pp. 104–10, 134–7, 146.

41. *Das individuelle Allgemeine*, pp. 152–6.

42. *Hermeneutics and Criticism*, p. 20.

43. *The Handwritten Manuscripts*, pp. 164, 195, etc. Cf. Frank, *Das individuelle Allgemeine*, pp. 310–11.

44. *On the Different Methods of Translation*, pp. 4–5, 25. Cf. *The Handwritten Manuscripts*, p. 206.

45. *On the Different Methods of Translation*, pp. 5–7. Cf. *The Handwritten Manuscripts*, pp. 99, 104, 148.

46. *On the Different Methods of Translation*, p. 25.

47. Ibid., p. 6.

48. Ibid., pp. 2–3. Cf. *Hermeneutics and Criticism*, p. 230; and, though more equivocally, psychology lectures, p. 509. As Frank mentions, Schleiermacher in this vein concedes that, as he puts it, mere *Wettergespräche* do occur (Frank, *Das Sagbare und das Unsagbare*, p. 209; cf. *The Handwritten Manuscripts*, p. 102).

49. Cf. *The Handwritten Manuscripts*, p. 57 on "authors in whose works one finds everything one expects and nothing else"; and *Das Leben Jesu*, at FSSW 1/6:11 on the many people who "stand entirely in the power of the collective life."

50. Cf. aesthetics lectures, p. 636, where Schleiermacher says that understanding is indeed in most cases only approximate but that in some cases "the expression can convey the thought quite identically into the other person."

51. See e.g. *Hermeneutics and Criticism*, pp. 69–70, 275–6; also, though more equivocally, psychology lectures, p. 509.

52. *Hermeneutics and Criticism*, pp. 276–7.

53. *On the Different Methods of Translation*, p. 25 (translation modified): "Every language . . . contains within it a system of concepts which, precisely because they touch each other in the same language, because they connect and complement each other, are a *whole* whose isolated parts do not correspond to any in the system of other languages, God and Being, the original noun and the original verb, hardly excepted."

54. For a discussion of the latter case, and of relevant literature, see my "On the Very Idea of Denying the Existence of Radically Different Conceptual Schemes." Interestingly enough, Schleiermacher himself

eventually recognized that color conceptualization shows striking variability (see psychology lectures, p. 509).

55. Kahn, *The Verb 'Be' in Ancient Greek*. Kahn characterizes the late introduction of a purely existential use of the verb *to be* as only a new *use* of the verb rather than a change in its *meaning*. However, if one follows Schleiermacher's equation of meaning with usage and his holism across usages, one will certainly be inclined to draw the more radical conclusion.

56. *Hermeneutics and Criticism*, p. 95.

57. Dilthey, "Schleiermacher's Hermeneutical System," p. 217; Kimmerle, at *The Handwritten Manuscripts*, p. 29.

58. *Introductions to the Dialogues of Plato*, pp. 2−3; *The Handwritten Manuscripts*, p. 104.

59. See e.g. *Introductions to the Dialogues of Plato*, pp. 2−3; *On the Different Methods of Translation*, pp. 7, 13; *The Handwritten Manuscripts*, pp. 92, 104, 171.

60. Eventually, Schleiermacher sharply distinguishes between psychological and technical interpretation in their turn, confining technical interpretation to the pursuit of the necessary development of a text's "seminal decision" over the course of the text (*Hermeneutics and Criticism*, pp. 102 ff.).

61. e.g., in 1829 Schleiermacher still writes that "there is no thinking without words" (*The Handwritten Manuscripts*, p. 193), and the 1830 and 1833−4 psychology lectures continue to assume a dependence of thought on language as well (see e.g. pp. 133−4, 140, 263, 539−40). Indeed, at one point in the 1830 psychology lectures he can still write of "the activity of thought in its identity with language" (p. 263).

62. See *Hermeneutics and Criticism*, pp. 30 ff.

63. See the aphorisms from 1805 and 1809−10, esp. at *The Handwritten Manuscripts*, p. 61; and above all, assuming that Virmond's dating is correct, the 1805 lecture on "technical" interpretation at *Hermeneutics and Criticism*, pp. 93 ff. Also relevant in this connection are the ethics lectures from the winter semester 1805−6.

64. Herder's key texts here are *On Thomas Abbt's Writings* and *On the Cognition and Sensation of the Human Soul*, where he adds psychology to Ernesti's purely language-oriented approach to interpretation. e.g., in the latter work he writes that the wise interpreter "attempts to read more in the spirit of the author than in his book; the deeper he penetrates into the former, the more perspicuous everything becomes."

65. Frank, *Das individuelle Allgemeine* and *Das Sagbare und das Unsagbare*.
66. See e.g. *Hermeneutics and Criticism*, pp. 94, 229–30; *The Handwritten Manuscripts*, p. 99; *On the Different Methods of Translation*, p. 6.
67. See *Hermeneutics and Criticism*, pp. 67–8.
68. See ibid., p. 237.
69. *The Handwritten Manuscripts*, pp. 70, 99, 149.
70. See e.g. ibid., pp. 97–8.
71. *Hermeneutics and Criticism*, pp. 254, 229. Skinner often puts his point not in terms of a need to fix an author's illocutionary intention but in terms of a need to fix his "illocutionary force." However, I prefer to avoid the expression "illocutionary force" here because of intimate connections that Austin gave it with performatives and with social "uptake" which do not seem helpful.

    Frank considers a rationale for psychological interpretation similar to that suggested above but articulated in terms of illocutionary force and rejects it for a different reason (*Das Sagbare und das Unsagbare*, pp. 187–8). His reason for rejecting it (both philosophically and as an interpretation of Schleiermacher) is that illocutionary force is conceived as purely conventional, not subject to originality. This objection does not seem to me a very strong one, though. For a theory of illocutionary force could surely accommodate as much originality in illocutionary force as it would be plausible to ascribe to people (even if particular versions of such a theory, for example John Searle's, happen not to). And if Frank means to object on the ground that authorial intentions are *always* unconventional, then that seems implausible (even if perhaps encouraged by the inferior a priorist strand of Schleiermacher's reflections on authorial individuality discussed earlier).
72. *Hermeneutics and Criticism*, p. 254.
73. See e.g. Friedrich Schlegel's *Athenaeum Fragments*.
74. *The Handwritten Manuscripts*, p. 202; cf. *Hermeneutics and Criticism*, p. 92.
75. See e.g. *The Handwritten Manuscripts*, pp. 50, 113.
76. See e.g. *Introductions to the Dialogues of Plato*, pp. 1–2; *Hermeneutics and Criticism*, p. 92.
77. See e.g. *Hermeneutics and Criticism*, pp. 28, 102 ff.; *The Handwritten Manuscripts*, p. 192.
78. It seems to be entirely absent from the version of 1805 (assuming this dating of Virmond's to be correct) (*Hermeneutics and Criticism*, pp. 94 ff.), and to be still only ambiguously present in the version of

1809–10 (ibid., esp. pp. 254–5). By contrast, it is central to the version of 1832 (ibid., pp. 101 ff.).

79. Dilthey, "Schleiermacher's Hermeneutical System," pp. 100 ff.

80. A minor but interesting illustration of this problem can be seen in the fact that in the *Introductions to the Dialogues of Plato* Schleiermacher's assumption of this model seduces him into committing one of his most spectacular errors of chronology concerning the Platonic dialogues: assuming this model as a basis for interpreting the Platonic corpus as a whole, he expects Plato's corpus to begin with a dialogue which already contains all of Plato's mature ideas in microcosm, and so he identifies the *Phaedrus* (!) as the earliest Platonic dialogue (see esp. pp. 67–8).

81. *Hermeneutics and Criticism*, pp. 102 ff.

82. Ibid., pp. 117, 132, 136.

83. Ibid., p. 136.

84. Ibid., pp. 102–3.

85. Ibid., p. 140.

86. Ibid., p. 136.

87. Ibid., p. 106.

88. Ibid., p. 140.

89. See e.g. *The Handwritten Manuscripts*, pp. 191 ff., 205.

90. Ibid., pp. 193–4.

91. Ibid., p. 192.

92. Note that in the *Dialectics* of 1811 (*Dialectic or The Art of Doing Philosophy* [Atlanta: Scholars Press, 1996]) Schleiermacher actually calls the closely related process of concept *formation* one of "induction" (pp. 54–7), and that in the *Dialectics* of 1822 he calls this "induction" a process of "comparative judgments" (ibid., p. 57 n.).

93. Dilthey, "The Rise of Hermeneutics," in *Hermeneutics and the Study of History*, pp. 248–9; H.-G. Gadamer, *Truth and Method*, pp. 186–7.

94. *Hermeneutics and Criticism*, pp. 92–3.

95. *The Handwritten Manuscripts*, pp. 64, 113.

96. *Hermeneutics and Criticism*, p. 23; cf. pp. 134–5.

97. Here I basically agree with Frank, *Das individuelle Allgemeine*, pp. 314, 331.

98. See esp. *The Handwritten Manuscripts*, p. 113.

99. Ibid., pp. 42, 150.

100. *Hermeneutics and Criticism*, p. 23. Cf. *Das Leben Jesu*, p. 8: "The maximum of [human-knowing] is a sort of *Prophetie*."

101. See e.g. *The Handwritten Manuscripts*, pp. 215–16; *Hermeneutics and Criticism*, pp. 17–18. (It is true that Schleiermacher is here mainly concerned to combat reliance on a presupposition that a text's *author* is divinely inspired, rather than reliance on a presupposition that its *interpreter* is. However, Ernesti had already forbidden the latter, and the spirit of Schleiermacher's remarks is to *extend* that prohibition to the former *as well*.)

102. See e.g. *The Handwritten Manuscripts*, p. 207.

103. For the latter point, see esp. *Das Leben Jesu*, pp. 6–8.

104. Cf. M. Frank, *Schleiermacher: Hermeneutik und Kritik* (Frankfurt am Main: Suhrkamp, 1999), p. 47.

105. *The Handwritten Manuscripts*, p. 207. Cf. Schleiermacher's characterization of "divination" in the context of *criticism* as a process of fallible conjecture (*Hermeneutics and Criticism*, pp. 177, 193). Frank similarly understands "divination" as for Schleiermacher a method of hypothesis (*Das individuelle Allgemeine*, pp. 332–3; *Das Sagbare und das Unsagbare*, pp. 66–7, 102). However, Frank's further claim that its probability cannot be assessed (*Das Sagbare und das Unsagbare*, p. 181) is quite misleading, especially in overlooking the important possibility of *falsification*.

106. See esp. *On Thomas Abbt's Writings* and *On the Cognition and Sensation of the Human Soul*.

107. See esp. Frank, *Das individuelle Allgemeine*, pp. 351–64.

108. As Frank emphasizes in this connection in *Das individuelle Allgemeine*, Schleiermacher does imply that meanings are irreducibly individual and hence strictly unattainable by interpreters, that the ("divinatory") method for approaching them is fallible and provisional, and that inquiry in general advances through the sort of communal approximation to truth described in the dialectics lectures. However, *pace* Frank, these doctrines, far from conflicting with, *presuppose* an objectivist assumption of the sort described here.

   More recently, in his edition of Schleiermacher's dialectics lectures, Frank has in effect conceded that his original attribution of a consensus theory of truth to those lectures in *Das individuelle Allgemeine* was a mistake, that they instead assume a realist, or correspondence, conception of truth (M. Frank, *Friedrich Schleiermacher: Dialektik* [Baden-Baden: Suhrkamp, 2001], 1:34, 41, 56). This is an admirable self-correction. However, notice that it also entirely pulls the rug out from under Frank's reading of Schleiermacher's hermeneutics in *Das individuelle*

Allgemeine as a position similar to Gadamer's. For the central strategy of that reading was to build on the ascription to Schleiermacher of a consensus theory of truth in general, an ascription to him of a conception of interpretation in particular as, likewise, an ongoing social construction of facts about meaning.

109. This sort of anachronism has indeed recently become something of a cottage industry in Germany. For example, Irmscher has similarly tried to read *Herder* as a sort of proto-Gadamer (in his essay "Grundzüge der Hermeneutik Herders").

110. See esp. Friedrich Schlegel, *Philosophy of Philology* (1797). Consequently, Frank is certainly right to reject Palmer's *equation* of art with science in Schleiermacher's position (*Das individuelle Allgemeine*, p. 341), but Frank *understates* the point.

111. This is not to deny that there remain important points of contrast between its employment in interpretation and in natural science. For example, whereas natural scientific hypotheses are always formulated, the hypotheses involved in interpretation are often not, and indeed may not even always be formul*able*. Nor, of course, does mathematics play the sort of role in interpretive hypotheses that it plays in natural scientific ones.

112. This, I take it, is the force of the contrast he often draws between divination and the merely "mechanical" (see e.g. *Hermeneutics and Criticism*, pp. 10–11, 229, 232). (As I mentioned earlier, he does think that plain induction plays *a* role in interpretation, namely as the "comparative" method which dominates in linguistic interpretation. But his idea is that in natural science it is the *only* method whereas interpretation also requires divination, or hypothesis.)

113. The exegetical argument just presented requires a little qualification. For Schleiermacher does not sustain the pictures of a sharp art vs. science opposition and of natural science's method as purely plain-inductive, or "mechanical," which I have just ascribed to him with complete consistency. Occasionally, he suggests a contrary picture of natural science as rather like art and as not merely mechanical but also involving imagination (see e.g. psychology lectures, pp. 467–8).

114. Examples of this are Dilthey, Weber, Heidegger, Gadamer, and Frank. A noteworthy exception is Helmholtz.

12

Herder, Schleiermacher, and the Birth of Foreignizing Translation

Translation can sound like a rather arcane and dry subject. However, when one recalls the enormous role that it plays in our lives—mediating most of our encounters with texts from the past and from contemporary cultures beyond our own, mediating most of our encounters with other peoples and their governments, and so on—one quickly realizes that it constitutes such a pervasive and important interface in our relations both to texts and to people that it surely deserves theoretical consideration.[1] Moreover, any initial sense that translation is a mechanical, unproblematic process, and hence a dry subject, dissolves quickly once the topic is actually investigated.

Schleiermacher is rightly famous for having developed what some more recent theorists have aptly called a "foreignizing" (as opposed to a "domesticating") methodology for translation.[2] He has especially been praised for this by two important recent translation theorists who are themselves sympathetic to such a methodology: Antoine Berman and Lawrence Venuti.[3]

It seems to me that Berman and Venuti have done a great service in drawing attention to the importance of Schleiermacher's theory, and that much of the detail of their accounts is very insightful as well. However, it also seems to me that their accounts are misleading in important respects—indeed, that they in a way miss what its inventors saw as, and what moreover actually is, the most fundamental nature, point, and value of the "foreignizing" approach altogether (leaving us with a case of *Hamlet* without the Prince). I therefore hope in this essay to explain the genesis and character of Schleiermacher's "foreignizing" approach in a way that substantially corrects and complements their accounts.

To be more specific: A first point that needs to be brought out in (albeit in this case fairly mild) opposition to their accounts is the enormous extent to which Schleiermacher's theory of translation is indebted to Herder's.

Berman does include a chapter on Herder as a forerunner to Schleiermacher,[4] but he gives no impression of a strong or detailed influence, and Venuti essentially leaves Herder out of the picture altogether. However, I believe that the true situation here is that Schleiermacher's key essay *On the Different Methods of Translation* (delivered as an address in 1813) owes its main theses concerning translation to Herder's early *Fragments on Recent German Literature* (1767–8).[5]

To say a little more about the general character of their relation: In other work, I have argued for roughly the following picture of Schleiermacher's theory of *interpretation* (or "hermeneutics"). The main lines of the theory are borrowed from Herder (in particular, Schleiermacher's central theses that "linguistic" interpretation needs to be complemented with "psychological" interpretation, and that the core method especially of the latter is one of "divination," or in other words tentative hypothesis, are both Herderian innovations), and where the theory departs from Herder it almost always does so for the worse rather than the better. That was the bad news about Schleiermacher, as it were. However, in this essay I want to counterbalance it by conveying some partially similar but much better news concerning his theory of *translation*. Here, a similar picture of massive continuity with and indebtedness to Herder emerges; but in this case Schleiermacher's innovations are for the most part *refinements*.

Turning to a more important area of disagreement with Berman and Venuti: They both see the main virtues of "foreignizing" over "domesticating" translation as lying in an *ethico-political* superiority of the former over the latter—particularly, in the facts that the former is superior to the latter as a means for developing the target language and culture in certain ways,[6] and that the former is consistent with a cosmopolitan respect for and openness to the Other, whereas the latter serves an imperialist domination and effacement of the Other. This is an important and valid theme (both in connection with Herder and Schleiermacher and intrinsically). However, Berman and Venuti develop it in a way that incorporates certain misunderstandings.

The first (and by far the gravest) of these lies in the fact that in emphasizing these ethico-political motives behind "foreignizing" translation to the extent that they do, Berman and Venuti obscure, and indeed implicitly negate, an even more fundamental motive behind it: that of *faithfully reproducing the original text's meaning*.[7] The *Concise Oxford Dictionary* defines "translate" as follows: "express the sense of (word, sentence, book) in or into another language." Historically speaking at least, this surely *has* been the most commonly accepted fundamental goal of translation.[8] Shortly before Herder and Schleiermacher wrote, this goal had been stated in emphatic terms by a man whom they both admired above virtually all others in connection with questions of interpretation and translation, Ernesti:

> The object of a version [i.e. a translation] from one language into another, is to express the sense of the author, without diminution, addition, or alteration.[9]

And at about the same period, another of Herder's great intellectual heroes, Lessing, had made a similar plea for semantic faithfulness in translation in the *Literaturbriefe* (the journal on which Herder's *Fragments* provided a sort of commentary). *Pace* Berman and Venuti, it seems to me that Herder and Schleiermacher both fully accept this traditional fundamental goal, and that their main achievement in translation theory essentially depends on this acceptance. Specifically, it lies in the fact that they reinterpret this goal in light of a new, revolutionary, and indeed broadly correct theory of meaning which they develop—a theory which identifies meanings with word-usages, but which also incorporates a revised form of the old empiricist intuition that sensations or feelings are internal to meanings—and on this basis argue for the necessity of adopting a certain foreignizing approach to translation if the goal in question is to be accomplished, namely an approach that employs two foreignizing strategies both of which are required in order faithfully to capture the original meaning as that task is now understood in light of the new theory: a "bending" of word-usages in the target language intended to reproduce or mimic those in the source language, and a reproduction of the original musical "form" or "tone" (which, among other things, communicates fine nuances of sensation or feeling).

Disregarding, and indeed dismissing, this traditional goal behind Herder and Schleiermacher's approach, and a fortiori their reinterpretation of it in light of a new theory of meaning, not only leads Berman and Venuti to overlook the approach's most fundamental, and I think also most compelling, motive. It also leads them to overlook its central "bending" strategy altogether (as indeed does most of the relevant secondary literature), as well as some of the deepest arguments behind the strategy of reproducing musical form; and to misunderstand, or only very imperfectly understand, many of its further features as well.[10]

The second (albeit less grave) shortcoming in Berman and Venuti's accounts of the ethico-political motives for preferring foreignizing over domesticating translation lies in their underestimation of the extent to which Herder and Schleiermacher were already driven by the sort of cosmopolitan motive of advancing respect for and openness to the Other that they themselves see as speaking strongly in favor of the foreignizing approach. Berman, while he recognizes such a motive in Schleiermacher,[11] depicts Herder's interest in translation as standing entirely in the service of his own language and culture.[12] Venuti denies the cosmopolitan motive to Schleiermacher as well, on the contrary accusing him of seeking German "global domination" and showing "chauvinistic condescension toward foreign cultures."[13] In fact, as we shall see, both Herder and Schleiermacher were already deeply imbued with, and motivated in their commitment to foreignizing translation by, a cosmopolitan concern for the Other.

I hope that this short critique of Berman and Venuti may have served to introduce some of this essay's main themes and to pique the reader's interest. However, the main purpose of the essay is not to pursue it further. Rather, it is to provide a positive account of the birth of the theory of foreignizing translation in Herder and Schleiermacher—in the course of which the critique should be vindicated along the way. Accordingly, section 1 will explain what I take to be the most important features of Herder's theory of translation; section 2 will then identify continuities between that theory and the theory that Schleiermacher presents in his justly famous essay *On the Different Methods of Translation* (1813); finally, section 3 will attempt to identify and explain the main refinements that Schleiermacher introduces into the theory.

1. Herder's Theory of Translation

Herder's theory of translation is found mainly in three places: the *Fragments on Recent German Literature* (1767–8); the essay "Would it be True that Shakespeare is Untranslatable?" in the *Popular Songs* [*Volkslieder*] (1774) (whose purpose is to demonstrate that Shakespeare *can* be translated); and (in a rather different, indeed contrary, spirit) Herder's discussion of translation in connection with his translations of the modern Latin poetry of Balde in the late *Terpsichore* (1796).[14]

Herder was also himself a prolific and accomplished translator. Indeed, Edna Purdie aptly describes him as "perhaps . . . the first translator of genius in Germany in the eighteenth century."[15] This point (which applies equally to Schleiermacher) is significant, for several reasons. First, to the extent that one accepts the plausible principle, later articulated by A.W. Schlegel, that adequate translation theory and adequate translation practice are interdependent,[16] it provides some ground to expect that Herder may have valuable things to say in his translation theory. Second, it allows one to complement scrutiny of his translation theory with consideration of his translation practice, as a means of more confidently and precisely interpreting the theory.[17] Third, his demonstration that his translation theory could be successfully implemented in practice was a considerable part of his contribution, and no small source of his theory's influence on others.

Let us, then, consider the main features of Herder's theory of translation. To begin with a principle that is fundamental both to his theory of interpretation and to his theory of translation: Eminent Enlightenment philosopher-historians from the middle of the eighteenth century such as Hume and Voltaire had still believed that, as Hume puts it, "mankind are so much the same in all times and places that history informs us of nothing new or strange."[18] Herder discovered (or at least saw more clearly and fully than anyone before him) that this was *false*, that peoples from different historical periods and different cultures vary *tremendously* in their concepts, beliefs (as well as other propositional attitudes), values, perceptual and affective sensations, and so on. He also saw that similar, albeit usually less dramatic, variations occur even between individuals within a single culture and period.[19] (We might call this fundamental Herderian insight for short his principle of *radical mental difference*.)

Herder recognized that, because of radical mental difference, and in particular because of radical *conceptual* difference, translation is bound in many cases to be an extremely difficult task, even to the point of being impossible without at least some distortion of the original text's meaning.[20] He believed (plausibly) that this is especially true when ancient texts are translated into modern languages. For example, he writes in the *Fragments*:

As little as the ancients could translate the language of our books and academic lectures can we translate [*nachsprechen*] them.

I have a complaint against those who want to read Homer in a translation, even if one as correct as possible. You are no longer reading Homer but something which *approximately* repeats what *Homer* said inimitably in his poetic language.[21]

By contrast, Herder believed (again plausibly) that translation from *modern* European languages normally presents a less severe challenge to the modern European translator because those languages are usually more closely related, and similar in mode of thought, to his own.[22] (We might call this whole position for short Herder's principle of the resulting *extreme difficulty of translation*.[23])

Another important and seminal step which Herder takes in the *Fragments* is to argue that as a result of radical mental difference translation typically faces twin dangers, the Scylla of "a too lax translation" and the Charybdis of "a too accommodating [*anpassende*] translation" (i.e. a translation which accommodates the language/thought of the target text too much to that of the source text), and that it ought to steer between those two extremes, but (like Thomas Abbt's translations) tend more towards the latter one:

I consider it the *finest* form of criticism to be able to show exactly the middle course "how a translator must not step a hair's breadth too close to his two languages, the one from which and the one into which he translates." A too lax translation, which our critics commonly call free and unforced, sins against both: the one it fails to satisfy, for the other it stirs no fruits. A too accommodating translation, which lightweight cheerful souls slavishly reprimand, is much more difficult, it strives on behalf of both languages, and seldom gets as valued as it should be. Since such an author must everywhere experiment, accommodate, dare, he earns from our censors with the high eyebrows that they decry him for three failed experiments, take everything daring in him to be linguistic error, and approach the attempts of an artist like a pupil's exercises of apprenticeship. This is what happened to Abbt with his *Sallust*. When a cheerful youth shows daring for his fatherland, then I wish him an old man of understanding by his side, only let the latter not go ahead; and if by chance the former has strayed too far, then may a genius, like an invisible friend of humanity, lead him back to his own people.[24]

What is Herder's complaint against the former extreme? As can be seen from the above passage, it is fundamentally twofold: first, that this extreme is semantically and otherwise unfaithful to the original text ("fails to satisfy" it), and second, that it also misses an opportunity to enrich the target language by importing conceptual and other novelties into it ("stirs no fruits" for it).

Whom does Herder have in mind as the representatives of this invalid approach to translation? He sometimes identifies this as the usual *French* approach to translation.[25] (The usual French approach *was* in fact extraordinarily, and indeed deliberately, faithless to original texts, both semantically and in other ways, at this period. One more scrupulous French critic had already famously complained that such translations were "belles infidèles.") However, he also has a much more formidable opponent in his sights: Luther. For another example of this sort of approach is the *Verdeutschung* in translation, or indulgence of the distinctive qualities of the German language, which Luther had championed in theory in his famous *Letter on Translation* (1530), and implemented in practice in his translation of the Bible. (Luther's translation of the Bible is often quite loose semantically and in other ways. Its semantic looseness can be seen in its rendition of Luke, chapter 6, containing the famous Sermon on the Mount, for example.[26]) Herder does not explicitly identify this formidable opponent in the *Fragments* (his general estimation of Luther is extremely high; and he was, after all, a Lutheran minister!). But one can see that he has Luther in his sights from such facts as the following: in the *Critical*

Forests he refers in the course of discussing translation to "an old German word whose strong use has become contemptible and ridiculous for us through many a bad execution: *Verdeutschung*";[27] when praising Luther's Bible translation in the *Fragments* he pointedly stresses that he does so for its *German writing* (i.e. rather than for its quality as a translation);[28] and in the *Letters concerning the Study of Theology* (1780–1) he says that Luther is only "almost" still the hero of Bible translation, that he "gets a lot of places wrong,"[29] and that his Bible translation should still be used but only with "corrections."[30]

Herder also explicitly discusses and criticizes a certain rationale that had commonly been used to justify such a domesticating approach to translation, since at least the time of Antoine Lemaistre (1608–50) and John Dryden (1631–1700): namely, that one should translate foreign texts by writing what the foreign author *would have* written had he originally written in the target language. In such a vein, Lemaistre had already argued in 1650: "You must render into our language all that is in the Latin and you should do that so well that if Cicero had spoken our language he would have spoken as we make him speak in our translation."[31] And more famously, Dryden had written in his *Dedication of the Aeneis* (1697): "I have endeavoured to make Virgil speak such English as he would himself have spoken, if he had been born in England, and in this present age."[32] This rationale had indeed already been at least hinted at by Luther.[33]

Herder objects to this rationale that at least in the case of an ancient author such as Homer it cannot be applied because such an author *could not* have written in our language:

[Ebert's] Young could, in German, in our time, in accordance with our morals and religion, still have written his *Nights* [i.e. *Night Thoughts*]. But [Homer, Aeschylus, and Sophocles] their works in our language? in our time? with our morals? Never! As little as we Germans will ever get a Homer who in all respects is for us what he was for the Greeks.[34]

Herder therefore argues that translation should err in the other direction, towards excessive accommodation to the source text, namely in the interests of achieving semantic and other forms of faithfulness to the source text and also exploiting the source text's resources for conceptually and otherwise enriching the target language.

But how is this to be accomplished? One important, albeit in a way obvious, principle which Herder derives from the situation of radical mental difference and the resulting extreme difficulty of translation is that, in order to be as semantically faithful as it *can* be, translation must (at least in the challenging cases) be based on the sort of scrupulous and arduous interpretive inquiry into the original text's meaning that he advocates in his elaborate theory of interpretation. He makes this point in the *Fragments* in the course of discussing the translation of ancient oriental (in particular, Hebrew) poetry, for example:

> The best translator must be the best exegete ... Where is a translator who is simultaneously philosopher, poet, and philologist? He should be the morning star of a new epoch in our literature![35]

(We might call this for short Herder's principle of the consequent *need for real interpretive expertise*.[36])

But how is even an interpretive expert going to overcome the obstacle of radical conceptual difference in translation and thereby achieve translation's most fundamental goal of accurately reproducing a source text's meaning in the target language? Herder's answer to this question constitutes one of his most important methodological contributions, and one of his deepest philosophical insights concerning translation. Some more recent philosophers have implied that such an ambition would be *incoherent*, that if conceptual scheme diversity existed, then translation *could not* succeed. For example, Donald Davidson has written that "the failure of intertranslatability is a necessary condition for difference of conceptual schemes."[37] However, this superficially plausible-sounding position involves a serious error, and one that Herder had already seen beyond.[38]

Herder would dismiss it as an error not only for the relatively obvious, and only partly satisfying, reason that translation may succeed in *approximately* expressing a text's meaning even if it fails to do so *exactly* (recall his remark about translation "which *approximately* repeats what *Homer* said inimitably in his poetic language"), but also for the following much less obvious and more important reason:

It is a fundamental, revolutionary, thoroughly modern, and broadly correct principle of Herder's philosophy of language that concepts or meanings are—not, as many philosophers before him had thought, referents, Platonic "forms," empiricist mental "ideas," or whatnot, but—*word-usages*. Accordingly, concerning the problem of overcoming radical conceptual difference in translation, Herder holds that when a translator encounters a significant difference between a word-usage and hence meaning in the source language and the closest word-usage and hence meaning currently available in the target language, i.e. a conceptual gulf, instead of simply leaving the target language as it is, he should *"bend," or modify, its word-usage and hence its meaning* in order to enable it to express (or at least better approximate) the meaning in the source language.

Such a strategy was not entirely new with Herder, for it had already been advocated by Thomas Abbt in the *Literaturbriefe*, from whom

Herder in the *Fragments* quotes the following passage where the strategy is implied:

The true translator has a higher intention than making foreign books intelligible to readers, an intention which raises him to the rank of an author . . . who really enriches the state. Now this intention is none other than fitting to his mother-tongue excellent thoughts after the model of a more complete/perfect language. Thus did Apollo cause Achilles' armor to fit Hector as perfectly as if it had been made on his body . . . One should [undertake the formation of one's language] through attempts on the model of a better language. This already represents to us clearly many concepts for which we need to look for words, and presents these concepts in such juxtapositions that we need new connections. Not to mention here euphony . . . What handsome advantages would accrue to our language if it learned to mold itself to [*sich anschmiegen an*] the Greek and Latin languages as much as possible, and showed its pliability to the eyes of the public . . . If our translators add to these ancients also some modern foreigners whose genius is proven and whose language is related with ours, what would we not have to be grateful to our translators for![39]

Similarly, Herder himself in the *Fragments* argues that the German language can learn from Greek authors more successfully than from Latin authors "because it can adapt itself more flexibly [*biegsamer*] to the Greek language than to the Latin," and that the translator from Greek into German needs to exploit "the flexibility [*Biegsamkeit*] of the German language."[40] Likewise, in the *Popular Songs* he remarks that his own translations of Shakespeare involve "bendings and enrichments of our language."[41]

How exactly would this technique work? Take a case which, as we saw, Herder regards as especially challenging, that of translating Homer. Consider, for example, the problem of translating Homer's word *aretê* into English. A translator working in Herder's "bending" manner will begin by selecting the single word in existing English which, in his estimation, comes closest to *aretê* in meaning, say the word *virtue* or *excellence* or *valor*. (The choice of a *single* word is essential to this approach; choosing several words would subvert it. So too would translating *other* Homeric words by whichever single English word is chosen.) However, the translator will recognize that, whichever of these words he chooses, the rule for use that governs it in existing English is still very different from that which governs Homer's word *aretê*, so that there is still a difference in meaning. For instance, if he chooses the word *virtue*, he will recognize that the descriptive component of the rule that governs the word *virtue* in existing English makes it a linguistic solecism to ascribe *virtue* to a habitual liar or a pirate,[42] but quite linguistically proper under certain circumstances to ascribe it to a physically weak man; whereas exactly the converse rule governs the word *aretê* in Homer—so that the two words are still quite sharply different in meaning. What, therefore, is the translator to do? He need not simply resign himself to accepting this semantic discrepancy. Instead, for the duration of his translation he will implicitly modify the rule governing the word *virtue* in order to make that rule agree (or at least more closely accord) with the one that governs the word *aretê*. For instance, he will implicitly drop the descriptive rule governing the word *virtue* which was just mentioned, and switch to its converse instead, consequently for the duration of his translation writing quite happily of certain habitual liars and pirates as having *virtue* (e.g. Odysseus and Achilles, respectively), but scrupulously avoiding describing any physically weak man as having it. He will thereby succeed in expressing (or at least come closer to expressing) the meaning of Homer's word *aretê* in English.

This sort of approach was not commonly used by translators in Herder's day, nor is it today, and adopting it would entail an extensive and radical change in the nature of translation practice. In advocating it, Herder was butting heads with Luther again, among other people. For, in addition to being semantically loose in other ways, Luther's translation of the Bible is so in particular by *failing* to use the sort of one-word-for-one-word approach that Herder champions here.[43] And the same discrepancy with Herder's policy is found in many recent translations as well. Consider, for example, Richmond Lattimore's translation of Homer's *Iliad* (certainly an excellent translation of its kind). Instead of translating the word *aretê* with a single English word, Lattimore employs an extraordinary motley of English words: "valor,"[44] "strength,"[45] "warcraft/courage,"[46] "manhood,"[47] "virtue,"[48] "power,"[49] "horsemanship,"[50] and "fleetness [of foot]."[51]

Herder's fundamental objection to this more common approach would be simple and radical: in failing to reproduce source language word-usages, it ipso facto fails to express source language meanings or concepts, and a fortiori cannot express the relevant source language propositions either; translation of this sort is therefore a house built on sand.[52]

By contrast, Herder himself (at least when practicing the strict sort of translation here in question) is pretty rigorous in giving the sort of one-word-for-one-word translations that he recommends.[53] This can be seen, for example, by analyzing his translations of Shakespeare in the *Popular Songs*, which in general both aim at and achieve a high degree of semantic faithfulness,[54] and which in particular almost always translate salient words consistently across multiple occurrences (at least within a particular excerpt). Consider, for instance, Herder's longish translation of the ghost scene from *Richard III*, act 5, scene 3.[55] In this case, words which occur in multiple locations are almost always translated uniformly across their multiple occurrences—including the words "soul," "despair," "murder(er)(ed)," "die," "sleep," "live," "flourish," "awake," "bosom," "dream," "villain," and "conscience" (which consistently become *Seele, verzweifeln, (Mord)/Mörder/Ermordeten, sterben, Schlaf/schlafen, leben, blühen, erwachen, Busen, Traum/träumen, Bösewicht,* and *Gewissen,* respectively).[56]

We might for short call this fundamental Herderian solution to the problem of bridging conceptual difference in translation his *"bending" strategy.*

Herder is well aware that this "bending" strategy will inevitably make for translations that are less comfortable to read than those that can be produced by a more domesticating approach (such as Luther's or Lattimore's). However, he sees this as a proper price to pay in return for translation's greater accuracy, its more exact reproduction of meaning. Thus he praises Abbt for practicing this approved sort of translation in the following terms:

> As far as I am concerned, Abbt's brevity can be a shortcoming or barbarism; I for myself turn back and fold my hands: "Holy Tacitus! give us more Abbts! or at least, please do not punish us any more with translators who smooth out your rough brevity" . . . [Abbt is an] estimable translator; he knows the essence [*das Schroot und Korn*] of our language and seeks to coin strong words, to seek out old vivid words [*Machtworte*], to guide the syntax in accordance with his purpose . . . Certainly, therefore, unusual to read, difficult to translate. But who wants to allow himself to be easily read and translated into Frenchified German?[57]

As I mentioned before, this "bending" strategy is not only fundamental to Herder's (and subsequently Schleiermacher's) foreignizing approach to translation, but is also one of the philosophically deepest aspects of his (and then Schleiermacher's) theory of translation. For example, it provides the resources for correcting the sort of seductive mistake that Donald Davidson makes.[58] Yet this strategy is more or less entirely overlooked by Berman and Venuti (and indeed, by most of the relevant secondary literature).

Let us turn next to a further, and in some ways better known, fundamental principle to which Herder subscribes. Several of Herder's recent predecessors in the German-speaking world had already argued that a translation needs to reproduce not only a work's semantic content but also its *musical form* (e.g. meter, rhyme-scheme, alliteration, and assonance). For instance, Breitinger had already done so in 1740 and Bodmer in 1746.[59] Similarly, as we saw in passing earlier, Abbt in his plea for a type of translation which molds itself to the original and hence enriches the target language had included not only a molding to concepts but also a molding to musical form ("euphony"). Famously, Herder himself likewise emphasizes the importance of reproducing a text's musical "form" or "tone" in translation.[60]

As Herder articulates this position, he can sometimes even seem to be espousing it at the cost of *abandoning* the traditional conception that the main goal of translation is one of faithfully reproducing meaning. For example, at points in the later *Popular Songs* (1778–9) he seems to advocate the reproduction of musical form or tone *at the expense* of reproducing semantic content.[61] However, it would be quite surprising if Herder really *had* abandoned that traditional goal—given its prominence in such deeply admired predecessors as Ernesti and Lessing; its retention in the versions of an insistence on reproducing musical form recently cited from Breitinger, Bodmer, and Abbt; and perhaps especially the sort of scrupulous concern to realize it that we have seen Herder showing so far. And accordingly, on closer inspection it turns out that his considered position *builds on* rather than repudiating the traditional one: it is that translation should aim *both* for an exact reproduction of meaning *and* (as an additional, but essentially secondary, desideratum) for a reproduction of musical form or tone.[62] This can be seen from two texts which stand at opposite chronological ends of his authorship, for example: In the *Fragments* (1767–8), where he discusses translation at length, he sets up as an ideal for translation a *combination* of the sort of philological exactitude which he sees as exemplified by Michaelis's translations and the sort of felicity in versification which he sees as exemplified by Cramer's.[63] And he shows that he prioritizes the reproduction of semantic content over the reproduction of musical form by *beginning* his central discussion of the challenges involved in translation with a discussion of *semantic* ones, and only *afterwards* going on to discuss ones which rather concern musical *form*.[64] Similarly, some thirty years later, in the *Letters for the Advancement of Humanity* (1793–7), he remarks:

Form is much in art, but not everything. The most beautiful forms of antiquity are animated by a spirit, a great thought, which makes the form into form and reveals itself in it as in its body. Remove this soul and the form is a husk . . . If I had to choose, thoughts without form or form without thoughts, I would choose the first. My soul can easily supply them with the form.[65]

Moreover, on closer inspection, Herder's seeming departures from this position turn out to be more apparent than real. In particular, his remarks in the *Popular Songs* which seem to play up musical form or tone at the expense of semantic content are immediately preceded in the text by a commitment to exactness in translation which evidently encompasses both.[66] And when his remarks are scrutinized closely, they turn out not to be offering any *general* counsel of semantic carelessness in translation, but instead to concern and depend on some very specific peculiarities of popular ballads which in Herder's view warrant a measure of it in this *particular* case: first, the fact that their intrinsic nature is more musical than semantic;[67] and second, the (connected) fact that *for the very traditions which produced them* their musical form was more important and invariant than their verbal-semantic content.[68] In sum, for Herder the traditional goal of faithfully reproducing meaning remains the primary goal of translation, and is not displaced but instead complemented by a (secondary) goal of reproducing musical form or tone.

But in fact (and here we come to another important aspect of Herder's position to which the scholarly literature has failed to do justice) even this way of putting things understates the degree of Herder's continuity with the traditional conception of translation's fundamental goal as one of faithfully reproducing meaning. For in his view translation's pursuit of an exact reproduction of musical form is not *independent* of, but instead largely *serves*, its pursuit of an exact reproduction of meaning. It is true that according to him reproducing musical form *in part* serves goals which are distinct from that of an exact reproduction of meaning: in particular, he believes that the musical form of a work of literature (like all music) expresses exact nuances of feeling or emotion, so that reproducing it is essential for this reason;[69] and perhaps more obviously, he also believes that it is vital to the beauty of a work, so that reproducing it is essential for this reason too.[70] But the exact reproduction of musical form is also in his view essential in important part precisely because it is required for a full and exact reproduction of meaning. For he espouses a position that musical form and semantic content are *not strictly separable*. Thus in the late *Terpsichore* (1796) he says that Balde's meters are "more than dress," that they are the "form of thoughts," and so must be reproduced as accurately as possible in translation,[71] and he describes the sort of nuanced prosody that the ancients used as a "music of the sense of words."[72] Indeed, already in a letter from 1770 he implies that it is essential to preserve Shakespeare's rhymes in translation in part because of a semantic content which only they convey exactly. Because the translator Wieland has never himself felt a Romeo-love,

the most beautiful hints in which love speaks more than through words have remained for him a quite unknown language. Also, Shakespeare has in this play [*Romeo and Juliet*] many rhymes which Wieland curses in his notes, like a donkey; rhymes which certainly can drive a translator's head and pen to distraction, but which in the original as much belong to the true romance-language of love as they, to be sure, can seem foolish to someone who is without feelings.[73]

Why does Herder hold such a position? He has, I think, two main reasons: First, the musical form of a work—for example, its meter and rhyme-scheme—typically carries its *own* semantic content. This is part of what he means when he says that the nuanced prosody of the ancients was a "music of the sense of words."[74] It also seems to be part of what he has in mind when he observes in the *Popular Songs* (in a remark that may help to clarify the longer passage quoted above) that "it was Shakespeare's favorite trick not to leave the dearest love without rhyme."[75] A crude example may serve to illustrate the point more effectively than subtler ones would: the meter and rhyme-scheme of the limerick carry immediate connotations of humor and bawdiness. Second, as I already mentioned, in Herder's view, musical form, in particular the musical aspects of poetry, reveals fine nuances of *feeling*.[76] But Herder also subscribes to a quasi-empiricist theory of meaning, according to which feelings are not sharply detachable from meanings, nor, therefore, the exact imaginative recapturing of feelings by a reader from his exact semantic understanding of a text. Consequently, for this reason too it is *semantically* necessary to reproduce the musical form of a text in a translation. To illustrate this point with a concrete example close to Herder's concerns: it might plausibly be argued that in order exactly and fully to understand the meaning of Juliet's words "Good night, good night! Parting is such sweet sorrow / That I shall say good night till it be morrow" (*Romeo and Juliet*, act 2, sc. 2, ll. 185–6), one needs to hear such musical features as the meter, the three modulated repetitions of "good night," the alliteration "such sweet sorrow," and the end-rhyme "sorrow/morrow."

This is another area in which Herder is at odds with his most formidable opponent on the subject of translation: Luther. Luther had not attempted to reproduce the verse forms of the Old Testament, instead resting content with a uniform prose translation. As one might expect given Herder's commitment to the principle just explained, there are strong signs of his dissatisfaction with that Lutheran approach. For example, in the *Fragments* he calls for a translation of the Old Testament which combines Michaelis's philological skill with Cramer's skill in versification; he himself long cherished a plan (never realized) to produce a new translation of the Old Testament; his own sample translations of the more poetic parts of the Old Testament, such as the Psalms, attempt to reproduce their musical forms;[77] and the very title of his greatest work on the Old Testament, *On the Spirit of Hebrew POETRY*, points in the same direction. Moreover, he occasionally ventures a more explicit swipe at Luther on this score. For example, in the *Letters concerning the Study of Theology*, just after the passage already mentioned in which he urges budding theologians to use Luther's translation of the Bible for the time being but to incorporate "corrections," he adds, "or if you want some practice, especially in the poetic books of the Old Testament, then work for yourself."[78]

In addition to espousing this ambitious ideal of reproducing musical form in *theory*, Herder also provides some impressive illustrations of it in his translation *practice*. His sample translations of the more poetic parts of the Old Testament are noteworthy in this regard. So too, as Purdie points out, are some of his translations of ballads in the *Popular Songs*.[79]

In sum, Herder's considered position is that the translator should complement translation's primary goal of reproducing a work's semantic content with a secondary goal of reproducing its musical form or tone as well, and this not only, or even mainly, as a *separate* goal, but also, and perhaps mainly, as an essential means to fully achieving the former goal. (We might call this for short his principle of *reproducing musical form, and thereby also exact meaning.*[80])

So far this account of the motivation behind Herder's foreignizing ideals of "bending" word-usages and reproducing musical form has focused mainly on their envisaged indispensability for, and contribution to, the realization of translation's traditional fundamental goal: faithfully reproducing the meaning of the original text. This consideration is central to his position. However, he also has additional important reasons for advocating these approaches to translation which should now be considered. (It is here that we come to the sorts of reasons that Berman and Venuti have rightly, though one-sidedly, emphasized.)

It will be recalled that Abbt, in the passage which Herder quotes in the *Fragments*, regards it as an important merit of the sort of approach to translation that he and subsequently Herder advocate that it promises to enrich the target language, especially by adding new concepts to it through "bending" its word-usages, but also by contributing new musical forms to it ("euphony"), and that he especially expects such advantages to accrue from the translation of the classical languages, Greek and Latin, while also envisaging them coming from modern languages. Herder basically agrees with Abbt about all this. Thus, he writes in the *Fragments*, "Let our language be formed by means of translation,"[81] and like Abbt he especially expects the envisaged benefits to come from the classical languages,[82] while also recognizing that translations from modern languages such as English and French have provided, and can continue to provide, beneficial enriching effects on German.[83] Likewise, later in the *Popular Songs* he recommends his own type of translation of Shakespeare as importing "enrichments of our language."[84] (We might call this Herder's principle of *enriching the target language in concepts and musical forms through "bending" and musical-form-reproducing translations.*)

Herder's position in this area is somewhat ambivalent and unsettled, however. Already in the *Fragments* he qualifies and even contradicts his fundamental endorsement of Abbt's stance in certain ways. For one thing, he has a more discriminating picture of which classical models should be used.[85] For another thing, and more startlingly, he at points questions the value of subjecting a modern language like German to the sort of enrichment in question at all.[86] Some of this ambivalence stems merely from pessimism about the broad practicability of the sorts of translations that it would require.[87] But a deeper and more principled source of such ambivalence lies in an impulse to preserve the *authenticity* of a language such as German. In this vein, Herder at one point goes as far as to question the whole idea of improving languages through translation, on the grounds that a language in its uninfluenced state has the superiority of a virgin in her purity—a proposition which he illustrates by reference to what he considers the essentially uninfluenced condition of ancient Greek in the period of its greatest intellectual vitality.[88] In this connection, he is especially concerned about what he perceives to have been, and still to be, a harmful dominating influence of Latin and French on the German language.[89] In later work he modifies his position yet again. For one thing, he evidently overcomes his reservations in the *Fragments* about the value of translation's enriching function (already anomalous within the *Fragments* itself), for he himself goes on to translate on a grand scale largely with that function in view (for example, in the *Popular Songs*). For another thing, beginning with the *Popular Songs* of 1774 he stops according the classical languages any privileged role as models for enriching modern languages, instead extending this function more or less equally to a broader range of languages.[90] One should therefore probably say that in the end Herder's considered position is that the sort of enrichment in question is indeed valuable, and that this function is by no means confined to translations from the classical languages.

The general idea that (the proper sort of) translation's role includes enrichment of the target language was less novel than it might be supposed. It reaches back to the Romans—for example, Horace and Cicero, for whom this was an important part of their conception of their translations from Greek into Latin.[91] It can also be found in Spanish and French translators and translation theorists from the sixteenth to eighteenth centuries such as Jean Luis Vives, Jacques Pelletier du Mans, Jean le Rond d'Alembert, and Jacques Delille.[92] In Germany it was indeed already a virtual commonplace by the time of Abbt and Herder (due in large part to the historical example of Luther's Bible with its obvious role in transforming the German language). However, these precedents do not, of course, reduce the principle's importance. And one should also note that (Abbt and) Herder's *specific* way of understanding it is less commonplace, especially in its conception that a "bending" of pre-existing word-usages in the target language eo ipso introduces new concepts into the target language and thereby makes these, and the thoughts that they can articulate, available to target-language users for the first time. Contrast this, for example, with du Mans's assertion, in the course of expressing the generic idea of target-language enrichment by translation, that "*ideas are common to the understanding of all men* but words and manners of speech are particular to different nations."[93]

Berman, in his brief account of Herder's translation theory, well notes this sort of culturally *self*-regarding motive concerned with the development of the target language and culture. Berman himself also has culturally *other*-regarding, cosmopolitan motives for advocating foreignizing translation.[94] But he does not attribute these to Herder. This picture of Herder is one-sided. It does reflect Herder's emphasis within the *Fragments*. However, it is not faithful to Herder's *oeuvre* as a whole. Herder in fact already at the time of the *Fragments* (1767–8) cherished cosmopolitan values (see, for example, his contemporaneous essay *On the Change of Taste* [1766]). By the time of the *Popular Songs* (1774) these play a strong role in his work. And they reach perhaps their fullest and finest flowering in the 10th collection of the *Letters for the Advancement of Humanity* (1793–7). Culturally other-regarding, cosmopolitan concerns were, moreover, clearly a central motive behind his project of translating and publishing the *Popular Songs*: he did this, not only out of intellectual curiosity about the songs in question and the light they throw on the inner lives of other peoples, or from a culturally self-regarding interest in using them as means for developing the German language and its literature (though both of these motives were certainly important to him), but also because of a *concern for the peoples involved themselves*—as an expression of respect for them, and as a means of cultivating similar cosmopolitan moral sentiments towards them among other Germans.[95] Moreover, it seems clear that for Herder the same culturally other-regarding, cosmopolitan motive dictates not only the general project of translating the *Popular Songs* but also the *manner* of their translation, namely that this should be the foreignizing sort of translation that has been explained above, incorporating both a "bending" of word-usages and a reproduction of musical forms in order to achieve semantic and musical faithfulness. His main line of thought here is that in order to serve effectively as an expression of respect for the peoples in question, and as a means of cultivating a similar respect for them in other Germans, translations of their songs must at least strive to be strictly *accurate*, and hence semantically and musically faithful. Thus in a preface to the *Popular Songs* he demands

that one give us *whole, faithful natural history* of peoples in their own *monuments* with some completeness, . . . not speak oneself, but *let them speak*, not always ask "what the good of that is" but, good or not good, *present* it, not *beautify*, not trim and distort it with the hood of religion or of classical taste, but give it *as it is*, and with faithfulness, joy, and love.[96]

By contrast, Herder sees *domesticating* translation, of the sort that was widely practiced and preached in his century, especially by the French, as profoundly incompatible with cosmopolitan goals: insufficiently respectful of the Other and unsuited to cultivating respect for the Other in readers—indeed, usually a vehicle for a contrary belittling, imperialist agenda. He already implies such a position in the following passage from the *Fragments*, for example:

> The French, too proud of their national taste, assimilate everything to it, instead of accommodating themselves to the taste of another time. Homer must come to France as *one conquered*, dress in their style, in order not to offend their eye; allow his venerable beard and old simple costume to be removed; he is supposed to adopt French customs, and where his rustic nobility still peeps forth, there he gets derided as a barbarian.—We poor *Germans*, on the other hand, still virtually without a public and without a fatherland, still without tyrants of a national taste, want to see him as he is.[97]

Turning now to some further points: One consequence that Herder draws from the whole extremely ambitious conception of the task of translation sketched above is that proper translation is bound often to be a much more demanding and creative task than it is commonly taken to be: "The translator must himself be a creative genius in order to do justice to his original."[98] This notion that translation requires a sort of creative genius was not in itself unprecedented. For example, Anne Dacier (1647–1720) had already championed it.[99] But with Herder the rationale for it is quite different from, indeed almost the very opposite of, hers: whereas she championed this quality as belonging to "free" but not to "servile" translations,[100] Herder champions it as belonging to translations which are, precisely, in a sense servile, namely servile to the requirements of reproducing as faithfully as possible both semantic content (in particular, by "bending") and musical form. For Herder, the need for genius mainly stems from the extraordinary difficulty of performing this double task, and the need for creativity from the linguistic-conceptual and musical innovations in the target language which doing so demands.

Finally, despite the centrality to Herder's theory and practice of translation of the model of translation explained above, he actually has a rather *liberal* theory and practice of translation (especially in his later period). Thus in the late *Terpsichore* he writes that there are "*many* sorts of translation, depending on who the author is on whom one works and the purpose for which one represents him."[101] Accordingly, as we have seen, when dealing with certain ballads in the *Popular Songs* (and even with the more lyrical parts of Shakespeare), he sometimes deliberately departs from his central model in the direction of sacrificing semantic faithfulness to faithfulness in musical form for reasons specific to the particular genre involved; in his versions of Balde's Latin poems in the *Terpsichore* he explicitly eschews "translation" proper in favor of what he instead calls "rejuvenation"; and in his translations from the *Greek*

Anthology in the *Scattered Leaves* (1785–97) he likewise explicitly renounces "literal translations" in favor of "imitations."

A little reflection suggests that this sort of liberalism is the only reasonable position to adopt. For the appropriateness of one sort of translation or another surely does depend to a great extent on the particular genre of literature in question,[102] and on which of a rather large range of possible purposes the translator is pursuing.[103] For example (to cite a case in which both factors are relevant), if one is dealing with Aristophanic comedy and one's purpose is to provide a version in English which can be successfully performed on the stage, one would be quite ill advised to offer a semantically scrupulous version (such as B.B. Rogers supplies) and much better advised to offer a semantically loose one which employs intelligible modern analogues for Aristophanes' more obscure and outdated jokes (such as W. Arrowsmith's *Clouds*).[104] On the other hand, if one's purpose is to help general academic readers or beginning classics students in their study of the plays, then the converse choice might make more sense (i.e. a semantically scrupulous version, perhaps supported by explanatory notes).

Still, Herder's considered position (at least in his earlier and better statements, such as the *Fragments*) seems to be that the ambitious foreignizing model of translation which has been explained above does enjoy a certain privileged position. Why? I suggest that his main reason is that only this model of translation promises to do justice to what has been and remains the most commonly accepted fundamental goal of translation, namely faithfully reproducing the original text's meaning. Moreover, I suggest that this is a very *good* reason for according the model in question such a privileged position.

2. Schleiermacher's Theory: Continuities

Herder's espousal of this ambitious foreignizing ideal in his translation theory and practice had an enormous impact on subsequent German translation theory and practice (and thereby on modern translation theory and practice more generally). This is especially true of his principle of complementing semantic with musical faithfulness.[105] This principle was taken over by Voss, who implemented it in his both semantically and musically-metrically scrupulous translations of Homer, published from 1781 on (in realization, moreover, of a quite specific call for this sort of translation of Homer that Herder had issued in the *Fragments* and the *Critical Forests*).[106] It was also espoused by A.W. Schlegel, both in his theoretical work,[107] and in his semantically and musically-metrically scrupulous translations of Shakespeare, published from

1797 on (the latter, moreover, again in response to a quite specific call for, as well as demonstration of the possibility of, this sort of translation of Shakespeare that Herder had presented in "Would it be True that Shakespeare is Untranslatable?" and in the main body of the *Popular Songs*).[108] Both directly and indirectly (i.e. via its theoretical adoption and practical implementation by Voss, A.W. Schlegel, and others), Herder also effected its theoretical adoption and practical implementation by Schleiermacher (in *On the Different Methods of Translation* from 1813), Wilhelm von Humboldt (in his 1816 translation of Aeschylus' *Agamemnon* and the theoretical essay prefacing it),[109] Goethe (in his *West-östlicher Divan* of 1819 and its appended notes),[110] and others. Herder's principle of "bending" word-usages in order to ensure semantic faithfulness was taken over by certain successors as well (albeit less widely)—especially by Schleiermacher in his 1813 essay and his translations of Plato, and later on by Rosenzweig and Buber in their theoretical writings and their translation of the Old Testament.[111] It is to Schleiermacher's appropriation and development of Herder's whole theory of translation—as the most impressive and influential among the theoretical appropriations of it just mentioned—that I shall now turn.

Schleiermacher's theory of translation is found primarily in his brilliant essay *On the Different Methods of Translation* (1813).[112] There are also some important remarks concerning the subject in his aesthetics lectures of 1825,[113] and in his 1831 address on Leibniz's notion of a universal language.[114]

As in the case of Herder (and for the same reasons), it is also important to note that Schleiermacher was a masterful *practitioner* of translation. The primary example of this is his epoch-making series of translations of the works of Plato, which are still widely respected and used in Germany to this day, two centuries after they were first done.

The central positions concerning translation that Schleiermacher presents in his 1813 essay are almost entirely indebted to Herder. However, he also elaborates and refines Herder's positions in some significant and fruitful ways. In the present section I shall indicate the main continuities between the two theories; in the next section, Schleiermacher's main elaborations and refinements.

For Schleiermacher, as for Herder, the principle of radical mental difference, including radical *conceptual* difference, between cultures and periods, and even to some extent between individuals belonging to the same culture at the same period, is fundamental, and constitutes the main challenge for translation (as it does for interpretation). Schleiermacher implies this situation in the central, profoundly influential picture that he sets forth in his essay of a deep gulf between the thought/language of the author and that of the translator's reader, a gulf which, he says, must be overcome either by bringing the thought/language of the reader closer to that of the author or conversely:

In my opinion there are only two [roads]. Either the translator leaves the author in peace, as much as possible, and moves the reader towards him; or he leaves the reader in peace, as much as possible, and moves the author towards him.[115]

Schleiermacher also implies it in his almost equally important picture of the translator's task as, more specifically, a double one of not only bridging a gulf between his reader's thought/language and the thought/language of the culture to which the author belonged but also conveying to his reader respects in which the author's thought/language departed from that of the author's own culture:

If [the translator's] readers are to understand, they must perceive the spirit of the language that was the author's own and be able to see his peculiar way of thinking and feeling; and to realize these two aims the translator can offer them nothing but his own language.[116]

Again like Herder, Schleiermacher sees this situation of radical mental difference as making translation an *extremely difficult* task in many cases, even to the point of rendering it impossible without at least some distortion of the original text's meaning.[117] And again like Herder, he sees this as especially true of translation from ancient (or otherwise culturally distant) languages, rather than from closely related modern ones—or as he puts it in more general terms, of translation between "all languages not so closely related that they can almost be considered different dialects only."[118]

Again like Herder with his central "too accommodating" vs. "too lax" choice, Schleiermacher argues that because of the mental, and in particular conceptual, gulf that the translator normally faces, he must choose between two alternative strategies of translation. He must either leave the, say, ancient author with his concepts and try to bring the modern reader closer to the ancient author's concepts, or leave the modern reader with his concepts and try to bring the ancient author closer to the modern reader's concepts:

Either the translator leaves the author in peace, as much as possible, and moves the reader towards him; or he leaves the reader in peace, as much as possible, and moves the author towards him.[119]

As Schleiermacher more specifically conceives the latter strategy, it allows the modern reader to retain his pre-existing concepts/language precisely as they already are (it "does not expect any labor or exertion on the part of the reader") and attempts to express the ancient author's thoughts as he would have expressed them had he used, not his own concepts/language, but instead the modern reader's concepts/language in their already existing form ("to show the author's work as it would have been if the author himself had originally written it in the reader's language").[120] This is essentially a domesticating strategy of the sort commonly advocated and practiced by the French, or by Luther with his *Verdeutschung*, but one supplied with Lemaistre's and Dryden's more specific rationale for it ("what the author would have written if . . . ").[121] However, like Herder, Schleiermacher argues that this strategy is unacceptable—partly because it forgoes translation for mere "imitation," or in other words abandons translation's fundamental duty of semantic faithfulness;[122] and partly because under the thought-experiment in question, neither the author nor his thoughts could survive the imagined transition.[123]

For Schleiermacher, as for Herder before him, therefore, only the former strategy is acceptable: leave the author in peace and move the reader towards him, or in other words leave the author with his concepts/language and bring the reader closer to the author's concepts/language.

But how is that to be achieved? Again like Herder, Schleiermacher argues that because of radical mental difference and the consequent extreme difficulty of translation, in order to be as faithful as it *can* be, translation will (at least in challenging cases) need to be based on the sort of scrupulous, arduous interpretive inquiry into the original text's meaning that he advocates in his elaborate hermeneutic theory. Thus he writes in *On the Different Methods of Translation*:

Whoever has mastered [the] art of understanding through the most diligent cultivation of a language, through precise knowledge of the whole historical life of a nation, and through the living representation of single works and their authors, he and he alone may wish to lay open the same understanding of the masterpieces of art and scholarship to his contemporaries and compatriots [i.e. in translations].[124]

A further, and even more striking, continuity with Herder lies in the fact that Schleiermacher takes over Herder's solution to the fundamental problem of how in translation to bridge the conceptual gulf that often exists between the source language and the target language, namely by "bending" word-usages and hence meanings in the target language. For Schleiermacher, as for Herder before him, meanings are—not referents, Platonic "forms," mental "ideas," or whatnot, but instead—word-usages, or rules of word use. Hence he writes in his hermeneutics lectures that "the . . . meaning of a term is to be derived from the unity of the word-sphere and from the rules governing the presupposition of this unity."[125] Accordingly, for Schleiermacher, as for Herder before him, the task of overcoming a conceptual gulf in translation can and should be achieved by, as Schleiermacher puts it, "bend[ing] the language of the translation as far as possible towards that of the original in order to communicate as far as possible an impression of the system of concepts developed in it,"[126] or as he also puts it, effecting "innovations and deviations . . . in such a way that their accumulation may . . . generate a certain characteristic mode of expression."[127] For Schleiermacher, as for Herder before him, this approach requires that a word in the source language be translated uniformly with a single word in the target language throughout, "so that one word does not acquire a number of wholly different representatives, or a colorful variety reign in the translation where the original has strictly related expressions throughout."[128] This approach is possible, according to Schleiermacher, because a person's language is not something immutable, but instead something plastic that can be modified in innumerable directions by altering the rules for use governing the words which it contains, and hence ipso facto their meanings: the translator can exploit this potential in his language, modifying for the duration of his translation the rules for use governing words, and hence their meanings, in order to make these resemble more closely the rules for use, and hence meanings, of words in the source language.[129] As we saw, this was (Abbt and) Herder's solution to the challenge of bridging conceptual distance as well.[130]

Schleiermacher implements this method fairly rigorously in his own translations of the Platonic dialogues (as Herder had done in his translations of Shakespeare). Consider, for example, his translation of epistemic words in the *Apology* (a good test-case both because of the multiple occurrences of the relevant words in the Greek and because of the co-presence of a number of closely related but different words in the Greek). There he follows the policy in question pretty strictly. For instance, *sophos* and *sophia* usually become *weise* and *Weisheit* respectively;[131] *eidenai* usually becomes *wissen*,[132] while its cognate *sunoida emautôi* becomes either *wußte von mir selbst* or the similar *bin mir bewußt*; *epistamai* and *epistêmôn* usually become *verstehen* and *sachverständig* respectively;[133] *phronesis* usually becomes *Einsicht*;[134] and *gignôskein* usually becomes *merken*.[135]

It was, I strongly suspect, largely Voss's *failure* to implement such a policy that occasioned Schleiermacher's reservations about his translations of Homer in *On the Different Methods of Translation*, particularly on the grounds of their insufficient semantic faithfulness.[136] For an examination of Voss's translations shows that, despite their more general striving for semantic accuracy, they *do not* implement the Herder-Schleiermacher "bending" strategy, with its central and essential feature of translating a single word in the source language uniformly across its various occurrences by means of a single word in the target language.

Voss instead translates in such a way that, precisely (to requote Schleiermacher's description of what in his view should *not* happen), "one word . . . acquire[s] a number of wholly different representatives, . . . a colorful variety" (very much as we previously saw Luther and Lattimore doing). Thus, to return to the Homeric example I discussed earlier, the word *aretê*, in Voss's translation of the *Iliad* this word is variously translated as *Tugend*,[137] *Tapferkeit*,[138] *Kraft*,[139] *Kampfeskunde*,[140] *Gedeihen*,[141] *Herrlichkeit*,[142] *Macht*,[143] and *vorzüglich [im Lauf]*.[144]

Again like Herder, Schleiermacher recognizes that the approved "bending" approach to translation will inevitably make for translations that are significantly less comfortable to read than those generated by a more domesticating approach, but he sees this as a proper price to pay in return for their greater accuracy, their more exact reproduction of meaning. Thus he notes that a translator working in this bending mode will "willingly force himself to appear in movements less light and elegant than those he is capable of, to seem brutal and stiff, at least at times, and to shock the reader."[145]

Again like Herder, Schleiermacher argues that, especially in the case of poetry and more artistic forms of prose, it is vitally important to attempt to reproduce not only the semantic content but also the *musical form or tone* of the original, and moreover that this is important in part because conveying the musical form or tone is required *in order* to convey the semantic content precisely:

In the field of poetry and more artistic prose . . . the musical element of language, which becomes apparent in rhythm and change of tone, also has a specific and higher meaning. Everyone feels that the finest spirit, the highest magic of art in the most perfect products is lost, or even destroyed, when this is not taken into account. Hence, what a sensible reader of the original observes as peculiar in this respect, as intentional, as influencing tone and mood of feeling, as decisive for the imitative and musical accompaniment of speech, that will also have to be translated by our translator.[146]

As can be seen from this passage, Schleiermacher's rationale for this requirement is also broadly the same as Herder's: the reproduction of musical form is necessary, not only for a precise communication of the feelings or emotions expressed by the original work ("tone and mood of feeling"), and for preserving the beauty of the original work ("the highest magic of art in the most perfect products"), but also for the precise communication of the original work's *meaning* ("the musical element of language, which becomes apparent in rhythm and change of tone, also has a specific and higher meaning").

Moreover, like Herder, Schleiermacher sees the reproduction of musical form as *semantically* essential in this way because he believes musical form and semantic content to be inseparable (especially in poetic works). Thus in his aesthetics lectures he says:

People have thought that one must be able to take away the whole poetic form of a poem and have the poem nonetheless remain; indeed, people have gone even further, in that they have thought that even if the poetic clothing is removed the poetry must lose nothing in it. But this view is quite perverse and contrary to the nature of the matter, for it actually presupposes that form and content do not belong together, and accordingly it appears as though the poet should first make the thought and then the poetic clothing, and draw the meter from that. Rather, form and content must be exactly grown into each other, and one must conceive it as arisen in one piece.[147]

Furthermore, while Schleiermacher is rather vague about this, it seems reasonable to infer that for him, as for Herder, the semantic significance of musical form derives from at least two sources: (1) Certain musical features, for example certain meters, themselves bear meanings. Thus A.W. Schlegel, a member of Schleiermacher's circle, had already written in 1803:

Since all metrical forms have a definite meaning, and their necessary character in a given language may very well be demonstrated (for unity of form and essence is the goal of all art, and the more they interpenetrate and reflect each other, the higher the perfection achieved), one of the first principles of the art of translation is that a poem should be recreated in the same meter, as far as the nature of the language allows.[148]

(2) The word-meanings in a text are often in essential part constituted by feelings whose precise expression is only achieved with the aid of the musical features of the text. Thus, just as we saw that Herder complements his conception of meanings as word-usages with a quasi-empiricist theory of concepts which underpins his version of such a position, so Schleiermacher complements his conception of meanings as word-usages, or rules of word use, with a conception of them as Kantian empirical schemata, or rules for the production of images, presumably including ones of feeling or emotion.[149]

For Schleiermacher, as for Herder, the main motives behind the two foreignizing translation strategies of "bending" word-usages and reproducing musical form that have been explained above assume the traditional fundamental goal of translation, namely faithful reproduction of meaning,[150] and justify the two strategies in light of their shared new and broadly correct theory of meaning as necessary means for realizing that goal. But again like Herder, Schleiermacher, in addition to the above semantically focused motives for advocating the sort of foreignizing translation that "bends" word-usages and reproduces musical form, also has two further important motives.

First, like Herder, he notes, and approves of the fact, that the translator working in this mode will enrich his own language—especially by developing new concepts,[151] but also by developing new musical forms.[152] Accordingly, he writes:

Just as our soil itself has no doubt become richer and more fertile and our climate milder and more pleasant only after much transplantation of foreign flora, just so we sense that our language . . . can thrive in all its freshness and completely develop its own power only through the most many-sided contacts with what is foreign . . . Much of what is powerful and beautiful in our language has in part developed through translations or has in part been drawn from obscurity by them.[153]

Second, contra Venuti's picture of Schleiermacher as a German nationalist bent on German world domination, Schleiermacher in fact shares Herder's cosmopolitan motive for advocating foreignizing translation. A Herderian cosmopolitanism was an early and enduring part of Schleiermacher's outlook.[154] Moreover, translation's role in expressing and cultivating cosmopolitan respect for other peoples is a central component of his case for its importance generally, and for the need to develop it in Germany in particular:

The fact that speech is translated . . . allows people to establish contact who were originally as far apart from each other as the length of the earth's diameter.[155]

Our nation may be destined, because of its respect for what is foreign and its nature, which is one of mediation, to carry all the treasures of foreign arts and scholarship, together with its own, in its language, to unite them into a great historical whole, so to speak.[156]

It is reasonable to infer from these statements that for Schleiermacher the same cosmopolitan motive also dictates that translation should be of the foreignizing sort that he advocates, since in his view this is required in order for it to be semantically (and musically) faithful, and semantic (and musical) faithfulness in the representation of foreign peoples' texts and ideas is obviously a necessary condition for showing such peoples "respect," and for establishing "contact" with them in the both intellectual and affective-moral sense that he has in mind in these passages.[157]

Moreover, like Herder before him, Schleiermacher in this connection sharply contrasts what for him is the paradigm of an imperialist nation, the French (by whom at the time of the 1813 essay German soil had recently been overrun), who, he says, never translate in this authentic way—"Who would want to claim that anything had ever been translated either from the ancient languages or from the Germanic languages into French!"—[158] with the mission of the Germans to do so, in their "respect for what is foreign."[159]

Again like Herder, Schleiermacher infers from this whole ambitious ideal for proper translation—especially, "bending" word-usages in order to achieve semantic faithfulness and complementing semantic faithfulness with a faithful reproduction of musical form—that such a translator needs to be a sort of creative genius: the superior sort of translator is an "artist."[160]

Finally, like Herder (though not to the same extent), Schleiermacher, despite his commitment to that ideal, is somewhat liberal in his conception of the forms that transference from one language into another may take. Admittedly, such liberalism is not much in evidence in his 1813 essay. There, on the contrary, he argues (1) that translation proper must take the foreignizing form which he advocates and really cannot take the domesticating form which initially seems to be an alternative to it (since it thereby turns into mere imitation, among other problems);[161] and (2) that such related forms as imitation and paraphrase fall short of being translation proper, and are moreover only results of a despair about the possibility of translation proper, a despair which is in the end unwarranted, and which they are in any case unable to assuage.[162] However, in his aesthetics lectures of 1825 he allows much more legitimacy to imitation than that implies, treating it as a valid and important genre.[163] And even in his 1813 essay, he at least allows that imitation and paraphrase have validity in a cultural context which is less advanced in its enthusiasm for and knowledge about the foreign than that of his own day.[164] So in the end his considered position seems to be that, while foreignizing translation of the sort that he champions enjoys a special status (warranting its monopoly over the honorific name "translation"), other sorts of interlinguistic transfer such as imitation and paraphrase have a certain legitimacy as well.[165]

Why does foreignizing translation enjoy such a privileged status? For Schleiermacher, as for Herder before him, this is primarily because only it promises to achieve translation's traditional fundamental goal of faithfully reproducing meaning (as well as musical form) to the greatest extent possible. Thus he says that "the actual purpose of all translation" is "the least possibly distorted enjoyment of foreign works,"[166] and that it is a condition of the establishment of foreignizing translation "that the understanding of foreign works be a familiar and desired condition";[167] whereas by contrast he distinguishes both imitation and paraphrase from translation proper on the grounds that they operate "not with a view to gathering [foreign works'] real artistic or linguistic sense [-sinn], but rather to fill a need and to contemplate spiritual art," so that "the concept of translation adduced here is completely abandoned."[168]

In short, like Herder's, Schleiermacher's considered position is basically liberal about different forms of interlinguistic transfer, but accords foreignizing translation a special status, and does so mainly because only it promises to realize, to the greatest extent possible, translation's traditional fundamental goal of faithfully reproducing meaning (as well as musical form).

To sum up this section in a sentence: all of the core features of Herder's theory of translation are preserved in Schleiermacher's theory, composing its core as well.

3. Schleiermacher's Theory: Refinements

However, Schleiermacher's theory also departs from Herder's in certain respects, and the departures include a number of significant refinements, or improvements. I would therefore like in this section to discuss what seem to me the most important of these.

Not all of Schleiermacher's deviations from Herder's theory constitute progress. Some of them are, rather, regressive, constituting particular respects in which Herder's theory is superior to Schleiermacher's. Let me briefly mention three of these. First, as we recently saw, Schleiermacher is usually less liberal than Herder about the forms that interlinguistic transfer may legitimately take—especially in *On the Different Methods of Translation*. But his arguments against liberalism are not convincing, and Herder's more decided liberalism seems the better position.

Second, in *On the Different Methods of Translation* Schleiermacher (unlike Herder) alleges that there is one major exception to the rule that conceptual incommensurability arises across languages thereby posing the main challenge for translation. His exception concerns the part of language that refers to or describes items of sensory experience. He basically argues that the meaning of such terminology is invariant across languages, and so can be mechanically and easily transferred from one language to another. He therefore distinguishes such transference from "translation [*Übersetzen*]" proper as mere "interpreting [*Dolmetschen*]."[169] However, his claim that there exists such an exception is very dubious. For instance, the ancient Greek term *Helios* and our term *sun*, while they both refer to the same sensible object, are sharply discrepant in sense (for one thing, the former term unlike the latter implies some sort of personhood); and color conceptualization (an area of language concerned with sensory experience if ever there was one) turns out to be a strong example of an area in which radical conceptual difference occurs, and in which translation therefore faces serious difficulties (the thoroughgoing distinctiveness of Homer's color vocabulary as compared with our own being a case in point).[170]

Third, in some works, especially the *Ethics* and *Dialectics* lectures, Schleiermacher (unlike Herder) implies, on the basis of an a priori argument about the very nature of reason (or meaning/understanding), that conceptualization can *never* be exactly the same between two people—which would immediately entail that there is a principled and immovable obstacle to translation *ever* fully succeeding. However, this argument is implausible—in its very a priori status, its specific details, and its highly counterintuitive consequence that people can *never* really understand each other. On the other hand, Schleiermacher's theory of translation should not be judged too harshly in this respect, for it is one of the virtues of *On the Different Methods of Translation* as compared with his other works that it *avoids* this implausible position.

Much more striking in Schleiermacher's theory of translation than such steps of regress are a number of steps of *progress*. Let us begin here with some of the foundations of Herder and Schleiermacher's theories: the principles of radical mental difference and of the consequent extreme difficulty of translation. The tendency of Schleiermacher's position is to *radicalize* these principles in certain ways (i.e. ways which are more legitimate than the dubious way just mentioned).

As we have already noted, like Herder before him, Schleiermacher sees the task of achieving semantic faithfulness, especially in the face of conceptual incommensurability, as presenting great challenges for the translator, and he sees the additional requirement on translations of poetry and more literary forms of prose that they reproduce the musical forms of the original as presenting further great challenges (so that translation is an "art"). But beyond these two sources of challenges which had already been identified by Herder, Schleiermacher also plausibly identifies several further sources of challenges confronting the translator.

A first, and rather obvious, one is the following. Surprisingly, Herder says little or nothing about *tensions between* the two tasks just mentioned (those of achieving semantic fidelity and fidelity to musical form). By contrast, Schleiermacher points out that serious and even unresolvable tensions are often bound to arise between them for a translator:

> But how often—indeed it is almost a miracle if one does not have to say always—will rhythmical and melodic fidelity not be locked in irreconcilable combat with dialectical and grammatical fidelity![171]

This point was not new with Schleiermacher; d'Alembert had already made it in his *Observations sur l'art de traduire* (1758),[172] and Lessing had wrestled with it as well.[173] Nonetheless, it is an important point, and Schleiermacher is right to emphasize it.[174]

A further plausible and interesting radicalization of Herder's fundamental principles that Schleiermacher effects stems from his development of a much more *holistic* conception of meaning than is yet to be found in Herder (this is the one major area in which Schleiermacher's philosophy of language both revises and arguably advances beyond Herder's). At least three aspects of the semantic holism in question can be distinguished: (1) As we saw in passing earlier, Schleiermacher espouses a doctrine of "the unity of the word-sphere." This doctrine in effect says that the various specific senses which a single word typically bears, and which will normally be distinguished by a good dictionary entry (for example, the different senses of "impression" in "He made an impression in the clay," "My impression is that he is reluctant," and "He made a big impression at the party"), form a larger semantic unity to which they each essentially belong (so that any loss, addition, or alteration among them entails an alteration in each of them, albeit possibly a subtle one).[175] (2) He holds that the nature of any particular concept is in part defined by its relations to a "system of concepts and their signs."[176] In this connection, the *Dialectics* lectures focus mainly on a concept's relations as a species-concept to superordinate genus-concepts, relations as a genus-concept to subordinate species-concepts, and relations of contrast to coordinate concepts falling under the same genus-concepts. However, other types of conceptual relationships would be included here as well—for example, both morphologically transparent ones, such as those between "to work," "worker," and "a work" in English;[177] and morphologically opaque ones, such as that between *physis* and *nomos* in Attic Greek.[178] (3) He holds that languages' *grammatical* systems vary—for example, one inflective language may employ a certain system of declensions, whereas another employs a different system, whereas yet another language, such as Chinese, lacks any system of declensions at all—and that a language's distinctive grammatical system is internal to, and partly constitutive of, the concepts expressed within the language.[179]

Schleiermacher argues, very plausibly, that such holistic features of meaning greatly exacerbate the phenomenon of conceptual difference across languages and the difficulty of bridging it in translation (by means of the "bending" method), to the point of often making complete bridging impossible because the holistic features of the source language cannot be exactly reproduced or mimicked in the target language:

If, in the case of two languages, one word in one language exactly corresponded to one word in the other, if it expressed the same concept to the same extent, if their declensions represented the same relationships . . . so that these languages were indeed different to the ear only—then all translation would be . . . mechanical . . . and it could be said of every translation that except for the effects produced by sound and melody, it puts the foreign reader in the same relationship to the author as the native reader. But the case with all languages not so closely related that they can almost be considered different dialects only is precisely the opposite, and the farther they are apart in time and genealogical descent, the less a word in one language corresponds completely to a word in another or a declension in one language comprehends exactly the same multiplicity of relationships as another in a different language . . . How does the translator propose to find a happy solution here, since the system of concepts and their signs in his language is totally different from that of the original language, and since roots of words do not cover each other in parallel, but rather cut through each other in the most amazing directions? It is therefore impossible for the translator's use of language to be as coherent as that of his author.[180]

Schleiermacher's novel recognition of such holism, and of the great obstacle to the success of translation that it represents, does not leave the translator *entirely* helpless in the face of it, either in Schleiermacher's view or in fact; there are certain things that the translator can do in response to it. For instance, part (1) of Schleiermacher's holism could motivate the translator to sustain the one-word-for-one-word policy even in cases where Herder would have seen two different occurrences of a word as involving homonymy and thereby absolving him of the need to implement that policy (e.g. the word "impression" in "He made an impression in the clay" and "My impression is that he is reluctant").[181] Similarly, part (2) of Schleiermacher's holism might motivate a response which can actually be seen fairly clearly in his translation practice: Herder tended to be content to implement the one-word-for-one-word policy in a merely minimalist way, giving uniform translations of *single words* indeed, but making little effort to reproduce *families of morphologically cognate words* from the source language in the target language. For example, in his translation of the ghost scene at *Richard III*, act 5, scene 3, the family of morphologically cognate words "die," "death," "deadly," "dead" becomes respectively *sterben, Tod, Mörder-, (–)* (i.e. "dead midnight" becomes simply "Mitternacht"); and the morphological cognates "wronged" and "wrongs" become respectively *verdrungen* and *Schuld*.[182] By contrast, Schleiermacher seems to work hard to reproduce such families of morphological cognates. For example, as we already saw, in his translation of the epistemic vocabulary of Plato's *Apology* the words *sophos* and *sophia* become *weise* and *Weisheit* respectively; *eidenai* and *sunoida emautôi* become respectively *wissen* and *wußte von mir selbst/bin mir bewußt*; and *epistamai* and *epistêmôn* become respectively *verstehen* and *sachverständig*.[183] Even part (3) of Schleiermacher's holism might be addressed by the translator to some extent, namely by "bending" grammatical features of the target language. This had in fact already been proposed even before Schleiermacher in connection with syntax.[184] Concerning declension, in cases where both the source language and the target language have systems of declension (especially if they are closely related and similar, as is true of Greek, Latin, and German for example) there may even be some prospect of "bending" declension in the target language (though this will be more or less precluded if the target language does not have a developed system of declension, as in the case of English or Chinese for instance).[185] Still, all that said, the extent to which the problem posed by semantic holism is going to be solvable by the translator seems bound to be quite limited, and Schleiermacher's pessimism about this therefore warranted.

Another plausible development which Schleiermacher effects in Herder's fundamental principles towards greater radicalism lies in his stronger emphasis on the fact that the conceptual distance with which the translator needs to cope is typically in a sense a *double* one. Often, when we translate, say, an ancient author, we need to deal, not only with the conceptual distance that exists between our modern language and the shared language of his ancient community, but also with a certain conceptual distance that has arisen between his community's language and his own due to conceptual modifications or innovations which he has introduced.[186] Schleiermacher argues that a translation should strive to make such conceptual innovations as apparent to the modern reader of the translation as they would have been to the ancient reader of the original:

> If [the translator's] readers are to understand, they must perceive the spirit of the language that was the author's own and be able to see his peculiar way of thinking and feeling.[187]

How could this possibly be accomplished? Schleiermacher suggests that, at least in principle, it both can and should be accomplished by using relatively older terminology from the target language to translate terms in the original author which were conceptually conventional but relative neologisms from the target language for terms in the original author which were conceptually innovative.[188]

However, he also recognizes that there are bound to be severe limits to the possibility of success in implementing this solution, since, for example, it may turn out that the best semantic approximation that we have to some concept innovated by the ancient author happens to be a relatively old term of ours, whereas the only relative neologisms of ours that might serve are less close semantically:

> How often a new word in the original will be best corresponded to by one that is precisely old and tired in our language, so that the translator, even if he wanted to show the language-forming aspect of the work there, would have to put an alien content in the spot and hence deviate into the realm of imitation! . . . How often, even when he can render the new by means of the new, the word that is closest in composition and derivation will nonetheless fail to render the sense most faithfully, and so he will

after all have to awaken other connotations if he does not want to harm the immediate connection! He will have to console himself with the thought that he can make good his omissions in other places where the author used old and well-known words, and that he will therefore after all achieve in general what he is unable to achieve in every particular case.[189]

In sum, the additional requirement that Schleiermacher here imposes on the translator is not one which the translator is *entirely* at a loss to cope with, but it does appreciably complicate his already complicated task (of reproducing semantic content and, where relevant, also musical form, and of doing both of these things together), and thereby makes the likelihood of complete success that much lower.

Another important innovation in Schleiermacher's theory is closely connected to the radicalizations of the difficulty of translation just discussed. Those radicalizations reduce the degree of success that Schleiermacher expects even the best translations to be able to achieve even below the already-low level envisaged by Herder. Indeed, Schleiermacher often seems skeptical that translations can ever fully achieve even the basic goal of semantic faithfulness, let alone that plus the goal of faithfully reproducing musical form plus the goal of faithfully reflecting authorial innovations. His position thus comes close to that held by a long tradition of skepticism about the very possibility of translation—a tradition that prominently includes, for example, Roger Bacon (who was concerned mainly about the non-reproducibility of semantic content),[190] and Dante (who was more concerned about the non-reproducibility of musical form).[191] However, he avoids falling victim to outright skepticism (or, for that matter, to an equally desperate renunciation of semantic equivalence as the primary goal of translation, such as one finds in Benjamin, Berman, and Venuti, for example), and he achieves this feat by means of one of his simplest but also most important innovations: As we saw earlier, Herder, when discussing the translation of Homer, had taken the position that, while any translation of Homer will perforce fall short of reproducing Homer's meaning and musical form exactly, such a translation should nonetheless strive to *approximate these as closely as possible.* Schleiermacher's colleague and friend Friedrich Schlegel (with whom he first co-developed the project of translating Plato, and probably also much of his theory of interpretation and translation) already articulated a more radical version of that conception in his *Philosophy of Philology* of 1797, arguing that the "immeasurable difference" that separates ancient or classical thought from our own makes translation of at least ancient or classical texts problematic for us even to the point of strict impossibility, but that we should not for that reason abandon their translation but should instead conceive it as an infinite task, one that can never be fully accomplished but in which we nonetheless can and should make progress:

Whether translations are *possible* is something no one has bothered himself with . . . Each translation is an indeterminate, infinite task.[192]

Schleiermacher shares, and if anything even further generalizes, that position: this is his conception of virtually *all* translation (properly so called). Thus, despite his severe, and arguably well-grounded, skepticism about the possibility of translation—as an activity aimed at the goals of faithfully reproducing semantic content, musical form, and an impression of the author's conceptual innovations—ever achieving full success, he can still consider it a worthwhile and important activity, holding that it should strive to realize these goals *as fully as possible*, and should use the method that will best enable it to do so:

These are the difficulties that beset this method [i.e. the favored reader-to-author method] and the imperfections inherent in it. But once we have conceded them, we must acknowledge the attempt itself and cannot deny its merit . . . Art must learn, as far as possible, to overcome its difficulties, something we have not tried to hide.[193]

His strong strain of skepticism therefore in the end entails nothing more destructive of translation than an insistence that even the optimal type of translation can only claim the character of a sort of vitally necessary evil.[194]

A further innovation for which Schleiermacher can arguably claim con-siderable credit is his sharp distinction between, and unambiguous judgment concerning, two possible forms that translation proper might take:

In my opinion there are only two [roads]. Either the translator leaves the author in peace, as much as possible, and moves the reader towards him; or he leaves the reader in peace, as much as possible, and moves the author towards him.[195]

Schleiermacher of course judges that only the former approach is acceptable.

As we have seen, this position builds on insights of Herder's—in particular, Herder's fundamental insight into radical mental difference, and his connected conceptions in the *Fragments* concerning the need for the translator to steer between the Scylla of a "too lax translation" and the Charybdis of a "too accommodating translation," and the preferability of a type of translation that errs towards the latter side.[196] However, Schleiermacher recasts this Herderian choice in starker terms. This has often been seen as a weakness in Schleiermacher, but it could, I think, be argued that it is a strength.

One arguable advantage of Schleiermacher's version of the position lies in the value of its sharper distinction as an analytical tool for clarifying what is going on at particular points within a translation, and for classifying translations into different types according as they tend more in the one direction or the other. These two virtues are (explicitly or implicitly) conceded even by many translation theorists who find fault with Schleiermacher's version of the position in other respects.[197]

But I would also suggest that the value of Schleiermacher's version of the position goes beyond that. Schleiermacher has often been criticized for his insistence that the translator make a clearcut choice between the two approaches, on the grounds that the translator should rather aim for a sort of *compromise* between them (as Herder had already held). Rosenzweig, Lefevere, and Huyssen all criticize Schleiermacher in this way, for example.[198] However, that criticism can perhaps be answered. As we recently saw, for Schleiermacher perfect translation is only an ideal which a translator will inevitably fall short of fully realizing in practice. Accordingly, Schleiermacher's considered view seems to be that the reader-to-author approach is part of that ideal (whereas the author-to-reader approach is not), but that in practice a translator will always fall some way short of fully realizing it, in particular by resorting to author-to-reader strategies at certain points. The net effect of this position is thus in one sense the same as that of a position like Herder's or Rosenzweig's which demands that the translator compromise but err in the direction of foreignizing: people who espouse the two positions will end up approving of and disapproving of more or less the same translations. But Schleiermacher's position seems different from and preferable to theirs in two respects: First, it keeps more clearly in view the fact that complete foreignizing, if it were only practicable, would be optimal, in particular because it is required for fully realizing translation's traditional fundamental goal of accurately reproducing meaning. Second, and relatedly, it thereby promises to work more effectively as a guide to practitioners of translation than an ideal of compromise would, keeping them more "on their toes" in pursuit of that traditional fundamental goal. (An analogy: if an athletics coach wants to make the long-jumpers on his team reach 20 feet, it may nonetheless be a more effective means of bringing this about to set the mark at 25 feet rather than at 20 feet.)

Another area of significant innovations is Schleiermacher's case against the one of the two options that he distinguishes which he regards as illegitimate, namely "leav[ing] the reader in peace, as much as possible, and mov[ing] the author towards him." Schleiermacher intimately associates this approach with the criterion of *what the author would have written if his native language had been the target language instead of the source language*: "the translation wants to let its Roman author, for instance, speak the way he would have spoken to Germans if he had been German"; it shows the author "as he, as a German, would have originally written in German"; it "show[s] the author's work as it would have been if the author himself had originally written it in the reader's language."[199] As we saw, this criterion had been popular as a rationale for domesticating translation at least since the time of Lemaistre and Dryden, and it had already been criticized by Herder in the *Fragments*. Schleiermacher's strategy against domesticating translation is mainly to argue that this rationale is invalid.

There is an immediate problem with this strategy, namely that it seems clear on reflection that this is only *one* possible rationale for the domesticating approach, and hence should not be simply *equated* with the latter—so that in defeating this rationale Schleiermacher would not, in fact, have defeated the domesticating approach itself.

Despite some genuine confusion on this score, Schleiermacher has resources for coping with this problem, however. For he also has a more fundamental complaint against the domesticating approach which promises to tell against *any* version of it: namely, that it turns translation into mere *imitation*, or in other words fails to realize translation's fundamental goal of semantic (and other forms of) faithfulness to the degree that is possible. Thus he writes concerning this approach:

> It is obvious that if the formula is faithfully followed in this field [of comedy], it will either lead to pure imitation or to an even more clearly repulsive and confusing mixture of translation and imitation . . . One can see . . . that this would not be translation, strictly speaking, and that its goal would not be the most precise possible enjoyment of the works themselves; it would become more and more imitation.[200]

I therefore suggest that Schleiermacher's case against the *what the author would have written if* . . . rationale should really be seen as an *additional* argument against *one* especially common and seductive rationale for the domesticating approach.

Now, Schleiermacher develops a very interesting argument against this rationale which in effect takes into account not only the original Lemaistre-Dryden version of it, in which, as we saw, the thought-experiment concerns what the author would have written if he had known the target language *instead of* the source language, but also a possible revised version of it (revised in order to cope with some serious problems which emerge for the original version) in which it rather concerns what the author would have written if he had *added* a grasp of the target language to his grasp of the source language. Let us consider these two parts of Schleiermacher's case in turn.

Concerning, first, the classic version of the rationale found in Lemaistre, Dryden, and others, it will be recalled that Herder had already objected to this idea of translating in such a way as to write what (say) an ancient author *would have* written had he written not in his own language but instead in our modern language, that an ancient author such as Homer *could not* have written in our modern language.[201] Schleiermacher takes over that objection but in effect develops it into two distinct objections between which Herder had remained ambiguous, both of them very plausible: (1) that the particular *thoughts* of the ancient author could not have been expressed if he had only had our modern language (as it already exists), and (2) that the ancient author could not even *himself* have existed without his language, possessing instead only ours (as it already exists). For both of these reasons, Schleiermacher argues, this rationale is implicitly incoherent. His argument, to explain it in a little more detail, goes as follows: Given the conceptual incommensurability between a translator's modern language (in its pre-existing form) and an ancient author's language,[202] and given that one can only have thoughts which one can express in one's language,[203] the identity of the thoughts expressed by the ancient author in a given text could not survive the removal of his language and its replacement by the translator's modern language (in its pre-existing form), for only the language which he actually used, not the modern alternative (in its pre-existing form), furnishes the concepts in terms of which the thoughts expressed in his text can be articulated. Nor could the ancient author even himself survive such a removal and replacement, for only the language which he actually used, not the modern alternative (in its pre-existing form), furnishes the concepts in terms of which the beliefs, desires, and so forth that in essential part made him the man he was can be articulated. Schleiermacher puts this whole argument as follows:

Can anyone who is convinced of the internal and essential identity of thought and expression—and the whole art of all understanding of speech and therefore also of all translation is based on this conviction—can such a person want to sever a man from the language he was born into and think that a man, or even just his train of thought, could be one and the same in two languages? . . . The aim of translating in a way such as the author would have originally written in the language of the translation is not only out of reach, but also null and void in itself, for whoever acknowledges the shaping power of language . . . must concede that every most excellent human being has acquired his knowledge, as well as the possibility of expressing it, in and through language, and that no one therefore adheres to his language mechanically as if he were strapped into it . . . and that no one could change languages in his thinking as he pleases the way one can easily change a span of horses and replace it with another . . . The question cannot even be raised of how [a man] would have written his works in another language.[204]

To claim that one had in one's modern translation the work that the ancient author would have written had he used not his own language but the language of the modern translation (in its pre-existing form) would therefore be like saying that one had

brought . . . the picture of the author just as he would have looked if his mother had conceived him with another father. For if the writer's particular spirit is the mother of works . . . , his national language is the father.[205]

However, to his considerable credit, Schleiermacher in effect notices that the classic form of the rationale in question might be revised in an attempt to enable it to cope with the objections just raised: the criterion could become, not what an ancient author would have written in the translator's modern language (as it pre-exists) if the author had *substituted* a grasp of this modern language for his grasp of his ancient language, but if he had *added* a grasp of this modern language to his grasp of his ancient language.

Schleiermacher spends several pages wrestling with this proposal, without great success. He argues that such cases of bilingualism are in fact extraordinarily rare, at least in a relevant form: one class of cases of authorial bilingualism turns out to concern subject-matters which the author could not have expressed in his primary language (e.g. cases such as Grotius and Leibniz, who wrote professionally in Latin or French in preference to their native tongue);[206] another class of cases turns out to concern courtiers' and diplomats' small talk, commercial transactions, and the like, which Schleiermacher considers too mundane and mechanically transferable to be the subject-matter of translation in the higher sense in which he is interested;[207] and when it comes to such fields as art and philosophy (the fields with which translation in that higher sense *is* concerned), he claims that bilingualism hardly ever occurs, and indeed should not occur.[208] He then infers that in such fields the paucity of examples of bilingualism deprives the proposed criterion ("what the author would have written if . . . ") of the empirical evidence that would be required in order for it to be implemented in a determinate way, leaving the translator who employs it without any real guidance: "If it is not possible to write something in a foreign language worthy of—and in need of—translation as an art, or if this is at least a rare and miraculous exception, we cannot set up as a rule for translation that it should imagine how the writer himself would have written in the language of the translator, for there is no abundance of examples of bilingual authors from which an analogy could be drawn for the translator to follow; rather he will be left almost totally to his own imagination for all works that do not resemble light entertainment or commercial transactions."[209] He therefore concludes that the applicability of such a criterion is "severely limited, . . . almost equal to zero," that it is "almost impossible to put into practice."[210]

These points are very problematic, however. One problem with them is that the sort of bilingualism that Schleiermacher considers vanishingly rare is arguably a lot commoner than he allows. This was already true in his own day, as cases close to home such as the Schlegels and Wilhelm von Humboldt illustrate. But in more recent terms: even if one sets the bar of fluency very high indeed, one still has such famous cases as Rilke (who was able to compose poetry in both German and French) and George Steiner (completely trilingual in German, French, and English), as well as myriad less-well-known scholars in American and other universities who are equally at home in English and another language or other languages, and so on. Another problem here is that in any case mere paucity of evidence for "what the author would have written if . . . " would not call into question that there was a *fact* of the matter; it would only make it difficult to *assess* whether or not this criterion had been satisfied by particular translations.

A different sort of problem—but also potential salvation for Schleiermacher—lies in the fact that he has overlooked a much more damning objection to the revised criterion in question: Hypothesizing that the author retains his original language, adds another language, and then composes his work in the latter certainly overcomes the initial objection that *he* would no longer exist, but it does nothing to overcome the initial objection that the *thoughts* expressed in his original work would fail to be expressed in the resulting work. It would only do so if the author were to switch from *original composition* in the new language (the case that the proposed revised criterion has in view) to a sort of *translation* into it from thoughts that he had first (at least mentally) articulated in the original language. So the original Lemaistre-Dryden criterion would in fact need to be revised still further, namely in the manner just indicated, if it were to have any chance of surviving *both* of Schleiermacher's initial objections.

Schleiermacher does not himself see this, nor does he consider such a further revised version of the criterion as a rationale for author-to-reader translation. Indeed, strangely enough, at one point in his essay he presents the new criterion in question here as a valid rationale for the *alternative*, reader-to-author approach: this "will be perfect in its kind when one can say that if the author had learned German as well as the translator has learned Latin, he would not have translated the work he originally wrote in Latin any differently than the translator has done."[211] However, the possibility that someone might instead appeal to this criterion in order to rationalize an author-to-reader approach is fairly obvious, and in fact one recent advocate of such an approach, Nida, has done just that (albeit without running through the several steps of argument given above which could lead towards doing so). Thus Nida offers as a rationale for "dynamic equivalence" (i.e. domesticating) translation: "a reproduction of the original, such as [the author] himself, if master of the English language, would have given."[212]

Although Schleiermacher fails to consider this further-revised version of the criterion as a rationale for the author-to-reader approach, his very failure to do so, and his use of it as a criterion for the reader-to-author approach instead, imply that he does not believe that it could work in that function. And it seems to me that he is correct in this implication. The following are some reasons for this which go beyond anything he says explicitly but which stay within the general spirit of his overall position. At least in the relevant cases, "what the author would have written if he had acquired the target language and himself translated into it" will surely depend on the nature of the author's own theory and practice of translation.[213] It may be that in such areas of discourse as courtiers' or diplomats' small talk or the language of commercial documents this sort of dependence will be minimal, or easily overlooked, because in such areas the ways of translating particular words and sentences tend to be heavily socially regulated (for obvious social-functional reasons).[214] But certainly where the fields that interest Schleiermacher are concerned (for example, literature and philosophy), the dependence seems inevitable.[215] This fact has two immediate consequences, both of which undermine the possibility of using the criterion in question as a general rationale for an author-to-reader approach (or for that matter, as a general rationale for a reader-to-author approach either): First, while an author whose translation theory and practice was domesticating would presumably re-write his work in his now added target language in the manner of a domesticating translator, an author whose translation theory and practice was foreignizing would presumably do so in the manner of a foreignizing translator—so that this criterion could be expected to favor *foreignizing* translation about as often as it favored domesticating translation. Second, many authors will not *have* a translation theory or practice, so that in their case the criterion will presumably deliver no determinate verdict at all, there will simply be no fact of the matter as to "what the author would have written if . . . "

Moreover, it is by no means clear that the author, even if he does have a particular translation theory and practice, so that the criterion would at least yield a determinate result in his case, has any *final authority* in the matter. Famously, it is one of Schleiermacher's central principles concerning *interpretation* that an interpreter ought to understand an author *better than he understood himself*, i.e. that the author's self-understanding is corrigible in certain ways. This principle might well *itself* call into question the authority of an author's manner of re-expressing his own work in another language. But more importantly, it also suggests a further reason for calling it into question:

Problems of self-understanding aside, even if the author, because he theorizes and practices translation in some definite manner X, would, had he acquired fluency in some second language, have re-expressed his work in that language in form Y, might it not be the case that his theory and practice of translation X is *misguided*, so that his re-expression Y lacks validity for *this* reason?

In sum, I suggest that Schleiermacher is in the end right to reject as a rationale for domesticating translation not only the original version of the "what the author would have written if . . . " criterion, but also the two possible revised versions of it which have been considered above, even if, as we have seen, his case for rejecting the latter versions stands in need of some revision.[216]

Let us turn now to Schleiermacher's *approved* method: moving the reader of the translation towards the author, in particular by "bending" word-usages in the target language. A first point to note here is that Schleiermacher develops two important defenses of the "bending" strategy against alternative strategies which might seem to call into question the need for it (and perhaps also the need for a reader-towards-author method generally, or even the very assumption of a conceptual gulf that undergirds the whole reader-towards-author-or-author-towards-reader choice).

As we saw from the examples of Luther, Voss, and Lattimore, one very tempting tack for a translator to take when faced with a difficult word in the source language might be, not to "bend" a single counterpart in the target language, but instead to use several words/concepts in the target language as it already exists, depending on which one of them seems best for a given context. As we also saw, however, Schleiermacher firmly rejects this approach, insisting on the importance of translating "so that one word does not acquire a number of wholly different representatives, or a colorful variety reign in the translation where the original has strictly related expressions throughout."[217]

On reflection, Schleiermacher's position here seems justified. Consider, for example, Homer's color-word *chlóros*, a word that Homer sometimes applies to things which we would classify as yellow (e.g. honey) and at other times to things which we would classify as green (e.g. healthy foliage). A translator who followed the alternative approach under consideration would probably translate this single word *chlóros* differentially according to different contexts (as Voss and Lattimore in fact do). For example, he might judge that in some contexts the best candidate for conceptual equivalence was our concept green and in others our concept yellow, and so translate the word as though it were homonymous, switching back and forth between *green* and *yellow* according to the context. Now such a procedure is certainly likely to be more comfortable than Schleiermacher's "bending" strategy for readers of the resulting English translation—for example, in this case it spares them grating passages about honey being *green* or healthy foliage being *yellow*. However, it only buys this arguably rather slight virtue of comfort at the cost of an arguably much more serious vice, namely that of severely distorting the meaning conveyed to readers of the translation—by, for example, giving them the quite false impression that Homer has *two familiar* concepts here whereas he in fact has *a single unfamiliar* one.

Another somewhat tempting alternative to "bending" which Schleiermacher considers and rejects is the approach of substituting for a problematic word in the source language a more complex phrase in the target language which aims at extensional equivalence, and thereby at capturing the original meaning. For example, in the case of *chlôros* the translator might substitute in all contexts the phrase *green or yellow*. Schleiermacher incorporates his description of and objection to such an approach into his description of and objection to the somewhat broader genre of *paraphrase* (of which this approach is one aspect). Herder had already criticized this genre (with special reference to biblical paraphrases such as Locke's paraphrase of the New Testament) in his *Letters concerning the Study of Theology* (1780–1), on the grounds that it loses the spirit of the original text and distorts the original text's thoughts or meanings.[218] Schleiermacher follows Herder in this general criticism, but also incorporates into it a more specific criticism, in the same vein, of the particular approach in which I am interested here. Thus he rejects paraphrase in general and this aspect of it in particular as inherently distorting of the spirit or the meaning of the original text, as follows:

Paraphrase strives to conquer the irrationality of languages, but only in a mechanical way. It says: Even if I do not find a word in my language which corresponds to that in the original language, I still want to try to arrive at its value as far as possible by adding restrictive and expansive definitions. Thus it clumsily works its way through between a vexatious too much and a torturous too little by a piling up of details. In this way it may possibly succeed in rendering the content with limited precision, but it totally abandons the impression [made by the original], for the living speech has been killed irrevocably . . . The paraphrast treats the elements of the two languages as if they were mathematical signs that could be reduced to the same value by means of addition and subtraction, and neither the spirit of the language transformed nor that of the original language can reveal themselves in this method.[219]

Once again, reflection suggests that Schleiermacher is right to reject this sort of approach as inferior to his own "bending" approach. For even if this sort of approach were to succeed in getting the *extension* of the original word right in the target language and thereby make progress towards capturing its meaning or intension in *this* way, it would inevitably end up distorting the word's meaning or intension in *other* ways (besides, more obviously, being aesthetically discrepant with the original wording and aesthetically displeasing). For example, the proposal to substitute for *chlôros* the phrase *green or yellow* throughout would suffer (not only from obvious aesthetic discrepancy with the original and aesthetic infelicity, but also) from the serious vices that, like the previous alternative approach, it imputes to Homer possession of the *two familiar* concepts of green and yellow whereas he in fact only has the *single unfamiliar* concept of *chlôros*; and that in addition it imputes to him a *disjunctive* concept whereas he in fact has a *non-disjunctive* one. (One might dub this sort of problem for the approach in question *the paradox of paraphrase*.)[220]

Schleiermacher also contributes a number of further significant points in defense, explanation, and justification of the "bending" approach. Let us begin with two of his defensive points. The first of these is the following. Herder (it will be recalled) had argued that the *oddities* that will inevitably result from the bending approach—e.g. honey being called "green" or, alternatively, healthy foliage "yellow"—are an acceptable price to pay for semantic accuracy. As we saw, Schleiermacher certainly agrees with that. But he also envisages them playing a more positive role. His reasoning is as follows. It seems crucial for the success of this sort of approach to translation that the reader be made *aware* both that and where the translator is conveying something conceptually unfamiliar to him by means of bending. But how is this to be accomplished? Schleiermacher observes, in effect, that it is to be accomplished by means of the very *oddity* of the translation in the relevant areas. Thus he writes that a translator working in this bending mode will "willingly force himself to appear in movements less light and elegant than those he is capable of, to seem brutal and stiff, at least at times, and *to shock the reader as much as is necessary to keep him aware of what he is doing.*"[221] For example, in our *aretê* and *chlôros* cases, such oddities in the translation as finding that someone like Odysseus who has been characterized as a habitual liar is nonetheless ascribed *virtue* or that an object which is paradigmatically yellow such as honey is nonetheless described as *green* will flag, and alert the reader to, the conceptual unfamiliarity of what is being expressed by means of these words, and the bending that is being employed in order to cope with it.[222]

A second defense of the "bending" (and also musical-form-reproducing) approach against potential criticism which Schleiermacher develops concerns the *conceptual (and musical-formal) enrichment* of the target language that it effects. It will be recalled that in the *Fragments* Herder was at points ambivalent about this due to concerns that the target language's authentic nature might be harmed by it. Schleiermacher himself voices similar concerns in his *Ethics* lectures of 1812−13.[223] However, by the time he presents *On the Different Methods of Translation* in 1813 he has come to the conclusion that such concerns are really misplaced. He does raise them in a provisional way in the course of the essay.[224] But towards the end of the essay he answers them with the observations that "we should not fear great harm to our language" from such translations because (1) "it must be established . . . that there is, in a language in which translation is practiced to such an extent, a field proper to translators, and that much should be allowed to them that probably ought not to emerge elsewhere," and (2) "we can rely on the assimilating process of language to discard again whatever has been accepted only because of a passing need and does not really correspond to its nature."[225] In other words, (1) a properly conducted practice of "bending" (and musical-form-reproducing) translation can and should incorporate a recognition that greater freedom is to be allowed to the translator than to other language users, and (2) there will normally be enough conservative inertia in a language to prevent it from being driven far or long from its natural course through the insertion into it by translation of alien concepts (and musical forms),[226] so that for both of these reasons Herder's worry in fact turns out to be unwarranted. On the whole, the evident reasonableness of treating translation as a special area permitted certain liberties that are not extended to other domains, and the actual history of languages' responses to innovations, suggest that this judgment is sound, and hence an improvement on Herder's moments of alarmism in the *Fragments*.[227]

Two further contributions which Schleiermacher makes concern the identification and explanation of some necessary conditions for successful implementation of the "bending" approach. First, he argues that in order for this approach to work, *considerable amounts* of material need to be translated in this manner:

This type of translation has no value whatsoever if it is practiced only by chance and in isolated instances in a given language. For that obviously falls short of the aim that a foreign spirit should blow toward the reader; on the contrary if he is to be given a notion . . . of the original language and of what the work owes to it, so that his failure to understand that language is somewhat made up for, he must not only be given a very vague impression that what he reads does not sound completely familiar; he must also be made to feel that it sounds like something different yet distinct. But that will only be possible if he is able to make massive comparisons . . . These comparisons are not available if only isolated works of masters of isolated genres are sporadically translated into a language . . . This method of translation must therefore be applied extensively, a transplantation of whole literatures into a language . . . Isolated works of this type are of value only as precursors of a more generally evolving and developing willingness to adopt this procedure. If they fail to arouse this, things will work against them in the language and the spirit of the time; they can then appear only as mistaken attempts and have little or no success in themselves.[228]

Schleiermacher's thought here has two main parts: One part is a concern that in order for readers to become sufficiently used to the "bending" type of translation so that they develop a tolerance for it and an ability to understand it, they need to see it practiced broadly. But another, and perhaps more prominent, part is a concern that in order for a reader to catch on to the specific conceptual peculiarities which the "bending" is attempting to convey to him, he will need to be exposed to multiple occurrences of the word whose usage is being bent, and in an appropriately wide variety of contexts (a mere isolated instance or two will be unlikely to succeed in conveying the original rule for use, or concept, to him). Both of Schleiermacher's concerns are valid ones, and his proposed solution to them, namely extensive (and for the latter purpose, also systematic) use of the "bending" approach, seems apt.[229]

Second, Schleiermacher notes that in order for the "bending" approach to work, the modern target language involved must not be too rigid to permit the necessary "bending." Thus he writes that "this method of translating cannot thrive equally well in all languages, but only in those that are not the captives of too strict a bond of classical expression outside of which all is reprehensible."[230] His concern here is not so much that there may be intrinsic inflexibility in the target language itself—for, as we saw earlier, he believes that *all* language is of its nature plastic—but rather that a people's attitude towards violations of customary usage may be implacably hostile.[231] For if a people reacts to "bending" with a sense of outrage or revulsion, translations which employ it are unlikely to be accepted. In this connection, Schleiermacher particularly identifies the French as a nation who are (currently) too rigid in their attitudes towards their own language to allow the "bending" sort of translation to thrive, but implies that by contrast the Germans are (currently) flexible enough in theirs to allow it to do so, and he links this difference with a difference in politico-ethical stance (roughly, French imperialist domineering vs. German cosmopolitan humility).[232]

Schleiermacher indeed believes that the viability of foreignizing translation depends on a rather specific and complex set of historical preconditions which includes not only this sort of flexible attitude towards language but also a reasonably widespread interest in, and knowledge of, works in foreign languages among at least the more educated part of the public.[233] A fairly specific and complex historical *kairos* is required—which he considers to have arrived in the Germany of his day, but not (yet) in France.[234]

A final noteworthy contribution which Schleiermacher makes to the theory of "bending" translation concerns its justification, the reasons for its importance. In addition to the reasons that he shares with Herder—namely, faithful reproduction of semantic content, conceptual enrichment of the target language, and the expression and promotion of cosmopolitan respect for the Other—he also supplies a further significant reason. In his 1831 address on Leibniz's ideal of a universal language he adds the consideration that, through its conceptual enrichment of target languages, "bending" translation contributes to the development of a shared conceptual vocabulary among peoples, which, besides generally facilitating intercommunal dialogue and mutual understanding,[235] in particular makes possible the pursuit of intersubjective agreement in the sciences—something that requires shared concepts as its precondition.[236]

4. Conclusion

In sum, it was Herder who first developed the main principles of a theory of foreignizing translation (borrowing heavily from predecessors such as Abbt). Schleiermacher then took over those principles to form the core of his own theory of foreignizing translation. However (unlike his theory of interpretation, or "hermeneutics," which was similarly indebted to Herder's but tended to worsen it), his theory of translation also developed Herder's in some ways that significantly refined and improved it. Between them, the two men developed a truly powerful conception of, and rationale for, foreignizing translation.

In the course of establishing these points, it should have become clear that Berman and Venuti's account of the birth of foreignizing translation requires substantial revision. In particular, the magnitude of Herder's contribution is far greater than they suggest; both Herder and Schleiermacher were already strongly motivated by the sorts of cosmopolitan ethico-political concerns that motivate Berman and Venuti themselves but which the latter largely deny to their predecessors; and above all, a factor that is quite missing from Berman and Venuti's account, namely translation's traditional fundamental goal of reproducing the meaning of the source text as accurately as possible, provided Herder and Schleiermacher with their most important argument for preferring the foreignizing approach, as well as with their conception of the specific techniques (such as "bending" word-usages) that it needs to employ.

Notes

1. For some reflections on the pervasiveness and importance of translation in human life, see Schleiermacher, *On the Different Methods of Translation*, pp. 1–2; G. Steiner, *After Babel: Aspects of Language and Translation* (Oxford: Oxford University Press, 1998); and H.J. Störig, *Das Problem des Übersetzens* (Stuttgart: Henry Goverts Verlag, 1963), introduction. For a salutary caution against the temptation to overstretch the concept of "translation" in making this point, however, see A. Berman, *L'Épreuve de l'étranger*, p. 292.

2. This is not to say that "foreignizing" translation *practice* never occurred before Schleiermacher and his age developed its methodology. For, aside from the fact that earlier anticipations of the methodology can be found, such practice could well have occurred before being richly theorized. For example, St Jerome's practice in his translation of the Bible actually had this character. Accordingly, the "birth" in my title does not mean the birth of the *practice* of foreignizing translation, but rather the birth of its methodology and practice guided thereby.

3. See esp. Berman, *L'Épreuve*, and L. Venuti, *The Translator's Invisibility: A History of Translation*. Even before Berman and Venuti's work, Schleiermacher's influence on modern translation theory was enormous. As might be expected, this influence is especially strong among theorists who are themselves sympathetic to his "foreignizing" approach—e.g., within the German tradition, Wilhelm von Humboldt, Goethe, Rudolf Pannwitz, Franz Rosenzweig, Martin Buber, Walter Benjamin, and Martin Heidegger; and beyond that tradition, such nineteenth-century British "foreignizing" translators and theorists as Newman and Browning, Ortega y Gasset in Spain, and even certain Chinese theorists. But his influence has been almost as strong even among theorists who are themselves uncommitted, or even hostile, to his "foreignizing" approach, in the sense that he nonetheless provided the fundamental theoretical framework within which they theorize (e.g. Eugene Nida).

4. *L'Épreuve*, ch. 2.

5. Cf. L.G. Kelly, *The True Interpreter: A History of Translation Theory and Practice in the West* (Oxford: Blackwell, 1979), p. 224: Schleiermacher's essay "owes its main themes" to Herder's *Fragments*.

6. As Berman puts it: in its proper, foreignizing form translation becomes "a creative act of decentering" (*L'Épreuve*, p. 40; cf. chs. 2 and 3).

Venuti tends to lend this function a left-wing political slant, but it is not *essentially* left-wing.

7. Berman consistently emphasizes ethico-political considerations both in exegesis of the historical figures he considers and in stating his own views. By contrast, he hardly mentions the historical figures' interest in reproducing the meaning of an original text at all. And when he comes to identify what he characterizes as "a conception of translation . . . which . . . is the object of a *consensus* at core sufficiently general . . . both among translators and among everyone interested in translation," he strikingly omits the most obvious candidate of faithfully reproducing the original text's meaning and instead identifies "poeticity," i.e. a translation's constituting a real text in its own right, and "ethicity," i.e. its showing "a certain respect for the original," which, however, he again strikingly declines to explain either wholly or partly in terms of faithfulness to the original text's meaning (A. Berman, *Pour une critique des traductions: John Donne* [Paris: Gallimard, 1995], p. 92; cf. p. 93 n. 117, where he does include a certain respect for the *letter* but again not for *meaning*; also his "Translation and the Trials of the Foreign," in L. Venuti ed., *The Translation Studies Reader* [London and New York: Routledge, 2000], pp. 596–7, where, though, his position is more ambiguous). Similarly, Venuti in *The Translator's Invisibility* plays up the ethico-political, and in particular anti-imperialist, virtues of foreignizing translation (pp. 19–21), but seems to question the traditional focus on reproducing meaning as a goal of translation (pp. 24–5), and cites Ezra Pound's foreignizing approach with evident approval for "privileging the signifier over the signified" (p. 200).

8. Cf. Kelly, *The True Interpreter*, p. 155: "No matter the period or genre, the basic lexical technique is formal equivalence" (i.e. reproducing semantic content). Berman too hypothesizes a transhistorical "idea" of translation which gets realized with different modulations throughout history, but mysteriously characterizes this "idea" as indefinable (*Pour une critique des traductions*, pp. 60–1). The former part of this position seems fairly plausible, but the obscurantism of the latter part quite unnecessary: if there is such an enduring "idea" of translation, then it is surely *reproducing the meaning of the original text in another language*.

9. J.A. Ernesti, *Institutio interpretis Novi Testamenti* (1761), trans. as *Ernesti's Institutes*, pp. 185–6.

10. Berman and Venuti evidently commit this rather large exegetical and philosophical sin of omission mainly due to their inclination to adopt uncritically a certain widespread and variegated twentieth-century

skepticism about the conception that the proper goal of (interpretation and) translation is to (grasp and) reproduce an original meaning, and indeed about the very notion of meaning itself. This sort of skepticism seems to me misguided. But even if it were more justified than it is, that would still not warrant radically distorting the interpretation of Schleiermacher and Herder in order to incorporate it.

11. *L'Épreuve*, pp. 236–41.

12. Ibid., p. 66.

13. Venuti, *The Translator's Invisibility*, p. 99; cf. pp. 109–10; also Venuti, *The Scandals of Translation* (London and New York: Routledge, 1998), pp. 184–5.

14. As tended to happen in several other areas of his thought, the later Herder moved towards different and largely inferior positions on translation. These will be de-emphasized in the present essay.

15. E. Purdie, *Studies in German Literature of the Eighteenth Century* (London: Athlone, 1965), p. 126.

16. See A. Huyssen, *Die frühromantische Konzeption von Übersetzung und Aneignung*, pp. 88, 91, 111.

17. This is at least possible in a case like Herder's (and subsequently Schleiermacher's) where a person's translation theory and translation practice tend to be impressively consistent with each other.

18. Hume, *Enquiry concerning Human Understanding* (1748), in Hume, *Enquiries concerning Human Understanding and concerning the Principles of Morals* (Oxford: Clarendon Press, 1975), p. 83.

19. These positions are prominent in many of Herder's works, including *On the Change of Taste* (1766), *This Too a Philosophy of History for the Formation of Humanity* (1774), and *On the Cognition and Sensation of the Human Soul* (1778). One important forerunner in commitment to them was Ernesti in his *Institutio interpretis Novi Testamenti* (1761). Another was d'Alembert.

20. As we shall see, besides the difficulties arising from conceptual difference, Herder is also concerned about difficulties arising from differences in available musical forms. In addition, he mentions difficulties arising from differences in syntax (G1:200, 645), idiomatic sayings (ibid.), and word-plays, such as puns (G1:585; cf. G5:1178–80).

21. *Fragments*, G1:199, 203.

22. Ibid., pp. 200, 205, 646.

23. An important forerunner here was d'Alembert, who in his *Observations sur l'art de traduire* (1758) already traced the main difficulty of translation to the distinctive "geniuses" of both languages and individual authors

(*Œuvres de d'Alembert* [Paris: Belin/Bossange, 1822], vol. 4, pt. 1, pp. 31 ff.).

24. G1:648–9.

25. See e.g. G1:307.

26. e.g., "kurios estin tou sabbatou ho huios tou anthrôpou [the son of man is lord over the sabbath]" becomes "Des Menschen Sohn ist ein Herr *auch* des Sabbats" (v. 5); "ho de epoiêsen, kai apekatestathê hê cheir autou" gets elaborated into "Und er tat's; da ward ihm seine Hand wieder zurechtgebracht, *gesund wie die andere*" (v. 10); "Ioudan Iskariôth, hos egeneto prodotês [Judas Iscariot *who became* a betrayer]" is turned into simply "Judas Ischariot, den Verräter" (v. 16); "kata ta auta gar epoioun tois prophêtais hoi pateres autôn [*for in the same way did their fathers behave towards the prophets*]" becomes simply "Desgleichen taten ihre Väter den Propheten auch" (v. 23); "hoti penthêsete kai klausete [because you will *grieve* and weep]" becomes "denn ihr werdet weinen und *heulen*" (v. 25); "katêrtismenos de pas estai hôs ho didaskalos autou [but when perfected each will be as his teacher]" becomes "wenn der Jünger ist wie sein Meister, so ist [er] vollkommen" (v. 40); and "kai tote diablepseis to karphos to en tôi ophthalmôi tou adelphou sou ekbalein [and then you will see clearly so as to remove the mote in the eye of your brother]" becomes "*besiehe dann, daß* du den Splitter aus deines Bruders Auge ziehest" (v. 42). (I have modernized Luther's spelling here, but not his wording.)

27. S3:127.

28. G1:381–2.

29. G9/1:247.

30. G9/1:599. It is true that later on, in the *Terpsichore* of 1796, Herder by contrast praises Luther as "the greatest master of translation in our language" (S27:276). But matters are complicated here by the facts that the *Terpsichore* is engaged in what Herder explicitly distinguishes from strict "translation [*Übersetzung*]" as mere "rejuvenation [*Verjüngung*]" (S27:275), and that it belongs to a period when Herder's commitment to strict translation had itself receded.

31. A. Lefevere, *Translation/History/Culture* (London and New York: Routledge, 1992), p. 60.

32. Quoted by S. Bassnett, *Translation Studies* (London: Routledge, 1988), p. 64.

33. In his *Letter on Translation* Luther at one point justifies his German translation of a passage from the Bible in which an angel greets Mary on the grounds that "that is the way he would have spoken if he had

wanted to greet her in German." (A. Lefevere, *Translating Literature: The German Tradition from Luther to Rosenzweig* [Assen and Amsterdam: van Gorcum, 1977], p. 9.)

34. *Fragments*, G1:205. As we shall see later, there are actually two good points lurking here between which Herder does not clearly distinguish: one concerning the impossibility of transferring the *thoughts*, the other the impossibility of transferring the *author*.

35. Ibid., pp. 292–3.

36. This principle was not entirely new with Herder. e.g. T. Huber, *Studien zur Theorie des Übersetzens im Zeitalter der deutschen Aufklärung 1730–1770* (Meisenheim am Glan: Anton Hain, 1968), p. 78 cites Venzky as a forerunner; and one could also mention, even earlier, Leonardo Bruni (1374–1444) (see Lefevere, *Translation/History/Culture*, p. 83).

37. D. Davidson, *Inquiries into Truth and Interpretation*, p. 190; cf. p. 184.

38. Consequently, when some Davidsonians argue that the phenomenon of successful translation shows that different conceptual schemes are not involved after all, this argument, despite a superficial air of plausibility, turns out to be fallacious.

39. *Fragments*, G1:199–200; cf. 645–6. Herder's perception of Abbt's virtues as a translator, his important methodological debt to Abbt identified here, and some further, related debts to Abbt in translation-theory to be discussed below together constitute a substantive reason for Herder's reverence of Abbt (which has sometimes puzzled commentators, such as Haym).

40. G1:205.

41. G3:26. A strategy very much like this Abbt-Herder strategy had already been advocated a little earlier by d'Alembert in his *Observations sur l'art de traduire* (1758) (see Lefevere, *Translation/History/Culture*, p. 112). Kelly implies that Cicero already saw the problem of conceptual incommensurability and advocated a bending approach for overcoming it in *De finibus* (Kelly, *The True Interpreter*, p. 221), but I am skeptical. For one thing, Cicero seems only to be concerned with incommensurabilities in a very limited sphere, namely technical terminology. For another, and more important, thing, his strategies for coping with them seem to be, *not* bending, but instead borrowing terms from the source language, introducing new coinages into the target language, and employing multiple words in the target language for a single problematic word in the source language.

42. I here borrow the useful distinction between an ethical term's "descriptive" and "prescriptive" meaning from R.M. Hare.

43. To return to the example of Luke, ch. 6: Even in the course of this relatively short stretch of text Luther fails to render many repeated words, including several rather salient ones, in a consistent fashion across occurrences, one-word-for-one-word. Examples (given here in the grammatical form of first occurrence) are *egeneto, exestin, eisêlthen, therapeuei, epoiêsen, proseuxasthai, ochlos, ekbalôsin, plên, huios,* and *sesaleumenon*.

    On the other hand, Herder is *followed* in his approach by the eminent twentieth-century translators of the Old Testament and theorists of translation Rosenzweig and Buber, who both argue forcefully for the necessity of using the one-word-for-one-word approach. See their contributions in Störig ed., *Das Problem des Übersetzens*, esp. pp. 244–7, 359 ff., 380.

44. *Iliad*, bk. 11, l. 763; bk. 13, ll. 275 and 277; bk. 14, l. 118; bk. 22, l. 268.

45. Ibid., bk. 8, l. 535; bk. 20, l. 242.

46. Ibid., bk. 13, l. 237.

47. Ibid., bk. 11, l. 90.

48. Ibid., bk. 9, l. 498.

49. Ibid., bk. 23, l. 578.

50. Ibid., bk. 23, l. 571.

51. Ibid., bk. 20, l. 411.

52. A Kantian or Fregean philosopher might be tempted to object to this line of argument that it essentially depends on a now-superseded conception that word-meanings are prior to sentence-meanings or propositions. As it happens, Herder does often tend to think in such terms (cf. C. Taylor, "The Importance of Herder," p. 58). However, his position here *need* not depend on any such dubious assumption. All that it needs to assume is that word-meanings are *inter*dependent with, rather than simply dependent on, sentence-meanings. And while there may be some philosophers in the Kantian-Fregean tradition who would want to question even that, doing so in fact looks philosophically implausible.

53. This approach must not be confused with the similar-sounding, traditionally controversial approach of translating "word for word" instead of "sense for sense." In that context, "word for word" primarily means giving one word for one word within each sentence and in the same order (see e.g. Hieronymus, "Brief an Pammachius," in Störig ed., *Das Problem des Übersetzens*, pp. 1 ff.; also Lefevere, *Translation/History/Culture*, pp. 3, 15, 62–3, 91–101, 104–5), often (or at

least, so the traditional complaint goes) at the cost of obscuring the sense (as in an interlinear version, for example). By contrast, Herder's approach is much less concerned, indeed probably neutral, about preserving the number and order of words within a sentence, and instead has the very different concern that words be translated consistently across multiple occurrences within a text. Moreover, it stands squarely in the *service* of reproducing the sense.

54. This is true of the more discursive passages at least. The more lyrical ones tend to be semantically looser.

55. *Popular Songs*, G3:42–5.

56. There are a few minor exceptions: while *soul* does in most occurrences become *Seele*, in a single occurrence it becomes *Geist* (probably an oversight on Herder's part); and "sleep thou a quiet sleep" becomes "*schlummre* sanften Schlaf" (obviously an aesthetically motivated choice on Herder's part).

57. *On Thomas Abbt's Writings*, G2:589, 595. Bending word-usages is of course only one aspect of the foreignizing for which Herder is here praising Abbt.

58. Davidson's error of course consists in not noticing that the principle that a difference in conceptual schemes requires a failure of intertranslatability is only true concerning intertranslatability of the languages involved *as they are at the time in question*—in not noticing that a difference in conceptual schemes is perfectly compatible with the languages involved *subsequently becoming* intertranslatable.

59. Concerning Breitinger, see Berman, *L'Épreuve*, pp. 64–5; concerning Bodmer, see Lefevere, *Translation/History/Culture*, pp. 127–8.

60. For a classic statement of this principle, see *Popular Songs*, G3:246–8. Unlike Herder's equally important "bending" technique, this principle has received considerable attention in the secondary literature. See esp. A.F. Kelletat, *Herder und die Weltliteratur* (Frankfurt am Main: Peter Lang, 1984), pp. 49, 54–6, 71–2, 172, 186–7, 197, 209–10; Berman, *L'Épreuve*, ch. 2; and Purdie, *Studies in German Literature of the Eighteenth Century*, pp. 124 ff. However, the secondary literature has failed to do justice to several of the finer points of this principle which I am about to discuss.

61. *Popular Songs*, G3:246–8.

62. Cf. Purdie, *Studies in German Literature of the Eighteenth Century*, ch. 6.

63. *Fragments*, G1:197; cf. 292–3.

64. Ibid., pp. 194–204. Cf. pp. 305 ff.: "A second, higher level: if there were translators who not only studied their author in order to transfer

the sense of the original text into our language, but also discovered his distinctive tone, who placed themselves into the character of his manner of writing, and expressed correctly for us the true distinguishing traits, the expression and color-tone of the foreign original, its governing character, its genius, and the nature of its poetic type."

65. S18:121–2.

66. *Popular Songs*, G3:243–4: "Each person has the freedom to translate, to beautify, to polish, to form, to idealize [these pieces] as he likes, so that nobody can any longer recognize the original; it is *his* and not *my* way, and the reader has the freedom to choose."

67. Ibid., p. 246: "The essence of the *Lied* is *song*, not depiction."

68. Ibid., p. 247. In some other cases where Herder seems to be advocating or practicing a neglect of semantic faithfulness this is because he is not concerned with translation proper [*Übersetzung*] at all but instead with what he explicitly distinguishes from it as rejuvenation [*Verjüngung*] or imitation [*Nachbildung*].

69. See e.g. *Terpsichore*, S27:170; *Popular Songs*, G3:45.

70. See e.g. *Fragments*, G1:258: "Poetry is almost untranslatable in its beauties because here euphony, rhyme, individual parts of speech, putting together of words, formation of sayings—everything—produces beauty."

71. S27:276–7.

72. S27:280.

73. G2:1159.

74. Cf. A.W. Schlegel: "Since all metrical forms have a definite meaning, and their necessary character in a given language may very well be demonstrated (for unity of form and essence is the goal of all art, and the more they interpenetrate and reflect each other, the higher the perfection achieved), one of the first principles of the art of translation is that a poem should be recreated in the same meter, as far as the nature of the language allows" (Lefevere, *Translation/History/Culture*, pp. 79–80).

75. G3:35.

76. See e.g., in addition to S27:170 and G3:45 (already cited), S15:529 on a text's musical aspects being internal to the images it expresses; and S22:326: "[Symbols'] sound and progress and rhythm do not only signify but *are* vibrations . . . of our sensations."

77. See e.g. *Letters concerning the Study of Theology*, G9/1:237–42.

78. Ibid., p. 599. The twentieth-century translation theorists and translators of the Old Testament Rosenzweig and Buber are again Herder's heirs

here. For they too argue that it is vital for a translator of the Bible to strive to reproduce not only its semantic content but also its musical form because the two are inseparable (Störig ed., *Das Problem des Übersetzens*, pp. 237–8, 351–2, 356–7, 380–1, 386).

79. Purdie, *Studies in German Literature of the Eighteenth Century*, pp. 125–7.
80. There are, though, some serious complications in this area which Herder himself anticipates and which should be briefly discussed. A first concerns the *practicability* of implementing such a reproduction of musical features in certain cases. Both in the *Fragments* and later in the *Terpsichore* Herder expresses something very close to despair about the possibility of reproducing *ancient* meters, especially due to the shift from quantitative or pitch-based meters in the ancient languages to accent-based ones in modern languages. He thereby anticipates Wilamowitz, who presents this as a damning objection to the ideal of reproducing musical form (see e.g. his "Die Kunst des Übersetzens," at Lefevere, *Translation/History/Culture*, pp. 33, 170–1). However, to inflate this worry into such an objection seems dubious. For one thing, there is room for disagreement about just how impossible the feat in question really is (for a claim that its difficulty has been exaggerated, see e.g. R. Humphries, "Latin and English Verse—Some Practical Considerations," in R.A. Brower ed., *On Translation* [Cambridge, Mass.: Harvard University Press, 1959]). But more importantly, this is supposed to be an *ideal* to which one *approximates* as closely as possible, and even in cases where it is impossible to reproduce a meter at all exactly, it may, and usually will, still be possible to provide one that is similar to it, i.e. at the very least more similar than others or than none at all (cf. Kelly, *The True Interpreter*, pp. 198 ff.). Analogous points apply to other musical features.

A different, and deeper, complication concerns the likelihood that the emotional and semantic connotations (as well as the aesthetic impact) of a given meter, or other musical feature, may *vary* quite dramatically across historical periods and cultures. Herder himself hints at this at *Terpsichore*, S27:277–8, where he implies that the relation between meter and emotional/semantic connotations varies between languages. Cicero apparently conceived of such connotations as natural, common to everyone (*De oratore*, bk. 3, ch. 57, sec. 216; Cicero was concerned with *emotional* connotations). But that seems highly doubtful. For example, Wilamowitz has suggested, plausibly, that a discrepancy in such connotations arises even between French and German Alexandrines, making reproduction of the former by the latter inappropriate ("Was ist übersetzen?" in Störig ed., *Das Problem des Übersetzens*, p. 149). And M. Herzfeld in a similar vein discusses the genre of Cretan *mandinadhes* (rhyming/assonant verse couplets), a genre which for Cretans tends to evoke clever, teasing insight, and serious emotional and semantic connotations, but whose meter and rhyme-scheme when he tried to reproduce them in English sounded like doggerel, and hence would tend to evoke intellectual dullness and naive or humorous emotional and semantic connotations for an Anglophone audience (M. Herzfeld, "The Unspeakable in Pursuit of the Ineffable: Representations of Untranslatability in Ethnographic Discourse," in *Translating Cultures*, ed. P.G. Rubel and A. Rosman [Oxford and New York: Berg, 2003], p. 125). Consequently, even where a reproduction of, or at least close approximation to, a meter (or other musical feature) *is* possible, there remains a serious question as to whether it is desirable, and whether some quite different one, or perhaps just plain prose, might not be preferable instead, as more effectively conjuring up the original emotional and semantic connotations (as well as the original aesthetic impression). It seems to me that this is a very difficult question, and one that it would be rash to try to decide here. However, I am inclined to think that the ideal of reproducing meter (and other musical features) can withstand this threat, for roughly the following reasons: (1) In such cases, it will generally be possible to educate a target audience's sensibilities by means of actual examples and supplementary explanations so that they learn to associate the right sort of emotional and semantic connotations with the meter (or other musical feature) in question, rather than the wrong sort. (2) It might be objected that that really amounts to a refusal to translate, analogous to deciding to leave the words of the original language and merely offering explanations of their meanings; but it seems to me that there is a significant difference between the two cases, in that the process of education involved here can normally be much easier and quicker. (3) One important reason for adopting this approach, rather than, say, switching to a different meter in the target language which already has the right, or more right, emotional and semantic connotations (as Wilamowitz in effect recommends in "Was ist übersetzen?"; see esp. pp. 149, 161–2), is that it promises to open up a field of fine grain in the emotional and semantic connotations of a work which would not be made available by such mere switching. (4) Nor is this rationale, as it might seem to be, inconsistent with the sort of education mentioned in (1), as though in order for that education to have taken place the fine grain in question would *already* have to have been communicated, so that the promise of providing it is after all empty. For the sort of education involved in (1) need only be rather coarse grained (e.g. in the Cretan case a shift from associating the meter and rhyme-scheme in question with stolid, naive, humorous connotations to associating them with clever, insightful, often serious ones).

81. *Fragments*, G1:187. As for Abbt, for Herder this is a matter of developing in the target language not only new concepts but also new musical forms (see e.g. ibid., p. 210, where he discusses the enrichment of German's musical forms through the translation of Horace).

82. For example, he claims that Heilmann has already had such beneficial effects on the German language through his translation of Thucydides (ibid., p. 207).

83. Ibid., pp. 239, 258–60.

84. G3:26.

85. In particular, he prefers Greek over Latin, sees Homer and other Greek poets as presenting almost insuperable obstacles, and regards Greek prose, such as that of Thucydides, as the most promising candidate—G1:201–7.

86. See e.g. G1:201 ff., 311–12, 351, 360, 375–7, 380, 384–5, 559–60, 645 ff.

87. See e.g. G1:201 ff.

88. G1:646–7.

89. See on this R. Haym, *Herder nach seinem Leben und seinen Werken*, 1:156–8.

90. The translations in the *Popular Songs* are themselves eloquent testimony to this step, but for a more theoretical expression of it within the work see G3:62–8.

91. See Bassnett, *Translation Studies*, pp. 49–50; Kelly, *The True Interpreter*, p. 213.

92. See Lefevere, *Translation/History/Culture*, pp. 37, 51, 53, 112.

93. Ibid., p. 53 (emphasis added). By contrast, already much closer to Abbt and Herder's position here were d'Alembert in his *Observations sur l'art de traduire* (ibid., p. 112) and Bodmer (Lefevere, *Translating Literature*, pp. 18–22).

94. See e.g. *L'Épreuve*, pp. 17, 288–9.

95. All of these motives are clearly evident in the preface which Herder wrote to the fourth book of the *Popular Songs* of 1774 (G3:59–68).

96. Ibid., p. 62.

97. *Fragments*, G1:307; cf. *Critical Forests*, S3:127. The close links of
foreignizing translation to cosmopolitanism, and of domesticating
translation to imperialism, first explored by Herder (and, as we shall
see, others immediately influenced by him, such as Schleiermacher),
have since his time been explored further by more recent translation theorists such as Nietzsche, Berman, Meschonnic, and Venuti.
I believe that their shared intuition about such links contains much
truth. Consider, for example, this revealing statement made by the
British domesticating translator of Persian poetry, Edward Fitzgerald,
at the height of British imperialism in the nineteenth century: "It is an
amusement to me to take what liberties I like with these Persians, who
(as I think) are not poets enough to frighten one from such excursions,
and who really do want a little Art to shape them" (quoted by Bassnett,
Translation Studies, p. 13). However, the shared intuition of the theorists mentioned also prompts certain questions which suggest the need
for important qualifications. For example, Nietzsche in *The Gay Science*
famously links Roman domesticating translation practice vis-à-vis the
Greeks with motives of imperial domination (see Lefevere, *Translating
Literature*, p. 96). But could a case not be made that the commonest
attitude of Roman translators was rather one of *admiration and awe*
of their Greek models, and that their domesticating approach was
less an expression of any imperialist disrespect than the result of the
fact that they were mainly writing for a restricted, educated audience
which already knew the Greek originals, and so were trying to vie
with rather than to reproduce the originals (cf. Bassnett, *Translation
Studies*, pp. 49–50)? Again, Henri Meschonnic postulates a motive of
imperialist domination behind the domesticating ("dynamic equivalence"), as opposed to foreignizing ("formal equivalence"), approach
advocated by the recent American translation theorist Eugene Nida
(H. Meschonnic, *Pour la poétique II* [Paris: Gallimard, 1973]). But,
while it seems likely that such motives do indeed play a role at points
in Nida's theory (e.g. vis-à-vis Judaism, as Meschonnic emphasizes;
and perhaps especially vis-à-vis the Third World recipients of the Bible
translations with which Nida is involved), is not the most striking
thing about Nida's theory rather that his domesticating approach to
translating the Bible stems from *love and awe* of the Bible and a desire
to see it *revered* (so that he goes as far as to set up equivalence of
behavioral response between readers of the translation and readers
of the original text as the ultimate goal of the sort of "dynamic
equivalence" translation that he advocates)? Such domesticating moves

recommended by Nida for Bible translation as switching the order of mention in a narrative in order to reflect chronological sequence, removing anthropomorphisms concerning God, and improving the rhetoric of Paul's speeches (E. Nida, *Toward a Science of Translating*, pp. 138–9, 224–6) thus seem to be mainly the result of motives that are the very opposite of those associated with domesticating translation by the Herder-Nietzsche-Meschonnic-Berman-Venuti tradition. (Note also that, unlike his arguable imperialist ambitions against Judaism, his more salient imperialist ambitions against the Third World recipients of Bible translations are directed against users, not of the *source* language, but of the *target* language.) Conversely, while it is probably true that foreignizing translation is usually advocated and practiced from broadly cosmopolitan motives, can one not at least imagine someone advocating and practicing it from the very opposite motive of making foreigners look silly? These points do not, I think, by any means destroy the basic Herder-Nietzsche-Berman-Meschonnic-Venuti intuition, but they do suggest that it requires qualification. In particular, it seems to me important to entertain the possibility, and indeed the likelihood, that, while the *overall social function* of domesticating translation is indeed usually imperialist, as they envisage, *individual* domesticating translators will in many cases be innocent of such motives, and will some-times even have quite contrary ones. (Concerning a similar situation in the theory and practice of *interpretation*, see my "On the Very Idea of Denying the Existence of Radically Different Conceptual Schemes.")

98. *Fragments*, G1:204; cf. 199; also Abbt's statement in the passage quoted by Herder in the *Fragments* that the good translator attains "the rank of an author."

99. Lefevere, *History/Translation/Culture*, pp. 12–13.

100. Ibid.

101. S27:275. Cf. Herder's rather more grudging concession earlier, in the *Popular Songs* of 1778–9, that, while his own method has been to avoid adding "correctness" to the originals, and at points even to sacrifice it where it would have injured the main tone of the pieces, "Each person is at liberty to give a version [*übertragen*] of them, beautify, hone, pull, idealize them as he likes, so that no one any longer recognizes the original; it is *his* and not *my* way, and the reader is at liberty to choose" (G3:243–4).

102. Cf. for an earlier version of this point Huetius (Lefevere, *Translation/History/Culture*, pp. 92–102).

103. Cf. H.J. Vermeer, "Skopos and Commission in Translational Action," in Venuti ed., *The Translation Studies Reader*, pp. 221 ff.

104. *Pace* some uncharacteristically obtuse remarks to the contrary by Schleiermacher at *On the Different Methods of Translation*, p. 26. Schleiermacher implausibly claims that a foreignizing translation of ancient comedy is better suited than a domesticating one to preserving the "lightness and naturalness" which he (more plausibly) considers to be essential to ancient comedy.

105. Cf. Kelly, *The True Interpreter*, pp. 195–7.

106. See esp. *Fragments*, G1:204–5, 306–8; also *Critical Forests*, S3:126 ff. Herder would later warmly praise Voss's *Odyssey* (S18:321). Cf. Berman, *L'Épreuve*, p. 82, who rightly notes that Voss then in his turn became a sort of model of translation practice for Goethe, Friedrich Schlegel, Wilhelm von Humboldt, and others.

107. See e.g. his *Geschichte der klassischen Literatur* of 1803 (as excerpted at Lefevere, *Translation/History/Culture*, pp. 78–80).

108. Cf. Kelletat, *Herder und die Weltliteratur*, pp. 41–6; Purdie, *Studies in German Literature of the Eighteenth Century*, p. 131; Huyssen, *Die frühromantische Konzeption von Übersetzung und Aneignung*, ch. 4.

109. For the most relevant parts of this essay, see Lefevere, *Translation/History/Culture*, pp. 137–8, 140–1. Humboldt's essay is heavily indebted to Schleiermacher's, presented publicly just three years earlier.

110. Goethe's treatment of translation in this work is probably indebted not only to his mentor Herder, but also to Schleiermacher's essay (*pace* Berman, who at *L'Épreuve*, pp. 95–7, 230 gets the debt the wrong way round through mistakenly dating Schleiermacher's essay to 1823 instead of 1813). A few years earlier, in *Dichtung und Wahrheit* of 1811–14, Goethe had by contrast argued in favor of *prose* translations of poetry (at least for young people and the general populace). His shift in the 1819 work to the principle of musical faithfulness, and also his strikingly historicized picture there of three types and epochs of translation, probably reflect Schleiermacher's intervening influence.

111. See the essays by Rosenzweig and Buber in Störig ed., *Das Problem des Übersetzens*.

112. *On the Different Methods of Translation* = *Über die verschiedenen Methoden des Übersetzens*, in FSSW 3/2:206 ff. Lefevere's translation is occasionally unreliable, and in particular omits an important long footnote concerning the role of musical-metrical faithfulness in the translation of poetry. So in what follows I shall mostly cite the translation, but sometimes instead the German text.

113. FSSW 3/7:702–8.

114. FSSW 3/1:138–49.

115. *On the Different Methods of Translation*, p. 9.

116. Ibid., p. 7.

117. Ibid., pp. 4–6, 14, 27.

118. Ibid., p. 5.

119. Ibid., p. 9.

120. Ibid., p. 19.

121. Schleiermacher's close association of the strategy with this rationale is anticipated and influenced by Herder, not only in the *Fragments* but also, and perhaps especially, in a review article from 1800 in which he too equates the two (S20:345). I shall criticize the closeness of the association between the two assumed by Schleiermacher (and the late Herder) below.

122. *On the Different Methods of Translation*, pp. 26–7.

123. Ibid., pp. 20 ff. Schleiermacher's arguments to this effect will be discussed in detail below.

124. Ibid., p. 7. Cf. pp. 3–5: the true translator needs a "scholarly knowledge of fact and language," "precise knowledge and . . . mastery of both languages." Schleiermacher's colleague and friend Friedrich Schlegel had already argued in his *Philosophy of Philology* (1797) that "translation belongs entirely to philology, is a thoroughly philological art" ("Friedrich Schlegels 'Philosophie der Philologie' mit einer Einleitung herausgegeben von Josef Körner," in *Logos*, 17 [1928], p. 47).

125. Schleiermacher, *Hermeneutics: The Handwritten Manuscripts*, p. 50. The specific notion of "the unity of the word-sphere" will be discussed below.

126. *On the Different Methods of Translation*, p. 25.

127. Ibid., p. 17.

128. Ibid., p. 14 (translation slightly modified).

129. Schleiermacher believes that in principle all language is plastic, or susceptible to modification, in this way, and that this is the key not only to adequate translation but also to authorial conceptual innovation: "Every freely thinking, mentally self-employed human being shapes his own language . . . The living power of the individual . . . creates new forms by means of the plastic material of language" (ibid., p. 6; on the basis of this conception, Schleiermacher in his 1831 address recasts Leibniz's idea of a universal language in a *prospective* spirit). A.W. Schlegel had already written in 1796 of the "much praised plasticity of our language [i.e. German]" which made translation possible (see Lefevere, *Translation/History/Culture*, p. 55).

130. Schleiermacher implies, with the realism of the experienced translator, that in practice this method will usually need to be restricted in its application to the more important words/concepts in a text rather than being applied to all of them indiscriminately, and that the reader will usually have to be satisfied if it is successfully implemented only in particular writings, or even particular parts thereof, rather than throughout an author's whole corpus (*On the Different Methods of Translation*, p. 14).

131. There are one or two exceptions, where *sophos/ia* get translated by forms of *sich verstehen auf*. Also, note that *sophistês* gets translated as *Sophist* rather than, say, as *Weise*.

132. There are one or two exceptions, where *eidenai* gets translated as *kennen*. Also, *epistamai* sometimes gets translated as *wissen*, and *epistêmê* as *Wissenschaft*, which blurs the distinction between *eidenai* and *epistamai*.

133. But see the previous note for a qualification.

134. But *phronimôs* becomes *vernünftig*. Also, note that *gignôskein* sometimes becomes *einsehen*, which, with its proximity to *Einsicht*, risks blurring a distinction.

135. But see the previous note for a qualification. Also, *aisthanomai* sometimes gets translated as *merken* as well, which again risks blurring a distinction.

136. In a footnote on the question of whether to translate poetry in prose or musically-metrically, Schleiermacher champions (at least, for his day) musical-metrical translations, such as (he says) Voss's translations of Homer and A.W. Schlegel's translations of Shakespeare. But he then goes on to add, more critically of Voss, a call for "a metrical translation [of Homer] of a sort that, to be sure, we perhaps do not yet possess," thus implying that Voss's translations are inadequate in some way (*Über die verschiedenen Methoden des Übersetzens*, p. 221). Also, later in the essay he complains, in terms which, though general, clearly seem (in light of the earlier footnote) to be targeted largely against Voss, about cases in which translators of poetry pay too much attention to reproducing musical form at the expense of semantic content (ibid., pp. 225–6).

137. *Iliad*, bk. 11, l. 763; bk. 13, l. 277; bk. 14, l. 118; bk. 23, l. 571.

138. Ibid., bk. 8, l. 535; bk. 13, l. 275.

139. Ibid., bk. 11, l. 90; bk. 13, l. 237.

140. Ibid., bk. 22, l. 268.

141. Ibid., bk. 20, l. 242.

142. Ibid., bk. 9, l. 498.

143. Ibid., bk. 23, l. 578.
144. Ibid., bk. 20, l. 411.
145. *On the Different Methods of Translation*, p. 16. Cf. pp. 15–17.
146. Ibid., p. 14. Cf. the long footnote at *Über die verschiedenen Methoden des Übersetzens*, p. 221, where Schleiermacher discusses Goethe's opinion in *Dichtung und Wahrheit* (1811–14) that prose translations even of poetic works are more apt for educating youth, and argues that although this applied to the age about which Goethe was writing, characterized as it was by a low level of interest in and knowledge of foreign languages and works, it *no longer* applies in Germany's present, more advanced stage of culture, whose youth and adults need metrical translations of poetic works, such as A.W. Schlegel has provided for Shakespeare and Voss for Homer. Cf. also Schleiermacher's *Aesthetics*, FSSW 3/7:702 ff., where he discusses the need to reproduce the prosody of ancient poetry in translation, though also the difficulty of doing so (in particular, he agrees with Herder—and like Herder, anticipates Wilamowitz—in noting that the shift from the quantitative meters of ancient poetry to the accentual meters of modern poetry presents a major obstacle to reproducing the musical form of ancient poetry in a modern translation). The same ideal had also been espoused, indeed even more emphatically and prominently, by A.W. Schlegel, for example in his essay *Etwas über Wilhelm Shakespeare bei Gelegenheit Wilhelm Meisters* (1796) (see Lefevere, *Translation/History/Culture*, p. 32). This ideal tends to play a somewhat less central role in Schleiermacher's theory than in either Herder's or A.W. Schlegel's, for several reasons. For one thing, unlike Herder and Schlegel, Schleiermacher is himself much more involved in the translation of prose than of poetry (his main translation activity concerns the Platonic dialogues). For another thing, in comparison with Herder and Schlegel, he is in general less focused on, and less secure in his judgments about, art, including poetry and music.
147. FSSW 3/7:704–5 (this passage may owe something to the editor, who is here summarizing the contents of Schleiermacher's lectures rather than simply reproducing them). Cf. A.W. Schlegel, *Die Kunstlehre* (Stuttgart: Kohlhammer, 1963), p. 247: in poetry there are no true synonyms "because the words have a different sound, because this sound appears to us involuntarily to refer to the meaning, and so gives to it different side-determinations, because even the form . . . of the word . . . affects the way in which its sense is grasped."

148. Lefevere, *Translation/History/Culture*, pp. 79–80.

149. Once again Schleiermacher's associate A.W. Schlegel seems committed to a version of this reason as well. For example, he says that "the sense of words is determined according to the intuitions which people are in the habit of associating with them; so that we are in constant danger of ascribing to the words of the Greek poets a quite different meaning than they had for them and their audience, even when we understand them grammatically as exactly as you please" (quoted by Huyssen, *Die frühromantische Konzeption von Übersetzung und Aneignung*, p. 89; cf. pp. 69 ff. on Schlegel's connected appropriation of Herder's interpretive method of *Einfühlung*).

150. Schleiermacher's commitment to this traditional goal is indeed if anything even stronger than Herder's. In his 1813 essay he in effect treats commitment to it as a necessary condition for something to count as a "translation" at all. For example, he distinguishes imitation and paraphrase as mere *pis aller* for translation rather than forms of translation on the grounds that they operate "not with a view to gathering [foreign works'] real artistic or linguistic sense [-*sinn*], but rather to fill a need and to contemplate spiritual art" (*On the Different Methods of Translation*, pp. 7–8).

151. Ibid., pp. 28–9.

152. Thus in the aesthetics lectures Schleiermacher notes that the translation and imitation of ancient verse forms, particularly ancient meters, in German has led to important developments in German: "Only since this turn of our language towards the ancient [verse] forms has a major development in our language been attained; and this should therefore be seen not as an error but as an element which has become constant" (FSSW 3/7:704).

153. *On the Different Methods of Translation*, p. 29. (In one of those small touches which, though of less importance in themselves, help an interpreter to be confident in pinning down an influence, Schleiermacher goes on at p. 30 to identify oratory as a potential alternative means for developing a target language, just as Abbt had done in the passage quoted by Herder at *Fragments*, G1:199–200.)

154. Already in early works such as *On What Gives Value to Life* (1792–3), *On Religion* (1799), and the *Soliloquies* (1800) Schleiermacher strongly championed a Herderian cosmopolitan ideal of "humanity." Cosmopolitan sentiments are evident in the 1813 essay on translation as well. For example, Schleiermacher says there that "in many ways . . . a human being only becomes cultured in a certain sense and a citizen

of the world through the understanding of several languages," and that "genuine" citizenship of the world does not suppress love of one's fatherland (*Über die verschiedenen Methoden des Übersetzens*, p. 236; cf. the passages quoted next here). And cosmopolitan sentiments are still present in Schleiermacher's latest works, for example his 1831 lecture on Leibniz's idea of a universal language. It is true that during the French invasion of Germany in the years leading up to the time of the 1813 essay Schleiermacher sometimes expressed sentiments which could be described as "nationalist" (especially in his sermons), but to confuse this basically cosmopolitan and defensive "nationalism" with the exclusive, aggressive forms of "nationalism" with which we are painfully familiar from later periods of German history, as Venuti does, is unjustified.

155. *On the Different Methods of Translation*, p. 1.

156. Ibid., p. 29. Concerning this "respect for what is foreign" and "mediation," note also Schleiermacher's remark elsewhere in the essay that it is an essential part of a "purely ethical outlook" that "the sense for what is less closely related [than what one encounters in one's own language and dialect] remain open too" (*Über die verschiedenen Methoden des Übersetzens*, p. 208; cf. Berman, *L'épreuve*, pp. 240–1).

157. Cf. A.W. Schlegel's position in his *Geschichte der romantischen Literatur* (1803) that the aim of faithful translation—or what he calls "objective poetic translation"—is "nothing less than to combine the merits of all different nations, to think with them and feel with them, and so create a cosmopolitan center for mankind" (Lefevere, *Translation/History/Culture*, p. 17); that a translator in this mold is "a messenger between the nations, a mediator of mutual respect and admiration" (quoted by Berman, *L'Épreuve*, p. 213).

158. *Über die verschiedenen Methoden des Übersetzens*, p. 243. (Lefevere mistranslates this sentence on p. 29 of his translation.)

159. *On the Different Methods of Translation*, p. 29.

160. Ibid., p. 3. Schleiermacher's colleague and friend Friedrich Schlegel had already emphasized the need for *creativity* and *art* in the translator in work from 1796–1800: "Translation is really linguistic creation. Only the translator is an artist who works in language"; "The translation of poets . . . has become an art" (Lefevere, *Translating Literature*, pp. 60–1).

161. *On the Different Methods of Translation*, pp. 9 ff.

162. Ibid., pp. 7–9.

163. FSSW 3/7:702 ff.

164. *Über die verschiedenen Methoden des Übersetzens*, p. 221.

165. A.W. Schlegel's considered position is similar: although he normally advocates and practices a type of translation which strives to be faithful to both semantic content and musical form—"objective poetic translation," as he calls it—he also allows that *imitation* is more appropriate in certain cases, and accordingly himself sometimes practices this, for example in connection with Sanskrit literature (see Lefevere, *Translating Literature*, pp. 54–5).

166. *Über die verschiedenen Methoden des Übersetzens*, p. 241. Cf. p. 242: "the most accurate possible enjoyment of the works themselves."

167. Ibid., p. 231.

168. *On the Different Methods of Translation*, pp. 7–8.

169. Ibid., pp. 2–4.

170. Concerning this, see my "On the Very Idea of Denying the Existence of Radically Different Conceptual Schemes." Schleiermacher's mistake here perhaps stems in part from a failure to recognize the sort of distinction between *sense* and *referent* which, under the influence of some remarks in Herder's *Ideas for the Philosophy of History of Humanity* (1784–91), was just beginning to be drawn clearly at this period by Wilhelm von Humboldt. Humboldt writes, for example: "Even in the case of purely sensible objects the terms employed by different languages are far from being true synonyms, and . . . in saying *hippos*, *equus*, or *cheval* one doesn't say exactly the same thing. The same holds true a fortiori in the case of non-sensible objects" (*Hellas und Latium* [1806]); "Even for [external physical objects that are plainly perceivable by the senses] the word is not the equivalent of the object that hovers before the sense, but rather the conception thereof through language-production at the particular moment of finding the word. This is a notable source of the multiplicity of expressions for the same objects; and if in Sanskrit, for example, the *elephant* is now called the twice-drinking one, now the two-toothed one, and now the one equipped with a single hand, as many different concepts are thereby designated, though always the same object is meant" (*On the Diversity of Human Language-Structure and its Influence on the Mental Development of Mankind* [1836]). This distinction would later receive its classic formulation in Frege's essay *On Sense and Reference*. Sameness of *referent* between pieces of referring/descriptive vocabulary by no means ensures sameness in their *sense*.

171. *On the Different Methods of Translation*, p. 14 (translation amended).

172. See Lefevere, *Translation/History/Culture*, p. 110.

173. See Purdie, *Studies in German Literature of the Eighteenth Century*, p. 115. This problem drove Lessing to prefer prose translations of verse to metrical ones.

174. Herder's theoretical neglect of this sort of challenge is surprising, given its prominence in d'Alembert and Lessing, the fact that (as we saw) he often discusses the need to marry semantic with musical fidelity (e.g. in his remarks about combining Michaelis's philological talent with Cramer's talent in versification), and the fact that he must have wrestled with it constantly in the stricter parts of his own translation practice (e.g. in his translations of Shakespeare). I suspect that the reason for his theoretical neglect of it lies in his official theoretical conviction in the inseparability of musical form and semantic content (as already discussed). This conviction may have inclined him to suppose that there can be no deep tension between the two tasks: to be semantically faithful *is* to be faithful to the musical form and vice versa. However, if that *is* his reason for neglecting this challenge, then it is a misguided one, and Schleiermacher (who, as we saw, shares Herder's conviction about the inseparability of form and content) has seen further. For, even if musical form bears its own meanings and also adds nuances to the meanings of the words in a work, this does not preclude irreconcilable conflicts of the sort in question. For example, if we are translating some word X in the original text of a poem, it will still often be the case that a word Y in the target language which would be the closest semantic counterpart to X will not be usable without disrupting the meter or the rhyme-scheme, whereas a word Z in the target language will preserve the meter or rhyme-scheme better but only at the cost of straying further from the semantic content of X, even if the semantic loss suffered by using word Z is *offset* by an accrual of original meaning pertaining to the meter or rhyme-scheme itself and an accrual to word Z or to other words of a shade of original meaning which the meter or rhyme-scheme supplies and which would have been lost without it. From a purely semantic point of view, this offsetting might outweigh, underweigh, or just exactly counterbalance the semantic loss incurred by using word Z, depending on the particular case; but the essential point is that whichever of these things happens, the semantic loss remains a real one.

175. For a fuller discussion of this position, see Essay 11. The modern translation theorist Nida introduces a strikingly similar conception in his discussion of a word's "semantic field" (Nida, *Toward a Science of*

Translating, pp. 37–40). Nida also implies an important point which is at least less clear in Schleiermacher, namely that what is essential to the specific word meanings is not only what—to use Schleiermacher's term—"the unity of the word sphere" *comprises* but also how it is *structured* (to the extent that these two things are distinguishable) (ibid., pp. 89 ff.).

176. *On the Different Methods of Translation*, p. 14; cf. p. 25.

177. See ibid., p. 14 concerning the need to reproduce an author's "use of related words and roots of words."

178. Ibid., p. 25: especially in philosophy "every language . . . contains within it a system of concepts which, precisely because they touch each other in the same language, because they connect and complement each other, are a *whole* whose isolated parts do not correspond to any in the system of other languages."

179. Ibid., p. 5: "The further [languages] are apart in time and genealogical descent, the less a word in one language corresponds completely to a word in another or a declension in one language comprehends exactly the same multiplicity of relationships as another in a different language."

Herder had not at the time of writing the *Fragments* (1767–8) yet clearly seen that the grammatical structures of languages vary in essential ways (in his *Treatise on the Origin of Language* [1772] he still treats grammar as essentially common to all languages, with the peculiar exception of Chinese). However, he went on to recognize this later, namely in *Ideas for the Philosophy of History of Humanity* (1784–91). And this position was then taken over and elaborated further even before Schleiermacher published his 1813 essay by his (sometime) colleague and friend Friedrich Schlegel, for whom it constituted one of the main rationales for a new discipline of "comparative grammar" which he proposed and began to develop (in his *On the Language and Wisdom of the Indians* [1808]). Shortly afterwards (and soon after the publication of Schleiermacher's essay), it would be taken over from Schlegel and developed even further by Bopp, Wilhelm von Humboldt, and other early contributors to the foundation of modern linguistics.

180. *On the Different Methods of Translation*, pp. 4–5, 14.

181. It may perhaps be that Schleiermacher's own translations actually differ from Herder's in this way, though determining whether this is so would require further analysis.

182. *Popular Songs*, G3:42–5.

183. For some later reflections on and developments of the Herder-Schleiermacher one-word(-family)-for-one-word(-family) approach,

see Störig ed., *Das Problem des Übersetzens*. In a cautious and rather critical discussion from 1826, A.W. Schlegel says that such an approach may work for certain kinds of texts, e.g. geometry textbooks and some sorts of philosophy books, but not for poetry, which cannot, he says, be treated like "a collection of algebraic signs." More specifically, in connection with translating such "incommensurable" (his own term) Indian words/concepts as *dharma* or *yoga*, he rejects both the approach of bending a corresponding word in the modern European target language (since the bending would have to be too severe in such cases) and the approach of simply leaving the Indian word untranslated, instead preferring the use of multiple target-language words (pp. 99–100). By contrast, Rosenzweig and Buber stay firmly committed to the one-word(-family)-for-one-word(-family) approach (which they discuss in connection with their translation of the Old Testament). Rosenzweig champions this approach as necessary not only for preserving the sense of the words involved, but also for preserving other textual effects, though he notes that its application has to be kept within the bounds of the linguistically possible (pp. 244–7). Buber is a firm champion of this approach as well, like Schleiermacher emphasizing that it needs to be applied not only to individual words but also to whole families of related words, and like Rosenzweig stressing that this is necessary, not only in order to preserve word-meaning, but also in order to preserve other textual effects, especially messages which are conveyed by a text not through explicit statements but through significant repetitions of what he calls *Leitwörter*; though he too notes that there are limitations to this approach's applicability, and in particular that it should not normally be used with non-salient words or in cases where the immediate context forbids (pp. 359 ff., 380).

184. As can be seen from the passage by Abbt that Herder quotes in the *Fragments* and that I requoted above ("new connections"), Abbt was already interested in bending the target language not *only* towards the source language's word-usages, but also towards its *syntax*. And Herder already shared that interest as well (for example, as we saw earlier, he praises Abbt for this at *On Thomas Abbt's Writings*, G2:589, 595; similarly, at *Fragments*, G1:309 he praises a translator for fitting Greek syntax to German). The question of bending syntax later became salient and controversial in an interesting way in connection with Voss's translations of Homer. While, as we saw, Voss was not scrupulous about bending word-usages, he did tend to import distinctive features

of Homeric syntax into German. And this became a focus of A.W. Schlegel's acute, though vacillating, critical attention—Schlegel at first strongly objecting to such importations that they were unnatural to German, then later, as the Germans got accustomed to Voss's work, retracting that objection and conceding that Voss's importations had been successful, before finally (but after the two men had fallen out for other reasons) returning to a more critical stance. See *August Wilhelm von Schlegels sämmtliche Werke*, ed. E. Böcking (Leipzig: Weidmann, 1846), 9:115–93. In the twentieth century Rosenzweig and Buber would again, in connection with their foreignizing translation of the Old Testament, regard faithfulness to the syntax of the Hebrew as an essential part of the translator's task (see Buber, "Zu einer neuen Verdeutschung der Schrift," in Störig ed., *Das Problem des Übersetzens*, p. 387).

185. A similar point applies to verb conjugations.

186. *On the Different Methods of Translation*, p. 6. (Schleiermacher indeed—though somewhat questionably—treats the presence of this sort of conceptual modification or innovation as a necessary condition of the significance of a work, and therefore of its worthiness of being translated in the first place.)

187. Ibid., p. 7; cf. pp. 13, 18. Ernesti and Herder had already recognized the phenomenon of double conceptual distance involved here, but they had not gone on to draw the consequence that it constitutes a special challenge for translation. Someone who *had* already done so was d'Alembert in his *Observations sur l'art de traduire* (1758) (*Œuvres*, pp. 31 ff.), to whom Schleiermacher is evidently indebted not only for his recognition of this challenge, but also for his conception of how it should be addressed.

188. *On the Different Methods of Translation*, p. 13. As I implied in the preceding note, Schleiermacher is indebted for this strategy to d'Alembert's *Obervations sur l'art de traduire* (see esp. *Œuvres*, p. 37).

   Notice that it is a consequence of Schleiermacher's commitment to this strategy that he could *not* accept an approach which has sometimes been advocated for the translation of certain texts, and which theorists have often tended to confuse with his own foreignizing approach (e.g., Bassnett, *Translation Studies*, pp. 70–5; Berman, *L'Épreuve*, pp. 266–78; and Venuti at points in *The Translator's Invisibility*), namely a general *archaizing*. His implicit rejection of such an approach can also be seen from the fact that he wants a translation of an ancient text to produce the same effect on a modern reader as the ancient text did on the ancient reader—for an ancient reader did *not* normally have any impression of archaicness. Archaizing in fact plays no essential role at all in Schleiermacher's approach to translation, as far as I can see: neither "bending" nor the reproduction of musical form essentially involves it, and it is by means of *these* techniques that he aims to produce a sense of what is foreign, not by using vocabulary or musical forms which are antiquated within the target language. Nor need it be the case that the "relatively older terminology" just mentioned is actually *archaic*.

189. *On the Different Methods of Translation*, pp. 13–14 (translation modified). The exact nature of the compensation envisaged in the last sentence is somewhat obscure. It *sounds* as though Schleiermacher is proposing to compensate for the weaknesses described by using target-language neologisms in places where the author was using "old and well-known words," but I doubt that he can really mean that, since, while that would no doubt indeed convey a quite general impression of innovation, it would subvert his fundamental strategy for conveying what is conceptually new and what not at the particular level. And if his point is instead that one compensates merely by using "old and tired" target-language vocabulary in the places in question, then that is not much of a *compensation*. A better version of his general line of thought here would perhaps be to say that while at the particular level there will be both some successes and some failures (both some cases where conceptual innovations do indeed receive relative neologisms in the translation and some cases where they do not; both some cases where well-worn concepts do indeed receive well-worn vocabulary in the translation and some cases where they do not), overall one can at least expect a reasonably accurate picture to be conveyed of *areas* in which the author was conceptually innovative and *areas* in which he was not.

190. See Lefevere, *Translation/History/Culture*, pp. 49–50.

191. Concerning this skeptical tradition, see Kelly, *The True Interpreter*, pp. 214 ff., 222–3.

192. F. Schlegel, *Philosophy of Philology*, pp. 16, 38–9, 42. His brother A.W. Schlegel holds a similar position (see Huyssen, *Die frühromantische Konzeption von Übersetzung und Aneignung*, pp. 76, 85, 92–3).

193. *On the Different Methods of Translation*, pp. 19, 29. This model of translation has close analogues in other areas of Friedrich Schlegel's and Schleiermacher's thought. Thus a prominent (though not, perhaps, the best) strand of Schleiermacher's *hermeneutics* adopts a similar position about the nature of *interpretation*: it is never possible fully to understand

what another person writes or says; still, one should not for that reason give up the goal of attaining such understanding (or for that matter, alter the traditional conception of interpretation's goal as grasping the interpreted subject's original meaning), but one should instead strive to come as close as possible to such understanding. Indeed, for Schlegel and Schleiermacher—working as they do under the influence of Platonic, Kantian, and Fichtean notions that an infinite striving towards unrealizable ends is the nature of human cognition and the human condition generally—such a conception of translation (and interpretation) is part of a more general picture of human cognition and the human condition as an infinite striving towards goals that are never fully realizable.

It is important, however, to see that one might accept this Schlegel-Schleiermacher model for *translation* without also endorsing their application of it to other areas. In particular, whereas the *hermeneutic* version of this model runs into serious philosophical problems, concerning how one could ever *know* that the situation it posits obtained, and indeed whether therefore it even really makes *sense* to suppose it does (cf. my *Wittgenstein on the Arbitrariness of Grammar*, esp. ch. 7), the *translation* version does not, for there is no implication in this case that an exact *understanding* of the original text is impossible (only an exact reproduction of its meaning in translation).

194. See *On the Different Methods of Translation*, pp. 27–8. Berman and Venuti strongly dislike such conceptions of translation as a sort of *pis aller* for comprehension of the original work in the original language. Berman develops several interesting arguments against them. One quite persuasive point that he makes concerns the historical centrality of translation to the literary "polysystem" (see e.g. *Pour une critique des traductions*, p. 54; think here, for example, of the central role that Bible translations have played in the development of the West's literature). But this is a point with which Schleiermacher would fundamentally agree (recall his emphasis on translation's role in enriching a target language and culture), and which he already takes into account in his conception that translation is a *necessary* evil. Berman also develops several more ambitious arguments. For example, he argues that original works only fully realize their essential natures in translation (ibid., pp. 39–43), that translation brings with it a sort of sui generis critical insight into original works which is not attainable in any other way (*L'Épreuve*, pp. 248–9, 271–3, 289–90), and that since *all* literature includes an element of foreignness, reading a translation is only different

in *degree* from reading the original text (ibid., p. 249). However, these more ambitious arguments all seem rather questionable.

195. *On the Different Methods of Translation*, p. 9. Schleiermacher argues that this distinction is more fundamental than and subsumes several more familiar distinctions, such as translation following the letter vs. translation following the sense, and faithful translation vs. free translation (ibid., pp. 10−11).

196. *Fragments*, G1:648−9. There is actually a longer historical story to be told about how Herder's position led to Schleiermacher's, involving some later work of Herder's and a discussion of translation by Goethe from 1813, but I shall not go into this here.

197. For example, Rosenzweig, although he criticizes Schleiermacher's conception that the translator must make a clearcut choice one way or the other and instead champions a form of compromise (like Herder), concedes the former of these two virtues (Störig ed., *Das Problem des Übersetzens*, p. 221; Lefevere ed., *Translating Literature*, p. 111). And the value of Schleiermacher's distinction as a principle for classifying different types of translation is (explicitly or implicitly) conceded not only by theorists such as Venuti who are sympathetic with his foreignizing choice (Venuti's fundamental distinction between "foreignizing" and "domesticating" forms of translation essentially just repeats Schleiermacher's), but also by many theorists who are agnostic about or even hostile to that choice. For instance, Nida's influential distinction between translation which aims for "formal equivalence" (i.e. foreignizing) and translation which aims for "dynamic equivalence" (i.e. domesticating) is essentially just a repetition of Schleiermacher's distinction (Nida, *Toward a Science of Translating*, pp. 25−6, 161−6, 183−4, 191−2).

198. For Rosenzweig's criticism, see Störig ed., *Das Problem des Übersetzens*, p. 221; Lefevere ed., *Translating Literature*, p. 111. For Lefevere's, see ibid., pp. 66−7. For Huyssen's, see *Die frühromantische Konzeption von Übersetzung und Aneignung*, p. 65.

199. *On the Different Methods of Translation*, pp. 10, 19.

200. Ibid., pp. 26−7.

201. *Fragments*, G1:205 (as quoted earlier).

202. *On the Different Methods of Translation*, pp. 4−5, 25.

203. Ibid., pp. 5−6, 20.

204. Ibid., pp. 20−1.

205. Ibid., pp. 24−5.

206. Ibid., pp. 21−2.

207. Ibid., pp. 22–3.

208. Ibid., pp. 23–4.

209. Ibid., p. 24.

210. Ibid., pp. 25, 28.

211. Ibid., p. 10.

212. *Toward a Science of Translating*, p. 167.

213. Concerning my conjunction here, "theory and practice," cf. Berman's apt remarks against the notion that translation is an *intuitive* process, and in support of its essential inclusion of an element of *reflection* which tends in the direction of theory (*L'Épreuve*, pp. 300–1).

214. Thus Schleiermacher observes that in the case of translations concerned with legal transactions within established institutions "their expressions in both languages are fixed either legally or through usage and reciprocal explanations" (*Über die verschiedenen Methoden des Übersetzens*, p. 210).

215. This asymmetry between the two sorts of cases of course reflects one in Schleiermacher's own argument.

216. Of course, *other* rationales for domesticating translation might be tried as well. For example, Nida, who in effect argues in favor of a domesticating rather than a foreignizing approach to translation (*Toward a Science of Translating*, pp. 25–6, 161–4), offers as his main rationale for domesticating translation the goal of producing a *similar behavioral response* in the target reader to that in the source reader (ibid., pp. 148–9, 159, 182–3). However, as stated, this seems hopelessly undiscriminating. For example, the criterion in question had better not include similarity in *linguistic* behavior, i.e. responding with the source language! And (despite what one infers to be Nida's underlying Christian-proselytizing motive for the rationale) it had also better not include similarity in such responses as evincing conviction or reverence, otherwise the proper English translation of *Mein Kampf* would have to be one that made the English reader sincerely echo its venomous assertions and show reverence for the *Führer*. One suspects that in the end the only even potentially defensible version of Nida's criterion would have to be something like: similarity between source reader and target reader in *those aspects of behavioral response which constitute semantic understanding*. But then, setting aside the problem that this assumes a questionable behaviorism about such states as understanding, it looks like a criterion that would much more plausibly be held to warrant *foreignizing* than domesticating translation.

217. *On the Different Methods of Translation*, p. 14 (translation slightly modified).

218. G9/1:351 ff.

219. *On the Different Methods of Translation*, p. 8 (translation modified).

220. There are certainly further alternatives to the "bending" approach which might be advocated as well as the two just considered. One would be simply to leave the problematic word from the source language untranslated. This is a common enough technique (e.g. English language translations will often leave *savoir faire* or *Zeitgeist* untranslated), and is often quite sensible. But of course it is as much a *refusal* to translate as a technique of translation. Another approach would be to neologize. This too is a common enough technique (e.g. with technical terms), and is sometimes appropriate, though not for all types of text, and not in large quantities. Another approach would be to translate the problematic word by means of a multiplicity of alternatives in different contexts (as Luther, Voss, and Lattimore do) *but always provide the original word in parentheses afterwards*. This is again a common enough technique and often sensible in certain sorts of texts. But it can only be used sparingly without taxing the reader's patience, and there are many sorts of texts for which it would not work (e.g. poems and novels). Moreover (and this is the most important point to note here), all three of these techniques arguably work, to the extent that they do work, in a *similar way* to the "bending" approach.

221. *On the Different Methods of Translation*, p. 16 (emphasis added). Cf. pp. 15–17.

222. Of course, it is possible for a reader to miss such clues. He might, for example, in the cases just mentioned simply infer that Homer has absurd views about who is virtuous and what is green, or alternatively, and even worse, that the translator is a bungler. However, such failures to perceive what is going on could be forestalled or at least minimized for all but the obtusest of readers by means of explicit discussion outside the translation itself concerning the principles on which the translation is being done and the particular cases in which they are being applied. In this general spirit, Herder had already called for "notes and explanations in a high critical spirit" to accompany any translation of Homer (*Fragments*, G1:307). And in Schleiermacher's case, not only his prefaces and notes to his translations of Plato, but also, and indeed especially, his essay *On the Different Methods of Translation* itself, perform this function for those translations. In more recent times, one of the

strongest and most articulate advocates of complementing foreignizing translation with ample notes and explanations has been V. Nabokov (the novelist and translator).

223. F.D.E. Schleiermacher, *Ethik (1812/13)* (Hamburg: Felix Meiner, 1981), pp. 115–16: "[Translations] can, though, have disadvantageous effects on the character of language. It is indifferent for the purity of the type whether one imitates a foreign contemporary language or a foreign dead language."

224. *On the Different Methods of Translation*, pp. 16–17.

225. Ibid., p. 29.

226. In his 1831 address on Leibniz's idea of a universal language, Schleiermacher argues that this conservative inertia is especially strong in the area of a nation's *poetry*: "Distinctiveness should remain preserved. For this purpose, as far as language is concerned, is stationed above all poetry, which stays at home to guard this holy hearth when the other drives of mankind wander through the whole territory of the spirit in order to see holy images abroad as well. Whatever they bring back from their wanderings, poetry only appropriates for its works what is expressible in native tones; poetry is most implacable in expelling invading foreigners, by which both constancy of sound and authenticity of representation are after all always endangered, as soon as they are replaceable by something native" (FSSW 3/1:144). Nonetheless, he also observes in the aesthetics lectures concerning alien musical-metrical forms which have been imported into German that some of them have passed the sort of test in question here and have thereby achieved a lasting enrichment of the German language: "Only since this turn of our language towards the ancient [verse] forms has a major development in our language been attained; and this should therefore be seen not as an error but as an element which has become constant" (FSSW 3/7:704).

227. Of course, one should be rather skeptical about some of the assumptions in terms of which Herder expresses his original worry and Schleiermacher this answer, such as that languages once existed in a pristine ("virginal") state, and that languages have "natures." However, both the worry and the answer could be easily enough recast without making such assumptions.

228. *On the Different Methods of Translation*, pp. 17–18.

229. This position is in tension with Schleiermacher's suggestion earlier in his essay that the "bending" approach should be applauded even if it is only successfully implemented in particular writings of an author or

even only in particular parts thereof rather than throughout his whole corpus (ibid., p. 14). One could perhaps reconcile these statements by saying that in the later context Schleiermacher is talking more about what "bending" translators need to do in order really to succeed, whereas in the earlier context he was talking more about what we ought to praise them for.

230. Ibid., p. 17. Cf. p. 19. A.W. Schlegel had already made a similar point in his *Homers Werke von Heinrich Voss* of 1796 (see Lefevere, *Translation/History/Culture*, p. 55).

231. In this spirit, A.W. Schlegel had written in his *Geschichte der klassischen Literatur* (1803) that although German had been uniquely successful in absorbing foreign musical forms, "Yet I do not want this to be considered an advantageous feature which just happens to be present in the composition of our language. Others could also open themselves to a great variety of influences; all it takes is resolve and hard work. This flexibility of ours finds its roots only in the fact that the German tries harder to participate in the movements and changes of the soul which correspond to those outside movements. The willingness of the German national character to translate itself into foreign ways of thinking and to abandon itself entirely to them finds expression in our language, which makes it the best translator and mediator for all others" (in Lefevere, *Translating Literature*, pp. 52–3).

232. *On the Different Methods of Translation*, pp. 28–9. Cf. Lefevere, *Translation/History/Culture*, pp. 76–9 for similar contrasts between the French and the Germans by Goethe and A.W. Schlegel.

Note that this is not simply a case of Germans badmouthing Frenchmen (though some of that may be involved too). D'Alembert had already made a similar point about the inflexibility of the French language in his *Observations sur l'art de traduire*, and Victor Hugo later would as well (see Lefevere, *Translation/History/Culture*, pp. 18, 108).

233. *Über die verschiedenen Methoden des Übersetzens*, pp. 220–1, 231. For a helpful discussion of Schleiermacher's conception of the historico-social preconditions for the success of foreignizing translation, see Berman, *L'Épreuve*, pp. 236–8.

234. Goethe, probably under Schleiermacher's influence, develops a similarly historicized conception of translation in his notes for the *West-östlicher Divan* of 1819, where he sketches an account of three different periods and types of translation culminating in the period of semantically and formally faithful translation. Rosenzweig basically takes over Goethe's historicized account (see Störig ed., *Das Problem*

des Übersetzens, pp. 227–9). Berman likewise adopts the conception that foreignizing translation requires a certain historico-cultural *kairos* (see *Pour une critique des traductions*, pp. 222–3).

235. Cf. *On the Different Methods of Translation*, p. 1: "The fact that speech is translated . . . allows people to establish contact who were originally as far apart from each other as the length of the earth's diameter."

236. FSSW 3/1:146–9. In Schleiermacher's view, this sort of intersubjective agreement is of vital importance, not only for more obvious reasons, but also because it is an essential criterion of genuine knowledge in the sciences. His discipline of dialectics is largely motivated by this conception. (For some further discussion of this, see Essay 10.)

Select Bibliography

Herder

Primary Texts

There are two main German editions of Herder's works:

Johann Gottfried Herder Sämtliche Werke, B. Suphan et al. (eds.), Berlin: Weidmann, 1877– .

Johann Gottfried Herder Werke, U. Gaier et al. (eds.), Frankfurt am Main: Deutscher Klassiker Verlag, 1985– . (This edition includes very helpful notes.)

Johann Gottfried Herder Briefe, W. Dobbek and G. Arnold (eds.), Weimar: Hermann Böhlaus Nachfolger, 1977.

Translations

On World History, H. Adler and E.A. Menze (eds.), Armonk, NY: Sharpe, 1996. (Contains short excerpts on history from a variety of works, prominently including the *Ideas*.)

J.G. Herder on Social and Political Culture, F.M. Barnard (ed.), Cambridge: Cambridge University Press, 1969. (Includes (partial) translations of Herder's 1769 *Journal*, *Treatise on the Origin*, *This Too a Philosophy of History*, the *Dissertation on the Reciprocal Influence of Government and the Sciences*, and the *Ideas*, plus a very helpful introduction.)

God: Some Conversations, F.H. Burkhardt (ed.), 1940; repr. Indianapolis: Bobbs-Merrill, 1962.

Outlines of a Philosophy of the History of Man, T. Churchill (ed.), London: J. Johnson/ L. Hansard, 1803. (This is a translation of the *Ideas*.)

J.G. Herder: Philosophical Writings, M.N. Forster (ed.), Cambridge: Cambridge University Press, 2002. (Contains full translations of *How Philosophy Can Become*, *Treatise on the Origin*, *On the Cognition*, and *This Too a Philosophy of History*, as well as other pieces.)

Sculpture: Some Observations on Shape and Form from Pygmalion's Creative Dream, J. Gaiger (ed.), Chicago: The University of Chicago Press, 2002. (This is a translation of *Plastic*.)

Reflections on the Philosophy of History of Mankind, F.E. Manuel (ed.), Chicago: University of Chicago Press, 1968. (Contains excerpts from Churchill's 1800 translation of the *Ideas*.)

The Spirit of Hebrew Poetry, J. Marsh (ed.), Burlington, Vt.: Edward Smith, 1833.

Johann Gottfried Herder: Selected Early Works, 1764–7, E.A. Menze, K. Menges, M. Palma (eds.), University Park, Pa.: Pennsylvania State University Press, 1992. (Contains several early essays, including *On Diligence in Several Learned Languages*, and selections from the *Fragments*.)

Selected Writings on Aesthetics, G. Moore (ed.), Princeton, NJ: Princeton University Press, 2006. (Contains the first and fourth books of the *Critical Forests*, the essays *Shakespeare* and *On the Influence of the Beautiful Sciences on the Higher Sciences*, and several other pieces on aesthetics.)

On the Origin of Language, J.H. Moran and A. Gode (eds.), Chicago: University of Chicago Press, 1986. (Contains a partial translation of *Treatise on the Origin*.)

German Aesthetics and Literary Criticism: Winckelmann, Lessing, Hamann, Herder, Schiller, Goethe, H.B. Nisbet (ed.), Cambridge: Cambridge University Press, 1985. (Contains two pieces of Herder's in aesthetics, including his important essay *Shakespeare*.)

General treatments (largely concerned with Herder's philosophy of language)

Beiser, F.C., *The Fate of Reason*, Cambridge, Mass.: Harvard University Press, 1987. (Ch. 5 covers several topics helpfully, including Herder's philosophies of language, mind, and religion.)

Berlin, I., *Vico and Herder: Two Studies in the History of Ideas*, New York: The Viking Press, 1976. (Concise and excellent.)

Clark Jr., R.T., *Herder: His Life and Thought*, Berkeley and Los Angeles: University of California Press, 1955. (Detailed and useful, though unimaginative.)

Haym, R., *Herder nach seinem Leben und seinen Werken*, Berlin: Gaertner, 1880. (A classic, detailed intellectual biography. Still by far the best general book on Herder.)

Irmscher, H.D., *Johann Gottfried Herder*, Stuttgart: Reclam, 2001. (A very good short introduction.)

Additional works concerned with Herder's philosophy of language

Huber, T., *Studien zur Theorie des Übersetzens im Zeitalter der deutschen Aufklärung 1730–1770*, Meisenheim am Glan: Anton Hain, 1968.

Irmscher, H.D., "Grundzüge der Hermeneutik Herders," in *Bückeburger Gespräche über J.G. Herder 1971*, Bückeburg: Grimme, 1973.

Kelletat, A.F., *Herder und die Weltliteratur*, Frankfurt am Main: Peter Lang, 1984. (A helpful treatment of Herder's interest in world literature, in particular his theory and practice of translation.)

Sapir, E., "Herder's 'Ursprung der Sprache,'" *Modern Philology*, 5/1 (1907). (An excellent discussion of the *Treatise* by an important twentieth-century linguist.)

Taylor, C., "The Importance of Herder," in E. and A. Margalit (eds.), *Isaiah Berlin: A Celebration*, Chicago: University of Chicago Press, 1991.

—— "Language and Human Nature," in his *Human Agency and Language: Philosophical Papers I*, Cambridge: Cambridge University Press, 1996.

Willi, T., *Herders Beitrag zum Verstehen des Alten Testaments*, Tübingen: J.C.B. Mohr, 1971. (A treatment of Herder's approach to interpreting the Old Testament.)

Literature on other topics

Barnard, F.M., *Herder's Social and Political Thought: From Enlightenment to Nationalism*, Oxford: Oxford University Press, 1965. (Chs. 3–5 cover Herder's political thought very well.)

Beiser, F.C., *Enlightenment, Revolution, and Romanticism*, Cambridge, Mass.: Harvard University Press, 1992. (Ch. 8 on Herder's political philosophy is excellent.)

Bollacher, M. (ed.), *Johann Gottfried Herder: Geschichte und Kultur*, Würzburg: Königshausen und Neumann, 1994.

Broce, G., "Herder and Ethnography," *Journal of the History of the Behavioral Sciences*, 22 (1986).

Ergang, R., *Herder and the Foundations of German Nationalism*, 1931; repr. New York: Octagon Books, 1966. (Helpful on Herder's political thought and his intellectual influence. Marred, however, by a false assimilation of Herder's nationalism to later German nationalism, and an unduly warm assessment of such a position.)

Gjesdal, K., "Reading Shakespeare—Reading Modernity," *Angelaki*, 9/3 (2004).

Irmscher, H.D., "Grundfragen der Geschichtsphilosophie Herders bis 1774," in *Bückeburger Gespräche über J.G. Herder 1983*, Bückeburg: Grimme, 1984.

Lovejoy, A.O., "Herder and the Enlightenment Philosophy of History," in his *Essays on the History of Ideas*, 1948; repr. New York: Capricorn Books, 1960. (Helpful and short.)

Meinecke, F., *Historism: The Rise of a New Historical Outlook*, New York: Herder and Herder, 1972. (Ch. 9 on Herder is very helpful.)

Mühlberg, D., "Herders Theorie der Kulturgeschichte in ihrer Bedeutung für die Begründung der Kulturwissenschaft," *Jahrbuch für Volkskunde und Kulturgeschichte*, 12 (1984).

Nisbet, H.B., *Herder and the Philosophy and History of Science*, Cambridge, Mass.: Modern Humanities Research Association, 1970. (A helpful account of Herder's views about science.)

Norton, R.E., *Herder's Aesthetics and the European Enlightenment*, Ithaca: Cornell University Press, 1991. (Helpful both on aspects of Herder's aesthetic theory and on Herder's general relation to the Enlightenment.)

Otto, R., and Zammito, J. (eds.), *Vom Selbstdenken: Aufklärung und Aufklärungskritik in Herders "Ideen zur Philosophie der Geschichte der Menschheit,"* Heidelberg: Synchron, 2001.

Purdie, E., *Studies in German Literature of the Eighteenth Century*, London: Athlone, 1965.

Sauder, G. (ed.), *Johann Gottfried Herder 1744–1803*, Hamburg: Felix Meiner, 1987.

Wiora, W., "Herders Ideen zur Geschichte der Musik," in E. Keyser (ed.), *Im Geiste Herders*, Kitzingen am Main: Holzner, 1953.

Zammito, J.H., *Kant, Herder, and the Birth of Modern Anthropology*, Chicago: University of Chicago Press, 2001. (An excellent, thorough study.).

Hamann

Primary Texts

There are two main German editions of Hamann's works:

Hamanns Schriften, F. Roth (ed.), Berlin: G. Reimer, 1820– .

Johann Georg Hamann Sämtliche Werke, J. Nadler (ed.), Vienna: Verlag Herder, 1949.

Johann Georg Hamann, *Briefwechsel*, W. Ziesemer and A. Henkel (eds.), Wiesbaden: Insel, 1955– .

Translations

Johann Georg Hamann's Relational Metacriticism, D.D. Dickson (ed.), Berlin: de Gruyter, 1995. (Includes translations of the *Socratic Memorabilia*, parts of the *Crusades*, *Philological Thoughts and Doubts*, and the *Metacritique*.)

Hamann: Writings on Philosophy and Language, K. Haynes (ed.), Cambridge: Cambridge University Press, 2007. (Includes translations of major parts of the *Crusades*, as well as the *Philological Thoughts and Doubts*, the *Metacritique*, and other pieces. Also contains very helpful explanatory notes.)

Hamann's Socratic Memorabilia: A Translation and Commentary, J.C. O'Flaherty (ed.), Baltimore: Johns Hopkins University Press, 1967.

General treatments (largely concerned with Hamann's philosophy of language)

Beiser, F.C., *The Fate of Reason*. (Ch. 1 on Hamann is very helpful.)

Berlin, I., *The Magus of the North: J.G. Hamann and the Origins of Modern Irrationalism*, New York: Farrar, Straus, and Giroux, 1993. (A short and helpful introduction, though not the product of deep scholarship on primary sources.)

Dilthey, W., "Johann Georg Hamann," in his *Gesammelte Schriften*, Stuttgart: B.G. Teubner and Göttingen: Vandenhoeck and Ruprecht, 1914– , vol. 11.

Nadler, J., *Johann Georg Hamann*, Salzburg: Otto Müller, 1949.

Unger, R., *Hamann und die Aufklärung*, Jena: Eugen Diederichs, 1911. (Probably still the best general book on Hamann, though too uncritical.)

Additional works concerned with Hamann's philosophy of language

German, T.J., *Hamann on Language and Religion*, Oxford: Oxford University Press, 1981. (Helpful on certain topics.)

Hacking, I., "How, Why, When, and Where Did Language Go Public?" and "Night Thoughts on Philology," both in his *Historical Ontology*, Cambridge Mass.: Harvard University Press, 2002. (Thoughtful and stimulating, though not scholarly.)

Mauthner, F., *Beiträge zu einer Kritik der Sprache*, 1902; 3rd edn., Berlin: Felix Meiner, 1923.

O'Flaherty, J.C., *Unity and Language: A Study in the Philosophy of Johann Georg Hamann*, 1952; repr. New York: AMS Press, 1966. (Somewhat disappointing.)

Unger, R., *Hamanns Sprachtheorie im Zusammenhange seines Denkens*, Munich: C.H. Beck, 1905. (Still by far the best book on the subject.)

Schleiermacher

Primary texts

There are two main German editions of Schleiermacher's works:

Gesamtausgabe der Werke Schleiermachers in drei Abteilungen = Friedrich Schleiermacher's sämmtliche Werke, Berlin: G. Reimer, 1835– .

Kritische Gesamtausgabe, H.-J. Birkner et al. (eds.), Berlin/New York: de Gruyter, 1980– .

(The latter edition will eventually supersede the former, but is still far from complete.)

In addition, the following editions are especially important for philosophers:

F. Schleiermacher: Hermeneutik. Nach den Handschriften neu herausgegeben und eingeleitet von Heinz Kimmerle, 1959; 2nd, rev. edn., Heidelberg: Heidelberger Akademie der Wissenschaften, 1974.

Schleiermacher: Hermeneutik und Kritik. Herausgegeben und eingeleitet von Manfred Frank, 1972; 7th edn., Frankfurt am Main: Suhrkamp, 1999.

Friedrich Schleiermacher: Dialektik. Herausgegeben und eingeleitet von Manfred Frank, 2 vols., Frankfurt am Main: Suhrkamp, 2001.

Aus Schleiermachers Leben in Briefen, 4 vols., L. Jonas and W. Dilthey (eds.), Berlin: G. Reimer, 1858– .

Translations

Hermeneutics: The Handwritten Manuscripts, J. Duke and J. Forstman (eds.), Atlanta: Scholars Press, 1986.

Hermeneutics and Criticism, A. Bowie (ed.), Cambridge: Cambridge University Press, 1998.

"On the Different Methods of Translation," in *German Romantic Criticism*, A.L. Willson (ed.), New York: Continuum, 1982.

Introductions to the Dialogues of Plato, Cambridge and London: Pitt Press, Deighton, and Parker, 1836.

Dialectic or The Art of Doing Philosophy, T.N. Tice (ed.), Atlanta: Scholars Press, 1996. (This contains Schleiermacher's first lecture notes on dialectics from 1811.)

Friedrich Schleiermacher's "Toward a Theory of Sociable Conduct" and Essays on Its Intellectual-Cultural Context, R.D. Richardson (ed.), Lewiston, NY: Edwin Mellen, 1995.

On the Highest Good, H.V. Froese (ed.), Lewiston, NY: Edwin Mellen, 1992.

On What Gives Value to Life, E. Lawler and T.N. Tice (eds.), Lewiston, NY: Edwin Mellen, 1995.

On Freedom, A.L. Blackwell (ed.), Lewiston, NY: Edwin Mellen, 1992.

Soliloquies, H.L. Friess (ed.), Chicago: Open Court, 1926.

On Religion: Speeches to its Cultured Despisers, R. Crouter (ed.), Cambridge: Cambridge University Press, 1988.

Christmas Eve: Dialogue on the Incarnation, T.N. Tice (ed.), San Francisco: Edwin Mellen, 1990.

The Life of Jesus, J.C. Verheyden (ed.), Philadelphia: Fortress, 1975.

The Christian Faith, H.R. Mackintosh and J.S. Stewart (eds.), Edinburgh: T. and T. Clark, 1928.

On the "Glaubenslehre," J. Duke and F. Fiorenza (eds.), Atlanta: Scholars Press, 1981. (This is a translation of Schleiermacher's two 1829 open letters to Lücke.)

Schleiermacher on Workings of the Knowing Mind, R.D. Richardson (ed.), Lewiston, NY: Edwin Mellen, 1998. (This includes a translation of Schleiermacher's 1799 review of Kant's *Anthropology*.)

General treatments

Berner, C., *La Philosophie de Schleiermacher*, Paris: Éditions du Cerf, 1995.

Dilthey, W., *Leben Schleiermachers*, 2 vols., M. Redeker (ed.), Berlin: de Gruyter, 1970.

Haym, R., *Die Romantische Schule*, 1870; 4th edn., Berlin: Weidmann, 1920, ch. 3.

Redeker, M., *Schleiermacher: Life and Thought*, Philadelphia: Fortress, 1973.

Scholtz, G., *Die Philosophie Schleiermachers*, Darmstadt: Wissenschaftliche Buchgesellschaft, 1984.

Works on Schleiermacher's philosophy of language (esp. hermeneutics and translation-theory)

Berman, A., *L'Épreuve de l'étranger*, Paris: Gallimard, 1984. (An excellent treatment of the translation-theory of Schleiermacher and some of his contemporaries.)

Boeckh, A., *Encyklopädie und Methodologie der philologischen Wissenschaften*, 1877; 2nd edn., Leipzig: B.G. Teubner, 1886.

Bowie, A., *From Romanticism to Critical Theory: The Philosophy of German Literary Theory*, London: Routledge, 1997.

Dilthey, W., "Schleiermacher's Hermeneutical System in Relation to Earlier Protestant Hermeneutics" and "The Rise of Hermeneutics," both in his *Hermeneutics and the Study of History*, Princeton, NJ: Princeton University Press, 1985.

Frank, M., *Das individuelle Allgemeine: Textstrukturierung und -interpretation nach Schleiermacher*, Frankfurt am Main: Suhrkamp, 1985.

—— *Das Sagbare und das Unsagbare: Studien zur deutsch-französischen Hermeneutik und Texttheorie*, Frankfurt am Main: Suhrkamp, 1990.

(These two books, especially the former, arguably constitute the most important secondary literature on Schleiermacher's hermeneutics.)

Gadamer, H.-G., *Truth and Method*, New York: Continuum, 2002, pt. 2. (A hostile but important treatment of Schleiermacher's hermeneutics.)

Gipper, H., and Schmitter, P., *Sprachwissenschaft und Sprachphilosophie im Zeitalter der Romantik*, Tübingen: Gunter Narr, 1985, pp. 92–8. (An excellent book.)

Hirsch Jr., E.D., *Validity in Interpretation*, New Haven and London: Yale University Press, 1967. (An important Anglophone appropriation of Schleiermacher's hermeneutics.)

Huyssen, A., *Die frühromantische Konzeption von Übersetzung und Aneignung*, Zürich and Freiburg: Atlantis, 1969.

Kimmerle, H., *Die Hermeneutik Schleiermachers im Zusammenhang seines spekulativen Denkens*, dissertation, Heidelberg, 1957.

Palmer, R.E., *Hermeneutics: Interpretation Theory in Schleiermacher, Dilthey, Heidegger, and Gadamer*, Evanston, Ill.: Northwestern University Press, 1969, ch. 7. (Helpful on Schleiermacher and other subjects.)

Patsch, H., "Friedrich Schlegels 'Philosophie der Philologie' und Schleiermachers frühe Entwürfe zur Hermeneutik," in *Zeitschrift für Theologie und Kirche*, 63 (1966). (A learned and important article.)

Ricoeur, P., "The Task of Hermeneutics," *Philosophy Today*, 17 (1973).

—— "Schleiermacher's Hermeneutics," *The Monist*, 60 (1977).

Szondi, P., "L'Herméneutique de Schleiermacher," *Poétique*, 2 (1970).

—— "Schleiermacher's Hermeneutics Today," in his *On Textual Understanding and Other Essays* = *Theory and History of Literature*, vol. 15, Manchester: Manchester University Press, 1986.

(Szondi's articles are consistently thoughtful and helpful.)

Venuti, L., *The Translator's Invisibility: A History of Translation*, London: Routledge, 1995. (Helpfully touches on, and works in the spirit of, Schleiermacher's theory of translation.)

Wach, J., *Das Verstehen: Grundzüge einer Geschichte der hermeneutischen Theorie im 19. Jahrhundert*, 1926–33; repr. Hildesheim: Georg Olms, 1966. (Learned and informative, though not exciting.)

The introductory materials in the two German editions of Schleiermacher's hermeneutics and in their English translations (all cited above) are also helpful.

Literature on other topics

Brandt, R.B., *The Philosophy of Schleiermacher: The Development of His Theory of Scientific and Religious Knowledge*, New York: Greenwood, 1968.

Burdorf, D., and Schmücker, R. (eds.), *Dialogische Wissenschaft*, Paderborn: F. Schöningh, 1998.

Faull, K.M., "Beyond Confrontation? The Early Schleiermacher and Feminist Moral Theory," in *Friedrich Schleiermacher's "Toward a Theory of Sociable Conduct" and Essays on Its Intellectual-Cultural Context*.

Guenther-Gleason, P.E., *On Schleiermacher and Gender Politics*, Harrisburg, Pa.: Trinity, 1997.

Kaulbach, F., "Schleiermachers Idee der Dialektik," *Neue Zeitschrift für systematische Theologie und Religionsphilosophie*, 10/3 (1968).

Lamm, J.A., *The Living God: Schleiermacher's Theological Appropriation of Spinoza*, University Park, Pa.: Pennsylvania State University Press, 1996.

Lehnerer, T., *Die Kunsttheorie Friedrich Schleiermachers*, Stuttgart: Klett-Cotta, 1987.

Niebuhr, R.R., *Schleiermacher on Christ and Religion*, New York: Scribner, 1964.

Odebrecht, R., *Schleiermachers System der Ästhetik*, Berlin: Junker und Dünnhaupt, 1932.

Sigwart, C. von, *Schleiermachers psychologische Voraussetzungen, insbesondere die Begriffe des Gefühls und der Individualität*; repr. Darmstadt: Wissenschaftliche Buchgesellschaft, 1974.

Wagner, F., *Schleiermachers Dialektik. Eine kritische Interpretation*, Gütersloh: 1974.

Wehrung, G., *Die Dialektik Schleiermachers*, Tübingen: J.C.B. Mohr, 1920.

Also helpful are M. Frank's introduction to his edition of the dialectics lectures and R. Crouter's introduction to his edition of *On Religion: Speeches to its Cultured Despisers* (both cited above).

Index

Lightning Source UK Ltd.
Milton Keynes UK
UKOW06f1623251116

288524UK00001B/1/P